PRESIDENTIAL POWER

POWER, CONFLICT, AND DEMOCRACY:
AMERICAN POLITICS INTO THE TWENTY-FIRST CENTURY
ROBERT Y. SHAPIRO, EDITOR

POWER, CONFLICT, AND DEMOCRACY:

AMERICAN POLITICS INTO THE TWENTY-FIRST CENTURY

ROBERT Y. SHAPIRO, EDITOR

This series focuses on how the will of the people and the public interest are promoted, encouraged, or thwarted. It aims to question not only the direction American politics will take in the twenty-first century but also the direction American politics has already taken.

The series addresses the role of interest groups and social and political movements; openness in American politics; important developments in institutions such as the executive, legislative, and judicial branches at all levels of government as well as the bureaucracies thus created; the changing behavior of politicians and political parties; the role of public opinion; and the functioning of mass media. Because problems drive politics, the series also examines important policy issues in both domestic and foreign affairs.

The series welcomes all theoretical perspectives, methodologies, and types of evidence that answer important questions about trends in American politics.

PRESIDENTIAL POWER

Forging the Presidency for the Twenty-first Century

Robert Y. Shapiro, Martha Joynt Kumar, Lawrence R. Jacobs
EDITORS

 COLUMBIA UNIVERSITY PRESS   NEW YORK

Columbia University Press
Publishers Since 1893
New York   Chichester, West Sussex

Library of Congress Cataloging-in-Publication Data
Presidential power / Robert Y. Shapiro.
    p. cm.—(Power, conflict, and democracy)
  ISBN 0–231-10932-6—ISBN 0-231-10933-4
    1. Presidents—United States. 2. Executive power—United States. I. Shapiro, Robert Y.,
  1953–II. Kumar, Martha Joynt. III. Jacobs, Lawrence R. IV. Title. V. Series.

  JK516.P73 2000
    352.23′5′0973—dc21   00–020655
  CIP

CONTENTS

PREFACE

Presidential Power: Forging the Presidency for the 21st Century has three objectives related immediately to its title. Political scientists still consider Richard Neustadt's *Presidential Power: The Politics of Leadership* (New York: Wiley, 1960) as the seminal book on the American presidency—the one that still influences not only their thinking and research about presidential power, but also that of presidents and their advisers who have come to learn directly or indirectly about Neustadt's advice—and warnings—for those in the White House.

One purpose of this volume is to examine critically the important themes and questions that *Presidential Power* posed—and still poses—for political scientists by presenting recent research by a new group of scholars in a way that does not simply reexamine and extend Neustadt's analysis and thinking, but questions and challenges it as well. In the end, while the volume's authors and editors (true to some of their Columbia University roots in the spirit of sociologist Robert Merton) think of themselves as standing on Neustadt's shoulders in trying to advance the study of the presidency, Neustadt takes some noticeable bruising as they climb up. Indeed, it is this intellectual process of beating and battering that may be the highest form of flattery.

The second purpose of this volume is to offer reflections and implications from what we have learned about presidential power as we move directly into the 21st century. The contributors have focused on identifying challenges facing the presidents of the new century not only within the White House and the executive branch, but also in Washington more generally and in the wide inter-

national world in the post-Cold War era. The volume also analyzes the changing character of presidential power and influence. While the position of chief
executive is a highly personal one—no other institution in American government is so singularly identified with one person, whether the president's name
is Ronald Reagan, George Bush, or Bill Clinton—it is clear that political and
new institutional developments condition what any president can accomplish.
The institution of the presidency is the prominent feature of this volume's
analysis, which comes as the world enters a new century and after the impeachment and near conviction of the country's last twentieth century president, Bill
Clinton.

One additional objective of this book is to fulfill its first two purposes in a
way that is useful to students and general readers interested in reading beyond
Presidential Power and other basic works on the presidency.

Earlier versions of nine of the main chapters were originally invited papers
(through a competitive review process) presented at a conference entitled
"Presidential Power: Forging the presidency for the 21st Century," which was
held on November 15–16, 1996, at Columbia University in New York. With the
1996 presidential election and the 35th anniversary of the publication of *Presidential Power* as its backdrop, the conference assembled junior and senior
scholars, including Richard Neustadt, to examine the current state of research
on the presidency. Borrowing on the experience of Neustadt, who was a member of President Truman's White House staff, wrote *Presidential Power* during
his years in Columbia's political science department and continued to serve at
the nexus of scholarship, politics, and policymaking, those attending the conference explored the problems facing the institution and its occupants. In addition, the conference addressed the relevance of scholarship to understanding
the policy issues facing presidents and their White House operations.

ACKNOWLEDGMENTS

First and foremost, we thank the sponsors of the conference for their support and assistance: The Presidency Research Group, which is an organized section of the American Political Science Association, and which convened the conference committee (see below for its members); The Academy of Political Science, founded in 1880, which through books and its principal publication, *Political Science Quarterly*, conducts and channels in understandable ways to political leaders and the general public scholarly examinations of political institutions, processes, and public policy; The Italian Academy for Advanced Studies in America, which participates in diverse intellectual activities on the Columbia campus; The Center for Political Leadership and Participation at the University of Maryland at College Park, which provided support for young scholars to attend the conference; and at Columbia University in the City of New York, support was provided by the Department of Political Science, the School of International and Public Affairs, the Center for the Social Sciences (recently renamed the Paul F. Lazarsfeld Center for the Social Sciences and now part of the Institute for Social and Economic Theory and Research), the Department of Political Science of Barnard College, and Columbia University Press.

In these organizations, at the time of the conference, thanks go to Demetrios (Jim) Caraley (President, Academy of Political Science; Barnard College and Columbia University), Georgia Sorenson (Center for Political Leadership and Participation at the University of Maryland), Lisa Anderson (Chair, Columbia's political science department), Michael Delli Carpini (Chair, Barnard's political science department), Douglas Chalmers (Acting Dean, School of International and Public Affairs), Richard Brilliant (Director, Italian Academy for Advanced Studies in America, Columbia University), Harrison White (Director, Center for the Social Sciences), and John Michel (Columbia University Press).

We owe special thanks for help in organizing the conference at Columbia to the political science department's Aida Llabaly; doctoral students Wynne Pomeroy Waller, John Lapinksi, and Charles Riemann; and the Center for the Social Science's Debra Gilchrest.

We are also enormously grateful to our fellow members of the conference committee for their work on the substance of the conference and for reviewing the original paper proposals:

Richard Brody, George Edwards, Karen Hult, Nelson Polsby, Bert Rockman, Georgia Sorenson, Robert Spitzer, Terry Sullivan, and Shirley Anne Warshaw.

We would also like to single out and thank our other colleagues who participated in the conference panels: Larry Berman, John Burke, Carl Cannon, Betty Glad, Fred Greenstein, Karen Hult, John Kessel, Bruce Miroff, Terry Moe, Richard Pious, Theda Skocpol, Terry Sullivan, Stephen Wayne, and James Sterling Young.

In addition to being a contributor, Natasha Hritzuk expertly assisted in putting together the entire volume. Last, we thank John Michel (for his good humor—and patience) and Leslie Bialler (for his editorial wizardry) and Kim L. Callihan (for her index) at Columbia University Press.

Robert Y. Shapiro
New York, New York

Martha Joynt Kumar
New Castle, Delaware

Lawrence R. Jacobs
Minneapolis, Minnesota

March 2000

CONTRIBUTORS

Charles M. Cameron is associate professor of political science at Columbia University. Formerly a National Fellow at the Hoover Institution and a Research Fellow at the Brookings Institution, he is the author of *Veto Bargaining: Presidents and the Politics of Negative Power*.

Matthew J. Dickinson is assistant professor in the government department at Harvard University, where he teaches courses on American political institutions, including Congress, the presidency, and the bureaucracy. His publications include *Bitter Harvest: FDR, Presidential Power and the Growth of the Presidential Branch*, a book that examines the origins of the presidential staff, as well as several articles examining different aspects of the American presidency. His current research assesses the sources of modern presidential power.

George C. Edwards III is Distinguished Professor of Political Science at Texas A & M University and Director of The Center for Presidential Studies in the Bush School. He is editor of *Presidential Studies Quarterly* and has authored dozens of articles and has written or edited seventeen books on the presidency, American politics, and public policymaking.

David Epstein is associate professor of political science at Columbia University. His research interests include game theory, legislative organization, redistricting, and comparative political institutions, and he recently published *Delegating Powers*, a book on delegation, jointly with Sharyn O'Halloran (Columbia University)

John G. Gunnell is Distinguished University Professor in the Graduate School of Public Affairs, State University of New York at Albany. His principal areas of research and teaching are political theory with a special emphasis on the philosophy and history of social science. His latest work includes *The Descent of Political Theory: The Genealogy of an American Vocation* and *The Orders of Discourse: Philosophy, Social Science, and Politics.*

Diane J. Heith is assistant professor of government and politics at St. John's University. She has written and co-authored recent articles on presidents and public opinion and the media. She is currently completing a book on public opinion and political leadership examining the use of public opinion polling in six presidential administrations.

Natasha Hritzuk is a doctoral candidate at Columbia University. She is doing research on the role of issues as catalysts to political activity, the effect of contextual variables on political participation by racial and ethnic groups, and press coverage of African Americans in the United States over the past twenty years.

Lawrence R. Jacobs is associate professor of political science at the University of Minnesota. He is author of *Health of Nations* and numerous articles on public opinion, the mass media, and substantive issues related to social security and health policy. He is coauthor, with Robert Y. Shapiro, of *Politicians Don't Pander: Political Manipulation and the Loss of Democratic Responsiveness.* (2000).

Martha Joynt Kumar is professor of political science at Towson State University and senior scholar at the Academy of Leadership at the University of Maryland. She has written extensively on the president and the media and is coauthor of *Portraying the President: The White House and the News Media* (1981) and author of *Wired for Sound and Pictures: The President and White House Communications Policies* (forthcoming). She currently is serving as the Executive Director of the White House Transition Project, funded by the Pew Charitable Trusts, aimed at smoothing the path to power for the new White House staff coming into office in 2001. She also serves as co-editor of the journal *Congress and the Presidency.*

Robert C. Lieberman is assistant professor of political science and public affairs at Columbia University. He is the author of *Shifting the Color Line: Race and the American Welfare State.*

Michael W. Link, Ph.D., University of South Carolina, has published several articles on the topics of presidential advisory networks and the psychological dimensions of relationships between presidents and their aides. Currently he is a survey director at the Research Triangle Institute in North Carolina.

Kenneth R. Mayer is associate professor of political science at the University of Wisconsin-Madison. His main interest in the presidency is the legal sources of presidential powers, especially executive orders.

Nolan McCarty is assistant professor of political science at Columbia University. He received his Ph.D. in political economy from Carnegie Mellon University and taught at the University of Southern California and has been a National Fellow at the Hoover Institution. His research interests include presidential and legislative politics as well as formal theory and research methodology. He has published numerous articles on executive-legislative relations. He is currently doing research on polarization, the dynamics of interest group access, and the development of separation of powers.

Richard E. Neustadt Douglas Dillon Professor of Government Emeritus at Harvard University is author of *Presidential Power* and coauthor of *Thinking in Time*, among other works. He was a White House assistant to President Truman and a consultant to Presidents Kennedy and Johnson. Neustadt's most recent book, *Report to JFK: The Skybolt Crisis in Perspective*, deals with one of his consulting assignments.

Sharyn O'Halloran is associate professor of political science and international affairs at Columbia University. Her research interests include trade policy, interbranch relations, the policy effects of racial redistricting, and the testing of formal models. She has published one book on trade policy, *Politics, Process, and American Trade Policy*, and another on delegation jointly with David Epstein, *Delegating Powers*.

Mark A. Peterson is professor of policy studies and political science at the UCLA School of Public Policy and Social Research, following previous appointments at Harvard University and the University of Pittsburgh. His publications on the presidency include *Legislating Together: The White House and Capitol Hill from Eisenhower to Reagan*. He is currently editor of the *Journal of Health Politics, Policy and Law*, a former guest scholar at the Brookings Institution, and a former American Political Science Association Congressional Fellow.

Richard M. Pious holds the Adolph and Effie Ochs Chair in American Studies and is chair of the department of political science at Barnard College. His books include *The American Presidency* (1979) and *The President, Congress, and the Constitution* (1984), coauthored with Christopher Pyle.

Thomas Preston is assistant professor of international relations in the department of political science, Washington State University. His published works in political psychology cover bureaucratic politics and group dynamics, presidential leadership style, personality, and foreign policy decisionmaking. In international security, his publications include pieces on nuclear proliferation, interstate security relationships, and the design and use of policy simulations.

Lyn Ragsdale is professor of political science at the University of Arizona. She has written numerous articles and three books on the American presidency, including *Vital Statistics on the Presidency*. She has been the president of the Western Political Science Association and is editor of the *Political Research Quarterly*.

Rose Razaghian is a doctoral student in political science at Columbia University. Her research focuses on empirical analysis of the development of the American bureaucracy.

Russell L. Riley is an academic program director with the Salzburg Seminar in American Studies, Salzburg Austria. He formerly taught American government at Georgetown and the University of Pennsylvania. He is the author of *The Presidency and the Politics of Racial Inequality: Nation-keeping from 1831 to 1965*.

Bert A. Rockman is the University Professor of Political Science at the University of Pittsburgh. He is a former president of the Organized Section for Presidency Research and has won the Richard E. Neustadt Prize for the best book on the U.S. Presidency, *The Leadership Question* (1984). Most recently he has co-edited (with Colin Campbell) and contributed to *The Clinton Legacy* and coauthored (with Joel Aberbach), *In the Web of Politics: Three Decades of the U.S. Federal Executive* (forthcoming).

Robert Y. Shapiro is a professor of political science at Columbia University. He is coauthor (with Benjamin I. Page) of *The Rational Public* (1992) and numerous articles on public opinion, political behavior, and American politics. He is coauthor (with Lawrence R. Jacobs) of *Politicians Don't Pander: Political Manipulation and the Loss of Democratic Responsiveness* (2000).

Renée M. Smith is assistant professor of political science at the University of Rochester. Her research on the American presidency and public opinion has been published in many books and journals.

Jeffrey K. Tulis teaches political science at the University of Texas at Austin. His publications include *The Presidency in the Constitutional Order* and *The Rhetorical Presidency*. He is currently completing a book on institutional deference among Congress, the President, and the Court.

Thomas J. Weko is associate professor of politics and government at the University of Puget Sound. He is the author of *The Politicizing Presidency* (1995) and a regular contributor to *The Presidency in the Political System*.

CHAPTER 1

Introduction: Presidential Power

Robert Y. Shapiro, Martha Joynt Kumar,
and Lawrence R. Jacobs

The frustration of Americans with government reached record highs from the 1970s to the end of the century, even as policymakers in Washington were intent on restructuring the federal government to make it more efficient and effective. This has stunningly continued in the wake of the scandal surrounding the impeachment and Senate trial of President Bill Clinton. The American presidency, which had been an institution with strong public support in 1960, has more recently been continually attacked by political partisans, organized groups and interests, and reports in the news media, as well as by the American public itself. As the nation moves on from the partisan politics of impeachment to new crises and challenges (those in Serbia, Kosovo, and East Timor at this writing), no individuals are going to be as enmeshed in Americans' frustrations and in policymakers' efforts to restructure government as are the president and the White House staff. Because of recent events and especially the great transformations that have occurred in domestic and international politics, the challenges of the American presidency are greater than ever. This volume examines the state of the presidency and presidential leadership as the century turns. The chapters that follow appraise the difficulties to be confronted and opportunities posed in the new century, and they examine the means available to the president to wrestle with these challenges.

The take-off point for the volume is the now classic account by Richard Neustadt in *Presidential Power* (*Presidential Power: The Politics of Leadership* (New York: Wiley, 1960). This account has continued to be the most widely assigned and read book on the subject and has been the cornerstone of far-reaching research on the presidency. This attests to Neustadt's success in communicating important themes about the nature and limits of power to multiple audiences—to students and teachers alike, and to presidents themselves.

Neustadt's core argument that not merely the use of formal authority but also the effective use of personal bargaining skill and tenacity must be considered when measuring presidential performance almost immediately generated a resonance in the study and debate about the power of the presidency. This argument raised a number of themes that stimulated a wide range of research—research in directions (with apologies to *Star Trek*) no scholars had gone before: research on White House organization, White House-Cabinet relations, presidential decision-making, presidential-congressional relations, other more general separation of powers issues, the role of the public's support for the president, and the importance of a president's relationship with the news media. While all of these topics are very familiar today, some were much less so before 1960.

In recent years there have been major changes in the problems facing the presidency. At the same time, the study of the presidency has shown signs of intellectual maturity and continuing innovative analysis. Presidential scholarship has stretched back historically and comparatively across multiple presidencies, for example, in the study of presidential rhetoric and the "institutional presidency"; it has elaborated upon the presidency's relationships with other institutions, including presidential-congressional relations, the presidency and the press, and the presidency and organized interests; it has demonstrated increasing—and increasingly complex—data gathering and statistical sophistication; and it has shown greater conceptual development, including, more recently, formal modeling of both the interpretive and mathematical variety (e.g., game theoretic and strategic approaches to presidential institution building, coalition building, interactions with bureaucratic agencies, vetoing). This volume brings together this range of scholarship to show the contributions of the field's analytical scope and increasing methodological rigor.

PLAN OF THE BOOK

Part I of the volume contains essays by George Edwards and John Gunnell, who review Neustadt's approach to the study of the presidency and Neustadt's place in political science and the study of American politics. Edwards describes Neustadt's emphasis on presidents' personal power and how this approach led presidential scholars to focus on the behavior of the "people within institutions and their relationship with each other rather than focusing primarily on the institutions themselves and their formalities." This tension between focusing on individuals versus institutions and institutional processes is a running theme throughout this volume; we will return to it in the concluding chapter. Gunnell's essay offers a broad and thoughtful examination of *Presidential Power* in the context of the development of the theory and practice of American political science and with regard to the tension between academic and public discourse. We—and Richard Neustadt himself—also return to this tension in the last section of the volume.

In reexamining *Presidential Power*, the essays that follow in parts II to V focus on major themes and the questions associated with them that have been raised but not resolved by Neustadt's work. Specifically, they cover four aspects of presidential power and the presidency: presidents as persuaders and the personalization of power; organizing and institutionalizing the presidency; the president in the political system; and the potential for leadership. While they can be listed separately, the first three are not mutually exclusive, and they can affect and interact with each other. The questions raised below concerning any one of these areas will have implications for the others as well. All three have ramifications for the potential for leadership.

In each of these four areas, Neustadt expanded the focus of study of the presidency to include the personal uses of power as well as the formal authority provided in the Constitution and in legislative enactments. In examining these aspects of the presidency, presidential scholars have advanced our understanding of presidential power by both building upon and also challenging Neustadt's approach. This process of applying and developing further the type of inquiry and analysis that impressed Neustadt, while at the same time asking new questions of arguably comparable importance that he did not address, is indeed a very high form of academic tribute.

PRESIDENTS AS PERSUADERS AND THE PERSONALIZATION OF POWER

Neustadt's most famous dictum is that presidential power is the power to persuade; this is personal power that involves the president's ability to influence others to achieve a political outcome. Neustadt depicted the president as operating in a pluralistic environment in which there are numerous actors with independent power bases and perspectives different from his. Thus, the president must marshal resources to persuade others (e.g., by arm-twisting, trading favors, and other means) to do as he wishes; a president cannot necessarily rely on expanding the institution's legal authority or adjusting its support mechanisms. Yet many scholars have emphasized the limitations of the president's persuasive potential, and others continue to stress the importance of institutional bases of command. What, then, is the potential of persuasion? Have we gone too far in deemphasizing the legal, institutional, and political bases of power, such as the organizational structure of the White House and executive branch, and the partisan balance in Congress (i.e., whether the president's party is the majority or minority party)? Or is personal leadership the core of the presidency. One of Neustadt's greatest contributions was expanding the vision of presidential scholars to include the dynamics of personal leadership. He viewed power more as a function of personal politics than of formal authority or position. Yet many authors have argued that attention from academics and the press has focused inordinately on the president's personal traits at the expense of the institutional environment in which he functions. Indeed, the Clinton scandal and the impeachment process directed attention toward both Clinton the person and the institutional environment and its attendant politics. What, then, is the principal source of presidential power? Is there an appropriate balance to be found balance between personality and institutional position?

ORGANIZING AND INSTITUTIONALIZING THE PRESIDENCY

One of Neustadt's richest legacies has been his discussions of decision-making processes and of presidents' relations with their staff and the responsibilities of presidents' aides. Yet it is not clear what we (and presidents) have learned. Presidents need to try to get organizational and institutional assistance, even if in the end they may still have to rely on themselves; that is, no level of organizational support or staffing can substitute for deficient leadership skills. Still, institutionalization can provide resources and assistance to presidents. Presidents regularly conclude that they must reorganize their staff and decision-making processes. Institutional memory in the White House can be fleeting. How, then, can presidents most effectively structure their office to accomplish their goals and compensate for their personal weaknesses?

THE PRESIDENT IN THE POLITICAL SYSTEM

Neustadt adopted a presidency-centered perspective to American government, viewing the presidency from over the president's shoulders and not from the perspective of the political system. Many academics and journalists have continued—implicitly or explicitly—to adopt the same orientation. Yet some authors readily conclude that the president is not and should not be the center of American government. They feel that Neustadt's approach neglected to examine the presidency from the perspective of the American separation of powers system; the implicit assumption is that the president should be the principal decision-maker in American politics. What, then, is the proper role of the president in American government, and what are appropriate expectations of the presidency? To what extent might a Congress-centered or party-centered approach provide further insight into presidential power and politics.

THE POTENTIAL FOR LEADERSHIP

The late twentieth century has witnessed a series of presidencies that have been criticized for lacking vision, inspiration (and honesty and moral character, in the case of Bill Clinton), and effectiveness. Ultimately, what is the potential of presidential leadership? Are presidents more likely to "act" or to "react"? Are there new means available to them, such as those that facilitate political communication involving the mass media and public opinion? Or are there new barriers to this? Can presidents move beyond facilitating transactions among policymakers and transform the public's thinking and the institutional setting in Washington? If presidents can engage in transformational leadership, should we expect them to do so, and how can we reconcile this with democratic governance?

The answers to all of the above questions are fundamentally important to understanding the presidency. Each set of questions resides at the core of scholarship on the presidency. The essays in this volume offer some answers and evidence bearing on them, and they suggest ways of further investigation of these fundamental concerns.

Parts II to V of the volume each include three essays based on research by members of a new generation of presidency scholars. Each part is introduced and appraised by a senior expert. The final section (Part VI) offers a commentary, "A Preachment from Retirement," by Neustadt; this is followed by an evaluation of the politics of impeachment from the perspective of Neustadt's *Presidential Power* and the social scientific study of the presidency; and, last, a synthesis and concluding perspective by two of the volume's editors.

The essays in this volume pay particular attention to how *Presidential Power* has led to advances in research and insight into the American presidency, not only through Neustadt's own vision, but through what scholars who have followed him—some more critical than others—thought he might not have fully appreciated. Criticism of Neustadt may seem a controversial subject in this volume. But judging from the conference at which many of the essays were originally presented and from Neustadt's own essay at the end of this volume, criticism is best handled by Neustadt himself. And as we began in the Preface: whatever Neustadt's successors and critics might claim, what would they have seen without the view from his shoulders?

PART 1

Richard Neustadt's Presidential Power and
American Political Science

CHAPTER 2

Neustadt's Power Approach to the Presidency

George C. Edwards III

Perhaps the best known dictum regarding the American presidency is that "presidential power is the power to persuade."[1] It is the wonderfully felicitous phrase that captures the essence Richard Neustadt's argument in *Presidential Power*.

This central insight provided scholars with a new orientation to the study of the presidency. When the book was published in 1960, this framework was strikingly different from those of Edward S. Corwin[2] and Clinton Rossiter[3] that had dominated presidential scholarship. These differences were to have important consequences for how the many scholars would examine the presidency over the next four decades.

Neustadt's political power approach to the study of the presidency can be contrasted with legal, institutional, psychological, and other approaches.[4] Neustadt's framework highlights the president's operational problem of *self-help* in thinking about influence strategically. The political power approach has had many consequences for analyzing and understanding the presidency. Neustadt saw the president operating in a pluralistic environment in which there are numerous actors with independent power bases and perspectives different from his. Thus the president must marshal resources to persuade others to do as he wishes (the operational problem). A president cannot only rely on expanding the institution's legal authority or adjusting its support mechanisms.

The emphasis on persuasion encouraged moving beyond Corwin and

Rossiter. In Neustadt's words, " 'powers' are no guarantee of power"[5] and "*[t]he probabilities of power do not derive from the literary theory of the Constitution.*"[6] Power, then, is a function of personal politics rather than of formal authority or position. Neustadt placed people and politics at the center of research.

Following Neustadt's lead, scholars have been encouraged to focus primarily on the people within institutions and their relationships with each other rather than on the institutions themselves and their formalities. It is not the roles of the president but the performance of those roles that matters. It is not the boundaries of behavior but the actions within those boundaries that warrant the attention of scholars.

The president's need to exercise influence in several arenas leads those who follow the power perspective to adopt an expansive view of presidential politics that includes both governmental institutions and actors, such as the Congress, bureaucracy, and White House staff, and those outside of government, such as the public, the press, and interest groups. Thus, what has to be explained in studying presidential interactions (the dependent variables) includes not only presidential decisions themselves but also congressional and public support for the president, press coverage of the White House, bureaucratic policy implementation, and sets of policy options prepared by the bureaucracy for the president.[7]

Because the power approach does not assume presidential success or the smooth functioning of the presidency, the influence of bureaucratic politics and other organizational factors in the executive branch are as important to investigate as behavior in more openly adversarial institutions such as Congress.

Power is a concept that involves relationships between people. By focusing on relationships and suggesting why people respond to the president as they do, Neustadt forces us into a more analytical mode. To understand relationships, we must explain behavior. Describing it is not enough, nor is storytelling about interesting but unrepresentative incidents—a temptation that is only natural when writing about the presidency. Neustadt, however, is concerned with the strategic level of power:

> There are two ways to study "presidential power." One way is to focus on the tactics . . . of influencing certain men in given situations. . . . The other way is to step back from tactics on those "givens" and to deal with influence in more strategic terms: what is its nature and what are its sources? . . . Strategically, [for example] the question is not how he masters Congress in a peculiar instance, but what he does to boost his chance for mastery in any instance.[8]

Neustadt, then, is less interested in what causes something to happen in one instance than in what affects the probabilities of something happening in every instance. To think strategically about power we must search for generalizations and calculate probabilities. Although he employed neither the language nor the methods of modern social science, Neustadt was clearly a forerunner. His emphasis on reaching generalizations about presidential power may have been his greatest contribution of all.

There is also an important prescriptive element in *Presidential Power*. Neustadt's central motivation for writing the book was to offer advice to presidents to help them help themselves with their strategic problem of power, and he remained interested in the challenges of governing. Indeed, tying scholarship to governing is important because governing is the primary reason we study politics (entertainment value aside).

Whether we are interested in explaining the consequences of efforts at persuasion or prescribing a strategy to obtain or maintain resources useful in persuasion, the critical questions are, "what is the potential of persuasion"—with Congress, the public, or others?"; and specifically, "what is the potential of various persuasive resources with those whose support the president needs"? Seeking answers to these questions inevitably leads to explanations and generalizations.

In this quest for answers, Neustadt's orientation to studying the presidency specifies little about how to measure concepts, test propositions, or analyze data. It does not by itself enforce rigor in our analyses. Nor does it prevent us from missing the big picture by focusing on tactical rather than strategic questions. Yet, Neustadt's approach does encourage a focus on the bigger questions and on explanation. As essays in this volume illustrate, others have picked up where Neustadt left off by attempting to measure concepts rigorously, to test propositions, to analyze data, and to challenge Neustadt's tendency to not go far enough in terms of broad theory and explanation.

In encouraging a new look at the presidency, Neustadt's political power approach did not supplant—indeed, it may have provoked—more traditional orientations to the study of the presidency; for example, there continue to be important legal studies of presidential powers,[9] and innumerable institutional histories.[10] Neustadt had no interest in supplanting this more traditional work.

Still, the political power approach cannot answer all the important questions about the presidency. Neustadt's emphasis on relationships does not lead naturally to investigations of the president's accountability, the limitations of the institution's legal powers, or the day-to-day operation of the presidency.

Nor does it explain the contribution to decisionmaking of the psychological makeup of the individual serving as president.

Some commentators are bothered by the top-down orientation of the power approach—that is, viewing the presidency from the perspective of the president.[11] They feel that this approach neglects to examine the presidency from the perspective of the American political system and that it carries the implicit assumption that the president should be the principal decisionmaker in American politics. These critics argue that such premises are too Machiavellian and that an evaluation of the goals and means of presidents must be added to analyses of power.

Others find exaggerated the depiction of the president's environment as basically confrontational, with conflicting interests of political actors creating centrifugal forces the president must try to overcome. Moreover, they claim that the heavy emphasis on power relationships may lead analysts to underestimate the importance of ideology or other influences on behavior.[12] Such issues continue to require more attention.

Neustadt's emphasis on the personal in politics has led some scholars to overlook the importance of the context in which the president operates as well as his institutional setting. For example, when *Presidential Influence in Congress*[13] was published in 1980, it contained an argument that presidential legislative skills such as bargaining, arm twisting, and personal appeals were rarely a decisive factor in determining the outcome of votes on the president's program. This argument was made when the tremendous productivity of the Great Society years—and the widespread attribution of this productivity to Lyndon Johnson's undoubted political skill—was still fresh in people's minds.

Although today a more modest view of the role of legislative skills has been developed and accepted, there was a substantial barrier of conventional wisdom to overcome. It would be unfair to argue that Neustadt erected an impediment to understanding the broader patterns of presidential influence; however, his emphasis on the person in the office certainly discouraged it, especially among his less discerning readers. Similarly, many scholars and other commentators on the presidency have fallen prey to the personalization of politics and have uncritically accepted, for example, an exaggerated concept of the potential for using the "bully pulpit" to go public.

The notion of the dominant president who moves the country and the government by means of strong, effective leadership has deep roots in our political culture. Those chief executives whom Americans revere—Washington, Jefferson, Jackson, Lincoln, Wilson, and both Roosevelts—have taken on mythical proportions as leaders. Even though the American public has been frequently disillusioned with the performance of presidents and has recognized that stalemate is common, it has eagerly accepted what appears to be effective presidential leadership, as with Ronald Reagan in 1981, as evidence on which to renew faith in the potential of the presidency. After all, if presidential leadership works some of the time, why not all of the time?

Behind such thinking is the implicit view that all it takes is the right person at the helm for the ship of state to sail smoothly. This perception directly influences expectations and evaluations of presidents. If it is reasonable to expect successful leadership from the White House, then failures of leadership must be personal deficiencies. If problems arise because leaders lack the proper will, skills, or understanding, then the solution to the need for leadership is straightforward and simple: elect presidents willing and able to lead. Because the system can respond to appropriate leadership, it will function smoothly with the right leaders in the Oval Office.

The public can indulge in high expectations of its chief executives and freely criticize them if they fail; for example, presidents may be chastised if they appear unable to bring around Congress or the public to their point of view. The blame lies clearly in the leader rather than the environment. Americans need not concern themselves with broader forces in American society that may influence presidential leadership. Because these forces are complex and perhaps even intractable, to focus on the individual as leader simplifies analysis and evaluation of the problems of governing.

On the other hand, presidential leadership may not be preeminent in American government. The national preoccupation with the chief executive may be misplaced and the belief in the impact of the individual leader may be largely a myth—a product of a search for simple solutions in an extremely complex, purposefully inefficient system in which the founders' handiwork in decentralizing power defeats, by constitutional design, even the most capable leaders.

If this is the case, the public should expect less of its presidents and be less disappointed when they are not successful in leading. In addition, the focus should be less exclusively on the president and more on the context in which the president seeks to lead. Major changes in public policy may then require more than just the "right" person in the job and may not turn on a president's leadership qualities. It does not follow, of course, that failures of presidential leadership may never be attributed to the White House or that presidents have no control over the outcome of their relations with other political actors. It does mean that we must continue to seek a better understanding of presidential power and leadership in order to think sensibly about the role of the chief executive in the nation's political system.

In sum, the approach to studying the presidency fostered by Neustadt is not and cannot be all things to all people; it does not ask all the important questions nor provide a guide to finding all the answers we seek. However, *Presidential Power* has remained the most influential, and most admired, book on the American presidency. And for good reason. Its focus on the influence relationships of presidents operating within the presidency was a critical intellectual breakthrough that forced us to broaden and clarify our thinking and encouraged us to emphasize explanation and generalization in our research. This is the legacy of *Presidential Power* into the 21st century.

NOTES

1. Richard E. Neustadt, *Presidential Power and the Modern Presidents* (New York: Free Press, 1990), p. 11.

2. Edward S. Corwin, *The President, Office and Powers, 1787–1957*, 4th rev. ed. (New York: New York University Press, 1957).

3. Clinton L. Rossiter, *The American Presidency*, 2nd ed. (New York: Harcourt, Brace, 1960).

4. For a discussion of these approaches, see Stephen J. Wayne, "Approaches," in George C. Edwards III and Stephen J. Wayne, eds., *Studying the Presidency* (Knoxville: University of Tennessee Press, 1983), pp. 17–49.

5. Neustadt, *Presidential Power*, p. 10.

6. Neustadt, *Presidential Power*, p. 37. Italics in original.

7. See, for example, George C. Edwards III, *At the Margins: Presidential Leadership of Congress* (New Haven: Yale University Press, 1989); *The Public Presidency* (New York: St. Martin's, 1983); and *Implementing Public Policy* (Washington, D.C.: Congressional Quarterly, 1980). Other examples of the political power approach include Fred I. Greenstein, *The Hidden-Hand Presidency* (New York: Basic Books, 1982); Bert A. Rockman, *The Leadership Question* (New York: Praeger, 1984); Terry M. Moe, "The Politicized Presidency," in John E. Chubb and Paul E. Peterson, eds., *The New Directions in American Politics* (Washington, D.C.: Brookings Institution, 1985); and Jeffrey E. Cohen, "Presidential Rhetoric and the Public Agenda," *American Journal of Political Science* 39 (February 1995): 87–107.

8. Neustadt, *Presidential Power*, p. 4.

9. Recent examples include Louis Fisher, *Constitutional Conflicts Between Congress and the President*, 4th ed., rev. (Lawrence: University Press of Kansas, 1997); Louis Fisher, *Presidential War Power* (Lawrence: University Press of Kansas, 1995);

and Mark J. Rozell, *Executive Privilege* (Baltimore: Johns Hopkins University Press, 1994).

10. Recent examples include Lawrence R. Jacobs and Robert Y. Shapiro, "The Rise of Presidential Polling: The Nixon White House in Historical Perspective," *Public Opinion Quarterly* 59 (Summer 1995): 163–195; Charles E. Walcott and Karen M. Hult, *Governing the White House* (Lawrence: University Press of Kansas, 1995); and Thomas J. Weko, *The Politicizing Presidency: The White House Personnel Office, 1948–1994* (Lawrence: University Press of Kansas, 1995).

11. See Bruce Miroff, "Beyond Washington," *Society* 17 (July/August 1980): 66–72.

12. See Peter W. Sperlich, "Bargaining and Overload: An Essay on Presidential Power," in Aaron Wildavsky, ed., *The Presidency* (Boston: Little, Brown, 1969), pp. 168–192.

13. George C. Edwards III, *Presidential Influence in Congress* (San Francisco: W. H. Freeman, 1980).

CHAPTER 3

Richard Neustadt in the History of American Political Science

John G. Gunnell

In this essay, I examine Richard Neustadt's *Presidential Power* in the context of the evolution of the theory and practice of American political science and with respect to the problem of the relationship between academic and public discourse which has been so central to the history of the discipline and profession. It is also important to relate Neustadt's work to the general political ambience in which it was situated.

Neustadt was clear about what we might call the intention of the book, that is, what his objective was in writing it. He was attempting to describe and explain how a president can make the powers of the office "work for *him*." The basic "theme" was "personal power and its politics: what it is, how to get it, how to keep it, how to use it."[1] Neustadt was, however, less explicit about the purpose of the work, the audience toward which it was directed, and the intellectual persuasion informing it.

In some respects, the book might, at first glance, appear as anomalous in the context of the dominant political science literature of the period since it did not represent the methodological and quantitative emphases characteristic of the behavioral movement, which was beginning to dominate political science. It is evident, however, that Neustadt, like the behavioralists, was rejecting what was understood as the traditional legal/institutional approach to political analysis; moreover, there are distinct dimensions in the work connecting it to the substantive images of politics that were emerging in the literature of political science as well as to some of the broader concerns of the discipline and profession. Although the book has been expanded in successive editions to account for the subsequent history of the presidency, the original text has been retained; and despite its perennial appeal it in many respects remains very much a work of its original time and place. The other chapters in this volume situate Neustadt's arguments within the research and literatures dealing more strictly with the presidency.

When, in the mid-1930s, John Dewey addressed the issue of liberalism, he employed the concept very broadly to refer to a certain range of beliefs and attitudes that, even though more prominent in the modern era, "might be traced back to Greek thought," but he also attempted to give liberalism a distinct contemporary historical identity.[2] In doing so, he did for academic discourse what Franklin D. Roosevelt had done in politics,[3] and there was a connection between the two efforts. Dewey's argument for the application of intelligence to human affairs and his plea for a "new liberalism" that would replace the *laissez-faire* variety, was in part an unmistakably philosophical underwriting of the New Deal legislative program. And, to some extent, Dewey saw in the modern presidency an answer to his concerns, voiced a decade earlier, about the eclipse or absence of a distinct public realm and a democratic public.[4] A quarter of a century after Dewey announced the new liberalism, the image of Roosevelt continued to inform Neustadt's account of presidential action which, in turn, adumbrated the Kennedy era. The book was a quintessential academic expression of both the theoretical and practical vision of liberalism with its image of vigorous leadership and interventionist government. But the book also both reflected and contributed to the emerging behavioral paradigm in political science and the basic theory of American politics that dominated the behavioral movement.

First, there was the emphasis on *interest, power,* and *process* which not only characterized the "realist" turn against formalism in Progressive political science after the turn of the century but was also at the core of the tradition manifest in the work of individuals such as Charles Merriam, Harold Lasswell, and G.E.G. Catlin; this new emphasis, in turn, became one the principal elements in the intellectual foundation of behavioralism. Although some, such as David Easton, argued that power was not an adequate core concept for a general theory of politics, his reconstitution of the image of politics as the "authoritative allocation of values" represented a similar range of phenomena and distribution of emphasis.[5] Second, there was the description of politics in terms of *pluralism* as well as the transformation of pluralism into a normative democratic theory. Pluralism involved a theory of power, but as both a prescriptive and empirical theory it required moving beyond the rudiments of the group theory of politics that had been evolving since the time of Arthur Bentley. What many pluralists, as well as their critics, became concerned with, however, was how the centrifugal forces of interest politics could be circumscribed and contained and how pluralism added up to a theory of democracy. Two basic and integrally related dimensions to the answer that emerged in pluralist theory were consensus and presidential action, and both dimensions were central to Neustadt's work.

One of the characteristics of behavioralism was not only a continued rejection of institutional analysis but also a depreciation of the idea of institutional checks and balances as an answer to the achievement of both stability and democracy. This was already apparent in David Truman's classic treatment of "political interests and public opinion"[6] which comprised part of the intellectual climate at Columbia University when Neustadt was writing *Presidential Power*. In several respects, Truman's work was the culmination of the evolution of the group theory of politics.[7] Although his primary emphasis was descriptive and explanatory, there was also a distinct effort to rehabilitate interest groups and demonstrate their role in representative democracy while recognizing some of the incipient pathologies such as "morbific" politics.

Truman, however, devoted considerable attention to what he called the "ordeal of the executive." Part of the reason for this concern was that the logic of pluralist theory led inexorably in the direction of an emphasis on both consensus and centralized authority. Many believed, in the wake of the work of historians such as Daniel Boorstin and Louis Hartz,[8] that a liberal consensus was an endemic element of American exceptionalism. Whether this consensus was the "genius" of American politics or a new form of "absolutism" might be debatable, but for all parties it provided an answer to the issue that attended American democratic theory since at least the time of de Tocqueville: how can there be a democratic polity without the relatively homogeneous democratic community that republican government seemed to require? From James Madison to Robert Dahl, there was a persistent belief that the social and institutional mechanisms of pluralist government and society might create a kind of virtual people, but from the nineteenth-century theory of the state to behavioralism, there was also a search for some deeper source of communal identity and sentiment. Despite claims about the dynamic equilibrium inherent in group politics, this kaleidoscopic universe, particularly given the complexities of the modern age and the need for an activist government, seemed to require constraints, both psychological and behavioral, that exceeded both tradition and the arena provided by formal governmental structures. The logic of pluralism, in effect, led to and entailed a new kind of concern with the presidency as both a creator of consensus and a master-bargainer; and it also pointed increasingly in the direction of the image of a plebiscitary theory of democracy as well as to a plebiscitary image of the presidency. All of this found expression in Neustadt's work.

Although Truman suggested that in "tranquil times" the presidency was largely another access point for group pressure, he emphasized that the extensive "exercise of discretion" and the increased role of the president in the initiation of legislation had resulted in the "gravitation of interest groups toward government" and, at the same time, had contributed to making "the most characteristic feature of twentieth-century government in the United States . . . the size and importance" of the Presidency. It had become "the most important and the most complex position in the governmental mechanism."[9] Truman placed great emphasis on the fact that neither the presidency nor its place in the "governmental process" could be understood in terms of constitutional and institutional structures. He argued that the president "must take the lead in effecting a continuous adjustment of the diverse interests within the nation," that the president's effectiveness "depends as much upon persuasion as upon force and legal authority," that the president "must appear to affirm the unity of the nation," that an "aggressive leadership has usually been demanded," that such leadership has been of a "highly personal character" and depended little on the cabinet and advisers, and that there had been an "enhancement of his ability to command a large public for his actions and utterances."[10] In many respects, Truman's general image of the president was a vessel to be filled with the kind of analysis that Neustadt offered.

When Neustadt's book first appeared, many scholars, particularly political theorists, likened it to the "great tradition" and the classic canon in political philosophy and particularly to the endeavors and concerns of Machiavelli.[11] Despite some obvious generic similarities, there is little to suggest that *The Prince* was the model for *Presidential Power*, even though in his analysis of the presidency, Neustadt was also laying out a "new route." Although both Machiavelli and Neustadt were concerned with how a pivotal politician gained and maintained "personal power" and with the complementarity between that vocation and the public good, and although there may be some interesting similarities with respect to both the analysis of power and the strategies recommended, there are distinct limits to comparing these works in terms of either their principal themes or the context of their production. First, the situation of the university social scientist, particularly in the United States, is considerably different from that of a displaced and frustrated sixteenth-century political actor engaging in a kind of literary surrogate politics in the context of the Florentine city-state. Both writers were ultimately concerned with practical matters, but while Machiavelli visualized the figure of the prince from the perspective of a landscape painter stationed far from the object, *Presidential Power* analyzed "the problem of obtaining personal power" by viewing "the Presidency from over the President's shoulder, looking out and down with the perspective of *his* place."[12]

Neustadt's work reflected the pluralist theory of politics that was emerging in mainstream political science by focusing on such phenomena as the *fungible character of power*, with multiple and competing centers, and the *transactional nature of power relations*; but, his work also contributed significantly to pluralist theory. The image of the president that emerges from Neustadt's work is that of an "expert," but one who is "not above politics" and who acts as the chief "bargainer" or power-broker in the pluralist system. Not unlike Mayor Lee in Dahl's *Who Governs?*,[13] the president is a professional politician, who works less from a position of given authority than from the accrual of prestige and the skill of persuasion in a world of diffused power. The president both holds the system together and moves it forward as an actor in the game yet to some extent outside it and who performs as both a teacher and facilitator. The president's personal pursuit of power and the success achieved consequently benefits both the office and the political order as a whole. In this context, it is in many ways the perception of the president that is crucial. While Neustadt placed much emphasis on the elements and strategies of power and interest, power ultimately seemed to emerge, as it did for someone such as C. Wright Mills,[14] as a symbolic commodity involving image, symbols, and reputation. Power becomes equated with the ability to persuade in a game of bargaining and exchange. But, maybe above all, the president creates and maintains what is at the core of the pluralist image of politics—consensus. In the same year that Neustadt's book was published, the authors of *The American Voter* noted both that "no democratic state has ever been governed by direct democracy" and that "the choice of a President has been the most important decision issuing from the electoral process."[15] But the question remained as to exactly how the presidency functioned in American democracy.

Dahl's early work, for example, did not indicate any clear attachment to the normative tradition of pluralism, and, in fact, he worried about a situation "where decisions are arrived at as a result of bargaining among a great variety of different groups." His primary concern was that this would lead to excessive presidential independence and power.[16] By the time of his collaboration with Charles Lindblom, however, Dahl had joined the growing chorus of those who believed that the American economic and political systems were a "polyarchy" consisting of self-correcting "countervailing powers" grounded in "social pluralism" and "bargaining" within a broad consensus on ends and means—and this was the essence of modern democracy.[17] As one leading study of presidential elections put it, "a pluralistic social organization must exist, and a basic consensus must bind together the contending parties." The same study also stressed that "twentieth-century political theory—both analytic and normative—will arise only from hard and long observation of the actual world of politics," and it concluded, much like the vision of Schumpeter, that democracy must be conceived in a plebiscitary manner.[18] But while pluralists were hard at work countering the claims of elitist theories of power, they were, at the same time, placing more emphasis on the role of elites within the process of pluralist politics.[19]

Dahl formalized the pluralist image of politics in *A Preface to Democratic Theory* and suggested that a "descriptive" account of the "American hybrid" also constituted a normative theory of democracy that was both derived from and described the operation of polyarchial political systems. Even more pointedly, he emphasized the "trivial" nature of constitutional structures in favor of "endless bargaining" within the all important matrix of "consensus." He argued that "what we ordinarily describe as 'politics' is merely the chaff. Prior to politics, beneath it, enveloping it, restricting it, conditioning it, is the underlying consensus" among those who are politically active.[20] Dahl challenged what he claimed to be Madison's emphasis on institutional checks and balances as a way of constraining Congress as well as what he alleged as Madison's failure to see the importance, and democratic implications of, the balance produced by "social pluralism" and other "extra-constitutional factors."

Dahl claimed that the Jacksonian belief that "the elected executive might be the true representative of the majority" had not been historically sustained, and the modern presidency, along with "decentralized bargaining parties" and "a decentralized bargaining legislature," had become a "decentralized bargaining bureaucracy." He noted, nevertheless, that in the American political system, "the dynamic center of power has proved to be the presidency,"[21] but the analysis of the presidency implied by this statement had not yet appeared. At the same time, however, critics of certain features of pluralism were also emphasizing the presidency, and to some extent Neustadt's book provided support for their position as well.

One of the earliest and most severe challenges to pluralism and the theory of interest group politics, as both a descriptive and normative thesis, was E. E. Schattschneider's *Semi-Sovereign People*, which appeared in the same year as

Neustadt's book. One of the casualties of the rise of pluralist theory, and the concomitant decline of a belief in the existence of a democratic public as the constituency of government, had been the idea of a substantive public interest. The public interest was construed as either policy outcomes or the sum total of identifiable interests. Schattschneider joined individuals such as Dahl in focusing on conflict and in jettisoning varieties of traditional idealistic democratic theory in favor of a "real" or descriptive account of democracy. He depicted democracy in a plebiscitary manner, that is, as "a competitive political system in which competing leaders and organizations define the alternatives of public policy in such a way that the public can participate in the decision-making process."[22] Yet he was less than happy with the pluralist theory of democracy.

Schattschneider maintained that there was a distinct difference between public and private interest—and between the exclusive, local, and privatizing tendencies of "pressure politics" and the inclusive democratic potential of electoral party politics and public authority as a way of articulating and nationalizing conflict and representing majorities. But in addition to parties as vehicles of democratic mobilization and representation, he stressed the role of the presidency:

> The rise of political parties and the extension of the suffrage produced the plebiscitary Presidency. The growth of presidential party leadership and the development of the Presidency as the political instrument of a national constituency have magnified the office tremendously. The Presidency has in turn become the principal instrument for the nationalization of politics.[23]

It is a short conceptual step from this proposition to Neustadt's suggestion that "what is good for the country is good for the President, and *vice versa*."[24] Soon other critics of pluralist theory and practice, such as Grant McConnell, would urge the view that both parties and the presidency were answers to the pathologies of group politics as well as a path to the realization of democracy. McConnell saw the president as both the major "centralizing element" in government and a basis for recovering the idea and possibility of "public interest:"

> The constituency of this majestic office is all the people. The prestige of its occupant is so great that when his power is husbanded and skillfully used he can make innovations of policy in the interest of those who are outside the pluralist scheme of rule.[25]

Neustadt's work cannot easily be identified as an integral part of either the pluralist or anti-pluralist literature, but it is difficult to read it outside the context of the pluralist image of politics, and debates about that image, that dominated the era. It represented to some extent an acceptance of the reality of pluralist politics as well as the pluralist account of power, but it was also a response to some of the difficulties inherent in a pluralist system. The question remains, however, of how the book fits into the more general discursive genealogy of American political science which during this period often seemed to eschew evaluation and prescription and the temptation to speak to political practice.[26] At a point when many were beginning to believe that the discipline had turned away from a concern with the practical dimensions of politics, Neustadt's intimations of advice to political actors may have seemed anomalous.

Many political scientists, such as Dahl, who had entered government service during the war were quick to return to the academy. While Dahl, like so many scholars including Easton, originally gravitated toward political science with a view toward practical political involvement, and had even looked with "disdain" upon a life of scholarship,[27] his participation in government service was short-lived. Neustadt, in sharp contrast, remained actively involved in public affairs. He entered public service (OPA) after receiving his Masters degree from Harvard (1941), and after serving in the Navy during the war, he joined the Bureau of the Budget while also working toward his Ph.D. His propensity for practical involvement in politics might have been, to some degree, a consequence of family background and an early immersion in the national politics of the period,[28] but he became a member of President Truman's staff in 1958 and, in his words, "became infected with politics in the Truman school." He wrote his dissertation on "Presidential Clearance of Legislation" (Harvard, 1951), and at the end of Truman's term, he moved to the academy, first as a visiting professor of public administration at Cornell (1953–54), and then as a member of the department of government at Columbia (1954–1964) where he wrote *Presidential Power*. More than most political scientists of this period, Neustadt would remain deeply involved with political life, but there is a greater affinity between his work and the scientism that characterized behavioralism than some might imagine.

Although most of those who spearheaded the movement for a more scientific political science eventually became exclusively academicians and remained insulated from public life, this was often not their original intention. Science had always been understood as a means rather than an end. From those who embraced the nineteenth-century theory of the state to Harold Lasswell's image of a policy science, the idea was that only by establishing its cognitive, that is, scientific, authority could political science achieve practical purchase. When the American Political Science Association was created in 1903, it set for itself a paradoxical agenda that symbolized the dilemma of the age. It committed itself to the scientific study of politics and to nonpartisanship, but the express purpose of this endeavor was to achieve what Frank Goodnow, the first president of the American Political Science Association, referred to as "practical authority" over politics. The same concern was evident in the Progressive agenda of political science after the turn of the past century and in the vision of Woodrow Wilson. And this spirit continued to animate the field from Charles Merriam's dream of a science that would speak truth to power to the behavioral "revolution." Behavioralism was initially rooted in an attempt to recapture, reconstitute, and defend the idea of a science of politics that would ultimately serve a practical purpose.

It has been tempting for commentators to suspect that during the 1950s behavioralism put a priority on pure science for a number of instrumental reasons, including funding sources, nationalism and conservative liberalism, and the fear of ideological contamination in the McCarthy era. The emphasis on pure science, however, also represented an extension of the basic goal of the discipline and its commitment to the idea that practical authority was ultimately a function of scientific status. This was, in part, reflected in the attempt of pluralists to extrapolate a normative theory of democracy from an empirical account of American politics. When many political scientists "went to war" in the early 1940s, which often involved working for the government, they often did not return to the academy dazzled by their practical experience. This surely occurred not only because many found the life of the academy personally preferable, but also because many, like Merriam before them, had found direct participation frustrating and less than efficacious.

Nowhere was political science's ambivalence about the priorities of pure science and practical relevance, and the problem of the relationship between the two, more evident than in Lasswell and Abraham Kaplan's extended and tortured analysis of the relationship between the "contemplative" and "manipulative" concerns of the field.[29] Sensitivity to this traditional issue was still very much present in Easton's 1951 critique of the discipline's intellectual dormancy and his plea for creative value and empirical theory.[30] Behavioralism, by the 1960s, could claim to represent mainstream political science, even if it enjoyed less than a plurality of supporters. Much of the criticism of behavioralism, however, revolved around its retreat from values and its passion for empiricism, and by the time that Dahl announced, although somewhat prematurely, the victory of the revolution in his "epitaph for a monument to a successful protest,"[31] there was little obvious discursive residue of the practical concerns that had propelled the scientific quest. In contrast, Neustadt's study of the presidency and his subsequent work must be read as an exception that retains the original faith of the discipline, a faith that still resonated in Easton's presidential address to the American Political Science Association in 1969[32] but that was often forgotten by the generation of scholars succeeding those who initiated the behavioral revolution.

More recently, the literary critic Stanley Fish disparaged those academicians who believe that what they do in their scholarly capacity has practical significance and consequences.[33] One of the books that he referred to as an example of such academic "megalomania" was Richard Neustadt's and Ernest May's *Thinking in Time*.[34] This book was, however, a poorly chosen target of criticism, since most of the material that Fish commented on was from various humanistic fields and represented individuals who fancied themselves radical and oppositional thinkers and who believed that their scholarly activities could be construed, and could function, as a mode of political action. Neustadt and May suggested something quite different. Their argument was that there could be practical "uses" of history, and they attempted to offer instructive case studies of political decision-making for policymakers. Fish had no sense of the tradition of discourse to which Neustadt belonged.

Even more explicitly than *Presidential Power*, *Thinking in Time* was "addressed to those who govern," that is, those who participate in "the practice of government service."[35] The book reflected Neustadt's activities at the Harvard University's John Fitzgerald Kennedy Institute of Politics, but it also expressed a continuing faith in the idea of usable knowledge. It was not the expression of some recent academic affectation about the relevance of theory for practice, but a vision deeply rooted in the history of American social and political science as well as the very idea of the American university.

NOTES

1. Richard Neustadt, *Presidential Power: The Politics of Leadership* (New York: Wiley, 1960), p. vii.

2. John Dewey, *Liberalism and Social Action* (New York: Putnam, 1935).

3. See Ronald D. Rotunda, *The Politics of Language: Liberalism as a Word and Symbol* (Iowa City: University of Iowa Press, 1986).

4. John Dewey, *The Public and Its Problems* (Denver: Swallow Press, 1954).

5. David Easton, *The Political System* (New York: Knopf, 1953).

6. David Truman, *The Governmental Process* (New York: Knopf, 1951).

7. See John G. Gunnell, "The Genealogy of American Pluralism: From Madison to Behavioralism," *International Political Science Review* 17 (1996).

8. Daniel Boorstin, *The Genius of American Politics* (Chicago: University of Chicago Press, 1953); Louis Hartz, *The Liberal Tradition in America* (New York: Harcourt, Brace, 1955).

9. Truman, *The Governmental Process*, pp. 395–398.

10. Ibid., pp. 399, 403, 422.

11. See, for example, William T. Bluhm, *Theories of the Political System* (Englewood Cliffs, N.J.: Prentice-Hall, 1971).

12. Neustadt, *Presidential Power*, p. viii.

13. Robert A. Dahl, *Who Governs?* (New Haven: Yale University Press, 1961).

14. C. W. Mills, *The Power Elite* (New York: Oxford University Press, 1956).

15. Angus Campbell, Philip E. Converse, Warren E. Miller, and Donald E. Stokes, *The American Voter* (New York: Wiley, 960, pp. 5, 7).

16. Robert A. Dahl, *Congress and Foreign Policy* (New York: Harcourt, Brace, 1950).

17. Robert A. Dahl and Charles E. Lindblom, *Politics, Economics, and Welfare* (New York: Harper, 1953).

18. Richard Berelson, Paul Lazarsfeld, and William McPhee, *Voting* (Chicago: University of Chicago Press, 1954), pp. 313, 323. See also Morris Janowitz and Dwaine Marvick, *Competitive Pressure and Democratic Consent* (Ann Arbor: Bureau of Government, Institute of Public Administration, University of Michigan, 1956).

19. See, for example, Floyd Hunter, *Community Power Structure: A Study of Decision-Makers* (Chapel Hill: University of North Carolina Press, 1953); Robert A. Dahl, "A Critique of the Ruling Elite Model," *American Political Science Review* 52 (1958); Nelson W. Polsby, *Community Power and Political Theory* (New Haven: Yale University Press, 1963).

20. Robert Dahl, *Preface to Democratic Theory* (Chicago: University of Chicago Press, 1956), p. 132.

21. Ibid., pp. 141, 144–145.

22. E. E. Schattschneider, *The Semisovereign People: A Realist View of Democracy in America* (Hinsdale, IL: Dryden Press, 1960), p. 138.

23. Ibid., p. 14.

24. Neustadt, *Presidential Power*, p. 185.

25. Grant McConnell, *Private Power and American Democracy* (New York: Knopf, 1967).

26. For an extended discussion of the historical relationship between American Political Science and politics, see John G. Gunnell, *The Descent of Political Theory: The Genealogy of An American Vocation* (Chicago: University of Chicago Press, 1993).

27. Robert Dahl in Michael Baer, Malcolm Jewell, and Lee Sigelman, eds., *Polit-*

ical Science in America: Oral Histories of a Discipline (Lexington: University of Kentucky Press, 1991). See also David Easton's oral history in this volume.

28. His grandfather was a Czech journalist and émigré, his father was a social security official and adviser to both Woodrow Wilson and Franklin Roosevelt, and his mother was a social worker. See *Current Biography* 1968, pp. 281–284.

29. Harold Lasswell and Abraham Kaplan, *Power and Society* (New Haven: Yale University Press, 1950).

30. David Easton, "The Decline of Political Theory," *Journal of Politics* 13 (1951). For a discussion of the relationship between the idea of an empirical science of politics and the practical concerns of political scientists, see John G. Gunnell, "Paradoxos Theoretikos," in Kristen Monroe, ed., *Contemporary Empirical Theory* (Berkeley: University of California Press, 1997).

31. Robert A. Dahl, "The Behavioral Revolution in Political Science: An Epitaph for a Monument to a Successful Protest," *American Political Science Review* 55 (1961).

32. David Easton, "The New Revolution in Political Science," *American Political Science Review* 63 (1969).

33. Stanley Fish, *Professional Correctness: Literary Studies and Political Change* (Oxford: Oxford University Press, 1995).

34. Richard E. Neustadt and Ernest May, *Thinking in Time: The Uses of History for Decision-Makers* (New York: Free Press,1986).

35. Ibid., pp. xi, xv.

PART 2

Presidents as Persuaders and the Personalization of Power

CHAPTER 4

Personal Power and Presidents

Lyn Ragsdale

Personal power in politics involves an individual's ability to influence other politicians to achieve a political outcome. Behind this relatively straightforward definition is fundamentally how people who work in Washington view Washington politics—it is a matter of personal action, personalities, and personal successes and failures. It involves people's assessments of each other as political players: who can get what done; who knows whom; and who they like and dislike. Personal power is also a matter of details. People in Washington relish the behind-the-scenes maneuvers that produce the often neat public pronouncements. People speculate over lunch about the personal, not policy, implications of decisions: Was it really the staff's call? Has someone won a major internal battle? Is one person angry at another? Personal power also moves on a quick time line. It is often measured hour by hour—who did what this morning sets up what others respond to in the afternoon. Politicians *know* that this is how politics works.

Neustadt's *Presidential Power* brought this approach to the study of the presidency: "The essence of a president's persuasive task is to convince [others] that what the White House wants of them is what they ought to do for their own sake and on their authority."[1] While many people have touted Neustadt for pioneering the personal perspective on politics, the perspective has been around as long as political decisions have been made. In 1960, Neustadt awoke presidential scholars to what now seems like an obvious way to study the office. His book shifted political scientists' attention away from an earlier constitutional approach with its concentration on presidents' legal precedents and judicial interpretations to a perspective centered on presidents' personal actions and power relations. In the first edition, he offered the account principally for Presidents Franklin Roosevelt, Harry Truman, and Dwight Eisenhower. With its most recent revision in 1990, the book continued to draw political scientists' attention to the personal decisions presidents make in their public policy choices with presidents through Ronald Reagan. This chapter examines Neustadt's application of the personal power approach to the presidency. It considers its advantages and disadvantages, both for presidents in the office and political scientists studying the office. In then introduces the analyses by Charles Cameron, Renee Smith, and Thomas Preston in their treatment of personal power.

Before *Presidential Power*

In 1960, Neustadt challenged the existing constitutional school of the presidency which focused on the legal-institutional significance of the office. According to that approach, the study of the presidency was not about personal power, but about constitutional power. It was less about politics than about law and history. Edward Corwin's leading text in the 1940s and 1950s focused on various conceptions of executive power and how presidents expanded specific constitutional powers: "The history of the presidency is a history of aggrandizement, but the story is a highly discontinuous one. Of the thirty-three individuals who have filled the office [as of 1957] not more than one in three has contributed to the development of its powers . . . But the accumulated tradition of the office is also of vast importance. Precedents established by a forceful or politically successful personality in the office are available to less gifted successors and permanently so because of the difficulty with which the Constitution is amended."[2]

Another leading scholar of the day, Clinton Rossiter, spoke of the multiple roles of presidents including chief of state, chief legislator, chief diplomat, chief executive, and commander in chief, most of which were derived from the enumeration of executive powers found in Article II of the Constitution. In addition, both Corwin and Rossiter wrote about the institution of the presidency. Rossiter observed that "The most notable development in the presidency in recent years is a change in the structure rather than a growth in power, although the latter is certainly the first cause of the change."[3] To be sure, the constitutional school did recognize the importance of individual presidents and their decisions: Corwin wrote that "what the presidency is at any particular moment depends in important measure on who is president"[4] But their primary emphasis and interest was not about the person but the Constitution.

The first several pages of *Presidential Power* sharply distinguished Neustadt's work from that of the earlier scholars: "My theme is personal power and its politics: what it is, how to get it, how to keep it, how to use it. . . . The search for personal influence is at the center of the job of being president" and "Presidential' means nothing but the president. Power means *his* influence."[5] Neustadt dismissed as too narrow a discussion of constitutional powers alone and insisted that institutional structures of the White House were of limited interest unless they were tied to a president's personal power gains and losses.

Aspects of Personal Power

What did Neustadt tell readers about the personal power of presidents? First, presidents' personal power is imperfect. The power is based on bargaining among politicians and although the president may have the upper hand in some games because of the stature of the office and his own acumen, there is no assurance that the president will win the games. Second, the power is quite personal. It does not transfer from one president to the next; nor can a close aide spend or acquire it on behalf of the president. Third, Neustadt's discussion offers a thoroughgoing descriptive account of individual presidents' decision-making. This provides a methodology for studying the presidency: the best way to study the office is to study its occupant and the best way to study the occupant is to rely on a series of case studies examining the president's use of personal power. These case studies revolve around the types of details Washington considers important—who does what to whom. There is a decided insider quality to Neustadt's accounts of various presidential decisions which underscores how the White House works and how Washington works. According to the personal power approach, it is necessary to know these insider details. Finally, the stories have a powerful prescriptive element coaching presidents about how, in practice, they should use power effectively.

One of Neustadt's examples helps clarify these four elements of personal power. Early in January 1957, President Dwight Eisenhower met with his cabinet to review the final fiscal year 1958 budget soon to be sent to Capitol Hill. The budget reflected a nod to "modern Republicanism," a message invoked during Eisenhower's reelection campaign. The $72 billion budget called for ample funding of key domestic programs including school construction and moderate increases in defense and foreign aid. With these priorities, no tax relief was in sight. Secretary of the Treasury George Humphrey interrupted the otherwise sedate gathering with concerns about the tax implications of the budget and suggested that he should issue a statement outlining those concerns with the release of the budget. Eisenhower and others felt a press conference rather than a written statement would be more appropriate. So on January 16, 1957, as Eisenhower's budget was unveiled to Congress, Humphrey made his prepared statement to the press which called for restraint by Congress to bring the budget total below the $72 billion mark. Then, in off-the-cuff remarks to reporters, he lamented the "terrific tax burden" and size of the federal budget and said, "I will predict that you will have a depression that will curl your hair." He also urged that "there are a lot of places in this budget that can be cut."

Humphrey's abrupt candor caused a firestorm in Washington over what the president's budget meant and whose signals to believe. While Humphrey himself acknowledged privately to Director of the Bureau of the Budget, Percival Brundage, that "I may have gone a bit overboard," Eisenhower held his own press conference the following week embracing Humphrey's efforts to cut the total budget estimates, but attempting to allay fears of any looming economic collapse. In the weeks that followed, congressional offices were deluged with letters from constituents who demanded budget cuts. The Bureau of the Budget directly requested cuts from agencies and departments. And Eisenhower continued to equivocate. He announced $1.3 billion in cuts from his own budget, but stated firmly that no further cuts could be made except at the "expense of the national safety and interest."[6]

This classic instance of personal politics and power in Washington vividly demonstrates the first aspect of personal power—its imperfections and limits. Even after an entire term in office, Eisenhower was nonetheless blind sided by

Humphrey's off-the-cuff remarks. As Neustadt wrote, "Nothing in the Constitution keeps a well-placed aide from converting status into power of his own, usable in some degree even against the president . . . The probabilities of power do not derive from the literary theory of the Constitution."[7] Second, the per-

sonal quality of power is evident as Humphrey's "curl your hair remark" gave him a distinct advantage over Eisenhower and others in the administration on budget politics. Third, Neustadt delved into this case study in considerable detail. The insider tale illuminates how the secretary of the treasury could move the president's position on the budget. This particular case is important for its lack of importance. While other cases that Neustadt studied—the Iran-Contra crisis, the Bay of Pigs, and Watergate— had lasting implications for the office, the ins and outs of the Humphrey press conference have been long since lost in the history of the presidency. So the case studies are important in underscoring the immediacy of presidential power and the importance of single moments in Washington politics. Finally, Neustadt attempted to tell Eisenhower and other presidents not to fall prey to a earnest adviser interested in promoting a public debate on policy decisions that were already technically made. Each of these aspects of personal power can be examined in greater detail.

POWER AS BARGAINING

While Neustadt's central thesis was that presidential power is a matter of political influence not constitutional language, he maintained that presidents' constitutional powers offer them advantages or vantage points from which they can attempt to persuade others. Moreover, the status and authority of the office, drawn partly from the Constitution, but also from the rituals of the nation, provided presidents with unique bargaining advantages that others in and out of the government cannot match.[8] What Neustadt called the presidential clerkship offered presidents additional advantages. The clerkship literally puts presidents "at the service" of the rest of the government—initiating most if not all of the policy and administrative efforts of the government. According to Neustadt, "Everybody now expects the man inside the White House to do something about everything . . . It merely signifies that other men have found it practically impossible to do their jobs without assurance of initiatives from him."[9]

However, the constitutional vantage points, the status of the office, and the clerkship carry presidents only so far. Neustadt concluded that beyond these bargaining advantages inherent in the office, presidents had two other key sources of influence: professional reputation, which involved the "expectations of those other men [sic] regarding his ability and will to use the various advantages they think he has" and public prestige which amounted to "those men's estimates of how his public views him and how their publics may view them if they do what he wants"[10] Together these three factors—advantages inherent in the office, professional reputation, and public prestige captured presidents' effective influence.

But others in Washington also have influence. By its very nature *political* influence involves reciprocal bargaining and mutual dependence between two or more politicians, regardless of whether one is the president. Ultimately, "the power to persuade is the power to bargain."[11] This is the give-and-take of real power rather than the formal design of constitutional power. Thus, presidents' political influence is never absolute, but always imperfect, limited by the influence of others. The presidential clerkship required Eisenhower to present a budget to the Congress. While the Congress was not likely to take the president's budget as the final word, the clerkship mandated that he offer it at least as the first word. While Eisenhower could have used this to his advantage to pave the way for modern Republicanism, instead Humphrey carried the day in the interest of budget cuts.

Personal Power

In the phrase "personal political influence" the word "personal" is just as pivotal as "political" for Neustadt in understanding the nature of bargaining. Influence for Neustadt is truly a matter of individual action. The president who has many aides and can delegate many decisions still retains his own personal influence. "We deal here with the president himself and with his influence on governmental action," Neustadt wrote. "In institutional terms the presidency now includes 2000 men and women. The president is only one of them. But *his* performance scarcely can be measured without focusing on *him*."[12]

For Neustadt the key question about personal influence was how a president "sees personal stakes in his own acts of choice."[13] If presidents fail to take into account their own personal interests they likely make choices that do not further their influence. The president's ability to see these stakes comes from human qualities: "a sense of purpose, a feel for power, and a source of confidence . . . The first two were conditioned by the third and that self-confidence was fashioned from experience and temperament."[14] Neustadt did not discuss personalities per se or dissect them into various types, but he evaluated an array of personal qualities including positive qualities drawn heavily from Franklin Roosevelt—self-confidence, drive, sociability, curiosity , mastery, sensitivity—and, in the later editions, a growing list of negative qualities—self-indulgence, compulsiveness, and insecurity—drawn from the personal failings of Johnson and Nixon which Neustadt saw as critical to the failings of their presidencies. Ultimately the principal generalization Neustadt offered about personal power is that each president approaches the office differently and some have personal qualities that allow them to be more successful than others.

Who Does What to Whom

Washington sees itself as a town run by behind-the-scenes steps and missteps and moment-to-moment politics. People who work in Washington are all but obsessed with knowing the sequence of events, personalities, and personal decisions behind a public choice. Neustadt represented this perspective well. It is difficult to underestimate the importance of portraying accurately the way Washington sees itself and coming to grips with why Washington sees these details as important and not simply a chronology of events. This not only makes for good reading but it also provides insights into how advisers, cabinet members, generals, members of Congress, and heads of state interact with presidents and how these other players may indeed get the upper hand. This approach captures Washington's view of itself, while it offers political scientists a methodology for studying the presidency. It suggests that understanding the details of a decision makes the difference. Without thorough knowledge of the details it is difficult to determine how the president's personal power unfolds or how this adds to the texture of the presidency.

PRESCRIPTIONS OF POWER

Amidst the descriptions of Washington of the 1950s through the 1980s, Neustadt offered a series of helpful comments to presidents about how to avoid the pitfall of personal bargaining. It this sense, the book is a primer for presidents to learn on the job. In many ways, as Neustadt himself asserts in a later chapter in this volume, the main audience of the book is not political scientists, but presidents and their advisers, many of whom come into Washington knowing little of the ways of the town. Many of the stories told are "dramatic incidents that were judged failures" in order to alert presidents that this could happen to them.[15] The prescriptions are based on a single metric of Franklin Roosevelt's actions in office. Neustadt believed that Roosevelt was the most careful user of personal power: "No president in this century has had a sharper sense of personal power, a sense of what it is and where it comes from; none has had more hunger for it, few have had more use for it, and only one or two could match his faith in his own competence to use it."[16] Since Neustadt's primary interest was what individual presidents do in office, the measure by which they are evaluated can only be another president.

FLAWS IN PRESIDENTIAL POWER

In each of these four respects, *Presidential Power* seems intuitively appealing. It is difficult to argue with the notion that politicians in Washington, including the president, bargain with one another to get what they want and that they do so ultimately as individuals unable to hide behind their staffs or to delegate the work to committees or commissions. It also makes sense that presidents are fallible figures. They make mistakes and the mistakes illuminate how problems can be avoided in the future. Neustadt's attention to case studies of presidents' actual personal influence rather than the constitutional and legal precedents they may have set provides empirical insights about Washington in the way people in Washington see the politics of the nation's capitol. Yet, there are two central problems with Neustadt's work and with its emphasis on personal power. First, Neustadt does not directly confront the presidency as an institution within which presidents work. Second, Neustadt's attention to detail provides limited ability to offer testable propositions across presidents.

Institutional Context

Neustadt does not fully consider the institutional context within which personal power operates. Later chapters in this volume build further on the role of institutions. To begin, the presidential institution involves a set of regular patterns of behavior and established structures that exist from one president to the next. These patterns and structures provide the boundaries within which individual presidents can craft deals and marshal their sense of personal power. As such, the boundaries promote similarities among presidents in the way they can behave and do behave. Neustadt's interest in the details of the inside story and the personal nature of power means that many of these similarities are missed. By their very nature, the inside stories are unique: no two episodes unfold in exactly the same way even for the same president. By its very nature, personal power varies from one president to the next. Yet in considering presidents within an institutional context many of the idiosyncrasies of individual presidents become less relevant. For instance, a good display of this similarity is the way in which presidents from Truman through Reagan held very similar foreign policy ideologies. While the names they used to distinguish one from the other were surely different, from Truman's talk of containment to Reagan's fury over the "evil empire," the essence of their decisions was the same: protect the world from communism. Institutional standards of policy choice—what was in the best interest of the country and the presidency—constrained presidents' personal influence on the choices they made.

The institution of the modern presidency has three features that figure heavily in how presidents can behave as individual players in office: the organization of the office, a mediated intimacy between the president and the public, and the symbolism of the office. These features have changed the office during the twentieth century shaping patterns that directly influence individual presidents' ability to exercise personal influence.

Presidential Organization. Neustadt came closest to considering the presidential organization when he discussed the presidential clerkship. Since presidents are suppose to initiate all things for all people, it follows that a large organization would be necessary to aid in this endeavor. He noted that the organization gave the president "a sporting chance to do the chores of office" but warned that this "will not automatically turn doing into influence. Helping a president perform his chores is a far cry from helping see personal stakes in his own acts of choice."[17] As noted above, his primary interest was to "treat the presidency as the president."[18] In part, this is a matter of scholarly attack. Neustadt made the bold statement about the presidency as president in order to show how different his approach is from those of Corwin and Rossiter in the constitutional school. But it is also more than Neustadt defining his disagreement with the earlier writers; he firmly believed that the keys to the presidency are individual presidents, their talents, and their choices. Because Neustadt focused so heavily on the personal side of personal influence, he neglected the way in which the office itself shapes this influence and makes it less personal and more institutional. What if the organization fundamentally shifts presidents' personal stakes and acts of choice?

Neustadt would likely suggest that the presidential organization is simply a vantage point or bargaining chip for presidents to use as they see fit. Presumably he would argue further that some presidents, like Franklin Roosevelt, ran it well and others, like Ronald Reagan, let it run them. But viewed as part of the presidential institution, the organization is no such vantage point. Instead, its size and shape—during the Clinton administration 1,600 people, 12 units, and a $217 million budget—fundamentally limit the amount of personal power that presidents have and provides a particular kind of personal power for them to use. This personal power is divorced from many of the decisions of the organization that go out under the president's name. It suggests that presidents have less ability to wield purely personal power now than they did earlier in the century. This is at least one reason why the Franklin Roosevelt metric adopted by Neustadt becomes so difficult for any other president to measure up to. Roosevelt served at a time when the presidential institution was emerging, particularly in budgeting, but it was not the leviathan that it later became. So it is not so much that presidents like Eisenhower, Johnson, and Nixon did not have the same hunger for personal power that Roosevelt had, but that personal power was a smaller commodity for the later presidents. Eisenhower's encounter with Humphrey indicates as much. Institutional players on the bud-

secretary of the treasury and the director of the Bureau of the Budget Office of Management and Budget)—had considerable clout regardless of who was president.

MEDIATED INTIMACY AND SYMBOLISM

American presidents' connections to the public is one of the most intricate aspects of the modern presidential institution. Neustadt studied this connection as public prestige. In the early edition of the book, he considered presidents' standing with the public, or their popularity, as an indirect source of influence filtered through other politicians' assessments of that popularity. He viewed the public's opinions of presidents as the brakes and accelerators for politicians' own judgments of the president, which he deemed professional reputation. While in the early edition Neustadt saw public prestige and professional reputation as distinctly different and out of step with one another, in the later editions he concluded that they had moved together and were more in sync. However, during Clinton's second term, Neustadt might well have reverted to his first stance—given Clinton's solid public approval ratings as numerous members of Congress called for resignation or impeachment over personal and public matters under investigation by a special prosecutor and grand jury (see Richard Pious's analysis of Clinton's impeachment and Senate trial in chapter 21).

But whether professional reputation and public prestige represent distinct or overlapping views of presidents misses a larger issue of public opinion as an independent source of influence for presidents that are *not* filtered through the judgments of members of the Washington community. The frequency and accuracy of polls in modern American politics permit them to serve as relatively indisputable political facts in Washington, a place where facts are always disputed. Public opinion is an independent source of influence not only because of the veracity of poll data but more fundamentally because it rests on two institutional foundations of mediated intimacy and symbolism which themselves further shape presidents' personal influence.

The first dimension of this public connection is what Murray Edelman termed "mediated intimacy."[19] Citizens feel they know presidents because, first, radio and, then, television news brought presidents live into people's living rooms. It is not just that presidents are typically the lead story on the news every night. It is not just that the president can appear live before a national audience to alert them to an impending crisis or lobby for their policy initiatives. The media story is also a personal story about presidents' private lives and their daily activities. This story has expanded and the mediated intimacy thereby grown in part because the White House has seen a distinct advantage in humanizing presidents. Images of Harry Truman taking his morning walk, Gerald Ford making his own breakfast, George Bush playing with celebrity dog Millie all create the impressions that people know the president as a person. The personal story has also expanded because the media find it a good one worth going after in considerable detail. Americans found out more about Bill Clinton's personal life, as he ran for office and as legal investigations unfolded, than they professed they wanted to know (see Martha Kumar's further analysis of presidents and the mass media in Chapter 18).

The second dimension, closely intertwined with the first, is the symbolism of the office. No matter what they may think of a given incumbent, Americans have particular views of the presidency as a symbol of the nation. This symbolism emerges in the first instance because the president is the only official elected by the entire nation. Thus, the office is the people's office. An emotional rather than in any way rational or practical understanding of the office and its occupant prevails. This reinforces and is reinforced by the intimacy of president-watching on television. It is drawn further from presidential campaigns in which candidates vie to be the one person to best solve the biggest problems of the country. It also rests on cultural assumptions in American politics about individualism, the importance of political heroes, and presidents as the nation's voice to the world. What these two dimensions do is make presidents' public prestige an independent factor in presidents' personal influence *for all presidents*. They are institutional features that all presidents must deal with; they are not optional bargaining advantages that presidents may or may not use depending on how they see their fortunes. Thus, personal power is confined within this institutional pattern of public and the central elements of personal power—options, strategies, and choices—are defined accordingly.

LOOKING AT THE DETAILS

Neustadt's interest in the details of personal power means that the degree to which he can generalize and theorize patterns across presidents is restricted. Many have complemented Neustadt for how well his theoretical argument has held up. What is missed is that the argument is an intuitive message of practical politics that is based on how politicians view politics. It is not theoretical in offering testable hypotheses about how presidents behave under certain circumstances and which factors that behavior. The intuitive message involves a series of generalizations of two types: those that cannot be disputed, but also

cannot be tested, and those that are testable, but are not actually tested. Among
the first type of nonfalsifiable generalizations, Neustadt writes:

> "The same conditions that promote his leadership in form preclude a guar-
> antee of leadership in fact"; "Powers are not guarantee of power; clerkship is
> no guarantee of leadership"; "In political government, the means can matter
> quite as much as ends; they often matter more"; "Bargaining advantages con-
> vey no guarantees. Influence remains a two-way street"; "His power is pro-
> tected by his choices"; "What other men expect of him becomes a cardinal
> factor in the president's own power to persuade"; "A president's decisive role
> in reputation-building is a source of opportunity as well as risk"; "Leeway
> guarantees one thing: avoidance of the trouble that can follow from its
> absence"; "To ask how he can guard his power stakes in acts of choice is thus
> to ask how clearly he perceives"; "A sensitivity to power's stakes and sources
> is not cure-all"; "Government power, in reality not form, is influence of an
> effective sort on the behavior of men actually involved in making public pol-
> icy and carrying it out."[20]

While these statements all make sense, they can do little to expand knowledge of the presidency and relations between presidents and other advisers,
because there is little way to test them. Neustadt does offer potentially testable
generalizations:

> "Everybody now expects the man inside the White House to do something
> about everything"; "The more an officeholder's status and his 'powers' stem
> from sources independent of the president, the stronger will be his potential
> pressure on the president";
>   "The professional reputation of a president in Washington is made or
> altered by the man himself"; "When men make judgments in the Washing-
> ton community they are no less concerned with what he is liked for, than
> with how many like him"; "Professional reputation is not popularity. Guard-
> ing one, therefore, is not equivalent to guarding the other"; "He can expect
> attention from them [the public] only when the things he need interpret to
> his benefit are on their minds for reasons independent of his telling"; "He
> teaches less by telling than by doing"; " Perhaps the quality of experience
> counts more than the quantity."[21]

While these are potentially testable, there have been few attempts by other
scholars to do so. In many ways, these generalizations stand much like the

other ones above. Students of the presidency have taken the statements as givens, and the field has had difficulty moving beyond them and asking other questions.

In addition, Neustadt's concentration on case studies of dramatic episodes of failure biases the understanding of the office and possible propositions that could be tested toward *politics as unusual* and away from the myriad of decisions that occur in which politics and presidential power is quite usual. Stories of presidential extremes are easy to pin on presidents' personal qualities and their vividly missed efforts to marshal their power choices. It is easy to suggest that the problems Bill Clinton faced with regard to his sexual relationship with a one-time White House intern Monica Lewinsky was the result of the president's own power failings based on personal qualities of self-indulgence and arrogance. But can the same be said for Clinton's efforts on budget balancing, welfare reform, gun control, the environment, terrorism, and relations with Russia? The concentration on spectacular negative episodes distorts the office and offers a lens that does not adequately look for patterns but instead looks for failures pinned on the idiosyncrasies of the participants. Neustadt's attention to the personal qualities of presidents and reliance on case studies makes it difficult to draw testable propositions about the office from the study of its individual occupants. Ultimately most presidential power may not be so fully personal. Instead, presidents' personal influence may take place within institutional mechanisms of the office that presidents reinvent or imitate in their own administrations.

New Approaches to Presidential Influence

The three chapters that comprise this section of the book ask questions Neustadt asked but in new ways. They also develop and elaborate theories of personal power that are examined empirically. In "Bargaining and Presidential Power," Charles Cameron writes about how presidential power is not the attribute of an individual but concerns of the outcome of a strategic interaction or "game." He is especially interested in how presidents interact with Congress in what can be characterized as "coordination games" and "bargaining games." Bargaining games, in particular, are central to the presidency in an era of divided party government.

Cameron illustrates the importance of bargaining games in this context by describing the nexus between a clearly formal presidential power—the veto—and the use of presidential reputation—how politicians perceive the president.

According to Neustadt, a president's professional reputation rests on how others perceive his past actions and, in turn, how they use these perceptions to predict future behavior. Neustadt maintains, but does not offer a direct test, that the president's reputation directly affects his ability to bargain in specific settings and under certain circumstances. The specific circumstance that interests Cameron is veto bargaining—the give and take between the president and Congress in efforts to fashion laws. The president uses the veto or the threat of a veto to attempt to get the legislation that he really wants from Congress. Cameron outlines three different types of veto bargaining: *sequential veto bargaining* in which Congress repeatedly passes a bill and the president repeatedly vetoes it; *veto threats* in which the president threatens a veto in order to extract certain modifications of the bill and may actually veto the bill if concessions from Congress are not forthcoming; and *blame game vetoes* in which Congress seeks to provoke a veto in order to damage the president's political prospects on other matters, including elections.

Reputation plays a role in these vetoes, according to Cameron, because the Congress writes a bill estimating what the president will accept. If the president threatens a veto or carries one out, the Congress must reconsider its impression of the president (his reputation). In turn, this leads to a reconsideration of the bill itself and Congress often (although not always) makes concessions. Cameron reviews the empirical evidence on the three types of veto bargains as well as formal mathematical models that have been developed for them. Thus, Cameron takes seriously Neustadt's notion of reputation and offers direct empirical measures of it in the veto process. While other scholars have examined reputation, they have done so by using imputed indicators of reputation—most often the number of times the Congress supports the president's position on legislation.[22]

Renee Smith writes about "The Timing of Presidential Speeches" in which she examines Neustadt's discussion of presidents as teachers of the public. While Cameron concentrates on Neustadt's concept of professional reputation, Smith turns her attention to his concept of public prestige. Smith targets the perceived costs and benefits of a presidential address to the president in acting as a public teacher and influencing public outcomes. Smith examines the effects of the president's approval ratings, as a measure of public prestige, along with economic conditions, war, and foreign and domestic political events on presidents' decisions to make major discretionary speeches to the nation. Surprisingly, and contrary to other research, Smith finds no effect of public approval on presidents' public speeches. It is difficult to know what to make of this. Neustadt's teacher analogy permits considerable loss in translation from the teacher to the students. In other words, the president's words might have little impact on public prestige, because the public pays little attention. But it is more difficult to understand why the public would not influence the presidents' own actions and ability to bargain. Smith suggests that differences between foreign and domestic policy environments provide some of the answers.

Thomas Preston's chapter "The President's Inner Circle: Leadership Style and the Advisory Process in Foreign Policy Decisionmaking" takes up Neustadt's interest in personalities and personal qualities. Like Neustadt, Preston maintains that their personal qualities lie at the center of presidents' personal influence. This is true of all leaders, not just presidents. Preston adopts a systematic comparative case study approach to capture the differences across presidents. Preston examines three dimensions to the personal qualities of presidents that are especially telling for personal influence: the need for power as a personality characteristic, the cognitive complexity of the individual, and the prior policy experience and expertise of the individual. Preston then devises a typology of presidential personal styles which are contingent on the relationships among the presidents' individual characteristics, their leadership styles, and their attentiveness to the external policy environment. Thus, presidents cannot be fit into neat boxes but instead the influence of their personality is contingent not only on the circumstance at hand but also the policy involved—foreign policy or domestic policy. This contingency approach moves beyond Neustadt because it explicitly recognizes the circumstances under which personal qualities matter and how they matter. It also offers a systematic treatment of these qualities across a number of presidents from Truman to Clinton (excluding Ford).

CONCLUSION

Professional reputation, public prestige, personal characteristics all affect the president's ability to personally persuade others. The three analyses that follow indicate the extent to which Neustadt's view of the presidency still stands. *Presidential Power* remains unquestionably the most influential book on the American presidency. But these new analyses also indicate the ways in which the view can be updated and made to better fit the institutional context within which individual presidents must operate.

NOTES

1. Richard Neustadt, *Presidential Power* (New York: John Wiley, 1960), p. 34.

2. Edward Corwin, *The President and Powers* (New York: New York University Press, 1957), pp. 29–30.

3. Clinton Rossiter, *The American Presidency, revised edition* (New York: Mentor Books, 1960), p. 121; see also Corwin, *The Symbolic Use of Politics*, 299–305.

4. Corwin, *The President and Powers*, p. 30.

5. Neustadt, *Presidential Power*, pp. vii-viii and 2.

6. Ibid., pp. 64–76, 108–123.

7. Ibid., pp. 42–43).

8. Ibid., p. 34.

9. Ibid., p. 6.

10. Ibid., p. 179.

11. Ibid., p. 36.

12. Ibid., p. 1.

13. Ibid., p.152.

14. Ibid., p. 203.

15. Ibid., p. ix.

16. Ibid., p.161.

17. Ibid., p.152.

18. Ibid., p. 2.

19. Murray Edelman, *The Symbolic Use of Politics* (Urbana, Illinois: University of Illinois Press, 1967), p. 33.

20. Neustadt, *Presidential Power*, pp. 7, 10, 47, 55–56, 60, 81, 90, 122, 150, 179.

21. Ibid., pp. 6, 42, 80, 87, 93, 100, 205.

22. Jon Bond and Richard Fleisher, *The President in the Legislative Arena* (Chicago: University of Chicago Press, 1990), and George Edwards, *At the Margins: Presidential Leadership of Congress* (New Haven: Yale University Press, 1989).

CHAPTER 5

Bargaining and Presidential Power

Charles M. Cameron

"Presidential power" is a deceptive phrase. It suggests that the capacity to shape policy is an attribute of the *president*, and a single attribute at that. But power is not an attribute of an individual, like her height or weight. Instead, "power" describes something about the outcome of a strategic interaction (a "game"). In particular, a president has power in a game when its outcome resembles what the president wants and he causes the outcome to be that way.[1]

This way of thinking about power shifts attention from the attributes of presidents to the characteristics of the games they play. Among these many games are the Supreme Court nominations game, the veto game, the executive order game, the treaty ratification game, the legislative leadership game, the agency supervision and management game, the commander-in-chief game, the staffing game, the executive reorganization game, the opinion leadership game, and the impeachment game. *Understanding the presidency means understanding these games.* I am tempted to add, "and that is all it means," but that would be too strong. Skill, personality, and charisma seem to matter, or so many people believe. But they always operate within the confines of specific games and strategic circumstances. Understanding the games presidents play is fundamental for understanding presidential power.

Presidents participate in so many games that it is hard to characterize them in a simple way. Broadly speaking, though, when presidents interact with Congress, they often play *coordination games* or *bargaining games*. Loosely speaking, coordination games require many players to act in one of several possible ways if they are to benefit themselves. If they do not all act in the same way, they work at cross-purposes. The politics of such games involve selecting the "focal points" coordinating the players' actions. A majority party setting its legislative agenda in Congress is a prime example of this situation, because many players—across committees in both houses and in the leadership—must focus on a few priorities if they are to accomplish much. Oft times, the selection of focal points involves loose norms and improvisation rather than formal procedures specified in law or the Constitution; this lies outside what Neustadt called the "literary theory of the Constitution," though hardly outside the reach of social science.

In contrast, bargaining games require players to divide among themselves a "pie," or set of benefits. The politics of bargaining involves gambits increasing one's share of the pie. Examples include haggling over the content of laws, pulling and hauling to determine the direction and vigor of agency decisions, and bickering over the appointment of executive officials and judges. These activities all involve give-and-take across the branches of government. Many bargaining games in which the president participates are quite formal, with a structure specified by the Constitution, by law, or by norms of long-standing precedent.[2]

In an era of divided party government, bargaining games become central to the presidency. The reason is twofold. First, coordination games require a convergence of interests among the players; otherwise, the players have little incentive to coordinate their actions. During divided government, the president's and Congress's interests are frequently too disparate for them to play coordination games. Second, the entrenchment of bargaining games in formal sources of authority allows the president to exploit them regardless of his opponents' wishes. However much Congress might want to disregard the president, it cannot—if his actions are grounded in an unassailable bargaining game. When it comes to the veto, for example, Congress has no escape clauses. At the end of the day, the veto pen awaits.

In this essay, I elaborate on these themes in several ways. In the first section, I explore the interaction of coordination games and bargaining games with unified and divided party government. The connection between bargaining games and divided party government is indeed a close one. In the second section, I review the empirical record on presidential bargaining games. I summarize findings from studies of appropriations, important legislation, bureaucratic activity, nominations, executive orders, and vetoes. I make a distinction between studies employing the "direct" method for studying presidential power and those employing an "indirect" method. The direct method relates the preferences of the president and other actors to the outcomes of bargaining games, such as the composition of the regulatory boards or the content of important laws. The indirect method examines indicators thrown up during the process of bargaining, such as the number of vetoes. Results from the direct method are often easy to interpret in terms of power relationships, though frequently these studies are hard to carry out because measuring governmental outputs is so difficult. In contrast, as I will shortly explain, interpreting process measures is deeply problematic absent explicit models of bargaining. Thus, the essence of the indirect method is to combine process measures, which are often easy to collect, with explicit models of bargaining. To give a flavor of the indirect method, I review some recent studies of the veto, including studies of veto threats, sequential veto bargaining, and blame game vetoes. Interestingly, explicit models of presidential bargaining games rehabilitate some concepts from *Presidential Power*, such as "reputation," which have largely fallen out of favor among contemporary students of the presidency. In the third section of the paper, I explore how the structure of bargaining games affects presidential power and helps to explain the variegated patterns in the empirical evidence. In the final section, I turn to a provocative topic: does the advent of the bargaining presidency mean an end to presidential greatness?

THE GAMES PRESIDENTS PLAY: COORDINATION VS. BARGAINING

Coordination games and bargaining games differ in important respects. In a coordination game, there are multiple equilibria (possible outcomes), for example, "drive on the left" or "drive on the right." In order to do well in the game, players must jointly focus on one of these equilibria and act accordingly. For instance, you don't want to be driving on the left when everyone else is driving on the right! Hence, the politics of coordination games turn on establishing common expectations—"focal points"—that coordinate the players' actions.[3] Conversely, in a bargaining game players struggle to divide a "pie." One should take an encompassing view of what constitutes the "pie" in political bargaining. It can include money or pork, but also the policy gains that may result from putting one person on a board rather than another. The structure of bargaining games often requires players to propose to one another splits of the pie. Sometimes only one player may propose the split, while the other can only accept or decline. Sometimes players alternate offers. Regardless of the exact structure of the game, the essential problem for players is to come to a speedy, efficient division of the pie, if there is one.

The different characteristics of coordination and bargaining games interact with the strategic context in which they occur to determine their importance to the presidency. A key variable is unified versus divided party government.

Coordination Games and Unified Party Government

During unified party government, the president's co-partisans control Congress. This does not mean that the president, his party's congressional leaders, and the rank and file in the majority party agree perfectly on common objectives. For much of the twentieth century, the Democrats' congressional party was ideologically heterogeneous in both the House and Senate, as was the Republicans' congressional party in the Senate.[4] Nonetheless, despite the dispersion of members around the parties' ideological cores, during unified party government the president and his co-partisans usually share broadly similar ideological objectives.[5] They are members of a team. This has been especially true in recent years, during which time congressional parties have moved toward ideological homogeneity.

Even when a single ideological team controls the presidency and both houses of Congress, governance is not simple. The team can direct its energies toward many different ends, all of them potentially worthy. But if the team's members do not focus their efforts on a few goals, they will accomplish little collectively. This is a consequence of the complex organization of Congress, which requires enormous effort from many different people within each chamber, extraordinary coordination across both chambers, and cooperation from the president.

In an environment like this, there is an opportunity for a special kind of leader, described by Kenneth Shepsle as follows: "Leaders are specific kinds of agents. They are relied upon by followers to coordinate their activities, to provide rewards and punishments for group objectives, to secure allies and defeat opponents, and generally to grease the skids for things the followers want."[6]

Leaders of this kind—*coordinative leaders*—establish focal points guiding what participants will do. These shared expectations are essential for effective, coordinated action. For instance, a president who leads a unified government will use his speeches to focus public expectations on specific policy innovations; if he is successful, he also establishes his congressional party's legislative priorities. Then, given this focal point inside and outside Congress, committee chairs in both chambers try to bring compatible proposals to the floor and to conference, to reap political credit from crafting and passing the legislation. Officials and experts from the executive branch may help them craft their proposals. Many case studies of lawmaking during unified government show this process at work.[7] As Shepsle's observation suggests, the leader may need to help matters along by allowing important actors to help select the focal points, by supplying useful information to participants, by punishing slackers and free riders, and by bribing holdouts with side payments, such as patronage or pork. There is no question that the process of selecting or creating focal points involves a deal of pulling and hauling, which scholars of the presidency often invoke by the phrase "bargaining." Nonetheless, the broad picture is one of coordinative leadership.[8]

Who will act as coordinative leader in the legislative leadership game? Because the Constitution fails to *confer* the role of governmental head on anyone, someone must *seize* that role if much is to happen. In modern times, the president has been in the best position to do that when government is unified. Most of the brilliant extraconstitutional improvisations of twentieth-century presidents—the "legislative program," the "executive budget," "going public" and the never-ending public relations circus, as well as the transformation of some constitutionally grounded activities, such as the State of the Union message—are vehicles by which the president can seize the role of intraparty (and thus interbranch) coordinator. Use of these devices is central to the "premier" model of the presidency forged by Theodore Roosevelt, Woodrow Wilson, and Franklin Roosevelt—all unified government presidents.[9]

What does a president look like when he is operating as a coordinative leader? We need look no further than Neustadt's *Presidential Power*. Neustadt's beau ideal, FDR, was the coordinative leader par excellence, at least in his first two terms. "Presidential power is the power to persuade" is the perfect motto for a coordinative leader working to establish focal points. Matthew Dickenson notes that prior to World War II, FDR spent three to four hours meeting with Congressional leaders *each day* during the legislative season.[10] Something similar was surely true of Lyndon Johnson during the legislative surge of the Great Society. This allocation of effort is a mark of a coordinative leader at work.

I have described one equilibrium of the legislative leadership game, a "president-dominant" equilibrium, where the president seizes the role of leader and his party chieftains in the House and Senate fall into line. But a second equilibrium is possible whereby a congressional leader (probably the Speaker of the House) seizes the lead. In the "Congress-dominant" equilibrium, the congressional leader establishes the focal points, the leadership in the other chamber tracks along, and the president must respond to their initiatives. We have not seen the Congress-dominant equilibrium during unified government since early in the twentieth century. But during divided party government, the president-dominant equilibrium is often unsustainable, at least much of the time.[11] The reason is the divergence in policy goals between the president and Congress. Given the divergence, the majority party in Congress will ignore the president's preferred focal points and establish its own, if it can. Thus, in 1994, when the Republicans gained control of Congress, Speaker Newt Gingrich used the "Contract with America" to create focal points inside and outside Congress that would coordinate action within the House and between the House and the Senate. Needless to say, Democratic presidential leadership of the rambunctious, conservative Republicans of 1994 was never an option. President Bill Clinton had to respond to congressional initiatives.

In a Congress-dominant equilibrium in the legislative leadership game, the president's extraconstitutional bag of tricks means little. His budget is "dead on arrival." His legislative program is a bootless prayer. His State of the Union message receives polite applause, but everyone knows its initiatives (if they are truly the president's) are bound for the waste basket rather than the statute books. Rather noticeably, the president does *not* spend four hours daily with the opposition party's congressional leaders, helping them maneuver their proposals through Congress. But the failure to establish a president-dominated equilibrium in the legislative leadership game during divided party government does not render the president powerless in other games—not by a long shot.[12]

Bargaining Games and Divided Party Government

Given a Congress-dominated equilibrium in the legislative leadership game, a divided party president will be driven back to constitutionally entrenched processes that Congress can neither alter nor ignore. Examples include the veto and appointment processes, in which the president is a potent actor whether Congress likes it or not. These processes partially determine the *content of legislation*, the *control of administrative agencies*, and the *composition of the courts*, all prizes worth fighting for.

Strikingly, many of these constitutionally entrenched processes are bargaining games. They involve a division of a policy "pie," with offers for dividing the pie coming from Congress and the president. Consider Supreme Court nominations. The president selects a nominee, in essence making Congress an offer about the composition of the Court. Congress may accept or reject the offer (the nominee) but cannot modify it; if it rejects, the president can make another offer (i.e., send up another nominee); and so on, until the vacancy is filled or the president leaves office.[13] Similarly, the veto game begins when Congress presents the president with a bill, in essence a policy offer. The president may accept or veto it, but cannot modify the bill. If he vetoes it and Congress fails to override, Congress may re-pass the bill in modified form, in essence making another offer. This process may continue until either the president accepts the offer, Congress overrides the veto, Congress desists from making further offers on that subject, or the president leaves office.

There are important bargaining games not grounded in the Constitution but nonetheless so well established that Congress cannot easily modify them and ignore the president, however much it wants to. In particular, the Administrative Procedures Act (APA) has a kind of quasi-constitutional status since it establishes ground rules for the federal bureaucracy's operations. Much of agency policymaking under the APA involves intensive interbranch bargaining.[14] This bargaining shapes the actions of bureaus and agencies during divided party government.

In short, when it comes to presidential bargaining games during divided government, Congress (like famed boxer Joe Louis's opponent) can run but it can't hide. It must deal with the president. Ultimately, Congress must present a bill, however cherished, to the president to sign or veto. Despite its fervent desire otherwise, Congress cannot choose a Supreme Court nominee. Only the president can do that. However much Congress would like to treat administrative agencies as appendages of its committees, it is unable to. They are part of the Executive Branch and the president will have his say about what they do.

THE IMPORTANCE OF BARGAINING GAMES FOR THE CONTEMPORARY PRESIDENCY

Neustadt had relatively little to say about specific bargaining games in *Presidential Power*, at least as I have defined bargaining games. The reason is not hard to find—he wrote near the end of a uniquely extended period of unified party government. Most of the divided party government with which he was familiar, during the Eisenhower Administration, was relatively nonconflictual (at least until after the 1958 election), because in those days the two congressional parties shared a great deal of common ground.[15] So one reading of *Pres-*

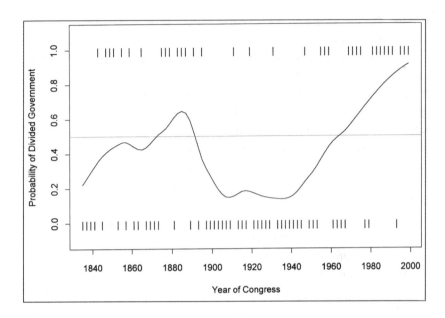

FIGURE 5.1.   Divided Government, 1835-2000

idential Power is that it is largely (though not exclusively) about rational presidential strategy in what I have called coordination games.

But things changed. To see how much, consider figure 5.1, showing the occurrence of divided party government from the 24th to 104th Congresses (1835 to 2000). In the figure, the hashmarks or "rug" at 0.0 indicate each Congress where unified government prevailed. The hash-marks at 1.0 show each Congress where divided party government occurred. The undulating line is the fit from a nonparametric, locally weighted regression model of the data.[16] Much the same effect would result from a running average of the 0–1 values but the local regression has superior statistical properties and is as easy to interpret. Given the scoring of the data, the line indicates the estimated probability that government will be divided at each point in time. For example, the model estimates as 50 percent the probability of divided government at the time of the 1871–72 Congress.

The data reveal three eras of unified and divided party control of the federal government since the emergence of the party system. First, there was a period stretching from the late 1840s to the election of 1896 in which the probability of divided government fluctuated around 50 percent or a little lower. (The dip just after 1860 results from the South's expulsion from Congress during and immediately after the Civil War.) This period was characterized by vigorous policy differences between the parties, first over slavery and civil rights, and later, as a rural agrarian nation struggled to transform itself into an urban, industrialized one, over labor laws, tariffs, and monetary policy.

The realigning election of 1896 ended the first era and ushered in the second—one of unified party government. Of course, the Republican Party held the government during most of the first part of this period, while the Democratic party dominated politics in the second half, following the New Deal realignment of 1932–36. Partisan and policy change was thus abundant during this period. What was rare was divided party government, whose probability the model estimates at less than 20 percent. In fact divided government occurred only three or perhaps four times, depending on how one dates the end of the era. The three clearcut cases are Taft and the Democratic House in 1911–12, Wilson and the Republican 66th Congress in 1919–20, and Hoover and the Democratic House in 1931–32. The remaining case is Truman and the Republican 80th Congress in 1947–48.

The regression model indicates that the great era of unified government drew to a close in the mid-1950s, shortly before Neustadt set pen to paper. By the early 1960s the probability of divided government passed the 50 percent mark. At this writing, April 1999, the probability of divided government is above 80 percent. The distribution of hashmarks at 1.0 strikingly shows that the latter part of the twentieth century constitutes the most concentrated such period since the 1880s and 1890s.

These data have profound implications for presidential politics. Perhaps the clearest is the greater importance of bargaining games for the contemporary presidency.

PRESIDENTIAL BARGAINING GAMES: WHAT DO WE KNOW?

Given the importance of bargaining games for the contemporary presidency, an obvious question is: What does the empirical record tell us about presidential bargaining games? This seems like it should be an easy question to answer, but unfortunately it is not. The problem is that data on the *process* of bargaining—the number of vetoes, of nominees rejected by Congress, the number of oversight hearings, the number of policy proposals in State of the Union messages, the number of bills introduced in Congress, the number of executive orders reversed by Congress, and so on—are relatively easy to collect but hard to interpret (I'll explain why shortly). Conversely, data on the *outputs* from bargaining games—for example, the number and content of important laws, executive orders, and treaties, the intensity and import of bureaucratic action, the ideological tenor and meaning of court decisions—are very hard to collect but much easier to interpret.

Why are process measures so much harder to interpret compared to output measures? The problem is that power in bargaining games often operates through *anticipation*. Congress anticipates a veto if it goes too far; in order to avoid the veto, it trims back a policy initiative. No veto occurs, but the president's preferences have altered what Congress would have done if could have operated without constraint. In other words, the game's structure allows the president to exercise power over the outcome, even absent a veto. As a second example, suppose the president anticipates a torrent of opposition if he nominates a controversial activist to head a regulatory agency. Accordingly, he eschews the controversial nominee in favor of a more moderate one, though he would prefer to put the activist in charge if he could do so without cost. The nomination then flies through Congress. In this case, the structure of the game allows Congress to exercise some power over the nominee's ideology even with no direct evidence of this in the public record.

Situations like this involve the "second face of power," power operating through anticipated response.[17] These situations are notoriously difficult to study using process measures since participants maneuver to avoid the most easily measured consequences of disagreement.

How can one find the traces of power when the second face of power is at work? There are two methods: the first direct, the second indirect. The direct method involves measuring policy outputs and relating them to the actors' preferences. If the president actually exercises power over the output, even without taking visible action, then a switch from a liberal president to a conservative one should result in a change in policy, *ceteris paribus*. If one collects data on policy outputs and proxies for preference changes (e.g., partisan affiliation of the president and key congressional actors), and the policy outputs change in a clear and simple way in response to changes in the preference proxies, then one has strong circumstantial evidence of power being exercised. Obviously, one needs to control for confounding influences, but the principle is clear enough.[18]

The indirect approach is more convoluted. It begins with process data, such as vetoes, rejected nominees, reversed executive orders, and blocked agency initiatives. The problem is interpreting such data. In order for events like vetoes to occur, there must be policy disagreement between the actors. But this is only a *necessary* condition. It is certainly not a *sufficient* condition, as arguments about the second face of power indicate. Instead, a process marker like a veto, a rejected nominee or treaty, or a reversed executive order, represents the impact of policy disagreement, *plus something else beyond mere disagreement.* Let us call this additional element "Factor X."[19] The essence of the indirect approach is to build an explicit model of bargaining *incorporating Factor X.* Using this model, one can interpret the process measures and even draw conclusions about presidential power. Absent such a model, all that can be concluded from process measures like counts of vetoes is that policy disagreement occurred—a very weak conclusion since policy disagreement may not trigger a veto without Factor X.[20]

In the next section, I review several studies employing the direct method to study presidential power, or that allow for interpretations of this kind. Then, I illustrate the indirect approach using recent studies of veto bargaining.

THE DIRECT APPROACH TO MEASURING PRESIDENTIAL BARGAINING POWER

Several recent studies attempt to measure policy outputs from presidential bargaining games. In almost all these studies, the measurement of the dependent variable—the output to be explained—is a critical issue because governmental outputs are so elusive. The strength of the conclusions depend critically on the validity of output measures but I will say little about this and other methodological issues. I group the studies by the policy-related dependent variable that they explain.

Appropriations

In a classic study, Kiewiet and McCubbins measure the impact the president has on appropriations.[21] The dependent variable is money actually appropriated by Congress to agencies, not money requested by the president. Kiewiet and McCubbins make inferences about where various presidents sought increases and cuts. Their statistical tests uncover an important maxim of veto bargaining, "you can't push on a string." Given a low "reversion point" (i.e., the default value for appropriations absent a new appropriations bill), presidents can use the veto to block large increases in small budget. Less frequently are they able to block cuts in large programs because this requires a high reversion point (e.g., a continuation at last year's appropriation). Only rarely can the veto force Congress to increase a small budget or cut a large budget more than it wants to. These require unusually favorable reversion points that are unlikely to arise. Taking into account the normal reversion points in the appropriations game, Kiewiet and McCubbins argue that that the veto gives the president strong power when he wants to cut budgets and much less power when he wants to increase them—you can't push on a string. Their statistical analysis of appropriations data supports their argument.

Enactment of Important Laws

One type of policy output is "important" laws. In an innovative study, David Mayhew devises two measures of "legislative importance," the first based on elite perceptions of the legislation at the time of its passage, the second based on retrospective judgments by policy experts.[22] Mayhew's statistical analysis suggests divided government does not decrease the production of important laws very much, if at all, a finding contradicting the conventional wisdom prevailing among many political scientists and journalists. His finding sparked considerable controversy about method and data.

Interpreting the Mayhew data from the perspective of presidential power may be problematic. Nonetheless, a reasonable intuition is that, for any given Congress, there may be policies that would be altered under unified government but remain in place during divided government because the president would use the veto power to protect them.[23] If so, a decrease in the production of important legislation during divided government may reflect the impact of the veto power. Howell et al. reconsider Mayhew's data, focusing on the contemporary perceptions series, and shows, using time series techniques, that production of important legislation decreases about 30 percent during divided government.[24] The effect is small enough to confirm Mayhew's skepticism regarding the conventional wisdom about "gridlock" but large enough to suggest—perhaps!—the traces of presidential power.

Policy Liberalism of Important Laws

A stronger test of presidential power comes when we shift attention from the number of important laws enacted to their policy content. Erikson et al. examine Mayhew's contemporary perceptions data, coding each law as "liberal," "conservative," or "neither."[25] They sum over each congress's production of important laws to yield a net liberalism/conservatism score for each Congress. They show that this score is related to public mood and the partisan composition of government. That is, unified Democratic governments produce liberal legislation, on balance; unified Republican governments produce conservative legislation, on balance; and divided governments produce a legislative record that on balance falls between the two extremes. This finding suggests that Republican presidents check the tendency of Democratic congresses to produce liberal legislation, while Democratic presidents check the tendency of Republican congresses to produce conservative legislation. The finding is hardly surprising. But it is important to know that simple, systematic evidence supports seemingly reasonable intuitions about presidential power and the content of legislation.

Statutory Delegation to Executive Agencies

Political scientists David Epstein and Sharyn O'Halloran engage in an even more ambitious attempt to study the effect of divided government on the content of legislation.[26] Again they study the laws identified in Mayhew's data as important. They undertake a content analysis of legislative histories, studying the extent to which Congress delegated discretionary authority to the executive. Their data show a pronounced divided government effect: Congress delegates more authority to a president of the same party. The results for presidential power are not entirely clear, since divided government presidents may be more aggressive in their use of their more limited discretion.[27] Nonetheless, the finding shows very clearly how equilibria in bargaining games can be very different under unified and divided government (see also the essay by Epstein and O'Halloran, chapter 15 in this volume).

Bureaucratic Activity

Two classic articles examine bureaucratic activity and the preferences of Congress and president. These studies largely created the "direct" method for studying presidential power. Weingast and Moran examine the activities of the Federal Trade Commission, and show that the activities of the agency seemed to reflect preferences within key congressional committees.[28] Moe reexamines this evidence and finds that presidential preferences also play an important role in the agency's output decisions.[29] Although these studies predate the new attention directed at divided government, taken in tandem they may suggest the importance of both actors' preferences in determining bureaucratic conduct.

Ideology of Supreme Court Justices

The identities of Supreme Court justices, and hence the ideological composition of the Supreme Court, are determined by the Supreme Court nominations game. The best quantitative study of presidential choices in this game provides evidence that presidents are strongly advantaged by the nominations process. Moraski and Shipan study presidential selection of nominees, focusing on their ideology.[30] The principal variable of interest to the authors is whether the nominee would be the "swing vote" on the Court, but they also study the impact of presidential and senatorial preferences on the president's choice. What they find is that Senate ideology has little effect on presidential choice of nominees. In other words, a president tends to nominate a person of the same ideological stripe whether the government is unified or divided government. An earlier study using less sophisticated models and weaker data comes to a similar conclusion, and historical evidence from case studies tends to confirm Moraski and Shipan's systematic analysis.[31] The structure of this particular bargaining game seems strongly to favor the president.

Number of Important Executive Orders

Moe and Howell's study of the effect of divided government on the number of important executive orders resembles Mayhew's analysis but measures a key output from the executive rather than legislative branch.[32] Like Mayhew, the authors uncover some counterintuitive results: the number of important executive orders appears to decrease during divided government, by about 20%–30%. In contrast, many analysts have suggested that the number of important executive orders might increase during divided government, as a substitute for the president's legislative proposals that have no prospect of success. The Howell and Moe results may suggest that divided government imposes constraints on the president even when he takes ostensibly "unilateral" action. An analysis of the net liberalism/conservatism of important executive orders, along the lines of Erikson et al.'s analysis of the Mayhew data, would be very interesting. It would be surprising if divided government did not operate as a moderating influence on the net liberalism/conservatism of presidential executive orders.

THE INDIRECT APPROACH: STUDYING VETO BARGAINING

Absent a model of vetoes (actual vetoes, not just veto power), any number of vetoes is equally compatible with little, some, or a great deal of presidential power over legislative outputs. No vetoes may mean that Congress has capitulated to the president, or the president has capitulated to Congress; or that Congress has made some compromises before submitting the bill to the president, who compromises somewhat by accepting it. Many vetoes are equally ambiguous. The lesson is a general one—data on process measures simply do not speak for themselves. The idea of the indirect approach is to combine process measures with explicit models of bargaining, in the hope the data will speak more distinctly.

Veto Threats

Matthews provides an elegant model of veto threats, beginning with a standard model of one-shot, take-it-or-leave-it bargaining over political issues.[33] Then he adds an explicit "Factor X"—congressional uncertainty about the president's policy preferences. In other words, Matthews assumes the president has a policy reputation, but the reputation is not so precise that Congress can predict with pinpoint accuracy the response of the president to every conceivable bill. Disagreement between the president and Congress, *plus* congressional uncertainty about how far it can push the president before triggering a veto, allows vetoes to occur within the model—they occur when the president turns out to be somewhat tougher (that is, more extreme) than Congress anticipated. Finally, Matthews allows the president to issue a veto threat before Congress writes a bill. Using quite sophisticated game theory, Matthews works out predictions about the behavior of Congress and president.

Within the confines of the model, one can evaluate the impact of the "institution" of the veto threat on presidential power. Broadly speaking, veto threats often enhance presidential power (relative to a world without veto threats), because they help the president and Congress strike bargains that they might not otherwise forge, for want of congressional concessions. Moreover, the concessions induced by threats often work to the advantage of the president.[34]

In our own research, my collaborators and I present systematic data on veto threats, congressional concessions after threats, and vetoes after threats, and use Matthews's model to interpret the data (and, to some extent, use the data to test the model).[35] The universe for the study consists of the 2,284 "nonminor" bills presented to the president between 1945 and 1992. We collected data on a random sample of 281 nonvetoed bills from the universe, stratified across three levels of "legislative significance" derived from an approach similar to Mayhew's. We also collected data on all vetoed bills in the universe, some 162 bills, for a total of 443 bills in all. We compiled data on threats and concessions from legislative histories of the bills, the public papers of the presidents, and newspaper accounts.

Statistical analysis of the data revealed the following patterns:

1. During unified government, veto threats rarely occur regardless of the significance of the legislation.
2. During divided government, veto threats occur frequently and increase in frequency with legislative significance. The frequency of veto threats for important legislation during divided government is surprisingly high: 34 percent of such bills received veto threats.
3. If a bill is not threatened, a veto is unlikely though not impossible.
4. If a bill is threatened, the probability of a veto increases dramatically, especially during divided government and at higher levels of legislative significance. But vetoes are not certain even after a threat.

5. Veto threats usually bring concessions.
6. Concessions deter vetoes. The bigger the concession the less likely a threatened bill is to be vetoed.

Although some of these findings lie outside the scope of Matthews's model (for example, the importance of legislative significance), for the most part these findings strongly resemble what the model predicts. Thus, the model "explains" the data, in the sense that it provides a detailed causal mechanism for the process. If one combines the import of the model—veto threats often enhance presidential power—with the data on the actual frequency of threats, one obtains a picture in which veto threats assume considerable importance in the armamentarium of presidents serving in periods of divided party government.

Sequential Veto Bargaining
Cameron and Elmes consider an extension of Matthews's model.[36] In this version of the model, the president does not issue a veto threat; however, Congress may pass multiple versions of a bill and the president may repeatedly veto it. The central question in this model of sequential veto bargaining is the ability of vetoes to extract policy concessions from Congress. As in Matthews's model, presidential policy reputation plays a key role. The president begins the game with a given reputation, and Congress makes an appropriate offer. But in response to a veto, Congress updates its beliefs and makes subsequent offers. The game has considerable strategic complexity, because the president may deliberately veto a bill in order to build a favorable reputation and extract concessions—and Congress knows the president may do this! Nonetheless, the model predicts that vetoes will usually bring concessions in re-passed bills. In addition, the model makes many other predictions about veto bargaining, some rather subtle. For example, the model predicts that vetoes are more likely for important bills than for less important ones, but that concessions will be smaller for important re-passed bills than in unimportant re-passed bills.

Cameron reviews extensive data on veto bargaining in the postwar period and uses it to test the model. Among the many empirical findings are the following:

1. The probability a bill was vetoed was fairly high (about 20%) when the legislation was important and government was divided.
2. Given a veto, sequential veto bargaining was quite rare for unimportant legislation but quite common for important legislation.

3. Vetoes almost always extract concessions in re-passed versions of the legislation.[37]

This is exactly the picture one would expect if the model captures important parts of interbranch bargaining. These findings are just a few of many that are explored in this book-length study of veto bargaining. Overall, the picture that emerges is one of intense bargaining, with the president using threats and actual vetoes to extract concessions from Congress. This process appears central to the legislative presidency in periods of divided party government.

Blame Game Vetoes

Groseclose and McCarty present an ingenious model of what they call "blame game" vetoes.[38] In these instances, Congress deliberately sends up legislation designed to provoke a veto. By carefully constructing the bill, Congress can force the president to act as if he were more extreme (more liberal or more conservative) than he actually is. The appearance of extremism alienates moderate voters, who judge the president's ideology by his actions. So again, incomplete information and policy reputation within the electorate are central to the model. However, the model focuses on the president's reputation within the electorate rather than in the Washington community.

The historical record shows that extremists in the congressional parties noisily advocate blame game vetoes during periods of divided party government. Also, there are notable examples of the strategy in action, most famously involving the congressional Democrats, President Bush, and the Family and Medical Leave Act of 1992.[39] The budget crisis and governmental shutdown of 1995 may well have been blame game vetoes at work.

Outstanding candidates for blame game vetoes are those that occurred in election years during divided party government, were relatively important (so that voters would take note), and that were hopeless cases for a veto override (i.e., the bills' authors probably knew their legislation had little chance of enactment). Table 5.1 displays all vetoes from 1945 to 1996 meeting these characteristics, seventeen vetoes in all.[40] This very conservative list, along with case studies, suggests that blame game vetoes may be an occasional and important partisan phenomenon during divided party government. Confirmation of this requires more systematic proof—which Groseclose and McCarty go on to supply.

A striking prediction of Groseclose and McCarty's model is that presidents will suffer a loss of popularity following vetoes of *important* legislation, *but only during periods of divided party government.* The hypothesis is very natural once one understands the model. They test the hypothesis with quarterly data

TABLE 5.1. Potential "Blame Game Vetoes," 1945–1996

Bill	Year	Override Votes	Description
H.R. 12	1956	202–211 (74)	Agricultural Act of 1956
S. 722	1960	45–39 (11)	Area Redevelopment Act
H.R. 3610	1960	249–157 (22)	Sewage treatment plant grants
H.R. 15417	1972	203–171 (47)	Labor, HEW appropriations
S.J. Res 121	1976	37–51 (22)	Milk price supports
H.R. 8617	1976	243–160 (26)	Hatch Act Revisions
H.R. 12384	1976	51–42 (11)	Military Construction
H.R. 13655	1976	41–35 (10)	Advanced Car Research
H.R. 1154	1988	272–152 (11)	Textile Apparel and Footware Trade Act
S. 3	1992	57–42 (9)	Campaign Finance and Electoral Reform Act
H.R. 2507	1992	271–156 (14)	Fetal Tissue Research
S. 5	1992	258–169 (27)	Family Leave
S. 323	1992	266–148 (10)	Family Planning
H.R. 1530	1996	240–156 (24)	Defense Authorization
H.R. 2076	1996	240–159 (26)	Commerce, Justice, State appropriation
H.R. 1561	1996	234–188 (48)	Foreign Aid and State Dept. authorization
H.R. 1833	1996	57–41 (9)	Late term abortions

on presidential popularity from 1953–1996 and discover exactly the predicted phenomenon. Moreover, it is surprisingly large in magnitude, exceeding the impact on popularity of macroeconomic variables like inflation and growth.

SUMMARY

The evidence in the preceding studies may seem dismayingly variable. In some games, like the Supreme Court nominations game, the president appears remarkably powerful despite divided party government. In others, like the statutory delegation game, the president seems quite vulnerable. In the veto game, perhaps the most intensively studied of all presidential bargaining games, presidential power depends on many different factors, including intangibles like the president's policy reputation inside and outside Washington. Why are the results so variegated? How can we make sense of them? I take up this subject in the next section.

PRESIDENTIAL POWER AND THE STRUCTURE OF BARGAINING GAMES

Over the last twenty years or so, social scientists have learned a great deal about bargaining. Game theorists have devised interesting models; experimentalists have examined bargaining under controlled circumstances; and empirical researchers have studied data from field settings.[41] There is a solid base of knowledge to draw on when trying to understand presidential bargaining game. That is the good news.

Unfortunately, there is some bad news as well. An important finding from bargaining theory is the following: When the bargainers do not disagree very much about how to divide the pie, then (not surprisingly) the fine structure of the bargaining game probably will not influence the outcome of the bargaining very much. Just about any sensible procedure will yield about the same outcome, absent a breakdown in the bargaining. But if the players have different preferences about the division of the pie, then *the fine structure of the bargaining procedure makes an enormous difference for outcomes.* Change the rules, even in subtle ways, and you may change the outcomes—and change them a lot.

The sensitivity of outcomes to the bargaining protocol is one reason why bargaining is so important to a president when government is divided. If the president has a favorable structure to work with, he can shape outcomes in the bargaining game regardless of Congress's desires. But the sensitivity of outcomes to procedural detail creates a problem for political scientists. There are not going to be many easy generalizations that hold over *all* the bargaining games that divided government presidents play. Political scientists will need to think hard about each one—almost as hard as presidents do. Presidential power resides in the details.

SOME CONSIDERATIONS IN ANALYZING PRESIDENTIAL BARGAINING GAMES

What details in bargaining games make a big difference to presidential power? The following rather tentative list of considerations provides a starting point.

Proposal Power vs. Veto Power

In many presidential bargaining games, one side (the "proposer") makes the other (the "chooser") a take-it-or-leave-it offer. The ability to do so often confers great power on the proposer, especially if the "leave it" option is unattractive for the chooser.[42] Of course, in some games, the president is the proposer and has the advantage; in others, he is the chooser and thus operates at a relative disadvantage. This simple observation goes a considerable way toward explaining the variation observed in empirical studies.

Here are some examples. In the legislation game, Congress has the proposal advantage. By carefully exploiting his veto power, the president can force Congress to compromise, perhaps quite a lot. But in general, proposal power gives Congress the edge. Thus, in the 80th Congress, President Truman opposed the Republican majority on tax cuts and labor policy. By repeatedly vetoing bills, Truman forced the Republicans to compromise to the point that they had veto-proof bills. Yet in the end, Congress cut the income tax and passed the Taft-Hartley Act. The latter dramatically reshaped labor policy in this country. Similarly, President Clinton extracted huge concessions from Congress in the battle over welfare reform (how large is often forgotten). But in the end, Congress reshaped welfare policy much more on its terms than the president's.

In the nomination game, the president has the proposal advantage. While Congress has sometimes rejected a president's nominee for the Supreme Court, the president has usually gone on to fill the seat with someone of comparable ideological stripe. For instance, Congress rejected two of President Nixon's nominees, Clement Haynsworth and G. Harrold Carswell. Nixon returned with Harry Blackmun, a jurist of similar ideology but with less inflammatory background. Blackmun successfully ascended to the seat.[43] The proposal power (and perhaps other features of this game) tends to create presidential power.

Not all presidential games have a simple ultimatum structure. For example, in the executive order game, the president can issue a order that becomes the new status quo. Congress can act to overturn the new status quo, by issuing its own policy bid (i.e., pass a bill). However, the president can protect the new status quo by vetoing the bill. So this game allows both sides some proposal power and some veto power. Working out the consequence of this structure demands an explicit model, such as those considered by Ferejohn and Shipan and by Howell.[44]

Regime Effects

A second structural element involves what might be called "regime effects." In the take-it-or-leave-it bargaining models I have discussed, the relative power of the president and Congress changes radically depending on where the status quo lies with respect to the favored policies of the two bargainers. This is the basis for the "can't push on a string" maxim in appropriations politics. Thus, even within a game with the same sequence of play and the same players, the president's power may vary dramatically given favorable and unfavorable status quos or reversion points, relative to the two bargainers' positions. This principle has been well understood by theorists[45] but has not always been appreciated by empirical researchers trying to make sense of field data from bargaining games. Some recent work, such as Moraski and Shipan's study, in which regime effects are central, points the way to a better treatment of a fundamental consideration in political bargaining.[46]

Uncertainty and Reputation

When the president is the chooser, his policy reputation can be an asset when dealing with a proposer. If the proposer is risk averse, its uncertainty about what the president will accept and reject may lead it to make a better offer then if it were certain what he would do. Under these circumstances, there is apt to be considerable strategizing around the president's policy reputation itself. The president may attempt to build a favorable reputation through his words and deeds, and his opponents may exert considerable effort to reduce their uncertainty.

The veto models demonstrate how policy reputation can make an important difference in presidential power when the president acts as chooser. In the threat model, congressional uncertainty about the president's policy preferences tends to advantage the president relative to a complete information world. In the sequential bargaining model, the president deliberately manipulates his reputation to extract better offers from Congress. But in the blame game model, Congress uses veto bait to damage the president's reputation with voters.

When the president is genuinely the proposer, as in the nomination or treaty games, his policy reputation many not buy him much. Only if the proposal is a signal about the president's future actions will it interact with reputational dynamics. But in many bargaining games, once the president's proposal is on the table, his most significant action in the game is over. In this case, reputational dynamics simply do not arise.

Two exceptions are worth mentioning. The first involves policy arenas that are linked or correlated. In this case, the president's action in one arena (e.g., health policy) offers a clue about his preferences in another (e.g., welfare policy).[47] The second exception involves third party observers, like the blame game configuration. In this situation, a third party—mostly importantly, voters—watches the bargaining between president and another player (e.g., Congress) and tries to deduce the president's policy preferences from his actions. Here, the president may be able to craft his proposals—for instance, treaties, nominees, agency policies, executive orders, and presidential discretionary actions in foreign policy—to cultivate a favorable reputation with voters.

The asymmetry in reputational dynamics associated with choosing and proposing is an elementary point that seems to have been overlooked. One source of confusion is the temptation to treat the president's legislative proposals as if they were genuine proposals. It is important to remember that the president's legislative proposals are not, from a formal viewpoint, proposals in a direct, legislative bargaining game. Instead, as I argued earlier, they are probably better thought of as bids to establish focal points in a subsequent coordination game. Unfortunately, from a theoretical viewpoint, the presidential-congressional focal point game remains largely terra incognita.

Repetition

Some presidential bargaining games approximate an ultimatum game. But in others, once a player makes an offer, another accepts or rejects it. If the offer is rejected, another offer is made and so on, possibly ad infinitum (in principle). In other words, the bargaining may extend through many rounds of play.

In bargaining games like this, the fine structure of the game is very important. To see this, note that it is easy to construct bargaining games of this form where all the power lies with the proposer, who always achieves his or her ideal policy.[48] It is also easy to construct games of this form where the power lies with chooser, who achieves his or her ideal policy.[49] It is also possible to construct games of this sort in which repetition has no effect; that is, the outcome with multiple rounds is no different than if there had been only one round of play.[50] It all depends, then, but on what? Despite much recent work on this type of game, the general principles remain elusive. At present, as these examples suggest, the devil is in the details. When repeated offers are part of a presidential bargaining game (at least potentially), analysts probably need to specify the game carefully and think hard about the opportunities for advantage implicit in the structure. This advice is not very helpful but at least it sends up a warning signal.

The End of Presidential Greatness?

Up to this point, I've stressed the details of presidential bargaining games because in an age of divided government, presidential power often resides in those details. But what does the advent of divided government and the rise of the bargaining presidency mean for the state of the institution, broadly conceived? I'll attempt one, provocative, answer.

There is a venerable tradition among historians of ranking presidents according to their "greatness." The source of this parlor game is a 1948 article by the distinguished historian Arthur M. Schlesinger. For his study, Schlesinger polled prominent historians and asked them to classify presidents as "great," "near great," "above average," "average," "below average," and "failures." Although the survey has been revisited several times, most presidents maintain fairly stable rankings in this system, especially those at the high and low ends of the scales. Recently, Arthur M. Schlesinger Jr. duplicated his father's survey, querying 32 noted scholars of the presidency.[51]

What do the ratings measure? Surely they tell us as much about the historians as the presidents. Scrutiny of the results suggests that the rankings reflect an ideal president, one with vision, boldness, and expansionary, activist achievement, not just in war but in peace. This is of course a modern ideal and one that some twentieth-century presidents—e.g., Taft, Coolidge, Harding—would have rejected. But it is also an ideal that is widely shared among contemporary Americans. The friends of the presidency often celebrate Lincoln, FDR, and Wilson when they contemplate the office's positive capabilities, and worry about Nixon, Grant, Harding, and Andrew Johnson when they reflect on its perils.

If we read the rankings this way—not as objective indicators of genuine "greatness" (whatever that might be) but as subjective reflections of one vision of what the office can be—then it might make sense to ask: what is the impact of divided party government and the bargaining presidency on this conception of presidential greatness?

As a first estimate at answering this question, I use the 1996 Schlesinger rankings, grouping presidents into "above average" (great, near great, and above average), "average," and "below average" (below average and failure). Then, I categorize the presidents by their partisan relationship with Congress. If a president served exclusively during unified party government, I classify him as "in the majority." If he served when his partisan opponents consistently held Congress, I classify him as "in the minority." All the other cases (i.e., unified government for a portion of a presidency, divided for the remainder, or one chamber held by co-partisans and one by opponents) I classify as "mixed." Table 5.2 shows the results. I focus only on presidents since the emergence of the party system in 1835, and of necessity I exclude a few presidents whose brief tenures defy ranking (e.g., William Henry Harrison).

The table reveals several patterns. First, the rankings distinguish activist, visionary, and bold presidents from less activist or disgraced ones. Perhaps the glaring exception is the "average" rating afforded Ronald Reagan, which has

TABLE 5.2   Partisan Status and Presidential Greatness

	Above Average	Average	Below Average	
In Majority	Lincoln, McKinley, TR, FDR, JFK, LBJ	Van Buren, Carter	Harding, Coolidge, Hoover	
	6	2	3	11
Mixed	Polk, Wilson, Truman, Eisenhower	Arthur, Cleveland, Harrison, Taft, Reagan, Clinton	Tyler Pierce Buchanan Grant	
	4	6	4	14
In Minority		Hayes, Ford, Bush	Taylor, Fillmore, A. Johnson, Nixon	
	0	3	4	7
	10	11	11	32

drawn adverse comment from conservatives.[52] It would be surprising if Reagan's score does not rise over time, as did Eisenhower's.

Second, there seems to be a relationship between the ranking and the partisan relationship of Congress and the president. Of the 11 presidents who served in the majority, more than half score as "above average." Of the 14 presidents who had mixed partisan status, a plurality cluster as "average" presidents. Of the 7 presidents who served in the minority, almost 60 percent scored as "below average," and none were "above average." A simple but very strict rule, "majority = above average, mixed = average, minority = below average," predicts 50 percent of the scores correctly. A slightly more permissive rule, "majority = above average or average, mixed = average, and minority = below average or average," predicts 66 percent of the scores correctly.

The first cut at the data is sufficiently intriguing to warrant a closer look. Figure 5.2 presents the data as a scatter plot, along with the predictions from a linear regression model relating partisan relationship to presidential ranking.[53] The 95 percent confidence intervals, shown as dotted lines, should be taken with a grain of salt since the variables are ordinal. But they help show the location of most of the observations. In the figure, the values of the observations are slightly jittered to make each point distinctly visible.

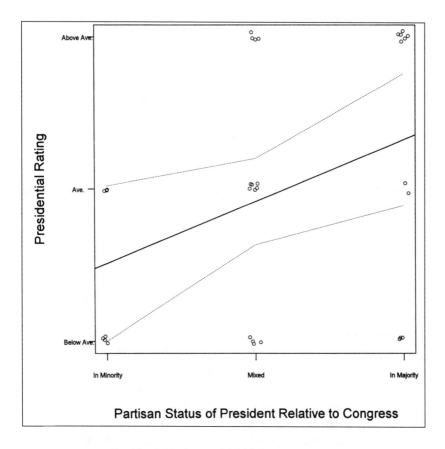

Presidential Ratings and Divided Party Government

The statistical model confirms that, on average, moving from minority status, to mixed status, to majority status substantially increases a president's ranking. The effect is both statistically significant and substantively important.

The principle lesson is quite clear: *an age of divided party government is unlikely to produce presidencies of the kind celebrated by historians as "great."* Of the 20 presidents who served in other than the majority, only 4, or 20 percent, beat the odds and scored "above average." All of these were "mixed" status presidents. For these four—Eisenhower, Truman, Wilson, and Polk—the legacy that so appeals to historians turns primarily or substantially on foreign affairs, and (excepting Eisenhower) much of it was achieved during intervals of unified party government. Of course, it may not be *impossible* for a minority status president to achieve the sort of presidency the historians celebrate as "above average." But the fact remains that no president in 165 years has pulled it off.

Why does divided party government so often sound the death knell for activist, visionary, pathbreaking presidencies? The first part of this essay suggests an answer. When the president enjoys majority status, he can shape the tide of events through coordinative leadership. By establishing focal points inside and outside Congress, he can move policy and the nation, sometimes breathtakingly. This sort of ostentatious achievement is crucial for the historian's preferred style of presidency. When the president is in the minority, he fights trench warfare, not the blitzkrieg. His achievements are measured in hard-fought inches. They depend on the clever use of bargaining games, playing each twist for advantage. In fairness we should probably accord bargaining presidents their own kind of greatness; but if we do, it will be rather different from the conception enshrined in Schlesinger's rankings.

David Mayhew has shown clearly that divided party government does not equal gridlock.[54] Even in its moments of partisan division, the separation of powers system can produce great legislation. It also produces presidents who exercise power through bargaining, a different mode than the coordinative leadership of unified government presidents. What the system does not produce during divided party government is great presidents—or only rarely, when the opportunities are unusually favorable. In fact, the absence of great presidents during divided party government may be the reason why so many political scientists and journalists mistakenly associate it with gridlock. If divided party government persists, as seems likely, then we must bid adieu to the office of Abraham Lincoln, Teddy Roosevelt, FDR, and Lyndon Johnson and welcome again the office of Chester Arthur, Grover Cleveland, Gerald Ford—and perhaps, Richard Nixon.

NOTES

1. This conclusion follows from the canonical definition of power: "power is a causal relationship between preferences and outcomes." For a thorough discussion, see Jack Nagal, *The Descriptive Analysis of Power* (New Haven: Yale University Press, 1975).

2. The distinction I am drawing between coordination and bargaining is rooted more in presidential politics than abstract game theory. For example, there are bargaining games in which coordination is critical (e.g., Nash bargaining games, with a multitude of equilibria). So I am not drawing a logical or mathematical distinction but instead pointing to the character of different activities.

3. Thomas Schelling, *The Strategy of Conflict* (Cambridge: Harvard University Press, 1960).

4. Keith T Poole and Howard Rosenthal, *Congress: A Political-Economic History of Roll Call Voting* (New York: Oxford University Press, 1997), especially pp. 82–84.

5. Using a method closely related to that of Poole and Rosenthal, Poole and McCarty shows that modern presidents tend to hold ideologies near the median of their congressional party (see Nolan M. McCarty and Keith T. Poole, "Veto Power and Legislation: An Empirical Analysis of Executive and Legislative Bargaining from 1961 to 1986," *The Journal of Law, Economic, & Organization*, Volume 11 (2): 282–312).

6. Kenneth A Shepsle and Mark S. Bonchek, *Analyzing Politics: Rationality, Behavior, and Institutions* (New York: Norton, 1997), p. 383.

7. See, for example, James L. Sundquist, *Politics and Policy: The Eisenhower, Kennedy, and Johnson Years.* (Washington, D.C.: Brookings Institution, 1968); or Theodore R. Marmor, *The Politics of Medicare* (New York, Aldine, 1973).

8. Studies of coordinative leadership include see Gary J. Miller, "Formal Theory and the Presidency," pp. 289–336 in George C. Edwards, John Kessel and Bert Rockman, eds., *Researching the Presidency: Vital Questions, New Approaches* (Pittsburgh: University of Pittsburgh Press, 1993), and Morris Fiorina and Kenneth Shepsle, "Formal Theories of Leadership: Agents, Agenda Setters, and Entrepreneurs," in Bryan Jones, ed., *Leadership and Politics* (Lawrence: University of Kansas Press, 1989).

9. Except Wilson in his fourth congress, the 66th Congress of 1919—1920, when his presidency unraveled. Of course, just because it is *possible* for unified government presidents to act as coordinative leaders, it does not mean it is easy for them to do so or that they will always be successful in their attempts.

10. Matthew Dickenson, *Bitter Harvest: FDR, Presidential Power and the Growth of the presidential Branch* (Cambridge: Cambridge University Press, 1997), p. 81. Dickenson relies on Arthur M. Schlesinger's *The Coming of the New Deal* (Boston: Houghton Mifflin, 1959).

11. I paint this picture with overly broad strokes, to show the main points clearly. There are occasions during divided party government when the president's and the congressional leadership's interests are close enough to sustain a president-dominated equilibrium. An example is foreign policy during the 80th Congress. Congress followed Truman's lead on the Marshall Plan and other initiatives—a very different picture from the brawl that was domestic policymaking on labor and tax policy.

12. Again, I paint in bold strokes for emphasis. Many caveats are necessary. For instance, the dynamic I describe is somewhat muted when congressional parties are not especially polarized, for example during the middle Eisenhower congresses. It is more evident when the parties are highly polarized, as in the late-nineteenth-century congresses or the contemporary one. Even then, a divided government

president sometimes can use the "bully pulpit" to put an item on congressional agendas, and steer the outcome somewhat via veto threats. Still, the difference between this and coordinative leadership should be clear.

13. Congress may also abolish the vacancy by manipulating the number of Supreme Court justices, as it did several times in the nineteenth century.

14. John Ferejohn and Charles Shipan "Congressional Influence on the Bureaucracy," *Journal of Law, Economics, and Organization* 6 (1990) (Special Issue) 1–20 and Martin M. Shapiro, *Who Guards the Guardians? : Judicial Control of Administration* (Athens : University of Georgia Press, 1988).

15. The only extended discussion of the veto in *Presidential Power* concerns Ike's vetoes after the 1958 election. This part of *Presidential Power* is remarkably prescient about the experience of later divided government presidencies, as the parties polarized in the late twentieth century.

16. The data are taken from CQ Inc., *Members of Congress Since 1789*, pp. 182–183, and Table 1–18 in *Vital Statistics on Congress*. In technical terms, the model shown was fit as a general additive model in the statistical language S-plus, employing the loess function lo (span = .4, degree = 2, family = binomial).

17. Peter Bachrach and Morton Baratz, "The Two Faces of Power," *American Political Science Review* (1962) 56: 947–952.

18. This method of studying power is laid out in the classics of the power literature, see Robert A. Dahl, *Modern Political Analysis*, 2nd ed. (Englewood Cliffs, N.J.: Prentice-Hall, 1970), and Jack Nagal, *The Descriptive Analysis of Power* (New Haven: Yale University Press, 1975). It was first applied to studying presidential power in Terry Moe, "An Assessment of the Positive Theory of 'Congressional Dominance' of Bureaucracy," *Legislative Studies Quarterly* (1987) 12: 475 and Barry R. Weingast, and Mark J. Moran. "Bureaucracy Discretion or Congressional Control? Regulatory Policymaking by the Federal Trade Commission." *Journal of Political Economy* (1983) 91: 765—800.

19. For those who don't like suspense: "Factor X" often turns out to be some type of uncertainty, including uncertainty about what others will do (e.g., in the form of mixed strategies) or what they want (e.g., incomplete information about actors' preferences) and thus what they will do.

20. One cannot even conclude that vetoes are evidence of the most important or most intense disagreements. Drawing that conclusion requires a model of vetoes in which the statement is true; absent the model, it is not a valid inference.

21. D. Roderick Kiewiet and Mathew D. McCubbins, "Presidential Influence on Congressional Appropriations Decisions," *American Journal of Political Science* 32 (1988): 713–736.

22. David Mayhew, *Divided We Govern: Party Control, Lawmaking, and Investigations 1946–1990* (New Haven: Yale University Press, 1991).

23. Using some simple game theoretic models, Keith Krehbiel shows that even this simple intuition is subject to important caveats (see Keith Krehbiel, *Pivotal Politics: A Theory of U.S. Lawmaking* (Chicago: University of Chicago Press, 1998).

24. William Howell, E. Scott Adler, Charles Cameron, and Charles Riemann, "Measuring the Institutional Performance of Congress in the Post-war Era: Surges and Slumps in the Production of Legislation, 1945–1994," *Legislative Studies Quarterly* (forthcoming).

25. Robert S. Erikson., Michael B. MacKuen, and James A. Stimson, *The Macro Polity* (Cambridge: Cambridge University Press, forthcoming).

26. David Epstein and Sharyn O'Halloran, *Delegating Powers: A Transaction Cost Politics Approach to Policy Making Under Separate Powers* (New York: Cambridge University Press, 1999).

27. Epstein and O'Halloran supply several formal models for studying delegation. Thus, they offer both direct and indirect studies of presidential power.

28. Barry R. Weingast, and Mark J. Moran, "Bureaucracy Discretion or Congressional Control?"

29. Terry Moe, "An Assessment of the Positive Theory of 'Congressional Dominance' of Bureaucracy,"

30. Bryon Moraski and Charles R. Shipan, "The Politics of Supreme Court Nominations: A Theory of Institutional Constraints and Choices," *American Journal of Political Science* 43 (4) (1999): 1069–1095.

31. Charles M. Cameron, Albert Cover and Jeffrey A. Segal, "Supreme Court Nominations and the Rational Presidency," paper prepared for the 1990 Annual Meetings of the American Political Science Association (San Francisco).

32. Terry Moe and William Howell, "The Presidential Power of Unilateral Action," Forthcoming, *Journal of Law, Economics, and Organization*.

33. Steven Matthews, "Veto Threats: Rhetoric in a Bargaining Game," *Quarterly Journal of Economics* (1989) 103: 347–69.

34. They don't always do so, for sometimes the concessions are inadequate to head off a veto. In this case, concessions don't actually advantage the president (neglecting veto overrides).

35. Charles M. Cameron, *Veto Bargaining: Presidents and the Politics of Negative Power* (New York: Cambridge University Press, 2000) and Charles Cameron, John S. Lapinski, and Charles Riemann. "Testing Formal Theories of Political Rhetoric." *Journal of Politics* (Forthcoming Winter 2000).

36. Charles Cameron and Susan Elves, "A Theory of Sequential Veto Bargaining," manuscript Department of Political Science and Economics, Columbia University, 1995. The model is presented in simplified form in Cameron, *Veto Bargaining* (see note 35).

37. Cameron, *Veto Bargaining: Presidents and the Politics of Negative Power.*

38. Tim Groseclose and Nolan McCarty, "Presidential Vetoes: Bargaining, Blame Game, and Gridlock," manuscript, Department of Political Science, Ohio State University, 1996.

39. Ronald D Elving, *Conflict and Compromise: How Congress Makes the Law* (New York: Simon & Schuster, 1995).

40. I count override attempts that failed by 10 or more votes as hopeless attempts. I include two others that failed by nine votes since they both seem reasonably clear instances of blame game vetoes.

41. For some review articles, see inter alia, John Sutton, "Non-Cooperative Bargaining Theory: An Introduction." *Review of Economic Studies* 53 (1986): 709–724. and Alvin E. Roth, "Bargaining Experiments," pp. 253–348 in *The Handbook of Experimental Economics.* John Kagel and Alvin Roth, eds. (Princeton: Princeton University Press, 1995).

42. For details, see the discussion of ultimatum games in Roth, "Bargaining Experiments." The basic reference in political settings is Thomas Romer and Howard Rosenthal, "Political Resource Allocation, Controlled Agendas, and the Status Quo," *Public Choice* (1978) 33: 27–44.

43. For an attempt to measure the ideology of Supreme Court nominees, see Jeffrey Segal, Charles M. Cameron, and Albert D. Cover, "A Spatial Model of Roll Call Voting: Senators, Constituents, Presidents, and Interest Groups," *American Journal of Political Science* 36 (1992): 96. They estimate a perceived liberalism score of .16 for Haynsworth, .04 for Carswell, and .12 for Blackmun.

44. Ferejohn and Shipan, "Congressional Influence on the Bureaucracy," 1990 and William Howell, *Unilateral Lawmaking: The Presidential Advantage.* Ph.D. dissertation manuscript, in progress, Department of Political Science, Stanford University (1999).

45. Krehbiel, *Pivotal Politics,* 1998.

46. Moraski and Shipan, "The Politics of Supreme Court Nominations," 1997.

47. McCarty proposes a veto model along these lines. In this model, the president's veto of a bill in arena x signals about his likely preferences in arena y (see Nolan McCarty, "Presidential Reputation and the Veto." *Economics and Politics* (1997) 9(1): 1–26. Thus, early establishment of a favorable reputation can extract better proposals from Congress in related policy arenas.

48. Examples of this kind are easy to construct if, for example, the chooser faces a per period cost from refusing offers.

49. Examples of this kind can be constructed if the chooser receives a per period benefit from delay while the proposer receives a per period cost from refusals.

50. Examples of this kind can be constructed, for example, when neither player faces per period costs or benefits but both discount the payoffs from the benefit received at the end of the game.

51. Arthur M. Schlesinger, Jr., "Rating the Presidents: Washington to Clinton," *Political Science Quarterly* (1996) 112(2): 179–191.

52. Alvin S. Felzenberg, "There You Go Again: Liberal Historians and the *New York Times* Deny Ronald Reagan His Due," *Policy Review*, March–April 1997.

53. Other techniques that take into account the ordinal nature of the variables (e.g., ordered probit) might be more attractive but OLS has the virtue of simplicity and robustness. I scored majority, mixed, minority as 1, 0, -1 respectively, and the same scores for above average, average, and below average. The resulting model was predicted ranking = -.08 + .41 status, with standard errors of .14 (t = -.6, p = .56) and .19 (t = 2.2, p = .04) respectively, R^2 = .14 on 30 degree of freedom.

54. Mayhew, *Divided We Govern*, 1991.

CHAPTER 6

The Timing of Presidential Speeches: Can the President Be an Effective Teacher

By Renée M. Smith

INTRODUCTION

Karlyn Kohrs Campbell and Kathleen Hall Jamieson argue that presidential rhetoric, whether written or oral, is one source of institutional power for the presidency. This power has been further enhanced in the information age "by the ability of presidents to speak when, where, and on whatever topic they choose, and to a national audience through coverage by the electronic media."[1] Similarly, Roderick Hart draws an explicit link between speech and power, calling presidential speechmaking a "tool" of modern governance.[2]

In recent years, presidential scholars have emphasized the literal and symbolic aspects of presidential speechmaking.[3] The trend toward a "public" or "plebiscitary" presidency,[4] in which the president increasingly seeks to influence public opinion by "going public" has been explained by Jeffrey Tulis as a consequence of the norms and pressures set in motion by Woodrow Wilson, who he says equated presidential leadership with rhetorical leadership.[5]

In contrast, Samuel Kernell argues that modern presidents choose to "go public" to promote themselves and their policies because of the incentives they face under the weakened party and coalition system associated with individualized pluralism. These arguments imply that presidents view speechmaking as a way to increase either general support for themselves or specific support for a public policy.[6] This link between presidential speechmaking, public approval of the president, and informal presidential power pervades much of the literature on both presidential approval and presidential speechmaking.[7] According to some authors, delivering a major address to the nation is one of the "levers" that presidents can pull in an attempt to manage their public approval levels.[8]

Because of the potential links among speechmaking, presidential approval, and presidential power, the question of how a president decides when to give a major address to the nation is an important one. As Neustadt argued, a president protects his prospects for power via the choices he makes.[9] And one decision presidents face is whether to address the nation on matters of domestic or foreign policy. Some conventional wisdom is that presidents are likely to deliver a major public speech when their job performance ratings are low. In her seminal work, Lyn Ragsdale argues that *any* change in a president's approval ratings increases the likelihood that a president will make a major public address.[10]

The purpose of this paper is to reexamine and expand conventional wisdom about presidential decisionmaking with respect to major public addresses. To do so, I develop an argument about the costs and benefits presidents consider when deciding whether to address the nation. I then examine the implications of the argument using data on presidential speechmaking from 1953 through 1994.

The President's Decision

I begin by assuming that presidents are rational or purposive decisionmakers whose goals revolve around getting reelected, making good public policy, and ensuring themselves favorable assessments in future historical accounts.[11] I assume also that each president's decision to speak to the public can be characterized as an unobserved propensity to address the public, which may vary by president. If we could observe this underlying attribute, we would, in effect, be observing the utility that each president expects to gain or lose from making a speech. The probability that a president gives a major address at a particular time is a function of the perceived costs and benefits of doing so. What, then, are the president's perceived benefits and costs?

Perceived Benefits

Neustadt argued that presidents confront five major constituencies as they attempt to exercise their power: executive officials and bureaucrats, members of Congress, partisans of the same party as the president, international leaders, and the mass public.[12] Executive officials and bureaucrats tend to take their cues from members of Congress and others in Washington. Members of Congress, in turn, rely both on their own assessments of a president's reputation and on evaluations of the president's job performance by the public at large (i.e., public prestige). Hence, when they decide to address the nation, presidents must consider the costs and benefits of doing so by assessing how a speech will affect each of these key constituencies. For instance, Kernell argues that direct appeals to the public on matters of public policy circumvent bargaining with members of Congress.[13] Such speeches may sway mass opinions[14] and, in turn, place pressure on members of Congress to vote in accordance with their constituents' preferences, to the benefit of the president.

With respect to public opinion, Neustadt argued that presidents face an indifferent audience that pays attention to the president only when its members "notice public trouble pressing on their lives."[15] For instance, "paychecks, grocery bills, children's schooling, sons at war are quite distinctly matters of real life" for which the public holds presidents accountable.[16] When the economy is performing poorly or when the United States is involved in a war, the public becomes attentive. At these times, a president may become a teacher who addresses the nation in an attempt to decrease public frustration with current conditions and to temper public hopes and expectations for the future. According to Neustadt, "The president as teacher has a hard and risky job. If he wants to guard his popular approval, he must give real-life experiences a meaning that will foster tolerance for him."[17]

Other important influences on a president's decision to address the nation are crises and other crucial events. As Neustadt noted, "happenings create his opportunities to teach. He has to ride events to gain attention."[18] He categorized these events as "outside events," over which the president has no control, and "self-made happenings" that a president can manufacture. Each can rouse public attention and thereby provide an attentive audience to the president as teacher. Moreover, members of the public expect presidents to take action when such events occur. For instance, respondents to a 1980 survey about the performance of an ideal president said they expected presidents to: provide strong leadership (75%), solve our economic problems (63%), avoid unnecessary wars (73.5%), and stand up for the U.S. in foreign affairs (54%).[19] As Neustadt suggested, "these 'oughts' of office underlie most short-run shifts in popular prestige," and hence, presidents must attend to these crises and events or face the consequences of a dissatisfied public.[20]

A president's decision to address the nation may also be affected by the length of a president's tenure in office. Paul Light suggests that presidents who want their legislative proposals to be passed by Congress must "move it or lose it"; presidents should push for passage of their domestic policy proposals during their first year in office.[21] Taken in conjunction with the argument that modern presidents face a system of individualized pluralism in which they have incentives to make public appeals to pressure Congress, this suggests that presidents should address the nation during their first year in office. Thus, presidents are likely to equate "moving it" with speaking to the public to enact proposed policies.

Perceived Costs

While speeches may bring benefits, a president may also incur costs when delivering a major address to the nation. Some of these costs are related to the degree to which presidents can suffer from public overexposure.

Kernell notes that, "Although major addresses can be the most dramatic and most effective approach for influencing public opinion, they also can be the most taxing. The public's attentiveness corresponds to the number of such appeals. . . . By potentially reducing the size and responsiveness of the audience for his next appeal, each prime-time address entails opportunity costs for the president."[22] Hence, a chief executive who addresses the nation too frequently may bore listeners and lose the public's attention.

Costs, Benefits, and Context

Because they face five different constituencies as they attempt to exercise power, presidents may place different weights on the perceived costs and benefits of making major addresses, depending upon the prevailing circumstances. In some cases, presidents care more about satisfying the concerns of international leaders and members of the House or Senate Foreign Relations committees. At other times, presidents may be concerned with responding to the public or to bureaucrats in an agency such as Health and Human Services. In the first case, presidents will more likely give a foreign policy address, and in the second, the likelihood of a domestic address increases. Because the decision to deliver a major address occurs in response to demands from different constituencies, the effects of the different influences can vary depending on whether foreign or domestic policies are central to the issue at hand.

A Model of the President's Decision

Taking these ideas together, the president's decision to address the nation depends upon at least five considerations: (1) the effect of a speech on the president's partisan, congressional, and public constituencies; (2) issues of peace and prosperity; (3) events and crises that the public expects a president to resolve; (4) the time elapsed in the president's term, and (5) the president's degree of under- or overexposure. Each of these factors influences the costs and benefits, and hence, the probability of a major presidential address, and can be compared collectively against available evidence.

Defining Major Speeches

For this study, I collected data on all major discretionary speeches made by presidents from 1949 through 1994. I distinguished between obligatory and discretionary speeches.[23] I defined discretionary speeches as those that are not constitutionally or traditionally mandated. Thus, my list of speeches does not include inaugural or farewell addresses nor State of the Union messages. I define major speeches as those that preempted regularly scheduled programming on at least one network and were aimed at a national rather than a specialized audience or constituency.[24] Table 6.1 summarizes these data, and Appendix A presents the full list.[25]

As shown in table 6.1, Truman and Bush gave fewer speeches on average than did other post-World War II presidents, while Nixon gave significantly more speeches than did the others. Using these data, I estimated a multivariate statistical model in which the dependent variable is coded as a 1 if the president

TABLE 6.1.   Major Discretionary Presidential Speeches, 1949–1994

President	Years	Speeches (N)	Yearly Average
Truman	1949–52	11	2.75
Eisenhower	1953–60	31	3.88
Kennedy	1961–63	13	4.33
Johnson	1963–68	24	4.80
Nixon	1969–74	34	5.67
Ford	1974–76	9	4.50
Carter	1977–80	14	3.50
Reagan	1981–88	34	4.25
Bush	1989–92	13	3.25
Clinton		10	5.00
Total		193	

gave a speech in month t, and is 0 otherwise.[26] The model estimates the effects of the explanatory variables on the likelihood over time of presidents giving major speeches.

EXPLANATORY VARIABLES

The discussion of the costs and benefits of presidential speech making suggested that five types of explanatory variables be included in the analysis of the model. The constituency variables were measured in three ways to reflect a president's national, partisan, and congressional constituencies. First, a president's standing with his national constituency was estimated by the percentage of individuals responding affirmatively to the Gallup Poll question: "Do you approve or disapprove of the way _____ is handling his job as president?"[27] Second, a president's standing with members of his own party was measured in terms of the percentage of partisans who said they approved of the president's job performance.[28] Finally, a president's standing with members of Congress was gauged by the percentage of times the House of Representatives and Senate, respectively, concurred with a president's position on legislation. Since these latter data were unavailable on an annual basis before 1953, the analysis was limited to the period from 1953 through 1994.[29]

The second set of variables bears on the effects of peace and prosperity on the probability that a president will give a major speech. First, to estimate the effects of war on the decision to deliver a speech, I examined four variables based on the number of battle deaths during the Korean, Vietnam, and Persian Gulf wars,[30] involving two separate measures for the Vietnam War— one each for the Johnson and Nixon administrations. The effects of Vietnam battle deaths may have been different for Johnson and Nixon because Johnson started the war while Nixon inherited it.[31] Second, to measure economic performance and its effects, I used the monthly level and the monthly change in the unemployment rate as well as the monthly rate of change in the Consumer Price Index, which commonly defines the nation's inflation rate.[32]

To measure the influence of events on the probability of a major presidential speech, I supplemented a list of presidential events published by Paul Brace and Barbara Hinckley,[33] ending in 1988, with entries from the yearly chronologies published in The World Almanac and Book of Facts. Since Brace and Hinckley categorized their events as either discretionary or nondiscretionary, paralleling Neustadt's distinction between uncontrollable "outside events" versus "self-made happenings," I used their decision rule to classify the 1989–1994 events as either discretionary or nondiscretionary.[34] A list of the 1989–1994 events and their classification appears in Appendix B. In addition to these measures of discrete events, I also used separate measures to capture the longer and more continuous events associated with the Watergate scandal and the Iran-Contra affair.[35]

To estimate the effects of a "move it or lose it" legislative strategy, I coded a dummy variable that takes the value of 1 during the first 12 months of each president's first administration and 0 otherwise. Finally, to measure the costs of executive overexposure to the public, for each month, I counted a running total of the number of days that had passed since the last major presidential address. All else equal, the more closely together in time that major presidential speeches occur, the more likely the president is to suffer from the costs of overexposure; whereas a greater time interval between major speeches represents a lower level of exposure and costs.

HYPOTHESES

Based on Neustadt, Ragsdale, and Kernell, I expect conventional wisdom to hold: decreases in support from the president's national, partisan, or congressional constituencies should tend to spur presidents to address the nation to bolster flagging evaluations and to shore up their political capital. Thus, I expect the multivariate coefficients or "effects" associated with these variables to be negative and significantly different from zero, indicating that as support from these constituencies decreases, the probability of a president giving a major speech increases.

Although Ragsdale found that military involvement decreased the likelihood that a president will address the nation, I had no *a priori* expectation about the effects of battle deaths on the probability of a presidential speech. Ragsdale's analysis included years in which the United States was involved in losing wars, whereas the current data include the Persian Gulf War, which the United States won. I do not expect the effect of battle deaths on the likelihood of a major speech to be the same for wars lost versus wars won.

With respect to the economy, I expect that as inflation or unemployment rises, the president will be more likely to address the nation. Although counter to some findings that presidents remain silent during economic downturns,[36] my expectation that presidents are likely to speak out as inflation or unemployment rises stems from evidence that these economic factors negatively affect a president's public prestige as measured by a president's approval rating.[37]

Hence, a proactive president would be likely to respond to increases in these economic indicators by giving a speech.

Because events grab the public's attention, the occurrence of discretionary and nondiscretionary events should increase the likelihood of a presidential speech: "Events determine audience attention for a president."[38] Moreover, if a president exercises his discretion and creates an event to gain public attention, I expect him to follow up that event with a presidential address.

Further, presidents have incentives to make many speeches in their first year in office as they attempt to get their legislative priorities passed by Congress. Thus, the coefficient estimated for the first year in office should be positive. Since a decrease in the number of days between major presidential addresses suggests possible overexposure, the impact of costs from public overexposure will produce a coefficient for the number of days between speeches that is positive and significantly different from zero.

RESULTS

Table 6.2 reports the estimated coefficients for the model of presidents' major addresses.[39] Contrary to conventional wisdom, neither the change nor the level of a president's national approval rating has a significant effect (i.e., statistically different from zero) on the likelihood of a president delivering a major address. The effects are likewise statistically insignificant for support from partisans and support in the House and Senate. The only variables that are statistically different from zero are discretionary foreign policy events and the measure of public exposure (the number of days since the last major address). Even the effect of Watergate is not statistically significant (using the appropriate two-tailed test). The overall lackluster performance of this model—that the occurrence of a major speech appears difficult to predict—corresponds with findings of other authors.[40]

One problem with this analysis, however, is that it treats all major discretionary presidential addresses in the same way. But the effects of these different variables could themselves vary depending upon whether speeches deal with domestic versus foreign policy. To examine this, I distinguished domestic speeches from foreign policy speeches. The separate analyses of these appear in tables 6.3 and 6.4.

I divided the explanatory variables into those more likely to influence the probability of a domestic policy speech and those more likely to affect the likelihood of a foreign policy speech. In many instances, this distinction was clear.

TABLE 6.2. Probit Model Estimates, All Major Discretionary Speeches, 1953–1994

	Coefficient[a]	Standard Error[b]	Coefficient/S.E
Constant	−0.079	0.964	0.082
Constituency factors:			
Level, National Approval	−0.038	0.037	−1.039
Change, National Approval	−0.003	0.031	−0.113
Level, Republican Approval	0.005	0.017	0.336
Change, Republican Approval	0.010	0.015	0.687
Level, Democratic Approval	0.013	0.023	0.578
Change, Democratic Approval	0.006	0.018	0.338
Level, Independent Approval	0.019	0.025	0.760
Change, Independent Approval	−0.003	0.021	−0.127
House Concurrence	−0.004	0.006	−0.617
Senate Concurrence	0.004	0.007	0.483
"Real Life" factors:			
Lagged level, Unemployment	−0.037	0.065	−0.568
Lagged change,Unemployment	0.301	0.320	0.943
Lagged level, Inflation	−0.012	0.019	−0.619
Korean Conflict	0.001	0.002	0.992
Vietnam, LBJ	−0.000	0.000	−0.613
Vietnam, RMN	0.000	0.000	0.043
Gulf War	0.998	0.732	1.363
Events:			
Discretionary Domestic	0.397	0.345	1.147
Nondiscretionary Domestic	0.101	0.231	0.435
Discretionary Foreign	1.200*	0.277	4.327
Nondiscretionary Foreign	0.174	0.321	0.542
Watergate	0.413	0.381	1.085
Iran-Contra Affair	−0.349	0.355	−0.985
Other factors:			
First-year	−0.027	0.181	−0.147
Exposure	−0.003*	0.001	−4.238
−2*LLR	52.067		$p < .001$
% Correctly Predicted (N=504)	84.52%		

a. Coefficients marked with an asterisk are statistically different from zero at a .05 (or better) alpha level for a one-tailed test.
b. These estimates have been corrected for heteroskedasticity using the White estimator.

The factors expected to affect the probability of a domestic policy speech include: indicators of prosperity such as the change in the unemployment and inflation rates; domestic scandals such as Watergate; discretionary and nondiscretionary domestic policy events; the measure representing the first-year "move it or lose it" strategy for domestic policy; and the time interval representing the degree of public exposure. With the exception of the level of national approval (which came the closest of all constituency factors in table 6.1 to obtaining statistical significance), variables that were statistically insignificant in table 6.1 were omitted from the analysis of domestic policy speeches.[41]

The factors expected to influence the probability of foreign policy speeches include: indicators of the effects of war; foreign policy-related scandals such as the Iran-Contra affair;[42] discretionary and nondiscretionary foreign policy events; and the time interval for the degree of the president's public exposure. The level of national approval was also included in the model, while the other variables that were statistically insignificant in table 6.1 were not.[43]

DOMESTIC POLICY SPEECHES

As shown in table 6.3, the level of presidential approval had no effect on the likelihood of a domestic policy speech. However, the probability of a domestic speech increased when the previous month's change in unemployment was positive, indicating that presidents were more likely to give domestic policy speeches in the face of worsening economic conditions. In contrast, the inflation rate had no statistically significant effect on the occurrence of major domestic speeches. The likelihood of a presidential address also increased during the first year of an administration.[44]

In addition, both discretionary and nondiscretionary domestic events positively affected the likelihood of a speech. Interestingly, the Watergate scandal increased the likelihood of Nixon addressing the nation. Although the coefficient for the degree of national exposure is statistically significant, its sign is opposite of that expected; the negative coefficient implies that the shorter the time between speeches the more likely a president is to give another address. There is no indication, then, that presidents have had a tendency to incur costs from public overexpose in terms of their major addresses on domestic policy. But this result is heavily influenced by the fact that beginning with Nixon, all presidents have given three or fewer speeches in their last year in office and have typically given their last major address months before leaving office.

TABLE 6.3. Probit Model Estimates, Major Discretionary Domestic Speeches

	Coefficients[a] (S.E.)[b]	Marginal Effects[c]
Level, National Approval	−0.010	
	(0.007)	0.0000
Lagged Change, Unemployment	0.798*	
	(.366)	0.0156
Lagged Level, Inflation	−0.031	
	(0.021)	0.0000
Watergate	0.573*	
	(0.347)	0.0129
Discretionary Domestic Events	0.780*	
	(0.368)	0.0175
Nondiscretionary Domestic Events	0.427*	
	(0.237)	0.0095
First year	0.378*	
	(0.180)	0.0085
Exposure	−0.002*	
	(0.001)	0.0004
Constant	−0.382	
	(0.464)	0.0000
−2*LLR	28.697	p < .004
%Correctly Predicted (N=504)	84.33%	

a. Coefficients marked with an asterisk are statistically different from zero at .05 (or better) alpha level for a one-tailed test.
b. These estimates have been corrected for heteroskedasticity using the White estimator.
c. The marginal effects are calculated as derivatives at mean, that is, by holding the means of all variables constant and taking the derivative with respect to the variable of interest.

The likelihood ratio statistic indicates that this model outperforms a simple model in which all cases are predicted as the modal category of no major domestic speech made (0). However, the percentage of cases correctly predicted is about the same for the simple model and the full model estimated here. This and the fact that the marginal effects for each variable are small indicate that there is need for further theorizing and additional explanatory variables.

TABLE 6.4.   Probit Model Estimates, Major Discretionary Foreign Policy Speeches

	Coefficients[a] (S.E.)	Marginal Effects[b]
National Approval	0.0040	
	(0.0057)	0.0000
Korean War	–0.0003	
	(0.0009)	0.0000
Vietnam-LBJ	–0.0005	
	(0.0003)	–0.0001
Vietnam-RMN	0.0003	
	(0.0004)	0.0000
Gulf War	1.5420*	
	(0.7357)	0.3680
Iran-Contra Affair	–0.6775*	
	(0.4148)	–0.1617
Discretionary Foreign Policy Events	1.1100*	
	(0.2701)	0.2649
Nondiscretionary Foreign Policy Events	0.6969*	
	(0.3175)	0.1663
Exposure	–0.0027	
	(0.0009)*	–0.0065
Constant	–0.9838*	
	(0.3434)	–0.2348
-2*LLR	39.474	p < .000
%Correctly Predicted (N=504)	82.54%	

a. Coefficients marked with an asterisk are statistically different from zero at a .05 (or better) alpha level for a one-tailed test.

b. The marginal effects are calculated as derivatives at mean, that is, by holding the means of all variables constant and taking the derivative with respect to the variable of interest.

FOREIGN POLICY SPEECHES

Table 6.4 reports a model for foreign policy speeches. First, note that the level of presidential approval is again statistically insignificant. Further, we see the different effects that battle deaths during times of war have had on the likelihood of a presidential speech. Neither the Korean War nor the Vietnam War during the Nixon administration had a statistically significant effect on the probability of a speech. Under Johnson, however, the Vietnam War variable has a negative coefficient that almost reaches statistical significance (for a two-tailed test, p < .065). In contrast, the Gulf War has a positive and significant effect, which could suggest that presidential speeches may be more likely when the United States is winning a popular war, as presidents use their addresses to claim credit for military achievements. But this finding may be peculiar to the Gulf War. Presidential speeches occur more frequently at the beginning of a war, so it is possible that the early victory in the Gulf War led to this finding.

The coefficient for the Iran-Contra affair, a scandal with foreign policy implications, is also statistically significant. In contrast to the Watergate scandal during the Nixon administration, the Iran-Contra affair made it less likely that President Reagan would address the nation on foreign policy. In addition, the coefficients for both discretionary and nondiscretionary foreign policy events are significant, showing that such events increase the likelihood of a major foreign policy address. As was found for domestic policy speeches, public exposure is again negative and statistically significant.

The estimates for marginal effects show that the Persian Gulf War had a large positive impact on the president giving a major foreign policy address, and the Iran-Contra affair had a moderate negative effect. Discretionary foreign policy events increased the likelihood of a major foreign policy speech by 26.5 percent while nondiscretionary events increased this probability by only 16.6 percent. The likelihood ratio shows that this model outperforms a simple model, but the fully specified model again predicts correctly the same number of cases as the simple model.

DISCUSSION AND CONCLUSION

The marginal effects of the explanatory variables are larger in the foreign policy model than for domestic speeches, which indicates that these variables affect foreign policy speeches more strongly than domestic speeches. This suggests that there are "two rhetorical presidencies." On the domestic side, the likelihood of a major address is only slightly affected by economic factors, domestic scandals, and discretionary and nondiscretionary domestic events. In foreign policy, however, discretionary events have a large and positive effect on major foreign policy addresses. This can be stated more strongly if we consider the Gulf War to be a series of discretionary events, since the war increased the probability of a presidential foreign policy address by 36.8 percent. The results in tables 6.3 and 6.4 are consistent with the hypothesis that a president makes tradeoffs in terms of which constituencies—domestic versus foreign policy—to satisfy.

For both domestic and foreign policy speeches, discretionary events—Neustadt's self-made happenings—have a stronger marginal impact than do nondiscretionary events on the likelihood of a major presidential address. Since the first step for a president as teacher is to gain the public's attention, the results in this essay are consistent with the idea that presidents can try to be effective teachers by creating events that will gain such attention. Because previous studies have shown that presidential speeches can boost approval ratings, it appears that some presidents are able to capitalize on these events and increase their general ratings. Considering both the evidence on the effects of speeches on presidential approval and the finding that discretionary events raise the probability of a major address, suggests that presidents can indeed be effective teachers who temper public frustration through their speeches. Ironically, the number of discretionary domestic and foreign policy events has remained small for each president, implying that presidents could be more effective teachers than they have been.

Thinking of the president as a teacher who tempers public expectations with realistic assessments of current and future conditions offers a solution to the much discussed "expectations gap."[45] Lowi argues that presidents face public expectations about the delivery of desired outcomes and services that are nearly impossible to meet. According to Lowi's Law of Outcomes, "The probability of failure is always tending toward 100 percent," and even partial successes look like failures when public expectations of the president run as high as they do today.[46] Lowi's proposed solution to the "expectations gap" is to strengthen political parties so that they can mediate the relationship between presidents and the public. But such mediating organizations are unnecessary if presidents exercise their abilities and opportunities to be teachers. As the analysis showed, both discretionary and nondiscretionary events increase the likelihood of a major presidential speech. And if used properly, such speeches could reset or influence public expectations, as suggested by Neustadt's characterization of the president.

In conclusion, however, there is no evidence that the level of, or changes in, presidential approval itself directly drives presidential speechmaking.[47] It may be time to revise conventional wisdom on this score. The decision to address the nation is more subtle and complex than previously believed. First, there are different factors that enter a president's decision calculus for domestic versus foreign policy speeches. Second, the effects of those factors common to domestic and foreign policy speech decisions vary across the two domains. Third, it is necessary to distinguish discretionary from nondiscretionary events to explain the conditions that affect the probability of a presidential speech. In short, explanations of presidential speechmaking are still incomplete; we need a better theory of presidential speechmaking. By ruling out certain extant hypotheses, the analysis offered here takes an initial step in that direction.

Appendix A. Major, Discretionary Presidential Speeches[48]

(All times are Eastern Standard Time)

Date	Time	Topic	Source[a]
Truman (11 speeches or statements)			
13 July 1949	NA	National economic policy	VS
19 July 1950	NA	Korean War	VS
1 September 1950	NA	Korean War	VS
9 September 1950	NA	Defense Production Act	VS
15 December 1950	NA	National emergency-Korean War	VS
11 April 1951	NA	Korean War/MacArthur recalled	VS
14 June 1951	NA	Inflation controls	VS
7 November 1951	NA	International arms reduction	VS
6 March 1952	NA	Mutual security program	VS
8 April 1952	NA	steel mills (nation)	VS
19 June 1952	NA	steel mills (Congress)	VS
Eisenhower (31 speeches or statements)			
19 May 1953	10:30 pm	National security costs	VS
3 June 1953	9:30 pm	Report with cabinet members	VS; BR
26 July 1953	10:00pm	Korean armistice signed	VS
6 August 1953	9:30 pm	Exec & cong achievements	VS
4 January 1954	9:30 pm	Admin goals and accomplishments	VS; BR
15 March 1954	9:00 pm	Tax program	VS
5 April 1954	8:30 pm	National goals and problems	VS; BR
23 August 1954	NA	Success of admin & 83rd Congress	VS; BR
15 July 1955	8:15 pm	Depart for Geneva conference	VS; BR

25 July 1955	10:30 pm	Return from Geneva	VS; BR
29 February 1956	10:00 pm	Decision on 2nd term	VS; BR
16 April 1956	evening	Farm bill veto	VS
3 August 1956	7:00pm	DDE and Dulles on Suez Canal	VS
31 October 1956	7:00 pm	Middle East, Eastern Europe	VS; BR
5 January 1957	NA	Middle East (Congress)	VS; BR
20 February 1957	evening	Middle East and United Nations	VS; BR
14 May 1957	9:00 pm	Government costs	VS
21 May 1957	8:30 pm	Mutual security programs	VS; BR
24 September 1957	9:00 pm	Desegregation in Little Rock	VS; BR
7 November 1957	8:00 pm	National security, technology	VS; BR
13 November 1957	evening	National security	VS; BR
23 December 1957	8:30 pm	Report on Paris NATO conference	VS
15 July 1958	NA	US troops to Lebanon	BR
16 March 1959	9:30 pm	W. Berlin/Soviet challenges to peace	VS; BR
6 August 1959	evening	Labor reform bill needed	VS; BR
10 September 1959	7:30 pm	Report on European trip	VS; BR
3 December 1959	7:15 pm	Departure on goodwill trip	VS; BR
21 February 1960	6:15 pm	S. America departure/national defense	VS; BR
8 March 1960	7:00 pm	South America return	VS; BR
25 May 1960	8:00 pm	Events at Paris summit	VS; BR
27 June 1960	7:30 pm	Report on trip to Far East	BR

Kennedy (13 speeches or statements)

25 May 1961	11:35 a.m.	National problems (Congress)	VS; BR
6 June 1961	7:00 pm	Return from European trip	VS; BR
25 July 1961	10:00 pm	Berlin crisis	VS; BR
2 March 1962	7:00 pm	Nuclear testing & disarmament	VS; BR
13 August 1962	7:00 pm	National economy	VS; BR
30 September 1962	NA	Univerity of Mississippi situation	VS
22 October 1962	7:00 pm	Cuban missile crisis	VS; BR
2 November 1962	5:30 pm	Cuban missile crisis	VS; BR
12 May 1963	9:00 pm	Birmingham Racial Strife	VS
11 June 1963	8:00 pm	Civil rights	VS
26 July 1963	7:00 pm	Nuclear Test Ban Treaty	VS

23 August 1963	NA	Mutual security authorization bill cut	BR
18 September 1963	7:00 pm	Nuclear Test Ban Treaty/tax cut	VS; BR

Johnson (24 speeches or statements)

27 November 1963	NA	Joint session	VS; BR
21 January 1964	11:30 am	Report on Geneva arms proposals	BR
9 April 1964	11:05 pm	Railroad labor dispute moratorium	VS
22 April 1964	6:55 pm	Railroad dispute settled	RU
2 July 1964	6:45 pm	Civil rights signing	VS
4 August 1964	11:36 pm	Vietnam/Tonkin Gulf	BR; RU
5 August 1964	NA	Tonkin Gulf (Congress)	BR
18 October 1964	8:30 pm	Events in Russia, China, UK	VS
15 March 1965	9:02 p.m.	US goals, civil rights (Congress)	VS; BR
26 March 1965	12:40 p.m.	Report on Ku Klux Klan arrests	BR
28 April 1965	8:40 p.m.	Troops to Dominican Republic	VS; BR; RU
30 April 1965	7:07 p.m.	Report on Dominican Republic	BR
2 May 1965	10:00 p.m.	Dominican Republic situation	BR; RU
30 August 1965	9:00 pm	Steel shutdown postponed	VS; BR
3 September 1965	6:30 pm	Steel settlement announced	VS; BR; RU
24 September 1965	1:35 pm	Panama Canal Treaty negotiations	BR
31 January 1966	10:00 am	Bombing of N. Vietnam resumed	RU
24 July 1967	11:58 pm	Troops sent to Detroit riot	VS
27 July 1967	10:30 pm	Civil disorder	VS; RU
26 January 1968	3:58 pm	Pueblo seized by N. Korea	VS; RU
31 March 1968	9:00 pm	Vietnam/ LBJ will not run again	VS; RU
5 April 1968	1:22 pm	Proclaims mourning for MLK	VS; RU
5 June 1968	10:07 pm	RFK assassination	VS; RU
31 October 1968	8:00 pm	Halts bombing of N. Vietnam	VS; RU

Nixon (34 speeches or statements)

14 May 1969	10:00 pm	Vietnam War	VS; RU; VA
8 August 1969	10:00 pm	Domestic programs	VS; RU
3 November 1969	9:32 pm	Vietnam War	VS; RU
15 December 1969	6:02 pm	Vietnam War: troop reductions	VS; RU
26 January 1970	9:00 pm	Veto of HEW bill	RU
23 March 1970	2:15 pm	Postal strike emergency declared	RU

20 April 1970	9:00 pm	Vietnam War: troop reductions	VS; RU; VA
30 April 1970	9:00 pm	Cambodian invasion	VS; RU; VA
3 June 1970	9:00 pm	Report on actions in Cambodia	VS; RU; VA
17 June 1970	Noon	Economic policy	VS; RU
7 October 1970	9:00 pm	Vietnam War: peace initiatives	VS; RU; VA
7 April 1971	9:00 pm	Vietnam War	VS; RU; VA
20 May 1971	Noon	SALT talks	VS; RU; VA
15 July 1971	10:31 pm	Trip to China announced	RU; VA
15 August 1971	9:00 pm	Economic policy: price freeze	VS; RU; VA
9 September 1971	12:32 pm	Economic stabilization (Congress)	VS; VA
7 October 1971	7:30 pm	Economic stabilization	VS; RU; VA
21 October 1971	7:31 pm	Supreme Court nominations	VA
25 January 1972	8:30 pm	Peace plan	VS; RU; VA
16 March 1972	10:00 pm	Busing	VS; RU; VA
26 April 1972	10:00 pm	Vietnam	VS; RU; VA
8 May 1972	9:00 pm	Vietnam	VS; RU; VA
1 June 1972	9:40 pm	Return from Soviet Union (Congress)	VS; VA
23 January 1973	10:01 pm	Paris peace accord	VS; RU; VA
29 March 1973	9:01 pm	Vietnam/domestic problems	VS; RU; VA
30 April 1973	9:01 pm	Watergate	VS; RU; VA
13 June 1973	8:30 pm	Price controls	VS; RU; VA
15 August 1973	9:00 pm	Watergate	VS; RU; VA
12 October 1973	9:06 pm	Ford to be nominated as VP	VS; VA
7 November 1973	7:30 pm	Energy shortage	VS; RU; VA
25 November 1973	7:00 pm	Energy policy	VS; RU; VA
17 January 1974	3:04 pm	Egyptian-Israeli agreement	S.O. 1989.
29 April 1974	9:01 pm	Watergate tapes	VS; RU; VA
29 May 1974	1:02 pm	Syria-Israeli agreement	S.O. 1989.

Ford (9 speeches or statements)

12 August 1974	9:06 pm	Joint session	VS
8 September 1974	11:05 am	Nixon pardon	VS; RU; VA
8 October 1974	4:02 pm	Whip Inflation Now policy (Congress)	VS
13 January 1975	9:00 pm	Energy and economy	VS; RU
29 March 1975	7:31 pm	Tax reduction bill signed	VS; RU

10 April 1975	9:04 pm	Foreign policy (Congress)	VS; VA
15 May 1975	12:27 am	Mayaguez rescue statement	RU
27 May 1975	8:31 pm	Energy programs	VS; RU
6 October 1975	8:00 pm	Tax and spending reductions	VS; RU

Carter (14 speeches or statements)

2 February 1977	10:00 pm	Fireside chat: national goals	VS; VA
18 April 1977	8:00 pm	Energy plan	VS; VA
20 April 1977	9:05 pm	Energy plan (Congress)	VS; VA
8 November 1977	9:00 pm	Update on energy plan	VS; VA
1 February 1978	9:00 pm	Fireside chat: Panama Canal	VS; VA
18 September 1978	8:06 pm	Camp David Summit (Congress)	VS
24 October 1978	10:00 pm	Anti-inflation program	VS
5 April 1979	9:00 pm	Energy: decontrol oil	VS
18 June 1979	9:03 pm	Vienna Summit, SALT II (Congress)	VS; VA
15 July 1979	10:00 pm	Crisis of confidence	VS; VA
1 October 1979	9:00 pm	Soviets in Cuba and SALT II	VS; VA
12 November 1979	2:01 pm	Boycott Iranian oil	VA
4 January 1980	9:00 pm	Soviets in Afghanistan	VS; VA
25 April 1980	7:00 am	Hostage rescue attempt	VS

Reagan (34 speeches or statements)

5 February 1981	9:02 p.m.	Economy	VS; VA
18 February 1981	9:00 p.m.	Economic recovery (Congress)	VS; VA
28 April 1981	9:05 p.m.	Economic recovery (Congress)	VS; VA
27 July 1981	8:01 p.m.	Tax reduction	VS; VA
24 September 1981	9:00 p.m.	Economic recovery	VS; VA
29 April 1982	8:00 pm	Federal budget	VS; VA
16 August 1982	8:02 pm	Tax and budget legislation	VS; VA
1 September 1982	6:00 pm	Middle East policy	VS.: VA
20 September 1982	5:00 pm	Marines to Lebanon	VS
13 October 1982	7:30 pm	Economy	VS; VA
22 November 1982	8:00 pm	Arms reduction and deterrence	VS; VA
23 March 1983	8:02 pm	National security	VS; VA
27 April 1983	8:04 pm	Central America (Congress)	VS; VA
5 September 1983	8:00 pm	KAL 007 shot down	VS; VA

27 October 1983	8:00 pm	Lebanon, Grenada	VS; VA
9 May 1984	8:00 pm	Central America	VS; VA
24 April 1985	8:00 pm	Budget and deficit reduction	VS; VA
28 May 1985	8:00 pm	Tax reform	VS; VA
14 November 1985	8:00 pm	Upcoming US-USSR summit	VS; VA
21 November 1985	9:20 pm	US-USSR summit (Congress)	VS; VA
28 January 1986	5:00 pm	Challenger explosion	VS
26 February 1986	8:00 pm	National security	VS; VA
16 March 1986	8:00 pm	Aid to Nicaraguan resistance	VS; VA
14 April 1986	9:00 pm	Air strike on Libya	VS
24 June 1986	Noon	Aid to Nicaraguan resistance	VS
14 September 1986	8:00 pm	Drug prevention (with Nancy)	VS; VA
13 October 1986	8:00 pm	Report on meetings with Gorbachev	VS; VA
13 November 1986	8:01 pm	Iran arms and Contra aid	VS; VA
2 December 1986	Noon	Iran-contra investigation	VS
4 March 1987	9:00 pm	Iran-contra controversy	VS; VA
15 June 1987	8:00 pm	Economic summit/arms control/deficit	VS; VA
12 August 1987	8:00 pm	Iran-contra and admin goals	VS; VA
10 December 1987	9:01 pm	US-Soviet summit	VS
2 February 1988	8:00 pm	Nicaragua	VS

Bush (13 speeches or statements)

5 September 1989	9:00 pm	Drug control strategy	VS; VA
20 December 1989	7:20 am	Panama	VS; Kernell 1993; VA
8 August 1990	9:00 am	Troops to Saudi Arabia	*Public Papers*
11 September 1990	9:09 pm	Persian Gulf/budget deficit (Congress)	VS; VA
2 October 1990	9:00 pm	Budget agreement	Kernell 1993; VA
16 January 1991	9:01 pm	Desert Storm air strikes begin	VS; Kernell 1993
23 February 1991	10:00 pm	Persian Gulf ground war begins	VS; VA
26 February 1991	9:48 a.m.	Iraqi withdrawal	VS; Kernell 1993
6 March 1991	9:12 pm	Persian Gulf conflict (Congress)	VS; VA
27 September 1991	8:02 pm	Nuclear arms reductions	VS; VA
1 May 1992	9:03 pm	Los Angeles riots	VS
1 September 1992	9:00 pm	Hurricane Andrew	VA
4 December 1992	12:32 pm	Somalia	VA

Clinton (10 speeches or statements)

15 February 1993	9:00 pm	Economic program	VS; VA
17 February 1993	9:10 pm	Administration goals (Congress)	VS; VA; TAMU
26 June 1993	7:40 pm	Missile strike on Iraqi headquarters	VA; TAMU
3 August 1993	8:00 pm	Economic program/budget	VS; VA; TAMU
22 September 1993	9:10 pm	Health care reform (Congress)	VS; VA; TAMU
7 October 1993	5:02 pm	Somalia	VA
15 September 1994	NA	Haiti	VS; VA; TAMU
18 September 1994	NA	Haiti	VS; VA
10 October 1994	NA	Iraq and Haiti	VS; VA; TAMU
15 December 1994	NA	Tax cuts	VS; VA; TAMU

a. Abbreviations VS, Ragsdale, *Vital Statistics*; VA, Vanderbilt Archives; TAMU, Texas A&M University archive; BR, *Broadcasting*; RU, Rutkus; S.O., Simon and Ostrom

APPENDIX B. EVENTS, SUPPLEMENTAL LIST

(D = domestic, F = foreign policy, DIS = discretionary, ND = nondiscretionary)

1953–1988

11/63	Kennedy assassination	(D-ND)
4/68	Martin Luther King assassination	(D-ND)
6/68	Robert Kennedy assassination	(D-ND)
7/73	Nixon imposes wage and price controls	(D-DIS)
9/74	Ford pardons Nixon	(D-DIS)
9/75	Two assassination attempts on Ford's life	(D-ND)
7/77	Bert Lance scandal	(D-ND)

1989–1994

1/89	Two Libyan jets downed by U.S. Navy	(F-DIS)
3/89	Senate defeats Tower nomination	(D-ND)
10/89	Bay area earthquake	(D-ND)
6/90	Bush reneges on tax pledge	(D-DIS)
8/90	Iraq invades Kuwait/U.S. troops deployed	(F-DIS)
10/90	Congress approves budget deficit plan	(D-ND)
11/90	UN authorizes force against Iraq	(F-ND)
10/91	Clarence Thomas controversy	(D-DIS)
12/91	Last U.S. hostages freed	(F-ND)

4/92	Rioting over Rodney King trial	(D-ND)
12/92	U.S. forces enter Somalia	(F-DIS)
2/93	World Trade Center bombing	(D-ND)
4/93	Religious compound burns at Waco	(D-DIS)
6/93	U.S. attacks Iraq to retaliate for plot to kill Bush	(F-DIS)
9/93	Israel and PLO sign accord in Washington, D.C.	(F-DIS)
11/93	NAFTA ratified	(D-ND)
7/94	Whitewater hearings open	(D-ND)
7/94	UN authorizes invasion of Haiti	(F-DIS)
9/94	Health care reform fails in Congress	(D-ND)

NOTES

1. Karlyn Kohrs Campbell and Kathleen Hall Jamieson, *Deeds Done in Words: Presidential Rhetoric and the Genres of Governance* (Chicago: The University of Chicago Press, 1990) p. 3.

2. Roderick P. Hart, *The Sound of Leadership: Presidential Communication in the Modern Age* (Chicago: The University of Chicago Press, 1987) p. 77.

3. Theodore Lowi, *The Personal Presidency: Power Invested, Promise Unfulfilled* (Ithaca, N.Y.: Cornell University Press, 1985), Barbara Hinckley, *The Symbolic Presidency: How Presidents Portray Themselves* (New York: Routledge, 1990), Samuel Kernell, *Going Public: New Strategies of Presidential Leadership*, 2nd ed. (Washington, D.C.: Congressional Quarterly Press, 1993), Paul Haskell Zernicke, *Pitching the Presidency: How Presidents Depict the Office* (Westport, CT: Praeger, 1994).

4. Lowi, *Personal Presidency*. George C. Edwards, *The Public Presidency* (New York: St. Martin's Press, 1983).

5. Jeffrey Tulis, "The Two Constitutional Presidencies" in Michael Nelson, ed., *The Presidency and the Political System* (Washington, D.C.: CQ Press, 1984).

6. Kernell, *Going Public*, p. 2.

7. For example, Kernell, *Going Public*, and Lyn Ragsdale, "The Politics of Presidential Speechmaking, 1949–1980," *American Political Science Review* 78: 971–984 (1984). Charles W. Ostrom, Jr., and Dennis M. Simon, "The Man in the Teflon Suit?" *Public Opinion Quarterly* 53: 353–387 (1989), Charles W. Ostrom, Jr., and Renée M. Smith, "Error Correction, Attitude Persistence, and Executive Rewards and Punishments: A Behavioral Theory of Presidential Approval," *Political Analysis.* 4 (1993): 127–183.

8. Charles W. Ostrom, Jr., and Dennis M. Simon, "Promise and Performance: A Dynamic Model of Presidential Popularity," *American Political Science Review* 79 (1985): 334–358.

9. Richard Neustadt, *Presidential Power and the Modern Presidents: The Politics of Leadership from Roosevelt to Reagan* (New York: The Free Press, 1990).

10. Ragsdale, "Politics of Presidential Speechmaking."

11. See also Richard F. Fenno, Jr. *Home Style: House Members in Their Districts* (Boston: Little, Brown, and Company, 1978).

12. Neustadt, *Presidential Power*, p. 8.

13. Kernell, *Going Public*, pp. 17–18.

14. Benjamin I. Page, Robert Y. Shapiro, and Glenn R. Dempsey. "What Moves Public Opinion?" *American Political Science Review* 78 (1987): 971–984.

15. Neustadt, *Presidential Power*, p. 84.

16. Ibid, p. 84. See also Donald R. Kinder and Susan T. Fiske. "Presidents in the Public Mind" in Margaret G. Hermann, ed., *Political Psychology* (San Francisco: Jossey-Bass Publishers, 1986).

17. Neustadt, *Presidential Power*, p. 89.

18. Ibid.

19. Donald R. Kinder, Mark D. Peters, Robert P. Abelson, and Susan T. Fiske, "Presidential Prototypes," *Political Behavior* 2 (1980): 315–337.

20. Neustadt, *Presidential Power*, p. 80.

21. Paul Light. *The President's Agenda: Domestic Policy Choice From Kennedy to Reagan*, revised ed. (Baltimore: Johns Hopkins University Press, 1991). See also Mark A. Peterson. *Legislating Together: The White House and Capitol Hill From Eisenhower to Reagan* (Cambridge: Harvard University Press, 1990).

22. Kernell, *Going Public*, p. 93.

23. Ragsdale, "Politics of Presidential Speechmaking." See also Lyn Ragsdale, *Vital Statistics on the Presidency: Washington to Clinton* (Washington, D.C.: Congressional Quarterly Press, 1996).

24. Ragsdale, defined a major speech as a live televised or broadcast address to the nation that preempts programming on all of the major networks (*Vital Statistics*, p. 165). While this implies that these speeches must occur during prime time, the list includes major speeches that do not fit these criteria. For instance, it includes an October 14, 1987, Reagan speech about Supreme Court nominee Robert Bork that the three major networks refused to broadcast. The list also includes a non-prime time Bush speech about the Iraqi withdrawal. Since the speeches compiled do not always follow from Ragsdale's definition, I developed my own, which does not require that speeches occur during "prime time," although a majority of them do. These speeches are listed in Appendix A. I do not include the Saturday radio addresses of Reagan, Bush, or Clinton.

25. Ragsdale, *Vital Statistics*, p. 164 reports the following distribution of speeches: Truman, 11; Eisenhower, 32; Kennedy, 11; Johnson, 15; Nixon, 30; Ford, 8; Carter, 13; Reagan, 38; Bush, 12; Clinton, 8. The largest discrepancies for these data

occur for the Johnson, Nixon, and Reagan presidencies where I find 9 more, 4 more, and 4 fewer speeches, respectively.

26. The following probit model is used to represent the president's decision about whether to give a major presidential address:

$$P(\ Y_t = 1) = \alpha_0 + \sum_{i=1}^{I} \beta_i\ C_{it} + \sum_{j=1}^{J} \delta_j\ R_{jt} + \sum_{k=1}^{K} \gamma_k\ E_{kt} + \pi\ T_t + \eta\ O_t + \varepsilon_t$$

where Y_t equals 1 if the president gives a major address in month t and is 0 otherwise; the C_{it} represent the president's standing with his key constituencies; the R_{jt} are indicators of "real life" concerns about economic and foreign affairs; the E_{kt} symbolize both uncontrollable "outside events" and "self-made happenings;" T_t is a measure of time into the president's term; O_t represents the degree of executive overexposure; and ε_t is a stochastic error term.

Under the assumption that the error term follows a standard normal distribution, the model is a nonlinear probit model. That is, the marginal effect of any variable on the propensity to give a major speech changes for each value of that variable rather than being constant as in linear regression. After obtaining coefficient estimates, to estimate and compare the marginal effects of each variable, I hold all other variables at their means.

27. These data are based on results reported in various editions of *The Gallup Poll Index*, the *Gallup Poll Monthly*, and data available from Roper's POLL database.

28. This variable is suggested by Michael Ault, "Arming the Prince: The Politics of Presidential Rhetoric, 1960–1992" unpublished manuscript (1996). I collected these data from various issues of the *Gallup Poll Monthly* and from George Edwards, *Presidential Approval: A Sourcebook*, (Baltimore: Johns Hopkins University Press, 1990).

29. These data are taken from Ragsdale, *Vital Statistics*. Data on concurrence with the president's position are percentages based on the number of congressional votes supporting the president's position divided by the total number of votes on legislation upon which the president took a position.

30. The number of battle deaths were culled from various editions of the *New York Times*, which reported weekly the U.S. Defense Department's announcements of the number killed in the Korean Conflict and the Vietnam War. These data represent the information that the public had at the time of a speech. Since the president is hypothesized to be responding to public dissatisfaction with the war, it is important, when possible, to use information that was publicly available at the time of the president's decision.

31. John E. Mueller, *War, Presidents, and Public Opinion* (New York: Wiley, 1973).

32. The economic data were obtained from the CITIBASE: Citibase economic database. 1946–1994. New York, Citibank, N.A., 1978.

33. Paul Brace and Barbara Hinckley. *Follow the Leader: Opinion Polls and the Modern Presidents* (New York: Basic Books, 1992). Brace and Hinckley's events are those that appeared in two of the following three annual summaries: *The World Almanac and Book of Facts, The Almanac of American History,* and *The Encyclopedia of Facts and Dates.* Brace and Hinckley's selection criteria seem more objective than those used in previous research (e.g. Ostrom and Simon, *Promise and Performance*). Brace and Hinckley's list may miss some events that others would include. I found their list incomplete in three ways. First, since they included the Reagan assassination attempt, I added four events that represented assassination attempts (or successes) on presidents. Second, I added Nixon's second imposition of wage and price controls since they included his first. And third, I included the Nixon pardon and the Bert Lance scandal, which seemed as important as other scandal-related events on their list. Adding these events did not change the substantive conclusions from my empirical results.

34. Based upon Brace and Hinckley, *Follow The Leader,* events were coded as discretionary versus nondiscretionary depending upon "whether the surface impression suggested some control by the president over the timing or occurrence of the event." As Brace and Hinckley acknowledge, this definition does not take into account covert activity in foreign affairs.

35. The Watergate variable takes on a value of 1 from February 1973 through July 1974 and 0 otherwise. The Iran-Contra variable takes on a value of 1 from November 1986 through the end of Reagan's term in 1988 and is 0 otherwise.

36. Ragsdale, "The Politics of Presidential Speechmaking" and Robert L. Dudley and Alan J. Rosenblatt, "When Silence is Golden: Presidential Speechmaking and Consumer Confidence," unpublished manuscript (1995).

37. Ostrom and Simon, "Promise and Performance"; Kernell, *Going Public*; Ostrom and Smith, "Behavioral Theory of Approval."

38. Neustadt, *Presidential Power,* p. 87.

39. Ragsdale, "The Politics of Presidential Speechmaking" and others have found that presidential speeches have a positive effect on a president's national approval rating. Given the conventional wisdom that the level of, or changes in, presidential approval affect the likelihood of a president delivering a major address, the potential endogeneity of presidential approval must be addressed. I checked my findings for the effects of endogeneity by reestimating the model using an instrumental variable to purge any effects of a reciprocal relationship between the occurrence of a speech and a president's approval rating. Each of the models discussed below was reestimated using an instrumental variable and in each case, presidential

approval remained statistically insignificant indicating that simultaneity has no effect on my statistical results.

40. Gregory L. Hager and Terry Sullivan, "President-centered and Presidency-centered Explanations of Presidential Public Activity," *American Journal of Political Science* 38 (1994): 1079–1103. To check the robustness of this finding, I also dropped all constituency variables except the level and change of presidential approval and reestimated the model, again finding neither the change nor the level of approval have a statistically significant effect. In addition, I reestimated the model for the period 1953 through 1984, under the assumption that the 1985 corporate takeovers of ABC, CBS, and NBC made it more difficult for the president to obtain air time, so that 1985 represented a structural break in the causal process. Again, neither the effects of a change in nor the level of presidential approval were statistically significant. For a different suggestion of structural change in the propensity of presidents to make major speeches, see Robert C. Turner, "The Popularity That Presidents Make: Going Public Then and Now" unpublished manuscript (1996).

41. None of the other constituency variables had a significant effect in the model for domestic speeches and thus were eliminated from the final model in table 6.3.

42. For evidence that support for Reagan after the revelation of arms sales to Iran was heavily affected by the public's views on U.S. involvement in Central American (implying that the Iran-Contra scandal falls under foreign policy domain), see Jon A. Krosnik and Donald R. Kinder, "Altering the Foundations of Support for the President through Priming," *American Political Science Review* 84 (1990): 497–512.

43. Because none of the other constituency variables had statistically significant effects in the model for foreign policy speeches, they were omitted from the final analysis shown in table 6.4.

44. See also Light, *The President's Agenda*; Peterson, *Legislating Together*.

45. Lowi, *The Personal Presidency*; Godfrey Hodgson, *All Things to All Men: The False Promise of the Modern American Presidency from Franklin D. Roosevelt to Ronald Reagan* (New York: Simon and Schuster, 1980).

46. Lowi, *The Personal Presidency*, p. 20.

47. See also Ault, "Arming the Prince" and Turner, "The Popularity that Presidents Make

48. Data compiled from: Kernell, *Going Public*; Ragsdale, *Vital* Statistics; Ostrom and Simon, "Promise and Performance"; Charles W. Ostrom, Jr., and Dennis M. Simon "The Man in the Teflon Suit?" *Public Opinion Quarterly* 53 (1989): 353–387; Dennis M. Simon and Charles W. Ostrom, Jr., "The Impact of Televised Speeches and Foreign Travel on Presidential Approval," *Public Opinion Quarterly* 53

(1989): 58–82; Denis Rutkus, "A report on simultaneous network coverage of presidential addresses to the nation" in Hearings, Subcommittee on Communications of the Committee on Interstate and Foreign Commerce, House of Representatives, Ninety-fourth Congress, 2nd session, March 2–3, 1976; a 1965 issue of Broadcasting magazine; and the online Vanderbilt Television (VA) and Texas A&M University presidential (TAMU) archives.

CHAPTER 7

The President's Inner Circle: Personality and Leadership Style in Foreign Policy Decision-making

Thomas Preston

I. LEADERSHIP STYLE: THE "ENABLER" OF PRESIDENTIAL POWER

Richard Neustadt observed that due to the inherent limitations on their institutional powers, presidents are forced to rely upon their interpersonal skills and arts of persuasion to carry out their policies. Although this description of presidential power appears to place individual presidents squarely into an institutional context that constrains most of their freedom of action, Neustadt's depiction of presidential power emphasizes the fundamental importance of the *personal presidency* as well. Neustadt views the personal characteristics (or qualities) of presidents as critical to successful presidential leadership—and to the ability of presidents to obtain the kind of "personal influence of an effective sort on governmental action" which he defines as *presidential power*.[1] However, before they can *persuade*, presidents must formulate and develop their policies, gather and analyze immense amounts of information, adapt their strategies and policies to a rapidly changing political environment, and surround themselves with advisers and advisory systems capable of effectively dealing with all of these difficult tasks. Across all of these areas, the individual characteristics of presidents play a critical role.

For Neustadt, the personal qualities necessary for successful presidents are those traits found in *"experienced politicians of extraordinary temperament,"*—ones possessing political expertise, unpretentious self-confidence in their abilities, and who are at ease with their roles and enjoy the job.[2] Noting that the

Presidency "is not a place for amateurs," Neustadt points to the importance of prior policy experience or expertise.[3] Further, Neustadt emphasizes the need for presidents to be active information-gatherers and to seek out multiple sources and differing perspectives on policy problems. This involves leaders cultivating enhanced "sensitivity" to the policy environment through "sensitivity to processes" (who does what and how in the political environment) and "sensitivity to substance" (the details and specifics of policy).[4] The clear message from Neustadt's work is that the personal qualities of leaders play a significant role in successful (or unsuccessful) presidential leadership—and that presidents who fail to effectively utilize their advisory systems, or who lack appropriate *sensitivity to the policy context*, are unlikely to develop the foundations of power necessary to persuade anyone.

This chapter presents a new typology of presidential leadership style which builds upon Neustadt's emphasis on the importance to policymaking of the personal qualities (or temperament) of presidents—an area he left largely unexplored. First, the relevant existing literature on leadership and personality is briefly reviewed. Next, a brief discussion of the research approach taken here is offered, followed by a presentation of the presidential leadership style framework itself. The application of this framework (linking the personal characteristics of presidents to their subsequent leadership styles in office) is then illustrated by examining the personality and leadership style of President Lyndon Johnson. The clear evidence from the archival record that Johnson's leadership style and decision behavior were consistent with his measured personality characteristics demonstrates the value of the theoretical framework and, more important, the utility of improving our understanding of the personal qualities of presidents.

Although there has been much debate over the merits of "president-centered" vs. "presidency-centered" research, I do not seek to fit into either camp directly, but to bridge the gap between them.[5] I take a "contingency-based" approach which accepts both president- and presidency-centered explanations (as Neustadt does implicitly in his definition of presidential power) and seek to establish criteria for determining when one type of explanation would be more appropriate than another. As Hargrove observes, the issue for presidential scholars should not be *whether individuals make a difference*, but *under what conditions* they make a difference.[6] In this sense, the framework presented here depicts the personality characteristics and styles of presidents as critical "enablers" of *presidential power* in the Neustadt-sense—that serve either to add or detract from the ability of presidents to perceive their policy environments and to navigate the treacherous shoals of the policy process.

II. THE POLITICAL PSYCHOLOGY OF PRESIDENTS, LEADERSHIP STYLE, AND INDIVIDUAL DIFFERENCES.

PRESIDENTIAL LEADERSHIP

Research on the impact of presidential personality or leadership style upon advisory arrangements and decisionmaking in the White House has taken on many forms. Some scholars have focused upon *aspects of the individual personalities of presidents* to understand their behavior in the White House.[7] Such treatments of the presidential personality range from early psychoanalytic studies exploring the "character" or psychological development of individual leaders[8] to more recent, nonpsychoanalytic techniques of content analysis derived from modern social psychology research which measure specific traits or characteristics of leaders to explain their behavior.[9] Other studies have developed portraits of presidential style through the use of archival evidence and interviews combining the personal qualities and backgrounds of leaders into distinctive styles in office.[10] Still other research, focusing more upon the differing organizational preferences of presidents, has analyzed the *strengths and weaknesses of different kinds of organizational arrangements.*[11] A common thread connecting these works, however, is the notion that *what individual presidents are like matters* and that their personal qualities can significantly affect decision making and policy.

INDIVIDUAL DIFFERENCES AND LEADERSHIP

A wealth of research also exists regarding the individual characteristics (or traits) of leaders and how these shape (both within and outside of groups) their styles of decisionmaking, interpersonal interaction, information processing, and management in office.[12] For example, among the psychological studies of the characteristics of leaders are ones examining personal needs for power,[13] personal needs for affiliation,[14] conceptual complexity,[15] locus of control,[16] achievement or task/interpersonal emphasis,[17] and self-confidence.[18] Recent archival research has found that three individual characteristics in particular—need for power, complexity, and prior policy experience—play a critical role in shaping presidential leadership style.[19] The framework presented in this chapter builds upon these findings. First, it is necessary to review these three central leader characteristics.

POWER

The need for power (or dominance) is a personality characteristic which has been extensively studied and linked to specific types of behavior and interactional styles.[20] Specifically, one would expect leaders with progressively higher psychological needs for power to be increasingly dominant and assertive in their leadership styles in office and to assert greater control over subordinates and policy decisions. For example, Fodor and Smith found that leaders with a high need for power were more associated with the suppression of open decisionmaking and discussion within groups than were low power leaders.[21] Similarly, a number of studies have found high power leaders requiring a far greater degree of personal control over the policy process and the actions of subordinates than do low power leaders.[22] In terms of interpersonal relationships, studies have also found that leaders high in the need for power exhibit more controlling, domineering behavior toward subordinates than low power leaders.[23]

Further, a study examining the characteristics and leadership styles of past U.S. presidents in cases of foreign policy decisionmaking, found that leaders high in the need for power preferred formal, hierarchical advisory system structures designed to enhance their own personal control over the policy process.[24] These leaders tended to centralize decisionmaking within tight inner-circles of trusted advisers and to insist on direct personal involvement and control over policy formulation and decisions. Their policy preferences tended to dominate both the policy deliberations within advisory groups and the nature of the final policy decisions. In contrast, low power leaders preferred less hierarchical advisory system structures and required less personal control over the policy process; their policy preferences tended not to dominate advisory group deliberations or final decisions. As a result, the input of subordinates played a far greater role in policymaking. Unlike these low power leaders, high power leaders were found to possess assertive interpersonal styles in which they would actively challenge or seek to influence the positions taken by their advisers; further, these leaders were also more likely to override or ignore the conflicting or opposing policy views of subordinates.

COMPLEXITY

The psychological literature has long argued that the cognitive complexity of decisionmakers is another individual characteristic which significantly affects the nature of decisionmaking, style of leadership, assessment of risk, and character of general information processing within decision groups.[25] For example, Vertzberger, among others, has noted that as the cognitive complexity of individual decisionmakers rises, they become more capable of dealing with complex decision environments and information that demand new or subtle distinctions.[26] When making decisions, complex individuals tend to have greater cognitive need for information, are more attentive to incoming information, prefer systematic over heuristic processing, and deal with any overload of information better than their less complex counterparts.[27] In terms of interactions with advisers and the acceptance of critical feedback, several studies have shown that complex individuals are far more interested in receiving negative feedback from others—and are more likely to incorporate it into their own decisionmaking—than are those who are less complex.[28]

Complexity has also been linked by scholars to how attentive or sensitive leaders are to information from (or nuances within) their surrounding political or policy environments.[29] Hermann notes that the more sensitive the individual is to information from the decision environment, the more receptive the leader is to information regarding the views of colleagues or constituents, the views of outside actors, and the value of alternative viewpoints and discrepant information.[30] In contrast, leaders with a low sensitivity to contextual information will be less receptive to information from the outside environment, will operate from a previously established and strongly held set of beliefs, will selectively perceive and process incoming information in order to support or bolster this prior framework, and will be unreceptive or close-minded toward alternative viewpoints and discrepant information. Vertzberger and Glad have noted that low complexity individuals tend to show symptoms of dogmatism, view and judge issues in black-and-white terms, ignore information threatening their existing closed belief systems, and have limited ability to adjust their beliefs to new information.[31]

One study found that highly complex leaders preferred more open advisory and information processing systems than did leaders lower in complexity—no doubt reflecting different needs for both information and differentiation in the policy environment.[32] High complexity leaders were far more sensitive than others to the external policy context, as well as to the existence of multiple policy dimensions or perspectives on issues. During policy deliberations, they also engaged in broad information search routines that emphasized the presentation of alternative viewpoints, discrepant information, and multiple policy options by their advisers. Such leaders focused substantial discussion within their advisory groups on future policy contingencies and the likely views or reactions of other policy actors in the environment. In addition, they were less likely to employ simplistic analogies, "black-and-white" problem representations, or stereotypical images of their opponents during policy deliberations. However, complex leaders had less decisive and more deliberative decision-making styles in office—a finding consistent with the heavy emphasis placed by such leaders upon extensive policy debate and information search within their advisory groups.

Less complex leaders—with their lower cognitive need for extensive information searches and examination of multiple policy perspectives—tended to be far less sensitive to both information and the external policy environment. This reduced sensitivity to information and to context manifested itself in limited information searches and in a diminished emphasis on the presentation by advisers of alternative viewpoints, discrepant information, and multiple policy options. Such leaders were more likely to rely upon simplistic analogies, "black-and-white" problem representations, or stereotypical images of their opponents during their policy deliberations. Further, given their limited interest in extensive policy debate or broad information searches, low complexity leaders were also found to have, according to the archival evidence, very decisive and less deliberative decisionmaking styles. It is important to emphasize, however, that complexity *does not* relate to either general intelligence or overall level of political sophistication. Complexity should not be seen as pejorative, since there are both advantages and disadvantages associated with leaders being either high or low in complexity. For example, there are many policy contexts, such as policy crises with limited decisionmaking time, in which the decisiveness of low complexity leaders would provide strong leadership and a sense of policy direction. Complexity refers simply to individuals' general, cognitive need for information and the degree to which they differentiate their surrounding policy environment.

However, complexity not only has the potential to affect how leaders process information, but may also influence their sensitivity to the interpersonal environment. Self-monitoring theory suggests that there are two characteristic interpersonal orientations: "high self-monitors" who are more sensitive and attuned to the nuances of the interpersonal environment than less sensitive "low self-monitors."[33] In terms of leadership styles, high self-monitors are more sensitive to the political situation (the views of constituents, political allies, opponents, the political climate, etc.); they actively seek information from advisers on the political situation; and they are "chameleon-like" in modifying their own behavior and policy decisions to conform to the existing environment. In contrast, low self-monitors place much less emphasis on the political situation in relation to their own behavior or policy positions; in this vein, they passively receive information on the political situation from advisers and are driven more by their own views and beliefs regarding policy than by a desire to conform to the existing political environment.[34]

PRIOR POLICY EXPERIENCE/EXPERTISE

Finally, the prior policy experience or expertise of leaders has a significant impact upon presidential style, the nature of advisory group interactions, and how forcefully leaders assert their own positions on policy issues.[35] Past experience provides leaders with a sense of what actions will be effective or ineffective in specific policy situations, as well as which cues from the environment should be attended to and which are irrelevant.[36] It influences how much learning must be accomplished on the job, the inventory of behaviors (standard operating procedures) possessed, and how confident the leader will be in interactions with experts. Leaders with a high degree of prior policy experience are more likely to insist on personal involvement or control over policymaking than are those low in prior policy experience, who will tend to be more dependent on the views of expert advisers.[37] Indeed, experienced leaders with expertise in a policy area are far less likely to rely upon the views of advisers or utilize simplistic stereotypes or analogies to understand policy situations. Such leaders are more interested in gathering detailed information from the policy environment, and they employ a more deliberate decision process than their less experienced counterparts. Similarly, leaders lacking experience or expertise find themselves far more dependent on expert advisers and more likely to utilize simplistic stereotypes and analogies when making decisions.[38] Knowing whether a leader is approaching foreign or domestic policy as a relative expert or novice provides insight into predicting how damaging such reliance upon analogy might be to a particular leader's information-management and information-processing styles.

III. THE RESEARCH APPROACH

The research underpinning this chapter's typology of presidential leadership style has been heavily influenced by recent scholarship emphasizing the need to study the presidency using only systematically collected data and explicit methodologies to test theoretical propositions.[39] Here, I briefly summarize how presidents' characteristics were measured in this typology and the empirical evidence on which I base my assumptions regarding the impact of leaders' characteristics on their decisionmaking behavior.

MEASURING LEADERS' CHARACTERISTICS

The individual characteristics of presidents have been measured using Margaret Hermann's (1983) *Personality Assessment-at-a-Distance* (PAD) approach. This method utilizes content analysis of the spontaneous interview responses by political leaders across differing time periods, audiences, and substantive topic areas to construct detailed personality profiles of individuals according to eight different traits: the need for power, need for affiliation, ethnocentrism, locus of control, complexity, self-confidence, distrust of others, and task/interpersonal emphasis.[40] This approach has previously been used to construct detailed profiles of more than one hundred political leaders in more than forty different countries.[41] These data for a sizable number of leaders not only allow us to set out the range of each characteristic, thereby demonstrating what constitutes high and low scores for leaders, but they also provide the means to compare empirically and interpret the scores for American presidents across these traits.[42] In gauging leaders' policy experience or expertise, an additional measure was developed to reflect factors such as the nature of each leader's previous policy positions, the degree to which leaders focused upon specific policy areas, and the extent to which they possessed other relevant policy experience.[43] Thus, in the typology of presidential leadership style presented below (see tables 7.1 and 7.2), presidents are placed into specific style categories based upon the PAD scores for their individual characteristics.

LINKING LEADER CHARACTERISTICS TO BEHAVIOR IN THE ARCHIVAL RECORD

The typology involves claims regarding the likely leadership styles and behavior of presidents with specific combinations of individual characteristics. Using the PAD technique, the individual characteristics of four modern American presidents—Truman, Eisenhower, Kennedy, and Johnson—were previously measured systematically and compared.[44] Hypotheses (based upon existing psychological and presidential research) regarding the behavioral implications of these characteristics for leadership style, decisionmaking, and advisory system preferences were tested against the archival record and presidents' actual foreign policy decisionmaking.[45] Since the focus was upon *per-*

sonal characteristics and their impact on leadership behavior, it was necessary to select presidents who varied in their personal characteristics in theoretically significant ways and for whom the relevant archival data were available.[46] Further, to have sufficient cases for comparison, a conscious decision was made to break down foreign policy cases into discreet units, called *Occasions for Interaction* (OCI). The OCIs were slices of time throughout each policy case, during which presidents and their advisers met (both formally and informally) and had the opportunity to formulate and debate policy and to make decisions.[47] As a result, the testing of the theoretical hypotheses involved assessing how well the individual characteristics of presidents (measured by PAD) predicted behavior (in terms of leadership style, decisionmaking, interpersonal interactions, and advisory preferences) in all the cases of interaction across policy cases and presidents.

IV. Toward a Typology of Presidential Leadership Style

Although many factors have been linked to leadership style,[48] archival research has suggested two dimensions of critical importance: (1) the leader's need for control and involvement in the policy process; and (2) the leader's need for information and general sensitivity to context.[49] In tables 7.1 and 7.2, these dimensions (*need for control* and *sensitivity to context*) combine to form the building blocks for a typology of presidential leadership style which takes into account the *contingent* nature of the relationships between leaders' individual characteristics, their leadership styles, and their attentiveness to the external policy environment.[50] The typology emphasizes the critical interaction between *static leader characteristics* (such as cognitive complexity and the need for power) and *nonstatic, changeable leader characteristics* (such as policy experience or expertise) in shaping presidential style. This distinction reflects the widely held view that basic *personality traits* in leaders, like power and complexity, remain stable over time.[51] In contrast, nonpersonality-based characteristics such as the degree of policy experience or expertise possessed by leaders in particular issue areas are, by their very nature, variable and not stable over time.[52] The interplay between these static and nonstatic attributes fundamentally shape not only the two critical dimensions of presidential leadership style, but also the degree to which the president will be attentive to (or influenced by) the external policy environment—whether in the form of outside institutional actors, advice, or information.

A. Leader Control and Involvement

The first dimension of leadership style is the leader's desire to personally control or be involved in the policy process in a given policy area. As the psychological literature on the need for power suggests, individuals differ greatly in their desire for control over their environments, with some insisting upon a more active role than others. According to table 7.1, leaders' needs for power interact with their prior policy experience or expertise to suggest an overall style regarding their need for control and involvement in the policy process.

The Director. Leaders with both extensive policy experience and a high need for power tend to have the activist presidential style of the Director. Because of their high need for personal control over the policy process, these leaders tend to centralize decisionmaking into a tight inner circle of advisers. Directors prefer direct personal involvement throughout the policy process (agenda-setting, formulation, deliberation, decision, and implementation), and generally insist on hierarchical advisory structures to enhance their personal control over policy. Although informal channels of advice and access will exist, formal channels will likely dominate the central site of decision. Given their high degree of experience and policy expertise, Directors tend to frame issues, set policy guidelines, and advocate strongly their own policy views within their advisory groups. They have the confidence to rely more on their own policy judgments than those of expert advisers. For Directors, the operative "decision rule" within their inner circle is that their own preferences dominate the policy process—with advisory group recommendations and final policy decisions usually reflecting these preferences. Presidents expected to exhibit Director leadership styles based on their high PAD scores on power and their extensive degree of prior experience in a given policy area, include Lyndon Johnson and Harry Truman in domestic policy and John Kennedy and Dwight Eisenhower in foreign policy.[53] This classification is also consistent with the views of historians and former presidential associates regarding both Johnson and Truman's mastery of domestic politics and their insistence upon maintaining personal control over this policy process.[54] It is also consistent with both Eisenhower and Kennedy's acknowledged expertise in the field of foreign affairs and their desire to retain personal control over the foreign policy process.[55]

The Administrator. Leaders with a low need for power but extensive policy experience tend to fit the activist presidential style of the Administrator. Unlike Directors, Administrators have less need for personal control over the policy process; as a result, decisionmaking tends to be less centralized and more colle-

TABLE 7.1   Presidential Need for Control and Involvement in the Policy Process.

Prior Policy Experience/Expertise in Substantive Area
(General Interest Level or Desire for Involvement in Policy)

	(High)	(Low)
(High) **Need for Power** (Desire for Control)	Director • Activist presidential style. • Decisionmaking centralized within tight inner circle of advisers. • Preference for direct personal control over final policy decisions. • Preference for direct personal involvement throughout policy process (i.e., agenda-setting, formulation, deliberation, decision, and implementation). • Preference for hierarchical advisory structures designed to enhance personal control (i.e., dominance of formal channels for decisionmaking, advice, and access). • Tendency to advocate own policy views, frame issues, and set specific policy guidelines. • Tendency for leader to rely more upon their own policy judgments than those of expert advisers. • *Inner Circle Decision Rule*: Leader's own policy preferences dominate the policy process. Final policy decisions and advisory group outputs reflect these preferences. *Examples of high need for power & high prior policy experience leaders:* Kennedy and Eisenhower—{Foreign Policy} Johnson and Truman—{Domestic Policy}	Magistrate • Relegative, less-activist presidential style. • Decisionmaking centralized within tight inner circle of advisers. • Preference for direct personal control over final policy decisions, but limited need for personal involvement throughout the policy process. • Preference for hierarchical advisory structures designed to enhance personal control (i.e., dominance of formal channels for decisionmaking, advice, and access). • Tendency to set general policy guidelines, but delegate policy formulation and implementation tasks to subordinates. • Tendency for leader to rely more upon the views of expert advisers than upon own policy judgments. • *Inner Circle Decision Rule*: Leader's own policy preferences dominate policy process, but these are heavily influenced by expert advice. Leader adjudicates between competing policy options presented by advisers to make final decisions. *Examples of high need for power & low prior policy experience leaders:* Kennedy and Eisenhower—{Domestic Policy} Johnson and Truman—{Foreign Policy}

gial, with the leader requiring less direct personal control over the process and the actions of subordinates. Administrators generally prefer informal, less hierarchical advisory structures designed specifically to enhance policy participation by subordinates. Like Directors, however, Administrators—with their high degree of personal policy expertise—tend to advocate strongly their own policy views, frame issues, and set specific policy guidelines within their advisory groups. They are also confident policymakers who rely more on their own policy judgments than those of expert advisers. For Administrators, the general

TABLE 7.1   Continued   **Prior Policy Experience/Expertise in Substantive Area**
(General Interest Level or Desire for Involvement in Policy)

	(High)	(Low)
Need for Power (Desire for Control)	Administrator	Delegator
	• Activist presidential style.	• Relegative presidential style.
	• Decisionmaking less centralized and more collegial, with leader requiring less direct personal control over the policy process and actions of subordinates.	• Decisionmaking less centralized and more collegial, with leader requiring little or no direct personal control over (or involvement in) the policy process.
	• Preference for informal, less hierarchical advisory structures designed to enhance participation by subordinates.	• Preference for informal, less hierarchical advisory structures designed to enhance participation by subordinates.
	• Tendency to actively advocate own policy views, frame issues, and set specific policy guidelines.	• Tendency to delegate policy formulation and implementation tasks to subordinates.
	• Tendency for leader to rely more upon own policy judgments than those of expert advisers in group.	• Tendency to rely upon (and adopt) the views of expert advisers when making final policy decisions.
	• *Inner Circle Decision Rule*: Leader's own policy preferences shape the nature of the general policy approach, but willing to compromise on policy specifics to gain consensus among advisers. ("majority rule" pattern)	• *Inner Circle Decision Rule*: Advisory group outputs and leader policy preferences reflect the dominant views expressed by either expert advisers or the majority of group members.
	Examples of low need for power & high prior policy experience leaders: Clinton—{Domestic Policy} Bush—{Foreign Policy}	*Examples of low need for power & low prior policy experience leaders:* Clinton—{Foreign Policy} Bush—{Domestic Policy}

decision rule within their inner circle is that their own policy preferences shape the general policy approach, but they are willing to compromise on specifics to gain consensus among their advisers. This tends to be reflected in a president's preference for a majority consensus within the inner circle before a decision is finalized. Presidents expected to exhibit behavior consistent with the Administrator style based upon their low PAD scores on power and high prior experience in a given policy area include Bill Clinton in domestic policy and George Bush in foreign policy.[56] This is consistent with scholars' views regarding Clinton's mastery of domestic politics and his insistence on maintaining personal control over the domestic policy process.[57] It is also consistent with Bush's acknowledged expertise in the field of foreign affairs and his insistence on maintaining personal control over the foreign policy process.[58]

The Magistrate. Leaders with a high need for power while lacking personal policy experience tend to exhibit the more relegative, less activist presidential style of the Magistrate. Similar to Directors, Magistrates have high need for personal control over the policy process and, as a result, tend to centralize decisionmaking into tight inner circles of advisers. Although Magistrates have a preference for direct personal control over final policy decisions, their lack of policy experience leads them to have limited need for personal involvement in the other stages of the policy process. As a result, while they set general policy guidelines for advisers, they tend to delegate policy formulation and implementation tasks to their subordinates. Further, their lack of policy expertise results in a tendency for Magistrates to rely heavily on the views of expert advisers in decisionmaking rather than on their own policy views. For Magistrates, the decision rule within their inner circle is that their preferences dominate the policy process—but that these views are also heavily influenced by other experts' advice. Essentially, like all good judges, Magistrates adjudicate between the competing policy options and views presented by their advisers before making final decisions. Presidents expected to exhibit behavior consistent with the Magistrate leadership style—based upon their high PAD power scores but low prior experience in a given policy area—include John Kennedy and Dwight Eisenhower in domestic policy, and Lyndon Johnson and Harry Truman in foreign policy.[59] This classification is consistent with the views of historians and former presidential associates regarding both Johnson and Truman's inexperience in foreign policy and dependence on expert advice in foreign policy decisionmaking.[60] It is also consistent with both Eisenhower and Kennedy's acknowledged inexperience in the field of domestic policy and their dependence on expert advice in domestic policymaking.[61]

The Delegator. Finally, leaders with both a low need for power and limited policy experience tend to show the relegating, less activist style of the Delegator. Given their low need for power and their limited expertise, Delegators are generally uninterested in policymaking and require little or no direct involvement or control over the policy process. Delegators prefer less centralized, more informal advisory structures designed to enhance participation by subordinates. In addition, their lack of policy expertise results in their tendency to 'delegate' policy formulation and implementation tasks to subordinates. Instead of relying on their own policy judgments in making final decisions, such leaders rely extensively upon (and usually adopt) the views of expert advisers. For Delegators, the operative decision rule within their inner circle is that advisory group policy recommendations (as well as the leader's) will reflect the dominant views expressed by either expert advisers or the majority of group members. Presidents expected to exhibit behaviors consistent with the Delegator leadership style—based upon their low PAD power scores and limited experience in a given policy area—include Bill Clinton in foreign policy and George Bush in domestic policy.[62] This classification is consistent with the views of scholars regarding Clinton's inexperience in foreign policy and dependence on expert advisers in foreign policymaking.[63] It is also consistent with Bush's acknowledged inexperience in the field of domestic affairs and his lack of interest and involvement in the domestic policy process.[64]

B. LEADER SENSITIVITY TO CONTEXT

The second dimension of leadership style is a leaders' general sensitivity to context (i.e., their general cognitive need for information, their attentiveness and sensitivity to the characteristics of the surrounding policy environment and the views of others). As the literature on complexity and experience illustrates, individuals differ greatly in terms of their general awareness of, or sensitivity toward, their surrounding environments. Indeed, individuals vary radically even in their general cognitive need for information when making decisions: some prefer a broad search before reaching conclusions, whereas others choose to rely more on their own existing views and other simplifying heuristics. In table 7.2, the leaders' cognitive complexity interacts with their prior substantive policy experience or expertise to produce an overall style regarding the need for information and sensitivity to external context.

The Navigator. Leaders characterized by both high complexity and extensive policy experience tend to fit the highly sensitive, vigilant style of the Navigator. Navigators tend to be active, vociferous collectors of information, and their expertise in policy leads to both greater sensitivity to potential outside policy constraints and the enhanced search for information and advice from relevant outside policy actors. Navigators use this information to conduct interpersonal relations, to map out the nature of the surrounding policy environment, and to identify the correct policy path to follow in their decisionmaking. As high self-monitors, Navigators are attentive to the political situation (the views of constituents, political allies and opponents, the political climate, etc.) and tend to be "chameleon-like" in modifying their own behavior and policy decisions to conform to this environment.

In their style of information processing navigators are "inductive experts." As such, because of their high complexity, they see the world in far less absolute terms than do their less complex counterparts, and subsequently rely less upon simple stereotypes and analogies to understand the policy environment. Further, because the world is perceived as complex, they place substantial empha-

TABLE 7.2   Presidential Sensitivity to Context
(e.g., to the policy environment, institutional constraints, the views of subordinates, etc.)

| | **Prior Policy Experience or Expertise in Policy Area**
(Sensitivity/Attentiveness to External Policy Environment) | |
	(High)	**(Low)**
(High) **Cognitive** **Complexity** (General need for Information & Sensitivity to Context)	Navigator • Vigilant, highly sensitive presidential style. • High general cognitive need for information and high personal interest/background in policy area. • Active collector of information from the policy environment (i.e., used to either make decisions or find correct policy path to follow). • Expertise in policy area results in greater sensitivity to potential outside constraints on policy and enhanced search for information and advice from relevant outside actors. • High self-monitor. • "Inductive Expert"—information-processing style. *Examples of high complexity & high prior policy experience leaders:* Kennedy, Eisenhower, and Bush—{Foreign Policy} Clinton—{Domestic Policy}	Observer • Less sensitive, spectating presidential style. • High general cognitive need for information, but limited personal interest/background in policy area. • Interested in information on policy specifics, but heavily dependent upon expert advice to make sense of situation and for policy recommendations. Limits personal role in the analysis of the data. • Limited personal expertise in policy area results in reduced sensitivity to potential outside constraints on policy and less awareness of (search for) information and advice from relevant outside actors. • High self-monitor. • "Inductive Novice"—information—processing style. *Examples of high complexity & low prior policy experience leaders:* Kennedy, Eisenhower, and Bush—{Domestic Policy} Clinton—{Foreign Policy}

sis on broad information search and the gathering of multiple and competing policy views. At the same time, because of their policy experience, they are more likely to trust their own instincts on policy matters—even in the face of opposition from expert advisers in their own inner circles. As a result, expert advisers, although fully included in policy deliberations, have far less influence on the final policy decisions of experienced presidents than they do on those of less experienced ones.

However, *inductive experts* share with *inductive novices* the tendency to possess deliberative, less decisive decision styles. Because such leaders recognize the complexity of the policy environment, they prefer to gather immense amounts of information and advice prior to making final decisions. As a result, although perhaps slightly faster than less experienced leaders, *inductive expert*

TABLE 7.2   Continued   **Prior Policy Experience or Expertise in Policy Area**

(Sensitivity/Attentiveness to External Policy Environment)

	(High)	(Low)
Cognitive Complexity (General Need for Information & Sensitivity to Context) **(Low)**	Sentinel • Vigilant, sensitive presidential style. • High personal interest/background in policy area, but low general cognitive need for information. • Expertise in policy area results in greater sensitivity to potential outside constraints on policy and enhanced search for information and advice from relevant outside actors. • Seeks to personally guide policy along path consistent with own personal principles, views, or past experience. • Avoids broad search for policy information beyond that deemed relevant given past experience or existing principle or views—especially information which is critical of or challenges these elements. • High self-monitor. • "Deductive Expert"—information—processing style. *Examples of low complexity & high prior policy experience leaders:* *Johnson, Truman—{Domestic Policy}*	Maverick • Less sensitive, unorthodox, independent-minded presidential style. • Low general cognitive need for information and limited personal interest/background in policy area. • Avoids broad collection of general policy information—instead, policy decisions are driven primarily by own personal, idiosyncratic policy views and principles. • Limited personal expertise in policy area results in reduced sensitivity to potential outside constraints on policy and less awareness of (search for) information and advice from relevant outside actors. • Low self-monitor. • "Deductive Novice"- information-processing style. *Examples of low complexity & low prior policy experience leaders:* *Johnson, Truman—{Foreign Policy}*

presidents tend to respond slowly to policy problems, make fewer absolute policy decisions, and be more willing to reconsider their views in the face of new evidence once a decision has been made. U.S. presidents expected to exhibit behavior consistent with the Navigator leadership style—based on their high PAD complexity scores and their high degree of experience in a given policy area—include John Kennedy, Dwight Eisenhower, and George Bush in foreign policy, and Bill Clinton in domestic policy.[65]

For example, the archival evidence, as well as former associates, support the view that President Eisenhower's style was characterized by broad information search, limited use of simplistic stereotypes/analogies, and a deliberative, less decisive decision style that is consistent with complex leaders.[66] Indeed, Eisenhower possessed an advisory system, centered around an elaborate National Security Council, geared to providing him with immense amounts of information and broad consideration of policy alternatives.[67] And, although willing to consider the views of expert advisers, Eisenhower had enough confidence in his own policy expertise that he was in no sense dependent on these advisers. Research on cases during the Eisenhower administration, particularly Dien Bien Phu, also support the contention that the president's style pattern was consistent with that of an inductive expert.[68]

Similarly, President Kennedy shared with Eisenhower an advisory system characterized by broad information search, multiple access points for advisers, limited use of stereotypes/analogies, and a deliberative, less decisive decision style.[69] Like Eisenhower, Kennedy demonstrated both a willingness to reconsider his policy views in light of new evidence and a flexibility enabling him to adapt to changing circumstances.[70] The greatest evidence of Kennedy's inductive style appears in the period between the Bay of Pigs and the Cuban Missile Crisis, during which many of his former associates note his incredible growth and learning.[71] Indeed, this kind of flexibility and adaptability is the hallmark of cognitively complex individuals and is indicative of a greater ability to learn on the job—especially when compared with less complex leaders.[72] Further, like Eisenhower, Kennedy was confident enough in his policy judgment to ignore expert advisers and rely on his own knowledge when these were in conflict—a characteristic well-illustrated by events during the Cuban Missile Crisis. And, although detailed archival research is not yet possible for President Bush, existing research and studies of his decisionmaking during the Gulf War strongly suggest that his behavior was consistent with the Navigator's inductive expert style.[73]

The Sentinel. Leaders characterized by low complexity, yet possessing extensive prior policy experience, reveal the vigilant presidential style of the Sentinel. They tend to avoid broad searches for policy information beyond what is deemed relevant given their own past experience, existing principles, or views. This is especially true if that information is likely be critical of these elements or challenge them. However, their expertise in policy does result in greater sensitivity to potential outside constraints on policy, as well as to enhanced sensitivity to information and advice from outside policy actors. They are highly self-monitoring and therefore attentive to the political situation (the views of constituents, political allies and opponents, the political climate, etc.) and tend to be "chameleon-like" in modifying their own behavior and policy decisions to conform to the existing environment. Sentinels also have a "deductive expert" style of information processing. Because of their low complexity, Sentinels see the world in absolute, black-and-white terms—and rely more heavily than do their high complexity counterparts on simple stereotypes or analogies to understand their policy environments. Further, since they perceive the world in a relatively straightforward way, they place less emphasis on both broad information search and gathering of competing opinions/views within their advisory systems. At the same time, their extensive policy experience leads Sentinels to trust their own instincts on policy matters—even in the face of opposition from expert advisers in their own inner circles. Due to their lower complexity, these deductive experts also possess decisive, less deliberative decision styles. As a result, one would expect such presidents to react quickly to policy problems, make firm policy decisions, and be generally reluctant to reconsider their views once an action had been taken. Presidents expected to exhibit behavior consistent with the Sentinel leadership style based on their low PAD complexity scores and high degree of prior experience in the given policy area include Lyndon Johnson and Harry Truman in domestic policy.[74] This classification is consistent with the view of historians and former presidential associates regarding both Johnson and Truman's tendencies to engage in black-and-white thinking, frequently use analogy, and get involved in limited information-search for dissonant advice (while actively seeking out information consistent with their views) typical of leaders low in cognitive complexity.[75]

The Observer. Leaders characterized by high complexity, yet possessing limited prior policy experience, exhibit the less sensitive, spectating presidential style of the Observer. Their limited policy expertise reduces their sensitivity to potential outside constraints on policy as well as to information and advice from relevant outside actors. Although observers are interested and seek to be informed by their subordinates about policy specifics, they are still heavily dependent on expert advice in their decisionmaking because of their lack of policy experience in the area, and tend to limit their own personal role to data analysis or weighing options. They want the expert advisers to make sense of the situation and recommend a direction. As low self-monitors, Observers also tend to pay attention to the political situation when determining their own behavior or policy positions.

Observers are "inductive novices" in their information processing. Because of their high complexity, such leaders see the world in far less absolute terms than their less complex counterparts, and subsequently rely less on simple stereotypes and analogies to understand the policy environment. Because they perceive their world as a complex place, they are interested in broad information search and gathering multiple and competing policy views—which can then be reported to them by their advisers. At the same time, however, because of their lack of policy expertise, such leaders tend to possess advisory systems in which expert advisers play a significant role shaping and formulating policies. Inductive novices also tend to possess a deliberative, less decisive decision style. Because they recognize the complexity of the policy environment, such leaders prefer to gather immense amounts of information and advice prior to making final policy decisions. As a result, one would expect such presidents to respond slowly to policy problems, to make fewer absolute policy decisions, and in the face of new evidence be willing to reconsider their views once a decision has been made. Presidents expected to exhibit behavior consistent with the *Observer* style based upon their high PAD complexity scores and inexperience in a given policy area include John Kennedy, Dwight Eisenhower, and George Bush in domestic policy, and Bill Clinton in foreign policy.[76] This is consistent with the view of historians and former presidential associates regarding the tendency of these presidents to engage in broad information searches (for both supportive and critical feedback) and their willingness to consider multiple perspectives or dimensions to problems. Their information-processing styles reflect high differentiation of their environments and avoidance of black-and-white thinking—qualities typical for leaders high in cognitive complexity.[77]

For example, Clinton was known for his emphasis on collecting diverse policy information from multiple sources and examining policy issues in great detail prior to making policy decisions. Indeed, there is clear evidence in Clinton's case of both his dependence on expert advisers and his willingness to accept their judgments on foreign policy matters. Further, while demonstrating substantial flexibility and a willingness to reconsider decisions or policies in the light of new evidence, Clinton was not known for either his rapid decisionmaking or decisiveness.[78]

The Maverick. Finally, leaders characterized by both low complexity and limited prior policy experience are less sensitive, independently minded (and often unorthodox) Mavericks. Because of their limited need for information and their limited policy experience, Mavericks tend to avoid broad collection of policy information. Their decisions are driven primarily by their own personal, idiosyncratic policy views and principles, which are often heavily influenced by simple decision heuristics (such as analogies). Their lack of expertise leads Mavericks to have reduced sensitivity to potential outside constraints on policy and to be less aware of information and advice from relevant outside actors. In determining their own behavior or policy positions, Mavericks tend to be low self-monitors and place much less emphasis on the political situation and environment than upon their own views and beliefs.

Concerning information processing, Mavericks are also "deductive novices." Due to their low complexity, they see the world in absolute, black-and-white terms and rely heavily on simple stereotypes or analogies to understand the policy environment. Perceiving the world in a relatively straightforward way, they place less emphasis upon searching broadly for information and gathering competing views from their advisory systems. At the same time, Mavericks tend to be very aware of their shortcomings in policy experience and, as a result, are more receptive to (and often dependent upon) the advice of expert policy advisers—despite their general tendency to possess relatively closed information-processing systems. Such leaders are also likely to have decisive, less deliberative decision styles and to spend less time than their more complex counterparts weighing information before making policy decisions. One would expect such presidents, then, to react quickly to policy problems, make firm policy decisions, and be generally reluctant to reconsider their views once an action had been taken. Based upon their low PAD complexity scores and low degree of prior experience in a given policy area, presidential *Mavericks* include Lyndon Johnson and Harry Truman in foreign policy.[79]

For example, typical of the Maverick, Truman developed a pattern throughout his administration of depending upon his Secretaries of State (James Byrnes, George C. Marshall, and Dean Acheson) to formulate the details of foreign policy and provide guidance. Both Truman's associates and the archival record point to his tendency to process information at a low level of complexity, often utilizing simplistic stereotypes and other shortcuts in reaching decisions. In fact, Truman would often not seek out competing views or additional information on policy proposals presented by individual advisers and would allow the emotions of the moment or the affective strength of negative stereotypes to take hold; further, he would make decisions without consulting the rest of his advisers. Of course, Truman's decisiveness is legendary, as is the degree to which he saw the world in black-and-white terms and used simple analogy to understand it.[80]

V. Assessing Overall Presidential Style: Composite Leadership Style Types.

By combining the two central dimensions of presidential style—the need for control and sensitivity to context—a more nuanced, composite leadership style can be described for each president which provides a better definition of style than that offered by previous typologies. As such, presidents may be distinguished from one another by more than just the unidimensional measure of their need for control and involvement in the policy process (as in the typologies of Barber and Johnson), but also by their general sensitivity to policy information and context. As illustrated in table 7.3, presidential leadership styles may take on any of 16 possible combinations, according to the leaders' individual characteristics measured by PAD across two dimensions (see tables 7.1 and 7.2).

In addition to providing greater variation in style types, the resulting typology provides greater analytical capability to study the impact of leadership styles across different policy domains by incorporating a more contingent notion of leadership style into the analysis of presidents. For example, a serious weakness of previous typologies has been their firm roots in either foreign policy or domestic policy, with presidential styles generally appearing to be incompatible between the two domains. Although personality traits (i.e., need for power and complexity) are stable in form over time within individuals and should have the same impact upon presidential behavior regardless of policy domain (foreign or domestic), this is not the case for non personality-based characteristics like prior policy experience or expertise.[81] In the typology presented here, leadership styles for presidents vary across foreign and domestic policy domains based on the leaders' degree of prior policy experience in the particular area. Table 7.3 compares the composite leadership style designations for a number of modern U.S. presidents across both foreign and domestic policy.

The Value of a Contingency Approach. It is important to recognize that presidential leadership styles can change over time, often as a result of a leader's increasing policy experience or expertise developed through involvement in the policymaking process. For example, scholars and associates of Kennedy have suggested that the learning experiences created by the Bay of Pigs fiasco fundamentally affected his behavior and leadership style during the Cuban

TABLE 7.3   Composite Leadership Style Types Among Profiled Presidents.

	Foreign Policy	Domestic Policy
Truman	Magistrate-Maverick	Director-Sentinel
Eisenhower	Director-Navigator	Magistrate-Observer
Kennedy	Director-Navigator	Magistrate-Observer
Johnson	Magistrate-Maverick	Director-Sentinel
Bush	Administrator-Navigator	Delegator-Observer
Clinton	Delegator-Observer	Administrator-Navigator

Missile Crisis.[82] This resulted in his transition to a more cautious, deliberative style that scholars have praised as an exemplar of good management.[83] Interviews with former presidential advisers support this notion that, despite consistency in a leader's general personality, decisionmaking and leadership styles often change over time as a result of learning and experience.[84] Therefore, it is essential that any typology created to accurately model presidential behavior adopt a contingent view regarding the evolving relationship between a leader's individual characteristics and style. In this way, one avoids casting presidents into "locked-in" styles, which allow for no learning over time.[85] Further, while remaining faithful to the view of many scholars that the basic characteristics of the leader's personality remain stable over time, this approach also acknowledges that some individual characteristics (such as *experience or expertise*) are by their very nature variable.[86]

Second, by focusing on the prior experience of leaders across policy areas, the typology introduces yet another contingent notion: that presidents will likely have a 'mixed' overall style of leadership, depending on their areas of policy experience or expertise. For example, when entering office, Bill Clinton had extensive domestic policy experience and expertise as a result of his tenure as Governor of Arkansas.[87] Clearly, such a policy background would have been expected to have a significant effect upon his leadership style in the White House, at least with regard to domestic policy. One would have expected Clinton to be a more self-confident leader and involved in the formulation of policy and possessing greater awareness of the need to attend to domestic political actors, while recognizing the constraints on successful policymaking. At the same time, Clinton entered the White House without significant experience in foreign policy. As a result, Clinton's foreign policy style would be expected to be characterized by greater dependence upon expert advice, increased willingness to delegate policy formulation to subordinates, and a tendency to be more tentative in foreign policymaking than would be the case in domestic policy. Indeed, as noted above, presidential scholars have observed such style differences for Clinton in domestic versus foreign policy,[88] a dichotomy not limited to Clinton alone.

For example, Eisenhower was seen as having a significantly different style of leadership in foreign policy—where he had immense personal expertise—than in the more unfamiliar territory of domestic policy.[89] In the former, he was self-confident regarding policy decisions, actively involved in policy formulation and debate, and less swayed by expert advice. In the latter, he was more tentative, less actively involved, and more dependent upon expert advice. Similarly, Truman's delegative leadership style in foreign policy, where he lacked significant expertise, noticeably differed from his domestic policy style, where he was supremely confident of his ability and political instincts.[90] This was also true of Lyndon Johnson, who possessed immense experience and expertise in domestic policy but little expertise in foreign affairs.[91] Given his unparalleled domestic policy experience (which was similar to Eisenhower's in foreign affairs), Johnson was supremely confident in his own policy views and instincts, and was actively involved in both policy formulation and debate.[92] Johnson's domestic experience taught him where to focus his attention within the external policy environment and to remain open to feedback regarding political opportunities and potential constraints concerning the successful implementation of his policies. In contrast, Johnson's lack of foreign policy expertise left him less aware of the external environment and more dependent on the views of expert advisers—a reliance that would later have serious consequences for his decisions on Vietnam.[93]

Third, a contingent approach provides a means for ascertaining "when" and "how" the external policy environment, whether in the form of institutional actors, advice, or information, is likely to influence presidential policymaking. Individuals vary greatly in the degree to which they are sensitive (or attend) to information or feedback from the surrounding environment. This entails the distinction, emphasized throughout the psychological literature, that individual behavior and decisionmaking are influenced not by the actual, "objective" nature of the surrounding policy environment, but instead by the individual's own awareness or perceptions of the nature of that environment.[94] People vary greatly in terms of their need for information and their sensitivity to context.[95] Thus, in the case of Harry Truman, who was less concerned about what other institutional actors thought and more concerned about his own view of the correctness of policy, focusing inordinately on the views or power distributions across other institutional actors does not explain much regarding his final policy decisions.[96] On the other hand, in the case of presidents more sensitive to the surrounding policy environment such as Dwight Eisenhower or Bill Clinton, it is necessary to take into account the political and institutional context at the time to explain their behavior.[97]

Of course, one implication of this contingent notion of leadership style is that during the course of an administration, presidential style within policy areas themselves can change. Although some presidents may continue to follow a pattern of low personal involvement and interest in a policy area throughout their term in office—thereby limiting the amount of policy expertise they could gain on the job—over time, some leaders clearly gain a great deal of policy experience in previously unfamiliar areas. Often, this occurs due to the existence of a critical policy problem, the very nature of which demands intense presidential attention and involvement day in and day out. A good example of this was Vietnam for Lyndon Johnson. Although Johnson entered office with a Magistrate-Maverick leadership style in foreign policy, by mid-1967/early-1968, it would be more accurate to describe Johnson's style as a more experienced Director-Sentinel. Although space limitations prohibit exploring how Johnson's leadership style changed over time, a brief review of the evidence illustrates Johnson's initial Magistrate-Maverick leadership style at the beginning of his administration.

VI. THE MAGISTRATE-MAVERICK: THE FOREIGN POLICY STYLE OF LYNDON JOHNSON.

PAD scores for Johnson's individual characteristics indicate that he had both a high need for power and low cognitive complexity.[98] Johnson's experience score shows a low degree of prior experience in foreign policy. Given these scores, Johnson's need for control and involvement in the policy process should resemble that of the Magistrate, while his general need for information and sensitivity to context corresponds to that of the Maverick. Available archival evidence reveals that the typology's predictions regarding Johnson's likely foreign policy behavior (i.e., the Magistrate-Maverick style) correspond with his actual behavior, according to historians and former-associates of the president.[99]

A. CONTROL AND INVOLVEMENT

The Magistrate style type would be expected to have a preference for direct personal involvement in the policy process, resulting in a tendency to centralize decisionmaking into a tight inner circle of advisers (see table 7.1). At the same time, however, the lack of prior policy experience/expertise results in a willingness to relegate many policy tasks to subordinates. Indeed, Magistrates are heavily dependent on experts for the formulation and design of policy itself, and one would expect to see such a leader's own policy views significantly shaped by those of expert advisers. Although Magistrates usually adjudicate between the competing policy views held by advisers, their final policy decisions will usually resemble the views held by the dominant faction of advisers within their inner circle. What evidence do we find in the archival record to support the description of Lyndon Johnson as a Magistrate (high in power needs, but low in foreign policy experience)?

1) Need for control over the policy process and the advisory system
In the White House, Johnson preferred a tightly hierarchical, centrally controlled organizational structure to enhance his dominance over the policy environment. This was a hallmark of his leadership style. As Senate Majority Leader, LBJ had often been accused of being a "dictator" by fellow senators, who resented his complete control over the machinery of the Senate, his constant pressure for unanimous-consent agreements, his persuasive "harassment," and his eagerness to cut off debate.[100] As president, Johnson's advisory system was structured to maximize both his control over policy and his authority over the White House. Specifically:

> His hierarchy was an orderly structure with many fixed relationships, but he alone was at the top with direct lines of communication and authority to the several men who occupied the level below. In Johnson's administration there was no Sherman Adams [Eisenhower's Chief of Staff]. The President was his own chief of staff: he made the staff assignments; he received the product of his staff's work and reconciled or debated between the competing reports; he set the pace of action and the tone of discussion.[101]

Johnson's need for control was widely noted by many of his advisers. In the foreign policy arena, former-Secretary of State Dean Rusk observed that Johnson insisted on maintaining a high degree of personal control over the formulation and implementation of policy within his advisory group.[102] Paul Nitze recalled that not only did Johnson demand "absolute loyalty" from his aides, but also "felt a need wholly to dominate those around him."[103] Secretary of Defense Robert McNamara remarked that Johnson exhibited an "autocratic style" on many occasions, while Joseph Califano observed that not only did Johnson want "to control everything," but also that "his greatest outbursts of anger were triggered by people or situations that escaped his control."[104]

Within his advisory system, Johnson drew decisionmaking and debate over policy into small, inner circles such as the Tuesday luncheons or other small groups, and avoided the use of larger gatherings, such as the Cabinet or NSC, for such purposes.[105] Indeed, Johnson demonstrated a preference for smaller groups early in his administration. He was personally more comfortable formulating and discussing policy within the Tuesday luncheons, surrounded by trusted, loyal colleagues than doing so in larger groups like the Cabinet where leaks were more likely.[106] Further, former-White House Press Secretary George Christian noted that if something required an urgent response, Johnson tended to make those decisions outside of the luncheons in still smaller meetings, with only a few of his closest advisers being present.[107] It was certainly the case that actors *outside* of Johnson's inner circle of advisers in the Tuesday luncheons were excluded from policy debate and from formulating decisions on foreign policy matters. Indeed, although there was actually a great deal of interaction between the president and his advisers on foreign policy within Johnson's advisory system, most of it occurred at the very top of the hierarchy without significant input from lower-level officials or outside actors.[108]

2) Prior foreign policy experience and dependence upon expert advice Although at times knowledgeable in certain areas, Johnson lacked significant expertise and experience in foreign policy and, like Truman, scored low on this characteristic compared to Eisenhower and Kennedy.[109] Commenting on Johnson's uncertainty and sense of insecurity in handling foreign policy, Townsend Hoopes observed:

> The President seemed, from the beginning to the end, uncomfortable and out of his depth in dealing with foreign policy. His exposure to the subject as a member of relevant House and Senate Committees had been long, but superficial. . . . The most exhaustive search of the Johnson record reveals no solid core of philosophical principle or considered approach to foreign policy—indeed no indication that he gave the subject much serious attention before 1964. There is only an erratic rhythm of reaction to those foreign crises that impacted upon the particular elements of domestic politics that had engaged his interest or his ambition.[110]

Further, Johnson had not gained much foreign policy experience during his time as Kennedy's vice president. As George Ball observed, with the exception of his involvement in the Ex Comm during the Cuban Missile Crisis, Johnson "was not at all close" to foreign policy decisionmaking during the Kennedy years and "was actually involved in very few of the decisions that were taken during that period" and in "very little of the discussion."[111] Even with regard to Johnson's behavior within the Ex Comm:

> He came into the meetings. He said relatively little. He didn't take a dominant part at all in the discussions. The rest of us did to a much greater extent. He was inclined to take quite a hard line, as I recall, but displaying at the

same time a kind of deference to the rest of the group, almost making it clear that he recognized that he didn't have the background and experience, that he had not been through this problem in as intimate a sense as most of the rest of us had been.[112]

Thus, just as it had with Truman, Johnson's lack of foreign policy expertise led him to be deferential toward the views of policy experts and less forceful in the exposition of his own views. As Paul Warnke observed, Johnson, with little background in foreign affairs, relied on his foreign policy advisers to a great extent and was dependent on them.[113] Clearly, Johnson's willingness to defer to experts differed greatly between the domestic and foreign policy realms. As Kearns noted:

> Confident of his mastery of domestic politics and matters of substance, he never hesitated to override or ignore counsel that contradicted his own judgment. In dealing with foreign policy, however, he was insecure, fearful, his touch unsure. In this unfamiliar world, he could not readily apply the powerful instruments through which he was accustomed to achieve mastery. . . . Thus Johnson, for whom the label "expert" meant almost nothing in domestic affairs, who knew just how wrong established wisdom could be, and how often unjustified a high "reputation" was, felt dependent on the wise experts of established reputation in foreign policy.[114]

Indeed, as Ball later commented, Johnson's foreign policy inexperience left him "out of his element in the Vietnam War" and lacking in the self-confidence needed to overrule his advisers at that critical moment in July 1965 when American involvement in the war was escalated.[115] Agreeing that the stereotype of Johnson—that he was more concerned with domestic matters and not very knowledgeable about foreign affairs—was "fairly true," Ball observed that "Lyndon Johnson understood America, but little of foreign countries or their history."[116] Instead, Johnson's great policy expertise was in domestic politics, Senate procedures, and in an insider's knowledge of how Washington really worked.

According to Warnke, while Johnson did not have very much foreign policy experience, he had a degree of confidence in both himself and his advisers that encouraged his active participation in the policy process but limited his willingness to challenge their views.[117] As Warnke noted:

> Lyndon Johnson was a man of immense self-confidence . . . And he had a lot of confidence in his foreign policy advisers. And I think that part of this was that he thought that John Kennedy was a foreign policy expert. And he kept

President Kennedy's foreign policy team. And, he thought that they were in total command of the situation. And he found it very, very difficult to figure that they may have been wrong.[118]

An example of Johnson's dependence on expert advisers and his reluctance to delve beneath the surface of their advice in foreign affairs is illustrated by the pattern of advising adopted by Johnson's close aides McNamara and Rusk. Given Johnson's well-known desire to consider policy problems only after his advisers had invested their "best effort," McNamara and Rusk made a "special effort to reach a common conclusion" on issues before approaching the president.[119] As Rusk later recalled, throughout their years in the Johnson administration, he and McNamara "almost never went to the president with a divided opinion."[120] This had the effect of reducing the level of conflict within the advisory group, but also served to limit the president's exposure to a full debate over policy alternatives. As Bundy observed, by meeting together prior to meetings with Johnson, McNamara and Rusk were able to decide in advance what issues really needed the president's attention.[121]

3) Johnson's adjudicating style with advisers
Johnson's advisory system emphasized a leader-dominant, competitive arrangement among his advisers that allowed the president to control the process and select advice flowing from multiple, overlapping advisory assignments.[122] In this way, Johnson obtained several options on a particular policy or several versions of a speech without being limited to input from any one adviser. As Christian observed, this was "Johnson's way of getting something out of more than one person so he could decide which version he wanted":[123] Further, when Johnson had a "really tough call" to make on a policy and felt that he really needed to have the pros and cons fleshed out, he sometimes "set up what amounted to a mini-debate between advocates, and he got two points of view on something."[124] On such occasions, advisers who sent opposing memos to Johnson on the topic, were summoned to debate the issue in front of the president, who would later make up his mind.[125]

McPherson observed that Johnson frequently utilized the tactic of, as one staffer described it, "taking an absurd position and making you drag him back from it."[126] As an example, McPherson recounted a story from Johnson's Senate days when Admiral Lewis Strauss was nominated to be Secretary of Commerce, a move vehemently opposed by a Senate ally of Johnson. Seeking a sense of where people stood and not wanting to reveal his views during such a messy fight, Johnson instructed his staff to prepare a memo on Strauss without an overall summation, focusing on the best pro and con arguments. Eventually,

Strauss was defeated by only a few votes and Johnson sent a congratulatory note to his staff for their good work. McPherson recalled:

> And we found out, later, that Johnson used that memo everyday when people came to see him about Strauss. He had the guys for Strauss read the con side, and not the pro, they'd just read the con side, and then he'd say, "You want me to support this man? After you've read that? Now, tell my why, how can I support a man like that, this is what my staff says!" As if we hadn't written anything else. And people who were against him, he'd show the pro to, and say, "Now look, here's this fine man, here's what my boys say! They've written out this memo that laid out the case for him, now you tell me why they're wrong!" So that was a traditional Johnson method. His M.O.[127]

Clearly, in terms of Johnson's need for control and involvement in the policy process, his leadership style resembled that predicted for the Magistrate.[128]

B.) SENSITIVITY TO CONTEXT

Given their low cognitive need for information and limited personal background in the policy area, Maverick leaders are expected to avoid broad collections of general policy information from throughout the environment (see table 7.2). Instead, their attention to context is driven primarily by their own personal, idiosyncratic policy views and principles, which are often heavily influenced by simple decision heuristics (such as analogy). Mavericks have a reduced sensitivity to potential outside constraints on policy, and they seldom seek out information and advice from relevant outside actors. Being low self-monitors, even while receiving information on the policy situation from advisers, such leaders will be driven more by their own views and beliefs regarding policy than by any desire to conform to the existing political environment. They will also exhibit a "deductive novice" style of information processing. What evidence do we find in the archival record of Johnson as a Maverick (low in both cognitive complexity and prior foreign policy experience/expertise)?

1) Style of information processing

As expected of an individual with low complexity, Johnson possessed a largely undifferentiated image of the world: he relied heavily on stereotypes and analogies and he processed most of his information about foreign affairs through relatively simple lenses. Johnson's natural "tendency" in the way he processed information about foreign affairs was "to think about the external world in the simplistic terms of appeasement versus military resolve."[129] Similarly, Johnson tended to view Vietnam in straightforward ideological terms, reducing the entire conflict to simple equations such as, freedom versus communism, or appeasement versus aggression.[130] Indeed, it has often been noted that Johnson tended to see "each country and all the people he met through an American prism" when either traveling abroad or contemplating foreign policy decisions as president.[131] Johnson's simplified worldview envisioned American values as not only having "universal applicability" abroad, but held that these values were so clearly correct that there was a worldwide consensus regarding their positive nature.[132]

Similarly, Johnson frequently employed simple analogies to understand events abroad. In the 1965 Vietnam case, the powerfully simple analogy of Korea, which, like the Munich analogy emphasized standing up to aggression to prevent further expansionism by a ruthless opponent, was more important in shaping Johnson's views on Vietnam than the more complex Dien Bien Phu quagmire analogy offered by George Ball.[133] In Johnson's worldview, the Korean analogy offered consistency with his existing beliefs about the situation, and suggested a successful outcome, which Dien Bien Phu did not. Such selective use of simple analogies that are consistent with existing beliefs and the avoidance of more complex ones is consistent with low complexity individuals.

Johnson heavily used simple analogies in his reasoning. For example, Johnson explained his inability to withdraw from Vietnam in terms of his belief that history told him that "if I got out of Vietnam and let Ho Chi Minh run through the streets of Saigon, then I'd be doing what Chamberlain did in World War II."[134] Similarly, Warnke noted Johnson's frequent use of analogies in understanding foreign events:

> I think that the principal analogy Johnson had was Munich. That there weren't going to be any more Munichs . . . He'd often talk in terms of, that he had to stop this threat at the very beginning. If we'd stopped Hitler before Czechoslovakia, it would have made a big difference.[135]

Another expectation of low complexity leaders is that they tend to see complex situations in simple terms, and frequently frame issues into "us" vs. "them" formulas. One would also expect low complexity leaders to personalize situations, and to exhibit a tendency to frame problems or challenges from external opponents as direct challenges to themselves. In this regard, Johnson appeared to possess these characteristics in his information-processing. Unlike Kennedy, who "approached people and decisions with cool detachment and calculation," Johnson "personalized almost every situation."[136] This observation is consistent with PAD scores which rank Kennedy and Johnson as, respectively, high and low complexity leaders.[137]

However, although Johnson's low complexity did leave him vulnerable to simplistic information processing, like Truman, it held the advantage of making him a more decisive decisionmaker. In fact, Clark Clifford argued that of all the presidents he had known, Johnson and Truman were the two who were the most willing to take on the "big issues" or the difficult questions, and then make tough decisions.[138] Similarly, McGeorge Bundy argued that Johnson was "very good" at making the tough decisions, being decisive, and not putting matters off.[139]

With regard to his style of information-processing, Johnson's associates and the archival record point to his tendency to process information at a low level of complexity, often utilizing simplistic stereotypes and other heuristics in reaching his decisions.[140] However, contrary to expectations for a low complexity leader, Johnson was a voracious consumer of information of all sorts, casting his net wide to gather as much information as possible from the policy environment. In his voluminous night reading load, Johnson reviewed all of the speeches given in Congress that day, a broad range of editorial comments from both the broadcast and print media, cable traffic from the State Department, as well as the various position papers and memoranda sent to him by his staff and Cabinet officers. And, although Johnson would only see one or two of the thousands of cables passing through the State Department daily, he insisted that a daily memorandum of principal developments in these cables be prepared by State and included in his night reading.[141]

This said, however, Johnson was very selective in the "type" of information he sought from his environment, focusing primarily on information that would assist him in passing or implementing a program. Information useful for gaining a "broad, brush-stroke," deep understanding of policy was less important to him.[142] As a result, Johnson's information-search routine tended to be very selective, and the same degree of emphasis that he placed on collecting detailed information on the domestic policy environment was not placed on obtaining similar data about the foreign policy environment. As Bundy observed, there is a great difference between the information you need when you're making up your mind and the information you need in making things come out your way, and "Lyndon Johnson was a legislator who was used to gathering information on how to build a majority, working his way towards decisions in ways that took into account this need."[143] And in many ways, this helps to explain the limited, if detailed, focus of Johnson's search for information in his policymaking. The need was for the type of information that would "make things turn out his way" rather than for that which would fully "flesh-out" an issue from every angle before a decision was taken. Again, this pattern is consistent with the information-processing style of a low complexity individual.

As was the case for Johnson's attention to domestic policy considerations, his use of this elaborate informal network of advisers was highly selective in both its nature and focus. Although Johnson did use outside advisers to broaden his network of advice, these were usually individuals on whose loyalty he could count, and who generally supported his policies. For example, Clifford notes that Johnson, wanting to draw on his experience in the Truman administration, arranged to consult with him from time to time as an outside adviser and counselor, an arrangement also established with another close Johnson confidant, Abe Fortas.[144] Both men were advisers with whom Johnson had a long personal history, and he felt confident of their loyalty and friendship and knew they were generally supportive of his policies. Thus, while LBJ pursued information in a manner somewhat reminiscent of a more open information-processing system, this was short-circuited by the low complexity manner in which he utilized and interpreted that information.

Johnson presents the paradox of a president who has a broad information network, who gathers and reviews a great deal of raw information personally, and who consults with a large number of outside advisers, but who does not seem to use all of this information or accept that which is contrary to his views. Although Johnson made heavy use of polls and sought out a great deal of information on the domestic environment when making foreign policy decisions, these did not necessarily govern his actions.[145] As Warnke observed, Johnson was a very "adroit politician" who was always responsive to domestic political considerations and attentive to Congress when making policy decisions, but these were never the "determining factor" of his policies.[146] Indeed, throughout his presidency, Johnson demonstrated an ability to be fully aware of the criticism of his policies within Congress and the public, but to still pursue a policy line he believed to be correct. This pattern is consistent with that of a low self-monitor in the policy area—the hallmark of the Maverick.[147]

VII. Conclusion.

This chapter argues that the essential building blocks of presidential power and persuasion reside in the individual characteristics, or qualities, of presidents themselves. In this regard, presidential leadership style plays a critical role creating the "foundations" for presidential power and influence, enabling a leader to either develop advisory systems that effectively gather information and assist in quality decisionmaking, or create ones that are serious impediments to their effective influence over governmental action. The theoretical framework presented, linking research on individual characteristics to their effect on presidential decisionmaking and leadership style, is a step toward improving our understanding of Neustadt's puzzle regarding the components of presidential power and influence. Two style dimensions (*need for control* and *sensitivity to context*) appear to be critical components of presidential leadership styles. A president's need for control and involvement in the policy process, for example, results in behaviors consistent with either the *Director, Administrator, Magistrate,* or *Delegator* styles. In contrast, a president's general sensitivity to information and awareness of the surrounding policy context gives rise to behaviors consistent with either the *Navigator, Sentinel, Observer,* or *Maverick* styles. Illustrating this framework and its application to understanding leaders, Lyndon Johnson's behavior in office was especially consistent with a Magistrate-Maverick leadership style.

It is hoped that this approach—and its sensitivity to the contingent nature of the importance of individual versus institutional variables—will contribute toward bridging the gap between explanations of presidential power that focus on institutional factors and those that focus on leaders themselves. For example, given high complexity/experienced leaders sensitive and attentive to their surrounding environments, it is essential to attend to the constraints (or other influences) on the president in the external policy environment, since such leaders are likely to seek out such information and use it actively in their decision-making. In contrast, in the case of low complexity/inexperienced leaders generally inattentive to their surrounding environments, understanding *what these leaders are like in terms of their personal characteristics* becomes critically important in predicting their behavior (and institutional variables correspondingly less important) because such individuals will likely pay limited attention to outside advice or the nature of the external environment when making decisions. Indeed, if one wants to understand the behavior and decisions of these leaders, it is necessary to know where to look and *in what contexts individuals matter.*[148]

NOTES

1. Richard E. Neustadt. *Presidential Power and the Modern Presidents: The Politics of Leadership From Roosevelt to Reagan* (New York: The Free Press, 1990) p.ix.

2. Ibid., pp. 207–208.

3. Ibid., pp. 152–153; 162.

4. Ibid., pp. 128–130.

5. See, George C. Edwards, John H. Kessel, and Bert A. Rockman. *Researching the Presidency: Vital Questions, New Approaches* (Pittsburgh: University of Pittsburgh Press, 1993); Gregory L. Hager, and Terry Sullivan, "President-centered and Presidency-centered Explanations of Presidential Public Activity," *American Journal of Political Science*, 38 (4) (1994): 1079–1103. President-centered studies of leadership focus upon the role of individual presidents themselves—whether in terms of character, personality, or management preferences—in shaping White House organizations and policy processes within their administrations. For examples, see James D. Barber, *The Presidential Character: Predicting Performance in the White House* (Englewood Cliffs: Prentice-Hall, 1972); Richard T. Johnson, *Managing the White House: An Intimate Study of the Presidency* (New York: Harper, 1974); Alexander L. George, *Presidential Decisionmaking in Foreign Policy: The Effective Use of Information and Advice* (Boulder: Westview Press, 1980). Fred I. Greenstein, *The Hidden-Hand Presidency: Eisenhower as Leader* (New York: Basic Books, 1982); Erwin C. Hargrove, *Jimmy Carter as President: Leadership and the Politics of the Public Good* (Baton Rouge: Louisiana State University Press,1988); Stanley A. Renshon, *High Hopes: The Clinton Presidency and the Politics of Ambition* (New York: New York University Press, 1996). In contrast, presidency-centered studies focus upon institutional or organizational variables within the presidency itself to explain the subsequent shape of White House organizations and policy processes. For examples, see Hugh Heclo, "The Changing Presidential Office," In A.J. Meltsner, ed., *Politics and the Oval Office: Towards Presidential Governance*, pp. 161–184; Paul C. Light, *The President's Agenda: Domestic Policy Choice from Kennedy to Carter* (Baltimore: John Hopkins University Press, 1982); Terry M. Moe, "Presidents, Institutions, and Theory," In G. Edwards, J. Kessel, and B. Rockman, eds., *Researching the Presidency: Vital Questions, New Approaches* (Pittsburgh: University of Pittsburgh Press, 1993), pp. 337–385; Martha S. Feldman, "Organization Theory and the Presidency," In G.Edwards, J. Kessel, and B. Rockman, eds., *Researching the Presidency: Vital Questions, New Approaches*, pp. 267–288; Charles E. Walcott, and Karen M. Hult, *Governing the White House: From Hoover Through LBJ* (Lawrence: University Press of Kansas, 1995); Shirley A. Warshaw, *Powersharing: White House-Cabinet Relations in the Modern Presidency* (Albany: State University of New York Press, 1996).

6. Erwin C. Hargrove, "Presidential Personality and Leadership Style," In Edwards, Kessel, and Rockman, eds., *Researching the Presidency: Vital Questions, New Approaches*, pp. 70–73. See also, Fred I. Greenstein, *Personality and Politics: Problems of Evidence, Inferences, and Conceptualization* (Chicago: Markham Publishing Company, 1969).

7. Alexander L. George,. and Juliette L. George, *Woodrow Wilson and Colonel*

House: A Personality Study (New York: Dover, 1964); Alexander L. George, and Juliette L. George, *Presidential Personality and Performance* (Boulder, CO: Westview Press, 1998); Barber, *The Presidential Character*; Betty Glad, *Jimmy Carter: In Search of the Great White House* (New York: Norton, 1980); Betty Glad, "Black-and-White Thinking: Ronald Reagan's Approach to Foreign Policy," *Political Psychology*, 4 (1983): 33–76; Margaret G. Hermann,. "Assessing Personality-at-a-Distance: A Profile of Ronald Reagan," *Mershon Center Quarterly Report*, Vol. 7 (Columbus OH: The Ohio State University, 1983b); Margaret G. Hermann, "Defining the Bush Presidential Style," *Mershon Center Memo* (Columbus, OH: The Ohio State University, 1989); Hargrove, *Jimmy Carter as President*; David G.Winter, Margaret G. Hermann, Walter Weintraub, and Stephen G. Walker, "The Personalities of Bush and Gorbachev Measured at a Distance: Procedures, Portraits, and Policy," *Political Psychology*, 12 (1991).: 215–245.

8. George and George, *Woodrow Wilson and Colonel House*; Barber, *The Presidential Character*; Renshon, *High Hopes*.

9. Hermann, "Assessing Personality-at-a-Distance" and "Defining the Bush Presidential Style"; David G. Winter, "Leader Appeal, Leader Performance, and the Motive Profiles of Leaders and Followers: A Study of American Presidents and Elections," *Journal of Personality and Social Psychology*, 52 (1987): 196–292; Winter et al., "The Personalities of Bush and Gorbachev Measured at a Distance"; Thomas Preston, *The President and His Inner Circle: Leadership Style and the Advisory Process in Foreign Policy Making*, Unpublished Ph.D. Dissertation at The Ohio State University, 1996; Thomas Preston, " 'Following the Leader': The Impact of U.S. Presidential Style Upon Advisory Group Dynamics, Structure, and Decision," In P. 't Hart, E. Stern, and B. Sundelius, eds., *Beyond Groupthink: Political Group Dynamics and Foreign Policymaking* (Ann Arbor: University of Michigan Press, 1997), pp. 191–248; Michael Lyons, "Presidential Character Revisited," *Political Psychology*, 18 (4) (1997): 791–811.

10. Greenstein, *The Hidden-Hand Presidency*; Hargrove, *Jimmy Carter as President*; Charles O. Jones, *The Trusteeship Presidency: Jimmy Carter and the United States Congress* (Baton Rouge: Louisiana State University, 1988); John P. Burke and Fred I. Greenstein, *How Presidents Test Reality: Decisions on Vietnam, 1954 and 1965* (New York: Russell Sage Foundation, 1991).

11. Johnson, *Managing the White House*; George, *Presidential Decisionmaking in Foreign Policy*; Roger B. Porter, *Presidential Decision Making: The Economic Policy Board* (Cambridge: Cambridge University Press, 1980); Colin S. Campbell, *Managing the Presidency: Carter, Reagan, and the Search for Executive Harmony* (Pittsburgh: University of Pittsburgh Press, 1986); Cecil B. Crabb, Jr.,. and Kevin V. Mulcahy, *Presidents and Foreign Policy Making: From FDR to Reagan* (Baton Rouge: Louisiana State University Press, 1986); Stephen Hess, *Organizing the Presidency*

(Washington, D.C.: Brookings Institution, 1988); Phillip G. Henderson, *Managing the Presidency: The Eisenhower Legacy—From Kennedy to Reagan* (Boulder: Westview Press; Burke and Greenstein, 1988); *How Presidents Test Reality*; Margaret G. Hermann and Thomas Preston, "Presidents, Advisers, and Foreign Policy: The Effect of Leadership Style on Executive Arrangements," *Political Psychology*, 15 (1) (1994a): 75–96; Margaret G. Hermann and Thomas Preston, "Presidents and Their Advisers: Leadership Style, Advisory Systems, and Foreign Policymaking," In E. Wittkopf, ed., *The Domestic Sources of American Foreign Policy: Insights and Evidence*, Second Edition (New York: St. Martin's Press, 1994b), pp. 340–356; Margaret G. Hermann and Thomas Preston, "Presidents, Leadership Style, and the Advisory Process," In E. Wittkopf and J. McCormick, eds., *The Domestic Sources of American Foreign Policy: Insights and Evidence*, Third Edition (New York: Rowman and Littlefield, 1998).

12. See, Ralph M. Stogdill and Bernard M. Bass, *Stogdill's Handbook of Leadership: A Survey of Theory and Research* (New York: The Free Press, 1981); Margaret G. Hermann, "Explaining Foreign Policy Behavior Using Personal Characteristics of Political Leaders," *International Studies Quarterly*, 24 (1980): 7–46; Margaret G. Hermann, *Handbook for Assessing Personal Characteristics and Foreign Policy Orientations of Political Leaders* (Columbus, OH: Mershon Center Occasional Papers, 1983a); Margaret G. Hermann, "Personality and Foreign Policy Decision Making: A Study of 53 Heads of Government," In D.A. Sylvan and S. Chan, eds., *Foreign Policy Decision Making: Perceptions, Cognition, and Artificial Intelligence* (New York: Praeger, 1984), pp. 53–80; Margaret G. Hermann, "Leaders' Foreign Policy Orientations and the Quality of Foreign Policy Decisions," In S. Walker, ed., *Role Theory and Foreign Policy Analysis* (Durham: Duke University Press, 1987a), pp. 123–140; Margaret G. Hermann, "Assessing the Foreign Policy Role Orientations of Sub-Saharan African Leaders," In S. Walker, ed., *Role Theory and Foreign Policy Analysis* (Durham: Duke University Press, 1987b), pp. 161–198; Yaacov Vertzberger, *The World In Their Minds: Information Processing, Cognition, and Perception in Foreign Policy Decisionmaking* (Stanford, CA: Stanford University Press, 1990); Winter et al., "The Personalities of Bush and Gorbachev Measured at a Distance"; Charles P. Smith, John W. Atkinson, David C. McClelland, and Joseph Veroff, eds., *Motivation and Personality: Handbook of Thematic Content Analysis* (Cambridge: Cambridge University Press, 1992); Hermann and Preston, "Presidents, Advisers, and Foreign Policy"; Hermann and Preston, "Presidents, Leadership Style, and the Advisory Process"; Preston, *The President and His Inner Circle*; Preston, "Following the Leader."

13. See, David G. Winter, *The Power Motive* (New York: Free Press, 1973); Winter, "Leader Appeal, Leader Performance, and the Motive Profiles of Leaders and Followers"; David C. McClelland, *Power: The Inner Experience* (New York: Irvington,

1975); Lloyd S. Etheredge, *A World of Men: The Private Sources of American Foreign Policy* (Cambridge: MIT Press, 1978); Hermann, "Personality and Foreign Policy Decision Making"; Hermann, "Assessing the Foreign Policy Role Orientations of Sub-Saharan African Leaders"; Robert J. House, "Power and Personality in Complex Organizations," In B. M. Staw and L. L. Cummings, eds., *Personality and Organizational Influence* (Greenwich, CT: JAI Press Inc, 1990), pp. 181–233).

14. See, R. P. Browning and H. Jacob, "Power Motivation and the Political Personality," *Public Opinion Quarterly*, 28 (1964): 75–90; David G. Winter and Abigail J. Stewart, "Content Analysis as a Technique for Assessing Political Leaders," in Hermann, ed., *A Psychological Examination of Political Leaders* (New York: Free Press, 1977), pp. 21–61; D. C. McClelland and R. E. Boyatzis, "Leadership, Motive Pattern and Long-Term Success in Management," *Journal of Applied Psychology*, 67 (1982): 737–743; Winter, "Leader Appeal, Leader Performance, and the Motive Profiles of Leaders and Followers."

15. See, Peter Suedfeld and A. D. Rank, "Revolutionary Leaders: Long-term Success as a Function of Changes in Conceptual Complexity." *Journal of Personality and Social Psychology*, 34 (1976): 169–178; Peter Suedfeld and Phillip Tetlock, "Integrative Complexity of Communication in International Crisis," *Journal of Conflict Resolution*, 21 (1977): 169–184; M. J. Driver, "Individual Differences as Determinants of Aggression in the Inter-Nation Simulation," in Hermann, ed., *A Psychological Examination of Political Leaders* (New York: Free Press, 1977), pp. 337–353; Phillip Tetlock, "Integrative Complexity of American and Soviet Foreign Policy Rhetorics: A Time-Series Analysis," *Journal of Personality and Social Psychology*, 49 (1985): 565–585; Hermann, "Personality and Foreign Policy Decision Making"; Hermann, "Leader's Foreign Policy Orientations and the Quality of Foreign Policy Decisions."

16. See, J. B. Rotter, "Generalized Expectancies for Internal Versus External Control of Reinforcement," *Psychological Monographs: General and Applied*, 80 (1966); W. L. Davis and E. J. Phares, "Internal-External Control as a Determinant of Information-Seeking in a Social Influence Situation," *Journal of Personality*, 35 (1967): 547–561; Hermann, "Personality and Foreign Policy Decision Making"; Hermann, "Leader's Foreign Policy Orientations and the Quality of Foreign Policy Decisions."

17. See, Winter and Stewart, "Content Analysis as a Technique for Assessing Political Leaders"; A. J. Rowe and R. O. Mason, *Managing With Style: A Guide to Understanding, Assessing, and Improving Decision Making* (San Francisco: Jossey-Bass, 1987); Hermann, "Leader's Foreign Policy Orientations and the Quality of Foreign Policy Decisions"; Paul C. Nutt, *Making Tough Decisions: Tactics for Improving Managerial Decision Making* (San Francisco: Jossey-Bass, 1990)

18. See, Hermann, "Assessing the Foreign Policy Role Orientations of Sub-Saharan African Leaders"; House, "Power and Personality in Complex Organizations";

Winter et al., "The Personalities of Bush and Gorbachev Measured at a Distance." Although this psychological research often operationalizes these traits differently, the basic meaning of the concepts remains consistent. The need for power concerns establishing, maintaining, or restoring one's power, i.e., one's impact, control, or influence over others. The need for affiliation is concerned with establishing, maintaining, or restoring warm and friendly relationships with other persons or groups. Conceptual complexity involves the ability to differentiate the environment (i.e., degree of differentiation a person shows in describing or discussing other people, places, policies, ideas, or things). The locus of control reflects the degree to which individuals perceive some degree of control over the environment (i.e., do they personally have the ability to affect outcomes or does the external environment play the main role in outcomes?). The task/interpersonal (or achievement) focuses upon the relative emphasis in interactions with others on getting the task done vs. focusing on feelings and needs of others (an interpersonal emphasis). Self-confidence involves the person's sense of self-importance or image of his/her ability to cope with the environment. For more detailed discussion of these traits, see Hermann, *Handbook for Assessing Personal Characteristics and Foreign Policy Orientations of Political Leaders*; Charles P. Smith, John W. Atkinson, David C. McClelland, and Joseph Veroff, eds, *Motivation and Personality: Handbook of Thematic Content Analysis* (Cambridge: Cambridge University Press, 1992).

19. Preston, *The President and His Inner Circle*.

20. T. W. Adorno, E. Frenkel-Brunswik, D. J. Levinson, and R. N. Sandord, *The Authoritarian Personality* (New York: Harper, 1950); Browning and Jacob, "Power and Motivation and the Political Personality"; R. E. Donley and D. Winter, "Measuring the Motives of Public Officials at a Distance: An Exploratory Study of American Presidents," *Behavioral Science*, 15 (1970): 227–236; Winter, *The Power Motive*; Winter, "Leader Appeal, Leader Performance, and the Motive Profiles of Leaders and Followers"; Winter and Stewart, "Content Analysis as a Technique for Assessing Political Leaders"; Etheredge, *A World of Men*; Hermann, "Explaining Foreign Policy Behavior Using Personal Characteristics of Political Leaders"; Hermann, "Assessing the Foreign Policy Role Orientations of Sub-Saharan African Leaders"; McClelland, *Power: The Inner Experience*; House, "Power and Personality in Complex Organizations."

21. Eugene M. Fodor and T. Smith, "The Power Motive as an Influence on Group Decision Making," *Journal of Personality and Social Psychology*, 42 (1982): 178–185.

22. See, Winter, *The Power Motive*; Winter, "Leader Appeal, Leader Performance, and the Motive Profiles of Leaders and Followers"; Etheredge, *A World of Men*; Hermann, "Explaining Foreign Policy Behavior Using Personal Characteristics of Political Leaders."

23. See, Browning and Jacob, "Power and Motivation and the Political Personality"; Winter, *The Power Motive*; Winter, "Leader Appeal, Leader Performance, and the Motive Profiles of Leaders and Followers"; Winter and Stewart, "Content Analysis as a Technique for Assessing Political Leaders"; Eugene M. Fodor and D. L. Farrow, "The Power Motive as an Influence on the Use of Power," *Journal of Personality and Social Psychology*, 37 (1979): 2091–2097; McClelland, *Power*.

24. See, Preston, *The President and His Inner Circle*. The *need for power* in this study was operationalized using Personality Assessment-at-a-Distance (PAD) content analysis of spontaneous statements and interviews by these leaders. In coding for power, the focus is upon verbs, which are coded for need for power if the verb context meets any of the following six conditions included in Winter's (*The Power Motive*), need for power coding scheme: (1) strong, forceful action; (2) giving of help when not solicited; (3) an attempt to control others; (4) an attempt to influence, persuade, bribe others; (5) an attempt to impress others; (6) concern for one's own reputation or position. The score for power is based on the percentage of verbs (out of the total in the passage) meeting these six criteria. Typically, around one hundred such passages (of at least 100 words in length) are randomly selected and coded to form a profile score on this trait for any particular leader. These leader scores and their relative value (high or low) are then determined using a larger, 94 world leader data set coded using PAD which provides a range reference for the scores. For more details, see Preston, *The President and His Inner Circle*.

25. See, Driver, "Individual Differences as Determinants of Aggression in the Inter-Nation Simulation"; Abraham Zaleznik, "Managers and Leaders: Are They Different?" *Harvard Business Review*, 55 (3) (1977): 67–78; P. D. Stewart, M. G. Hermann, and C. F. Hermann, "Modeling the 1973 Soviet Decision to Support Egypt," *American Political Science Review*, 83 (1) (1989): 35–59; Tetlock, "Integrative Complexity of American and Soviet Foreign Policy Rhetorics"; M. D. Wallace and P. Suedfeld, "Leadership Performance in Crisis: The Longevity-Complexity Link," *International Studies Quarterly*, 32 (198): 439–452; Hermann, "Explaining Foreign Policy Behavior Using Personal Characteristics of Political Leaders"; Hermann, "Assessing the Foreign Policy Role Orientations of Sub-Saharan African Leaders"; Vertzberger, *The World In Their Minds*.

26. Vertzberger, *The World In Their Minds*, p. 134. See also, W. A. Scott, "Cognitive Complexity and Cognitive Balance," *Sociometry*, 26 (1963): 66–74; J. Bieri, "Cognitive Complexity and Personality Development," in O. J. Harvey, ed., *Experience, Structure and Adaptability* (New York: Springer, 1966), pp. 13–37; "Revolutionary Leaders"; Suedfeld and Tetlock, "Integrative Complexity of Communication in International Crisis."

27. See, H. Schroder, M. Driver, and S. Streufert, *Human Information Processing*

(New York: Holt, 1967); Rudy V. Nydegger, "Information Processing Complexity and Leadership Status." *Journal of Experimental Social Psychology*, 11 (1975): 317–328.

28. See, Nydegger, "Information Processing Complexity and Leadership Status"; R. C. Ziller, W. F. Stone, R. M. Jackson, and N. J. Terbovic, "Self-Other Orientations and Political Behavior," in M. G. Hermann, ed., *A Psychological Examination of Political Leaders*, pp. 337–353.

29. Hermann, "Personality and Foreign Policy Decision Making"; Preston, "Following the Leader."

30. Hermann, "Personality and Foreign Policy Decision Making," pp. 54–64.

31. Vertzberger, *The World in Their Minds*, p. 173. Glad, "Black-and-White Thinking," p. 38. See also, M. Rokeach, "The Nature and Meaning of Dogmatism," *Psychological Review*, 61 (1954): 194–204; R. E. Kleck and J. Wheaton, "Dogmatism and Responses to Opinion-Consistent and Opinion-Inconsistent Information," *Journal of Personality and Social Psychology*, 5 (1967): 249–252.

32. See, Preston, *The President and His Inner Circle. Cognitive complexity* was operationalized using the PAD content analysis of spontaneous statements and interviews by these leaders. In coding for complexity, one looks within the content of passages for a set of words indicating a high degree of differentiation or high complexity words (e.g., may, possibly, sometimes, tends) and for words indicating a low degree of differentiation or low complexity words (e.g., always, only, without a doubt). The complexity score is based on the percentage of all high plus low complexity words that were high complexity in each passage. These leader scores and their relative value (high or low) are then determined using a larger, 94 world leader data set coded using PAD which provides a range reference for the scores. For more details, see Preston, *The President and His Inner Circle.*

33. Mark Snyder, *Public Appearances, Private Realities: The Psychology of Self-Monitoring* (New York: W. H. Freeman and Company, 1987) p. 33.

34. Snyder, *Public Appearances, Private Realities.*

35. See, Barber, *The Presidential Character*; George, *Presidential Decisionmaking in Foreign Policy*; Margaret G. Hermann, "Ingredients of Leadership," in M. G. Hermann, ed., *Political Psychology: Contemporary Problems and Issues* (San Francisco: Jossey-Bass, 1986), pp. 167–192; House, *"Power and Personality in Complex Organizations."* Research by House suggests that the greater an individual's task expertise in a policy area, the more frequently they will attempt to assert power and the more likely they will be successful in asserting control, p. 148.

36. Hermann, "Ingredients of Leadership," p. 178.

37. Preston, *The President and His Inner Circle.*

38. Y. F. Khong, *Analogies At War: Korea, Munich, Dien Bien Phu, and the Vietnam Decisions of 1965* (Princeton, N.J.: Princeton University Press, 1992); Jack S. Levy, "Learning and Foreign Policy: Sweeping a Conceptual Minefield," *Interna-*

tional Organization, 48 (2) (1994): 279–312; Preston, *The President and His Inner Circle*.

39. See, for example, John H. Kessel, *The Domestic Presidency: Decision-Making in the White House* (North Scituate: Duxbury Press, 1975); John H. Kessel, "The Structure of the Reagan White House," *American Journal of Political Science*, 28 (1984): 231–258; Alexander L. George, *Case Studies and Theory Development*, paper presented to the Second Annual Symposium on Information Processing in Organizations. Carnegie-Mellon University, 1982; George C. Edwards and Stephen J. Wayne, *Studying the Presidency* (Knoxville: The University of Tennessee Press, 1983); Bert A. Rockman, *The Leadership Question: The Presidency and the American System* (New York: Praeger, 1985); Gary King and Lyn Ragsdale, *The Elusive Presidency: Discovering Statistical Patterns in the Presidency* (Washington, D. C. : Congressional Quarterly Press, 1988); George C. Edwards, "The Quantitative Study of the Presidency," *Presidential Studies Quarterly*, 11 (1981): 146–150; George C. Edwards, *At the Margins: Presidential Leadership of Congress* (New Haven: Yale University Press, 1989); Edwards, Kessel, and Rockman, *Researching the Presidency*; Gary King, Robert O. Keohane, and Sidney Verba, *Designing Social Inquiry: Scientific Inference in Qualitative Research* (Princeton: Princeton University Press, 1994). This emphasis upon methodological considerations is especially critical for studies which center on the role played by personality in presidential style, in view of the long-standing criticism of such research as composed primarily of descriptive case studies, in which leadership styles identified by authors were left unoperationalized, untested, or unsystematically studied. See, for example, Fred I. Greenstein, *Personality and Politics: Problems of Evidence, Inference, and Conceptualization* (Chicago: Markham Publishing Company, 1969); Moe, "Presidents, Institutions, and Theory"; Barbara Sinclair, "Studying Presidential Leadership," in Edwards, Kessel, and Rockman, eds., *Researching the Presidency: Vital Questions, New Approaches*, pp. 203–232.

40. For definitions and coding categories for personality characteristics in PAD, see Hermann, *Handbook for Assessing Personal Characteristics and Foreign Policy Orientations of Political Leaders*; Preston, *The President and His Inner Circle*.

41. The PAD technique has a long track record of use in previous research on political leaders. For examples, see Hermann, "Explaining Foreign Policy Behavior Using Personal Characteristics of Political Leaders"; "Assessing Personality-at-a-Distance"; "Personality and Foreign Policy Decision Making"; "Leaders' Foreign Policy Orientations and the Quality of Foreign Policy Decisions"; "Assessing the Foreign Policy Role Orientations of Sub-Saharan African Leaders"; "Defining the Bush Presidential Style"; Walker et al., "The Personalities of Bush and Gorbachev Measured at a Distance"; Preston, *The President and His Inner Circle*; Preston, "Following the Leader," The 94 world leader data set compiled utilizing PAD and a

broader argument linking the characteristics to the foreign policy orientations for these leaders is presented in Margaret G. Hermann, Thomas Preston, and Michael D. Young, *Who Leads Matters: Individuals and Foreign Policy*. Unpublished manuscript.

42. Hermann, Preston, and Young, *Who Leads Matters: Individuals and Foreign Policy*.

43. For example, presidents scoring high in foreign policy experience/expertise included Eisenhower, Bush, Nixon and Kennedy. Truman, Johnson, Reagan, and Clinton had low scores. See Preston, *The President and His Inner Circle*, for a more detailed discussion of this measure.

44. Preston, *The President and His Inner Circle*.

45. A controlled-comparison case study approach was employed to ensure that archival documents were coded consistently and systematically to make possible comparisons across presidents and cases of decisionmaking (See, George, *Case Studies and Theory Development*). Archival documents covering all aspects of presidential interaction with advisers and decisionmaking in foreign policy cases were collected from the presidential libraries, including minutes of NSC or Cabinet meetings, memoranda between advisers and the president, diaries and memoirs chronicling interactions, telephone conversations, reports, etc. When possible, interviews with advisers were also conducted to provide both clarification of the archival record and independent assessments of the leader's personal characteristics being explored by the research.

46. The secondary literature strongly suggested that the presidents were very different from one another in both personality and leadership style. See, Donovan, *Conflict and Crisis*; Donovan, *Tumultuous Years*; Ambrose, *Eisenhower*; Sorensen, *Kennedy*; Schlesinger, *A Thousand Days*; McPherson, *A Political Education*; Clifford, *Counsel to the President*; Burke and Greenstein, *How Presidents Test Reality*—a view which subsequent PAD and archival analysis in Preston, *The President and His Inner Circle* confirmed empirically.

47. Each OCI begins with the start of any formal meeting of the president's main advisory group (such as the NSC, Cabinet, etc.). It continues on throughout all subsequent formal and informal interactions between the leader and their advisers until the beginning of the next meeting of the main advisory group. For more details, see Preston, *The President and His Inner Circle*.

48. Hermann and Preston, "Presidents, Advisers, and Foreign Policy."

49. Thomas Preston and Paul 't Hart. "Understanding and Evaluating Bureaucratic Politics: The Nexus Between Political Leaders and Advisory Systems," *Political Psychology* Vol. 20, No. 1, March 1999, pp 49–98.

50. Though a contingency approach may be less parsimonious than some critics of individual approaches prefer for the purposes of theory-building, it more

THE PRESIDENT'S INNER CIRCLE

accurately reflects the empirical evidence regarding how static leader characteristics (such as complexity or need for power) interact with nonstatic variables (such as policy experience or expertise) to affect both style and overall sensitivity to the environment.

51. See, Greenstein, *Personality and Politics*; Winter, *The Power Motive*; Winter and Stewart, "Content Analysis as a Technique for Assessing Political Leaders"; Margaret G. Hermann, "Comments on Foreign Policy Makers Personality Attributes and Interviews: A Note on Reliability Procedures," *International Studies Quarterly*, 24 (1980b): 67–73; Robert R. McCrae, "Moderated Analyses of Longitudinal Personality Stability," *Journal of Personality and Social Psychology*, 65 (3) (1993): 577–585.

52. Preston, *The President and His Inner Circle*; Preston and 't Hart, "Understanding and Evaluating Bureaucratic Politics."

53. For example, Johnson's (as Senate Majority Leader) and Truman's experience in the Senate focused principally on the domestic policy arena, whereas Kennedy (Senate Foreign Relations Committee) and Eisenhower's (Supreme Allied Commander WWII and NATO Supreme Allied Commander) experience was strongly geared towards foreign policy. All four presidents have a high need for power (based on PAD scores and ranges for the 94 leaders). In addition, in terms of measures of prior experience in Preston, *The President and His Inner Circle*, Johnson and Truman scored high in domestic policy, Eisenhower and Kennedy high in foreign policy. Thus, their scores place them in the Director style.

54. See, for example, Harry McPherson, *A Political Education* (Boston: Little, Brown, 1972); Doris Kearns, *Lyndon Johnson and the American Dream* (New York: Harper, 1976); Robert J. Donovan, *Conflict and Crisis: The Presidency of Harry S. Truman, 1945–1948* (New York: Norton, 1977); Robert J. Donovan, *Tumultuous Years: The Presidency of Harry S. Truman, 1949–1953* (New York: Norton, 1982); Clark Clifford, *Counsel to the President* (New York: Random House, 1991); Joseph A. Califano, Jr, *The Triumph and Tragedy of Lyndon Johnson: The White House Years* (New York: Simon and Schuster, 1991); David McCullough, *Truman* (New York: Simon and Schuster, 1992); Preston, *The President and His Inner Circle*. The view of Johnson and Truman as having far greater experience or expertise in domestic policy (as opposed to foreign policy) and their insistence upon maintaining personal control and involvement over domestic policymaking was also emphasized during interviews with former presidential advisers George Elsey, George Christian, Paul Nitze, Paul Warnke, Arthur Schlesinger, Jr., Harry McPherson, Walt Rostow, and McGeorge Bundy.

55. See, for example, Arthur M. Schlesinger, Jr, *A Thousand Days: John F. Kennedy in the White House* (Boston: Houghton Mifflin, 1965); Theodore C. Sorensen, *Kennedy* (New York: Harper, 1965); Greenstein, *The Hidden-Hand Presi-*

dency; Stephen E. Ambrose, *Eisenhower: Soldier and President* (New York: Simon and Schuster, 1990); Dean Rusk, *As I Saw It*, edited by Daniel S. Papp (New York: Norton, 1990); Burke and Greenstein, *How President's Test Reality*; Preston, *The President and His Inner Circle*. The view of Kennedy as having far more foreign than domestic policy experience or expertise, as well as his insistence upon maintaining personal control and involvement in the foreign policy process, was also emphasized during interviews with former presidential advisers Arthur Schlesinger, Jr., McGeorge Bundy, Walt Rostow, and Paul Nitze.

56. Both presidents have a low need for power (based on PAD scores and range references based upon the 94 leader data set). In addition, in terms of prior experience, Clinton scores high in domestic policy, Bush high in foreign policy, which places them in the Administrator style.

57. See, David Maraniss, *First in His Class: A Biography of Bill Clinton* (New York: Simon and Schuster, 1995); Margaret G. Hermann,. "Advice and Advisers in the Clinton Presidency: The Impact of Leadership Style," in S. Renshon, ed., *The Clinton Presidency: Campaigning, Governing, and the Psychology of Leadership* (Boulder, CO: Westview Press, 1995), pp. 149–164; Fred I. Greenstein. "Political Style and Political Leadership: The Case of Bill Clinton,"in S. Renshon, ed., *The Clinton Presidency: Campaigning, Governing, and the Psychology of Leadership*, pp. 137–148; Renshon, *High Hopes*; Hermann and Preston, "Presidents and Their Advisers"; Hermann and Preston, "Presidents, Leadership Style, and the Advisory Process."

58. See, for example, Bob Woodward, *The Commanders* (New York: Simon and Schuster, 1991); Thomas Preston and Michael D. Young "An Approach to Understanding Decision Making: The Bush Administration, The Gulf Crisis, Management Style, and World View," paper presented at the International Studies Association Meeting, Atlanta, 1992; Hermann, "Defining the Bush Presidential Style"; Hermann and Preston, "Presidents and Their Advisers"; Hermann and Preston, "Presidents, Leadership Style, and the Advisory Process."

59. All four presidents have a high need for power. In terms of prior experience, Johnson and Truman score low in foreign policy, Eisenhower and Kennedy low in domestic policy. These scores place them in the Magistrate style.

60. See, for example, Kearns, *Lyndon Johnson and the American Dream*; Donovan, *Conflict and Crisis*; Donovan, *Tumultuous Years*; George W. Ball, *The Past Has Another Pattern* (New York: Norton, 1982); Larry Berman, *Planning a Tragedy: The Americanization of the War in Vietnam* (New York: Norton, 1982); Larry Berman, *Lyndon Johnson's War: The Road to Stalemate in Vietnam* (New York: Norton, 1989); Clifford, *Counsel to the President*; McCullough, *Truman*; Robert S. McNamara, *In Retrospect: The Tragedy and Lessons of Vietnam* (New York: Random House, Inc., 1995); Preston, *The President and His Inner Circle*; Preston, "Following the Leader." The view of Johnson and Truman as having far less experience or expertise in for-

eign policy (as opposed to domestic policy) and their dependence upon expert advice in foreign policymaking was also emphasized during interviews with former presidential advisers George Elsey, George Christian, Paul Nitze, Paul Warnke, Arthur Schlesinger, Jr., Harry McPherson, and McGeorge Bundy.

61. See, for example, Schlesinger, *A Thousand Days*; Sorensen, *Kennedy*; Greenstein, *The Hidden-Hand Presidency*; Ambrose, *Eisenhower*; Clifford, *Counsel to the President*; Preston, *The President and His Inner Circle*. The view of Kennedy as having far more foreign than domestic policy experience or expertise, as well as his dependence upon expert advice in domestic policymaking, was emphasized during interviews with former presidential advisers Arthur Schlesinger, Jr., McGeorge Bundy, Walt Rostow, and Paul Nitze.

62. All three presidents have a low need for power . In terms of measures of prior policy experience, Clinton scores low in foreign policy, Bush low in domestic policy, which places them in the Delegator style.

63. See, for example, Maraniss, *First in His Class*; Hermann, "Advice and Advisers in the Clinton Presidency"; Greenstein, "Political Style and Political Leadership"; Renshon, *High Hopes*; Hermann and Preston, "Presidents and Their Advisers"; Hermann and Preston, "Presidents, Leadership Style, and the Advisory Process."

64. See, for example, Hermann, "Defining the Bush Presidential Style"; Ryan J. Barilleaux, "George Bush and the Changing Context of Presidential Leadership," in R. Barilleaux and M. Stuckey, eds., *Leadership and the Bush Presidency: Prudence or Drift in an Era of Change?* (London: Praeger, 1992), pp. 3–23; Hermann and Preston, "Presidents and Their Advisers"; Hermann and Preston, "Presidents, Leadership Style, and the Advisory Process."

65. All four presidents measure high in terms of their prior policy experience (i.e., Kennedy, Eisenhower, and Bush in foreign policy and Clinton in domestic). Further, all four also have high cognitive complexity scores (based on PAD scores and range references based upon the 94 leader data set), which place them in the Navigator style.

66. See, Henry Cabot Lodge, *As It Was: An Inside View of Politics and Power in the '50s and '60s* (New York: Norton, 1976); Andrew J. Goodpaster, Oral history interview, October 11, 1977, Eisenhower Library; Andrew J. Goodpaster, Oral history interview, January 16, 1978, Eisenhower Library; Greenstein, *The Hidden-Hand Presidency*; Arthur S. Flemming, Oral history interview, June 2–3, 1988, Eisenhower Library; Harold Stassen and Marshall Houts, *Eisenhower: Turning the World Toward Peace* (St. Paul: Merrill/Magnus, 1990); Ambrose, *Eisenhower*; Burke and Greenstein, *How President's Test Reality*; Preston, *The President and His Inner Circle*.

67. Greenstein, *The Hidden-Hand Presidency*; Anna Kasten Nelson, "The 'Top of the Policy Hill': President Eisenhower and the National Security Council," *Diplomatic History*, 17 (4) (1983): 307–326; Preston, *The President and His Inner Circle*.

68. Melanie Billings-Yun, *Decision Against War: Eisenhower and Dien Bien Phu, 1954* (New York: Columbia University Press, 1988); Burke and Greenstein, *How President's Test Reality*; Preston, *The President and His Inner Circle*.

69. Preston, *The President and His Inner Circle*.

70. Schlesinger, *A Thousand Days*; Sorensen, *Kennedy*; Ball, *The Past Has Another Pattern*; Preston, *The President and His Inner Circle*.

71. Schlesinger, *A Thousand Days*; Sorensen, *Kennedy*; Clifford, *Counsel to the President*; Preston, *The President and His Inner Circle*.

72. Preston, *The President and His Inner Circle*.

73. Hermann, "Defining the Bush Presidential Style"; Preston and Young, *An Approach to Understanding Decision Making*; Hermann and Preston, "Presidents and Their Advisers"; Hermann and Preston, "Presidents, Leadership Style, and the Advisory Process."

74. These presidents measure high in terms of their prior policy experience in domestic policy. However, they also score low in cognitive complexity (based on PAD scores and range references based upon the 94 leader data set), placing them in the Sentinel style category.

75. See, Kearns, *Lyndon Johnson and the American Dream*; Donovan, *Conflict and Crisis*; Donovan, *Tumultuous Years*; Clifford, *Counsel to the President*; Preston, *The President and His Inner Circle*; Preston, "Following the Leader"; Thomas Preston, "Lyndon Johnson and the 1965 Decision to Escalate U. S. Involvement in Vietnam," in M. Hermann, C. Hermann, and J. Hagan, eds., *Leaders, Groups, and Coalitions: Decision Units and Foreign Policy Making*, unpublished manuscript. The view of Johnson and Truman as exhibiting a pattern low complexity information-processing characteristics (i.e., black-and-white thinking, use of analogy, selective search for confirming and limited search for dissonant advice/information, etc.) was emphasized during interviews with former presidential advisers George Elsey, George Christian, Paul Nitze, Paul Warnke, Arthur Schlesinger, Jr., Harry McPherson, Walt Rostow, and McGeorge Bundy.

76. While all four presidents measure low in terms of their prior policy experience (i.e., Kennedy, Eisenhower, and Bush in domestic policy and Clinton in foreign), they also have high cognitive complexity scores which place them in the Observer style.

77. See, Schlesinger, *A Thousand Days*; Sorensen, *Kennedy*; Clifford, *Counsel to the President*; Hermann, "Advice and Advisers in the Clinton Presidency"; Preston, *The President and His Inner Circle*; Hermann and Preston, "Presidents, Leadership Style, and the Advisory Process." The view of Eisenhower and Kennedy as exhibiting a pattern of high complexity information-processing characteristics (i.e., broad information search, substantial differentiation of their environments, avoidance of black-and-white thinking and use of simplistic analogy, etc.) was emphasized in

interviews with former presidential advisers Arthur Schlesinger, Jr., Harry McPherson, Walt Rostow, and McGeorge Bundy.

78. See, A. Mitchell, "Panetta's Sure Step in High-Wire Job," *New York Times*, August 17, 1995, p.A16; A. Mitchell and T. S. Purdum. "Clinton the Conciliator Finds His Line in Sand," *New York Times*, January 2, 1996, pp. A1 and A8; Hermann and Preston, "Presidents, Leadership Style, and the Advisory Process."

79. The view of Johnson and Truman as exhibiting a pattern of low complexity information-processing characteristics (i.e., black-and-white thinking, use of analogy, selective search for confirming and limited search for dissonant advice/information, etc.) and little prior foreign policy experience or expertise was emphasized in interviews with former presidential advisers George Elsey, George Christian, Paul Nitze, Paul Warnke, Arthur Schlesinger, Jr., Harry McPherson, Walt Rostow, and McGeorge Bundy.

80. See, Donovan, *Conflict and Crisis*; Donovan, *Tumultuous Years*; Rusk, *As I Saw It*; Clifford, *Counsel to the President*; Preston, *The President and His Inner Circle*; Preston, "Following the Leader."

81. See, Winter, *The Power Motive*; Hermann, "Comments on Foreign Policy Makers Personality Attributes and Interviews"; McCrae, "Moderated Analyses of Longitudinal Personality Stability"; Preston, *The President and His Inner Circle*.

82. See, Sorensen, *Kennedy*; Schlesinger, *A Thousand Days*; Graham T. Allison, *Essence of Decision* (Boston: Little, Brown, 1971); Erick K. Stern, "Probing the Plausibility of Newgroup Syndrome: Kennedy and the Bay of Pigs," in P. 't Hart, E. Stern, and B. Sundelius, eds., *Beyond Groupthink: Political Group Dynamics and Foreign Policymaking* (Ann Arbor: University of Michigan Press, 1997), pp. 153–189.

83. See, Irving L. Janis, *Victims of Groupthink* (Boston: Houghton Mifflin, 1972); Alexander L. George, "The Cuban Missile Crisis," in A. L. George, ed., *Avoiding War: Problems of Crisis Management* (Boulder, CO: Westview Press, 1991), pp. 222–268.

84. According to observations by former presidential advisers George Elsey, Harry McPherson, George Christian, Paul Warnke, Paul Nitze, McGeorge Bundy, Walt Rostow, Richard Neustadt, and Arthur Schlesinger, Jr.. See, Preston, *The President and His Inner Circle*.

85. Useful discussions of the importance of learning and experience upon decisionmaking and cognition can be found in Khong, *Analogies At War*, and Levy, "Learning and Foreign Policy."

86. Greenstein, *Personality and Politics*; Barber, *The Presidential Character*; Winter, *The Power Motive*; Winter and Stewart, "Content Analysis as a Technique for Assessing Political Leaders"; Hermann, "Comments on Foreign Policy Makers Personality Attributes and Interviews"; McCrae, "Moderated Analyses of Longitudinal Personality Stability."

87. See, Maraniss, *First in His Class*; Renshon, *High Hopes*.

88. See, Hermann and Preston, "Presidents, Leadership Style, and the Advisory Process"; Greenstein, "Political Style and Political Leadership"; Renshon, *High Hopes*.

89. Arthur Larson, *Eisenhower: The President Nobody Knew* (New York: Scribner's, 1968); Greenstein, *The Hidden-Hand Presidency*; Ambrose, *Eisenhower*; Preston, *The President and His Inner Circle*.

90. This point was also emphasized in interviews with former-Truman advisers George Elsey and Paul Nitze. See also, Donovan, *Conflict and Crisis*; Donovan, *Tumultuous Years*; Rusk, *As I Saw It*; Clifford, *Counsel to the President*; Preston, *The President and His Inner Circle*; Preston, "Following the Leader."

91. Kearns, *Lyndon Johnson and the American Dream*; McPherson, *A Political Education*.

92. McPherson, *A Political Education*; Califano, *The Triumph and Tragedy of Lyndon Johnson*.

93. This point was emphasized during interviews with former-Johnson advisers McGeorge Bundy, Walt Rostow, Harry McPherson, Paul Warnke, Arthur Schlesinger, Jr., and George Christian. See also, Kearns, *Lyndon Johnson and the American Dream*; McPherson, *A Political Education*; Ball, *The Past Has Another Pattern*; Burke and Greenstein, *How Presidents Test Reality*; Califano, *The Triumph and Tragedy of Lyndon Johnson*; Clifford, *Counsel to the President*; Preston, *The President and His Inner Circle*; Berman, *Planning a Tragedy*; Berman, *Lyndon Johnson's War*; McNamara, *In Retrospect*.

94. Harold Sprout and Margaret Sprout, *Man-Milieu Relationship Hypotheses in the Context of International Politics* (Princeton: Center of International Studies, Princeton University, 1956); Michael Brecher, *The Foreign Policy System of Israel* (Oxford: Oxford University Press, 1972); Robert Jervis, *Perception and Misperceptions in International Politics* (Princeton: Princeton University Press, 1976); George, *Presidential Decisionmaking in Foreign Policy*; Hermann, "Ingredients of Leadership"; Vertzberger, *The World in Their Minds*.

95. Hermann, "Personality and Foreign Policy Decision Making"; Vertzberger, *The World in Their Minds*.

96. Donovan, *Conflict and Crisis*; Donovan, *Tumultuous Years*; Preston, "Following the Leader."

97. Billings-Yun, *Decision Against War*; Preston, *The President and His Inner Circle*; Hermann and Preston, "Presidents, Leadership Style, and the Advisory Process."

98. See, Preston, *The President and His Inner Circle*.

99. In Preston, *The President and His Inner Circle*, a study was conducted of all facets of Johnson's decisionmaking between September 1967 and March 1968 during the debate over a partial-bombing halt in Vietnam. Analysis of the archival evidence—consisting of all available documents, from minutes of meetings to memos

and other documents—showed a strong correlation (between 67–75% match across OCIs examined) between the behavior expected of individuals with Johnson's personal characteristics (high power, low complexity, low policy experience/expertise) and Johnson's behavior according to the archival record.

100. McPherson, Harry. 1972, *A Political Education*. Boston: Little, Brown, p. 169.

101. Doris Kearns, *Lyndon Johnson and the American Dream* (New York: Harper and Row, Publishers, 1976) pp. 239–240.

102. Oral history interview, Dean Rusk, July 28, 1969, pp. 38–39, Johnson Library.

103. Paul H. Nitze, *From Hiroshima to Glasnost: At the Center of Decision* (New York: Grove Weidenfeld, 1989) p. 261.

104. Robert S. McNamara, *In Retrospect: The Tragedy and Lessons of Vietnam* (New York: Random House, 1995), pp. 294, 305–309; Joseph A. Califano, Jr, *The Triumph and Tragedy of Lyndon Johnson: The White House Years* (New York: Simon and Schuster, 1991), pp. 10 and 25–26.

105. Oral history interview, Clark Clifford, December 15, 1969, p. 19, Johnson Library; David C. Humphrey, "Tuesday Lunch at the Johnson White House: A Preliminary Assessment," *Diplomatic History* 8 (1) (Winter 1984).

106. Humphrey, "Tuesday Lunch at the Johnson White House," p. 90.

107. Interview with George Christian conducted by Thomas Preston, August 4, 1993.

108. Interviews with McGeorge Bundy, Walt Rostow, Paul Nitze, Harry McPherson, and Paul Warnke.

109. Preston, *The President and His Inner Circle*.

110. Townsend Hoopes, *The Limits of Intervention* (New York: McKay, 1969),pp. 7–8.

111. Oral history interview, George Ball, July 8, 1971, pp. 2–3, Johnson Library.

112. Ibid., p. 3, Johnson Library.

113. Interview with Paul Warnke conducted by Thomas Preston, July 6, 1995.

114. Kearns, *Lyndon Johnson and the American Dream*, p. 256.

115. George W. Ball, *The Past Has Another Pattern* (New York: Norton, 1982), p. 375.

116. Ibid., p. 426.

117. Interview with Paul Warnke conducted by Thomas Preston, July 6, 1995.

118. Ibid.

119. Oral history interview, Dean Rusk, July 28, 1969, p. 9, Johnson Library.

120. Ibid.

121. Interview with McGeorge Bundy conducted by Thomas Preston, November 18, 1993.

122. Interview with George Christian conducted by Thomas Preston, August 4, 1993.

123. Ibid.

124. Ibid.

125. Ibid.

126. Interview with Harry C. McPherson conducted by Thomas Preston, July 7, 1995.

127. Ibid.

128. Additional archival evidence supporting Johnson's style classification as a Magistrate is found in content analysis of Johnson's actual behavior during Vietnam decisionmaking from 1967–1968. Across all forty-four indicators of need for personal control and involvement in the policy process, Johnson behaved in a Magistrate-consistent manner 77 percent of the time (across all formal and informal interactions). See Preston, *The President and His Inner Circle.*

129. Hoopes, *The Limits of Intervention*, p. 7.

130. Kearns, *Lyndon Johnson and the American Dream*, p. 257.

131. Ibid., p. 194.

132. Ibid., p. 194.

133. Yuen Foong Khong, *Analogies At War: Korea, Munich, Dien Bien Phu, and the Vietnam Decisions of 1965* (Princeton, N.J.: Princeton University Press, 1992) pp. 97–147.

134. Ibid., p. 181.

135. Interview with Paul Warnke conducted by Thomas Preston, July 6, 1995.

136. Clifford, *Counsel to the President*, p. 304.

137. Preston, *The President and His Inner Circle.*

138. Clifford, *Counsel to the President*, p. 655.

139. Interview with McGeorge Bundy conducted by Thomas Preston, November 18, 1993.

140. Johnson's use of analogy as a decisionmaking heuristic is illustrated in Khong, *Analogies At War.*

141. Oral history interview, Dean Rusk, July 28, 1969, p. 8, Johnson Library.

142. Interview with Harry C. McPherson conducted by Thomas Preston, July 7, 1995.

143. Interview with McGeorge Bundy conducted by Thomas Preston, November 18, 1993.

144. Oral history interview, Clark Clifford, August 7, 1969, p. 6, Johnson Library.

145. Based upon interviews with George Christian, Paul Warnke, and Harry McPherson in Preston, *The President and His Inner Circle.*

146. Interview with Paul Warnke conducted by Thomas Preston, July 6, 1995.

147. Additional archival evidence supporting Johnson's style classification as a Maverick is found in content analysis of Johnson's actual behavior during Vietnam decisionmaking from 1967–1968 in Preston, *The President and His Inner Circle*, p.

438, which found that across nineteen critical indicators of his sensitivity to context and pattern of information-processing, Johnson behaved in a Maverick-consistent manner 68 percent of the time across all formal and informal interactions. This research disaggregated Johnson's interactions within his advisory system utilizing analysis of Occasions for Interaction (OCI) discussed earlier in this chapter. See Preston, *The President and His Inner Circle*.

148. Hargrove, "Presidential Personality and Leadership Style," pp. 70–73.

PART 3

Organizing and Institutionalizing the Presidency

CHAPTER 8

Staffing and Organizing the Presidency

Bert A. Rockman

In appraising the presidency at mid-century, Richard Neustadt asked, "What does the President, himself, contribute to the conduct of the Presidency?"[1] For Neustadt the answer was choice and persuasion.[2] The unique role of the president was to lead, although he noted that the presidency was becoming something more broad-reaching than the person of the president. The growing magnitude of government and its complexity, the need for presidential assertion in the midst of that, and the extension of presidential power through surrogate presidential agencies were both justifying and confirming processes of institutional regularity.[3]

The important task of staffing and organizing the presidency was a mixed blessing for presidents. Clearly, it became increasingly difficult to cope without institutionalization in the presidency. Further, while presidents needed help with management of the presidency, the core of the presidency for Neustadt was leadership not management.[4] In the end, no amount of staffing or organizational resources would be able to substitute for deficient leadership skills. The presidency may not be the same as the president, but no presidency can have a chance of success without a skilled president. That is the essence of the Neustadtian canon.

That being the case, staff and organization in the presidency can potentially constrain presidential power as much as facilitate it. Neustadt noted that power relations were the product of mutual dependencies, the implications of which I examine in terms of staffing and organizing the presidency. The key principle for staffing resulting from these mutual dependencies is competitive uncertainty. Apart from the president's political sensibilities and goals, however, the application of Neustadt's principles is fraught with ambiguity. Next, I discuss central issues regarding Neustadt's theory of organizing and staffing the presidency, particularly those concerning possible contradictory tendencies in staffing functions, presidents' styles and goals, and the changing nature of the environment in which they work. Finally, I note the ways in which the chapters by Kenneth Mayer and Thomas Weko (chapter 9), Matthew Dickinson (chapter 10), and Michael Link (chapter 11) can help us further understand issues pertaining to staffing and organizing the presidency.

Mutual Dependencies

The process of leadership involves a recognition of reciprocities and mutual dependencies. These features mean, as Neustadt told us, that a president cannot command. Thus, with limited means at his disposal, a president must seek to persuade others to see things as he would like them to be seen. Staff assistants can both help and hinder this process. No one except the president can truly speak the president's mind; yet others who do the daily work of the presidency gain leverage by saying they do.

In reality, presidents (like all of us) rarely know precisely what they want. Their views are often incompletely formed so they typically want the widest possible latitude to keep their options open. Options begin to close when undecided matters prematurely reach the Oval Office, if only because an aide or spokesperson is placed in controversy's way; further, anyone dependent on others for help can be undercut by deliberately or inadvertently misspoken, or prematurely spoken, words signaling intent. In the face of ambiguity, aides are queried to say something, and their remarks can foreclose the president's options.

While it is certainly true that a president has a need to know, it is equally true that those who act in his name also need to know. The problem is this: how can a president preserve his options while communicating his choices and preferences? Keeping others in the dark preserves choice but produces chaos. Such a strategy (if it is indeed one) may allow for optimal levels of intelligence to reach the president yet may foreclose presidential options by defaulting choices to those who must say or hint at what they think is on the president's mind. A massively curious press wants to know what the president will do. Ever present is the prospect that someone in the administration will misspeak or, equally problematic, speak before a particular choice is revealed to the president.

None of this even touches on the notion that those who act on behalf of the president may have their own fish to fry. The helpers, Neustadt notes, can set up shop for themselves. Aides may wish to ensure that a president who does not communicate what is on his mind will be compelled to follow their lead. Such a possibility should not be discounted, but even if it were, no president can hope to control at all times those speaking on his behalf. The difficulty of such control is multiplied by the conditions through which, in Neustadt's conceptualization, presidential options are preserved. Principally, they are retained through a process of competitive uncertainty.

COMPETITIVE UNCERTAINTY

To management theorists, staffing functions to accomplish what no one person can do alone. For the most part, its purpose is to bring order from complexity, to obtain a bottom line from a multitude of vignettes, and to systematize decisionmaking and make explicit what had previously been ad hoc and implicit.

Nothing could be farther from the Neustadtian theory of presidential management, which is the ultimate un-system. Who the principal is at the center of it matters deeply. Neustadt's president, at least the one with a feel for power, is a hands-on leader, but not a linear one. That was Harry Truman's problem—everybody knew where he was coming from, making him easy to resist.

Eisenhower may well have been a nonlinear leader in Fred Greenstein's rendition,[5] but he was not a hands-on type. It is not clear that Eisenhower believed staffing was the route to presidential salvation, but his style was assuredly more organized and attentive to details and options set forth before the relevant administration actors. Apparently, Eisenhower believed that what he knew should be common knowledge to those compelled to act on behalf of his administration.

Truman's theory of staffing was simple enough: "The buck stops here," implying the president was both responsible and accountable. This outlook was rich in honesty and public virtue but anemic in guile. Eisenhower's staffing system implied that the president had partners in governance who had best be taken into confidence. Eisenhower's conception of staffing was coincident with the idea that he was an indispensable part of an enterprise that could not be managed by one person or through ad hoc methods. Compared to some bouts of presidential megalomania featuring Lyndon Johnson and Richard Nixon, the Eisenhower model seemed to possess the virtue of propriety. Neustadt's conception of American government, however, makes orderliness, guileless- ness, and, by implication, propriety, presidential liabilities.

The problem of achieving effective leadership goes beyond the peculiarities of American government. Neustadt noted that in all systems, if in different ways, the forces of resistance are always strong.[6] Messiness can persist beyond a facade of order, though the magnitude of messiness and its modalities may vary from place to place. Messiness is justified, however, as the theory of Amer- ican government. True as this may be, American presidents are often asked to impose order on disorder, not to contribute to it. The problem, then, lies in how presidents can achieve a preferred order.

One approach emphasizes the orderly processes of information gathering and assessment, inviting collegial participation in ordered ways. Neustadt thinks of this as a chairman of the board style or model. It is clear that Neustadt thinks little of this as a means of preserving a leader's stakes. In this vein, he concluded that the chairman of the board model Eisenhower chose for himself did nothing to enhance his power or further his goals—assuming knowledge of them was evident.

In sum, orderliness, as Neustadt saw it, was no virtue.

Systems of management are for business school curricula not for political leaders. Accruing power necessitates limiting the potential of others to do the same. Two consequences arise from this: first, competition and uncertainty of mission keeps staff and their existing units off-balance; none can hold a critical monopoly over intelligence or implementation. And secondly, such a process should enable intelligence to improve qualitatively to produce more diversity of options.[7]

Systems for Neustadt do not substitute for judgment, which is, after all, the product of astuteness. The only system that can work is a system (meaning a nonsystem) of competition.[8] But such a process merely has the potential for giving a president what he needs (intelligence); it cannot assure him what he wants (compliance).

From Neustadt's perspective, the chairman of the board approach cannot work because it fails to provide presidents with unpredictable information. Clear lines of intelligence coincide with organizational and other biases; a pres- ident dependent exclusively on such information will soon be dependent upon the sum of preexisting biases. In the end, Neustadt presumes a president of intense curiosity, angling to know what his options are—not as they appear immediately, but as they constrain his future choices and political resources.

Astuteness lies in far-sighted self-interest. In that regard, a president had better be his own best helper. But such a (largely hypothetical) president must not only have a well-honed taste for power but must also be extraordinarily (perhaps impossibly) wise.

Interpreting Neustadt's analysis of presidential-staff relations is nothing if not subtle and nuanced. There are pieces for the reader to stitch carefully together, inferences there for the taking, possibilities to be pondered, but little that says explicitly "do this; don't do that." If judgment is the pivotal idea, it is hard to conceptualize or quantify. In this sense, Neustadt's corpus of work on the subject of presidential power is like a great piece of art, music, or literature. The general contours can be quickly made knowable to the relatively uninitiated, but interpretive nuances inevitably differ. Neustadt worried greatly that he could be misinterpreted. One of Nixon's aides, later convicted in the Watergate scandal, paid him perverse heed, by claiming that *Presidential Power* provided the guiding precepts for Nixon's indicted co-conspirators.[9] Neustadt's concerns about being misinterpreted tell us, among other things, how subjective and nonformulaic much of his guidance really is.

Its basic outline is that political instinct is crucial. An instinct for power, among other things, leads to political self-preservation. Political aptitude also creates the possibility of wise choices, defined obviously in terms of self-preservation but also more generally on behalf of advancing a president's objectives. But it is less clear just precisely what this instinct is and how it ought to be manifested other than by arguing backward from success. Ideally, a president lacking astuteness probably ought not to be in office; but many lacking this critical trait continue to occupy the post. What can be done for them, if anything? Neustadt's tools are of little help to those unable to use them.

We know also that a president needs resources beyond his wits in dealing with other actors. Yet we know too that Neustadt was attuned to the potential for internecine conflict within presidential administrations and to the prospect that staffing could impede, not just serve, the making of judicious choices. Put to proper use, though, the staffing function could widen the frequency of what presidents might hear and extend their range of vision. So armed, they would be better able to avoid pitfalls that inevitably would be played out as pratfalls, damaging a president's standing in Washington and beyond. Done properly with the right people, the resourceful use of staffing could help a president know more, perceive future risks, and enable him to more skillfully exploit his vantage points. The right stratagem is, as noted, one of overlapping and competitive roles in the presence of strategic purpose and tactical flexibility. It is not clear how this would work in the absence of "Mr. Right." And it is not clear whether such a theory of staffing could in any way be separated from Neustadt's ideal incumbent. Would not this incumbent intuitively know to follow Neustadt's recommendations?

ISSUES IN NEUSTADT'S THEORY OF STAFFING

Neustadt's theory gives the essentials of the way a president may become master of his staff and the administration's organizations. These elements cannot be separated from Neustadt's more general arguments about presidential power. They lead to four interrelated questions: (1) Does Neustadt's theory of staffing emphasize learning and intelligence functions at the cost of implementing or doing? (2) Does this theory imply an active president and an active presidency and, hence, bias against a reactive president and a conserving presidency? (3) Inevitably overlapping with 2: is Neustadt's theory of staffing able to accommodate diverse presidential styles? and (4) Is this theory even possible today?

LEARNING VS. DOING

A savvy president, according to Neustadt, keeps others off balance to enhance his ability to gain information—information that he will need to bargain. For Neustadt, information is not the equivalent of power, but feeds power. A president reliant on predictable sources of information can be manipulated and cut off from what he needs to know. But just what does he need to know? Clearly, he cannot know everything, and if he could, he would not be in need of staff. Moreover, knowing too much can lead to a lack of focus or incisiveness in reaching a bottom line (summarized in the aphorism that analysis leads to paralysis). Knowledge or its absence can therefore affect a president's bargaining leverage.

It is daunting how much a president needs to know, especially for those who come to office ill-prepared for its intensely political nature. No president totally ignorant of or uninterested in the details of public policy can expect to fare well in bargaining. Yet, a president must be hypersensitive to political information. Policy analysts and specialists abound in the bureaucracy and even on his staff. The president may have reason to need them and even possibly heed them, but they need him even more. The president must know who is coming from where, with what interests at stake, and how he may appeal to enough of them to pull together a coalition or avoid a serious mishap.

Neustadt began with the proposition that the U.S. political system was resistant to command and that a president's power to persuade was largely a function of his bargaining leverage. In the main, Neustadt is still correct. However, Neustadt's emphasis on the competitive uncertainty principle and the use of staffing to generate political intelligence may well conflict with the ability of presidents to implement their objectives. Keeping everyone a bit off-stride certainly implies implementation will be equally uncertain. Those to whom tasks are delegated may be uncertain of their responsibilities. Good, Neustadt might say. But it is unclear whether presidents would or should strive for a disorganized mess with little cooperation across units. Whatever else, one source of a president's leverage is to appear to run a tight ship. But this is unlikely to happen in a system designed mainly for intelligence functions and hands-on presidential administration. Staffing that aids the chief executive's ability to gather intelligence will likely hinder him when implementing policy, and vice versa.[10] This is so partially because intelligence requires openness and even ambiguity regarding intent whereas implementation requires clarity and certainty. Therein lies the presidential staffing dilemma.

While the president's staffing needs are surely multiple, it is critical that what is done corresponds with the president's intentions. While delegation is power, how can that power be controlled and monitored? And how can it be coordinated? These are very central questions the answers to which certainly impact presidential success or failure. Yet, as the presidency evolves, government becomes more complex, and the press makes transparent what was previously opaque, it has clearly become more difficult, if not impossible, for the president to play the role of chief-of-staff.

If there is any single proposition commending itself to managing the presidential apparatus, it is that poor management gets presidents into trouble, making them appear disorderly and inept. Nothing, of course, can substitute for judgment. In that, Neustadt is right. But judgment is a concept inevitably filled with ambiguity, and it cannot be reduced to a formula.

At some point, though, clarity is essential if others are to follow. In broad terms, that was the secret of Ronald Reagan's presidency—a presidency successful in every respect emphasized by Neustadt. Reagan achieved his central goals not only for his time but into the future, and was adjudged to be a political success. Reagan's professional reputation may have fared less well, but others operating in his name achieved that for his presidency. Was there, in the end (or for that matter the beginning or the middle), any secret as to what the Reagan presidency was about?[11] It was obviously about doing and spending less, except for defense and fighting crime.

The Reagan presidency was not staffed around the idea of acquiring information. It knew very well what it wanted to do, and it organized itself around ensuring its goals would be met.[12] Of course, the Reagan administration can arguably be faulted for failing to heed sound policy advice. The Reaganites, however, found such "sound policy" advice inconsistent with both their policy objectives and political advantages. Rejecting, even suppressing, such advice was hardly a problem for the Reagan people (even if it later might be for the American people). The Reagan presidency had no need to be organized around variety or to find ways of promoting it. To the contrary, it was organized around the goals it wished to see attained and the processes that would ensure their efficient implementation.[13]

A single case neither makes nor refutes a theory, but if the Reagan case cannot be considered successful, it is hard to know what could be. It would be fair to say that the Reagan staffing arrangements and the principal himself were not congenial to Neustadt's original arguments about how to run an administration.[14] The point, of course, is not that Neustadt's scheme is wrong and Reagan's right. Rather, the main point is that the hands-on style of Franklin Roosevelt and the more remote delegating style of Ronald Reagan reflected two different sorts of presidents. Their ideas and goals were in different stages of formation, and their needs, as well as political personalities, were different. Yet, by Neustadt's own criteria, presidents operating differently could be considered successes regardless of how we view the content of their policy goals. The obvious conclusion is that organization and staffing arrangements are contingent. One of the things they are contingent on is a president's goals and his steadfastness in their pursuit.

ACTIVE AND REACTIVE PRESIDENCIES

Neustadt's notions of a hands-on president who keeps his aides uncertain, encourages competition between them and promotes crosscutting lines of communication, seems ill-fit for a certain style of presidency, namely a conserving and reactive or process oriented presidency. By contrast, an active presidential style driven by policy goals seems to be most obviously appropriate for Neustadt's prescriptions.

Of course, imputing goals is a difficult business. No one can truly say what the model activist president, Franklin Roosevelt, wanted. Undoubtedly, Roosevelt himself was not always aware of that or, at least, had fairly fluid and changeable objectives as events altered his calculus. It would be equally hard to figure out exactly what Eisenhower wanted, a point on which neither Neustadt nor Fred Greenstein, two eminent scholars of the presidency, were able to read-ily agree. Nonetheless, presidents come to office with more or less of a pro-grammatic orientation, even if they remain uncertain about the details of the specific programs. At least those who come with a more programmatic orien-tation leave us their legislative proposals or inspired rhetoric; those who come with less leave us to wonder why they sought office in the first place. Theirs is a Tory (preservationist) concept of government, if not necessarily by intent, at least by default.

Ironically, although the American political system best accommodates a low profile president (wish not, get not), the odds are stacked against a conserving or reactive presidency. In analyzing the Bush presidency, David Mervin asked whether it was possible for a president of Bush's "guardian" style to be success-ful, given expectations, especially on the part of the media, of what a president should do.[15]

I do not know if there is a Tory (preservationist) theory of staffing since the concept itself is a modern invention. However, it would seem a Tory theory of governing would be predicated on providing orderly processes of review and communication based on a relatively austere public agenda. The Tory theory of leadership (a virtual oxymoron) assumes that showing up truly is the biggest part of the role. Ronald Reagan was no Tory, nor were most American presi-dents, with Eisenhower and Bush emerging as the exceptions, and in the lim-ited time we could observe him, Gerald Ford. These presidents assumed trou-ble would find them; they did not need to stir up any. Order appeared to suit them fine.

Contestably, Eisenhower's presidency increasingly has come to be seen as the most effectively organized in the era of modern presidential staffing.[16] No team, even winning ones, pulls together all of the time. Still, it may be said of Eisenhower's administration that processes of reviewing and vetting took place regularly. Eisenhower may have been a chairman of the board, but he wanted processes and people in place whom he could trust to act together when he needed them to. Even his wildly unpopular Secretary of Agriculture, Ezra Taft Benson, lacked popularity mainly because he followed Eisenhower's preferred policies of reduced price supports for farmers. Eisenhower seemed also to have a decent respect for, and ability to reach accommodations with, the congres-sional opposition. His was an administration of settled ideas and settlements. Being above the fray was part of the style Eisenhower wanted to project, and was largely compatible with his rather limited agenda and icon status. Besides, whatever threats or deals Eisenhower needed to make on his behalf could be handled through his chief-of-staff, Sherman Adams.

The other Tory president, George Bush, like Eisenhower, put together a team of "knowns" well-versed and experienced in government or, at least, in the arts of governance. Despite this, Bush got into trouble, precipitated in part by different and more partisan times under divided government and by his lack of the personal stature that enabled Eisenhower to pass through and recover from his troubled times. Further, Bush's troubles reflected the fortunes of ill-timing with his bad news coming late in his term, leaving him little room from which to come back. Nevertheless, his problems also reflected poor political judgments regarding those whom he chose to be members of his inner corps of aides. Like Eisenhower, Bush appointed a former Governor of New Hampshire who helped his political prospects in the state's first-in-the-nation primary election. In Bush's case, this turned out to be John Sununu,[17] whose arrogance and contempt for other actors—both within and outside the administration—served his principal poorly. Unlike Eisenhower's staff, whose lines to Congress flowed well, Bush's people sought to disconnect their president to the greatest extent possible from Congress. Not only Sununu, but especially C. Boyden Gray, the President's Counsel, and to a lesser extent, Richard Darman, the OMB director, tried to operate beyond Congress's reach and even above the law.[18] If Bush wanted an accommodative presidency, he chose the wrong inner circle for that purpose, though his staff arrangements elsewhere largely worked well.

Similarly, Bush's judgments after his great triumph in the Gulf War could be said to have lacked wisdom. With his popularity at a zenith, Bush could have sought at least symbolic accommodative arrangements with the Democratic majorities in Congress. He chose instead to confront the Democrats to bolster his standing within his own party and regain its confidence after he broke his "no new taxes" pledge in the fall 1990 budget bill.

Bush's problems were not staffing arrangements but personnel misjudgments; he placed people in critical but improperly situated roles, given his administration's emphasis on rounding sharp edges. More important, his problems, at least those he could control, had to do with judgment. This bob-and-weave president chose to slug it out just at the point his levers and resources were turning southward. Looking reasonable, as he did in the first two years, would at least have bought him time. In the end, and especially to the extent that Bush could control his own fate, Neustadt's emphasis on the person in office (despite Bush's impressive vitae) is well-placed. His emphasis on organizing a presidency is misplaced mainly because presidents differ in what they want out of their presidencies.

PRESIDENTIAL STYLE

The above issues lead directly to questions of variation in presidential style. Typically, characteristics of style and modes of conducting oneself in office are closely related, with the former usually inferred from evidence about the latter. Change-oriented presidencies, whatever the direction of change, are likely to have active agendas; reactive presidencies less so. That is now old news. However, at least one president was remarkably passive in the face of his quite activist presidency (Reagan). Another stayed highly involved as his presidency became less committed to change (Clinton). The person in office does not always match the ambitions of his presidency.

The people who hold the office also differ in their curiosity, their abilities to separate fact from credible fiction, and the ways in which they prefer to deal with people including their aides. They differ too in the knowledge and experiences they bring to office. Do these differences make a difference? Some, like Neustadt, think yes. Others, like Terry Moe, think not.[19] The obvious way to conceptualize the difference personal differences make, to use the jargon of social science, is to define a dependent variable or at least a phenomenon to be explained and a set of independent "style" variables. This may not always be possible operationally, but it is helpful to think about the matter in this way. In all likelihood, the more large scale the dependent variables, the less personal variables will matter. But this does not mean they are unimportant. One might analogize to voting behavior where we often know the predilections of the vast majority of the electorate long before the election. Only a small proportion of the electorate will turn the tide of a winner-take-all election in a competitive race. Similarly, large forces lead many presidents to face similar conditions or pressures, but personal differences make for variant behaviors, or at least varied presentations of similar behavior.

Large trends do, after all, affect a number of presidents.[20] In this regard, as described in the next section, the conditions prevalent since Neustadt wrote in the 1950s have made it harder for presidents to manage the government and to cut deals with other insiders. The personal variables, however, are the value added (or subtracted) from trends, cyclical regularities, and situations that any president may face. No matter how much is determined, nor how limited the president's freedom of action, it is he who ultimately decides how to expand, accommodate, or even shrink from constraints. Neustadt did not—and he knew he did not—focus on the most substantial circumstantial determinants of presidential power. Those matters, he knew, largely lay beyond the president's power to control. He did, however, focus on how different presidents might react to similar circumstances. What was their feel for power in these situations? What did or could they know to deter them from incurring ruinous costs and, thus, mortgaging their presidencies? No single factor view of the world can, except in the mind of its beholder, plausibly render this unimportant.

What is, then, the difficulty for Neustadt's arguments regarding staffing and organization? It is that Neustadt's preferred style of operating the presidency doesn't accurately fit with some presidents. One would be hard put, for example, to see Reagan managing a presidency as Neustadt recommends. It is difficult to imagine placing an active verb behind Reagan's name during his presidency. One might conclude that Neustadt could hardly envision a man of such limited curiosity and intellectual energy in the presidential office. But Reagan could be said to have had Harry Truman's willingness to stand behind principle with greater political intuition and skill than Truman had, and a greater ability to deflect responsibility on matters for which he did not wish to be held responsible.

However and by whomever Reagan's management procedures were organized, at the very least he had to sign off on a system that was best for him. Such a system delegated authority, regularized coordinative practices, and placed the White House chief of staff in a position to oversee it. The first Reagan administration had in James Baker a skilled political manager at the head of the process, whereas the second Reagan administration suffered from a John Sununu-like business executive, Donald Regan, at least until after the Iran-contra operation, when Nancy Reagan's opposition apparently sealed his fate. Surely, whatever Reagan knew, he knew what kind of man he was—and he was not likely to be reading briefing books into the night or checking in on who was doing what at some agency. He was there to be scripted and consulted. Still, he knew what he wanted and did not want. When Baker brought him a tax increase deal that congressional leaders had agreed to, Reagan knew he did not want it. Quite possibly, he was merely inattentive to the process unfolding before him, but conceivably he allowed the exercise of negotiation to continue in order to show Baker who was president after all. In sum, the management style has to fit the president.

Organization can complement presidential style and it may, at its best, compensate for the deficiencies of the principal. Lyndon Johnson's style tells us that hands-on intervention can be at least as disastrous as any other mode of operation. Neustadt correctly maintained that it comes down to the person holding office, but there is no formula for managing or ensuring success in office.

Whatever Johnson lacked, it was hardly a lust for power nor was it inex
in Washington. Indeed, with Johnson and Nixon, the basic problem
each lusted for power too much, at the cost of prudence. In each ca
them, and, above all, the country, dearly.

WASHINGTON AT CENTURY'S END

Political Washington has changed markedly since Neustadt first wrote *Presidential Power*. Since then there has been a shift to a more public politics and
governing process (which Neustadt noted in subsequent editions of the book),
a wider array of key players and less comity between them, a heightened partisan atmosphere, and a more complex government deemed by the public to be
untrustworthy. Deference has been replaced by cynicism. Cutting deals is
harder to do. Private vulnerabilities among politicians, their appointees, and
associates are now instantly public. Conflict within administrations is more
readily exploited. Leaking, always prevalent, is more routine as actors seek to
advance their interests or prevent them from being incurred upon. Governing,
in a word, is harder; more so, if a president actually has a program. Looking
good has increasingly replaced doing good. The Clinton presidency, in this
regard, has perhaps been a parable for its times. It amply fulfilled its political
goals (reelection and high approval ratings) without advancing its advertised
policy goals. The fate of the Clinton presidency makes that of the Reagan presidency all the more remarkable. The Reagan presidency, after all, looked good
(most of the time) accomplishing at least the outlines of a far-reaching agenda.
Ironically, after the 1994 elections that produced the Republican Congress, it
was left to Clinton to fill in much of the Reagan agenda.

The typically difficult-to-control process of governing is now even harder to
control. "To spin" is a new verb in the American political lexicon, and has
spawned the new noun and role of spinner. The consequence is that what a
president most needs (or at least wants) from his staff is to look good, part of
which requires getting good spin from top rate news spinners. The problem is
that what presidents may want and need most for the public interest is potentially in conflict. Enamored with spin, a president can get himself (and the
country) in deeper trouble, as attested to by Clinton's deceptions about the
Lewinsky affair, leading to his impeachment by the House.

No doubt, as part of the general growth in cynicism toward government,
contemporary political scientists are much less likely than at mid-century to
equate the well-being of the president to that of the country (as did Neustadt).

As everything has become more complicated, from lines and modalities of political communication to government itself, presidents are often in need of insulation from, rather than exposure to, the pressures these complications generate. Some presidents may still wish to be their own chief-of-staff, but everything in their environment tells them this is no longer possible. Carter and Clinton eventually succumbed, realizing that they could not be both president and chief-of-staff. This tells us something about how both the presidency and the political environment within which it is situated have evolved. Mistakes are more readily picked up and picked upon. Media coverage has grown, its deference to the president has diminished, and it has developed a fine sense for hunting down gaffes and scandals (see Martha Kumar's essay— chapter 18—for more on presidents and the news media). Moreover, numerous advocacy groups searching for the opportunity to advance, and deter damage to, their cause are often fed leaks and they, in turn, often force action. Under these conditions, all presidents are apt to want to run a tighter ship— sooner or later.

Neustadt's conceptions of staffing seem especially appropriate to an entrepreneurial, experimental presidency whose president has a ravenous appetite for both policy options and political intentions. Of all our subsequent presidents, Lyndon Johnson and Bill Clinton, notably both Democrats, probably have come the closest to the FDR model. Johnson had an insatiable need to know about political options and to keep his staff and administration off-balance. But in the end, he did not make use of the knowledge that was there.[21] He was a prisoner of his political assumptions. Clinton came to office more educated and sophisticated about policy than Johnson and much less a captive of past assumptions. In addition, he had qualities of political astuteness, though his were different from Johnson's. Johnson knew the game and the players. By Clinton's time, the game had changed and the number of players had expanded. His efforts were directed outward toward public legitimacy. Whatever the qualities of Clinton's political instincts, they have not run in organizational directions. Clinton and his people could ask questions endlessly (sometimes they were even interested in the answers), but they could not bring matters to resolution. The 104th Congress and its successor helped Clinton with this problem by bringing their agenda to him.

Arguably, the most successful president since Roosevelt in Neustadt's terms was Ronald Reagan. No two people could be more unalike than Roosevelt and Reagan, and no two presidents could be more different in the ways they organized their presidencies. That alone should tell us that there is no robust approach to presidential staff management across different political personalities nor across time. That is discouraging for theory at first blush. But what it means is that we have to keep our eye on the changing incentives in the political system and on the way these interact with the levels of curiosity, sensitivity, drive, and the goal orientation of the person in office. I think this would be consistent with the spirit in which Neustadt wrote even if not wholly consistent with his exact words.

New Work On Staffing and Organizing the Presidency

Michael Link and Matthew Dickinson each contribute important empirical evidence, respectively, to the ways in which presidents make use of their staffs and administrations and to explaining the growth of presidential staffing. Kenneth Mayer and Thomas Weko look especially at the institutional means by which presidents seek to enhance their power.

Dickinson's analysis suggests that staff growth is a function of a changing and more politically complicated and difficult environment which presidents must navigate. In his analysis, he argues that the costs of staff growth, nonetheless, yield marginal benefits to presidents in reducing their bargaining costs with other actors. Staffing increases presidential resources for bargaining. To keep pace, an environment of greater complexity necessitates an institutionalized growth of presidential resources.

The enlargement of the presidency does not mean that the president has acquired larger powers. It means that presidents have been trying to find ways of coping with the complications arising in their midst.

Link examines the ways in which presidents use their administrations. He evaluates the impact of three factors: personal style, and institutional and situational influences. In turn, he connects these influences to the expansiveness or concentration of presidential communication networks. Though seeking larger generalizations, Link focuses on two presidencies, Jimmy Carter's and the first term of Richard Nixon's. His evidence shows that all three factors come into play influencing presidential communication networks. Individually, presidents may begin differently but, based on the Nixon-Carter comparison, they look more similar over time as expansiveness gives way to concentration. Institutionally, the inner core of presidential contacts tends to be with senior White House officials—a reflection of the institutional significance of these roles. Finally, particular events on Link's policy "kaleidoscope" tend also to concentrate presidential contacts with a particular set of advisers. In sum, all these conditions come into play. This result may satisfy the proponents of each body of theory or perhaps dissatisfy them equally.

Link's findings suggest ordered contingency in a world we might like to grasp more easily. "Keep it simple, stupid" seems to be the motto for the age, though perhaps keeping it simple assures also that the "it" will be stupid. This may have been a lesson Neustadt was trying to teach us.

Mayer and Weko, alternatively, argue that there are powerful uniformities at work in the president's motivations used to control the fate of their presidencies. Individual presidents differ in style but all, they argue, seek to alter to their advantage the institutional basis of governance. If Neustadt noted that an instinct for power was necessary to overcome the limits of institutional power among presidents, Mayer and Weko claim, in the context of recent institutional theory, that presidents cumulatively seek to alter the institutional balance of power in their favor. We are thus confronted with at least superficially conflicting perspectives each based on the imperatives of institutional weakness. One perspective tells us that individual instinct and prowess is critical to overcoming the institutional frailties of presidential power (Neustadt). The other tells us that all presidents find the means to cumulatively alter the institutional balance of power (Mayer and Weko). Thus there may be significant tensions between the themes in this essay and elements of the next three chapters. Which of these notions has greater validity is fundamental to how we think about the organizational presidency and its place in the presidential tool kit.

Ultimately, the organizational presidency and staff growth are ways of coping with complexity. Do they hinder or help presidents? Effective staffing compensates for weaknesses of the individual incumbent. Poor staffing reinforces the weaknesses. But who knows one's own personal weaknesses? In the end, how a White House is organized and with whom it is organized has much to do with the president in office despite the obvious accumulation of presidential organizations.

ACKNOWLEDGMENT

I am grateful to the Swedish Collegium for Advanced Study in the Social Sciences, Uppsala, Sweden for providing me the hospitality and time to write this chapter. I am also grateful to Joel D. Aberbach for his comments on an earlier draft.

NOTES

1. Richard E. Neustadt, "The President at Mid-Century," *Law and Contemporary Problems* 21 (Autumn 1956): 615.

2. Ibid., p. 617.

3. Richard E. Neustadt, "Presidency and Legislation: The Growth of Central Clearance," *American Political Science Review 48 (September 1954)*: 641–671.

4. Neustadt, "The Presidency at Mid-Century," p. 645.

5. See Fred I. Greenstein, *Eisenhower As Leader: The Invisible-Hand Presidency.* (New York: Basic Books, 1982).

6. Richard E. Neustadt, "White House and Whitehall," *The Public Interest* (Winter 1966): 55–69.

7. There is nothing particularly new in Neustadt's formulation since typically tyrannical leaders of the past, ancient and modern, used similar methods to consolidate their grip on power. Keeping one's associates off-balance and in competition with one another kept down the odds of their forming a coalition against the ruling tyrant. It also enabled the tyrant to gain intelligence on his associates. To be sure, none of this is meant to suggest that Neustadt's purpose was to advance tyranny. Hardly. It was only to suggest that elements of Neustadt's formulation for dealing with staff has roots in the leadership precepts of some not too savory leaders.

8. Neustadt's philosophy may be appropriately summarized in the following passage: "Reorganization . . . is obviously useful, often essential, as a supplement to the appointive power in building or in equalizing institutionalized competitions. . . . [But] it cannot be enough to reorganize. . . . In their relations to each other and the President, his official associates need stirring up . . . just enough so that they are never absolutely confident in unchecked judgment of their chief's own judgment, or of their colleagues either." (Neustadt, "The Presidency at Mid-Century," p. 644.)

9. Neustadt recounts in the 1990 preface to *Presidential Power* his concern about being misinterpreted by White House staff personnel who came to government innocent of governmental experience and by journalists and college students who came to the book innocent of history (pp. xvi-xvii). The risks are apparent. What lessons could one learn about, let us say, the music of Brahms or the poetry of Pound without a tutored ear or eye? Little, I would think. Herein is the problem in interpreting Neustadt's theory of presidential power—he asks us to share in his suppositions without clearly stipulating what those might be. He tells us explicitly, however, that if the presidency cannot be made to work, the system will not work. If one is a president or even an aide, that is pretty heady stuff. It is natural for interested parties to turn to Neustadt's work to justify their own purposes.

10. For further elaboration of this, see Bert A. Rockman, "Organizing The White House: On A West Wing And A Prayer," *Journal of Managerial Issues*, 5 (Winter 1993): 453–464.

11. See Aaron Wildavsky, "President Reagan as a Political Strategist" in Charles O. Jones ed., *The Reagan Legacy: Promise and Performance* (Chatham, NJ: Chatham House, 1988), pp. 289–305.

12. See here Joel D. Aberbach and Bert A. Rockman (with Robert M. Copeland), "From Nixon's *Problem* To Reagan's *Achievement*: The Federal Executive Reexamined" in Larry Berman, ed., *Looking Back On The Reagan Presidency* (Baltimore: The Johns Hopkins University Press, 1990), pp. 175–194.

13. For an assessment of the Reagan administration management style, see Colin Campbell, *Managing The Presidency: Carter, Reagan, and the Search for Executive Harmony* (Pittsburgh: University of Pittsburgh Press, 1986).

14. Some things did go awry in the Reagan administration, chief among them the Iran-contra episode. Nevertheless, in this and some other cases, what went awry was the administration's persistence in pushing, if necessary, its schemes beyond the bounds of legal recognition. There is no indication that this was merely the work of uncontrolled zealots acting on behalf of the administration.

15. David Mervin, *George Bush And The Guardian Presidency* (London: MacMillan's, 1995).

16. For example, Walter Williams, whose policy sympathies could fairly be said to lie closer to Democratic than Republican presidents, claims that after Eisenhower, organizational incompetence has been the hallmark of subsequent presidencies. See Walter Williams, *Mismanaging America: The Rise of the Anti-Analytic Presidency* (Lawrence, KS: University Press of Kansas, 1990).

17. For a revealing discussion of the Sununu problem, see Colin Campbell, "The White House and Cabinet Under the 'Let's Deal' Presidency" in Colin Campbell and Bert A. Rockman eds., *The Bush Presidency: First Appraisals* (Chatham, NJ: Chatham House, 1991), pp. 185–222.

18. The view is naturally biased to some extent—the author being former Deputy Counsel to the U.S. House of Representatives. Nevertheless, see Charles Tiefer, *The Semi-Sovereign Presidency: The Bush Administration's Strategy for Governing Without Congress* (Boulder, CO: Westview, 1994).

19. Neustadt, of course, emphasizes the importance of style. See his chapter for criteria in appraising presidential performance (chapter 9) in the latest edition of *Presidential Power* (1990). By contrast, Terry Moe emphasizes the influence of contemporary conditions on presidential needs to concentrate and institutionalize power. See, for example, Terry Moe, "The Politicized Presidency" in John E. Chubb and Paul E. Peterson, eds., *The New Direction in American Politics* (Washington, DC: The Brookings Institution, 1985), pp. 235–271, and Terry Moe, "Presidents,

Institutions, and Theory" in George C. Edwards III, John H. Kessel, and Bert A. Rockman, eds., *Researching The Presidency: Vital Questions, New Approaches* (Pittsburgh: University of Pittsburgh Press, 1993), pp. 337-385. At the outset of his chapter in the latter volume, Moe tells us that everyone has a style and asks what difference it makes. Obviously, he thinks very little.

20. In this regard, see Bert A. Rockman, *The Leadership Question: The Presidency and the American System* (New York: Praeger, 1984).

21. See Leslie Gelb and Richard Betts, *The Irony of Vietnam: The System Worked* (Washington, DC: The Brookings Institution, 1979).

CHAPTER 9

The Institutionalization of Power

Kenneth R. Mayer and Thomas J. Weko

Richard Neustadt's observation in *Presidential Power* that "the probabilities of power do not derive from the literary theory of the Constitution,"[1] revolutionized research on the U.S. presidency. The power of the presidency did not stem directly from the legal authority of the office; instead, Neustadt argued, that power is a function of an individual president's "personal capacity to influence the conduct of the men who make up the government,"[2] and is brought into execution by persuasion, not command. Rather than falling back solely on constitutional and statutory grants of power, presidents found their influence in extralegal sources: reputation among others with power in the Washington community; standing with the mass public outside the nation's capital; and an ability to act strategically.

Presidential Power transformed presidency studies. It led a generation of scholars away from traditional legal and historical modes of analysis, which had come to be seen as static and atheoretical,[3] and laid the intellectual foundations for scholarship that explored the informal and personal bases of presidential leadership. The study of the presidency expanded to include analysis of presidential personality, the president's standing with the mass public, and the president's strategies and accomplishments as a legislative leader. While Neustadt's view of presidential leadership and power has been criticized[4] and creatively amended,[5] its basic premise that "presidential power is the power to persuade" continues to be the starting point for a great deal of presidential scholarship.

Neustadt's model viewed the institutional setting of the presidency as more or less given. Although American politics had been buffeted by war (both hot and cold) and conflicts over the scope of the welfare state, presidents were constrained by the routines and responsibilities of the modern presidency. Truman and Eisenhower preserved and even elaborated on the presidency they inherited from Franklin Roosevelt. Presidential leadership was a function of the institutional setting in which chief executives found themselves, and successful presidents explored how best to exploit the limited opportunities for personal leadership that these institutions afforded.

This is not to say that institutions are unimportant—indeed, Neustadt recognized the significance of structure and process in several major essays he wrote in the 1950s[6]—but they were viewed as setting limits on the exercise of power rather than providing opportunities.

In this essay we argue that a renewed focus on institutions as a *source* of presidential power offers some new insight into the evolution of the modern presidency. The institutional focus we set out in this chapter differs in two ways from the conception of presidential leadership presented in *Presidential Power*. First, we argue that presidents do not take the presidency as fixed and invariable. Rather, presidents look beyond specific decisions and existing structures and regularly try to explore the limits of the office, and to reshape it to make the office they inherited more responsive to their leadership. Second, we posit that presidents can exercise influence not only by personally intervening to influence "the conduct of the men [and women] who make up the government," but also by actively working to mold and alter the institutions within which these men and women work.

As an application of what has been called "the new institutionalism" or the "new economics of organization," our approach argues that the presidency as *an institution* has multiple opportunities for presidents to exercise leadership through the "politics of structure,"[7] rather than through the case-by-case application of personal influence. Following those who study formal organizations and human cognition,[8] we argue that the routines and organizations that make up the modern "institutionalized presidency"[9] permit presidents to shape outcomes through their ability to affect structures, processes, and personnel. That is, presidents can wield influence over policy by exerting control over the organizations and institutional processes that produce those decisions, and by choosing the people who will make those decisions.

But which presidents will so choose to alter the presidency, bolstering their institutional capabilities for the exercise of power? All of them will. Although individual presidents differ in their proclivities to exploit and augment the institutional bases of presidential leadership, each is held accountable for the performance of the national government, and has powerful incentives to structure processes and institutions to create an environment that is amenable to presidential influence.[10] The chief motivation for institutional development and centralization is the mismatch between presidential preferences and responsibilities on and the resources at the chief executive's disposal. To be sure, the process of institution building is affected by the preferences and choices of individual presidents: some presidents may be more inclined to take advantage of opportunities to expand the limits of their power, while others may be more likely to work with the status quo.[11] In the long run, however, the setting of the presidency pushes presidents to centralize.

Although all presidents are driven by the weight of public and elite expectations to structure the presidency in ways that make it more congenial to their leadership, they face serious constraints and will often fail. The first constraint that presidents face stems from the national government's constitutional structure, in which power is shared among separate institutions (this phrasing is Neustadt's). Major institutional changes usually—though not always—require the president to obtain congressional approval, or at least congressional acquiescence. A second constraint arises from the various sources of political power outside government—from political parties, interest groups, the news media, and elite opinion. Presidents do not, by any stretch, have a monopoly on the ability to structure and organize institutions. Their efforts will sometimes be constrained and rebuffed—or even reversed. For example, Ronald Reagan's aggressive centralization of political appointments sometimes yielded retaliation from Congress that diminished the president's institutional capacities for bureaucratic leadership. In response to Reagan's packing of the Civil Rights Commission with conservative appointees, Congressional Democrats passed a 1983 statute circumscribing the president's authority over the Commission, authorizing him to appoint only four of its eight commissioners. In the 1970s, Congress enacted a wave of institutional and legal constraints on the presidency in an effort to reassert its prerogatives and take back ground that had been lost during the excesses, in particular, of the Nixon Administration. Among these were the Budget and Impoundment Control Act and the creation of the Congressional Budget Office, to the War Powers Act, the creation of an Independent Counsel, and modifications to the Freedom of Information Act making it more difficult for the president to keep information secret.

Despite these constraints, however, presidents continue to enjoy three distinct advantages—over Congress in particular—in their quest to reshape the presidency. The first advantage is asymmetric information. In a world of perfect information, institutionalizing interactions (through formal organization) offer no efficiencies over case by case bargains. Bureaucrats or legislators, when facing a proposal to alter existing institutional arrangements or procedures, would know how those changes would affect their own interests and react accordingly. But perfect information does not exist, and even presidents can be surprised at the unintended consequences of their actions. Yet presidents are in a better position than others to understand the impact that their proposals will have: they have critical informational advantages, not only about their own preferences (information they will guard), but also about the possible consequences of their proposals.

The history of the presidency's institutionalization is replete with stories of legislators or bureaucrats who seriously misjudged the consequences of reform, and of presidents who attempted to obscure the true nature of their motivations. The two most important presidential institutions, the Bureau of the Budget (BoB, which evolved into the Office of Management and Budget in 1971) and the Executive Office of the President (EOP), were established amid poorly understood intentions, unplanned consequences, and even intentional obfuscation. The chief architect of the EOP, Louis Brownlow, admitted that when he wrote the initial drafts of Executive Order 8248 (which established the EOP), he purposely obscured language that established a unit called the Office of Emergency Management (OEM), which was to serve as the legal foundation for multitudes of presidential wartime agencies.[12] Since the first reorganization bill (in 1937) generated such intense opposition from critics—who saw it as "evidence of Roosevelt's dictatorial ambitions"—Brownlow was sensitive to how the press and public might react had they known the full implications of the order's language.[13] Though Brownlow acknowledged that his plan contained "novel and unprecedented feature[s]," he presented it "to Congress and the public in a way that sought to camouflage its constitutional implications."[14]

Brownlow likened the OEM provision to a "rabbit stowed in the hat": when the order was issued,"the little rabbit came out . . . but was so disguised in small print, with no capital letters, that it occasioned no remark on the press or in [general discussions].[15] OEM was listed as the sixth organizational unit with the Executive Office of the President; it was not identified by name; and the remainder of the order said nothing about its structure or functions (the other five units were all explicitly defined in section II of the order). It was not until May 1940, when Hitler invaded the Low Countries, that Roosevelt activated the OEM, thus "[pulling] the rabbit out of the hat for keeps."[16]

The same is true for the BoB, which was enthusiastically endorsed in Congress despite expressed fears that it would lead to an excessive growth in executive power. In this case, Congress simply misjudged what the institution would mean, even though proponents of the Bureau were hardly quiet about its implications for presidential power. While there were some fears of presidential encroachment on legislative powers, the act was neither intended nor expected to alter the balance between the two branches and was largely viewed by Congress as a means to help rationalize its own previously chaotic budgetary process. What proved to be a truly important reform in the development of American political institutions was feasible precisely because its far-reaching political consequences were unanticipated."[17]

Presidents' second major advantage is that on many questions of structure they can simply take the initiative and leave it up to Congress or the courts to stop them.[18] Congress most often retains the ultimate authority, but it will typically have a difficult time working through the cumbersome legislative process to reverse a presidential action. Moreover, during the twentieth century, Congress ceded more and more power to the president, particularly through delegating legislative authority to the Executive Branch. This practice has significantly enhanced the president's discretionary authority to make policy. The tremendous growth in federal government powers and responsibilities in the twentieth century has presented presidents and Congress with numerous opportunities to grapple over the question of who should control these new powers and institutions. As problems arose, a struggle often ensued over which branch would have the most influence, and the shape solutions would take.[19]

Finally, presidents possess not only superior information and the advantage of going first, but also the opportunity to exploit "residual decision rights" within an environment that has been increasingly hospitable to their exercise. Many of the informal constraints that once hemmed in their exercise of power—most especially the claims of party and policy networks—have sharply receded, permitting contemporary presidents to reshape the presidency in ways their mid-century predecessors would have envied. In sum, the expectations facing presidents are incentives for each of them to mold institutions more amenable to their leadership; these advantages have made it possible for them to substantially realize their aims, and to create structural capacities for the exercise of power vastly different from those which existed before.[20]

Below we examine three ways that twentieth-century presidents have vastly added to the structural capacity for power. These cases were chosen because they involve powers notoriously lacking in the early-twentieth-century presidency, but widely seen to be central to the creation of the modern presidency: control over political appointments, budgeting, and regulation.

A Structural Capacity For The Exercise of Power: The Case of Presidential Appointments

One of the clearest ways to gain understanding of an institutional account of presidential power is to focus on major presidential appointments. The claim made here is simple: contemporary presidents at the end of the twentieth century possess a far greater capacity to exercise influence over these choices than did their mid-century predecessors—*not because of their personal capacity to influence the conduct of the men and women who vie with them for control over these decisions—but instead because a series of presidents have dramatically altered the presidency's structural capacity for the exercise of power* .

Where did this institutional capacity come from? In part, the new institutional environment of presidential appointments was obtained by statute, such as the Civil Service Reform Act of 1977.[21] For the most part, though, this new structural capacity was created through the use of "residual decision rights": presidents used their discretionary authority to promulgate executive orders about the civil service system,[22] and, most importantly, to create a large and specialized staff in the White House Personnel Office, with which they centralized—and presidentialized—the selection of political appointees.

Formally endowed with the capacity for unilateral action, presidents have nonetheless had to reckon with a host of informal constraints. The process of issuing executive orders to remove administrative posts from civil service protection brought with it charges of "politicization." Expanding the size and reach of the White House staff—permitting it to poach on the traditional prerogatives of parties, interest groups, or cabinet secretaries—proved to be a risky undertaking, and was sometimes rebuffed. However, the expectation that presidents would be the leader of their administrations in reality as well as name has induced all modern presidents to create new institutional arrangements for the selection of appointees. The net result of their efforts has been a sharply expanded institutional capacity for presidential leadership in staffing the executive branch.

This argument about the emergence of an institutional capacity for presidential leadership in the making of political appointments[23] can be illustrated by briefly comparing four presidencies: those of Truman, Kennedy, Johnson, and Carter. Truman, Kennedy, and Johnson each tried to create institutional arrangements that were more congenial than those they had inherited. Kennedy and Johnson were bolder and more successful than Truman in re-creating institutional arrangements: they operated within an increasingly plebiscitary environment that more weakly constrained how they put their unilateral powers to use. The steps these presidents undertook to create more advantageous institutional arrangements were not the product of the president's personal predilection. Rather, the quest to create a appointment process that was more centralized and "presidentialized" was necessitated by the weight of public and elite expectations. The cumulative results of presidents' efforts have been unmistakable: by the end of the twentieth century the making of political appointments had become a far more presidential process than it had been at mid-century, *regardless of the skills and aptitudes of those who occupy the White House* .

TRUMAN

Although the power to nominate executive officials is one of the most important formal powers awarded presidents by the Constitution, until late in the twentieth century presidents had precious little control over who served as executive officials. Virtually all appointments in the executive branch were only nominally "presidential." In practice, nearly all decisions about staffing were made outside of the White House: they were the product of negotiations among cabinet secretaries, congressmen from the president's party, party officials, and clientele groups. Appointments to positions in the field offices of federal agencies (e.g., postmasters and U.S. attorneys) constituted the vast majority of presidential appointments, and these appointees were chosen not by the president, but by senators and officials from the president's party. Senators nominated candidates directly to the executive departments; departments, in turn, submitted slates of candidates to the White House—which confirmed the senators' choices. In short, the constitutional order was stood on its head.[24] Only a thin layer of subcabinet appointments, roughly 100, linked the president to the bureaucracy. Here, too, the role of the president was very modest. Most of those who served in policymaking positions were in fact chosen outside of the White House by department heads—and they, in turn, were heavily influenced by the claims of congressional committee leaders and clientele groups with whom their departments had ongoing relationships.

Although President Truman presided over an executive branch with roughly 22,000 appointive posts, he initially relied on one aide, Donald Dawson, to assist him with nominations. How could Truman meet the burden of making these appointments with such modest assistance? By leaving these choices to others. Lacking an institutional capacity to independently recruit and evaluate candidates, the Truman White House leaned heavily upon clientele groups and their congressional allies or department executives to furnish it with candidates and political intelligence. Politicians outside the White House either selected candidates and Truman ratified their choices, or they created a "short list" from which the president made his choices. To be sure, Truman could occasionally intervene on an *ad hoc* basis to influence *particular* decisions: that is, he could exercise personal power of a sort described in *Presidential Power*. This sort of intervention, though, yielded an administration that was Truman's in name only: in fewer than one in ten appointment decisions did Truman and his White House aide play "a leading role,"[25] and many who held posts in the Truman administration were far less attached to the outlook and fortunes of their president than they were to the congressional committees and organized interests to whom they owed their tenure in office.[26]

Truman and his aides were not content merely to exercise personal power by intervening selectively in appointment decisions; they also explored ways in which the institutional structure of appointment politics could be turned to the president's advantage. Spurred by a dearth of desirable candidates "percolating up" from this highly decentralized process, in the winter of 1950 Truman directed his aides to devise improvements in the staffing of the executive branch. In March 1950, Dawson assembled a "Committee on Executive Personnel," staffed by five assistant secretaries, "young men on their way up who were bright, vigorous, not afraid of new ideas and who did not particularly come out of a political milieu" (in other words, they were not representatives of Democratic machine politics). The committee's members, assisted by academic experts, met throughout the spring and summer of 1950, and by October 1950 they completed their work: a plan to assist the president in staffing the government, which they dubbed "Operation Best Brains." Various members of the committee proffered different recommendations; common to each, however, was the ambition to create a structural capacity for presidential leadership that had previously been absent. Assistant Secretary of Labor Philip M. Kaiser, for example, proposed "to establish in the White House, under Dawson, a personnel unit headed by a staff director and composed of several top-flight assistants" and clerks. It was envisioned that this expanded staff would create an inventory of presidentially appointed posts in the executive branch, keep track of vacant posts, solicit recommendations from civic and political leaders around the country, and, when vacancies arose, submit a slate of candidates to the president. In short, the "residual decision rights" of the presidency would be put to use to create a new set of institutions that were more responsive to presidential leadership.

Although the reorganization of the president's personal staff may be a unilateral discretionary action, Truman's aides clearly understood that creating a
new set of institutional arrangements would circumscribe the prerogatives and
limit the influence of those outside of the White House—particularly party
leaders and cabinet secretaries (and, indirectly, the constituencies linked to
their departments). Throughout its deliberations the committee was keenly
aware that "party officials were watching us with a jaundiced eye," and it continually weighed the possible reactions of party leaders to its proposals. Hence,
the committee was careful to keep its proposal confidential, "because of the
controversy that its recommendations might have aroused" among party officials. As the committee neared the completion of its work, its staff prepared
talking points for a cabinet presentation of its proposal. As the talking points
show, Dawson assiduously sought to defuse the fears of party officials. His
planned talk did not begin with a statement of the changes "Best Brains" would
introduce but with an inventory of what the plan would not do:

> First let me tell you about that the plan recommended by the Committee
> *does not do.* (1.) It does not provide for the selection of appointees by anyone
> but the president. (2.) It does not locate candidates for cabinet positions. (3.)
> It does not alter the requirement of political acceptability or circumvent the
> Democratic National Committee in any way. (4.) It does not substitute tech-
> nicians for leaders. (5.) It does not substitute external judgments for those
> responsible agency officials.[27]

As the "Best Brains" committee completed its deliberations, party officials
weighed in with their views, making it clear that they saw the committee's plan
for a fortified presidential staff as a threat, an unwarranted "layer of expertise
interposed between the national committee, the congress, the local and state
political organizations, and the president."[28]

It was not simply party notables who hemmed in the president's staff. It was
also department heads and the "policy networks" to which they were linked.
After promising not to "circumvent the Democratic National Committee in
any way," Dawson promised not to "substitute external [White House staff]
judgments for those of responsible agency officials." Assurances notwithstanding, department heads were no more receptive to Dawson's plan than were
party officials. As two Brookings scholars reported following an interview with
an assistant to Donald Dawson, Martin Friedman, "Friedman indicated [that
following] general agreement with the proposition that there was a kind of
undeclared war between Cabinet members and White House staff members on
the matter of presidential appointments. Within their fields, Cabinet members

tried to control decisions on appointments themselves and tried to avoid initiative from the White House on such appointments." In this "undeclared war" department heads and their allies consistently won the battles, and they had no intention of ceding their advantage to the White House by permitting it to develop a larger and more powerful staff. "Best Brains," Dawson later recollected, had been unwise because it was "too ambitious" and threatened to create "too much of an intermediary layer [staff] between the president and responsible [departmental] officials"—a judgment with which any cabinet officials would concur. In the end, Dawson never presented this talk or the committee's final report to the cabinet. Rather, in light of the hostile response with which it was met, Dawson and his team opted to reject the study's recommendations—and decided it would be unwise to even reproduce the report. Truman and his aides were dependent on the assistance that department heads and party notables could provide, and the potential costs of putting the president's discretionary authority into play were sufficiently large to deeply constrain its use. His Democratic successors, less restricted in their exercise of formal powers than he, would be able to make very different choices.[29]

KENNEDY AND JOHNSON

In the spring of 1961, more than a decade after the plans of "Operation Best Brains" emerged stillborn, John Kennedy and his staff were faced with the same choice: whether to expand the size and influence of their appointments staff, thereby threatening the prerogatives of party notables and department executives, or to eschew this course. They chose to build a White House staff for political appointments similar to the staff Truman's aides could only furtively contemplate.

John Kennedy first signaled that he was alert to the possibility of restructuring the institutional setting of political appointments during his transition. Kennedy built a large retinue of personal aides, collectively dubbed the "Talent Hunt," and solicited their support in staffing top administration jobs to ensure the bureaucracy would be responsive to the president. Working alongside the secretaries-elect, these aides marshaled their own slates of candidates for cabinet secretaries to consider and reviewed the choices of cabinet secretaries, eyeing them for their fitness as "New Frontiersmen." To be sure, Kennedy and his aides did not centralize the staffing of the administration during the transition; in fact, they were quite some distance from this goal. Nonetheless, they did succeed in leaving a deeper presidential imprint on the administration than had any previous president A study of presidential appointments estimated that

Kennedy and his staff played a significant role in 54 percent of the appointments made during the first year of the administration—a figure nearly three times that of Eisenhower's first year .[30]

After the transition, however, Kennedy's appointment screening process reverted to the practices used by previous presidents. Yet only a few months into the Kennedy presidency, voices were raised throughout the administration urging the president to make the transition practices permanent. Budget Bureau Director David Bell, senior White House aide Fred Dutton, and Civil Service Commissioner John Macy—a veteran of Operation Best Brains— urged that a new staff be established outside of the Office of Congressional Relations so that appointments could be "depoliticized" and put to use to serve the managerial needs of the presidency. Kennedy and his inner circle embraced the idea, and by August of 1961 they had set to work to restructure the president's capabilities. Two weeks into his work, John Kennedy's newly recruited aide, Dan Fenn, clearly saw the implications of this new White House staff for the exercise of presidential leadership. "In the broadest sense," Fenn observed, "the objectives of this effort are to . . . suggest highly competent people who share the President's fundamental political and operating philosophy for major governmental positions, thereby to strengthen the president's control over the government [and] improve the management of the government."[31]

Although Kennedy's aides did not shrink from using the president's "residual decision rights" as Truman's had, they were aware that their efforts were viewed with suspicion outside of the White House. Hence, they proceeded cautiously, building a small staff (of four young aides borrowed from the BoB and Civil Service Commission) and confining their attention to about one-third of the vacant posts during 1962, their first year of operation. Though aiming to increase the president's institutional presence in appointment decisions, Kennedy's aides made an indirect and tentative advance rather than a frontal assault on the prerogatives of party notables in appointment politics. For example, in deference to the constraints that party claimants continued to impose on the White House, Kennedy's aides made no efforts to extend their reach to the two remaining bastions of local job patronage, the Justice Department and the Post Office Department. Moreover, Kennedy's aides clearly understood that departments and agency heads would be loathe to cede control over staffing decisions—control they had used to further their working relationships with Capitol Hill and their clientele, and to enhance their own policy agendas. Here, too, they proceeded with caution. Describing his role to an agency head, appointments aide Dan Fenn wrote, "By and large we have moved into this on the basis of "Can we help you out?" We have established a staff service to departments and agencies and . . . to the President."[32]

Where Kennedy had a keen interest in a post, or when a cabinet secretary had proven unable to manage his department without White House guidance, Kennedy's nascent appointments staff played a leading role in staffing decisions. At HEW's Office of Education, for example, both these conditions were met. HEW Secretaries Abraham Ribicoff (1961–1962) and Anthony Celebrezze (1962–1964) were seen by White House aides to be weak and incompetent leaders. Remarked one aide, "Tony Celebrezze didn't know the Office of Education from Cleveland City Hall, and as far as he was concerned, whatever Ralph Dungan [appointment chief] wanted was all right with him. He didn't have any ideas at all [about the post]." Conversely, Kennedy's White House staff ceded control over choices to those outside the White House under the opposite circumstances.[33]

Like Kennedy before him, Lyndon Johnson probed and reshaped the institutional arrangements he inherited from his predecessors, turning them to his advantage. Building on precedents forged during the Kennedy presidency, Johnson eagerly expanded the size, competence, and reach of the president's appointments staff. At Johnson's direction *all* departmental recommendations on appointments were to flow through his personnel office, headed by John Macy, and the president instructed department heads to collaborate with Macy in "seeing candidates for presidential appointments." Moreover, Johnson admonished Macy that all senior appointees were to be "the president's people," that the president is "the appointing officer, and they are part of *his* administration." Macy responded by tripling the size of the appointments staff, and by establishing a rudimentary specialization among his staff (paralleling that of the BoB). By and large, Macy's staff was remarkably successful in bringing a presidential perspective to bear on choices that were previously immune to his influence. In roughly eight out of ten cases, Macy's staff either suggested candidates for vacancies or offered the president its *own* evaluation of candidates proposed by departments and agencies, evaluations that it solicited from a national network of contacts across the nation and throughout the EOP (especially the BoB). In the estimation of HEW's Wilbur Cohen, a handful of White House staffers were equivalent in stature to cabinet secretaries, including John Macy: "I rank him with them [cabinet heads], because when it comes to the personnel side, John Macy is . . . extremely important."[34]

In 1950, the president's senior appointment aide quietly retreated rather than "interpose" himself between the president and party and cabinet leaders. By the 1960s, presidents and their senior aides chose to make unprecedented use of their control over the White House Office, turning its staff into an institutionalized instrument of presidential power. What produced this change? None of the presidents and staffers described here took the institutional setting of the presidency as fixed and invariable; each recognized it to be (partially) endogenous. What distinguished Truman from his successors was the far greater discretion with which the later presidents could use their unilateral powers. Between the 1950 and the mid-1960s the hold of party organizations over presidents declined swiftly as presidential elections became increasingly personalized.[35] Hence, the costs also diminished of spurning their prerogatives and ignoring their wishes about the organization of the White House appointments. Accustomed to the practices of Roosevelt and Truman, veteran Democratic party figures, such as Jim Farley, Jim Rowe, and John Bailey (the titular head of the Democratic National Committee) were stunned and angry at Johnson's efforts to wrest control of appointments from them. From Johnson, however, party leaders received no solicitude: this was precisely the president's aim. In fact, they were sometimes chastised by Johnson for "interfering" with the White House personnel staff.[36]

The relationships of interdependence linking presidents to executive departments also began to change during these years. Able to employ the strategy of "going public" with greater ease and success, presidents in the 1960s became less dependent on reciprocal relationships with the leaders of "policy networks" or "protocoalitions"—that is, department and agency heads—to win support for their policies.[37] This change, along with the accretion of staff resources inside the White House, rendered "domestic cabinet members far more dependent upon the president's support and services than he upon theirs."[38] With their dependence on cabinet departments slowly waning, Kennedy and Johnson found it less costly than Truman to extend their reach over appointment choices by pulling them into an expanded White House staff, gradually undercutting the prerogatives of departmental leaders and their network allies.

The presidents following Johnson would each probe and prod the institutional arrangements structuring political appointments, seeking to extend and institutionalize their control over political appointments—chiefly through the aggrandizement of their White House staff. In the quarter century after Johnson's presidency, the president's personnel staff quadrupled in size, developed its own hierarchy, established a stable and elaborate division of labor, and garnered its own name: the Presidential Personnel Office (or, alternatively the

White House Personnel Office).[39] Only briefly during this quarter century would presidents and their aides *eschew* efforts to create a structural capacity for the exercise of power over appointments: both Nixon and Carter did during the first eighteen months of their presidencies, and both came to rue—and reverse—their initial decision. That they did so provides us with strong evidence that it is the general pressures that presidents face, *not* the individual leaders' proclivities or aptitudes that lead presidents to exploit their formal powers to create and adapt institutional structures more hospitable to presidential leadership.

CARTER

Campaigning for the presidency in the shadow of the Watergate affair, Jimmy Carter fashioned himself as a mirror image of the discredited Nixon, pledging to disperse the power that Nixon had illegitimately accumulated in the modern White House Office. If elected, Carter promised, he would reduce the size of the White House staff by 30 percent, eliminate the Chief of Staff, bar his aides from interposing themselves between the president and cabinet secretaries, and reinstitute a system of cabinet government.

Carter kept his promise. One year into his administration the president's appointments staff was smaller than any since Johnson's, and altogether inexperienced in the politics of the executive branch. Recounted one aide: "I had no real background for the job I got. I had no recruiting background, and I didn't know what a lot of agencies did. I was 29 years old and had no prior governmental experience. I even drove a moped to work. The guards at the White House just laughed at me when I came to work." Worse still, so did Secretary of HHS Joe Califano. "Califano found the White House staff, including us, to be unprofessional, unskilled, laughable, and so forth. He had deep contacts in Washington, and he wanted no direction from us. He thought that he knew much better than us—and in many ways he did."[40] Carter's small and inexperienced staff came to play a role in the staffing of executive departments that was wholly ministerial, and through them Carter exercised less influence over staffing of the executive branch than any president since Eisenhower. Carter succeeded in reestablishing the traditional personnel practices of mid-century presidents, but this retrograde structure would not last.

Faced with strong opposition from department heads and their clientele groups, Carter and his senior aides reluctantly concluded that their decision to decentralize staffing decisions had both undermined the president's political fortunes and weakened his policy leadership of the executive branch. Decentralizing the personnel process resulted in department heads staffing the government with men and women loyal to them. Lacking strong personal, programmatic, or ideological ties to the president, Carter's appointees "pursued their own agendas, cut their own deals on the Hill, and worked against the president."[41] In short, Carter and his aides believed they were losing control over their own administration, and that they supervised an executive branch filled with appointees who "didn't feel that they worked for Jimmy Carter"[42] and within whose ranks dissension was commonplace. This "multiplicity of voices . . . embarrassed the administration" and, when amplified by news organizations, "put the administration in an unfavorable light and contributed to doubts about the president's leadership ability."[43]

Regardless of his own inclinations, Carter learned, the president must be "the master of his own house"—and clearly he was not. Speaking at a conference of White House Personnel heads, Carter's top appointments aide, Arnie Miller, reflected:

> Carter thought that he could return to that earlier decentralized approach, but he failed to understand how interwoven the fabric of the presidency is. You pull a little string here and everything unravels. He tried to cut back on the size of the Presidential Personnel Office staff. He bumbled it. Midway through his presidency he realized that he had given away the store. The expectations are still there on a president. The demands are so concentrated now on the president. . . . in order to countervail all that out there, you've got to build your own in the White House.[44]

Thus, slowly and grudgingly, and against his personal preferences about how to organize his staff, Jimmy Carter did "build his own in the White House" during the final two years of his presidency, abandoning his commitment to cabinet government. In a supremely ironic move, Carter's aides sought out the advice and assistance of veterans of the *Nixon* personnel office, and by the third year of Carter's presidency his aides had come full circle: from reviling the Nixon White House to emulating its structure and routines. Although Carter's appointments staff never equaled Nixon's in size or influence, it changed dramatically between 1977 and 1979, tripling in size, and growing in specialization, competence, and influence. All of Carter's successors—Reagan in particular, though Clinton showed less mastery—have embraced the premise that "you've got to build your own in the White House" and acted accordingly, sustaining and sometimes sharply expanding the White House Personnel Office's capacity to "presidentialize" the appointment of executive officials.[45]

Studying the federal bureaucracy in the late 1930s, Arthur McMahon and John Millet found in its upper echelons only a few dozen presidential appointees, many of whom were veterans of party politics far more interested in quiet sinecures than in prodding the bureaucracy to support a presidential program. The assistant secretaries scattered across the federal departments, they lamented, were merely "idling cogs in the national machine"[46] Contemporary presidents—regardless of their personal skills and aptitudes—are endowed with an institutional capacity to staff agencies with men and women whose loyalties are far more presidential in focus. Top-level appointees arrive at their posts through the initiative (or with the approbation) of the president's staff. No mere "idling cogs," they are often keenly loyal to the president they serve, and aggressively promote his agenda. Presidents' efforts to reshape the routines and organizations for staffing the government have been uneven and sometimes fruitless, but in the long run they have molded a set of institutions far more amenable to presidential leadership than those of decades past.

Building institutional bases of presidential power over government staffing has been only one avenue for presidents to redress the imbalance between their capabilities and the demands imposed upon them; the pursuit of power has led presidents to build institutions that expand their control over other decisions that are central to governing, most importantly, to budgeting and regulation.

INSTITUTIONALIZATION OF THE BUDGET POWER

The development of the Bureau of the Budget is our second case study of how presidents tried to create, and also adapt, institutions and processes to enhance responsiveness. In many ways, BoB's creation and expansion were the archetype of the institutional dynamic we see as central to presidential power. The presidential budget followed a central pattern: societal and political pressures served as the impetus for a new government capability; Congress and the president competed over the question of control; the president prevailed and used the new capability in unanticipated ways to develop even more power, with Congress hard-pressed to stop him. Over time, the new powers—once so controversial—became institutionalized as routine and an accepted part of the presidency. This pattern has played out across presidents and eras, and has had less to do with who presidents have been as individuals than the relative positions and institutional characteristics of Congress and the presidency.

The national budget and the organization created to administer it evolved into centerpieces of presidential power after 1921. The two presidents involved in early efforts to create budgetary institutions—Taft and Wilson—immediately recognized that the new capability would provide a significant advantage over Congress in controlling executive branch activity. Both men saw that significant separations of powers questions were at stake, and outside pressure for a national budget was part of a broader effort to replace legislative parochialism and chaos with the "neutral competence" of scientific presidential management. Although, to Congress, the act was "a means of helping to rationalize its own previously chaotic budgetary process,"[47] there were clear signs from this period that legislators would be giving up much more than they believed at the time. Proponents of the budget system made no secret of their view that it would enhance presidential power, and some wanted to strip Congress of the power to amend presidential budget requests altogether.[48]

The sharp rise in expenditures around the turn of the century revealed flaws in the existing budget process. The trend during this period is well documented; expenditures more than doubled between 1880 and 1904, an increase attributable to spending on rivers and harbors, pensions, the Spanish American War, and construction of the Panama Canal.[49] At the same time, changes in congressional procedures in 1880 and 1885 decentralized spending authority to numerous committees, stripping the Appropriations Committee (itself established in 1865) of its power to control distributive pressures in the legislature.[50] Presidential control was lacking as well. Traditionally, each executive department developed its own budget, often in close contact with relevant appropriating committees in Congress. These budget estimates were then sent to the Treasury Department, which did little more than compile the individual documents into a Book of Estimates and transmit the result to Congress. There was nothing in the way of centralized presidential control, no coordination among agencies, and no attempt to relate expenditures to revenues. One consequence of such a loosely constructed process was that the budget estimates were frequently wrong. Agencies would often run out of money halfway through the year and require supplemental appropriations to avoid deficiencies. Congress, unhappy with what it saw as both carelessness and lack of respect for its own powers of the purse, began in the early twentieth century to enact more detailed budget legislation, as well as laws (such as the Anti-Deficiency Act in 1906) designed to limit executive branch leeway.

The consensus within Washington, D.C., was that the budget process was broken and needed reform. The question was how reforms would affect control of administrative activities and policies. The existing system placed Congress at the center and gave executive agencies a high degree of autonomy from the president; giving the president more control would necessarily reduce the influence of those who benefited from this arrangement. Congressional concerns were heightened because of earlier disputes over presidential control of the executive branch. In 1910, Taft issued an executive order prohibiting any department officials from asking for legislation or appropriations without the approval of the department head; this order also prohibited officials from providing any information to Congress without departmental approval. Congress responded by cutting "deeply into [Taft's] budget requests, forcing him to come back later for supplemental appropriations."[51] As part of his broader effort to gain control over administration, in 1910 Taft asked Congress for funds to establish a commission to study government administration and recommend improvements. From the outset, however, Taft anticipated that one of the recommendations of the Committee on Economy and Efficiency would be an executive budget.[52] To Taft, budgeting was a central executive function. In a letter to the Secretary of the Treasury, he outlined his position. "If the President is to assume . . . any responsibility for either the manner in which business of the Government is transacted," Taft wrote, " . . . it is evident that he cannot be limited by Congress to such information as that branch may think sufficient for his purposes. In my opinion, it is entirely competent for the President to submit a budget, and Congress cannot . . . prevent it. . . . And this power I propose to exercise."[53]

Congress not surprisingly took a different view, seeing its spending power as a cornerstone of its constitutional position in government. When Taft attempted to follow through on the Commission's recommendation for an executive budget, the result was nothing short of a constitutional confrontation between Congress and the president over who would control the vital budget function. Already chafing against Taft's efforts to control the expanding civil service, Congress was in no mood to cooperate on the budget; to many legislators, presidential control of the budget was an abdication of one of Congress' basic constitutional responsibilities, as well as an abandonment of its best method of constraining excessively energetic presidents. The prospect of an executive budget posed a direct challenge to congressional authority and autonomy. To House Speaker Joe Cannon, "an executive budget would signify the surrender of the most important element of representative government," and to others the presidential budget was "a step toward autocracy and a Prussian style military state."[54] When Taft proposed to submit a draft executive budget in 1912, Congress enacted a law that prohibited executive branch officials from preparing any budget documents except those that were specifically required by law. Taft responded by directing agency heads to submit the draft budget proposals in accordance with his instructions anyway, the law notwithstanding.[55]

Although Congress paid no attention to the budget submitted in this form, Taft's actions had a significant impact on the forces which ultimately resulted in the establishment of a presidential budget system in 1921. One account of Taft's impact maintained that although Congress rejected his attempt to implement the key recommendations of his Commission on Economy and Efficiency, his efforts still constituted "a great service in raising this important issue and focusing the attention of the public, as a whole, on this problem. It also furnished the supporters of the National Budget System the ground-work with which they could carry on the fight."[56] For a president generally considered to be weak, especially in the shadow of Theodore Roosevelt, Taft still managed to play a key role in, at a minimum, laying the foundation for a major expansion of executive power.

As has so often happened in the development of presidential power, war proved a crucial catalyst.[57] As the pressures of World War I served to increase federal expenditures dramatically, legislators recognized that to avoid total paralysis Congress would have to provide the president with some sort of budget power. Even so, Congress moved cautiously and the attempts to set up a presidential budget contained several key provisions that restricted presidential control. First, the newly established Comptroller General, an officer of Congress responsible for auditing executive branch spending, would be immune to presidential removal. President Wilson vetoed the first budget act in 1919 because of this provision. Two years later, Congress passed a revised act without this provision, signed into law by Harding. The second provision was the location of the Bureau of the Budget in the Department of the Treasury, the executive department considered most faithful to congressional sentiment. By putting the BoB there, Congress ensured some check on presidential influence. According to Milkis, the Budget Act of 1921 did significantly enhance the president's authority to oversee the expenditures of the executive departments and agencies, but the effect of this legislation was blunted by the placement of the newly created budget Bureau in the Treasury Department rather than directly under the supervision of the president himself. This choice tended to circumscribe the administrative power of the president and to retain the autonomy of executive departments and agencies from the oversight of the White House.[58]

The Treasury Department had a long history in the crossfire of presidential congressional disputes. In the 1830s, President Jackson and Congress repeatedly clashed over who had the authority to direct the Secretary of the Treasury to handle the nation's finances: "Congress frequently treated the Secretary of the Treasury as its agent, delegating to him—rather than the president—the responsibility for placing Government money either in the national bank or in State banks."[59]

The supporters of the executive budget took pains to minimize its impact on congressional prerogatives. The Committee report on the first version of the bill argued that "This bill does not in any way abridge the authority of Congress over appropriations. Congress will be at liberty, as now, to revise or increase the budget estimates or add new items to them. What attitude Congress takes on this question is not a matter of legislation but of rule. It is within the sole province of each House of Congress to decide whether it will modify the existing rules and committees established for the consideration of appropriations bills."[60]

Congressional intent notwithstanding, from the outset the new BoB took on responsibilities going well beyond simple budget preparation by coordinating the activities of a range of agencies disposing of surplus property from World War I. The assumption of these duties was no accident, since "increased control over administration was the Bureau of the Budget's ambition from its inception. From the beginning, [the first BoB Director Charles] Dawes understood the bureau's potential as an executive weapon. Despite the fact that the new law was not to take effect until fiscal year 1923, the Harding administration quickly devised a budget for fiscal year 1922. This was done without formal authority and rested on President Harding's orders, implemented through the new bureau."[61]

Dawes's diary of his activities during the first year of the BoB is an account of his ambitious attempts to make full use of BoB's potential.[62] Dawes cited as one of his accomplishments, "the reorganization of the routine business of government through the President of the Budget Bureau as an agency of executive pressure, and the creation by executive orders of coordinating machinery out of the body of the existing business organization."[63]

The new bureau immediately tried to expand its control to include general legislative clearance, by serving as the intermediary between agency officials and the president on all legislative recommendations that originated in the departments.[64] Because of agency objections, however, the effort was watered down. Nonetheless, within a few years, the BoB under Coolidge successfully "built a strong and well enforced, if narrowly defined accessory to central budgeting," requiring central clearance on all legislation with clear budgetary implications.[65] FDR repeatedly expanded BoB's clearance authority to include executive orders (1933), all agency legislative proposals (1934), and coordination of agency recommendations on enrolled bills (1939).[66] In 1954, Neustadt described the expansion of central clearance this way: "For more than thirty years now, central clearance has persisted, its history marked by a long series of 'accidental,' unforeseen accretions. Nothing once absorbed has been wholly displaced; each new element somehow encompasses the old. . . . overall, here is a record of great growth, successful adaptation—this under six successive presidents, through every variation in national and governmental circumstance since Harding's term of office."[67] The BoB staff increased by more than 1300 percent between 1924 and 1992, to carry out these increasingly diverse and complex functions.[68]

In contemporary politics, of course, both presidential control over the budget and the centrality of the Budget Bureau (now OMB), to the president's ability to control executive branch policy are routine.

Presidential Control Over Regulatory Policy

The push for a presidential budget parallels in rough outline a dispute that was to occur sixty years later over presidential attempts to reign in newly empowered regulatory institutions. Again, the pattern was the same: social and political pressures resulted in a new set of institutions and governing capabilities with a corresponding struggle over who was to control them. In this case the question was control of a rapidly expanding regulatory capacity in the 1960s and early 1970s. Beginning with Nixon, every president has tried to assert control over the new institutions and processes, issuing a series of executive orders imposing procedural requirements on agencies when they issued new regulations, with each successive presidential order putting more substantive procedural constraints in place.

The history of presidential efforts to control regulatory agencies actually goes back much further, although the scope of the problem emerged in sharp relief only as the capacity of these agencies expanded rapidly in the 1960s and 1970s. Regulatory agencies have posed unique problems, because unlike Cabinet departments they have been purposely insulated from presidential control; this insulation has typically been achieved by protecting high-level agency officials from removal.[69] The Brownlow Committee saw these agencies as a "headless fourth branch" of government lacking accountability to the president, and Eisenhower requested a memorandum detailing his authority over the operations of regulatory commissions (the report concluded that the president's authority was ambiguous, probably extending to the executive functions of the agencies but not their quasi-legislative or quasi-judicial functions).[70]

The problem of control grew acute in the early 1970s after Congress created a raft of new organizations; most of the concern revolved around the activities of the Environmental Protection Agency (EPA), which was established in 1970. Starting with Nixon, presidents moved to exert some control. Nixon began by establishing within the newly formed Office of Management and Budget a "Quality of Life Review," targeting EPA regulations.[71] Under the review program, EPA had to submit major regulations for interagency review thirty days prior to publication in the Federal Register. OMB did little more than "[coordinate] the review process by circulating draft regulations to all interested agencies," and "did not wield any decision making power."[72] Ford instituted the first formal procedures, issuing an executive order mandating an "inflationary impact analysis" of major regulations (Executive Order 11821, November 27, 1974). Carter replaced the Ford order with one of his own which required an analysis of the cost of each major regulation, an evaluation of alternatives, and approval of the least burdensome form of regulation (Executive Order 12044, March 23, 1978). Carter also established two organizations to monitor compliance and direct the regulatory review efforts (the Regulatory Analysis Review Group and the Regulatory Council).

The problem with all of these efforts to enhance presidential control over rulemaking was that they lacked teeth: they were "either essentially hortatory interagency advisory and review systems lacking centralized control and enforcement authority, or ad hoc intercessions into particular rulemakings by the president or White House staff at his behest."[73] Regulatory agencies remained free to promulgate regulations, whether or not they were consistent with the president's broader policy priorities. Nevertheless, the lack of any clear congressional guidance on the question left the territory open for a presidential assertion of prerogative.[74]

President Reagan made that assertion and dramatically altered the debate with his regulatory order, issued in February 1981. Executive Order 12291 required executive branch agencies to justify proposed rules and regulations using cost-benefit analysis, and it prohibited regulatory action unless "the potential benefits to society for the regulation outweigh the potential costs" [EO 12291, [2(a)]. Agencies had to prepare a Regulatory Impact Analysis and submit it to the Office of Management and Budget for review, and OMB had the authority to "recommend the withdrawal of regulations which cannot be reformulated to meet its objections."[75] Review authority was placed in The

Office of Information and Regulatory Affairs (OIRA), a unit within OMB created by the Paperwork Reduction Act of 1979 to coordinate agency efforts to collect data from business.

Reagan's order gave new power to OMB, and it "went way beyond the Nixon, Ford, and Carter administrations in applying cost-benefit analyses . . . to stymie agency rule making."[76] In practice, OMB review served to shield the rulemaking practice from public view, as initially officials did not keep written records regarding OMB contacts with either agencies or other interested parties regarding OMB's central clearance function: the review process, argue Cooper and West, "operated largely through informal, off the record contacts. Indeed, [OMB] not only has kept much of its written comments confidential, but it has usually preferred oral communications over the phone or through small staff conferences to written correspondence."[77] This centralized presidential control further, as it limited the possibilities of judicial review.

Executive Order 12291 had elements of the "unintended consequences" that derived from presidential interpretations of statutes. Congress created OIRA to limit the amount of data that the government could force business to provide. James Miller, Reagan's first OIRA director, noted his intent to use the Paperwork Reduction Act provisions to limit the regulatory power of independent agencies (to which the order did not apply):

> nearly every substantial regulation involves, as part of its enforcement mechanism, a requirement for filling out forms or maintaining specific records. And under the new paperwork act, all agencies, including the independents, must clear all the forms they wish to use through OMB.—specifically, by delegation, with the administrator of the Office of Information and Regulatory Affairs, which means me. . . the act does give OMB considerable authority.[78]

The order also demonstrated the impact of presidential initiative, as it altered existing institutional arrangements unilaterally and forced Congress to take active measures to try and recapture the ground it had lost to the president. One reason Reagan took the executive order route is that Congress would have refused to voluntarily grant such a measure of control, and attempts to seek legislative reform of regulatory institutions failed throughout the Reagan presidency.[79] The chronology suggests that a legislative alternative to 12291 was never considered. The order was issued on February 17, 1981, less than one month after Reagan was inaugurated; the Office of Legal Counsel in the Justice Department issued its opinion on the proposed order on February 13. Administration officials had been planning the order from the earliest days of the transition, and it could not have been thought of as a contingency plan pending failure to get legislation through Congress. It was a preemptive move, motivated by the assumption that legislation would have failed, and it was designed to take effect before a sixty-day freeze on regulations ended.[80] Once the tenor of the Administration's regulatory approach became clear, it could not expect any support from a Democratic Congress responsible for the regulatory structure that the order attempted to undermine.

By taking action unilaterally, Reagan put Congress in a defensive position. Executive Order 12291 is a textbook case of Congress's inability to countermand unilateral executive action, especially in contingent or ambiguous areas of constitutional authority. Despite intense Democratic opposition, Congress was unable either to alleviate the order's impact or undercut OIRA's authority, through either the legislative or appropriations processes. The only concession Congress won was an agreement in 1986 to require Senate confirmation of OIRA's head, and increased public disclosures of OIRA activities. These concessions were arguably minor: "were legislators and groups really able to exercise power, they could have put OIRA out of business. The president clearly had the upper hand. The regulatory review system churned on, shaping and delaying regulations, and infuriating groups and agencies."[81] Moreover, the reforms left undisturbed "manifold opportunities for informal communication and influence."[82] Even after legislative authorization for OIRA lapsed in 1989, both Bush and Clinton were able to get funding for it every year since.[83]

President Bush left in place the basic structure of the Reagan order, but created yet another organization to enhance presidential control and further insulate the centralization efforts from congressional interference. Under the authority of Executive Order 12291 and 12498, Bush transferred OIRA's regulatory review power to the "Council on Competitiveness," located in the White House and chaired by the Vice President. The Council, according to its critics, "undermine[s] the most basic precepts of democratic government" by operating in relative secrecy and providing opportunities for *ex parte* contacts outside the normal channels of the regulatory process.[84] Despite the intense controversy of the Reagan and Bush regulatory review efforts—one account of the ongoing struggle concluded that "no feature of modern U.S. government has been more controversial over the last decade than review of agency rules" by OMB[85]—White House influence in agency activities has now become an accepted part of the regulatory process. Although Clinton abolished the Council on Competitiveness upon taking office, he "most assuredly did not get rid of regulatory review. Indeed, he saw [it] as an essential to presidential leadership."[86] Clinton issued his own Executive Order on regulatory review (Executive Order 12866, September 30, 1993) which made some procedural changes to OMB review but "maintain[ed] much of the substantive focus of the Reagan orders, including the emphasis on cost-benefit analysis as the basic foundation of decision."[87]

The parallels between regulatory review and the national budget are clear enough. In both cases, the creation of a new capability or the need for new administrative structures produced a struggle between the president and Congress over control. Indeed, George Eads, who chaired Carter's Regulatory Analysis Review Group (RARG), saw both in "budgetary" terms: "In a real sense, [Executive Order 12291] marks the final emergence of regulation as a governmental function deserving the same level of attention as the raising and spending of money. We do not yet have a formal regulatory budget, but enough basic budget-like controls are now in place, at least on paper, to permit the president to shape regulatory programs singly and overall."[88]

CONCLUSION

In contrast to *Presidential Power's* view of presidents as leaders who work within exogenous institutions, this essay has shown that presidential leadership has been and can be substantially *institutional*: presidents exercise enduring influence over the "conduct of [those] . . . who make up the government" by altering the structure and procedures—i.e. the institutions—within which they (and others) act. The conduct of civil servants who promulgate regulations, the loyalties of the men and women who serve in appointive posts, and the budgeting decisions of agency heads have become—by design—far more closely harnessed to presidential aims than they were at the twentieth century's outset.

Presidents' efforts to develop a structural capacity for the exercise of power have not gone unchallenged. Presidents have consistently struggled with Congress to create institutions through which they can control budgeting and rulemaking within the executive branch. They have struggled, too, with extralegal claimants, such as parties, to create institutions through which they can exercise control over the selection of political appointees. As we have shown, presidents have engaged in these struggles throughout the twentieth century, not because of their personal predilections, but because the institutional resources for leadership with which they are endowed fall well short of the leadership expectations with which they are burdened. In the long run, presidents have prevailed in these struggles. Advantaged by superior information and by the capacity to act unilaterally or "go first," modern presidents have succeeded in creating institutional capabilities for influence—over budgets, over agency rulemaking, and over appointments—that have far surpassed those of their predecessors.

NOTES

1. Richard E. Neustadt, *Presidential Power and the Modern Presidents* (New York: Free Press, 1990), p. 37.

2. Ibid., p. 4.

3. An outstanding example of the public law tradition which preceded *Presidential Power* is Edward S. Corwin, *The President: Office and Powers* (New York: New York University Press, 1957).

4. Peter Sperlich, "Bargaining and Overload: An Essay on *Presidential Power* ," in Aaron Wildavsky, ed., *The Presidency* (Boston: Little, Brown 1969).

5. Samuel Kernell, *Going Public: New Strategies of Presidential Leadership*, 3rd ed. (Washington, D.C.: Congressional Quarterly Press, 1997).

6. Richard E. Neustadt, "Presidency and Legislation: The Growth of Central Clearance," *American Political Science Review* 48 (3) (September 1954); Richard E. Neustadt, "Presidency and Legislation: Planning the President's Program," *American Political Science Review* 49 (4) (December 1955).

7. Terry Moe and Scott A. Wilson, "Presidents and the Politics of Structure," *Law and Contemporary Problems* 57 (2) (Spring 1994).

8. James G. March and Herbert A. Simon, *Organizations* (New York: Wiley, 1958).

9. John Hart, *The Presidential Branch*, 2nd ed. (Chatham, N.J.: Chatham House, 1995); John P. Burke, *The Institutionalized Presidency* (Baltimore: Johns Hopkins University Press, 1992).

10. Moe and Wilson, "Presidents and the Politics of Structure."

11. Lyn Ragsdale and John J. Thiess, III, "The Institutionalization of the American Presidency, 1924–92," *American Journal of Political Science* 41 (4) (October 1997).

12. In between the expiration of the Reorganization Act of 1939 (in January 1941), and the passage of the First War Powers Act in January 1942, FDR used executive orders in the absence of legislative authority to establish wartime agencies within OEM. Emmerich goes on to note: "The Senate sub-committee on Appropriations did not like this method of creating new agencies, and senators, at a hearing in 1941, raised sharp questions as to whether they had been legally authorized." Roosevelt was able to rely on the prestige of the first director General of the Office of Production Management, William Knudsen, to neutralize opposition. When Knudsen entered the room at a Senate hearing to discuss OPM appropriations,

"senators rose to greet him, forgot their inhibitions, and passed the appropriations for the whole array of emergency agencies. . . . If there had been any doubt about the authority for creating these agencies, the act of appropriating funds gave a sanction to their legality and we were in business." Herbert Emmerich, *Federal Organization and Administrative Management* (Tuscaloosa, Alabama: University of Alabama Press, 1971), p. 72.

13. Alan Brinkley, *The End of Reform: New Deal Liberalism in Recession and War* (New York: Vintage Books, 1995), p. 22.

14. Sidney Milkis, *The President and the Parties: The Transformation of the American Party System Since the New Deal* (New York: Oxford University Press), pp. 429, 114.

15. Louis Brownlow, *A Passion For Anonymity* (Chicago: University of Chicago Press, 1958), pp. 427–29.

16. Ibid., p. 429.

17. Terry M. Moe, "The Politicized Presidency," in, John E. Chubb and Paul E. Peterson, eds., *The New Direction in American Politics* (Washington DC: Brookings Institution, 1985), p. 247.

18. Moe and Wilson, "Presidents and the Politics of Structure"; Kenneth R. Mayer, "The Importance of Moving First: Executive Orders and Presidential Initiative." Paper prepared for the 1996 Annual Meeting of the American Political Science Association, San Francisco.

19. At times, the courts have stepped in to mediate these battles, but most of the time they come down on the president's side. An exception is the recent Supreme Court decision that invalidated the line-item veto, an authority Congress had granted the president in 1997; see *Clinton v. New York* (No. 97–1374, June 25, 1998).

20. Terry M. Moe, "Presidents, Institutions, and Theory," in George C. Edwards, III, John H. Kessel, and Bert Rockman, eds., *Researching the Presidency: Vital Questions, New Approaches* (Pittsburgh: University of Pittsburgh Press, 1993), p. 378.

21. In this case presidents swiftly ended up using the Civil Service Reform Act (CSRA) in ways that lawmakers and civil service reformers hadn't anticipated—but Congress found itself unable to reverse how presidents made use of their newfound formal powers under the CSRA.

22. Dwight Eisenhower created a new category of political appointees, "schedule C" posts, by issuing an executive order; Thomas J. Weko, *The Politicized Presidency: The White House Personnel Office, 1948–1994* (Lawrence: University Press of Kansas, 1995), p. 37.

23. The pages that follow are drawn largely from Weko, *The Politicized Presidency* . We have chosen to examine four Democratic presidencies between 1948 and 1980 because they were affiliated with the New Deal regime (and its administrative

apparatus) rather than opposed to it. They, among all modern presidents, should have been the most satisfied with the *status quo ante*—and reluctant to engage in building a capacity for control over appointments. Their efforts to establish control over appointments through the elaboration of new institutional arrangements provides strong support for our claim that *all* presidents are driven by imbalance between resources and responsibilities to augment their structural capacities for leadership.

24. Dorothy Fowler, "Congressional Dictation of Local Appointments," *Journal of Politics* 7 (1) (February 1945); Joseph Harris, *The Advice and Consent of the Senate: A Study in the Confirmation of Appointments by the U.S. Senate* (Berkeley: University of California Press, 1953).

25. Dean Mann, and Jameson Doig, *The Assistant Secretaries: Problems and Processes of Appointment* (Washington DC: Brookings Institution, 1965), p. 87–88.

26. As James Rowe noted in a December 1946 memo to Harry Truman, the "personal loyalties of the administrators to those legislators instrumental in securing their appointments [and the power of the purse] . . . ensure that "even in the best of times control of the departments is difficult." "Cooperation or Conflict: The President's Relationship to an Opposition Congress," contained in James H. Rowe Oral History, Truman Library, p. 120.

27. Talking Points, "Presentation to the Cabinet," (Martin Friedman Papers, Truman Library, n.d.). Emphasis in original.

28. Weko, *The Politicized Presidency*, p. 51.

29. Ibid., p. 51.

30. Mann and Doig, *The Assistant Secretaries*, p. 88.

31. Weko, *The Politicized Presidency*, p. 55.

32. Ibid., p. 55.

33. Ibid., p. 56.

34. Ibid., p. 60.

35. John H. Aldrich, *Why Parties? The Origin and Transformation of Political Parties in America* (Chicago: University of Chicago Press, 1995).

36. Weko, *The Politicized Presidency*, pp. 32–35.

37. Kernell, *Going Public* .

38. Neustadt, *Presidential Power*, p. 194.

39. For example, in September 1993 the Clinton personnel staff consisted of roughly sixty aides. The staff was led by a director and assistant director, who in turn supervised the work of seven associate directors. Each of the seven associate directors—whose portfolio of departments and agencies was organized to parallel that of OMB associate directors—was assisted, in turn, by staff of five deputy directors.

40. Weko, *The Politicized Presidency*, p. 71.

41. Dom Bonafede, "Carter's Recent Staff Shakeup May Be More of A Shakedown," *National Journal*, June 17, 1978, p. 1852.

42. Personal interview, Carter White House aide.

43. Bonafede, "Carter's Recent Staff Shakeup May Be More of A Shakedown," p. 1852.

44. National Academy of Public Administration, *Recruiting Presidential Appointees: A Conference of Former Presidential Personnel Assistants* (Washington, DC: NAPA, 1984), p. 39

45. James P. Pfiffner, *The Strategic Presidency: Hitting the Ground Running*, 2nd ed. (Lawrence: University Press of Kansas, 1996).

46. Arthur W. McMahon and John D. Millet, *Federal Administrators* (New York: Columbia University Press, 1939), p. 302.

47. Moe, "The Politicized Presidency," p. 247.

48. Charles Wallace Collins, "The Coming of the Budget System." *The South Atlantic Quarterly* 15 (4) (October 1916): 314–15.

49. Louis Fisher, *Presidential Spending Power* (Princeton: Princeton University Press, 1975), p. 27.

50. David Brady and Mark A. Morgan, "Reforming the Structure of the House Appropriations Process: The Effects of the 1885 and 1919–20 Reforms on Money Decisions," in Mathew D. McCubbins and Terry Sullivan, eds., *Congress: Structure and Policy* (New York: Cambridge University Press, 1987).

51. Fisher, *Presidential Spending Power*, p. 29.

52. Stephen Skowronek, *Building a New American State: The Expansion of National Administrative Capacities, 1877–1920* (New York: Cambridge University Press, 1982), p. 187.

53. Cited in Peri Arnold, *Making the Managerial Presidency: Comprehensive Reorganization Planning 1905–1980* (Princeton: Princeton University Press, 1986), p. 46.

54. Fisher, *Presidential Spending Power*, p. 33.

55. "Copy of Letter Sent By The President to the Secretary of the Treasury Relative to the Submission of a Budget to Congress," September 19, 1912. Series 6, File No. 3868, Reel # 447, Papers of William Howard Taft.

56. E. E. Naylor, *The Federal Budget System in Operation* (Washington DC: The Hayworth Printing Co., 1941), p. 25).

57. Edward S. Corwin, *The Presidency: Office and Powers, 1787–1948* (New York: New York University Press, 1948).

58. Milkis, *The President and the Parties*, p. 104.

59. Fisher, *Presidential Spending Power*, p. 16.

60. U.S. Congress, Senate Special Committee on the National Budget, *National Budget System* (66th Cong., 2d sess., report no. 524., 1920), p. 6.

61. Arnold, *Making the Managerial Presidency*, p. 54.

62. Charles G. Dawes, *The First Year of the Budget of the United States* (New York: Harper, 1923).

63. Dawes, *The First Year of the Budget of the United States*.

64. Neustadt, "Presidency and Legislation: The Growth of Central Clearance," p. 644–654.

65. Ibid., 645–46.

66. In 1939 the Bureau was transferred from Treasury to the newly created Executive Office of the President, making it an even more effective instrument of presidential control.

67. Neustadt, "Presidency and Legislation: The Growth of Central Clearance," p. 668.

68. Ragsdale and Thiess, "The Institutionalization of the American Presidency, 1924–1992," p. 1296.

69. The Supreme Court upheld these protections in *Humphrey's Executor v. United States*, 295 U.S. 602 (1935), ruling that agencies with "quasi-legislative" or "quasi-judicial" powers could be independent of direct presidential control.

70. "Memorandum: The President's Powers Over Independent Regulatory Commissions." White House Office, Office of the Staff Secretary. Subject Series, White House Subseries. Folder: Rockefeller Committee on Reorganization of the Government [1956–1958] [1]. Dwight D. Eisenhower Presidential Library, Abilene, KS.

71. This summary is taken largely from Frank B. Cross, "Executive Orders 12, 291 and 12, 498: A Test Case in Presidential Control of Executive Agencies," *Journal of Law and Politics* 4 (3) (Winter 1988). President Nixon created the Office of Management and Budget in a series of reorganization orders issued in 1970. The change reflected the increasing policy and administrative responsibilities of the former BoB, in addition to the former Bureau's budget and accounting responsibilities; see Larry Berman, *The Office of Management and Budget and the Presidency, 1921–1979* (Princeton: Princeton University Press, 1979).

72. Caroline DeWitt, "The President's Council on Competitiveness: Undermining the Administrative Procedure Act with Regulatory Review," *The Administrative Law Journal of the American University*, 6 (1993), p. 769.

73. Morton Rosenberg, "Presidential Control of Agency Rulemaking: An Analysis of Constitutional Issues that May be Raised By Executive Order 12, 291," *Arizona Law Review* 23 (4) (1981): 1200*n* .

74. Kevin Whitney, 1982. "Capitalizing on a Congressional Void: Executive Order No. 12, 291." *The American University Law Review* 31 (1982).

75. Joseph Cooper, and William West, "Presidential Power and Republican Government: The Theory and Practice of OMB Review," *Journal of Politics* 50 (4) (November 1988), p. 871.

76. Robert F. Durant, *The Administrative Presidency Revisited: Public Lands, the BLM, and the Reagan Revolution* (New York: State University of New York Press, 1992), p. 49.

77. Cooper and West, "Presidential Power and Republican Government," p. 881.

78. Antonin Scalia, "Deregulation HQ: An Interview on the New Executive Order with Murray L. Weidenbaum and James C. Miller III," *Regulation* (March/April 1981), p. 23.

79. Alan B. Morrison, "OMB Interference with Agency Rulemaking: The Wrong Way to Write a Regulation," *Harvard Law Review* 99 (1986): 1063.

80. Staffing Memorandum, February 3, 1981, "Executive Order on Regulatory Management." WHORM Subject File, Folder: FG Federal Government Operations (000167) [1 of 2]. Ronald Reagan Presidential Library, Simi Valley, CA.

81. Moe and Wilson, "Presidents and the Politics of Structure," p. 40.

82. Cooper and West, "Presidential Power and Republican Government," p. 882.

83. Moe and Wilson, "Presidents and the Politics of Structure," pp. 40–41.

84. DeWitt, "The President's Council on Competitiveness," p. 795.

85. E. Donald Elliott, "TQM-ing OMB: Or Why Regulatory Review Under Executive Order 12, 291 Works Poorly and What President Clinton Should Do About It," *Law and Contemporary Problems* 57 (2) (Spring 1994), p. 167.

86. Moe and Wilson, "Presidents and the Politics of Structure," p. 41.

87. Richard H. Pildes and Cass R. Sunstein, "Reinventing the Regulatory State," *University of Chicago Law Review* 62 (1) (Winter 1995), p. 6.

88. George Eads, "Harnessing Regulation: The Evolving Role of White House Oversight," *Regulation* (May/June 1981), p. 19.

CHAPTER 10

Staffing the White House, 1937–96: The Institutional Implications of Neustadt's Bargaining Paradigm

Matthew J. Dickinson

INTRODUCTION

Although Richard Neustadt's *Presidential Power* (hereafter *PP*) remains a work of enduring influence, scholars have for the most part overlooked its institutional implications.[1] In fact, the *PP* paradigm helps explain the growth of what Nelson Polsby labels the "presidential branch": the large, White House-centered advisory staff system, functionally specialized and hierarchically arranged, that has played an increasingly prominent role in presidents' exercise of power during the post-Hoover, "modern" presidential era.[2]

Scholars typically attribute the growth in presidential branch size and influence to a variety of factors. These range from individual-based causes, particularly changes in presidential management preferences and operating styles, to more systemic forces including a growth in the presidential workload coupled with a weakening of the political constraints that once limited presidential staff aggrandizement.[3] These explanations undoubtedly tell an important part of the story. But they also overlook a fundamental implication of Neustadt's argument: *that presidents also institutionalize staff support to reduce bargaining uncertainty.*[4]

Neustadt's core argument in *PP* is that a president's bargaining exchanges with other actors and institutions constitute the primary means by which he (someday she) exercises influence. To bargain effectively, however, presidents need information and the expertise to interpret this information. "A president," he says, "is helped by what he gets into his mind. *His first essential need is information*" (italics added).[5] To Neustadt, it is a president's personal attributes, particularly a sense of purpose, "feel" for power, and self-confidence, that largely determines this leader's skill at gathering and interpreting bargaining-related information. Differences in these personal qualities help explain why some presidents bargain more effectively than do others.

Although Neustadt's unit of analysis in much of *PP* is individual presidents, his argument has broader institutional implications. To understand why this is so, consider on whom presidents characteristically relied for bargaining information and expertise in the time period examined in the first edition of *PP*. In the years 1933–60 a president's primary sources of bargaining-pertinent knowledge were members of what Neustadt labeled the Washington "community" (identified by bargaining interest, not locale): Congress, executive officials, a president's partisans, foreign governments, and other interested "publics." It was through repeated interaction with these actors and institutions that presidents developed an understanding of their respective needs and preferences, and thus of the likely consequences of making particular bargaining choices.

As several scholars point out, however, Neustadt wrote *PP* during an era when governing was a more insular affair than now.[6] The ensuing three decades witnessed the "atomization" of the American political system.[7] Political power became less concentrated within "the beltway," and its exercise more subject to public scrutiny and debate. It is hypothesized here that this fragmenting of public authority reduced the utility of Neustadt's traditional Washington community as information providers; members of this community became less able to provide the knowledge presidents needed to gauge accurately the most likely consequences of their bargaining choices. To compensate for this knowledge gap, presidents began to institutionalize expert help within the White House Office itself.

This essay's central argument, then, is that the growth of the presidential branch since FDR's presidency has occurred, in part, due to the increasing bargaining uncertainty fueled by the changing roles of institutions and actors in the American political system. To test this claim, staff developments during the 60-year period from 1937–1996 are compared with changes in the composition and behavior of key elements within the Washington community. The findings from multivariate statistical analysis support the argument that presidents' efforts to reduce bargaining uncertainty vis-à-vis key groups, particularly Congress, members of the president's electoral coalition, the mass public, and the executive branch, drive their acquisition of staff support.

These results have at least three important implications. First, they suggest an alternative explanation for the different staffing strategies adopted historically by Republican and Democratic presidents. Rather than a function of differences in presidential temperament, operating style, and prior administrative exposure, as several scholars surmise, these partisan tendencies are more likely rooted in the different bargaining contexts that Republican and Democratic presidents predominantly faced. Specifically, Republican presidents more often served when their party was in a minority on Capitol Hill, and hence found it more difficult to acquire bargaining-pertinent information from members of Congress. As a consequence they tended to embrace larger, more functionally specialized and hierarchical staffing arrangements than did Democratic presidents.

Second, the findings indicate why efforts to reduce, restructure, or otherwise reorganize the presidential branch have for the most part been unsuccessful.[8] Reforms have not been grounded in a full understanding as to why presidents decide to institutionalize staff assistance. In order to wean presidents from dependence on a White House-centered specialized staff system, reformers must provide alternative sources of information and expertise for recurring bargaining exchanges.

Finally, the hypothesis that bargaining uncertainty drives staff institutionalization helps integrate recent studies of the presidential branch with an earlier body of evidence inspired by Neustadt's original work that primarily focus on the determinants of presidential bargaining success. The synthesis of these two research tracks should produce a more complete understanding of the exercise of presidential power in the American political system. In this way, *PP* continues to guide important research on developments in the American presidency—further testimony to the seminal nature of Richard Neustadt's original contribution.

ANALYSIS: PRESIDENTS, BARGAINING AND STAFF

To assess the claim that uncertainty in bargaining fueled the growth of the presidential branch, the salient characteristics of that growth must first be specified. Although scholars have conceptualized staff institutionalization in a variety of ways,[9] this essay refers to the growth of the presidential branch in terms of three related trends: increases in White House staff size, its functional specialization, and its internal hierarchy.

The increase in the number of White House personnel has probably been the most researched aspect of staff institutionalization. It has also been the one that has engendered the least scholarly consensus because estimates of staff growth can vary considerably depending on how "staff" is defined. Some scholars have counted only full-time budgeted employees, while others also include part-time workers and those detailed to work in the White House while on another agency's payroll. Still others have looked mainly at the growth in senior-level staff who have direct access to the president, or have focused primarily on aides who dealt in the substance of policy or politics as distinct from clerical aides who primarily handled administrative duties. Moreover, there is disagreement regarding whether to focus only on the White House Office, or to include other staff components within the Executive Office of the President.[10]

Whatever the measure, however, the growth in staff size does not capture the full impact of what scholars mean by staff institutionalization. Increases in staff functional specialization and in internal staff hierarchy are also important.[11] Several studies have shown that the flow of information and the decisionmaking processes within bureaucracies is critically affected by differences in staff functional expertise and internal staff arrangements.[12] Critics of the growth in White House staff specialization complain that more specialized aides are less likely to serve a president's broader bargaining needs.[13] At the same time, there has been increasing concern that the internal layering of political appointees in the executive branch has diffused accountability and eroded performance.[14]

Ideally, then, to describe fully the growth in the presidential branch during the last six decades, a measure that accounts for the combined increase in staff size, internal hierarchy, and functional specialization is needed. One such measure can be derived from the White House staff listings presented annually in the *U.S. Government Manual*. Every president beginning with Franklin Roosevelt has published a yearly list of staff, composed primarily of senior political aides who worked in the White House Office.

Using these lists, the number of staff titles, the degree of internal staff hierarchy, and the extent of staff functional specialization were calculated for each year in the period 1937–1996, that is, from the first year of FDR's second term through the end of Clinton's first term.[15] These three indices were then combined to form a yearly index of staff institutionalization.[16]

Measuring the number of staff titles proved straightforward; it closely tracked, but was not the same as, the total number of staff listed each year.[17] To calculate functional staff specialization, aides with similar substantive duties, as identified by titles, were grouped into functional categories. Thus, for example, each aide whose title included the phrase "legislative affairs" collectively constituted one functional area. All aides with reference to "public liaison" in their titles constituted a second functional area. Those dealing with the press or the media were a third locus of specialization. Based on this approach, FDR's staff in 1937 was divided into three functional areas composed of political secretaries, the executive clerk's office, and the president's personal secretaries. In contrast, under Clinton in 1996 there were forty distinct functional advising areas, including but not limited to: chief of staff, legal counsel, domestic policy, national security, media, communications, intergovernmental relations, and speechwriting.

To measure internal staff hierarchy, the maximum number of links between levels of advisers, ranging from the lowest aide to the president, was counted. Thus, under FDR in 1937, there was one chain of hierarchy, since all of the clerks, secretaries, and personal secretaries listed in the *U.S. Government Manual* for that year reported directly to the president.[18] In contrast the Clinton staff was organized into a five-link hierarchy, ranging from special assistants to deputy assistants (one link) to assistants (two) to deputy chiefs of staff (three) to the Chief of Staff (four) who reports directly to the President (the fifth link).

When listings proved difficult to interpret, other sources were used that described staff operations in more detail.[19] Nevertheless, the index is not a perfect measure of staff institutionalization. First, as conceptualized it understates the impact of hierarchy: the index accords a single change in hierarchy no more weight than the addition of one staff title or specialized function, even though changes in hierarchy affect many aides at once.[20] Second, the index inevitably contains some measurement error: although listings do show consistency across administrations, there are no written guidelines telling the president whom to include in the *U.S. Government Manual*. Consequently, different presidents and their aides may have used slightly different criteria in compiling these lists.[21]

There is strong evidence, however, to suggest that the *Manual* is a valid source of comprehensive, continuous data regarding the institutionalization of significant staff support since FDR's presidency. Most important, the changes in the annual index, as shown in Figure 10.1, comport well with conventional historical accounts of presidential staffing trends. Based on the index, staff institutionalization increased incrementally under FDR and Truman, took a larger jump under Eisenhower, receded somewhat under JFK and LBJ, then increased steeply again during Nixon's first term. This was followed by Nixon's aborted second-term effort to scale back the White House bureaucracy. Thereafter staff institutionalization jumped again under Ford and Carter before dropping and then leveling off somewhat under Reagan and Bush.[22] Finally,

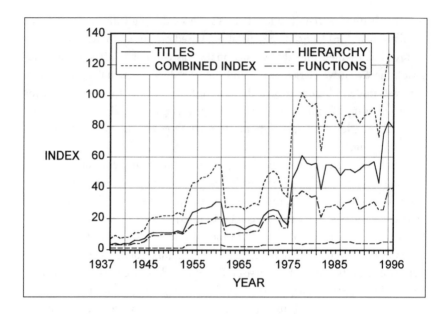

FIGURE 10.1.   Index of Staff Institutionalization, 1937-1996
Source: U.S. Government Manual (successive editions)

after an initial dip in Clinton's first year, the index subsequently took another large jump and remained at this level through his first term.[23]

Additional evidence that the index accurately measures what many scholars mean by a growth in the presidential branch is presented in Table 10.1 The mean levels of staff institutionalization for Republican and Democratic presidents from 1937–96 are significantly different, with Republicans' staffs 50 percent more institutionalized than Democrats' staffs. This is consistent with what

TABLE 10.1.   Differences in Democratic and Republican Presidents' Degree of Staff Institutionalization, 1937—1996

	Obs	Mean	Std. Dev.
Democratic Presidents	32	40.13	37.61
Republican Presidents	28	66.39	22.54
Total Observations	60	52.30	33.92

t = –3.22 with 58 d.f., p = 0.00 (Assuming equal variances)

other scholars have found using qualitative evidence.[24] It raises the question, however, as to the cause of these partisan differences. Do Republican and Democratic presidents employ different staffing strategies? Or are the differences a function of some other factor or factors that differentially affect Republican and Democratic presidents?

EXPLAINING PRESIDENTIAL BRANCH GROWTH

The characteristics of the index of staff institutionalization, then, are consistent with the staffing picture presented in the existing primary and secondary historical sources. But what explains this growth in size and complexity since 1937? The claim made earlier is that staff institutionalization is driven in part by increasing presidential uncertainty regarding the likely consequences of presidential choices on preferred outcomes. That uncertainty is fueled by changes within the president's chief bargaining transactors—Neustadt's Washington community—that makes them less useful as purveyors of information and expertise. Confronted with a loss of traditional sources of bargaining intelligence, presidents turn to other experts possessing the requisite knowledge and incorporate them into the presidential staff.[25]

To test this claim, the annual *percentage change* (see figure 10.2) in the index of staff institutionalization is regressed against annual percentage changes in the composition of the major presidential bargaining groups. These groups include Congress, "executive officialdom," party members, interest groups and the public.[26] The model predicts that as these groups become more fragmented, or more dominated by interests opposed to the president, it will become more difficult for presidents to extract the necessary bargaining information from them.

The annual *change* in the variables, rather than their yearly levels, is employed because several of the measures, including the measure of staff institutionalization, trend upward across the full time series. By differencing the variables, they are made stationary; that is, the underlying mean and variance of the dependent variable conditional on the explanatory variables is held constant throughout the time series.[27] This minimizes the likelihood of spurious results.[28] And by using the *percentage* annual change, rather than the change in absolute levels, the measures control for the impact of a growth in the size of the variables through time.[29]

From the president's bargaining perspective, Congress is undoubtedly the most important member of the Washington community. However, this bar-

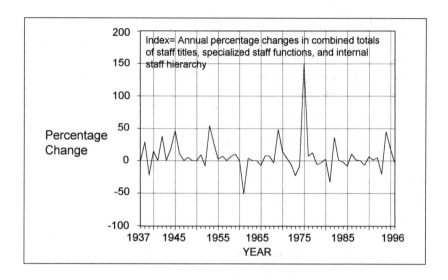

FIGURE 10.2.   Annual Percentage Change in the Index of Staff Institutionalization

gaining relationship has been characterized in the post-World War II era by the existence of divided government, with the presidency and the majority of one or both houses of Congress occupied by opposing parties. Divided government has meant diminished congressional political support for presidents and thus, presumably, a reduced flow of bargaining-relevant information from Capitol Hill.

To capture changes in the "cost" to presidents of extracting bargaining information from Congress over time, the yearly change in the percentage of seats in the Senate held by the president's party was used.[30] As this percentage increases, it should become comparatively easier for a president to extract the information and expertise needed to bargain effectively with Congress because there are more legislators who share the president's policy and political preferences. When this percentage declines, however, the model predicts it will become more difficult for a president to ascertain the likely outcome of bargaining on Capitol Hill, because members of the opposition party are more likely to conceal information and otherwise engage in strategic bargaining. Hence this variable should be negatively correlated with staff institutionalization.

A second recurring bargaining arena encompasses the president's "partisans" both in his party and among the general public. One of the biggest changes in American politics since Neustadt first wrote *PP* in 1960 is party leaders' declining ability to control the selection of presidential candidates and to run presidential campaigns.[31] As a result, rather than depend on the loose federation of state, local, and national party leaders who traditionally provided electoral expertise, presidents have resorted to creating their own "presidential" party of pollsters, consultants, and political strategists.[32]

To estimate the declining electoral influence of the party leadership, the number of party voters who participated in presidential primaries every four years was multiplied by the percentage of the president's party delegates selected through these primaries. This measure is premised on the idea that increased primary participation by the party rank-and-file together with the eclipse of the party caucus by primaries as the chiefs mean of selecting convention delegates reduces party leaders' control of the presidential nominating process. The index of staff institutionalization, then, should be positively correlated with the annual percentage change in this measure of party decline.[33]

A third important presidential bargaining exchange is with members of the executive branch. Several scholars argue that as the executive branch expands in response to a growth in demands for governmental services, presidents seek to maintain some semblance of administrative control by increasing the number of political appointees they make to the executive branch.[34] Scholars differ, however, concerning whether this strategy goes hand-in-glove with efforts to centralize administrative control over the executive branch through an expanded White House staff, or instead is typically employed by presidents as an *alternative* to centralized administrative control within the White House.[35]

The yearly percentage change in the number of presidential political appointees confirmed by the Senate is used to gauge presidents' efforts to control the executive branch.[36] If White House staff centralization and executive branch politicization operate in tandem, the number of political appointees should be positively associated with an increase in the index of staff institutionalization. If, on the other hand, presidents use them as competing strategies, the annual change in political appointees will be negatively associated with staff institutionalization. The analysis included a variable to control for a president's first year in office when the bulk of his political appointments to cabinet departments and agencies are made. This takes the value of 1 during each president's first year in office, and 0 otherwise.

After *PP*'s initial publication in 1960, anecdotal and survey evidence indicates that the number and influence of interest groups increased exponentially.

A kaleidoscope of PAC's, issue networks, and single-issue lobbies was overlaid on the relatively tidy world of iron triangles, peak associations, and hegemonic trade organizations that dominated policymaking 30 years ago.[37] It is expected to become increasingly costly for presidents to bargain with these groups due to both the rapid growth in the overall number of interest groups and the failure of many of the newer organizations to align along traditional party lines.[38] Presidents are thus expected to institutionalize staff in response to the growth and fragmentation of the interest group universe.

Unfortunately, it is difficult to construct a reliable measure of interest group elaboration across the entire time period considered here; most relevant studies have data going back only to the 1960s. Instead of counting actual interest groups, then, the annual change in the number of pages in the *Federal Register* is used as a proxy for interest group elaboration. The assumption is that an increase in the number, scope, and complexity of federal rules and regulations will provide more incentive for groups to organize and lobby.[39] The number of pages in the *Federal Register* likely reflects other trends as well, particularly a general growth in governmental programs, complexity, and size. Indeed, the annual number of pages closely tracks the increase in federal employees and budget outlays across the same time period, so it is likely capturing government growth in the executive branch as well as interest group elaboration. To partially control for this growth in government, the model included a variable measuring the annual percentage change in federal budgeted outlays in constant dollars.[40]

The fifth bargaining relationship considered here is that between the president and the public. A number of scholars have argued that presidential power is increasingly dependent on a president's ability to marshal public support via speechmaking and other public activities.[41] To gauge the impact of popular support for the president on staff institutionalization, the model includes a six-month trend variable measuring the change in the president's popularity between January and June of each year, as indicated by monthly Gallup poll results.[42] If presidential popularity falls significantly in this period, one expects presidents to institutionalize staff with the expertise to help them shore up their diminishing popular support. To control for the *level* of popularity, the model also includes a measure of the president's Gallup Poll standing as of June.

The extent of a president's bargaining uncertainty, of course, is not solely dependent on the behavior or characteristics of the actors and institutions with whom he is bargaining. It also reflects variations in presidents' bargaining skills due to differences in their professional training and experiences, and in their innate qualities such as temperament and intelligence. Following this reasoning, some presidency scholars argue that Republican presidents tend to embrace staff institutionalization more than Democrats (see table 10.1 above). This is typically attributed to partisan-related differences in presidents' governing philosophy and background. Neustadt argues that, beginning with FDR, Democratic presidents were more likely to view their White House aides as a *personal* staff, and thus to limit it to only those aides who dealt with some aspect of the president's daily workload.[43] In addition, Stephen Hess claims that Democrats tend to recruit aides with broad political experience who are more comfortable working with informal advising arrangements. Republican presidents, in contrast, rely more heavily on aides with business backgrounds, and thus tend to adopt "corporate" staff structures. Moreover, Democratic presidents tend historically to place greater emphasis on policy innovation, which also creates incentives to adopt more fluid advising structures.[44]

As noted above, however, the partisan staffing difference could instead be an artifact of the different political eras in which Republicans and Democrats have typically governed. To test what explains the partisan difference in staffing, the analysis includes a variable that took the value of 1 if the president is a Democrat and 0 if otherwise. If staffing does differ on the basis of a president's party affiliation, the coefficient for this variable should be statistically significant even when controlling for differences in political context.

The model also includes a variable to control for a significant upward spike in the annual change in the index of institutionalization for the year 1975 (see figure 10.2 above). This spike coincides with several Watergate-related "shocks" to the American political system that could conceivably have created unprecedented levels of presidential bargaining uncertainty just as President Gerald Ford began restructuring the White House for his 1976 presidential campaign. These shocks include a more adversarial White House press corps; more stringent campaign finance fundraising and reporting requirements due to the 1974 Federal Election Campaign Act (FECA); an increase in the number and influence of political action committees because of the new FECA rulings; and Ford's own unprecedented political standing as an appointed president seeking election in his own right, while facing a likely intra-party challenge from Ronald Reagan.

If these shocks collectively changed the nature of presidential bargaining in fundamental respects, a failure to account for them would decrease the fit of the regression estimation regarding the causes for changes in staff institutionalization. Accordingly, the equation includes a variable that takes the value of 1 in 1975, and 0 otherwise.[45]

RESULTS AND INTERPRETATION

As shown in Table 10.2, the full model explains more than 60% of the variance in yearly percentage change in the index of staff institutionalization (adjusted $R^2 = .63$). More importantly, the coefficients for five of the six variables created to gauge the impact of changes in the Washington community on staffing levels are significant at the $p < .05$ threshold, with signs in the expected direction. The t-value of the sixth variable, measuring a growth in pages in the Federal Register, is just above the $p < .05$ significance threshold ($p = .06$), but its sign is not in the predicted direction.

A significant part of the total variance in staff institutionalization as defined here is explained by the Watergate-induced shocks indicated by the dummy variable that takes the value of 1 in 1975. It accounts for a one-time jump of more than 160 percent in the index of institutionalization, suggesting that Gerald Ford's presidency demarcated the beginning of a new political era characterized by significantly higher levels of bargaining uncertainty.

The remaining variables designed to gauge changes in Congress, in the public, in the president's party, and in the executive branch also prove statistically significant predictors of staff institutionalization. Of these four variables, the two measuring changes in a president's partisan standing in Congress and in his public approval had the largest coefficients, predicting a 1.03 percent and a .74 percent yearly decrease in the index of staff institutionalization for a one-percent increase in the respective explanatory variables ($p < .05$).[46]

Interestingly, it appears that when controlling for these changes in bargaining groups, Democratic and Republican presidents do *not* vary in their tendency to institutionalize staff support. The variable for Democratic presidents is not a significant predictor of changes in staff institutionalization.[47] Instead, it appears much more likely that the partisan staffing differences observers have noted reflects the impact of divided government since 1937. Simply put, because Republican presidents typically governed with less party support in the Senate than did Democratic presidents, they faced higher bargaining costs and thus were more likely to institutionalize staff support.[48]

A six-month decline in Gallup poll ratings, controlled for the level of popular approval in June, is the third largest predictor of staff institutionalization

TABLE 10.2 Explaining Staff Institutionalization, 1937–1996
(Dependent Variable: Annual Percent Change in Index of Staff Institutionalization)

	Coef.[a] (Std. Err)	Impact[b]
1975 (reform dummy)	1.62***	.03
	(.17)	
Senate Party Support	−1.03***	−.004
	(.36)	
6 month popularity trend (January——June)	−.74**	−.02
	(.30)	
Party Erosion (%delegates*voters)	.11**	.01
	(.05)	
Senate Confirmed Political Appointees	−.05**	−.02
	(.02)	
Federal Regulations (#pages in Federal Register)	−.24*	−.01
	(.12)	
Federal Budget (in constant dollars)	.13	.01
	(.09)	
Popularity (June Gallup Poll)	.36*	.00
	(.19)	
First Year in Office (dummy)	.09	.02
	(.08)	
President's Party (Democrat 1)	.03	.02
	(.05)	
Intercept	.19	NA
	(.11)	
N:560, Adjusted R²: .63	Durbin-Watson: 2.19	

*** = significant at the .01 level **5 significant at the .05 level.
*= significant at the .10 level.

a. Unstandardized OLS coefficients; b's indicate percentage change in annual index of institution-alization caused by one percent annual change in variable. For dummy variables, b's indicate percentage change in annual index of institutionalization caused when variable = 1.

b. Calculated by multiplying mean annual change of variable across 60 observations with its regression coefficient.

behind the 1975 reforms and Senate support. As noted above, for every one-per-cent drop in approval ratings over a six-month period, the index of staff institu-tionalization increased by .74 percent ($p < .05$). It does appear, then, that presi-dents who experience a long-term decline in popular support are more likely to institutionalize staff assistance, much as Bill Clinton did by hiring David Gergen as a media adviser early in his first term in reaction to a precipitous drop in approval ratings. Next to support on Capitol Hill, then, the trend in a president's public standing appears to be the most important predictor of presidential branch growth (when controlling for the 1975 reforms).[49]

The erosion in party control of the presidential campaign is the fourth most important explanation for the growth of the presidential branch since 1937. When controlling for other factors, a one percent annual increase in this vari-able was associated with a .11 percent annual increase in staff institutionaliza-tion. It appears that the growth of the primary-based, media-dominated elec-toral system increases the incentives for presidents to institutionalize staff support within the White House.[50]

As Richard Nathan argued in his study of the Nixon and Reagan presiden-cies, presidents do appear to pursue executive branch politicization as an *alter-native* to White House staff institutionalization, but the impact is not particu-larly large; an increase of one percent in the annual number of Senate-confirmed political appointees is associated with about a .05 percent decline in staff institutionalization.[51] Presidents who can season the executive branch with political loyalists are evidently slightly less inclined to exercise administrative control by creating a White House counter-bureaucracy.[52]

The coefficient for the annual growth in the pages of the *Federal Register*, designed to capture the impact of interest group growth on presidential staffing, is not quite statistically significant ($p = .06$), and the sign of the coef-ficient is not in the expected direction. It may be that yearly changes in this measure do not accurately reflect changes in interest group pressure. But it is possible that its explanatory impact is being masked by the inclusion of the variable for the 1975 reforms; there is a significant jump in the number of pages in the *Federal Register* that year and, as an indication of the growing influence of interest groups, Ford is the first president to formally establish an office of public liaison to conduct outreach to interest groups.

It is also possible, however, given the negative relationship between the two variables, that presidents view White House staff institutionalization and the issuance of administrative rules and regulations (as stipulated in the *Federal Register*) as alternative means of influencing policy and political actors. That is, the growth in the *Federal Register* might be an indication of presidents' increasing reliance on administrative procedures as a way to manage a growing bureaucracy. This would support Nathan's contention that presidents see the "administrative presidency" as an alternative to overseeing the executive branch via a White House counter-bureaucracy.

Finally, the annual percentage change in the federal budget was not a statistically significant predictor of staff growth, suggesting that the growth in the federal government is not causing presidents' acquisition of specialized staff.

Conclusion

The results of the statistical analysis support the central claim of this paper: that Neustadt's bargaining paradigm can help explain the growth of the presidential branch. Presidents who encounter an increase in bargaining uncertainty, as defined here, with respect to a particular set of political actors are more likely to institutionalize White House staff support. Additional support for this claim is found in the numerous qualitative studies documenting the growth of the presidential branch. Although typically not meant to be theoretically explicit, these works are largely consistent with the argument here. Thus, John Hart traces Reagan's creation of the Office of Political Affairs to changes in presidential campaigns dating back to the post-1968 electoral reforms that diminished the influence of the party elite in the nominating process.[53] Stephen Hess argues that Nixon's decision to hire White House aides for investigatory purposes was made because "he needed information that he did not trust the usual mechanisms of the permanent government or his political party to supply."[54] Karen Hult and Charles Walcott note that the Office of Congressional Relations, as created by Eisenhower in 1953 and expanded by later presidents, "devoted considerable effort to gathering information about legislative activities."[55] Similar arguments can be made about the creation of a public liaison office by Ford, an office for intergovernmental affairs under Carter, and a communications office under Nixon. In each instance presidents institutionalized staff to reduce bargaining uncertainty with a key constituency.

However, several caveats to the argument are worth noting. To begin, the analysis is incomplete in a number of respects. It does not address the impact of bargaining changes in the international arena on staff institutionalization. Although the Assistant to the President for National Security Affairs and a handful of his senior assistants are included in the White House Office listings in the *U.S. Government Manual*, lower-level NSC aides are not listed because they are not officially a part of the White House Office. To evaluate the impact of an

increase in bargaining costs with foreign governments on staff institutionalization, the staffing index would need to include national security staff as well.[56]

Similarly, the analysis does not capture the impact on staff institutionalization of changes in the media's coverage of the presidency. Presumably the presidential office has developed in response to the growth in, and changing norms
of, White House press coverage. It is difficult to test this claim, however,
because there is no accurate way to gauge trends in media coverage since 1937;
the official listings of the size of White House press corps are incomplete and
thus misleading.[57]

Third, in addition to ignoring bargaining exchanges with the international
community and with the press, the evidence reported here does not take into
account the impact of increasing levels of staff institutionalization on its
annual change. That is, the model ignores the administrative difficulties posed
by an increasingly large and internally complex presidential branch. At some
point presidents may resist institutionalizing more staff support, even when
faced with increases in bargaining uncertainty, in order to avoid incurring
additional management costs. A fully specified statistical model, then, would
incorporate the administrative cost to presidents of managing presidential
staffs. Those costs are an unavoidable function of the responsibility presidents
must shoulder for what aides do in their name, whether authorized by the
president or not.[58]

Fourth, the argument says little about internal staff structures pertaining to
management and communication. As Neustadt warns, the mere acquisition of
specialized staff is no guarantee that pertinent bargaining expertise will reach
the president: "On the one hand [a president] can never assume that anyone or
any system will supply the bits and pieces he needs most; on the other hand, he
must assume that much of what he needs will not be volunteered by his official
advisers."[59]

Administrative methods must therefore be devised to ensure that aides provide the necessary information to the president in a timely fashion. How advisers are organized influences their usefulness in reducing presidential bargaining uncertainty.[60]

Fifth, the analysis does not address the political costs to presidents of institutionalizing staff. Presidents do not necessarily acquire staff support in a
political vacuum; this sometimes requires negotiating with Congress and even
the relevant interest groups and executive branch agencies.[61] For the most part,
however, as Hart documents, except in the aftermath of a staff-related scandal
(Watergate, the Iran-contra Affair) or issue-based political crisis (the Sputnik
launch, control of the nation's trade policy, or drug use among the nation's

youth), Congress has proved reluctant to dictate how the EOP—particularly the White House—is to be organized.[62] Nevertheless, presidents must anticipate the likely cost of staff institutionalization, particularly outside the White House Office, and act accordingly.

Finally, the essay presumes that presidents do recognize "information" gaps and react appropriately. Given sufficient time, one expects stable levels of bargaining certainty to create a semblance of institutional equilibrium, in which staff functions and positions remain largely unchanged across presidencies.[63] Equilibrium, however, is an analytic concept and, in practice, presidents cannot always know if staff expertise has reduced bargaining uncertainty to acceptable levels until after the bargaining exchange has been consummated. History suggests that it takes presidents up to a term in office before they understand their staffing needs. Consequently, although staff institutionalization will fluctuate around an equilibrium point, there will be frequent variation depending on both contextual factors that affect bargaining uncertainty and staff management costs, as well as differences among presidents in their administrative experience.[64]

In summary, Neustadt's conceptual foundation provides a stepping-stone toward a more complete understanding of the growth of the presidential branch. While there is much more to be done, the research and evidence described in this essay is nonetheless noteworthy.[65] In part, it suggests that to significantly reduce presidential staff size and functional specialization, given the current presidential workload, requires a fundamental restructuring in the president's relationship to other actors and institutions in the American political system. In particular, effective staff reform must be coupled with a corresponding effort to reduce the pervasive growth in presidential bargaining uncertainty that has characterized the post-FDR era. This may require presidents to reconstruct bargaining coalitions similar to those characteristic of an earlier political time, or to find substitutes for those coalitions through new institutional arrangements. Whether and how that can be done in the current political system is a complicated issue. But recent presidencies, with Watergate, Iran-contra, and lesser staff-related mishaps, suggest the endeavor is well worth pursuing.

NOTES

1. Indeed, Neustadt has been criticized for unduly "personalizing" the study of the presidency. See Terry Moe, "Presidents, Institutions and Theory" in George C. Edwards III, John H. Kessel, and Bert A. Rockman, eds., *Researching the Presidency:*

Vital Questions, New Approaches (Pittsburgh: Pittsburgh University Press, 1993). The irony of such charges is that almost none of the research inspired by *PP* examines individual presidents. Instead, it predominately focuses on testing Neustadt's argument, as laid out in *PP*'s first five chapters, regarding the sources and limits of presidential power. The clarity and power of Neustadt's argument in these chapters tends to obscure his more fundamental point regarding the importance of *information acquisition* to bargaining effectiveness. By overlooking this link, scholars have also missed the institutional ramifications of Neustadt's argument. See Richard E. Neustadt, *Presidential Power and the Modern Presidents: The Politics of Leadership from Roosevelt to Reagan* (New York: The Free Press, 1990).

2. Nelson W. Polsby, "Some Landmarks in Modern Presidential -Congressional Relations," in Anthony King, ed., *Both Ends of the Avenue* (Washington, D.C.: American Enterprise Institute, 1983). See also Fred Greenstein, "Changes and Continuities in the Modern Presidency" in Anthony King, ed., *The New American Political System* (Washington, D.C.: American Enterprise Institute, 1978), pp. 45–85. Some scholars date the origins of the presidential branch even earlier, to Hoover [Charles Walcott and Karen M. Hult, *Governing the White House: From Hoover Through LBJ* (Lawrence: University Press of Kansas, 1995)], Harding [Lyn Ragsdale and John Theis "The Institutionalization of The American Presidency, 1924–92," *American Journal of Political Science* 41 (4) (1997): 1280–1318], or—in the case of staff to deal with the press—to Theodore Roosevelt's presidency [Martha Kumar, "The Relationship Between the White House and the Press: One Hundred Years in the Making" (Paper prepared for delivery at the 1997 Annual Meeting of the Midwest Political Science Association)].

3. John P. Burke, *The Institutional Presidency* (Baltimore: Johns Hopkins University Press, 1992); Alfred Dick Sander, *A Staff for the President: The Executive Office, 1921–52* (New York: Greenwood Press, 1989); John Hart, *The Presidential Branch (From Washington to Clinton)* 2nd ed. (Chatham, N.J.: Chatham House Publishers, 1995); Thomas E. Cronin "The Swelling of the Presidency: Can Anyone Stop the Tide?" in Peter Woll, ed. *American Government: Reading and Cases*, 8th ed. (Boston: Little, Brown, 1984); Stephen Hess, *Organizing the Presidency* 2nd ed. (Washington, D.C.: The Brookings Institution, 1988); Ragsdale and Theis, "The Institutionalization of the American Presidency"; Terry Moe "The Politicized Presidency" in John E. Chubb and Paul E. Peterson, eds. *The New Direction in American Politics* (Washington, D.C.: The Brookings Institution, 1985), pp. 235–274; Samuel Kernell, "The Evolution of the White House Staff" in John E. Chubb and Paul E. Peterson, eds. *Can the Government Govern?* (Washington, D.C.: The Brookings Institution, 1989).

4. This is not all that presidential aides do, of course; in addition to reducing bargaining uncertainty by providing information and expertise, aides also perform

other critical duties for presidents, including handling clerical tasks (e.g., appointments and correspondence) and lending emotional support. The focus in this paper, however, is strictly on the *informational* prerequisites for effective bargaining.

5. Neustadt, *Presidential Power*, pp. 128–29.

6. Kernell, *Going Public*; Heclo, "Presidential Power and Public Prestige: 'a snarly sort of politics . . . ,'" Paper prepared for "Presidential Power Revisited" Conference, Woodrow Wilson Center June 13, 1996, pp. 1–27.

7. Anthony King, "The American Polity in the Late 1970s: Building Coalitions in the Sand," in King, ed., *The New American Political System* (Washington, D.C.: American Enterprise Institute, 1978); and the articles in Chubb and Peterson, *Can the Government Govern?*

8. Moe, "The Politicized Presidency"; Harold Seidman, *Politics, Position and Power (The Dynamics of Federal Organization)* 5th ed. (New York: Oxford University Press, 1998).

9. Lester G. Seligman, "Presidential Leadership: The Inner Circle and Institutionalization" *The Journal of Politics* 18 (1956): 410–26; Robert S. Gilmour, "The Institutionalized Presidency: A Conceptual Clarification" in Norman Thomas, ed. *The Presidency in Contemporary Context* (New York: Dodd, Mead, 1975) pp. 147–59; John P. Burke, "The Institutional Presidency" in Michael Nelson, ed. *The Presidency and the Political System*, 4th. ed. (Washington, D.C.: Congressional Quarterly Press, 1995), pp. 365–89; Hart, *The Presidential Branch*; Ragsdale and Theis, "The Institutionalization of the American Presidency," pp. 1280–1370; Margaret Jane Wyszomirski, "The Discontinuous Institutional Presidency" in Colin Campbell and M. Wyszomirski, eds., *Executive Leadership in Anglo-American Systems* (Pittsburgh: University of Pittsburgh Press, 1991), pp. 85–108; Paul C. Light, *Thickening Government: Federal Hierarchy and the Diffusion of Accountability* (Washington, D.C.: The Brookings Institution Press, 1995), pp. 1–31.

10. Bradley Patterson, *Ring of Power: The White House Staff and Its Expanding Role in Government* (New York: Basic Books, 1988); Hart, *The Presidential Branch*; Cronin, "The Swelling of the Presidency," pp. 377–390.

11. Burke, *The Institutional Presidency*; Hart, *The Presidential Branch*.

12. Thomas H. Hammond, "Agenda Control, Organizational Structure, and Bureaucratic Politics" *American Journal of Political Science* (May 1986): 379–420; Thomas H. Hammond and Gary J. Miller "A Social Choice Perspective on Expertise and Authority in Bureaucracy" *American Journal of Political Science* 29 (1) (February 1985): 1–28; Gary J. Miller, *Managerial Dilemmas: The Political Economy of Hierarchy* (New York: Cambridge University Press, 1992).

13. Hess, *Organizing the Presidency*, pp. 171–191; Matthew J. Dickinson, *Bitter Harvest: FDR, Presidential Power and the Growth of the Presidential Branch* (New York: Cambridge University Press, 1997), pp. 19–41.

14. Light, *Thickening Government*, pp. 61–95.

15. The beginning date for tracing the growth of the presidential branch was determined by the Brownlow Committee Report of January, 1937, which provided a partial blueprint for the Executive Office of President.

16. A factor analysis indicated that the three variables from which the staff institutionalization index was constructed indeed tapped a single factor (first factor eigen value 2.71, second factor -.02). The variable loadings on this factor were: staff titles, .97; functional specialization, .97; and hierarchy, .91.

17. This occurred because two or more individuals occasionally shared the same title. Only substantive positions were tallied, e.g., the president's physician, ushers, or other aides whose role is not integral to presidential bargaining were excluded, as were members of the Vice President's Office. Both military aides and members of the First Lady's staff were included, however, because in past years they occasionally played substantive bargaining roles. For instance, Clark Clifford began his stint in the Truman White House as a military aide. And First Ladies dating back to Eleanor Roosevelt were often important sources of bargaining information.

18. Dickinson, *Bitter Harvest*, pp. 86–116.

19. For past presidencies, useful sources included memoirs and secondary accounts from former staff members. For the Clinton administration, *The National Journal*, *The New York Times*, and *The Washington Post* proved most helpful.

20. A conservative approach was adopted in which hierarchy was added to, rather than multiplied by, titles and functions because of the difficulty in gauging, using secondary sources including the *U.S. Government Manual*, the extent of internal hierarchy across bargaining arenas. This approach lessened the risk of biasing the results by overstating the impact of hierarchy on the staffing index. An alternative staff institutionalization index, in which annual staff titles and functional specialization were *multiplied* by levels of internal hierarchy, was also considered and tested. The statistical results did not differ markedly from when hierarchy was added to staff titles and functional specialization to form the staff index; the specific regression coefficients changed, but the relative importance of the explanatory variables dealing with changes in Congress, the public, campaigns, and the 1975 reforms, did not (these are discussed below). Only the variable for Senate-confirmed presidential appointments was significantly affected when hierarchy was multiplied by titles and functions; it became statistically insignificant.

21. Clinton's White House staff listing for 1995 illustrates this point. It included 153 names, far more than any other president. Upon closer inspection, it turned out that most of these were junior members of the National Security staff who were not included in prior White House Office listings. Moreover, most of these names were left off the 1996 staff list, suggesting that the 1995 list was an aberration. Because the

NSC staff is not officially part of the White House Office, this analysis excluded all lower-level NSC aides from all yearly indices. By excluding these aides, Clinton's 1995 staff index was reduced to 127 which was more in line with the figures from his other years as president.

22. The relatively high levels of institutionalization under Ford and Carter may seem surprising, since both presidents made well-publicized efforts to reduce White House staff size. However, each also increased staff functional specialization, titles and internal hierarchy, which accounts for the comparatively high index during their presidencies.

23. Patterson, *Ring of Power*; Hess, *Organizing the Presidency*; Hart, *The Presidential Branch*; Burke, *The Institutional Presidency*.

24. Richard Tanner Johnson, *Managing the White House: An Intimate Study of the Presidency* (New York: Harper, 1974); Hess, *Organizing the Presidency*, pp. 187–189; Neustadt, *Presidential Power*, p. 219.

25. Dickinson, has argued that the decision to incorporate staff into the White House Office also reflects the frequency with which presidents engage in bargains requiring a particular kind of political or policy-related information; when bargains that require a certain expertise repeatedly recur, presidents opt to institutionalize the relevant experts into the president's staff (*Bitter Harvest*, pp. 220–26). This aspect of institutionalization is not examined further here.

26. Neustadt, *Presidential Power*; Lester G. Seligman and Cary R. Covington, *The Coalitional Presidency* (Chicago, Illinois: The Dorsey Press, 1989). Neustadt also includes foreign governments within the Washington community. However, they are excluded from this study because most of the president's national security aides, who provide foreign policy bargaining expertise, are not included among the White House listings in the *U.S. Government Manual*.

27. The differenced variables were then tested for stationarity using an Augmented Dickey-Fuller (ADF) test. This involved regressing the variable against its lagged value, its lagged annual difference across the two previous years, and a yearly trend variable. The ADF test indicated one could reject the presence in each variable of a unit root indicating nonstationarity at the .01 probability level.

28. A failure to make the variables stationary invalidates OLS regression analysis which is premised on the assumption that the probability of a change in the mean of the dependent variable as a result of the impact of the explanatory variable(s) does not change through time. By differencing the variables, of course, one loses some information regarding the long-run relationship between the variables, but it prevents an otherwise misleadingly high R^2.

29. The effect of using percentages is to exaggerate the importance of changes in the staff index and other variables when they are smallest, which occurs at the beginning of the time series, that is, during Roosevelt's term in office.

30. Presidential party support in the Senate, rather than the House, is used because it is the Senate that confirms presidential appointments to the executive branch, and the model tests whether presidents use executive branch appointments as an alternative to White House staff institutionalization. However, the equation was also estimated using a variable for presidential party support in the House along with the variable for support in the Senate, with no substantive difference in the results (the coefficient for House support was statistically insignificant).

31. Austin Ranney, "The Political Parties: Reform and Decline" in Anthony King, ed. *The New American Political System*, (Washington, D.C.: American Enterprise Institute, 1978), pp. 213–48; Paul S. Herrnson, *Party Campaigning in the 1980s* (Cambridge: Harvard University Press, 1988); Martin P. Wattenberg *Decline of American Parties, 1952–1992* (Cambridge: Harvard University Press, 1994), pp. 73–89.

32. Kathryn D. Tenpas and Matthew J. Dickinson, "Campaigning and Governing: An Electoral Connection?" *Political Science Quarterly* (Spring 1997).

33. For modeling purposes, it was assumed that changes in the degree of party control over the presidential election campaign influenced staff institutionalization only during the year of the presidential election. In those cases in which the incumbent ran unsuccessfully for reelection (1980 and 1988), the party variable changed in the following year to measure the degree of party erosion in the winning candidate's campaign. In all other years (and in any election year when an incumbent president was ineligible to run for reelection) this variable took a zero value.

34. Light, *Thickening Government*, pp. 32–60.

35. Compare Moe, "The Politicized Presidency," pp. 235–271 and Richard Nathan, *The Administrative Presidency* (New York: Wiley, 1983). Neither claim makes any presumption regarding whether the political appointees are political or policy experts; it matters only that the individual is a political appointee rather than a civil servant, and hence is hired (and can be more easily fired) by the president.

36. Appointment figures for 1937–1961 are derived from David T. Stanley, Dean E. Mann and Jameson W. Doig, *Men Who Govern: A Biographical Profile of Federal Political Executives* (Washington, D.C.: The Brookings Institution, 1967); for 1962–81 from the National Academy of Public Administration's appointee data base (NAPA Appointee Data Base: National Academy of Public Administration, 1985); for 1981–91 from a report of the General Accounting Office (U.S. Government General Accounting Office, "Political Appointees: Turnover Rates in Executive Schedule Positions Requiring Senate Confirmation," *GAO Office Report GGD-94–115FD*, 1994); for 1992, Lyn Ragsdale, *Vital Statistics on the Presidency: From Washington to Clinton* (Washington, D.C. Congressional Quarterly Press, 1996); and for 1993–96, from figures supplied by the Office of Personnel Management. Although each ana-

lyzes Senate-confirmed political appointees, the criteria for inclusion in each study may vary. Hence the numbers must be used with caution.

37. Jack L. Walker, *Mobilizing Interest Groups in America: Patrons, Reforms and Social Movements* (Ann Arbor: University of Michigan Press, 1990); Kay L. Schlozman and John T. Tierney, *Organized Interests in American Politics* (New York: Harper, 1986), pp. 58–87.

38. Hugh Heclo, "Issue Networks and the Executive Establishment," in Anthony King, ed., *The New American Political System* (Washington, D.C.: American Enterprise Institute, 1978), pp. 87–124.

39. To test the validity of this measure, the annual number of federal regulations was matched against a measure of interest group "elaboration" for the years 1953–1986, constructed by Mark Peterson for his book *Legislating Together*. They were highly correlated (.84). The measure also closely correlates (.89) with the yearly number of lobbyists registered in Washington under the 1946 lobbying act.

40. To measure government growth, earlier versions of the model also included variables measuring the combined yearly percentage change in the number of cabinet departments, independent and regulatory agencies, and government corporations, and percent changes in the annual number of federal employees. Neither proved significant and were subsequently dropped from the analysis. Because this equation only used differenced variables, however, it may underestimate the long-term impact of the variables measuring government growth on the levels of staff institutionalization.

41. Theodore Lowi, *The Personal President* (Ithaca, N.Y.: Cornell University Press, 1985); Samuel Kernell, *Going Public* 3rd ed. (Washington, D.C.: Congressional Quarterly Press, 1995).

42. This six-month period was chosen because the *U.S. Government Manual* is published in the fall of any given year, based on figures submitted during the summer to the Government Printing Office by the White House. Thus it is unlikely that the staff listings would reflect changes in presidential approval after midsummer. All public approval measures from 1945 on are based on responses to the question, "Do you approve or disapprove of the job [name of president] is doing as president?" Prior to then, survey questions designed to measure presidential approval used slightly different wording. Also, the question was asked much less frequently during FDR's presidency than in later years, which means that in some years there was no approval rating in either June or January, or both. When either of these two monthly polls was missing, the closest poll result in time was substituted when calculating the trend for that year. This only affects the popularity measures for FDR. Monthly poll results were found in George Gallup, *The Gallup Poll: Public Opinion 1935–71*, vol. 1 (New York: Random House, 1971); George C. Edwards *Presidential Approval: A Sourcebook* (Baltimore: John Hopkins Press,

1990); and Ragsdale, *Vital Statistics on the Presidency*; and, for 1995–96, individual Gallup polls.

43. Neustadt, *Presidential Power*, p. 222.

44. See Hess, *Organizing the Presidency*, p. 189, and Neustadt, *Presidential Power*, pp. 218–29.

45. When the multivariate equation is estimated without the observations for 1975, none of the coefficients of the remaining explanatory variables are significantly affected, but the equation's overall R^2 is lowered by almost half.

In earlier versions of the model a lag of the dependent variable was included to control for the possibility that the annual change in staff institutionalization in any given year is also a function of the prior year's change. It was not statistically significant, and was subsequently excluded. Earlier versions also included a measure for the impact of a president's time in office; the variable took a value of 1–4, corresponding to the year of the presidential term, but it also did not prove significant and was excluded.

46. To get a better sense of the explanatory importance of specific variables, impact measures were calculated by multiplying the mean annual change of each variable during 1937–1996 by its regression coefficient. For example, the mean annual change in Senate party support during the period 1937–96 is only -.4 percent. This means that the average annual impact of changes in Senate party support on staff institutionalization during this period is less than .5 percent (-.004). See table 10.2.

47. Note, however, that the partisan difference in staffing observed by scholars may be primarily a function of Republican presidents' greater emphasis on internal staff hierarchy, rather than a tendency to increase staff titles or functional specialization. The staff index used here likely underestimates the impact of hierarchy, and thus may underestimate the importance of partisan differences in this regard.

48. Among Democratic presidents since 1937 only Clinton, beginning in 1995, and Truman in 1947–48 faced an opposition majority in either branch of Congress. If the variable for presidential Senate support is dropped from the equation, the dummy variable for the president's party (Democrat or Republican) remains statistically insignificant, and the overall adjusted R^2 for the equation drops to .58. Thus, the inclusion of the Senate measure is not likely masking the influence of a president's party affiliation on the staffing index.

49. Note that the *level* of presidential popularity, as measured by the June Gallup Poll and controlling for the six-month trend in popularity, is positively correlated (p = .07) with an increase in staff institutionalization as indicated by a regression coefficient of .36.

50. Tenpas and Dickinson, "Campaigning and Governing: An Electoral Connection?," *Political Science Quarterly*.

51. Richard Nathan, *The Administrative Presidency* (New York: Wiley, 1983).

52. Note that the dummy variable controlling for a president's first year in office was not a statistically significant explanation for staff institutionalization.

53. Hart, *The Presidential Branch*, pp. 126–28.

54. Hess, *Organizing the Presidency*, p. 113.

55. Walcott and Hult, *Governing the White House*, p. 43.

56. To my knowledge there is no single source listing annual changes in the NSC staff. Using archives at presidential libraries, however, it should be possible to construct such a list, and to incorporate it into the staff index examined here.

57. Although lists of correspondents accredited to the White House do exist, they tend to undercount the actual number of White House press correspondents and they do not cover every year back to 1937. Earlier versions of the statistical model estimated here included a measure of the growth in the Congressional press corps to serve as a proxy for White House press growth. It was not a significant predictor of White House staff institutionalization.

58. For the argument that the growth in staff institutionalization inevitably imposes management costs on the president, see Dickinson, "Neustadt and New Institutionalists: New Insights on Presidential Power?," Occasional Paper, Center for American Politics Studies (Cambridge: Harvard University, 1996). These management costs are a function of the president's control (actual and perceived) over the presidential assistant's job-related incentives (pay and other material benefits, job tenure, and jurisdiction), and the divergence between president and aides regarding bargaining preferences (and the expertise for achieving them). Thus, the more accountable a president is held for staff behavior, and the greater the expertise and/or preference gap between the two, the more resources the president must expend to ensure that staff aides are working on the president's behalf.

59. Neustadt, *Presidential Power*, p. 129.

60. This argument is developed more fully in *Bitter Harvest*, which argues that FDR's use of "competitive adhocracy," whereby aides were pitted against one another in a bid to win his favor and access to the Oval Office, proved to be a particularly efficient way for FDR to manage his advisers, and thus to enhance his bargaining effectiveness (Dickinson, *Bitter Harvest*).

61. Terry Moe "The Politics of Bureaucratic Structure" in John Chubb and Paul Peterson, eds. *Can the Government Govern?* (Washington, D.C.: The Brookings Institution). For example, Congress rejected the Brownlow Committee's suggestion to place the Civil Service Commission under FDR's control. Conversely, Congress has occasionally created advising structures despite presidential objections, as it did when establishing the Council of Economic Advisers and the National Security Council. Both were initially resisted by Truman.

62. Hart, *The Presidential Branch*.

63. Compare to Kenneth Shepsle, "Institutional Equilibrium and Equilibrium Institutions," in Herbert Weisberg, ed. *Political Science: The Science of Politics*, (New York: Agathon Press, 1986).

64. Earlier versions of the multivariate model, however, included dummy variables for each of the presidents, which did not have statistically significant effects.

65. One additional way to examine the conceptual approach proposed here is to compare the staffs of chief executives operating in other political systems (for instance, at the state level in the United States, or cross-nationally). By identifying bargaining arenas and associated informational needs, one should be able to predict the pattern of institutional development in these contexts.

CHAPTER 11

The Presidential Kaleidoscope: Advisory Networks in Action

Michael W. Link

Presidential choice is the central theme in Richard Neustadt's *Presidential Power.* The continuous stream of decisions made by the president is the only true resource within his limited control through which he can attempt to achieve success in office.[1] Yet, the modern presidency is no longer the province of a single individual. It is instead a "plural" institution composed of hundreds of officials in the various executive branch departments and agencies.[2] Decisions about whom to rely on for information and advice have become, therefore, among the most important choices a president makes. The type and quality of information and advice a president receives are a direct reflection of those he surrounds himself with. In turn, the caliber of the information or advice directly affects the political and policy choices the president makes. Because the president's appointees and his relationships with them will have a direct bearing on his ability to exert control over the executive branch bureaucracy, there is need for a systematic understanding of the men and women who constitute the modern presidency and how they interact with the chief executive.

The key role advisers and staff play in the presidency raises a number of important questions concerning the interaction between a president and his aides: Who does the president see? When does he see them? In what types of forums (e.g., telephone, one-on-one, groups, etc.) does interaction tend to take place? Larger questions evolve from these: Why does the president meet with particular sets of individuals and not others? How do these sets of individuals change over time? What are the primary factors affecting these patterns?

Although Neustadt addressed some of these questions in *Presidential Power* (albeit indirectly), staffing arrangements and advisory relations were not the central focus of that work. As Rockman notes in chapter 8, what Neustadt offers in this area is a set of guiding principles, not a coherent theory. The basic theme concerning advisory relations in *Presidential Power* is that presidents should develop a dynamic system of information gathering and decisionmaking that will allow them to gather and exert "power" within the governmental system. Neustadt placed little emphasis on formal hierarchy and orderliness in presidential advising, suggesting instead that the president find a mode of operation allowing him to operate in a manner he finds effective.

This perspective differs considerably from that taken in more recent works on organizational theory, which often emphasize the need for a more systematic process for decisionmaking to achieve efficiency and effectiveness in large organizations. For example, Terry Moe suggests that in the area of advisory relations, presidents should ultimately be concerned with developing a "unified, coordinated, centrally directed bureaucratic system" which can be controlled from the top.[3] A president's success in accomplishing this task will determine, to a large degree, the level of autonomy he has from other institutions with which he must share power. In essence, it gives him greater latitude to act and make choices which will build his political capital and increase his chances of being viewed as a "successful" president.

Neustadt and Moe present two differing perspectives on how presidents should operate vis-à-vis their advisers and staff. Neustadt suggests the need for a loosely structured, more fluid system; Moe calls for a more centralized approach. Anyone who has spent much time studying presidential advisory systems will recognize elements of both perspectives at work. On the one hand, the modern presidency has become a highly structured, centralized, hierarchical institution. On the other hand, advisory relations—particularly at the top of this hierarchy—often appear marked by fluidity and even organizational chaos. This point is illustrated in Figure 11.1, which shows excerpts from the daily schedule of President Carter on March 21, 1978. Within nine hours, the president interacted with dozens of individuals, among them heads of state, school teachers, members of Congress, as well as his own personal staff. Presidential contact, therefore, does not always take place in accordance with the president's own desires, but rather is heavily influenced and dictated by the institutional roles to which the president must adhere. Finding an adequate model for studying such a complex process is challenging. Presidential advisory relations rarely follow a clockwork pattern, reflecting neatly meshed gears operating synchronically. Yet, how can social scientists study systematically a

From	To	Activity
5:00		The President received a wake up call from the White House signal board operator
5:36		The President went to the Oval Office
7:15	7:20	The President met with his Assistant for National Security Affairs, Zbigniew Brzezinski
7:32	7:38	The President talked with senator Russell B. Long (D-LA)
7:45	7:55	The President met with his Assistant for Congressional Liaison, Frank B. Moore
8:00	9:00	The President hosted a breakfast meeting for Democratic Congressional leaders
9:20	9:25	The President met with his assistant, Hamilton Jordan
9:30	9:48	The President telephoned the Chief of Government of the Republic of Panama, Brig. Gen. Omar Torrijos Herrera
9:33	9:46	The President met with: Warren M. Christopher, Deputy Secretary of State Stephanie R. van Reigersberg, Dept. of State interpreter Mr. Lordan
9:46	10:00	The President met with: Rex. L. Granum, Deputy Press Secretary Jerrold L. Schecter, Associate Press Secretary, NSC
10:30	10:45	The President participated in an arrival ceremony in honor of the Prime Minister of Israel, Menachem Begin
10:48	1:00	The President participated in a meeting with U.S. and Israeli officials
1:00	1:04	The President met with Mr. Brzezinski
1:04	1:30	The President met with Vice President Walter F. Mondale
1:30	1:53	The President met to discuss urban policy with: Richard G. Hatcher, Mayor (D-Gary, IN) Lee A. Alexander, Mayor (D-Syracuse, NY) Henry W. Maier, Mayor (D-Milwaukee, WI) Stuart E. Eizenstat, Assistant for Domestic Affairs and Policy Jack H. Watson, Jr. Assistant for Intergovernmental Affairs Bruce Kirschenbaum, Associate for Intergovernmental Affairs
2:15	2:27	The President participated in a ceremony to present the National Teacher of the Year Award to Mrs. Henry (Elaine) Barbour of Montrose, Colorado

FIGURE 11.1.   Excerpts from President Carter's Daily Diary of Activities (March 21, 1978)

phenomenon that in many respects seems to undergo continual change over time?

While no metaphor can capture completely the dynamics and complexity of the advisory process, the idea of a "kaleidoscope" is very useful. Relationships between a president and his advisers can be viewed as a kaleidoscopic *network* of individuals in that they are "complex and varied, changing form, pattern, color . . . continually shifting from one set of relations to another; rapidly changing."[4] When a kaleidoscope is in motion, the patterns formed change in their variety, color, and shape, yet do so within certain constraints. While kalei-doscopes often differ in the color combinations and variegated patterns they present, they operate under similar mechanical principles. This metaphor for behavior applies when we step back and take a look at the evolution over time of advisory networks both within and across presidencies.

Presidential Advisory Networks

"Network analysis," whether used metaphorically as an organizing concept or employed formally to refer to the use of graph and matrix theory in the exam-ination of social or political structures, is the analysis of a set of actors (or nodes) and the set of relations (connections or ties) among these actors.[5] Con-ceptualizing presidential advisory systems in network terms, while not new, has been underutilized since its initial use in studies of communication and influ-ence patterns among presidential aides.[6] A presidential advisory network, "encompasses the president and individuals (e.g., the national security assis-tant), subunits (such as the White House Office of Political Affairs), and orga-nizations (e.g., the CIA) that provide input into presidential decisions."[7] Embedded within this broader array of contacts is a smaller, yet still extensive network of direct ties we shall refer to as the president's *personal network* of contacts. Borrowing from Neustadt's perspective of viewing the presidency "from over the president's shoulder, looking out and down with the perspective of his place," the research presented here focuses on the president's advisory network as the president views it.[8]

Presidential daily diaries, which log, minute by minute, phone conversa-tions and in-person meetings, are a fertile and detailed source for studying presidential networks. These are not to be confused with presidential public appointment lists sometimes published in major newspapers. Rather, the information contained in the daily diaries records is complied using a number of diverse sources, including Oval Office and Executive Office Building logs and telephone records, Secret Service shift reports, and the personal logs of key officials such as the chief of staff, national security adviser, domestic policy adviser, and press secretary. These records have been used by presidential scholars to examine presidential reactions to stress in foreign policy decision-making, presidential learning in office, trends in contacts with key advisers, and comparisons of different Oval Office management styles.[9]

The analysis presented here examines the Nixon (first term) and Carter administrations to illustrate the kaleidoscopic nature of the development and evolution of advisory networks. While these two presidencies were linked closely in time, they were headed by two very different individuals. The data are drawn from the daily diaries of Richard M. Nixon (located at the Nixon Project) and Jimmy Carter (housed at the Jimmy Carter Presidential Library).[10] The analysis itself draws upon elements of two common approaches to studying the presidency: the *personalistic approach*, which stresses the importance of the unique characteristics and predispositions of each president and the *institutional approach*, which sees the organizational properties inherent in the office of the presidency as the most important.[11] Key features of both these approaches are used to highlight critical facets of advisory network operation.

The research shows that—like a kaleidoscope—advisory networks are complex and dynamic, blending organizational mechanics and personal operating style. In effect, presidential advisory networks are the products of factors that can both promote and confound a president's desire to establish functional relationships with the permanent bureaucracy and the political system at large. The networks contain elements of stability and centralization as well as fluidity and complexity. The result is a series of information flows toward and away from the president.[12]

STABILITY AND CENTRALIZATION IN PRESIDENTIAL NETWORKS

If presidents are actors motivated in large part to maximize their control over executive branch institutions by developing a stable, centralized network, there are a number of implications for how and why presidents should interact with the rest of the "plural presidency."[13]

THE INSTITUTIONAL PRESIDENCY: THE NETWORK TEMPLATE

First, presidents will be motivated to develop strong working connections that give them as much autonomy from the rest of the political system as possible. Moreover, presidents will have incentive to institutionally centralize them where they have the most control—in the White House Office (WHO).[14] Those who work in the WHO are not subject to Senate confirmation and thus tend to be the president's most loyal contingent. By establishing strong ties to key advisers and structures within the WHO, the president can, in large measure, bypass the permanent bureaucracies, many of which are structured to operate antithetically to presidential leadership.[15] For example, in 1969 Richard Nixon established the Council for Urban Affairs ostensibly to help him develop and coordinate domestic policies. When that structure failed to perform as he had hoped, Nixon abolished it and created the Domestic Council in its place. John Ehrlichman, by then one of Nixon's top advisers, was placed in control of this body, while Arthur Burns (Counselor to the President) and Daniel Patrick Moynihan (Assistant to the President for Urban Affairs), who had initially shared oversight of domestic policy, were assigned other duties. (Note: a listing of names and official titles for Nixon and Carter administration personnel referred to by name in this study is provided in the appendix).

Second, in seeking control over the many organizations of the executive branch (all of which have some level of autonomy), presidents will be motivated (and statutorily committed) to place their own agents in the top posts of these organizations. Politicization of bureaucratic leadership positions has been a major tactic used by presidents in their attempt to exert control over these institutions.[16] In essence, these appointees serve as intermediaries between the president and the permanent bureaucracy, so that the president's contact with these agencies is often limited to the president's personal agents (i.e., cabinet secretaries and agency heads), rather than career civil servants of the permanent bureaucracy.[17]

Yet, presidential control over these appointees is not as extensive as it is over WHO staff. This can create problems for the president. First, these officials may be "co-opted" by the bureaucracy, and may ultimately pursue the agency's goals over the president's objectives. Second, some appointees may seek to establish an independent power base and use this autonomy to advance their own objectives over the president's. In each case, the result is an erosion of trust between the president and the agent, which can lead to a distancing of the official from the president or his/her outright dismissal. Jimmy Carter's problems with Joseph Califano, his first Secretary of Health, Education, and Welfare, is a case in point. Califano was ultimately viewed by many in the administration as undermining some of the president's positions by his vocal criticisms in the press. The situation ultimately grew to such proportions that Carter fired Califano. The lesson, therefore, is that while presidents seek to optimize control over executive branch agencies by placing their own agents in positions of authority, the imperfect level of control they have over these officials can sometimes lead to chaos rather than stability in the president's advisory network.

Third, the presidency as an institution has a stabilizing effect on presidential networks. As the duties and expectations of the American president have expanded, so too has the apparatus created to assist him in carrying out his duties. Organizational growth necessitates differentiation both horizontally, in terms of separate units, and vertically, in terms of formal hierarchy. Differentiation defines roles and tasks within the formal advisory system (for both units and individuals). As these divisions become fixed, an organizational culture or set of beliefs and expectations develops concerning how this differentiated system should work.[18] Potential power spots within the system are identified. For instance, foreign policy has historically been viewed as an area of presidential dominance because of the president's formal role as commander-in-chief and the early recognition by other political actors that the United States should speak with one voice in foreign affairs.[19] We should, therefore, expect presidents to develop much stronger ties to organizations dealing directly with foreign policy issues (e.g., Department of State, Department of Defense, Central Intelligence Agency) than with other Cabinet level departments (e.g., departments of Labor, Commerce, Education). Moreover, as stated previously, these contacts should be focused at the top of the formal organizational hierarchy. In effect, organizational differentiation serves to define which positions are traditionally the most important and hence which are the most likely to have the president's attention. The formal structure of the executive branch, therefore, serves as a template upon which new presidents build their advisory networks and prioritize their contacts.

In order to examine these expectations against reality, all of the advisers and staff included in this study of Nixon (285 total) and Carter (501 total) were categorized in terms of their organizational affiliation (particular department or agency) and their position in the formal organizational hierarchy (director, cabinet secretary, staff assistant, etc.). The "inner" and "outer" Cabinet distinctions made by Thomas Cronin were extended to the non-WHO agencies of the Executive Office of the President (EOP). Organizational affiliations were then categorized as White House Office, "inner" and "outer" EOP units, and "inner" and "outer" Cabinet departments.[20] Similarly, the formal hierarchy was categorized as "top tier," "middle tier," and "lower tier."[21] While finer distinctions could be made, these broad categories were more than adequate to examine the suppositions posited above. The average number of minutes per week spent by advisers with the president in these various affiliation-hierarchy combinations are shown over time for the Nixon Presidency (table 11.1) and the Carter Presidency (table 11.2).

There are a number of important patterns and trends concerning the relationship between institutional structures and presidential access. First, not surprisingly, both Nixon and Carter spent more time, on average, with senior level staff personnel in the WHO than with any other type of adviser. This pattern holds for both presidents and across time within administrations, bolstering the assertion that presidents develop their strongest affiliations with personnel in the most centralized organizational structures.

TABLE 11.1 Average Number of Minutes per Week Advisers Spent with
President Nixon[a] by Unit Affiliation, Position in Hierarchy, and Year
(Average Number of Minutes per Week)

Position in Hierarchy[c]	Unit Affiliation[b]						
	WHO	Inner EOP	Outer EOP	Inner Cabinet	Outer Cabinet	N^d	$Sig.^e$
1969							
Top Tier	241	74	14	99	57	27	.001
Middle Tier	25	14	1	12	5	46	n.s.
Lower Tier	6	0	1	4	7	55	n.s.
1970							
Top Tier	221	47	11	51	48	29	.05
Middle Tier	16	3	0	6	4	47	n.s.
Lower Tier	3	1	2	2	3	47	n.s.
1971							
Top Tier	204	38	12	97	42	25	.05
Middle Tier	28	1	3	11	3	55	.05
Lower Tier	5	6	1	4	3	56	n.s.
1972							
Top Tier	236	29	10	34	11	24	.05
Middle Tier	19	6	9	3	3	43	.01
Lower Tier	4	0	5	1	2	39	n.s.

Notes:
a. Access levels are mean weekly access levels in minutes for members of each group. Figures are
rounded to nearest whole number.
b. Inner EOP units include BOB/OMB, CEA, and CIA; inner Cabinet departments include State,
Defense, Treasury, and Justice.
c. Top tier officials include Cabinet secretaries, EOP directors and chairmen, and senior White
House staff; middle-tier officials include under, deputy, and assistant secretaries, deputy directors,
and special assistants to the president; lower-tier officials include all others.
d. N is the number of advisers in each row.
e. Significance is based on an F-test of mean values across units for each level and year examined.

Comparisons of average numbers of minutes across unit affiliations which are not statistically significantly different at the .05 level are denoted by n.s.

TABLE 11.2 Average Number of Minutes per Week Advisers Spent with President Carter[a] by Unit Affiliation, Position in Hierarchy, and Year (Average Number of Minutes per Week)

Position in Hierarchy[c]		Unit Affiliation[b]					
	WHO	Inner EOP	Outer EOP	Inner Cabinet	Outer Cabinet	N^d	$Sig.^e$
1977							
Top Tier	191	143	26	112	80	31	.01
Middle Tier	33	18	0	11	10	52	.01
Lower Tier	11	14	2	3	6	150	.05
1978							
Top Tier	138	79	31	121	44	26	.05
Middle Tier	19	0	0	6	6	45	.01
Lower Tier	8	7	6	2	3	123	.05
1979							
Top Tier	227	95	33	114	30	39	.05
Middle Tier	19	3	0	11	7	50	n.s.
Lower Tier	9	3	5	3	1	70	.05
1980							
Top Tier	123	45	6	59	10	32	.05
Middle Tier	11	1	0	8	2	37	n.s.
Lower Tier	5	1	0	2	1	52	.05

Notes:

a. Access levels are mean weekly access levels in minutes for members of each group. Figures are rounded to nearest whole number.

b. Inner EOP units include BOB/OMB, CEA, and CIA; inner Cabinet departments include State, Defense, Treasury, and Justice.

c. Top tier officials include Cabinet secretaries, EOP directors and chairmen, and senior White House staff; middle-tier officials include under, deputy, and assistant secretaries, deputy directors, and special assistants to the president; lower-tier officials include all others.

d. N is the number of advisers in each row.

e. Significance is based on an F-test of mean values across units for each level and year examined. Comparisons of average numbers of minutes across unit affiliations which are not statistically significantly different at the .05 level are denoted by n.s.

Second, access levels were next highest for top-level inner cabinet personnel (the lone exception being the first year of the Carter administration when long-time Carter friend Bert Lance was at the helm of the OMB, pushing the inner EOP access levels higher). These departments (i.e., State, Defense, Treasury, and Justice) have traditionally been considered more exclusively "presidential" territory than the other departments and hence command greater presidential attention. Yet, despite their importance, inner cabinet personnel steadily lost access to the president over time in comparison to WHO officials. For instance, in 1969, the senior White House staff spent an average of 241 minutes per week with President Nixon compared to just 99 minutes per week for inner cabinet secretaries. By 1972, senior WHO advisers had seven times greater access to the president in comparison to the inner cabinet secretaries (236 minutes per week versus 34 minutes per week). The trend was not for WHO staff to gain greater access per se, but rather, the access of cabinet officials was significantly curtailed. A similar, but less extreme trend occurred for the Carter administration.

Third, there are similar patterns for top-level outer cabinet, inner EOP, and outer EOP personnel. In each case, these officials had much less access to the president in general, and over time they lost considerable ground (or access) in comparison with WHO personnel. These findings buttress the supposition that over time, presidents distance themselves from the less centralized elements of their advisory networks. Finally, presidential contact with middle- and lower-tier personnel dropped considerably (the latter by and large being permanent bureaucrats). It is difficult to separate out whether these patterns were due to turnover in the president's advisory network, as some officials moved on to other jobs and others joined the administration, or if this simply reflected a more general trend of wanting (and needing) less contact with staff and advisers over the course of a presidency. As discussed below, both Nixon and Carter experienced considerable turnover in their advisory networks, yet each also met with fewer advisers and spent less time in meetings with staff and advisers at the end of their presidencies than at the beginning.

It is also important to note, however, that with the exception of the final year of each administration, access levels for Cabinet secretaries (both inner and outer) as well as inner EOP directors tended to be greater than access for middle- and lower-tier WHO officials. This indicates that the battle for access to the president is not between the Cabinet and the White House staff per se, but rather between the *cabinet secretaries* and the *senior staff*. Given that the senior staff is housed directly in the White House and often consists of individuals with close, long-term personal relationships with the president, it is a battle in which cabinet secretaries stand little chance of prevailing. In sum, there is a strong relationship between formal position and pecking order in presidential networks, with White House senior staff (the most centralized and responsive set of personnel) having a significant advantage over all other groups in their access to the president.

INTERACTION STYLE: THE NETWORK "LENS"

While the institutional presidency provides a stable base upon which to build presidential advisory networks, presidents themselves play a crucial role in determining how these networks function. Each president comes to office with his own style. That style can offer a degree of stability in presidential networks. Presidential management style has received considerable scholarly attention both as a general concept and as it applies to specific presidencies.[22] Much of this focuses on the distinctions between the "formalistic" and the "collegial" modes of operation. The formalistic mode (usually associated with Eisenhower, Nixon, and Reagan) is hierarchically structured and highly centralized around a few top aides (primary among them the president's chief-of-staff). In contrast, the collegial mode (usually associated with Ford, Carter, and Clinton) is usually characterized by a wider ring of advisers having direct access to the president and by a greater degree of interplay among these actors.

In truth, however, all presidential advisory systems are hierarchically structured and centralized around the president. The real differences occurs in the number of people with regular, direct access to the president and in the types of forums (group vs. one-on-one) in which presidents prefer to meet with advisers. In other words, presidents have preferred *interaction styles* or general ways in which they prefer to interact with others in their *personal networks of contacts* (that is, the set of individuals with whom a president directly interacts). This preference is not limited to interactions with WHO staff, but rather reflects a general preference for how presidents like to organize their interaction with the broad array of executive branch officials. Here we examine the effects of interaction style on network operations, highlighting (1) the interplay between presidents and their "inner circle" of advisers and (2) the different types of forums in which presidents meet with their advisers.

PRESIDENTIAL CONTACT WITH "INNER CIRCLE" ADVISERS

Interaction style has its most recognized impact on patterning how presidents meet with their top advisers—those in their inner circle. Multidimensional scaling techniques were used to depict the pattern of interaction between President Nixon and the advisers he had the most contact with in the first (1969) and third (1971) years of his presidency (see figures 11.2 and 11.3).[23] The figures provide a snapshot of the president's inner circle at the outset of his administration (when relationships and interaction patterns were first forming) and a few years later, during a period when the president should be more comfortable with his job and staff and making the final push on his legislative agenda before the fourth year re-election period.[24]

The figures show that while Nixon kept a small cadre of close advisers (i.e., Haldeman, Ehrlichman, Kissinger, Schultz, Mitchell, and Ziegler), he would often bring new people into the inner core of his network for varying periods of time (such as Harlow, Colson, Connally, and Rogers). The figures also show two basic patterns persisting over time: (1) reliance on a relatively small number of advisers (particularly in comparison to the much broader Carter inner core), and (2) an emphasis on dyadic (one-on-one) rather than group interac-

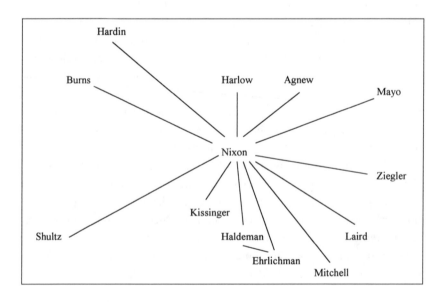

FIGURE 11.2. Interactions Among Nixon and His Closest Advisers, 1969
During the first year of his administration, Nixon maintained a number of close ties with his top foreign, domestic, and economic policy advisers as well as his vice president and top White House aides. With the exception of the Haldeman-Ehrlichman pairing, the pattern of interactions was dyadic rather than small group or collegial.

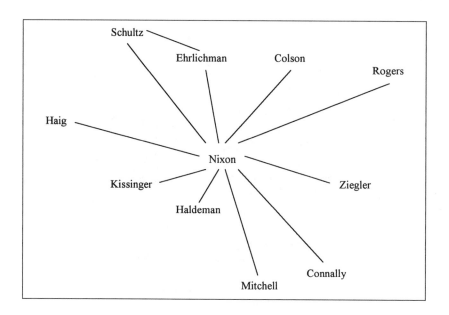

FIGURE 11.3.   Interactions Among Nixon and His Closest Advisers, 1971
The Nixon administration's focus on foreign affairs and the Vietnam War is obvious
during this period, as the president's advisory network was dominated by his top foreign policy and political advisers.

tions (denoted by the scarcity of strong adviser-adviser ties). Moreover, the figures show how the Nixon inner circle was dominated by WHO personnel. With
few exceptions (such as Hardin and Mayo in 1969), the only non-WHO officials in Nixon's inner core were close political allies or personal friends of the
president's (such as Mitchell, Schultz, and Connally).

Looking at the evolution of the Carter inner advisory core (see figures 11.4
and 11.5), we find a different scenario. During his first year in office (1977),
Carter's inner core was nearly twice the size of Nixon's during his first year (22
versus 12 advisers). There were also a larger number of strong adviser-adviser
linkages, reflecting Carter's preference for meeting with these advisers in moderate to large groups. Unlike the Nixon inner core, Carter initially included a
number of inner and outer Cabinet secretaries in his inner circle. Carter's pattern of meeting with his inner circle evolved somewhat by 1979, showing greater
policy-area differentiation (as evidenced by the clear policy-based groupings of
advisers at this time). Three basic groupings could be found during this period:
a foreign policy grouping (Brzezinski, Vance, Brown, Mondale, and Jordan), an

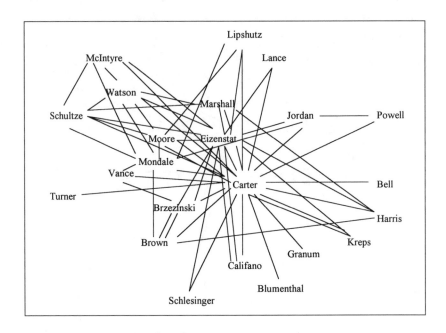

FIGURE 11.4.   Interactions Among Carter and His Closest Advisers, 1977
Carter's desire for a collegial advisory system at the outset of his administration is evident in this depiction of his inner advisory core. The network was comprised of 22
senior level advisers from the Cabinet, agencies of the EOP, and top White House assistants, who often met together in moderate to large size groups.

economic grouping (Kahn, McIntyre, Schultze, Mondale, and Eizenstat), and a
domestic policy/politics grouping (Eizenstat, Powell, Jordan, and Moore). The
figure also highlights the key roles Mondale, Jordan, and Eizenstat played as
"bridges" within the administration, serving as key links between these inner
circle network groups. As was true in the Nixon administration, by its third year
the Carter inner circle was dominated by WHO staff. Overall, these figures document Carter's transition from a very broad to a more narrow interaction style
as well as his movement away from maintaining strong ties with his cabinet secretaries to an emphasis on a WHO and foreign policy-based network.

Preferred Forums of Interaction

Next, looking at the effects of interaction style from a different perspective, we
find that over time both Nixon and Carter altered the way in which they met

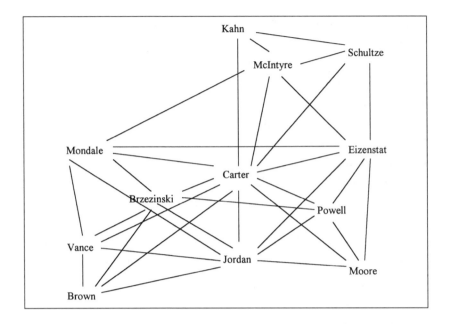

FIGURE 11.5. Interactions Among Carter and His Closest Advisers, 1979
The top of the Cater advisory network in 1979 was defined by three basic clusters of
advisers: foreign affairs, economic policy, and domestic politics. Chief of Staff Hamilton Jordan served as a bridge between the foreign affairs and domestic politics advisers, while the president's domestic adviser, Stuart Eizenstat, served as a common link
between the political and economic advisers.

with advisers(see table 11.3). Both presidents tended to move away from group
meetings (particularly formal meetings) to meetings with smaller groups as
well as more one-on-one interaction in person and by telephone. Both Nixon
and Carter have written about their growing impatience in office with formally
scheduled meetings, such as Cabinet and, in Nixon's case, Urban Affairs Council meetings.[25] This frustration apparently resulted in movement by both presidents away from formal group meetings.

Looking at specific changes in each president's network, we find substantial
differences as well. Although Nixon started his administration by emphasizing
informal group meetings as his preferred forum of interaction, he quickly
shifted during the course of his first term to meeting with advisers one-on-one.
By 1972, he was spending more than half of his meeting time in face-to-face
meetings with individual advisers and nearly 20 percent in telephone conversations with advisers and staff. Just over one quarter of his time was spent in infor-

TABLE 11.3   Percentage of Time Spent with Advisers by President, Type of Contact, and Year

	Percentage of Time Spent			
Nixon Administration	*1969*	*1970*	*1971*	*1972*
Telephone Contacts	12.4%	19.9%	18.1%	19.0%
One-on-One Meetings	33.1%	37.7%	45.9%	52.9%
Formal Group Meetings*	10.9%	4.2%	4.5%	2.9%
Other Group Meetings	43.6%	38.2%	31.5%	25.2%
(Total Time in Minutes)	(14,020)	(15,023)	(14,633)	(15,928)

Differences are significant at .001 level using Chi-Square test.

Carter Administration	*1977*	*1978*	*1979*	*1980*
Telephone Contacts	7.0%	11.4%	10.7%	19.8%
One-on-One Meetings	27.1%	23.0%	24.3%	24.6%
Formal Group Meetings*	10.3%	9.9%	8.1%	2.7%
Other Group Meetings	55.7%	55.8%	57.0%	52.9%
(Total Time in Minutes)	(9,766)	(8,918)	(10,627)	(7,130)

Differences are significant at .001 level using Chi-Square test.

*'Formal' group meetings are those officially designated in the daily diaries as a meeting of an official group (i.e., meeting of the Cabinet, National Security Council, Domestic Council, etc.).

Note: these percentages are based on yearly aggregates of the sampled data.

mal group meetings and less than 3 percent of his time was spent in formal group meetings (such as Cabinet or National Security Council meetings). These trends reflected Nixon's increasing preference for a narrower interaction style.

In contrast, Carter continually relied on informal groups, spending more than 50 percent of his time in such forums, while spending approximately one-fourth of his time in one-on-one meetings. Carter did, however, spend less time in formal group meetings and increased his use of telephone contacts. Further analysis (not shown here) indicates that this change had a significant effect on the access of outer-Cabinet (e.g., Commerce, HEW, HUD) and outer-EOP officials (e.g., Council for Environmental Quality, Office of Science and Technology). This fits with the earlier observation that over time, presidents may distance themselves from many of the more independent, less centralized elements of their advisory networks.

In sum, interaction style is a crucial element in determining presidential access patterns. While these styles may differ across presidencies, they tend over time to produce within these networks rather stable interaction patterns. For instance, Nixon maintained a relatively narrow network of contacts during his first four years in office. Carter, by comparison, moved from a very broad to a less broad style, yet his network of contacts in his final year in office was still considerably larger and reached deeper into the executive branch than Nixon's. Additionally, we find in both networks a reduction over time in the use of formal meetings (and for Nixon a reduction in group meetings of any type) and a greater reliance on more personal (and presumably more efficient) one-on-one interactions.

The Nixon and Carter presidencies suggest that presidents do seek to develop centralized and stable advisory networks, but such stability does not preclude some modification in these patterns over time. Formal differentiation of the executive branch, both in terms of hierarchy and separate organizational entities, serves as a template upon which presidents build and organize their networks of contacts. Personal interaction style leads to patterns of how and where these interactions take place. While there is evidence of changing interaction patterns in both administrations, the overarching trend was movement over time toward more personalized networks of contacts.

FLUIDITY AND COMPLEXITY IN PRESIDENTIAL NETWORKS

Although presidents may be motivated to seek efficiency and stability, advisory networks have remained in many respects extremely fluid. How fluid have they been? One answer can be found in presidential network turnover rates. *Network turnover* refers to the percentage change in network members from one time period to another; for instance, the percentage of advisers with presidential contact in one year who did *not* have contact the following year. Table 11.4 shows that the yearly turnover rates within the Nixon and Carter networks were remarkably high: averaging more than 60 percent per year for each. This means that six of every ten advisers in each president's personal network of contacts in one year were not members of the network the following year. At the individual adviser level, therefore, presidential networks are networks in flux.

Not surprisingly, turnover rates varied considerably according to the level of contact an adviser had with the president. Advisers were categorized *based on their level of access to the president* (not their formal positions) into one of three

TABLE 11.4   Network Turnover Rates by Administration, Access Level, and Year

Turn Over Rate*

	Nixon Network			Carter Network		
	69-70	*70-71*	*71-72*	*77-78*	*78-79*	*79-80*
Network:	64.3%	63.4%	69.9%	60.8%	70.8%	66.0%
	(83/129)	(78/123)	(95/136)	(141/232)	(143/202)	(105/159)
Inner Core:	58.3%	16.7%	50.0%	40.9%	33.3%	18.2%
	(7/12)	(1/6)	(5/10)	(9/22)	(5/15)	(2/11)
Outer Core:	33.3%	52.4%	61.1%	41.9%	71.9%	86.2%
	(4/12)	(11/21)	(11/18)	(13/31)	(23/32)	(25/29)
Periphery:	68.6%	68.8%	73.2%	66.5%	74.2%	65.6%
	(72/105)	(66/96)	(79/108)	(119/179)	(115/155)	(78/119)

*Turn over rate for each category is calculated as:

$$\frac{(\textit{\# network members in year 1 who were NOT in year 2})}{(\text{\# network members in year 1})}$$

These Ns are shown in the parentheses under the turn over percentage rates.

"circles" centered on the president: the inner core, outer core, and periphery. *Inner core* advisers had extraordinary access to the president, estimated as access (in minutes of contact with the president per year) one standard deviation or greater above the mean level of access for a given time period; *outer core* advisers had above average access levels (up to one standard deviation above the mean); and *peripheral* advisers had below average access levels.

Inner core turnover in the Nixon network ranged from 16.7% to 58.3% per year. The periods of high turnover reflected Nixon's shift to a smaller set of advisers during the 1969–70 and 1971–72 time periods. The lower rate stems from the opposite trend—an expansion of his inner core during the 1970–71 period. In contrast, turnover tended to be lower in Carter's inner core and it declined markedly over time, ranging from 40.9% (1977–78) to 33.3% (1978–79) to 18.2% (1979–1980)—reflecting a trend for Carter toward a somewhat smaller inner core. As the number of inner core members became smaller, the Carter network attained greater stability at its center. Ultimately, in each administration it was the "outer" cabinet personnel who tended to lose "inner" circle status. By the fourth year of each presidency, the Nixon and Carter inner cores were dominated by WHO staff.

For the outer core and periphery of each network, changes in turnover, on average, were higher and tended to escalate over time. In the Nixon network, outer core turnover ranged from 33.3% (1969–70) to 61.1% (1971–72). In the Carter network, turnover in the outer core jumped from 41.9% (1977–78) to 86.2% (1979–80) as Carter came to rely more on a smaller inner core, pushing some former insiders toward the periphery. Similarly, turnover was extremely high among peripheral advisers in each network (on average, just under 70%).

These turnover rates have two implications. On the one hand, presidents must deal with a diverse set of problems and demands—issues that require a tremendous amount of information. One way of handling this is to tap into a range of viewpoints and perspectives, particularly those of specialists in particular areas. As new problems arise, presidents call upon the appropriate personnel for the information they need. The result is a pattern of limited contact and high turnover for such officials. On the other hand, in terms of network efficiency and effectiveness, such high turnover rates (particularly toward the center of the network) would seem at some point to become problematic for the decisionmaking process, overloading the president with too many perspectives and inhibiting continuity. Overall, the high turnover rates associated within these networks underscore the extremely fluid nature of the advisory process at the presidential level.

Conclusions

Did the interactions of these two presidents and their advisers more closely follow the advice given by Moe (i.e., more unified and centrally directed networks of advice) or Neustadt (i.e., more dynamic systems with less emphasis on formal hierarchy and orderliness)? Nixon's and Carter's advisory networks clearly reflected both perspectives.

Both networks exemplified the institutionalization of the presidency. Each was arranged hierarchically and differentiated horizontally. Access was granted to individuals in units most closely affiliated with the president, in terms of both loyalty and geographic distance. Many advisers in units outside of the White House Office—no matter what their formal position in the executive branch hierarchy—gradually lost access to the president over time. These patterns occurred in both the Nixon and Carter networks.

Each president's preferred interaction style also had a stabilizing effect *within* each presidency, while producing different patterns *across* presidencies. Nixon began and ended his first term with a preference for one-on-one meetings with small numbers of advisers in a narrow interaction style. In contrast, Carter preferred to meet with larger numbers of advisers in group settings.

While he decreased over time both his number of group meetings and the number of advisers he met, he continued his broad interaction style until his final days in office. In short, both the institutionalization of the presidency and each president's own style helped to develop rather stable, centralized advisory networks.

Even with institutionalization, the Nixon and Carter networks were dynamic, as reflected in the high turnover rates for persons within these networks. Neither president was shy when it came to bringing in new individuals. The yearly turnover rate for their networks was over 60%, meaning that fewer than four of every ten advisers maintained contact with the president from one year to the next. The reasons for such a high turnover rate include retirement from office, lack of a further need for a particular adviser's expertise, and falling out of favor with the president. In short, while there were a number of stable patterns in the Nixon and Carter advisory networks, the participants in these networks were not a fixed group.

Unlike their predecessors, twenty-first-century presidents will engage in wide ranging interaction stretching throughout the executive branch. These advisory networks have elements of stability and centralization as well as fluidity and complexity. They are structured by institutional norms and precedents, shaped by the personal preferences of the individual holding the top office, and buffeted by both the demands of the office and the environment in which the presidency operates. If a president wants to enhance his chances of success in office he must bring with him certain skills which will enable him to build an anchored, yet dynamic network for information and to facilitate control over the executive branch. To do so effectively, an incoming president needs to find a mode of operation with which he is most comfortable and which accommodates institutional norms, yet allows the president to be responsive to environmental demands. Presidents need to operate effectively at the center of the advisory kaleidoscope.

APPENDIX: KEY TO ADMINISTRATION PERSONNEL NAMED IN THE STUDY

NIXON ADMINISTRATION PERSONNEL AND OFFICIAL TITLES:

Agnew, Spiro T.	Vice President
Burns, Arthur F.	Counsellor to the President/Chair, Federal Reserve Board
Colson, Charles	Special Council to the President

Connally, John	Secretary of the Treasury
Ehrlichman, John	White House Counsel
	Assistant for Domestic Affairs
Haig, Alexander	Deputy Assistant for National Security Affairs
Haldeman, H.R.	White House Chief of Staff
Hardin, Clifford M.	Secretary of Agriculture
Harlow, Bryce	Assistant to the President for Congressional Relations
Kissinger, Henry	Assistant for National Security Affairs
Laird, Melvin R.	Secretary of Defense
Mayo, Robert P.	Director, Bureau of the Budget
Mitchell, John	Attorney General
Rogers, William P.	Secretary of State
Shultz, George	Secretary of Labor
	Director, Office of Management and Budget
	Secretary of Treasury
Ziegler, Ronald	Press Secretary

CARTER ADMINISTRATION PERSONNEL AND OFFICIAL TITLES:

Bell, Griffin	Attorney General
Blumenthal, W. Michael	Secretary of Treasury
Brown, Harold	Secretary of Defense
Brzezinski, Zbigniew	Assistant for National Security Affairs
Califano, Joseph	Secretary of Health, Education, and Welfare
Eizenstat, Stuart	Assistant for Domestic Affairs and Policy
Granum, Rex L.	Deputy Press Secretary
Harris, Patricia R.	Secretary of Housing and Urban Development
Jordan, Hamilton	Assistant to the President
	White House Chief of Staff
Kahn, Alfred	Chair, Council on Wage and Price Stability
Kreps, Juanita M.	Secretary of Commerce
Lance, Bert	Director, Office of Management and Budget
Lipshutz, Robert J.	White House Counsel
Marshall, F. Ray	Secretary of Labor
McIntyre, James T.	Deputy Director, Office of Management and Budget
	Director, Office of Management and Budget
Mondale, Walter	Vice President
Moore, Frank B.	Assistant for Congressional Liaison
Powell, Jody	Press Secretary

Schlesinger, James	Assistant to the President
	Secretary of Energy
Schultze, Charles	Chair, Council of Economic Advisers
Turner, Stansfield	Director, Central Intelligence Agency
Vance, Cyrus	Secretary of State
Watson, Jack H.	Assistant for Intergovernmental Affairs

ACKNOWLEDGMENTS

I thank Bert Rockman, John Kessel, John Burke, Terry Moe, Bill Mishler, George Krause, and Jerel Rosati for their comments. This research was funded in part by a grant from the National Science Foundation (SBR-9510327). Any opinions, findings, and conclusions expressed in this article are those of the author and do not necessarily reflect the views of the National Science Foundation.

NOTES

1. Richard Neustadt, *Presidential Power and the Modern Presidents* (New York: The Free Press, 1990), pp. 150–151.

2. Gary King and Lyn Ragsdale, *The Elusive Executive: Discovering Statistical Patterns in the Presidency* (Washington, D.C.: CQ Press, 1988).

3. Terry M. Moe, "Presidents, Institutions, and Theory," in George C. Edwards III, John H. Kessel, and Bert A. Rockman, eds., *Researching the Presidency* (Pittsburgh: University of Pittsburgh Press, 1993).

4. *The Random House Dictionary of the English Language*, unabridged edition, Jess Stern, ed. (New York: Random House, 1967). p. 778.

5. David Knoke, *Political Networks: The Structural Perspective* (Cambridge: Cambridge University Press, 1990).

6. The mix of formal and informal relationships that defined the Nixon and Carter advisory networks are captured here using quantitative network analysis techniques. This analysis builds directly upon the pathbreaking work of John Kessel, who used detailed interviews to examine communication and influence relationships among staff members in the Nixon, Carter, and Reagan administrations (see John H. Kessel, "The Structures of the Reagan White House," *American Journal of Political Science* 28 (1984): 231–258; John H. Kessel, "The Structures of the Carter White House." *American Journal of Political Science* 27 (1983): 431–463; John H. Kessel, *The Domestic Presidency: Decision-making in the White House* (North Sci-

tuate, MA: Duxbury, 1975). Kessel's work is extended here in three important ways. First, he focused solely on relationships among presidential aides and advisers; the president himself was not included in the analysis. The perspective here, however, peers over the president's shoulder to look at *his* network of contacts. Second, where Kessel used in-depth interviews to define perceptions of interaction among staff members, this research relies on a more unobtrusive source for documenting contacts: the president's daily diary. Last, Kessel's analysis presented a snapshot of relationships within these administrations; in contrast, the use of the daily diaries provides a longitudinal look at network development and its dynamics. The research here also differs from that of others who have used daily diary data (noted in text above) in that it attempts to provide a more comprehensive explanation of network development and its dynamics over time using the advisory "kaleidoscope" as a model and demonstrating key aspects of this framework for the Nixon and Carter administrations.

7. Karen M. Hult, "Advising the President," in George C. Edwards III, John H. Kessel, and Bert A. Rockman, eds., *Researching the Presidency* (Pittsburgh: University of Pittsburgh Press, 1993), p. 113.

8. Neustadt, *Presidential Power*, p.xxi. A more complex picture of executive branch operations beyond the president's personal network is offered by Charles Walcott and Karen Hult, who examine the evolution of White House staff structures from 1929 to 1968 (see Charles E. Walcott and Karen M. Hult, *Governing the White House From Hoover Through LBJ* (Lawrence: University of Kansas Press, 1995). From their perspective, staff structures emerge as strategic responses to demands from the external political environment; in effect, they serve as coping mechanisms for the administration. Once in place, however, these structures can exercise an independent influence over behavior in the White House.

9. See Lee Sigelman and Dixie Mercer McNeil, "White House Decision-Making Under Stress." *American Journal of Political Science* 24 (1980): 652–653; James J. Best, "Who Talked with President Kennedy? An Interaction Analysis," *Presidential Studies Quarterly* 22 (1992): 351–369; James J. Best, "Presidential Learning: A Comparative Study of the Interactions of Carter and Reagan," *Congress and the Presidency* 15 (1988): 25–48; James J. Best, "Who Talked to the President When? A Study of Lyndon B. Johnson," *Political Science Quarterly* 103 (1988): 531–545; Robert J. Thompson, "Contrasting Models of White House Staff Organization: The Eisenhower, Ford, and Carter Experiences," *Congress and the Presidency* 19 (1992): 101–124. The diaries do have some limitations. While they provide a record of nearly all direct contacts between the president and his advisers, the diaries only allow analysis of adviser-adviser interactions in the presence of the president. Interactions among the advisers outside the purview of the president cannot be determined. Second, they do not allow analysis of indirect contacts. For example, we cannot determine

when an adviser is meeting with the president on his own behalf or if he is acting instead as an intermediary for a third party. Finally, the diaries do not contain sufficient information about the actual content of the meetings. Despite these constraints, the diaries remain the single, best source for documenting presidential interaction patterns.

10. A sampling strategy was employed in selecting data for cross-time analyses. Anticipating the use of time-series techniques to analyze these data (which require equal intervals between data points), a systematic sample of weekly data was drawn at six-week intervals resulting in the collection of 34 weekly blocks of data across each four-year term. All meetings were initially classified into one of six basic categories: "one-on-one," "formal group," "informal group," "boundary-spanning," "travel," and "social/ceremonial." One-on-one meetings consist of all bilateral interactions between the president and an adviser, including telephone calls and exclusive executive-adviser meetings. Informal group meetings are those involving the president and a relatively small number of advisers in ad-hoc meetings as well as semi-formal gatherings like working breakfasts or lunches. Formal organizational meetings involve more institutionalized processes, such as Cabinet or National Security Council meetings. Boundary-spanning meetings are those contacts in which the president meets with nonexecutive branch individuals, such as members of Congress, foreign dignitaries, or other governmental officials (excluding those meetings of a purely social or ceremonial nature). The travel and social/ceremonial categories are self-explanatory. Only meetings in the first three categories were included in this analysis as these were the forums in which most of the substantive interactions were expected to have taken place.

Each meeting was then coded as to the date, times, type of interaction, and persons attending the meeting. Dichotomies were used to denote the presence or absence of each executive branch member in these meetings. This study focused on individuals most likely involved in advising the president on policy matters or helping the president to perform as chief executive. Individuals playing traditionally administrative or facilitative roles (e.g., personal secretaries, interpreters, notetakers, etc.) were not included in the analysis; they account for less than 2 percent of the recorded contacts in the diaries. The overall data contained information on 3,399 meetings with 285 advisers and staff during the Nixon administration (1969–72) and 2,399 meetings with 501 advisers in the Carter administration (1977–81).

Previous research indicated that the total amount of time an adviser spent with the president is a better predictor of perceived influence in presidential advisory networks than are the frequency of contact or total time adjusted for intimacy (see Michael W. Link, *The Presidential Kaleidoscope: Advisory Networks in the Nixon and Carter Administrations*, Dissertation Research (University of South Carolina, 1996);

see also Michael W. Link and Charles W. Kegley, Jr., "Is Access Influence? Measuring Adviser-Presidential Interactions in Light of the Iranian Hostage Crisis," *International Interactions* 18 (1993): 343–364. Total time is used here to measure the levels of affiliation within these networks. Each dichotomous (present/absent) variable was weighted by multiplying it by the total time (in minutes) spent in each meeting. These weighted measures provide an indication of the *strength* of the connection between pairs of individuals in the network—not simply their coincidence in meetings. The weighted actor-in-meetings data were used to create a series of affiliation or actor-by-actor matrices, with each cell of the matrix representing the level of contact (measured in minutes) between all pairs of individuals in the network. These matrices as well as the initial meetings data were analyzed here.

11. For examples of research emphasizing the personalistic approach see Neustadt, *Presidential Power*; Irving L. Janis, *Groupthink* (Boston: Houghton Mifflin, 1982); Alexander George, *Presidential Decision-Making in Foreign Policy: The Effective Use of Information and Advice* (Boulder, CO: Westview Press, 1980); John Burke and Fred Greenstein, *How Presidents Test Reality: Decisions on Vietnam 1954 and 1965* (New York: Russell Sage Foundation, 1989); and Betty Glad and Michael W. Link, "President Nixon's Inner Circle of Advisers," *Presidential Studies Quarterly* 26 (1996): 13–40. Examples of the institutional approach can be found in Gary King and Lyn Ragsdale, *The Elusive Executive: Discovering Statistical Patterns in the Presidency* (Washington, D.C.: CQ Press, 1988); John Burke, *The Institutional Presidency* (Baltimore: Johns Hopkins University Press, 1992); and Terry M. Moe, "Presidents, Institutions, and Theory."

12. Advisory networks can serve more than a president's information needs. Oftentimes advisory networks can provide emotional and political support (see George, *Presidential Decision-making in Foreign Policy*). Studies have shown that during times of personal political crisis—when presidents feel under siege from external forces—presidents may turn to advisers who psychologically bolster them in their role, while at the same time turn away from advisers who offer concrete political advice that challenges the president's view of the situation (see Michael W. Link and Betty Glad, "Exploring the Psychodynamics of Advisory Relations: The Carter Administration's 'Crisis of Confidence,'" *Political Psychology* 15 (1994): 461–480. The Nixon advisory system sometimes contained and other times promoted the "dark impulses" of Nixon's personality (see Glad and Link, "President Nixon's Inner Circle of Advisers").

13. Moe has offered a provocative critique, arguing that the "personal presidency" has become akin to a doctrine of faith in presidential research (see Moe, "Presidents, Institutions, and Theory"). "The notion is that an acceptable explanation of presidential behavior," he asserts, "whatever its initial level of abstraction, must eventually be anchored in an understanding of why individual presidents

make the specific decisions they do" (p 342). While presidential personality and individual management style clearly affect presidential behavior, they are poor foundations upon which to build generalizable theories. The result has been a stifling of theory building in the study of the presidency. As an alternative, Moe proposes a rational actor approach, built around the institutional aspects of the presidency: in particular, a theoretical framework built on the politics of "structural choice" whereby presidents employ their formal powers to "provide themselves with a structural capacity for leadership," building institutions to meet their needs. This article borrows loosely from some of Moe's theoretical ideas.

14. See Burke, *The Institutional Presidency.*

15. See Moe, "Presidents, Institutions, and Theory."

16. Terry M. Moe, "The Politicized Presidency," in John E. Chubb and Paul E. Peterson, eds., *The New Direction in American Politics* (Washington, DC: Brookings, 1985).

17. Colin Campbell, *Managing the Presidency: Carter, Reagan and the Search for Executive Harmony* (Pittsburgh: University of Pittsburgh Press, 1986).

18. Moe, "Presidents, Institutions, and Theory"; Burke, *The Institutional Presidency.*

19. I. M. Destler, Leslie H. Gelb, and Anthony Lake, *Our Own Worst Enemy: The Unmaking of American Foreign Policy* (New York: Simon and Schuster, 1984).

20. Cronin classified cabinet departments as "inner cabinet" and "outer cabinet" based on their relative importance and relationship to the president (see Thomas E. Cronin, *The State of the Presidency,* 2nd ed. (Boston: Little, Brown, 1980). The "inner cabinet" departments—State, Defense, Treasury, and Justice—have historically (in one form or another) been a part of the executive branch since the Washington Administration. Similarly, the agencies of the Executive Office of the Presidency were classified here into "inner EOP" and "outer EOP" based on their historical importance to past presidents. For this analysis, "inner EOP" agencies included the Office of Management and Budget (OMB), the Council of Economic Advisers (CEA), and the Central Intelligence Agency (CIA). All other agencies were categorized as "outer EOP" agencies.

21. Two difficulties arose in categorizing these officials. First, a number of them changed positions over time, moving either to another department or moving up (or down) within an agency. In these cases, officials were classified according to the unit affiliation and position they held for the longest period of time during a given calendar year. Second, questions of comparability arose when trying to classify officials into top, middle, and lower tiered positions, particularly within the White House Office. There can be considerable variation in how presidents choose to title their top aides and assistants. A "special assistant to the president" in one administration may not mean the same thing (i.e., be in the same tier) in another adminis-

tration. For this reason, memoirs and other historical documentation were closely consulted when classifying "top tier" (i.e., senior staff) and "middle tier" WHO personnel. The "lower tier" personnel, therefore, were all of the remaining individuals who did not fit into the "top" or "middle" categories. Given the access distributions for these levels (as shown in table 11.1), the categorizations do capture the variations in access we would expect for these three classes of officials.

22. For examples of more general works on presidential style, see George, *Presidential Decision-making in Foreign Policy*; Richard T. Johnson, *Managing the White House* (New York: Harper, 1974); and Roger B. Porter, *Presidential Decision Making* (New York: Cambridge University Press, 1980). Studies of the styles of particular presidents include Burke and Greenstein, *How Presidents Test Reality*; and Fred I. Greenstein, *The Hidden Hand Presidency* (New York: Basic, 1982).

23. These figures were initially constructed using multidimensional scaling techniques to plot the interaction matrix of the president and his advisers in two-dimensional space. In some instances the initial plots were modified to provide the reader with a clearer view of the relationships among advisory group members. The lines connecting pairs of individuals indicate that they spent considerable time together in meetings with the president. Empirically, these lines indicate levels of interaction one standard deviation or more above the mean level of access for all advisers during a given year. The figures are used here to illustrate the basic pattern of interaction between each president and his "inner core" advisers as well as interactions among core members in the presence of the president.

24. Paul C. Light, *The President's Agenda* (Baltimore: Johns Hopkins University Press, 1991).

25. Richard M. Nixon, *RN: The Memoirs of Richard Nixon* (New York: Simon and Schuster, 1990); Jimmy Carter, *Keeping Faith: Memoirs of a President* (New York: Bantam Books, 1982).

PART 4

The President in the Political System

CHAPTER 12

The President in the Political System:
In Neustadt's Shadow

Jeffrey K. Tulis

Presidential Power's status as a classic account of American politics is due less to Richard Neustadt's insightful interpretation of "the presidency at mid-century," than it is to the fact that he articulated an entirely new way to think about presidential politics.[1] Neustadt's influence is evidenced by our own inclination to think about the presidency with categories he constructed, as well as by our inability to see how formative those categories have become.

In the Preface, Neustadt describes his purpose as "to explore the power problem of the man inside the White House." His innovation was to describe and analyze the power problem from the perspective of the president himself.

> To analyze the problem of obtaining personal power one must try to view the Presidency from over the President's shoulder, looking out and down with the perspective of *his* place. This is not the way we conventionally view the office; ordinarily we stand outside it, looking in. From outside, or from below, a President is "many men" or one man wearing many "hats," or playing many "roles." Conventionally we divide the job of being President according to the categories such a view suggests, "Chief Legislator," "Chief Administrator," "Chief of Party," and the like, and analyze the job by treating chieftanships in turn. For many purposes, however it becomes a block to insight. The President himself plays every "role," wears every "hat" at once. Whatever he may do in one role is by definition done in all, and has effects in all. When he attempts to make his wishes manifest, his own will felt, he is one

man, not many. To analyze this aspect of his job we need a frame of reference as unlike the usual categories as the view from inside out is unlike that from outside in.[2]

Neustadt sought to replace systemic perspectives with a presidential perspective. This way of thinking may be labeled "institutional partisanship," because it is not just the replacement of systemic thinking, but also a new view of the political system itself from the perspective of the presidency. Neustadt's analysis of presidential power is simultaneously a picture of the American political system as a whole. Previous scholars' accounts of the presidency were colored by their vantage point "outside," from one or other version of the system. Neustadt's account of the system is colored by his view of it "from over the president's shoulder." Thus, for example, Neustadt tends to equate presidential success with systemic success, and to treat presidential failure as deleterious for the polity.

Neustadt found "nothing has been harder" than his effort to escape from systemic points of view.[3] It is a measure of his success that contemporary students of the presidency may find nothing more difficult than an effort to escape from the institutionally partisan, strategic concerns that Neustadt established. Two relatively new communities of scholars appear to be trying to transcend Neustadt's categories of understanding and thereby reestablish the significance of systemic concerns. Both communities of scholars are sometimes labeled "new institutionalists" but they are very different from each other. One group is historically oriented and seeks to redescribe political patterns and practices across time. Another group treats presidential politics as a site suitable for the elaboration and application of rational choice theory. The chapters that follow by Lieberman, Epstein and O'Halloran, and McCarty and Razaghian, are useful illustrations of the promise and the limits of each of these new institutionalisms to establish a systemic point of view.

HISTORY AND PRESIDENTIAL POLITICS

Robert Lieberman offers a cautious critique of the most important book produced by the new historical community, Stephen Skowronek's *The Politics Presidents Make*.[4] It is helpful here to sketch the main themes of Skowronek's book by contrasting them with Neustadt's *Presidential Power*.[5]

Neustadt included three formative observations or premises that effectively reshaped the study of this institution: (1) that the leadership tasks of recent presidents are fundamentally different from those of past presidents, (2) that the experiences of Truman and Eisenhower exemplify the full range of approaches to modern leadership tasks, and (3) that the fundamental leadership problem is to strategically husband power. Skowronek's book challenges each of these commonplaces.

Against the notion that the "modern" presidency marks a distinct break with the past, Skowronek shows how the basic leadership problems have persisted over two centuries despite enormous changes in economic, social, and organizational arrangements. Presidents often have more in common with some nineteenth-century president than with an immediate predecessor or successor. To show this, Skowronek develops a notion of "political time." Presidents find themselves facing different obstacles to leadership depending upon their relation to a party/policy "regime." Presidents who build regimes are more like other builders than they are like presidents who consolidate or repudiate or merely articulate an existing regime.

To counter the notion that Truman and Eisenhower exhaust the viable leadership possibilities today, Skowronek thus offers four basic types of leaders and leadership situations: (1) presidents who find themselves opposed to a vulnerable regime (Jefferson, Lincoln, or FDR), a situation Skowronek calls the politics of reconstruction; (2) presidents who find themselves affiliated with a vulnerable regime (Adams, Pierce, Buchanan, Hoover, or Carter), a circumstance called the politics of disjunction; (3) presidents who must oppose a resilient regime (Tyler, Andrew Johnson, Wilson, Nixon), a politics of preemption; and (4) presidents who are affiliated with a resilient regime (Monroe, Polk, Theodore Roosevelt, LBJ, and Bush), labeled the politics of articulation. The requisites for success, indeed the very standards of success, are different for presidents in each of the four leadership situations.

The most interesting aspect of the book is the way it refutes the commonplace about power. According to Skowronek, presidents in different leadership situations face different obstacles in their attempts to create warrants for their authority. The key idea here is that authority is more crucial to presidential success than is power. One could say that Skowronek has redescribed presidential leadership in a way that locates its problems at the juncture of institutional maneuvers and cultural ethos, or of partisan bargaining and public philosophy, or of thought and politics.

Against this background, Skowronek compares presidents along two dimensions. He compares presidents to others situated similarly in political time, and he compares them, as well, to others situated proximate to them in chronological (historical) time. He does not so much refute Neustadt's account as substantially modify it.

Robert Lieberman tries to demonstrate that Neustadtian problems of coalition building are more common to recent presidents (Eisenhower, Nixon, Kennedy, and LBJ) than Skowronek allows. Moreover, he illustrates the ways in which Eisenhower and Nixon are especially successful notwithstanding their oppositional relation to the prevailing regime, while Kennedy and LBJ face a number of obstacles notwithstanding their affiliation with a governing regime. To the extent that Lieberman finds such patterns, he confirms Skowronek's animating insight that the dynamics of opposition and affiliation are different, while he offers an alternative interpretation of the content of those differences. Lieberman's critique of Skowronek is also muted by the fact that Skowronek himself does not abandon Neustadt's concerns, but rather supplements them. Skowronek could hardly disagree with Lieberman's conclusion that "to lead successfully, presidents must consider not only the broad structural nature of their authority but also the narrower quotidian problems of presidential power that Neustadt identified a generation ago. . ."[6]

Stepping back from the particular arguments Lieberman and Skowronek advance to the historical perspective that they share, one can't help but be struck by the fact that Neustadt's institutional partisanship continues to shape their efforts. Success, for Lieberman and for Skowronek is still measured by the preferences of the presidency rather than by the needs of the polity. Presidents are judged by the extent to which they succeed in accomplishing their partisan objectives rather than the extent to which they serve the interests of the polity. Like Neustadt, Skowronek and Lieberman assume that presidential accomplishment of partisan agendas is in the interest of the polity as a whole. For all the talk of regimes, structures and larger entities outside of the presidency, the world is still viewed from over the president's shoulder. Emblematic of this, "regimes" are partisan coalitions for these scholars rather than the constitution of a whole polity in the classic Aristotelian sense.

RATIONAL CHOICE AND PRESIDENTIAL POLITICS

Lieberman and Neustadt remind us of the importance of the president's bargaining skills for securing substantive legislative agendas. David Epstein and Sharyn O'Halloran argue that much public policy is constructed in the executive branch itself rather than through the legislative process. In writing the rules that give effect to legislation, members of the executive branch, including those appointed through the process McCarty and Razaghian describe, are legislators themselves and it is through the construction of regulations and rules that most of governmental policy is advanced. Thus, they argue, the president's ability to secure his own agenda is affected more by the extent of discretion bestowed upon him by Congress than by his ability to achieve a substantive legislative agenda in Congress.

Congress may grant presidents more or less discretion and they may locate discretionary authority in agencies closer or farther from the president's control. The burden of Epstein and O'Halloran's essay is to show that these variables are affected more by structures outside the presidency than they are by the president's bargaining skills. Specifically, they hypothesize that under unified government presidents will be given more discretion and more control, while under divided government presidents will be granted less discretion by Congress, and discretion that is delegated will be placed in agencies farther from the presidents control.

The ideas animating this argument are these: one who holds power might find it efficient to delegate it to someone else, given the press of other business or the need to accomplish many objectives in a relatively short time; the power holder will choose to delegate more power to the extent that the agent of that delegation shares the policy preferences of the delegator. Among political scientists and economists who employ this sort of reasoning, this is known as a principal/agent model. In Epstein and O'Halloran's account, Congress is the principal and the president, the executive agencies, and other units of government, such as the states, are the agents.

Epstein and O'Halloran test their hypotheses by examining the extent and location of delegation in legislation enacted between 1947 and 1990, a period that traverses episodes of unified and divided government. For the most part their data confirm their hypotheses. Congress tends to be more generous with presidents who share the majority's partisan perspective.

This confirmation is not perfect and it is useful to reflect upon the most striking counterexample to their argument. Under unified and divided governments Congress has delegated substantial budget control authority to the President and to the executive's Office of Management and Budget. In the case of budget control, the Congress has available to it its own agency, the Congressional Budget Office, which it has declined to employ in a series of budget control acts. No executive agency could be as closely controlled by Congress as its own budget office. Why does a Republican Congress cede so much power to a Presidency controlled by Democrats? There appear to be no easy hypotheses that readily explain this outcome, but other attempts to do so may be more interesting than those provided thus far by rational choice theories.[7]

Clearly, Epstein and O'Halloran move us away from the presidency-centered institutional partisanship characteristic of Neustadt's perspective. Their attention to structural variables might therefore lead one to believe that they had succeeded in recovering a systemic perspective. Rather, they have replaced presidency-centered institutional partisanship with a Congress oriented perspective. Conceiving of the Congress as principal and the president as agent privileges a view of the Constitution as one in which the legislative branch is supreme and it invites the reader to think about American politics from the legislative perspective.

Congress-centered institutional partisanship poses difficulties analogous to Neustadt's presidency-centered view. Just as Neustadt might be, and has been, criticized for not reflecting upon the appropriateness of presidential power, so might Epstein and O'Halloran be criticized for not reflecting upon the legitimacy of Congressional delegation of power. It should never be assumed that politics is "efficient" to the extent that Congress secures its preferences. Sometimes frustrating legislative will is systemically desirable.

When is delegation of power responsible and when does it represent an abdication of responsibility? One can only raise and answer this question from a systemic perspective, a perspective upon, not from, Congress's point of view. Viewing the political world from the legislative point of view downplays the enormous literature on the "nondelegation doctrine" as well as the growth of delegation in the twentieth century compared to earlier eras.[8] This is not solely a normative issue; it is an empirical problem as well. Epstein and O'Halloran are correct to suggest that Congress delegates power when it serves its interests to do so, but it should also be stressed that what Congress takes its interests to be is decisively shaped by the constitutional order in which it operates. Until we have a systemic or constitutional theory, we can not account for the origins and meanings of legislative and presidential preferences.

Like Epstein and O'Halloran, Nolan McCarty and Rose Razaghian are interested in the institutional processes that constrain the president's control of the bureaucracy. McCarty and Razaghian focus upon the politics of nomination and appointment to higher civil service positions in domestic agencies. Their most interesting finding is that presidents do not enjoy a "honeymoon period," as is conventionally assumed, in which public opinion supportive of newly elected presidents ensures that presidential preferences are endorsed by the legislative branch. Instead, presidents tend to nominate their least controversial appointments first and delay appointments for which they anticipate political contestation. Thus, what looks like a honeymoon is actually an exercise in strategic anticipation. Presidents don't escape conflict with the legislature over the composition of the bureaucracy. Rather, they strategically delay conflict that is present—thought not publicity noticed—from the beginning of their administrations.

"Strategic anticipation" is offered as an alternative to "bargaining persuasion" in Neustadt's formulation. Yet their study elaborates, more than it refutes, Neustadt's theory since they retain Neustadt's emphasis upon strategy understood from the president's point of view. As they state, "The goal for new presidents is to find the most able candidates who will still be responsive to their wishes." In the shadow of Neustadt, they seek ways to steer presidents clear of the "hazards of transition."

Just as Epstein and O'Halloran do not reflect upon the legitimacy of power, McCarty and Razaghian do not consider the merits of systemic theories of bureaucratic responsibility. Their account trades on a notion of presidential success that assumes the domestic bureaucracy should be staffed to efficiently carry out presidential preferences. Yet since the creation of the bureaucracy in the first Congress, alternative theories of bureaucratic organization and control have been advanced and continue to inform our separation of powers system. For example, for some purposes it may be important that the bureaucracy carry out Congressional, not presidential, will. For other purposes, it may be necessary for bureaucrats to have enough distance and discretion to resist Congressional and presidential preferences. A truly systemic point of view would accommodate these competing requisites of constitutional governance. Without a constitutional theory, one can't assess the appropriateness of the constraints on presidential appointment that McCarty and Razaghian identify so clearly.

Constitutional Thinking

Although the three essays in this section of our volume function within the shadow of Neustadt's paradigm, they also implicitly raise several issues that advance a systemic perspective. For example, Epstein and O'Halloran see an intellectual payoff from their study to be placing "the personal victories and failures of individual presidents within their proper context in our separation of powers system."[9] The issue of delegation, which animates their study, highlights the relation of the executive and the legislature in a way that presupposes their differences as institutional entities. Neustadt had done much to efface those differences by recasting the American system as "separate institutions sharing power."[10] Neustadt's formulation implied that power was a single kind of entity, like energy, over which multiple institutions competed. The issue of delegation reminds us that there are multiple kinds of power, captured in the many particular delegations, as well as in the very notion of delegation itself.

The delegation issue also raises a deeper theoretical problem. It is commonly thought that the engine of American politics is the competition for political turf between the President, Congress, and at times, the Supreme Court. In The Federalist, this idea was referred to as "ambition counteracting ambition."[11] In that famous defense of the Constitution, it was argued that self-interest of ambitious politicians could be tethered to institutional prerogatives and thus tamed and channeled for the public good. But tendencies toward delegation or deference in our time suggest an institutional culture in which ambitious politicians cede authority and responsibility rather than seek to advance it. The meaning and logic of separation of powers is thus ripe for reformulation.

McCarty and Razaghian's chapter provides a useful occasion to reconsider the logic of bureaucratic organization. Their data show that presidents delay nominations for second and third tier positions, not just to postpone conflict, but also to give their principal appointees the opportunity to recruit loyal lieutenants. This reflects a theory of bureaucratic organization first articulated by President Andrew Jackson in debate with Daniel Webster. Against Jackson, Webster argued that the bureaucracy should not be thought of as a hierarchy responsible to a president, but rather as an arrangement of offices independently responsible to law. The recent debate over the independent counsel statute has again raised this issue, as have the development of independent regulatory agencies. To the extent that *some* of our bureaucratic agencies reflect Webster's constitutional view, the constraints upon presidential preference may sometimes reflect the different kinds of functions performed by the contested offices. To the extent that the committee structure of Congress resembles the bureaucracy's functional differentiation, McCarty and Razaghian's prediction that some committees will be more partisan than others may actually be a proxy for this more fundamental constitutional fact.

Lieberman's elaboration of Skowronek's study raise an interesting implication for the status of executive leadership in a constitutional system. Neustadt gave us the most articulate expression of the idea that there is an ideal form of executive leadership. Political obstacles may vary, tactics may change, but a president should always seek to husband power in order to advance a positive partisan agenda. By showing that presidents face different leadership prospects at different stages of "political time," Skowronek raises the possibility that there are several ideals of leadership, not just one. For example, a President in an oppositional stance like President Clintons facing a Republican Congress in 1995 might seek to modify, ameliorate, contest, and improve the Republican agenda rather than to advance a coherent agenda of his own. I believe this is in fact what Clinton did, but he continued to seek to be a Neustadtian President; he sought to leave a legacy like other Presidents who stood at reconstructive moments of political time. By not knowing the kind of leadership he in fact provided, he undercut his ability to provide it well, he did not give the people occasion to understand his accomplishment, and he diminished the possibility of a flattering legacy. Skowronek's book provides the empirical basis for a constitutional defense of multiple forms of leadership even as he, and Lieberman, continue to privilege the reconstructive ideal at the heart of the modern presidency.

NOTES

1. Richard E. Neustadt, *Presidential Power* (New York: Wiley, 1960).

2. Ibid., p. vi.

3. Ibid.

4. Stephen Skowronek, *The Politics Presidents Make: Leadership from John Adams to George Bush* (Cambridge: Harvard University Press, 1993).

5. This synopsis is drawn from my essay, "On the Politics Skowronek Makes," *Journal of Policy History* 8 (1196) 2: 248–49.

6. Chapter 13.

7. For a superb critique of rational choice theory in political science, see Donald P. Green and Ian Shapiro, *Pathologies of Rational Choice Theory* (New Haven: Yale University Press, 1994). I am grateful to Jasmine Farrier for educating me about the anomalies of budget politics. She is currently working on a dissertation on that subject.

8. See especially, Theodore Lowi, *The End of Liberalism* (New York: Norton, 1969) and Sotirios A. Barber, *The Constitution and the Congressional Delgation of Power* (Chicago: University of Chicago Press, 1975).

9. Chapter 14.

10. Neustadt, *Presidential Power*, pp. 26–29.

11. *The Federalist*, No. 51.

CHAPTER 13

Political Time and Policy Coalitions: Structure and Agency in Presidential Power

Robert C. Lieberman

In *The Politics Presidents Make*, Stephen Skowronek upends Neustadt's personal model of presidential power. Since Franklin Roosevelt, Neustadt argues, presidents have faced a constant and enduring challenge of leadership.[1] Occupying an office of limited formal powers and facing a fragmented and often recalcitrant political system, presidents must persuade others to do their bidding. The skills and attributes that make for successful leadership—reputation, prestige, perception, and judgment—have, in Neustadt's picture, remained constant throughout the modern presidential era.[2] By contrast, Skowronek situates the presidency in a recurring regime pattern in American political development. Presidents come to power within regimes: "commitments of ideology and interest embodied in preexisting institutional arrangements."[3] The leadership challenge a particular president faces depends on his position within the prevailing regime; it may or may not be the same as that of his predecessors and successors. Consequently, Skowronek's analysis draws attention not to individual presidents and their personal styles and skills but to the structural pattern of regime change and the cycle of presidents within regimes—a pattern of "political time."

The contrast between Neustadt and Skowronek poses a formidable challenge for analysts both of presidential power and of American political institutions.[4] Which picture more accurately accounts for the contours of presidential leadership in American history? Which offers a better guide for would-be leaders? Where should we look for evidence about the character of presidential leadership: to particular and personal portraits of individual presidents, or rather to general and structural accounts of the historical moments in which presidents are situated? These antinomies of presidential power recapitulate a more general dilemma in the social sciences, between structure and agency—between more or less deterministic patterns of social reality and the creative potential of individual human actors. In this essay I argue that neither Neustadt's agency-centered model nor Skowronek's structural model fully explains presidential leadership. Rather, I advance a theory of presidential leadership that emphasizes moments of structured choice, opportunities for strategic presidential action within structurally defined and delimited situations.[5] I begin by contrasting Neustadt's and Skowronek's theoretical frameworks and sketching an alternative. I then explore this alternative through a focused account of presidential leadership in social policy in the post-New Deal era, from Eisenhower to Nixon. I conclude by discussing the broader theoretical implications of a structured choice approach and offering some reflections on Bill Clinton's presidential leadership.

CONFIGURATION AND CHOICE IN PRESIDENTIAL LEADERSHIP

The central concept motivating Skowronek's analysis of presidential power is the "regime"—the particular configuration of institutions, interests, and ideas that organizes politics and policymaking during a given era.[6] While the constitutional structure of American government has changed little in two centuries, the way Americans and their leaders understand and interpret that structure and translate it into actual governing practice has changed dramatically. Regimes in American political development comprise arrangements at this subconstitutional level that are relatively stable. Regimes are constituted at a variety of levels, from formal institutions (such as the structure of Congress or the administrative state) to the social bases of politics (such as party alignments and coalitions and patterns of interest representation); from ideas (such as prevailing beliefs about the proper role of government) to informal norms (such as patterns of congressional behavior). Nested within these broadly defined institutional arrangements are commitments to particular policies which become the touchstone for political action and conflict for leaders and would-be leaders over the course of a generation or more.

Except for those rare moments of opportunity when a regime is ripe for reconstruction, a president comes to power within a prevailing regime, which largely shapes the nature of his leadership. Presidents are either affiliated with the prevailing regime—products of its dominant community of interests and adherents of its ideology and policy commitments—or they are opposed to it. An affiliated president such as Lyndon Johnson, Skowronek argues, takes his cues from the regime itself and engages in a "politics of articulation"—finishing the unfinished work of his predecessors, extending the scope and reach of policies associated with the regime. A president opposed to the regime, such as Richard Nixon, however, finds himself in treacherous waters. His very basis for leadership is necessarily rooted in his opposition to the regime, and he may rightly see his own claim to the presidency itself as the expression of public dissatisfaction with what has come before.[7] Such a president cannot simply kowtow to the prevailing regime, but any attempt to repudiate it runs the risk of political implosion. His leadership will constitute a "politics of preemption," "an unabashedly mongrel politics," cobbling together elements of regime and opposition into a hybrid that falls between the simple regime-opposition categories.[8] For Skowronek, these regime orientations create structured contexts for presidential leadership that recur, defining what he calls "political time," so that even consecutive presidents can face dramatically different political and institutional challenges. What defines a president's leadership is his place in political time rather than his own skill in facing down an undifferentiated string of challenges.

Nevertheless, these boundaries contain within them a large space where presidents must act—must, as Neustadt would have it, *choose* how to act in order to meet particular, momentary, situational imperatives. These situations in which presidents act are, as Skowronek's analysis captures, determined by historically articulated institutional configurations. But although these configurations determine context, they do not altogether determine action.[9] Part of the disjunction between Skowronek's and Neustadt's analyses of presidential power arise from the different levels of generality at which they aim their explanations: Skowronek at the broad pattern, taking administrations whole, and Neustadt at the more particular, focusing on moves presidents make within their administrations. A comprehensive approach to presidential leadership should be able to account for both levels. The configurational regularities that Skowronek identifies across American political history account splendidly for the similarities he quite ingeniously coaxes us to see among similarly situated presidents. Thus "articulators"—Monroe, Polk, Theodore Roosevelt, Lyndon Johnson—resemble one another, as do "preempters"—Tyler, Taylor, Andrew Johnson, Cleveland, Wilson, Eisenhower, Nixon, and Clinton. The macro-configurational scheme, however, is less successful at explaining more fine-grained differences *among* similarly situated presidents—why and how do Eisenhower and Nixon differ? Johnson and Kennedy?

To account for such differences in presidential leadership, we need an approach that, while keeping the macrohistorical context in view, pays more direct attention to the specifically individual problems of presidential leadership, particularly the problems of building and sustaining governing coalitions. Governance in the American political system depends on the ability to form coalitions again and again in a context where no institutions—not even parties—can maintain stable coalitions for long.[10] In fact, it is the very absence of party government and concentrated political responsibility in American politics that creates the dynamic interplay between regimes and presidents and requires presidents to attend regularly to the problems of building and maintaining coalitions across parties and even across the regime-opposition boundary.[11] Moreover, the presidency is perhaps the most changeable element of the American political system. Affiliated and opposition presidents may come and go in quick succession, but the other institutions of government do not reverse their courses so easily. Even when the presidency changes parties, most of the rest of the government remains in the same hands. While a very small change in presidential voting, for example, might mean the difference between an affiliated and an opposition president, similar shifts in congressional voting may not produce such dramatic change in the composition of Congress.[12] Similarly, the courts respond to electoral outcomes only slowly and by accretion, as presidents fill vacancies and precedents are modified. Except for the very top layers, the bureaucracy remains in the same hands, making it very hard for presidents to effect major administrative change.[13] Outside of government, the same array of organized interests, public moods and opinions, mass media, and other forces that faced one president remains to confront his successor, regardless of party or regime orientation.[14]

The imperatives for presidential leadership in such a system, then, arise not only from the general status of the prevailing regime and the president's place in it, but also from the more particular forces that a president faces at each moment of his presidency. At such moments, presidents face strategic choices—choices given by institutionally configured situations, but choices nonetheless. Presidents make choices about policy and political strategy: what issues to take up, which policy initiatives to pursue and when to pursue them, which party or faction or interest group leaders to court and which to shun, and so forth. For example, Franklin Roosevelt chose in the middle of his first term to recast his political strategy for economic reconstruction, moving away from the business-government partnership approach of the National Industrial Recovery Act and the Agricultural Adjustment Act and toward a more populist agenda focusing on welfare state policies, labor rights, and aggregate economic management.[15] Buoyed by Democratic gains in the 1934 congressional elections and facing challenges from the courts, labor, and business, Roosevelt chose to embrace an emerging coalition and welcomed the contempt of the "economic royalists" whose favor he had courted in the first years of his presidency. In fact, this might be, to paraphrase former *Washington Post* editor Ben Bradlee, the essential act of presidential leadership: presidents choose.[16] In making their choices, presidents weigh such forces as the partisan composition of Congress and the fault lines within parties, the president's own standing among the Washington establishment and the country, the opinions and moods of the public, and historical happenstance. These forces not only shape the choices facing presidents but also define the very nature of the regime itself. If these factors sound familiar, it is because they echo precisely the characteristics of the political system that Richard Neustadt identified in 1960 as the cornerstones of presidential power.

In his later reflections on the presidency, Neustadt points to a president's "purpose,"—the issues that, over the course of a presidency, draw from him "words and acts that lead to irreversible commitment." It is such purpose, not ideology or passion or private desires or even initial intentions, that draws presidents to cast their lots for or against aspects of a regime. Presidential purpose comes not from a president's own predilections but from the decisions he makes "taking the real world as he finds it." "Franklin Roosevelt," Neustadt writes,

> did not enter office bent on becoming a "traitor to his class." Truman did not swear the oath with any notion that he was to take this country into the Cold War. Lincoln certainly did not assume the Presidency to gain the title of "Great Emancipator." Johnson's massive victory of 1964 surely was not intended as a prelude to the Vietnam War we know today.[17]

Rather, the political and historical identity of these presidents emerged from discrete and politically considered actions, choices (or series of choices) that presidents made to cope with and manage politically constructed crises of leadership. The task for analysts of presidential power is to locate these strategic moments which lie at the intersection of regimes and choices, of structure and agency.

PRESIDENTS AND THE NEW DEAL WELFARE STATE

The remainder of this essay explores this structured choice approach through an examination of the domestic policy initiatives of a sequence of modern presidents, from Eisenhower to Nixon. These four consecutive administrations are ideally situated to compare this perspective with both the regime and personalistic views of presidential leadership. Together they mark the long post-World War II ascendancy of the New Deal order, which was a regime of relatively stable—if internally riven—partisan alignments, group allegiances, ideological fault lines, and organized interests.[18] These administrations include two affiliated presidencies (Kennedy and Johnson) and two opposed presidencies (Eisenhower and Nixon) with two abrupt shifts—from opposed to affiliated in 1960 and back to opposed in 1968. While the period of these administrations saw, at least until Vietnam, a broad Cold War consensus in foreign policy, this was a period of sharp disagreement about domestic policy. The essential national policy commitments of the New Deal—labor rights, Keynesian macroeconomics, and the welfare state—were hotly contested during this period.[19] While these commitments enjoyed basic support, there were substantial disagreements about whether they should be expanded, maintained, reduced, or even eliminated altogether. In none of these broad policy areas was the postwar period a steady-state era. In the case of labor, the rights granted by the Wagner Act of 1935 were sharply curtailed by the Taft-Hartley Act, passed by a Republican Congress over President Truman's veto in 1947. Keynesian economic policies, which relied on government spending to maintain and stabilize the economy, meandered in and out of the national debate from the 1930s until the 1960s, when they were finally adopted by the Kennedy administration, albeit in a form more circumscribed than their original conception. The welfare state expanded, but often in surprising ways, with both support and resistance often coming from unexpected quarters.

The regime perspective on presidential leadership suggests a broad pattern of differences and similarities among these four presidencies. As "orthodox-innovators" affiliated with a resilient regime, Kennedy and Johnson were expected to celebrate the New Deal and try to complete its unfinished business after the Eisenhower interregnum. This stance, Skowronek suggests, points to a characteristic set of dilemmas arising from the need to keep moving forward while maintaining a fractious coalition.[20] As "preemptive," or "third-way," leaders opposed to a resilient regime, Eisenhower and Nixon had to perform a different balancing act, weighing their opposition to the New Deal against the need to confront its still dominant adherents. The result, according to Skowronek, should have been a highly individual mix of support for and opposition to the regime's policy initiatives and commitments. Certainly the broad outlines of these four administrations lend credence to the regime perspective. Eisenhower and Nixon ducked and weaved, lending often surprising support

to New Deal initiatives but using these moments to highlight and attack incipient conflicts within the New Deal regime. Kennedy and Johnson both supported the expansion and extension of New Deal policies, but often in selective
and surprisingly constrained ways. These regularities suggest the limitations of
Neustadt's individual view of presidential power.

Nevertheless, placing these presidents into these broad categories emphasizes certain similarities and differences at the expense of others. First, the policy leadership of Kennedy and Johnson was more similar to that of Eisenhower
and Nixon than the regime perspective might suggest, hinting that the differences between orthodox-innovation and preemptive leadership are not so
sharply etched. All of these presidents faced fundamentally similar political
and institutional conditions for building policy coalitions—party and interest
alignments, congressional and administrative politics, public opinion. Each
came to power under the broad umbrella of the New Deal, with its particular
configuration of institutional components: the dominant Democratic party,
composed of a volatile mixture of rural white South and urban multiracial
North; the Congress, mostly in Democratic hands, dominated by powerful
committee chairmen; the expanding administrative state; and the growing network of interest groups that was beginning to displace the party system as the
central representative mechanism of American politics. In every policymaking
instance, then, all four presidents were confronted with a similar array of coalition-building options. Although they viewed these options through different
regime lenses, their situations had much in common, institutionally speaking.
At the same time, the differences between Eisenhower and Nixon and between
Kennedy and Johnson were sharper than the regime perspective might suggest.
Although faced with a common set of elements for coalition building, each
president's opportunities for choice were different. A structured choice perspective emphasizes these moments of particular choice, in which presidents
seek to assemble, reassemble, or dismantle coalitions using these same elements, while weighing them against the background of regime politics. Within
the broad structure of the New Deal regime, each president chose differently.

This essay considers in particular the social welfare policy initiatives of these
four administrations, particularly regarding the programs created by the Social
Security Act of 1935. Franklin Roosevelt aspired to create a national, "cradle-to-
grave" system of economic security for all Americans. Due to the fragmentation of the American national state and the distinctive racial, class, and sec-
tional divisions of the Democratic Party, the New Deal welfare state fell
somewhat short of Roosevelt's ambitions.[21] Although the Social Security Act
may not have been the beginning of the American welfare state, it certainly

embodied the New Deal regime shift in national welfare policy. It expanded the reach of national authority for social provision well beyond any historical precedent. It established the basic structure of the American welfare state that remained in place for sixty years: nationally funded and administered social insurance programs for working people and federal grants to states for public assistance programs for the poor. The three basic components of the act were Old-Age Insurance, now commonly called Social Security, a mandatory, contributory system of pensions for retired workers; Unemployment Insurance, a system of compensation for previously employed workers; and a variety of means-tested public assistance programs for the elderly, the blind, and children (the last of these being Aid to Dependent Children, later Aid to Families with Dependent Children, the program most commonly called "welfare").

In the generation following the New Deal, these policies were all subjects of vigorous debate and frequent and competing proposals for expansion, adaptation, and retrenchment. The New Deal's heirs sought to fulfill, more or less gradually, Roosevelt's original aspiration for a fully national, universally inclusive welfare state, which he articulated most fully in his call for an "economic bill of rights" in his penultimate state of the union message in 1944.[22] This essay, however, is intended neither to explain surges and slumps of significant welfare enactments nor to present a comprehensive history of social welfare policy in the postwar era. The question, rather, is how presidents and their initiatives entered into those debates between the early 1950s and the early 1970s, and whether these presidents of different persuasions took strikingly different directions. The four presidencies are considered in two paired sequences. The first, Eisenhower and Kennedy, highlights Eisenhower's acceptance of much of the New Deal and Kennedy's somewhat surprising restraint. The second, Johnson and Nixon, emphasizes Nixon's ironic articulation of New Deal social policy aspirations. The conclusion then reflects on the later transition from Ronald Reagan and George Bush to Bill Clinton.

EISENHOWER AND KENNEDY: MODERATION AND RESTRAINT

Considering the Eisenhower and Kennedy presidencies in separate regime categories conceals surprising similarities between them. Considering them together suggests both the power and the limitations of the regime perspective. An anomalous president in many ways, Eisenhower was not, of course, a New Deal enthusiast but neither was he the New Deal nemesis that many of his supporters hoped and expected he would be.[23] His administration failed to roll back the welfare policies of the New Deal, and indeed in some critical instances Eisenhower led the fight for their expansion—the classic preemptive stance. Kennedy, who spent the 1950s as one of the leaders of a vocal Senate faction for expansion of some key New Deal welfare policies, was much more circumspect as president, appearing often to be articulating Eisenhower's legacy rather than Franklin Roosevelt's. A key exception to these general observations was Medicare, which Kennedy supported and Eisenhower did not.[24]

Eisenhower was elected president in 1952 as an anti-New Deal figure, "the leader," as Skowronek notes, "of a resurgent opposition out to find an alternative course that could still stand the test of legitimacy."[25] Both temperamentally and politically skeptical of the New Deal's expansive vision of government activity, he had been initially hopeful about the New Deal when Franklin Roosevelt was first elected. By 1934, however, he was "lambasting" Roosevelt and his program in conversations with his brothers.[26] When he entered the political fray to run for president as a Republican, he did so out of a sense of public obligation to help put the brakes on the New Deal after twenty years. "I was persuaded," he wrote in his diary shortly after taking office, "that I had a duty to turn to another task, that of offering myself as a political leader to unseat the New Deal-Fair Deal bureaucracy in Washington."[27] In his first state of the union message, Eisenhower attacked what he called Roosevelt's belief that, "all other things being equal, the federal government deserved first opportunity and had the right to solve any major problem that might arise in the nation." His response was both philosophical and stylistic. "I wanted to make it clear," he wrote in his presidential memoirs, significantly titled *Mandate for Change*, "that we would not be simply a continuation of the New Deal and Fair Deal, either in purpose or execution." Philosophically, he promised fiscal orthodoxy as an antidote to the profligate spending of the preceding administrations. On his political style, he commented in terms that clearly marked the contrast with his former commander-in-chief:

> In initiating a reversal of trends based on such beliefs—trends which by 1953 were twenty years old—we were setting in motion revolutionary activity. We suffered no delusion that such a revolution could become a reality through the frenzied drama of a first one hundred days, or that it would be the work of improvisation, however clever.[28]

Eisenhower clearly stood as a political leader opposed not only to the policy commitments of the New Deal but also to the haphazard, experimental approach to policymaking that it seemed to represent.

But Ike's opposition to the New Deal was not that of the orthodox, hard-line wing of the Republican party. He was drafted to run for president by party leaders who felt that the heir presumptive to the Republican nomination, Senator Robert Taft, could not be elected, not least because he represented a "reactionary" wing of the party. Eisenhower himself wrote in his diary in June 1951 that Taft was a "disciple of hate."[29] In an important campaign speech in Boise, Idaho, in August 1952, the nominee distanced himself both from "the Reactionary Right and the Radical Left."[30] Eisenhower's identity as a leader derived in large part from his and his party's opposition to the New Deal. Nevertheless, moving too far and too fast against popular New Deal policies and robust New Deal interests could easily undermine his legitimacy. This balancing game forced on Eisenhower a series of strategic choices in policy situations where the imperative was to build coalitions for presidential initiatives. The cumulative result of these choices was a stance of carefully considered moderation—cognizant of both the New Deal's resilience and his own party's opposition to it—that defined the limits of Eisenhower's opposition to the New Deal. In making these choices, he not only effectively reinforced much New Deal policy but also protected it from its attackers on the flanks of his own party.

The earliest social policy fights in the Eisenhower administration occurred over Old-Age Insurance. A Social Security amendment adopted in 1950 had increased benefits and extended coverage to many new workers, greatly improving the program's political standing and long-term prospects after substantial uncertainty in the 1940s.[31] But with the election of Eisenhower along with Republican majorities in Congress, opponents of Social Security thought they had their long-awaited opportunity to destroy the program. The House Ways and Means Committee created a special subcommittee on Social Security, chaired by Representative Carl T. Curtis of Nebraska, who had long been a burr under Social Security's saddle. The highlight of the subcommittee's fall 1953 hearings was Curtis's attempt to browbeat recently retired Social Security Commissioner Arthur Altmeyer, testifying under subpoena, into admitting that Old-Age Insurance was not really "insurance."[32] Curtis's hostile intentions fit hand-in-glove with a proposal being floated by the U.S. Chamber of Commerce to recast Social Security as a truly universal program in which pensions for all the aged would have been funded out of current revenues. The Chamber proposal would have ended the link between contributions and benefits that ensured the program's political support, and Social Security supporters saw it as a conservative scheme to do away with the program altogether.[33] Fueling their fears, the Secretary of the new Department of Health, Education, and Welfare (HEW), Oveta Culp Hobby, convened a secret advisory group of outside Social Security "experts" that was stacked with businessmen who supported the Chamber's plan. When word of the so-called "Hobby lobby" leaked to the press (through the good graces of Wilbur Cohen, a central figure in Social Security politics and a thoroughgoing creature of the New Deal), Hobby had to expand the advisory group and the administration was left with egg on its face.[34]

In his first state of the union message, however, Eisenhower had quite clearly advocated expanding Social Security coverage, and he flagged this proposal to congressional leaders in the first weeks of his term as "must" legislation.[35] To the public, and especially to apprehensive supporters of Social Security, it was not clear whether this meant expansion of the existing program or a reorganization along the lines of the Curtis-Chamber proposal.[36] In retrospect, however, it seems doubtful that Ike ever intended to ditch the program that had become the cornerstone of the American welfare state and a central pillar of the New Deal regime. To Republicans who opposed Social Security, Eisenhower was not soothing. "It would appear logical," he wrote to stockbroker E. F. Hutton, who called Social Security "tyranny," "to build upon the system that has been in effect for almost twenty years." The alternative, unacceptable to Eisenhower, was "turning it completely upside down and running the very real danger that we would end up with no system at all," which was precisely what many believed the Chamber of Commerce wanted.[37] In private he was blunt and withering about such Republicans. "Should any political party attempt to abolish social security," Eisenhower wrote his brother Edgar in 1954, "you would not hear of that party again in our political history." He added that only "a tiny splinter group" of right-wingers believed that the Republicans should take such a position, "but their number is negligible and they are stupid."[38] In his diary, Eisenhower reflected on his surprisingly good relations with Senator Taft, who died in July 1953. "In some things," Ike wrote, "I found him extraordinarily 'leftish.' This applied specifically to his attitude toward old-age pensions. He told me that he believed every individual in the United States, upon reaching the age of sixty-five, should automatically go on a minimum pension basis, paid by the federal government."[39]

This episode presented Eisenhower with a clear strategic choice. Although Republicans held majorities in both houses of Congress, they were divided between hard-core opponents of Social Security, behind Curtis, and more moderate supporters of maintaining the program; they could pursue neither course without forming a coalition with part of the Democratic minority. Democrats, too, were split between Northerners who supported expansion of Social Security and Southerners who opposed extending coverage to farm workers and servants, groups comprising the lion's share of African-American workers in the American economy.[40] Eisenhower had several options, any of which could have produced a politically viable Social Security policy coalition. Opposing Social Security expansion, or even altering the program altogether was a possible option, although one that Hobby and her clumsy tactics probably foreclosed. Nevertheless, right-wing Republicans and Southern Democrats formed a numerically and ideologically substantial core for a potential coalition against Social Security expansion.[41] Eisenhower, however, proposed another major expansion of Social Security that protected the program's structure and extended coverage to farmers, farm and domestic workers, and others previously excluded. The bill passed although Republicans required help from Democrats for it to pass in the House.[42] In choosing this course, Eisenhower opted to construct a broad moderate coalition that excluded those most reliable opponents of New Deal commitments, foregoing an opportunity to create what might have been the nucleus of an alternative governing coalition that would have hewed closer to the anti-New Deal impulses of his leadership. Although the contours of the choice were created by Eisenhower's oppositional regime stance, the choice itself was not wholly determined by the regime. Instead, Ike responded to the cross-partisan, institutional imperatives of coalition-building in a particular situation. In so doing, he helped not only to redefine his own stance toward the New Deal but also, ironically, to strengthen New Deal social policy itself and perhaps to foreclose future oppositional possibilities. What is important to note is that either choice would have been consistent with the preemptive leadership that was Eisenhower's structurally determined lot; each option would have drawn part of the New Deal coalition—Southern or Northern Democrats—toward Eisenhower's oppositional camp.

In other areas of New Deal social policy, Eisenhower faced similar choices and followed a similar, if less expansive, approach. Anxiety ran high during the 1950s over unemployment, and although poverty per se was not yet on the national agenda, problems of "structural unemployment" and permanently depressed areas and populations received attention from policymakers and the public.[43] In these areas, as on Social Security, Eisenhower took a decidedly moderate position, preferring to accommodate and even modestly expand New Deal commitments rather than reject them. While he resisted Democratic proposals for more assertive action—twice vetoing depressed areas legislation, for example—he promoted policies that helped shape, and even expand, the other pillars of New Deal social policy.

One of these pillars was Unemployment Insurance (UI), which Eisenhower consistently supported, albeit modestly, as a way to promote economic stability. In 1954, Congress passed legislation offered by the administration to extend UI coverage to approximately four million workers by covering employees of smaller firms that had previously been eligible. As with the Social Security extension of the same year, the administration had to rely on Democratic votes, even in a majority-Republican Congress, to pass the bill.[44] In the deep recession of 1958, Unemployment Insurance faced a more serious crisis. High unemployment meant that many workers were exhausting their UI benefits before finding work again. A group of liberal Democratic senators, led by John Kennedy and Eugene McCarthy, proposed a sweeping revision of the Unemployment Insurance program to cover nearly all workers and extend benefits permanently by creating national standards (to replace state-by-state determination of benefits). Eisenhower responded with a proposal to provide a temporary extension of benefits to workers who had exhausted their benefits during the recession. To finance these temporary extended benefits, the federal government would advance money to the states which would be repaid to the federal treasury over several years. In the House Ways and Means Committee, Chairman Wilbur Mills engineered the adoption of a bill much closer to the Kennedy-McCarthy proposal than the administration plan. In a rare rebuke to Ways and Means, the House defeated the committee's proposal and adopted instead a substitute very much like the Eisenhower plan, which was supported by a coalition of Republicans and Southern Democrats. In the Senate, Kennedy's bill was defeated in favor of the House bill, and the temporary extension of benefits was enacted.[45] While he resisted liberal efforts to expand Unemployment Insurance dramatically, Eisenhower not only supported its basic programmatic structure but also expanded it and assimilated it into his pro-business, Republican philosophy. "Far from disparaging the program as an unattractive remnant of the New Deal," historian Edward Berkowitz has noted, Eisenhower's economic advisers "credited unemployment compensation with preventing the 1957–58 recession from spiraling into depression."[46] At the same time, the contrast between Eisenhower's moderate acceptance of Unemployment Insurance and Kennedy's expansive position created expectations about what might happen to the program under a Democratic administration.

The Eisenhower administration took little direct action on public assistance, the third major component of the Social Security triad. Policymakers assumed, as they had since the 1930s, that social insurance would eventually eclipse public assistance as the primary mode of public social provision and that programs for the poor would simply wither away. There was, however, growing attention to structural problems in the economy. Certain regions and populations—African-Americans in the South, for example, and whites in

Appalachia—were clearly not benefitting from the general economic expansion the United States was enjoying; as a result, many Americans were unable to acquire skills and find jobs that would lift them beyond the need for public assistance. Here, too, Eisenhower's program consisted not of repudiating the New Deal approach of government involvement in the economy but of adjusting it. The New Deal and the Fair Deal, he believed, "did not have a monopoly on the goals of a good society," and he sought social welfare programs that would be both economical and effective at bringing the structurally unemployed—those who lacked skills or access to jobs—into the mainstream of the economy.[47] The approach his administration hit on was vocational rehabilitation, and in 1954 the administration proposed, and Congress passed, an expansion of federal vocational training efforts. Later in the administration, greater efforts took shape in the Democratic Congress to promote job training as a way of reducing the welfare rolls, particularly programs such as area redevelopment and the Youth Conservation Corps, which deliberately echoed the Civilian Conservation Corps of the early New Deal. Eisenhower was lukewarm toward these programs at best, but in principle he did not oppose federal involvement in vocational rehabilitation as a way to attack poverty.

While Eisenhower did not fully embrace the New Deal social policy regime, he certainly did not reject it. His general opposition to the New Deal framed, but did not wholly determine, his approach to policy leadership. He came to the presidency with Republican majorities in both houses of Congress, but even under these apparently propitious circumstances he did not choose to attack the New Deal head on. Rather, he cautiously assembled a moderate bipartisan coalition, eschewing more stridently oppositional possibilities, to expand New Deal welfare state commitments in some areas and contain them in others. Later in his administration he clashed more directly with liberals—notably John Kennedy—who sought much greater expansion of the New Deal welfare state. But even when he took on a clearly oppositional role, as in the area redevelopment vetoes, he never fully repudiated the New Deal. Rather, he sought to assimilate its elements into his own brand of Republicanism. As I. F. Stone noted rather caustically in 1955,

Dwight Eisenhower has occupied a most peculiar role in American politics. Through him, exploiting his fame as a soldier and his personal charm, the Eastern seaboard moneyed interests who direct the Republican party achieved a number of purposes. They attracted enough of the independent vote to win the 1952 elections from the Democrats, who have since 1932 been the majority party. They put into effect a program which accepted the main accomplishments of New Deal and Fair Deal but sought to establish a climate favorable to big business, notably in the control of basic resources and fiscal policy.[48]

Thus when Kennedy was elected president in 1960, the New Deal welfare state was hardly on the ropes. Still, Kennedy's stance in the Senate, as a leader of a faction that stood for the forceful articulation of New Deal welfare commitments, portended a dramatic turn in presidential leadership in social policy upon his move to the other end of Pennsylvania Avenue.

Kennedy's election signaled the restoration of the New Deal order after an eight-year hiatus. In short order, he broke the logjam that Eisenhower had created for several social policy initiatives that had originated in the Democratic Congress of the late 1950s. He signed the Area Redevelopment Act in 1961 and the Manpower Development and Training Act the following year.[49] His administration also represented a substantial departure from the Eisenhower years in its general approach to economic policy. For the first time, Keynesian principles found their way explicitly into the counsels of power, in this case the Council of Economic Advisors, to which Kennedy appointed a trio of card-carrying Keynesians: Walter Heller, Kermit Gordon, and James Tobin. However, the consumption-oriented "commercial" Keynesianism of the 1960s was in many ways a far cry from the more structural "social" Keynesianism that had emerged in the 1930s and 1940s; Kennedy's Keynesians urged passive rather than active fiscal intervention, tax cuts rather than spending, to stimulate the economy. Moreover, the Keynesians in the White House were partially offset in the administration by the appointment of an orthodox Republican, C. Douglas Dillon, as Secretary of the Treasury.[50] Most significant, Kennedy actively supported government health coverage for the elderly and the poor, a New Deal aspiration that Eisenhower had opposed.

Despite these notable differences with Eisenhower in economic philosophy and legislative advocacy, Kennedy's exercise of presidential leadership on social policy did not depart tremendously from Eisenhower's. Consider the new president's political situation. He was, to be sure, affiliated with the New Deal regime which had demonstrated its resilience through eight years of opposition rule, and he had been one of its champions in the Senate. However, he was elected by only the slimmest of margins, and although the Democrats held majorities in both houses of Congress, they actually lost seats in the House of Representatives in 1960 as the Republicans rebounded from the midterm drubbing they had taken in 1958. Kennedy's own party contained Northern and Southern wings that were growing steadily apart, particularly on policy matters touching on labor and race, as social policy issues increasingly did.[51] Despite his New Deal affiliation and the liberal tone of his earlier public career, and despite the élan that he and his family brought to the White House, the institutional conditions Kennedy faced were quite similar to those that had confronted his predecessor, and in order to lead he was forced to reach out beyond the circle of New Deal enthusiasts.[52] As with Eisenhower, Kennedy's affiliated regime stance as an orthodox-innovator shaped, but did not entirely determine, the choices he faced as president.

Kennedy entered office in January 1961 during another recession, and the new administration quickly swung into action, offering a "Program to Restore Momentum to the American Economy." This was a rather grandiose title for a package of executive and legislative action intended to stimulate the economy and attack unemployment, including important initiatives such as manpower training, the minimum wage, Medicare, and federal aid to education. To address the short-term problems of the unemployed, the administration also offered amendments to the core New Deal welfare policies dating from the Depression. There is, perhaps, little surprise in finding a Democratic president relying on New Deal policies as the basis for his own anti-recession program. What is surprising, however, is the restraint with which Kennedy pursued the articulation of these policies.

The most pressing need in 1961, as in the 1958 recession, was relief for the unemployed who had either exhausted or were not eligible for Unemployment Insurance benefits. Here Kennedy faced a strategic choice that paralleled those that Eisenhower had faced. As a senator, Kennedy had been one of the principal champions of the permanent expansion of UI, and the recession once again put the program's flaws and limitations on the national agenda; now as president, he had a seemingly golden opportunity to again present his sweeping proposal for change. Expansion of Unemployment Insurance also fit the Keynesian consensus among Kennedy's economic advisers, since it was a countercyclical spending program that pumped money into the economy during downturns.[53] Kennedy, then, had an opportunity to propose a broad extension of an important New Deal policy and at least to signal his intention to reconstitute the New Deal's cross-class and cross-regional coalition that gave rise to national social policies. Instead, however, he offered only another temporary extension of UI benefits on the Eisenhower model. He continued to advocate more comprehensive reform of Unemployment Insurance, encompassing broadened coverage and mandatory national benefit standards, but it was never an administration priority and Congress never even began to take action on the proposal. In fact, even the temporary benefit extension pushed

Kennedy's presidential leadership to the limits in a particularly revealing way when the administration requested a continuation of the temporary UI extension in 1962. This request was thwarted in the Ways and Means Committee by a quartet of Southern Democrats, signaling quite clearly that a serious presidential proposal to overhaul the permanent Unemployment Insurance structure would meet insurmountable resistance even in the party of the New Deal.[54]

In Unemployment Insurance, the New Deal apparently had no more room to grow. As with Eisenhower's situation, both of Kennedy's options were consistent with his regime position as an orthodox-innovator. Either he could keep true faith and advocate wholesale social policy expansion and risk not only losing but also inflaming increasingly raw wounds within his nominal governing coalition (not to mention squandering precious leadership resources for future policy battles), or he could assemble a coalition for more modest reform, at the risk of alienating his (and the regime's) most ardent supporters. Kennedy chose the latter course, apparently influenced primarily by the limits of his immediate institutional and political environment. As a result, his proposals wanly echoed Eisenhower's.

As part of its anti-recession package in 1961, the administration also proposed an extension of Aid to Dependent Children (ADC), giving states the option of providing ADC benefits to two-parent families in which one parent was unemployed, although Kennedy himself was unenthusiastic about the proposal.[55] The resulting program, ADC-UP (for unemployed parent) became one of the bases for the Public Welfare Amendments of 1962, which was one of the centerpieces of Kennedy's domestic program and the first of the welfare reform waves that later washed up like so much driftwood on the shores of American politics at more or less regular intervals. Here, too, Kennedy's proposals were not particularly bold, nor did they go far beyond the Eisenhower approach to public welfare. The central premise of the Public Welfare Amendments of 1962 was, in fact, strikingly familiar: vocational rehabilitation.[56] The legislation expanded funding for states to offer social services and vocational training to welfare recipients to move them off the welfare rolls and into the labor force.

While the social services community hailed the passage of welfare reform in 1962, not least because it enhanced the importance of rehabilitation and of the social workers who provided it, the Public Welfare Amendments of 1962 in many ways represented not an articulation of the New Deal welfare regime but at least the beginning of a retreat from that regime. First, the emphasis on work within AFDC (Aid to *Families* with Dependent Children, as the program was renamed by the 1962 amendments) reversed the original, maternalist conception of public assistance for children, which had been to enable single mothers to rear their children in their own homes rather than surrendering them to institutions such as orphanages.[57] Second, during Congress's consideration of the bill, Kennedy consistently failed to support initiatives aimed at asserting stronger national control over state public assistance programs in order to even out discrepancies among states and increase benefits. To this end, a group of Democrats on the House Ways and Means Committee sought to increase the federal share of ADC payments. Kennedy opposed this amendment, since it contradicted the rehabilitation thrust of the legislation. Republicans on the committee opposed the increased federal grants, shrewdly citing the president's opposition.[58] Kennedy thus found himself in a political position parallel to Eisenhower's, forming coalitions with elements of the opposing party in order to fend off one flank of his own. While Eisenhower joined with Democrats to repel the extreme anti-New Deal impulses of the Republicans, Kennedy joined with Republicans to undermine the fullest possible articulation of the New Deal in order to stave off the beginnings of decay in his own governing coalition. Like Eisenhower, Kennedy faced strategic choices among policy and political options that were all consistent with his prescribed regime role. And like Ike, he chose the path that was lit most clearly by the immediate, situational imperatives of coalition building in Congress, in the Washington community, and in the country at large. Because these underlying political forces were broadly similar in the 1950s and early 1960s, the clash of opposites over the New Deal regime had produced startlingly little variation in the character of presidential leadership on social policy. As a result, in November 1963, the New Deal welfare state looked very much as it had at the beginning of the Eisenhower administration. All that would appear to change with Kennedy's assassination and Lyndon Johnson's dramatic ascension to the Oval Office.

JOHNSON AND NIXON: THE IRONIES OF EXPANSION

Lyndon Johnson was the great innovator of the New Deal regime (aside from Roosevelt himself, of course), and it was during his administration and under his leadership that New Deal social policy found its truest extension and articulation. The litany of Johnson's accomplishments is long and distinguished—from the Civil Rights and Voting Rights Acts to the War on Poverty and all its attendant programs, from Medicare to Model Cities, from federal aid to education to open housing. Johnson's presidency clearly marked a tremendous departure both from Eisenhower's cautious mediation between the New Deal and its opponents and from Kennedy's circumspection in the face of constraints. He was, as Skowronek notes, the "orthodox-innovator" par excellence, the president affiliated with a resilient regime striving both to maintain the New Deal's fundamental commitments and to put his own personal stamp on them.[59] Even more than Kennedy, Lyndon Johnson owed his political career to the New Deal, having benefitted from Roosevelt's political patronage on more than one occasion, although as his career advanced he was as much an agnostic as an enthusiast.[60] As Senate Democratic leader during the Eisenhower years, he was the brilliant mastermind of legislative compromise between the New Deal regime and its opposition, and more than any American political figure of the 1960s he understood clearly the limits of the regime and the coalition that sustained it.[61] Still, for all of Johnson's deep personal and political affiliation with the New Deal and all his political acumen, the regime perspective by itself identifies only the boundary conditions—the structural context for choice—of Johnson's presidential leadership. While both Kennedy and Johnson were supporters of the New Deal regime, Kennedy seemed the more stalwart during the 1950s. Both sought to use their presidencies to advance and extend the regime's reach, and also to use the New Deal to define their own presidencies. Yet where Kennedy had been cautious and incremental in his social policy leadership, Johnson was bold and sweeping. Wherein lay the difference? Johnson himself identified three conditions for leadership that he suggested were uniquely met at the beginning of his administration: the need for action, the willingness to act, and the disposition to lead.[62] The need for action on social problems that remained unsolved since the 1930s was hardly new, nor was the disposition to lead, which all presidents possess by the very nature of their office.

What had changed was the willingness to act on the part of others in the political system and, hence, the strategic opportunities for choice that were available to Johnson. Like Kennedy an orthodox-innovator, Johnson faced similar pressures—at once to extend the reach and finish the building of the New Deal welfare state, and to prevent the fraying New Deal coalition from unraveling. Johnson's options were also similar to Kennedy's: whether to stress orthodoxy or innovation. He could either promote the fulfillment of Roosevelt's vision for the postwar world of a national, universalistic welfare state, keeping the faith but straining the coalition to the breaking point; or he could move slowly and deliberately, finessing internal conflict but disappointing true believers. Once again, a president faced an array of strategic paths consistent with his regime position, and it was left to him to make choices within the framework of the politics of articulation. Only now the circumstances of the choice had changed utterly.

Johnson cited two events that underscored the need for forceful national action on domestic problems. One was the launching of Sputnik in 1957, which brought domestic needs, particularly education and science and technology, into sharp relief and allowed domestic policy advocates to cite the Cold War as justification for strong national action. This circumstance, of course, shaped Kennedy's presidency as well. The second event was the assassination of Kennedy, which elevated Kennedy, who had been in political hot water before his death, to the status of a martyr for a cause. Seizing the moment to bask in Kennedy's posthumous halo, Johnson invoked his predecessor's memory to forge a link between Kennedy's legacy and the unfinished business of the New Deal and to press ahead with Kennedy's program—the New Deal program—with a boldness and dispatch that had eluded Kennedy himself.[63]

Kennedy's death raised the political cost of opposing initiatives associated with the late president, and Johnson capitalized on the new political landscape in shaping his own presidential leadership. Other political conditions as well made the moment ripe for bold action. Having successfully shattered Jim Crow in the South, the civil rights movement had reached what was perhaps its climax in August 1963 with the March on Washington, which was designed to press the national government not only to protect civil rights but also to promote equal economic opportunity.[64] And in 1964, Johnson was reelected in an earth-shattering landslide, bringing with him a Congress that was more heavily Democratic than any since the early years of the New Deal itself. To be sure, toward the end of his presidency, Kennedy himself had begun to take bolder action in the face of mounting social pressure by proposing civil rights legislation and charging his economic advisers to put together an antipoverty program.[65] There is no telling what direction Kennedy might have taken had he lived, nor is there any point in rehearsing once again the cycle of speculation that has generated both a hagiography and a countervailing demonology.[66] The fact remains that the institutional and political conditions for presidential leadership and the formation of policy coalitions were changing in the early 1960s—change that was surely accelerated by the assassination—and Johnson seized on those changes to differentiate himself from Kennedy while wrapping himself in Kennedy's mantle, and Roosevelt's.

The centerpiece of Johnson's program of welfare policy was the War on Poverty, declared in his first state of the union address in January 1964 and consummated in the Economic Opportunity Act of that year. Much in the War on Poverty was new, but in many ways it blended the New Deal social policy tradition with the notion of rehabilitation that was the hallmark of welfare policy in the Eisenhower and Kennedy administrations. Like the New Deal, the War on Poverty sought to unmoor the American welfare state from its reliance on local relief and create a national presence. The New Deal went partway in this effort, creating national social insurance programs but settling for parochial public assistance policies. The Economic Opportunity Act sought to take this effort further, creating direct links between the federal government and the poor in local communities through the Community Action Program and the doctrine of "maximum feasible participation."[67] At the same time, the Economic Opportunity Act, and particularly the Community Action Program, represented the pinnacle of the rehabilitation approach to welfare reform. Like the limited progress of the Eisenhower years and the Public Welfare Amendments of 1962, the War on Poverty promoted access to social services for the poor so that they could get jobs and leave the welfare rolls for good.

Despite its sweeping nature, the War on Poverty was also constrained in its conception and execution by the political exigencies of the moment in Congress, in the bureaucracy, and ultimately in state houses and city halls around the country.[68] In constructing the Economic Opportunity Act, Johnson faced a choice between pushing welfare policy further in a national, unified direction and offering a more restrained, although still expansive, proposal. Many forces from within his own governing coalition were pushing hard for the former course. For example, welfare officials in the Department of Health, Education, and Welfare tried to promote a variety of national guaranteed income schemes, and many of his close circle of advisers advocated a more thoroughgoing move toward a national redistributive policy.[69] Johnson also had advisers counseling restraint. Once again, either course would have been consistent with Johnson's regime position as orthodox-innovator. The key legislative problem for the President in pressing the Economic Opportunity Act was overcoming the opposition of Southern Democrats, particularly in the House, who threatened to oppose the program if it involved too much federal interference in local affairs and if it were defined as a program of redistribution rather than rehabilitation. Johnson's strategic response was to expand the nationalizing reach of the welfare state but to squelch any possibility of expanding the legislation beyond rehabilitation, thereby limiting its potential for political harm. When, for example, Sargent Shriver suggested paying for an expanded jobs program with a cigarette tax, he was met with a frigid silence from the president and he dropped the idea. Tactically, the administration's response was to prevail on a conservative Southerner, Representative Philip Landrum of Georgia, to sponsor the bill in the House rather than the controversial Representative Adam Clayton Powell Jr. of Harlem, who chaired the Education and Labor Committee.[70]

In order to keep Southerners on board, the administration had to hew fairly closely to an established model of welfare programming and funding, even if the comprehensive conception and scope of the War on Poverty outstripped anything that had come before. Landrum was, perhaps, not far off when he called it " 'the most conservative bill I've ever seen,' because it aimed at taking people off the welfare rolls and making them into 'taxpayers instead of tax-eaters.' "[71] The dramatic, innovative turn of welfare policy in the Johnson years, then, owed much to the extraordinary political circumstances of the mid-1960s, but also to the orthodoxies of a restricted postwar consensus that constrained Johnson's ability to extend the New Deal regime more fully. By the time Johnson's presidency was brought down by another of his wars, in Vietnam, his domestic war was already largely moribund, the victim, apparently, of a resurgent coalition against his attempt to bypass state and local governments and nationalize the welfare state.

The election of Richard Nixon to succeed Johnson in 1968 could easily be read as a sign of the triumph of the decentralized view of the welfare state and as a harbinger of a serious attempt to draw back from national social policy commitments.[72] But Nixon quite unexpectedly proposed not only to repudiate the rehabilitation orthodoxy that had taken hold in the Eisenhower administration, in which he served as vice president, but also to create a national presence in welfare policy beyond anything a New Deal-affiliated president had proposed. Like Eisenhower, Nixon was a thoroughgoing anti-New Dealer. From his very first political speech as a prospective congressional candidate in 1945, he had defined his career in opposition to Roosevelt's approach to government. In preparing for his presidential campaign in 1968, he set the Great Society squarely in the New Deal tradition, and opposed them both. "The Great Society," he wrote, "was created by liberal academics and bureaucrats steeped in the myths of the New Deal. When its theoretical high-mindedness ran up against the self-interested toughness of the people it was intended to serve, there was certain to be conflict." Nixon clearly entered office as a leader opposed to a New Deal regime that remained resilient, if rocky. "From the first days of my administration," he declared, "I wanted to get rid of the costly failures of the Great Society—and I wanted to do it immediately. . . . The worst offender was the welfare system."[73] Upon Nixon's election, it seemed that the New Deal welfare state was in trouble.

The regime perspective, however, suggests that Nixon's would be a "third-way" presidency—neither altogether resolute in opposition to the still-resilient New Deal nor doctrinaire in proposing a coherent program of its own. In fact, Nixon followed the third-way script to the letter and presided over the continued articulation and expansion of much of the New Deal welfare state. Nixon was, after all, a minority president, having received only 43 percent of the national vote in 1968, and he faced a Congress still dominated by the Democrats. As a result, much of Nixon's domestic policy leadership constituted an attempt to draw political advantage out of New Deal and Great Society issues and out of a coalition that remained loyal to the New Deal aspiration of a strong, national administrative state. In many areas, from environmental protection to consumer safety to occupational health, the Nixon administration produced major legislation.[74] Despite his vaunted "Southern strategy," Nixon promoted affirmative action early in his presidency with an eye toward competing for African-American votes.[75] In many areas of social policy as well, Nixon promoted the extension of the New Deal approach, presiding over the indexing of Social Security benefits to the cost of living and the nationalization of public assistance programs for the elderly and disabled into Supplemental Security Income.[76] But above all, he proposed the ultimately unsuccessful Family Assistance Plan (FAP), which in many ways outstripped anything Kennedy or Johnson ever contemplated in their articulation of New Deal principles and commitments. Here, at long last but from a surprising source, was a welfare program that seemed true to Roosevelt's economic bill of rights.

Nixon's views on welfare policy were largely unformed before 1968, but his approach to welfare reform was quite clearly motivated by disgust with the New Deal-Great Society approach and the enormous national state apparatus that these eras had spawned as well as the rehabilitation, social-service ethos that had engulfed national welfare policy over the fifteen years before he took office. As he put it in characteristically scornful fashion, "I abhorred snoopy, patronizing surveillance by social workers which made children and adults on welfare feel stigmatized and separate."[77] But rather than turn against welfare entirely, he proposed a negative income tax—essentially a system of national welfare standards that would provide a guaranteed minimum income to all Americans through a system of tax credits and refunds. This was a guarantee that liberal Democrats had long sought. Eugene McCarthy, for example, had proposed a guaranteed income during his 1968 presidential campaign, and welfare officials in the Johnson administration had tried without success to persuade Johnson to adopt such a plan.[78]

But for all of his loathing of the Great Society and the New Deal welfare state, Nixon ran into trouble when he tried simply to tear down Johnson's programs. He attempted to dismantle the Office of Economic Opportunity through a concerted program of executive reorganization, budgetary impoundments, and deft management, but these maneuvers provoked deep conflict with the Democratic Congress.[79] In formulating his approach to welfare reform, however, Nixon was careful not to repudiate the social goals of his predecessors, even if he rejected their means, echoing Eisenhower's belief that the New Deal regime "did not have a monopoly on the goals of a good society."[80] In his 1968 campaign he had advocated national welfare standards even while attacking Johnson's own attempts at nationalizing the New Deal welfare state.

As a new president opposed not only to the previous administration but also to a resilient prevailing regime, he needed to find a positive program by which he could be true to his own oppositional stance and at the same time address the needs of his own time and sustain the fundamental commitments of the New Deal regime. Unlike orthodox-innovators, who have the outlines of a program given to them by the very nature of their affiliation, opposition presidents react to the regime and must work harder to create positive, rather than negative, political and policy goals. Several of Nixon's political advisers suggested that a national guaranteed income was one of the few issues that could do this for him. As the brainchild of Milton Friedman and other conservative economists, it could unite the disparate wings of his own party; at the same time, it had obvious appeal to many Democrats as well.[81] Nixon's welfare leadership was calculated to make the most of his strategic political situation. Once again, a president was faced with an opportunity in which multiple options were consistent with his regime position; his options, in fact, varied even more widely than Johnson's because he was not expected to be true to any particular policy vision. Either he could play to the solid mass of his own party and continue to resist national commitments in welfare policy, probably bringing along Southerners and other conservative Democrats, or he could come at the problem the other way, appealing to a more centrist coalition of liberal Republicans and moderate (and, perhaps, liberal) Democrats with a more concerted program of national welfare policy. Either way, he would make both friends and enemies on both sides of the regime-opposition ledger. Ever the schemer—and the paradigmatic third-way president—Nixon did both, first proposing the Family Assistance Plan and then quietly dropping it.

Many of Nixon's chief policy advisers on welfare policy were either Democrats or had close links with Democratic policy networks.[82] Chief among them was Daniel Patrick Moynihan, one of the very "liberal academics and bureaucrats" he so distrusted. Nixon's openness to such cross-partisanship in generating his welfare policy seems surprising in restrospect, especially in light of the circumstances of his downfall after Watergate, but given his strategic situation in 1969, it made perfect sense. Moynihan likened Nixon to Benjamin Disraeli, the Tory prime minister who undertook bold social reform in the name of traditional conservatism.[83] Many Democrats were surprised and delighted to find receptive ears in the new administration to their pet proposal. "I couldn't believe," said Alice Rivlin, assistant secretary of health, education, and welfare under Johnson, "that I was sitting there talking to a Republican administration that seemed eager for this new solution that six months before I hadn't been able to convince Wilbur Cohen [Johnson's last secretary of HEW] was the right thing to do."[84] What became the Family Assistance Plan was even originally called the Family Security System, hardly an accidental reference to Social Security.

Nixon's conservative advisers were appalled. White House domestic counselor Arthur Burns, an old Eisenhower hand, said, "it ran counter to everything I knew about Dick Nixon."[85] Like Kennedy and Johnson before him, Nixon found himself following a very different script as president than he had followed on his way to the Oval Office. Along with other conservatives in the White House and the Treasury Department, Burns counseled Nixon to abandon the Family Assistance Plan, arguing instead for imposing new national requirements to improve existing state AFDC benefits in return for general revenue sharing. Ironically, the conservative forces in a Republican White House now supported maintaining and strengthening the existing structure of the New Deal welfare state. The FAP's advocates thus convinced Nixon that by supporting national welfare standards and a guaranteed income he was truly repudiating the New Deal-Great Society welfare tradition, and that Burns's alternative would "lock the . . . administration into an affirmation of the past."[86] Thus Nixon faced a choice: either propose, in the name of anti-New Deal principles, a warmed-over updating of AFDC, or break boldly with the past and thereby outdo Franklin Roosevelt and Lyndon Johnson in shaping a truly national welfare state. Either way, a clean break with the past was not possible; each choice looked both forward and backward. Simply opposing the New Deal regime did not point Nixon in a single direction; rather, the particular politics of coalition building took over.

The FAP was aimed at a moderate coalition of Republicans and Democrats who were dissatisfied with the state of welfare policy after the Great Society but were unwilling to jettison the national government's role altogether. It ended the assumption that employment and welfare were mutually exclusive options but said nothing about wages, job creation, or training. It amounted to an antipoverty strategy that was entirely compatible with the respectable, mainstreet business interests that formed the backbone of the Republican party. The plan drew the ire of conservatives and liberals alike, the former because it amounted to a "megadole," the latter because it was too stingy and, because of its emphasis on low-wage work, punitive.[87] The administration's bill was passed in the House by a middle-of-the-road coalition under the leadership of Republican leader Gerald R. Ford and Democratic Ways and Means Chairman Wilbur Mills, but it collapsed in the Senate, where conservative Republicans, liberal Democrats, and Southerners teamed up to defeat it in the Finance Committee.

Liberals, behind Senator Abraham Ribicoff, later tried to pass an expanded version of the FAP. Nixon faced another strategic choice within the preemptive mode—whether to compromise with Ribicoff to pass a bill or to hold fast to his moderate position, which was sure to lose in the Senate. He chose the latter course, preferring to reclaim conservative support for his ultimately successful bid for reelection in 1972.[88] In playing his preemptive role, zigging to promote expansive welfare reform and then zagging to oppose it, Nixon played shrewd coalition politics, using moments of strategic choice both to advance his own leadership and to undermine the dominant regime coalition to which he remained opposed. More than any other president in this era, Nixon demonstrated the power of a structured choice approach to presidential leadership: within the structural constraints imposed by the configuration of the New Deal regime, he chose a political course, at least in the welfare policy arena, that was carefully attuned to the concrete problems of building coalitions (whether to enact or defeat policy proposals)—and to the preservation of his own future choices and prospects for power.

REGIMES, COALITIONS, AND PRESIDENTIAL POWER

"One of the persisting anomalies of American as of British democracy," Daniel Patrick Moynihan wrote, "is that the party of ardor is frequently the one to make the cold decisions that come along in political life, while the party of reserve is not less commonly entrusted with the generous initiatives."[89] But the history of presidential leadership during the New Deal era suggests that such a pattern, far from being an anomaly, is the normal course of American policymaking. The model underlying Moynihan's statement is that of party government, in which a single party, upon gaining control of an institutionally unified government, is able to adopt its program wholesale. Under such institutional conditions, as in Britain, it would indeed be an anomaly for "the party of ardor" to pursue policies of restraint and for "the party of reserve" to enact social reforms, as Disraeli did in the nineteenth century. In a party government model, a change of government is equivalent to a regime transformation, as one set of ideological dispositions, policy commitments, interests, and electoral bases displaces another.[90] In such a system, an "opposition" leader is by definition out of power. Once the leader of the opposition comes to power, he is no longer an opposition leader; he and his party command a majority and thus constitute the government and, hence, the regime.[91]

But in the United States, with its "separated institutions sharing powers," in Neustadt's famous formulation, these institutional conditions do not obtain.[92] Leaders opposed to the prevailing regime do not automatically lose their status as opposition leaders upon assuming the presidency. It is possible, even usual, for parties to come and go in control of one or more national governing institutions without entailing a regime transformation. Rarely do presidential elections instigate intense periods of policy change, even in the instances—rare since World War II—that they produce unified party control of the national government.[93] Even when the presidency changes hands, the other elements of the political system generally remain more or less the same, or at least change only gradually. The anomalies in American politics are precisely those moments when national elections coincide with similar change in the rest of the system. Then and only then does the "party of ardor" appear—a momentarily unified coalition behind a leader who sweeps away the fragments of an old order and sets about to create a new one—and only then does an opposition leader truly shed his opposition status and become a regime leader in his own right. Such reconstructive leaders are uniquely free from the constraints of prior arrangements. Under normal circumstances, during the stretches between such junctures of reconstruction, presidents must govern from under the weight of old commitments, whether they share these commitments or not, and putative "presidents of ardor" are often led to make the cold decisions, while "presidents of reserve" are equally likely to be generous.[94] It is the broad patterns of leadership (and of constraints on leadership) arising from this fact that Skowronek elucidates.

This broad pattern, however, merely sharpens, rather than contradicts, the dilemmas of presidential leadership that Neustadt explores in *Presidential Power*. As Skowronek points out, Neustadt emphasizes similarities among presidents and their political situations within an era, while Skowronek simultaneously emphasizes differences within eras and often surprising similarities across eras that explode Neustadt's notion of a distinctively modern presidency.[95] Nevertheless, even presidents in very different political situations, with different institutionally defined leadership projects, are given the same raw materials of politics—also institutionally defined—with which to work: Congress, political parties, the Washington community, the administrative state, interest groups, and, ultimately, the public. These forces and institutions thrust onto presidents, regardless of their regime position, fundamentally similar dilemmas, opportunities, or moments of choice—not uniform, undifferentiated choice, but *structured* choice, delimited by configurations of institutions, ideology, and interest. The contours of these choices, the array of plausible options, and the leadership aspirations that presidents load onto these choices depend on the regime politics specified by political time. Nevertheless, choose they must, and making these choices poses precisely Neustadt's problem of presidential power: how to make choices that make future choices possible. To do this, to make sustained leadership possible in the ambiguous world of regimes and opposition, presidents must contend with the everyday politics of compromise and incremental adjustment and with the mundane problem of creating and sustaining coalitions within the confines of the prevailing regime. To do these things successfully, a president must recognize his regime position and its attendant limitations and possibilities, but he must also recognize that his leadership depends on his ability to manage precisely the political forces that Neustadt describes and to deploy his power of persuasion to move these forces as far as possible in the direction he wants them to go. The new challenge for analysts of presidential power is to join structure and agency to explore further the structured choices that presidents face. Superimposing Skowronek's insights onto Neustadt's can enable them to develop a perspective on presidential leadership that combines broad institutional patterns with particular configurational and situational details to provide explanations of, and prescriptions for, not only large patterns of leadership but particular moments of decision as well.

Bill Clinton's signing of welfare reform legislation in 1996 illustrates once again the pattern of structured choice that suggests the way toward such a perspective. Clinton was cast in the role of preempter, the first opposition counterweight to the Reagan revolution. Like Nixon a minority president, the Janus-faced Clinton defeated George Bush largely by attacking the policies of the previous twelve years—thus defining his own leadership project not affirmatively but negatively, against what he portrayed as the foreign adventurism and domestic lassitude of the Reagan-Bush years. At the same time, Clinton promised to be a "new Democrat," signaling his rejection of the New Deal orthodoxy that had died with Reagan's election. Entering office with tenuous majorities in both houses of Congress, he faced a series of strategic choices— over gay men and lesbians in the military, deficit reduction, economic stimulus, and free trade, among others—with which he began to shape his leadership and to feel out the possibilities for assembling a congressional coalition with which to govern. His most spectacular choice (and most spectacular failure), of course, was health insurance reform, in which Clinton's act of repudiation was simultaneously an attempt to recapture both the spirit and the substance of the New Deal. In pursuing health reform as he did, Clinton grossly miscalculated the tolerance both among the public and in the Democratic Congress for such sweeping reform; he both took his victory in 1992 too seriously as a mandate to repudiate the Reagan era and misread the coalition-forming possibilities in the euphoria of the first unified government since the Carter administration. Lying in wait for just such a miscalculation, conservatives in the Republican party used the health care episode as a platform to capture control of Congress, demonstrating the resilience of the Reagan regime and its skepticism toward government, and presenting Clinton with an entirely different political environment in the second half of his first term. Even the most obtuse observer could not miss these signals.[96]

In this milieu, Clinton came into his own, no longer as a would-be neo-New Dealer but as a preemptive neo-Reaganite, declaring in his 1996 state of the union address that "the era of big government is over." In this setting, he pursued another campaign pledge, to "end welfare as we know it." Here again, Clinton faced a strategic choice within the confines of his preemptive role: whether to join with Republicans and seek truly reforming change in the welfare system, alienating his liberal supporters, or to seek more modest and marginal changes while protecting the core received commitments of AFDC. Like Nixon, he moved in several directions in quick succession, often baffling and dismaying supporters and detractors alike. But the problem of coalition formation that Clinton faced imposed more stringent limits than Nixon (or Eisenhower) confronted. Nixon's Congress had two parties each divided into conservative and liberal wings, giving him a more "modular" set of coalition building blocks. By contrast, Clinton's Congress was extremely polarized, with fewer intraparty divisions and an unusually disciplined Republican majority, giving Clinton less opportunity to play the middle and the extremes against each other.[97] His initial welfare proposal, which combined punitive with expansive measures, went nowhere. The bill he ultimately signed (after two vetoes) included the more conservative elements of his own plan without its more liberal aspects and ceded nearly all control over welfare policy to the states.[98]

Liberal Democrats, who had been heartened by the two vetoes, were crestfallen; Republicans were outwardly ecstatic, although Clinton's embrace of "their" welfare bill robbed them of a potent issue in the 1996 campaign. Like other third-way presidents, Clinton shrewdly made political hay out of circumstances that seemed to be stacked against him by joining a cross-partisan coalition that abolished AFDC, effectively surrendering the New Deal aspiration of an inclusive, national welfare state and compressing two generations of anti-New Deal agitation into a few strokes of a ceremonial pen. Clinton's situation thus resembled that of Nixon and Eisenhower in its tension between president and regime; where it differed was in the particular coalitional configuration that framed Clinton's immediate opportunity for choice, narrowing his options. Unlike Nixon, he was ultimately unable to have it both ways, supporting sweeping welfare reform with one hand while killing it with the other (as Nixon did with FAP). Clinton's choice was to out-Reagan Reagan, and he won reelection handily.

Like the earlier episodes of New Deal-era presidential leadership, Clinton's course points to a perspective on presidential leadership that considers structure and agency—regimes, historical configurations, and choice—to explore both the general outlines and the particular paths of presidential action. What presidents do is a composite of what they must do and what they choose to do. Presidential imperatives—what they must do—are shaped largely by the structural forces of political time. Within the constraints of political time, presidential choices are shaped by their immediate political situations—their prospects for constructing winning coalitions on winning issues. But as both Skowronek and Neustadt suggest, leadership consists not simply in such coalition building in one instance or several, but in sustaining coalitions over the course of a presidency. To do this, to lead successfully, presidents must consider not only the broad structural nature of their authority but also the narrower, everyday problems of presidential power that Neustadt identified a generation ago: how to confront, day after day and month after month, the relentlessly elusive organs of power arrayed about them.

ACKNOWLEDGMENTS

I am especially grateful to Stephen Skowronek for his generous comments on an earlier version of this essay. For their help and advice, I also thank Charles Cameron, Fred Greenstein, Lauren Osborne, John Skrentny, Jeffrey Tulis, Stephen Wayne, and the editors and conference participants.

NOTES

1. Richard E. Neustadt, *Presidential Power: The Politics of Leadership* (New York: Wiley, 1960).

2. For a wise and illuminating discussion of judgment and political leadership, see Isaiah Berlin, "Political Judgment," in *The Sense of Reality: Studies in Ideas and their History* (New York: Farrar, Straus and Giroux, 1997).

3. Stephen Skowronek, *The Politics Presidents Make: Leadership from John Adams to George Bush* (Cambridge: Harvard University Press, 1993). The quotation is on page 34.

4. See Jeffrey K. Tulis, "On the Politics Skowronek Makes," *Journal of Policy History* 8 (1996): 248–52.

5. See William H. Sewell Jr., "A Theory of Structure: Duality, Agency, and Transformation," *American Journal of Sociology* 98 (1992): 1–29; Rogers M. Smith, "If Politics Matters: Implications for a 'New Institutionalism,'" *Studies in American Political Development* 6 (1992): 1–36; Pierre Bourdieu and Loïc J. D. Wacquant, *An Invitation to Reflexive Sociology* (Chicago: University of Chicago Press, 1992).

6. For useful discussions of the concept of regimes, see Stephen D. Krasner, "Structural Causes and Regime Consequences: Regimes as Intervening Variables," in Stephen D. Krasner, ed. *International Regimes* (Ithaca: Cornell University Press, 1983); Clarence N. Stone, *Regime Politics: Governing Atlanta, 1946–1988* (Lawrence: University Press of Kansas, 1989), 3–9; Mary Ruggie, *Realignments in the Welfare State: Health Policy in the United States, Great Britain, and Canada* (New York: Columbia University Press, 1996), pp. 13–22. For a clear and helpful elucidation of regimes in American political development, see David M. Hart, "Institutional Interference Patterns: Technology and Industrial Policy Since the 1920s" (Paper presented to the American Political Science Association, Washington, 1997).

7. See Morris P. Fiorina, *Retrospective Voting in American National Elections* (New Haven: Yale University Press, 1981).

8. Such "third-way" leaders are the subject of the Afterword of the second edition of *The Politics Presidents Make: Leadership from John Adams to Bill Clinton* (Cambridge: Harvard University Press, 1997).

9. Ira Katznelson, "Structure and Configuration in Comparative Politics," in Mark Irving Lichbach and Alan S. Zuckerman, eds. *Comparative Politics: Rationality, Culture, and Structure* (Cambridge: Cambridge University Press, 1997).

10. See Jessica Korn, *The Power of Separation: American Constitutionalism and the Myth of the Legislative Veto* (Princeton: Princeton University Press, 1996).

11. Charles O. Jones, *The Presidency in a Separated System* (Washington: Brookings Institution, 1994); David R. Mayhew, *Divided We Govern: Party Control, Lawmaking, and Investigations, 1946–1990* (New Haven: Yale University Press, 1991).

12. Although for most of the postwar era Republicans failed to get a majority of the national vote in congressional elections. When they did, in 1994, they won a majority of the House. Gary C. Jacobson, *The Electoral Origins of Divided Govern-*

ment: *Competition in U.S. House Elections, 1946–1988* (Boulder, CO: Westview Press, 1990).

13. Hugh Heclo, *A Government of Strangers: Executive Politics in Washington* (Washington: Brookings Institution, 1977).

14. Benjamin I. Page and Robert Y. Shapiro, *The Rational Public: Fifty Years of Trends in Americans' Policy Preferences* (Chicago: University of Chicago Press, 1992).

15. Ellis W. Hawley, *The New Deal and the Problem of Monopoly: A Study in Economic Ambivalence* (Princeton: Princeton University Press, 1966); Colin Gordon, *New Deals: Business, Labor, and Politics in America, 1920–1935* (Cambridge: Cambridge University Press, 1994); Alan Brinkley, *The End of Reform: New Deal Liberalism in Recession and War* (New York: Knopf, 1995).

16. Ben Bradlee, *A Good Life: Newspapering and Other Adventures* (New York: Simon and Schuster, 1995), p. 423. Bradlee himself may have been paraphrasing his friend John F. Kennedy's maxim that "to govern is to choose." Daniel P. Moynihan, *The Politics of a Guaranteed Income: The Nixon Administration and the Family Assistance Plan* (New York: Random House, 1973), p. 14.

17. Richard E. Neustadt, *Presidential Power and the Modern Presidents: The Politics of Leadership from Roosevelt to Reagan* (New York: Free Press, 1990), pp. 169–72.

18. David Plotke, *Building a Democratic Political Order: Reshaping American Liberalism in the 1930s and 1940s* (Cambridge: Cambridge University Press, 1996); Steve Fraser and Gary Gerstle, eds., *The Rise and Fall of the New Deal Order, 1930–1980* (Princeton: Princeton University Press, 1989); Karen Orren and Stephen Skowronek, "Regimes and Regime Building in American Government: A Review of Literature on the 1940s" *Political Science Quarterly* 113 (1998–99): 689–702. See also Theodore J. Lowi, *The End of Liberalism: The Second Republic of the United States* (New York: Norton, 1979).

19. Neustadt's characterization of this period as one of "emergencies in politics with politics as usual" thus seems defensible at the level of particular policy debates and coalitional conflict. Skowronek's counterargument, that there is no such thing as "politics as usual," is also true at the level of presidential orientations toward these commitments and the consequent differences in presidential leadership. Therein lies much of the disjunction between the two. Neustadt, *Presidential Power*, p. 5; Skowronek, *Politics Presidents Make*, p. 41.

20. Skowronek, *Politics Presidents Make*, pp. 41–43.

21. Robert C. Lieberman, *Shifting the Color Line: Race and the American Welfare State* (Cambridge: Harvard University Press, 1998).

22. Franklin D. Roosevelt, " 'Unless There Is Security Here at Home, There Cannot Be Lasting Peace in the World'—Message to the Congress on the State of the Union, January 11, 1944," in Samuel I. Rosenman, ed., *The Public Papers and Addresses of Franklin D Roosevelt* (New York: Harper, 1950), vol 13, pp. 32–42.

23. On Eisenhower and the regime perspective, see Skowronek, *Politics Presidents Make*, pp. 45–49; and the Afterword to the second edition.

24. Lawrence R. Jacobs, *The Health of Nations: Public Opinion and the Making of American and British Health Policy* (Ithaca: Cornell University Press, 1993).

25. Skowronek, *Politics Presidents Make*, p. 6.

26. Stephen E. Ambrose, *Eisenhower* (New York: Simon and Schuster, 1983), vol. 1, pp. 88, 100.

27. Robert H. Ferrell, ed., *The Eisenhower Diaries* (New York: Norton, 1981), p. 231.

28. Dwight D. Eisenhower, *Mandate for Change, 1953–1956* (Garden City, N.Y.: Doubleday, 1963), pp. 120–21.

29. Ferrell, *Eisenhower Diaries*, pp. 202–3, 195.

30. Eisenhower, *Mandate for Change*, p. 51.

31. See Edwin Amenta, Bruce G. Carruthers, and Yvonne Zylan, "A Hero for the Aged? The Townsend Movement, the Political Mediation Model, and U.S. Old-Age Policy, 1934–1950," *American Journal of Sociology* 98 (1992): 308–39.

32. Arthur J. Altmeyer, *The Formative Years of Social Security* (Madison: University of Wisconsin Press, 1966), pp. 221–35, 298–301.

33. Martha Derthick, *Policymaking for Social Security* (Washington: Brookings Institution, 1979), pp.144–56.

34. Edward D. Berkowitz, *Mr. Social Security: The Life of Wilbur J. Cohen* (Lawrence: University Press of Kansas, 1995), pp. 81–85.

35. Ferrell, *Eisenhower Diaries*, p. 228.

36. Berkowitz, *Mr. Social Security*, p. 79.

37. Quoted in Berkowitz, *Mr. Social Security*, p. 95.

38. Quoted in Fred I. Greenstein, *The Hidden-Hand Presidency: Eisenhower as Leader* (New York: Basic Books, 1982), p. 50. See also Mark H. Leff, "Historical Perspectives on Old-Age Insurance: The State of the Art on the Art of the State," in Edward D. Berkowitz, ed. *Social Security After Fifty* (Westport, CT: Greenwood Press, 1987), pp. 33–34.

39. Ferrell, *Eisenhower Diaries*, p. 269.

40. Lieberman, *Shifting the Color Line.*

41. On Southern Democrats and the conservative coalition, see V. O. Key Jr., *Southern Politics in State and Nation* (New York: Knopf, 1949); and Ira Katznelson, Kim Geiger, and Daniel Kryder, "Limiting Liberalism: The Southern Veto in Congress, 1939–1950," *Political Science Quarterly* 108 (1993): 283–306.

42. *Congressional Quarterly Almanac* 10 (1954): 54–56, 188–94.

43. See James L. Sundquist, *Politics and Policy: The Eisenhower, Kennedy, and Johnson Years* (Washington: Brookings Institution, 1968).

44. *Congressional Quarterly Almanac* 10 (1954): 223–25, 54–56.

45. *Congressional Quarterly Weekly Report* 16 (1958): 561–63.

46. Edward D. Berkowitz, *America's Welfare State: From Roosevelt to Reagan* (Baltimore: Johns Hopkins University Press, 1991), pp. 64–65.

47. Edward D. Berkowitz and Kim McQuaid, *Creating the Welfare State: The Political Economy of Twentieth-Century Reform*, rev. ed. (Lawrence: University Press of Kansas, 1992), p. 180.

48. I. F. Stone, *The Haunted Fifties, 1953–1963* (Boston: Little, Brown, 1989), pp. 104–5.

49. Irving Bernstein, *Promises Kept: John F. Kennedy's New Frontier* (New York: Oxford University Press, 1991), p. 181.

50. Margaret Weir, "The Federal Government and Unemployment: The Frustration of Policy Innovation from the New Deal to the Great Society," in Margaret Weir, Ann Shola Orloff, and Theda Skocpol, eds. *The Politics of Social Policy in the United States* (Princeton: Princeton University Press, 1988); Brinkley, *The End of Reform*; Bernstein, *Promises Kept*, pp.121–23.

51. Katznelson, Geiger, and Kryder, "Limiting Liberalism"; Lieberman, *Shifting the Color Line.*

52. Carl M. Brauer, "John F. Kennedy: The Endurance of Inspirational Leadership," in Fred I. Greenstein, ed. *Leadership in the Modern Presidency,* (Cambridge: Harvard University Press, 1988).

53. Bernstein, *Promises Kept*, p. 122.

54. *Congressional Quarterly Weekly Report* 17 (1961): 270–79, 875. *Congressional Quarterly Weekly Report* 20 (1961): 431–32, 1448–49.

55. Berkowitz, *Mr. Social Security*, pp.146–47.

56. See Berkowitz, *America's Welfare State*, pp.106–11; Sundquist, *Politics and Policy*, pp.125–30.

57. Theda Skocpol, *Protecting Soldiers and Mothers: The Political Origins of Social Policy in the United States* (Cambridge: Harvard University Press, 1992); Michael B. Katz, *In the Shadow of the Poorhouse: A Social History of Welfare in America* (New York: Basic Books, 1986); Linda Gordon, *Pitied but not Entitled: Single Mothers and the History of Welfare* (New York: Free Press, 1994).

58. *Congressional Quarterly Almanac* 18 (1962): 212–18; Lieberman, *Shifting the Color Line;* Sundquist, *Politics and Policy*, pp. 129–30; Gilbert Y. Steiner, *Social Insecurity: The Politics of Welfare* (Chicago: Rand McNally, 1966), pp. 40–47.

59. Skowronek, *Politics Presidents Make*, pp. 325–60.

60. See Robert Dallek, *Lone Star Rising: Lyndon Johnson and His Times, 1908–1960* (New York: Oxford University Press, 1991); Robert A. Caro, *The Years of Lyndon Johnson: The Path to Power* (New York: Knopf, 1982).

61. Skowronek, *Politics Presidents Make*, p. 334. See also Dallek, *Lone Star Rising*.

62. Lyndon B. Johnson, *The Vantage Point: Perspectives on the Presidency, 1963–1969* (New York: Holt, Rinehart and Winston, 1971), pp. 70–71.

63. Skowronek, *Politics Presidents Make*, pp. 335–36; Irving Bernstein, *Guns or Butter: The Presidency of Lyndon Johnson* (New York: Oxford University Press, 1996).

64. David J. Garrow, *Bearing the Cross: Martin Luther King, Jr., and the Southern Christian Leadership Conference* (New York: William Morrow, 1986), pp. 265–86.

65. Johnson, *Vantage Point*, pp. 69–75; Sundquist, *Politics and Policy*, pp. 112–13.

66. For a brief survey of the literature on Kennedy's domestic policy performance as president, see Bernstein, *Promises Kept*, pp. 3–7.

67. Sundquist, *Politics and Policy*, pp. 134–49; Lieberman, *Shifting the Color Line*; Daniel P. Moynihan, *Maximum Feasible Misunderstanding: Community Action in the War on Poverty* (New York: Free Press, 1969).

68. Susan Abrams Beck, "The Limits of Presidential Activism: Lyndon Johnson and the Implementation of the Community Action Program" (Ph.D. dissertation, Columbia University, 1985).

69. Vincent J. Burke and Vee Burke, *Nixon's Good Deed: Welfare Reform* (New York: Columbia University Press, 1974), p.11.

70. Johnson, *Vantage Point*, pp. 77–81; Bernstein, *Guns and Butter*, pp. 106–7; Sundquist, *Politics and Policy*, pp. 146–49.

71. Johnson, *Vantage Point*, p. 80.

72. See Joan Hoff-Wilson, "Richard M. Nixon: The Corporate Presidency," in Greenstein, ed. *Leadership in the Modern Presidency*.

73. Richard Nixon, *RN: The Memoirs of Richard Nixon* (New York: Grosset and Dunlap, 1978), pp. 34–35, 267, 424.

74. See Mayhew, *Divided We Govern*.

75. Paul Frymer and John David Skrentny, "Coalition-Building and the Politics of Electoral Capture During the Nixon Administration: African-Americans, Labor, Latinos," *Studies in American Political Development* 12 (1998): 131–61. See also Edward G. Carmines and James A. Stimson, *Issue Evolution: Race and the Transformation of American Politics* (Princeton: Princeton University Press, 1989).

76. Derthick, *Policymaking for Social Security*, pp. 349–68; Martha Derthick, *Agency Under Stress: The Social Security Administration in American Government* (Washington: Brookings Institution, 1990).

77. Nixon, *RN*, 426; Joan Hoff, *Nixon Reconsidered* (New York: Basic Books, 1994), pp. 116–17.

78. Moynihan, *Politics of a Guaranteed Income*, 61; Burke and Burke, *Nixon's Good Deed*, p. 11.

79. Hoff, *Nixon Reconsidered*, pp. 61–65; James L. Sundquist, *The Decline and Resurgence of Congress* (Washington: Brookings Institution, 1981), pp. 203–7.

80. Berkowitz and McQuaid, *Creating the Welfare State*, p. 180.

81. Moynihan, *Politics of a Guaranteed Income*, pp. 64, 69; Hoff, *Nixon Reconsidered*, pp. 116–17.

82. Hoff, *Nixon Reconsidered*, pp. 119–21; Moynihan, *Politics of a Guaranteed Income*, pp. 68–69; Burke and Burke, *Nixon's Good Deed*, p. 41.

83. Moynihan, *Politics of a Guaranteed Income*, p. 215; Berkowitz, *America's Welfare State*, p. 127.

84. Burke and Burke, *Nixon's Good Deed*, p. 39.

85. Hoff, *Nixon Reconsidered*, pp. 124; Nixon, *RN*, pp. 426–27.

86. Hoff, *Nixon Reconsidered*, p.125.

87. Michael B. Katz, *The Undeserving Poor: From the War on Poverty to the War on Welfare* (New York: Pantheon, 1989), pp.102–105; Frances Fox Piven and Richard A. Cloward, *Poor People's Movements: Why They Succeed, How They Fail* (New York: Pantheon, 1977), pp. 335–49; Nixon, *RN*, p. 427.

88. Nixon, *RN*, p. 428; Jill Quadagno, *The Color of Welfare: How Racism Undermined the War on Poverty* (New York: Oxford University Press, 1994), p. 133; Piven and Cloward, *Poor People's Movements*, pp. 341–42; Burke and Burke, *Nixon's Good Deed*, pp.184–85.

89. Moynihan, *Politics of a Guaranteed Income*, p. 61.

90. Although, as Paul Pierson shows, previous policies make retrenchment hard even in unified parliamentary systems. Paul Pierson, *Dismantling the Welfare State?: Reagan, Thatcher, and the Politics of Retrenchment* (Cambridge: Cambridge University Press, 1994). See also R. Kent Weaver and Bert A. Rockman, eds., *Do Institutions Matter?: Government Capabilities in the United States and Abroad* (Washington: Brookings Institution, 1993).

91. Or, as Hannah Arendt puts it, in the Westminster system, "one party always represents the government and actually rules the country, so that, temporarily, the party in power becomes identical with the state." Hannah Arendt, *The Origins of Totalitarianism* (New York: Harcourt, 1951), p. 252. I am grateful to Ira Katznelson, who suggested this reference in a public lecture, "A Seminar on the State" (Columbia University, 1998).

92. Neustadt, *Presidential Power*, p. 26. See also Jones, *The Presidency in a Separated System*.

93. David R. Mayhew, "Presidential Elections and Policy Change: How Much of a Connection Is There?," in Harvey L. Schantz, ed. *American Presidential Elections: Process, Policy, and Political Change* (Albany: State University of New York Press, 1996).

94. See Miroslav Nincic, "The United States, the Soviet Union, and the Politics of Opposites," *World Politics* 40 (1988): 452–75.

95. Skowronek, *Politics Presidents Make*, pp. 4–6.

96. Theda Skocpol, *Boomerang: Clinton's Health Security Effort and the Turn Against Government in U.S. Politics* (New York: Norton, 1996); Haynes Johnson and David S. Broder, *The System: The American Way of Politics at the Breaking Point* (Boston: Little, Brown, 1996).

97. Nolan M. McCarty, Keith T. Poole, and Howard Rosenthal, *Income Redistribution and the Realignment of American Politics* (Washington: AEI Press, 1997).

98. David T. Ellwood, "Welfare Reform As I Knew It," *American Prospect* 26 (May–June 1996): 22–29; Frances Fox Piven, "Was Welfare Reform Worthwhile?," *American Prospect* 27 (July-August 1996): 14–15; William Julius Wilson, *When Work Disappears: The World of the New Urban Poor* (New York: Knopf, 1996).

CHAPTER 14

The Institutional Face of Presidential Power: Congressional Delegation of Authority to the President

David Epstein and Sharyn O'Halloran

INTRODUCTION

For Neustadt the president is an individual and the presidency is a series of individuals trying to exert influence over public policy. Presidential power, according to this view, is limited and circumscribed by constitutional man-dates, and therefore the president must rely on his powers of persuasion to place his stamp on policy. The ability to persuade stems from a variety of sources, including personal reputation, bargaining skills, staff resources, and the ability to match a legislative program to the public mood. The extent that a president can use these resources to his advantage is the extent to which a pres-ident will be successful.

Where Neustadt conceives of presidential power in individual terms, we would place the presidency in its institutional context: the president is the head of the executive branch, and as such sits at the apex of a bureaucracy whose pri-mary function is the execution of laws. In the modern administrative state, where the scope and reach of federal activity far exceeds anything that the Founders originally envisioned, much of the president's influence over policy derives not from constitutional privilege, but from authority delegated by Con-gress to the executive branch. Thus, the president's ability to rise above the status of a mere clerk in the execution of laws is dependent on the amount of discre-tionary leeway to set policy that Congress is willing to cede the president and his agencies. To the extent that bureaucratic agents have discretionary authority in the interpretation and implementation of public laws, and to the extent that the president exerts control over these agents, the president has institutional power.

If the power of the president resides as much in his ability to gain discretionary authority as in his ability to push through legislative programs, the next step is to ask, when does Congress delegate authority to the executive? A Neustadtian approach (as adopted by, for instance, Barbara Kellerman and discussed further in this volume) would stress the personal bargaining power of the president and his ability to extract favorable deals from legislators regarding executive branch discretion.[1] The more adept is the president in these types of personal interactions, the more power will be delegated to executive branch actors.

In contrast, our approach emphasizes structural factors that influence delegation, more in line with the views expressed by Jon Bond and Richard Fleisher.[2] Our argument begins with the observation that executive branch policymaking is in part a *substitute* for legislative policymaking. That is, the details of public policy can either be explicitly spelled out in the implementing statute, or they can be left to the executive branch to fill in.[3] Seen from this perspective, policymaking involves a set of tradeoffs from the legislators' points of view: is it better for legislators to devote their own scarce time and resources to specify policy details, or would they rather leave these decisions to executive agencies, which are often better equipped to address complex issues but may not share legislators' policy goals? Are there some issues on which Congress prefers to delegate in order to escape the political heat? And if Congress decides to delegate, where within the executive branch will authority reside: with cabinet-level departments close to the president's control, or with more independent commissions? Or will Congress bypass the executive branch altogether and choose to delegate authority to the courts, the states, or even local actors?

Our approach implies that legislators will give more authority to executive agencies that share their policy agenda than to those that do not. If we can take party as a rough measure of policy preferences, then the president's institutional power should be regulated by such external factors as the presence of unified or divided government. We predict that the greater the differences in policy goals between the two branches, the more legislators will vote to restrict executive discretion and the more authority will be delegated to agencies farther from the president's control. Thus, presidents have other routes to political power besides reputation and bargaining, but their opportunity to exercise delegated authority will diminish as policy conflict with Congress increases.

An example will help illustrate our point. Ever since the 1934 Reciprocal Trade Agreements Act, Congress has delegated some degree of tariff-setting authority to the executive. But Congress has not delegated this authority in an unconstrained manner; rather, it has consistently imposed time limits on these delegations, requiring renewal of the president's negotiating authority at least once during every postwar administration. If one examines the changes in executive negotiating authority since the Truman administration, a striking pattern reveals itself: every time that Congress renewed delegation under unified government, the president's authority was expanded, and every time that delegation was renewed under divided government, the president's authority was restricted.[4] This occurred even though some minority party presidents such as Gerald Ford and Ronald Reagan have been characterized as good bargainers with strong interpersonal skills, and some majority party presidents such as Jimmy Carter and John F. Kennedy have been characterized as less skilled in these areas. In other words, a simple institutional model focusing on interbranch conflict explains changes in the president's institutional power in the realm of trade policy well, while the Neustadtian approach emphasizing personal skills performs less well.

The next section of this essay presents in greater detail the logic of our approach to presidential power, and elucidates the predictions that follow. We then examine these propositions with evidence on major postwar legislation, focusing on the amount of discretionary authority delegated to the executive branch and the location of this delegated authority. We conclude by suggesting how our insights relate to the broader debates on presidential power and policy outcomes.

THE POLITICS OF DELEGATION

The politics of delegation has two components: how much discretionary authority will Congress cede to the president, and where within the executive branch will decisionmaking authority reside? Our approach to these questions is illustrated in figure 14.1, which identifies two modes of policymaking. First, Congress can rely on its own internal decisionmaking procedures, where committees consider legislation and report out bills which must then be approved by majorities in both the House and the Senate. Second, legislators can sketch the broad details of policy and delegate the finer points to the executive branch. This means, however, that the president will have a much larger role in making policy, since it is the president who appoints the chief administrators of executive agencies.

What are the advantages and disadvantages associated with each alternative? Congress can write detailed laws that spell out every facet of public policy, but

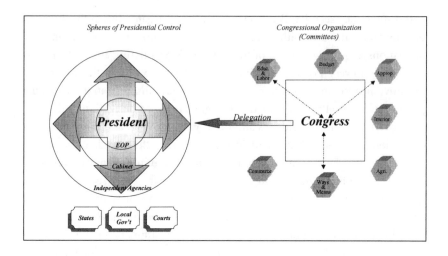

FIGURE 14.1.   Delegation and the Policymaking Process

the necessary information to make well-formed policy may be costly to obtain, and legislators have only a limited amount of time to spend on each piece of legislation. Plus, some policy areas—airline safety comes to mind—may carry the risk of significant political costs without many potential benefits. Alternatively, Congress can lighten its burden by delegating authority to the executive branch, but the bureaucrats who receive this authority may be motivated as much by the desire to pursue their own policy goals, inflate their budgets, and increase their scope of control as by their desire to follow congressional intent. Neither option is without its faults, but in different circumstances one or the other may be relatively more attractive from legislators' point of view.

Given this approach, we first ask how policy conflict between Congress and the president affects the amount of authority delegated. To begin with, presidents, in general, prefer more discretion to less as this gives them additional avenues to influence policy. And if bureaucrats had preferences identical to those of legislators, Congress could assure itself of favorable outcomes simply by delegating to the executive branch with unfettered discretion. As bureaucrats' preferences diverge from those of legislators, though, Congress will rationally place tighter constraints on the use of delegated authority through restrictive administrative procedures. Since the president appoints agency heads, who in turn direct agencies' actions, the implication is that legislators will grant more leeway to bureaucrats under unified than divided government; that is, when the president comes from the same party as the congressional majority rather than the minority.

Two contrasting examples illustrate this argument. When constructing the landmark 1965 Voting Rights Act, Congress delegated considerable amounts of authority to the Department of Justice. The Attorney General determined when federal examiners were needed to assist in voter registration, when a jurisdiction had employed literacy tests that brought it under the preclearance provisions of the act, when local election officers had fulfilled their duties regarding the enrollment of new voters, and so on. Legislators were willing to accede to executive requests for broad authority partly because they were convinced that the Johnson Administration strongly supported the act.

On the other hand, when Congress enacted the 1970 Clear Air Act, legislators, wary of the Nixon Administration, worried that bureaucrats would not enforce the act's provisions vigorously. They therefore wrote the law so as to give the executive branch very little discretion, spelling out in excruciating detail the standards and requirements that the EPA had to enforce, and giving citizens' groups ample opportunities to challenge EPA decisions in the courts. Again, the degree of agency discretion was closely related to legislative-executive policy differences.

How does interbranch conflict affect the location of delegated authority? Political actors, it has been emphasized, carefully calibrate the means by which policymaking power is ceded to the executive branch. As Terry Moe writes:

> Structural choices have important consequences for the content and direction of policy, and political actors know it. When they make choices about structure, they are implicitly making choices about policy. And precisely because this is so, issues of structure are inevitably caught up in the larger political struggle. Any notion that political actors might confine their attention to policymaking and turn organizational design over to neutral criteria or efficiency experts denies the realities of politics.[5]

As illustrated in figure 14.1, one important structural choice that Congress makes concerns the particular actors to whom authority is delegated: the executive office of the president (EOP) and cabinet departments, over which the president has a fair degree of control; independent agencies and commissions that are further removed from presidential influence; or state-level actors, local governments, and the courts, which are independent from the executive branch altogether. Legislators must first decide whether to give authority to the executive or to the states—this is the *federalism* question. And if authority will be located in the executive branch, Congress must choose the particular executive actor to receive the delegated authority—this is the *locational* question. Both are crucial threshold decisions in the delegation of regulatory authority.

Whatever the reason for choosing independent agencies over more politically responsive executive departments, Congress's tendency to use more independent actors should increase as the level of policy conflict between Congress and the president rises. Assume, for instance, that moving from independent agencies to cabinet departments makes policy outcomes more predictable at the cost of greater presidential control. During times of divided government, then, congressional preferences over the structure of delegation will shift, so that more authority will be given to executive actors further from the president's political reach; or Congress will delegate to the states and circumvent the executive altogether.

In sum, an institutional theory of delegation based on interbranch conflict predicts that under divided government, Congress will delegate less discretionary authority and move it farther from the president's reach. A Neustadtian theory, on the other hand, would predict that discretionary authority will tend to flow to presidents with strong negotiating skills and interpersonal abilities. We now turn to examining these predictions with evidence from major legislation in the postwar era.

PARTY VOTING OVER DELEGATION

Data

We analyze a sample of laws that come from David Mayhew's book *Divided We Govern*, in which he defines important legislation in a two-step—or as he calls it, a "two-sweep"—process.[6] The first sweep of legislation includes those bills reported in the year-end roundups of both *The New York Times* and *The Washington Post*. This sweep captures contemporary judgments about the productivity of national government and identifies those pieces of legislation that were thought to be of historic significance. The second sweep captures those laws that historians and political observers, in hindsight, identify as being of lasting importance.

Mayhew's data include 267 enactments over the 1947 to 1990 period, of which 64 were chosen in sweep one, 56 came from sweep two, and 147 were identified in both sweeps. Starting from this list we added important legislation in 1991 and 1992, but deleted constitutional amendments, treaties, and laws for which sufficient legislative summaries were unavailable, bringing us to a total of 257 public laws. We then examined all the rollcalls associated with the passage of these laws on the floor of the House of Representatives.[7] This includes rollcall votes on rules, amendments, procedural motions, final passage, conference reports, and veto overrides. The House recorded a rollcall vote on all but 8 of the laws, which produces a total sample of 249 bills. On these bills there were a total of 1,314 recorded rollcall votes.

We next classified each rollcall in terms of whether or not the vote was over executive discretion, defined as the latitude that an agency has to move policy away from the status quo. Executive discretion can be constrained in a number of ways: by Congress setting spending limits, by specifying impermissible actions, or by limiting the range of policies that an agency can set. Our purpose here is not to specify the particular mechanisms for limiting agency discretion, but rather to identify those measures on which members sought to alter the terms of delegation either by increasing or decreasing executive authority.

The procedure we adopted was as follows. First, for each rollcall vote, we read the corresponding *Congressional Quarterly Weekly Report* brief to determine if the motion was over delegation.[8] If not, then the rollcall was eliminated from the data set. This left us with 479 rollcall votes over delegation. The next step was to determine if the motion increased or decreased discretion. To code each rollcall, we first determined the relevant alternative to the motion being considered. For example, if the vote was on an amendment, the alternative was the unamended bill. If the vote was on final passage, the appropriate reference was existing law. If the vote was on a conference report then the relevant status quo was the version of the bill passed by the House. Given a motion and its relevant alternative, we determined which gave the executive greater discretionary authority. Of the 479 rollcalls over delegation, 266 sought to raise the executive's discretion and 213 sought to lower it.

Finally, for each rollcall over delegation, we recorded each House member's individual vote. This yielded a total sample of 187,385 member-votes.[9] We also included member-specific information, such as whether the legislator was on the committee that reported the bill or held a leadership position within the chamber. We also noted each member's seniority and partisan affiliation. In addition, we recorded the president's position on each rollcall: whether he favored, opposed, or had no announced position. These data are summarized in table 14.1.

INDIVIDUAL VOTING OVER DELEGATION

Our prediction is that members will support delegation to the executive more when they share similar policy goals; that is, when the president belongs to the same party. The Neustadtian approach predicts that presidents with better bargaining skills will receive more votes in support of delegation. To examine

TABLE 14.1 Descriptive Statistics and Data Sources

Variable	Description	Mean	Std. Dev.	Sources
Raise-or-Lower	1 if the measure would increase executive discretion; 0 if the measure would decrease executive discretion.	0.55	0.49	*Congressional Quarterly Weekly Report*, various years.
Vote	1 if the member voted Aye; 0 if the member voted Nay.	0.66	0.47	ICPSR Roll Call Vote Data
Pro-Delegation Vote	1 if Vote = Raise-or-Lower; 0 otherwise.	0.58	0.49	Authors' classification
President Support	1 if the president supported the position of greater delegation; 0 if the president had no announced position; and −1 if the president supported the position of less delegation.	0.21	0.64	Authors' classification
President	1 if the president is a Republican; and 0 otherwise.	0.560	0.496	Authors' classification
President Same	1 if the member was of the same party as the president; 0 otherwise.	0.509	0.499	Authors' classification
Party	1 for Republicans ; 0 for Democrats.	0.396	0.489	ICPSR Roll Call Vote Data
On Committee	1 if the member was on the committee that reported the bill; 0 otherwise.	0.112	0.315	Nelson, Garrison, 1993, Committees in the U.S. Congress, Washington, D.C.: *Congressional Quarterly Press.*

(Continued)

Variable	Description			Source
Committee Leader	11–13: committee chair; 21–24: ranking minority member; 0 otherwise.	0.685	3.33	Nelson, *Committees*
Party Leader	31–51 for Speaker, Majority leader, and Majority Whip; 61–71 for Minority leader, and Minority Whip; and 0 otherwise.	0.605	5.74	Nelson, *Committees*
Seniority	Total number of terms served in the House of Representatives	5.34	4.05	Nelson, *Committees*
Seat share	Avg. percent of House and Senate seats held by the party opposite president.	−0.016	0.107	Calculated by authors
Executive Order	Ranking of agency by the degree of independence; 1 is least independent, 5 is most.	2.24	0.84	Calculated by authors from *Congressional Quarterly* legislative summaries
Presidential Bargaining Skill	Ordinal ranking of presidential bargaining ability; 1 = Highest Skill, 9 = Lowest Skill	4.97	2.93	Calculated from Bond and Fleisher, *The President in the Legislative Arena*
Activism	(Year-1960) for years 1961–68; (1977-Year) for years 1969–77; 0 otherwise.	1.33	1.51	Calculated by authors
Start term	1 if the first two years following a presidential election; 0 otherwise.	0.58	0.50	Mayhew, *Divided We Govern*
Deficit	U.S. federal budget deficit over total federal outlays.	−0.075	0.097	*Economic Report of the President*, 1997, Washington: GPO

these hypotheses, we first constructed a new measure called Pro-Delegation Vote, which was set equal to one if a member voted Aye on a proposition to raise the executive's discretionary authority, Nay on a vote to lower discretion, and zero otherwise. So a vote in favor of delegation is a vote in favor of increasing or against decreasing the president's discretion.

Distributions of this variable disaggregated by party and administration are shown in figure 14.2. The horizontal axis in each graph indicates the proportion of votes in which an individual member supported greater delegation. The vertical axis shows the proportion of members with a given pro-delegation voting score. The distribution marked with crosses indicates Democrats, while the circles denote Republicans. These graphs provide a useful way to compare partisan support for executive delegation across administrations. During the Truman administration, for instance, Republicans generally voted against measures that increased executive discretion, with the modal Republican voting in favor of increased discretion only about 25 percent of the time. Democrats, on the other hand, were much more disposed to grant the executive greater discretion, with a mode of close to 80 percent support.

These nine graphs exhibit a clear partisan pattern in voting over delegation. When Republicans held the presidency, the Democrat and Republican distributions look nearly identical, so that both parties supported delegation at about the same rate. But when Democrats were in the White House, the Democrat distribution is considerably more supportive of delegation than the Republican distribution. This indicates that during times of unified government—the Truman, Kennedy, Johnson, and Carter administrations—voting patterns over delegation polarized, with Democrats quite willing on average to give discretionary authority to executive branch actors, and the Republicans rather wary of delegating such power. Thus a simple interbranch policy conflict approach predicts well these basic patterns of voting over delegation.

The president's position on each rollcall vote was used to create a delegation support measure, which took on the value of 1 if the president supported a motion to increase discretion or opposed a motion to decrease authority, -1 in the opposite cases, and zero if the president had no announced position. Not surprisingly, presidents in general supported greater executive discretion. Of the rollcalls on which they took positions, Democratic presidents supported greater delegation on 97 occasions and less delegation on only 24. For Republican presidents, the corresponding figures are 64 instances of support and 35 of opposition.

These data were further analyzed to see how well partisan characteristics

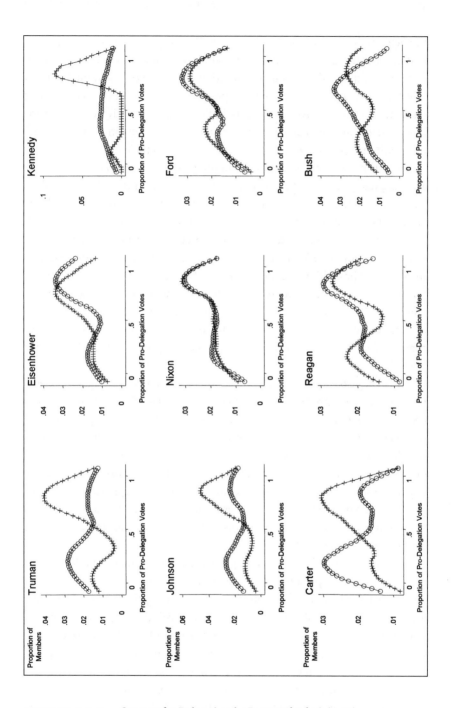

FIGURE 14.2. Support for Delegation, by Party and Administration

predicted individual votes over delegation. We use probit analysis for the estimation, which is a standard statistical technique employed when the phenomenon to be explained—voting on delegation—takes on only a limited number
of values. In this case, we had only two possibilities: a vote for or against greater
discretion. Thus positive coefficients indicate that a positive change in the
independent variable makes a member more likely to vote in favor of delegation, with the opposite interpretation for negative coefficients.

The estimates shown in the first column of table 14.2 reveal that Democrats
are more likely to support delegation than are Republicans, and that members
were more likely to vote for propositions supported by the president (and vote
against those that he opposed). The first of these findings accords well with
the conventional wisdom that Democrats prefer bigger government (insofar
as the expansion of federal authority usually means giving more discretion to
the executive branch), while the second must be interpreted with some care. It
may indicate that presidents sway members' voting decisions by taking a pre-
announced position, but it may also indicate that presidents are careful to
only announce a position one way or the other when they have a reasonable
chance of success, thus avoiding embarrassing legislative defeats whenever
possible.

The table also shows that more senior members tend to vote against delegation. Again, two interpretations come to mind. The first is that members
become more attached to the institution over time and guard its policymaking
prerogatives more jealously against executive incursions, whereas more junior
members focus more on passing policy, even if it means handing over some
discretionary authority to the executive branch. The other possibility is that the
best way for legislators to assure themselves continued reelection is to make
sure that Congress retains control over as many policy levers as possible, and
that the members who understand this better are those who stay around long
enough to accrue seniority.

In addition, even after controlling for these effects, members do support
delegation more to presidents of their own party. Our basic hypothesis that
interbranch conflict affects members' votes over delegation is thus supported;
legislators are more willing to cede presidents institutional power when they
share similar policy goals. Moreover, a comparison of the standardized coefficients from Model 1 indicates that the effects of a member's party, the president's support for a measure or lack thereof, and interbranch conflict are
roughly equivalent in determining a member's voting pattern, so interbranch
conflict is as important as a member's partisan affiliation in influencing voting
behavior.[10]

TABLE 14.2 Probit Estimates of House Members' Support for Delegation
Dependent Variable: Pro-Delegation Vote

Var.	Model 1	Model 2	Model 3	Model 4
Party	−0.20	−0.13	−0.20	−0.14
	(-32.94)**	(−20.26)**	(-33.25)**	(-22.45)**
President's Support	0.20	−0.13	0.20	−0.13
	(43.05)**	(−19.83)**	(43.18)**	(−20.37)**
Seniority	−0.002	−0.003	−0.002	−0.004
	(−3.29)**	(−4.18)**	(−3.15)**	(−5.70)**
President Same	0.21	0.07	0.20	0.10
	(36.06)**	(11.69)**	(32.48)**	(16.10)**
President Same×		0.66		0.65
President Support		(69.71)**		(69.22)**
On Committee×			0.10	
President Same			(7.09)**	
On Committee×			−0.0005	
President Opposite			(−0.04)	
President†				
Truman				−0.013
				(−0.74)
Eisenhower				0.15
				(9.24)**
Kennedy				0.20
				(10.14)**
Johnson				0.049
				(3.51)**
Nixon				0.048
				(3.77)**
Ford				0.08
				(4.98)**
Carter				-0.21
				(−15.26)**
Reagan				0.004
				(0.28)
Constant	0.16	0.20	0.16	0.19
	(25.09)**	(31.04**)	(24.14)**	(15.22)**
χ^2	4,070	9,003	4,121	10,342
No. Obs.	187,385	187,385	187,385	187,385

t-statistics in parentheses; robust linear estimates. * $\alpha<.10$; ** $\alpha<.05$.
†The omitted category is the Bush administration.

This finding is supported even more strongly in column 2, where an interactive term is added between the president's position and the variable indicating whether or not the president is of the same party. The coefficient on this term is positive and significant, suggesting that partisan divisions intensify on those rollcalls for which the president has announced a position beforehand. This finding has several explanations. One is that on pieces of legislation important enough for the president to take a position, party members rally in his support. Alternatively, the president may strategically take positions on issues that are controversial and divide the political parties.

Next, we investigate the relation between whether a member was on the committee that reported a given bill and that member's rollcall votes over delegation. Column 3 shows that committee members of the same party as the president support greater delegation, while the coefficient on committee members from the opposite party is statistically insignificant. This result highlights the tacit collusion or "iron-triangle" type behavior that may at times take place between agencies and the committees that oversee them; i.e., committees give agencies greater authority, which the bureaucrats then exercise to promote committee members' policy goals. Therefore, all else being equal, committee members who share the same policy preferences as executive branch actors should favor greater agency discretion.

Finally, to ascertain whether a Neustadtian theory of presidential bargaining power explains members' voting over delegation, column 4 includes variables representing each postwar presidential administration (with the Bush Administration as the reference or excluded category). Following Jon Bond and Richard Fleisher,[11] who review much of the secondary literature and gather overall assessments of individual bargaining skill, we divide presidents into three groups:

1. *Highly Skilled*: Johnson, Reagan, Ford;
2. *Mixed Assessments*: Eisenhower, Truman, Kennedy; and
3. *Unskilled*: Bush, Nixon, Carter.

The coefficients on each of the administration variables in Model 4 indicate the increased or decreased probability that a House member voted in favor of executive discretion during that administration. If the bargaining skill theory were to work well, and if this ranking of presidents is accurate, then the coefficients for each presidential administration should rank the presidents in an order similar to the list above. However, as shown by the ordering of the coefficients in the table, the actual ranking of presidents from most to least skilled is: Kennedy, Eisenhower, Ford, Johnson, Nixon, Reagan, Bush, Truman, and

Carter. Given the statistically significant differences between this ordering and the bargaining skill ordering above, we conclude that the personal skills theory alone is limited in its ability to explain members' votes over executive discretion.[12] Clearly the interbranch conflict theory adds much to our understanding of the president's institutional power.

Another key to presidential success is the extent to which the president can convince party and congressional leaders to support his legislative agenda. The ability to acquire this support can do much to determine the amount of discretionary authority that Congress cedes the president. For instance, early in 1994, House Majority Leader Richard Gephardt (D-MO) stated that he would not request renewing the controversial "Super-301" provision, which constrains the executive by mandating presidential retaliation against certain unfair trade practices used by other countries. As reported in *Congressional Quarterly Weekly Report*, "A long-time proponent of an aggressive trade policy, Gephardt said the change in his approach is the result of having a Democrat in the White House."[13] Two weeks after this announcement, President Clinton himself renewed the Super-301 clause (on less restrictive terms than those proposed by Gephardt) via an executive order.

To examine the impact of party and committee leadership, table 14.3 separates out party and committee leaders' support for delegation by party and administration. The data in the table reveal some interesting patterns. For

TABLE 14.3   Roll Call Support for Delegation by Party, Leadership Status, and Administration Dependent Variable: Pro-Delegation Vote

	Democrats			Republicans		
Administration	Party Leaders	Committee Leaders	All Members	Party Leaders	Committee Leaders	All Members
Truman	68.75	58.09	63.43	40.00	41.71	45.94
Eisenhower	64.18	57.07	61.10	66.67	58.14	64.63
Kennedy	90.90	82.77	80.76	57.14	47.77	51.26
Johnson	74.15	66.41	70.74	50.00	51.20	51.74
Nixon	60.49	59.09	58.51	61.35	62.00	58.86
Ford	74.07	63.94	59.55	66.04	63.88	60.44
Carter	60.28	60.68	56.52	35.29	49.26	43.79
Reagan	55.77	56.41	55.03	55.44	61.19	58.09
Bush	60.65	59.07	56.87	56.36	51.88	55.22

Democrats as a party, overall trends in support follow clearly partisan divisions. The order of presidents from most to least supported is: *Kennedy, Johnson, Truman*, Eisenhower, Ford, Nixon, Bush, *Carter*, and Reagan, with Carter as the one obvious outlier (Democratic presidents are in italics).

Relative to these scores, Democratic party leaders consistently demonstrate higher support levels. Since Democrats were the majority party for all but two Congresses in this period, higher support levels could indicate institutional incentives attached to majority party leadership. These incentives may reflect, as Richard Bensel suggests, implicit collusion with the executive to share power over important decisions.[14] Or alternatively, it may reflect the party leaders' task of building coalitions to pass legislation, meaning that they have less room to be partisan, particularistic, or protective of congressional prerogatives.

Democratic committee leaders, on the other hand, are at times more and at other times less supportive of delegation when compared to the average Democratic floor voter. Inspection of the table shows that committee leaders were less supportive in the Truman, Eisenhower and Johnson Administrations, and more supportive in all others. The fact that three of the first four administrations appear as periods of lower committee support suggests that a time trend may be at work. Committee leaders were more protective of congressional institutional goals during the 1950s and 1960s, which were by all accounts the high water mark of committee power in the twentieth century. As the barricades of seniority were slowly eroded through congressional reforms in the 1970s and as internal rifts in the Democratic party eased due to conversion of conservative southern districts to the Republican party, these members acted less like *committee* leaders and more like committee *leaders*—they protected their individual policy areas less and spent more energy trying to pass legislation.

On the Republican side, similar partisan patterns emerge with aggregate party voting. The ordering from most to least support for delegation is: Eisenhower, Ford, Nixon, Reagan, Bush, *Johnson, Kennedy*, and *Truman*, with *Carter* again bringing up the rear. That is, Republican members uniformly supported Republican presidents at higher rates than they supported Democratic presidents.

With Republican committee and party leaders, the patterns are less clearcut. In all likelihood, this is due to the Republicans' minority status in the House throughout most of the postwar period. For committee leaders, no obvious patterns appear in the data. Party leaders, though, generally follow a more consistent partisan tack than do rank-and-file members. They were more supportive of Bush, Eisenhower, Ford, and Nixon than the average Republican floor member, and less supportive of Truman, Johnson, and Carter. The only deviations from the pattern come with Kennedy, who was opposed more by the average Republican member than by the Republican leadership, and Reagan, who was more supported by the rank and file. Note that in none of these circumstances does a Neustadtian bargaining approach alone appear to offer much leverage in explaining voting patterns over and above an institutional partisan-based approach.

PARTY VOTING OVER DELEGATION

We next examine the rollcall data from a slightly different angle, taking each rollcall and determining the percentage of Democrats and Republicans voting Aye. All else being equal, we expect that members from the same party as the president will be more likely to support measures that delegate than will members of the opposite party. If the partisan voting hypothesis is correct, then we should observe the following four patterns in overall partisan voting:

1. Democrats will vote to lower discretion more when Republicans control the presidency than when a Democrat is president;

2. Democrats will vote to raise discretion more when the Democrats control the presidency than when Republicans control the office;

3. Republicans will vote to lower discretion more when Democrats control the presidency than when they do; and

4. Republicans will vote to raise discretion more when Republicans control the presidency than when there is a Democratic president.

In short, members will vote to increase the institutional power of presidents from the same party, and decrease the power of presidents from the opposite party.

We test these hypotheses by dividing the sample into eight possible cases, broken down by party of the president, by congressional majority party, and by whether the vote was to raise or lower executive discretion. Figure 14.3 illustrates these eight possible cases. The four hypotheses above can be translated into the following predictions: the value (percentage) in Case 3 will be greater than Case 1, Case 2 greater than Case 4, Case 5 greater than Case 7, and Case 8 greater than Case 6.

Table 14.4 summarizes the percentage of members voting Aye in each of the eight cases. For instance, on rollcalls to raise discretion, House Democrats voted Aye 81 percent of the time when a Democrat controlled the White House and 69 percent of the time when a Republican was in office. The bottom half of

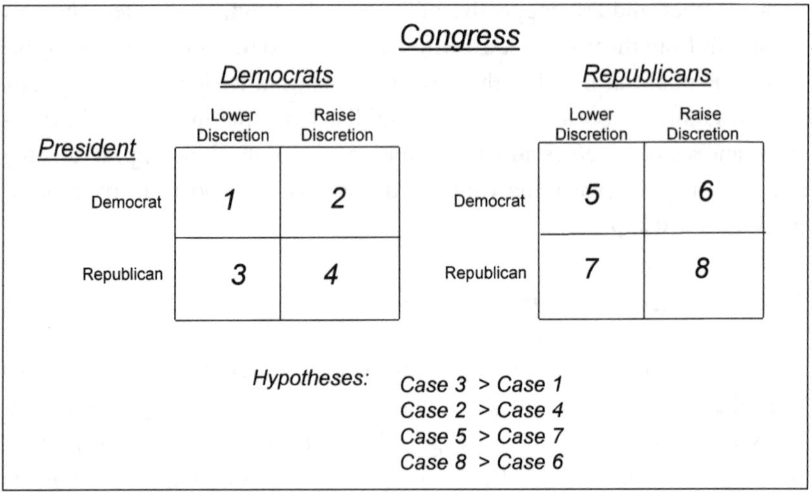

FIGURE 14.3   Hypotheses to Be Tested

TABLE 14.4   Percent of House Members Voting in Favor of a Roll Call to Delegate Authority, Divided by Party, Party of the President, and Whether to Raise or Lower Discretion

	Congress			
	Democrat		Republican	
President	Lower	Raise	Lower	Raise
Democrat	53%	81%	70%	64%
	(1)	(2)	(5)	(6)
Republican	57%	69%	60%	73%
	(3)	(4)	(7)	(8)

Note: N = 479;
    Cases from figure 15.3 referenced in parentheses.

Partisan Voting over Discretion

Alternative Hypotheses

Hypothesis	F-statistic	$P > F_{n-k}^k$
Case 3 – Case 1 = 0	1.16	0.246
Case 2 – Case 4 = 0	11.35	0.0008
Case 5 – Case 7 = 0	6.55	0.011
Case 8 – Case 6 = 0	5.91	0.015

table 14.4 reports the results of statistical tests on each of the four hypotheses stated above. In three of the four cases, the difference in voting patterns was in accordance with our predictions and statistically significant. In the one case in which the difference was not significantly different from zero—Case 1 vs. Case 3—the difference was in the hypothesized direction; it seems that Democrats are loathe to vote against executive discretion no matter who occupies the White House. Thus the patterns that emerge at the individual level reappear in aggregate party voting: members support delegation to presidents of their own party more than to presidents of the opposite party.

SPHERES OF PRESIDENTIAL CONTROL: TO WHOM DO YOU DELEGATE?

Next, we test our theory of structural choice, where the claim is that divided government should lead Congress to move decisionmaking authority to spheres further from presidential control. A Neustadtian theory, on the other hand, would argue that presidents with greater bargaining skill would retain more direct control over delegated authority. For our purposes here, two questions guide our inquiry. First, does divided government (congressional-executive conflict) influence where within the executive branch authority is delegated; and second, does divided government lead Congress to delegate authority to actors outside of the federal bureaucracy?

LOCATION OF DELEGATED AUTHORITY

As shown in figure 14.1 above, we can think of the president's influence over executive branch actors as consisting of a set of concentric circles. As authority is delegated to layers further from the president's core group of cabinet heads and EOP staff, presidential control wanes and becomes more diffuse. If this is true, then the logic of our approach would predict that as congressional-executive conflict increases, we should see Congress delegate authority to independent agencies and commissions that are less directly controlled by the president.

To investigate this claim, we identified the agencies mentioned in the *Congressional Quarterly* legislative summaries for each of our 257 public laws. All executive branch actors were then classified into one of the following five categories, using contemporaneous *U.S. Government Manuals* as a reference:
  1. Executive Office of the President;
  2. Cabinet Departments;

3. Independent Agencies;
4. Independent Regulatory Commissions;
5. Government Corporations.

Table 14.5 provides the frequencies of these observations by category, along with their relative frequency under divided and unified government. On average, each law identified about four different executive branch actors to receive authority, for a total of 961 agency-law observations. The table shows that cabinet departments were the most frequent recipients of delegated authority, comprising close to 60 percent of all observations. Government corporations were the least used of all categories; only 2.6 percent of the time did Congress delegate authority to these independent entities. The table also shows some indication of strategic delegation: the first two categories, EOP and cabinet, are used relatively more frequently under unified government, while independent agencies and commissions are used more often under divided control.[15]

These categories are listed in decreasing order of presidential control, or increasing order of independence. The Executive Office of the President, including for instance the Office of the United States Trade Representative, the National Security Council, and the Council of Economic Advisers, contains the president's personal staff as well as his closest advisers. The cabinet departments, such as Agriculture, Defense, and Labor, have more elaborate hierarchi-

TABLE 14.5   Agency Location, Discretion and Bureaucratic Structure under Unified and Divided Government

Recipients of Delegated Authority	All	Unified	Divided
Executive Office of the President	126	53	73
	(13.1%)	(13.4%)	(12.9%)
Cabinet Departments	573	254	319
	(59.6)	(64.3)	(56.4)
Independent Agencies	184	61	123
	(19.2)	(15.4)	(21.7)
Independent Regulatory Commissions	53	17	36
	(5.4)	(4.3)	(6.4)
Government Corporations	25	10	15
	(2.6)	(2.5)	(2.7)
Totals	961	395	566
	(100.00)	(100.00)	(100.00)

cal structures, but the president appoints all agency and division heads with the consent of the Senate and can remove them at will. Moreover, their budgets are submitted to Congress as part of the president's budget plan.

Independent agencies, by contrast, can submit their own budgets directly to Congress. Examples include the Central Intelligence Agency and the Environmental Protection Agency. Heads of independent regulatory commissions— such as the Federal Trade Commission and the Interstate Commerce Commission—are appointed by the president, but they serve for fixed terms. And government corporations, including Amtrak and the Post Office, get a proportion of their budget from market operations as opposed to direct federal government transfers.

We emphasize, though, that the choice is not necessarily one of presidential versus congressional control of agencies. Independent agencies may be exactly that: independent from both legislative scrutiny and executive interference. The correct view is therefore one of bias versus variance: Congress chooses between the biased but relatively certain policy outcomes that result from delegation to presidentially influenced actors, and less biased but more uncertain outcomes that result from delegation to independent agencies.[16]

An example of the greater uncertainty associated with delegating authority to independent commissions is illustrated by the battle in 1997 between the Clinton Administration and Federal Maritime Commission over the imposition of trade sanctions on Japanese ships. The commission's action was precipitated by a long-running dispute between the United States and Japan over the expensive fees and restrictions imposed on U.S. shipping fleets operating in Japanese ports. Events were unfolding at a leisurely diplomatic pace when suddenly the small, almost unknown Maritime Commission entered the fray by ordering the Coast Guard to bar Japanese cargo ships from U.S. ports. The commission threatened to impose sanctions after Japanese shipping companies, on order from their government, refused to pay $4 million in fines that had been imposed in an effort to relax Japanese port rules. The commission's actions sent top administration officials scrambling as they sought to work out an agreement with the Japanese that would persuade the Federal Maritime Commission to forego the embargo. In the end, a compromise was reached between the Clinton Administration and Japanese officials, averting the spectacle of Coast Guard cutters hunting down Japanese freighters, at least for the time being.[17] This episode illustrates how even the most obscure independent commissions can have profound effects on government policy and the potential uncertainty raised by their autonomy.

To estimate the relation between divided government and agency independence, the general strategy is to again use multivariate analysis. In this case, an ordered probit is appropriate since the location of delegated authority can take on one of five inherently ordered values, with the EOP being the least independent and government corporations the most. The data in table 14.5, however, show only the frequency with which each category occurred under divided and unified control. If certain categories were used in laws that delegated little overall authority, then we should count them less heavily in our analysis. Therefore each agency observation was weighted by the amount of discretionary authority delegated in the given law.[18]

Furthermore, the hypothesized patterns of delegation might show up most clearly in those instances where a new agency was created, as it is in these circumstances that legislators have the most leeway over the placement of delegated authority. Therefore we also conducted the analysis separately for all newly created agencies (these accounted for 202 out of our 961 observations). Finally, we measured interbranch conflict by seat share, which is the percent of seats held by the party opposite the president (see table 14.1).

The results of the estimation, shown in table 14.6, support our hypothesis. Model 1 uses only seat share as an independent variable, indicating that as the percent of seats held by members of Congress of the opposite party from the president increases, Congress tends to move authority away from the president's direct control and to the outer layers of the concentric circles of presidential influence. Model 2 shows that this statement continues to hold even when we control for other factors that may affect policymaking, such as the beginning of a presidential term, policy activism, and the size of the federal deficit. The seat share measure is statistically significant and in the predicted direction, and these effects become more pronounced when examining only those newly created agencies. These results have significant substantive implications as well: for instance, the probability of delegating to an EOP actor rises nearly 20 percent due to a switch from divided to unified government, and the probability of delegating to an independent commission falls from 13 percent to 7 percent.[19]

In Model 3 of table 14.6, we include a Presidential Bargaining Skill variable as well. This measure represents judgments concerning presidents' ability to bargain effectively with Congress; it was developed from Bond and Fleisher's rankings given above, with 1 representing the most highly skilled president (Johnson), and 9 the least skilled (Carter). A Neustadtian theory would predict that this variable will be positively and significantly related to the location of delegated authority, as more skilled presidents can retain more direct control

TABLE 14.6 Ordered Probit Estimates of Agency Location for All Laws
Dependent Variable: Executive Order

	All Agencies			New Agency Created		
	Model 1	Model 2	Model 3	Model 1	Model 2	Model 3
Seat Share	0.86	0.66	0.68	1.66	1.69	2.20
	(2.51)**	(1.81)*	(1.78)*	(2.23)**	(2.14)**	(2.52)**
Start Term		−0.055	−0.053		0.21	0.23
		(−0.74)	(−0.71)		(1.23)	(1.35)
Activist		−0.005	−0.005		0.090	0.082
		(−0.20)	(−0.21)		(1.68)*	(1.59)
Deficit		-0.59	-0.58		−2.13	−1.93
		(−1.47)	(−1.45)		(-2.12)**	(−1.90)*
Presidential			−0.002			−0.039
Bargaining Skill			(−0.17)			(−1.36)
μ_1	−0.63	−0.73	−0.73	−0.81	−0.42	−0.39
μ_2	1.03	0.93	0.93	0.91	1.33	1.38
μ_3	1.91	1.82	1.82	1.67	2.11	2.16
μ_4	2.36	2.27	2.27	2.42	2.87	2.92
χ^2	6.29	9.66	9.69	5.00	11.62	13.46
Num. Obs.	961	961	961	202	202	202

Note: z-statistics in parentheses; * $\alpha < .10$; ** $\alpha < .05$.

over agencies exercising discretionary authority. But as shown in the table, the coefficient on the bargaining skill variable is negative and insignificant in all cases. Thus once again the presidential skills model performs less well explaining the president's institutional power than a simple interbranch conflict model.

NON-EXECUTIVE DELEGATIONS

We next investigate when Congress circumvents the federal bureaucracy altogether by delegating to state agencies, local authorities, and the courts. To answer this question, for each law in our database we counted the percentage of actors outside of the executive branch to whom authority was delegated. For instance, the 1990 Clean Air Act contained 26 provisions that delegated to nonexecutive actors, out of a total of 213 provisions that delegated substantive authority. So the nonexecutive delegation ratio for this law is 26/213, or 12.2 percent.

TABLE 14.7   Two Sample t-test with Equal Variances of Percent Non-Executive
Delegations by Divided and Unified Government

Variable	Mean	Std. Err.	Number	t-statistic	P > |t|*
Unified	0.021	0.004	115		
Divided	0.035	0.006	142		
Difference	-0.014	0.007	257	-1.89	0.059

*Note: two-tailed test

Table 14.7 shows the results of a difference of means test comparing the percent of provisions that include delegation to nonexecutive entities under divided and unified government. During times of divided control, an average of 3.5 percent of all provisions delegate authority to bodies other than the federal bureaucracy, compared to 2.1 percent when the same party controls Congress and the presidency, a difference of 1.4 percentage points. As shown, nonexecutive actors do receive a greater percentage of delegations during divided government, thus supporting our hypothesis.

On the other hand, there is an alternative explanation for these findings. Divided government during the period studied was almost entirely due to a Democratic Congress and a Republican president. Republicans, as a party, oppose large federal government and favor the devolution of power to the states. Thus, a model predicting that greater Republican control leads to greater delegation to nonexecutive actors would essentially perform as well as ours.

EXAMPLE: SOCIAL SECURITY

The recent debate over the Social Security Administration will help illustrate the politics of structural choice. A cornerstone of Franklin Roosevelt's New Deal, Social Security was initially administered by an independent board, which was replaced in 1946 by the Social Security Administration (SSA). It continued as an independent agency until 1953 when the Republican-controlled Congress supported Eisenhower's move to consolidate the social services under the newly created Department of Health, Education and Welfare. This agency subsequently became Health and Human Services (HHS), thereby lodging the SSA firmly within the cabinet-department hierarchy.

On August 15, 1995, this all changed when the Social Security Administration was extracted from its place in the Department of Health and Human Services and once again became an independent agency. The reshuffling of administrative personnel was not simply a card trick; it was accompanied by real changes in the daily operations of the agency. Previously, the administrative head was designated by the Secretary of HHS and could be removed by the president. Under the new arrangement, the commissioner of the SSA was to be appointed by the president with Senate confirmation, and was then to serve for a fixed six-year term. Also, the agency's budget was no longer one of many items in the HHS department requests; rather, the reorganization required that each year the president send to Congress two budgets for the agency, including the president's final request as well as the agency's original proposal to the White House.

The move to create an independent agency was the brainchild of Senator Patrick Moynihan (D-NY). In an effort to aid pensioners and strengthen the Social Security program, Moynihan had argued for years that the SSA should be made independent as a way to "heighten its visibility and isolate it somewhat from the political party that controlled the White House, giving it more autonomy to direct and protect the Social Security Trust Fund, which paid social security benefits."[20] Three bills to this effect, though, had died in the Senate after passing the House in 1986, 1989, and 1992. The Clinton Administration initially opposed the reorganization of the SSA, as had the Reagan and Bush Administrations before it, maintaining that Social Security was best left under the purview of HHS. Secretary of HHS Donna Shalala, like her GOP predecessors, argued that making SSA an independent agency would "seriously dilute the attention and support it will receive at the highest level of our government."[21]

Nonetheless, Moynihan garnered sufficient support to pass the bill by voice vote in the Senate, picking up some support from Republicans (who no longer had the GOP White House position to defend) without losing Democratic backing. Likewise, the House considered the bill under expedited procedures and passed the measure by a vote of 413–0. The question, however, is why was Moynihan successful in 1995 when he had failed thrice before?

The answer comes from the logic of interbranch conflict. All presidents have incentives to retain control over Social Security, one of the country's most popular social programs, so that their policy preferences can be represented as more conservative along this dimension than those of either the House or the Senate. Democrats, in general, support an independent SSA as a means of curtailing political influence over an important social program. Republicans had no such policy motivations, and while a president of their own party occupied the White House, the Republicans were content with the status quo. In other words, any attempt to make the agency independent would be vetoed by the president and this veto could not be overridden, thus precluding policy movement.

Once a Democrat gained control of the White House, however, the situation took a new twist. Congressional Democrats maintained their stance in favor of independence, but now were joined by Republicans eager to impair presidential influence over social security once a Democrat controlled the White House. This paved the way for Moynihan's measure to sail through with large, veto-proof majorities in both houses. In sum, legislative and executive preferences over the SSA polarized, leading Congress to move the agency further from executive control.

CONCLUSION

By Neustadt's reckoning, to understand changes in presidential power over time one must examine changes in the president's individual characteristics, including bargaining skill, the ability to maintain a reputation, the lieutenants that the president assembles, and so on. This is the personal side of presidential power.

But there is another side to this story, which is the institutional aspect of presidential power. The president sits at the apex of the federal bureaucracy, a large hierarchical organization. And from time to time, Congress will invest executive branch actors with the ability to make important policy decisions. As we have shown, this type of power follows an identifiable pattern according to the degree of policy conflict between the two branches, both in the amount of authority delegated and in the type of actors that receive discretionary authority. Furthermore, none of the statistical tests that incorporated a proxy for presidential bargaining skills evinced clear and systematic support for the Neustadtian view.

Much of the variation in the president's institutional power, therefore, is not directly attributable to the president's bargaining ability or personal characteristics, but instead to more fundamental policy and political concerns. At the very least, this would appear to be an important baseline from which to judge presidential success. Many apparent presidential victories in the policy bargaining game can be ascribed to the fact that Congress and the president shared broadly similar policy goals, as with Johnson's Great Society programs. Conversely, presidential defeats may have been inevitable given the level of interbranch policy conflict; President Bush's failure to maintain his "no new taxes" pledge during the 1990 budget negotiations is a case in point, as was Clinton's inability to obtain fast track authority for expanding the North American Free Trade Agreement to Chile in 1997. Once we better understand the institutional dimensions of presidential power, we can better place the personal victories and failures of individual presidents within their proper context in our separation of powers system.

NOTES

1. Barbara Kellerman, *The Political Presidency: Practice of Leadership* (Oxford: Oxford University Press, 1984)

2. Jon Bond and Richard Fleisher, *The President in the Legislative Arena* (Chicago: University of Chicago Press, 1990).

3. This trade off is also recognized in Theodore Lowi, *The End of Liberalism* (New York: Norton, 1969). Lowi equates delegation of decisionmaking authority to either committees or the executive branch with an abdication of congressional legislative responsibilities. In contrast, we see delegation as a decision made by rational legislators trying to make policy in a complex environment. See, David Epstein and Sharyn O'Halloran, *Delegating Powers: A Transaction Cost Politics Approach to Policy Making Under Separate Powers* (New York: Cambridge University Press, 1999) Chapter 4 for a formal model of Congress's decision to delegate.

4. See Sharyn O'Halloran, *Politics, Process, and American Trade Policy* (Ann Arbor: University of Michigan Press, 1994), Chapter 5 for details.

5. Terry, Moe, "The Politics of Bureaucratic Structure," in J. Chubb and P. Peterson, eds., *Can the Government Govern?* (Washington, D.C.: Brookings Institution, 1989),p. 268.

6. David Mayhew, *Divided We Govern: Party Control, Lawmaking, and Investigations, 1946–1990* (New Haven: Yale University Press, 1991).

7. We use only the House of Representatives in our rollcall analysis since many Senate votes were taken by voice vote or by division rather than recorded rollcalls.

8. In most cases, it was clear when the motion under consideration sought to limit discretion. If in doubt, we referred to the *Congressional Quarterly* legislative summaries surrounding the passage of the bill. If still in doubt, we went to the *Congressional Record* and read the debates pertaining to the motion's passage.

9. These data were compiled from the ICPSR rollcall data set, as updated in Keith T. Poole and Howard Rosenthal, *Congress: A Political-Economic History of Roll-Call Voting* (Oxford: Oxford University Press, 1997). In the analysis we examined only Yea and Nay votes, leaving out announced, paired, or present votes.

10. The standardized coefficients on the variables Party, President's Support, and President Same are 0.098, 0.128, and 0.104, respectively.

11. Bond and Fleisher, *The President in the Legislative Arena*, pp. 198–201.

12. A Wilcoxon matched-pairs signed-ranks test confirms that the difference between these orderings is statistically significant at the 5 percent level.

13. *Congressional Quarterly Weekly Report* (February 26, 1994): p. 464.

14. Richard Bensel, "Creating the Statutory System: The Implications of a Rule of Law Standard in American Politics," *American Political Science Review* (1980) 74:734–744.

15. A chi-square test on table 14.5 yielded a Pearson chi-square(4) statistic of 9.11, with an associated probability of 0.058. Because the chi-squared value is significant, one could claim that the location of delegated authority and divided government are not independent events. The magnitude and direction of this effect will be estimated more precisely below.

16. This is the view expressed in Morris Fiorina, "Legislator Uncertainty, Legislative Control, and the Delegation of Legislative Power," *Journal of Law, Economics, & Organization* (1986) 2:33–51. Fiorina, however, characterizes the problem solely in terms of delegation to biased agencies as opposed to direct legislation, which is then interpreted by a series of luck-of-the-draw court decisions.

17. For a discussion of these events see Steven Lee Myer, "An Obscure Maritime Panel Gets Tough," *New York Times*, October 18, 1997, and David Sanger, "Japan Nears Pact with U.S. on Threat to Bar its Ships from U.S. Ports," *New York Times*, October 18, 1997.

18. Discretion is calculated as the percent of provisions that delegated authority, less the number of administrative procedures placed on the president's use of this authority. See Epstein and O'Halloran, *Delegating Powers*, for a detailed explanation.

19. These probabilities are calculated from the cutpoints μ_1 to μ_4 reported at the bottom of the first column in table 14.6, according to the logistic formula: Prob(category i) = $1/(1+\exp(\mu_i)) - 1/(1+\exp(\mu_{i-1}))$, where $\mu_0 = $ -infinity by definition.

20. *Congressional Quarterly Almanac*, 1993, Washington, D.C.: Congressional Quarterly Press, p. 381.

21. *Congressional Quarterly Almanac*, 1993, p. 381.

CHAPTER 15

Hitting the Ground Running: The Politics of Presidential Appointments in Transition

Nolan McCarty and Rose Razaghian

INTRODUCTION

The degree of personnel turnover associated with each shift of executive power in the United States is remarkable when compared with turnover in most democracies.[1] Upon entering office, each new president would like to quickly translate the vague promises of an electoral campaign into a concrete policy agenda. In order to realize the formulation and implementation of his agenda, the president depends heavily on subordinates throughout the White House and the rest of the executive branch. Although in many cases subject to advice and consent of the Senate, the president has the exclusive prerogative to appoint the high-level positions of the executive branch. The number of such appointments has grown into the hundreds for each administration. By securing positions for those who are loyal to him or share his policy views, the president can greatly increase the likelihood that his agenda will be carried out.

This presidential quest to "politicize," "presidentialize," or "control" the bureaucracy through appointments has received much scholarly attention, but it has rightly focused on the hurdles incurred by this strategy.[2] Not only has the challenging task of identifying loyal candidates been complicated by the declining role of parties in the organization of politics, but also the scrutiny of executive personnel by Congress, interest groups, and the mass media presents a number of new hurdles for each executive transition.[3] New presidents must strive to ensure that appointments neither antagonize supporters nor arm opponents. The result is a highly politicized process in which the success or failure of the president's agenda is at stake.

The literature on presidential transitions seems to offer two distinct, but perhaps conflicting, pieces of advice to new presidents who wish to make the most of their constitutional powers of appointment. One viewpoint articulated most vigorously by James Pfiffner is that presidents must "hit the ground running" to avoid missing the "window of opportunity."[4] Regarding the strategy of appointments:

> The importance of timeliness to the success of a presidency should not be underestimated. During a transition of the presidency, the permanent career bureaucracy continues to operate the government. But the governmental machinery is in neutral gear. Routine operation will go on without many problems, but new directions in policymaking will not be undertaken. Leadership is required that can only be provided by appointees of a new president. The longer the bureaucracy drifts the longer it will be before the president's policies and priorities can be implemented.[5]

Other scholars, however, question the need for speed. In the 1990 update of *Presidential Power*, Richard Neustadt focuses intensively on the "Hazards of Transition."[6] According to him, the problems related to presidential power have deepened through the "atomization" of the American government. Dispersed congressional power, a sprawling executive establishment, and the proliferation of interest groups have outstretched the president's ability to lead by persuasion.[7] As the complexity of the president's environment is intensified by these processes, the greater the likelihood of "transition hazards associated with newness in office, also newness to it" (p. 239). According to Neustadt, not only does a hurried transition lead to neophyte mistakes, but also early success is neither necessary nor sufficient for future success.

In this chapter, we wish take a further step toward understanding the politics of presidential transitions by examining how presidents reconcile these two pieces of conflicting advice when it comes to appointments. That is, how do presidents proceed quickly with caution? To this end, we examine a large number of transition appointments to analyze the strategies employed by new administrations to gain control of political positions in the executive branch. By transition appointments, we simply mean the first appointment to each existing position during the period of the new administration's inauguration.

Therefore, these appointments include not only those made during the period of transition, but also those made much later to replace incumbents of the previous administration or acting heads from the career service. The large number of appointments we study gives us a handle on the important decision that presidents face, on whether and how long to retain the previous administration's appointments or whether to select a new person.

The main question we tackle explores the strategies presidents employ in timing their first nomination for each available position. This allows us to examine in more detail the important tradeoff during the transition between speed and caution. Specifically, we explore how the tactics of new administrations are conditioned by the strategies of a particular set of political actors in the separation of powers system: the senators who must consent to presidential appointments. Although the Senate is not the only source of support or opposition in the political system for the president's choices, much of the opposition to the president's transition appears during the Senate confirmation process. So whether the ultimate source of opposition comes from outside groups or voices in the media, this opposition should be reflected in the way the Senate treats nominees. Even internal opposition from career officials in existing federal agencies should be reflected in opposition from the agency's friends in the Senate. To measure opposition, we compare the amount of time the Senate takes to reach a decision on confirmation.[8] All things equal, we postulate that longer confirmation processes compared to shorter ones reflect greater opposition to the president's program and appointees.

In turn, we argue that presidents seeking to seize control of the bureaucracy through smooth transitions of personnel must rationally anticipate areas of political opposition to avoid the "hazards of transition." In order to gain control quickly without dissipating political support, presidents should normally seek to make their relatively less controversial appointments earlier while saving more difficult ones until after the transition takes hold.

In our analysis, we find strong evidence that presidents are generally quite responsive to potential Senate opposition when making choices about the timing of particular transition nominations. In particular, we find that presidents tend to delay making nominations that are most likely to generate substantial scrutiny from the Senate. Thus, at least part of the advantage that early nominees appear to have in the confirmation process is due to strategic anticipation. These results provide additional evidence of the centrality of institutional procedure as a source of presidential power, an important theme in recent studies of the presidency, as reflected in previous chapters of this volume.[9]

The Politics of Transition Nominations

The process of staffing presidential administrations has increasingly centered around the president and the White House.[10] During the transition, the president-elect and his close advisers begin the process of identifying candidates for cabinet-level and other senior positions. The goal for new presidents is to find the most able candidates who will still be responsive to their wishes. However, from the president's perspective, the optimal staffing of the bureaucracy is hampered by a number of constraints.

One of these constraints that has somewhat diminished is that of national party organizations. The centralization of the appointments process has come at the expense of party leaders who once viewed as their domain patronage and the distribution of administration jobs. However, as the hold of these leaders on the presidential nominating process has waned, presidents have felt less compelled to seek their input on appointment matters.[11]

Conversely, many other constraints have intensified over recent years. Specifically, scrutiny of ethical lapses and personal behaviors has been increasingly emphasized during the appointment process. In spite of more intense screening, which throughout the period studied has included FBI background checks and extensive prenomination vetting, nominees have repeatedly arisen with ethics problems. In fact, the only cabinet-level appointments that failed during this period were primarily due to problems of ethics and personal behavior.[12]

During the transition, the transition team must be concerned with identifying not only able candidates who support the new administration, but also those that placate the new president's critical constituencies. The importance of regional, ethnic, and gender balance among appointees has been well recognized.[13] However, less attention has been paid to the need to accommodate allies on policy matters. Failure to do so often ignites opposition from both foes and friends of the administration. This phenomenon was clearly important in many of Carter's transition cabinet appointments. Three of his cabinet secretaries encountered the most vociferous opposition from liberal Democrats and interest groups.[14] Nixon HEW designate James Allen was primarily opposed by conservatives who questioned his support for court-mandated busing plans.[15]

Although placating friends and ethical guardians is obviously critical, the most daunting opposition comes from ideological opponents of the administration. All the presidents that we examine below faced significant opposition to some nominees due to policy differences. These conflicts have often been reflective of the important party cleavages of the era. During the Kennedy transition, opposition in the Senate Finance committee emerged because two nominees, HEW Secretary Wilbur Cohen and Assistant Treasury Secretary Stanley Surrey, appeared to advocate tax increases.[16] Similar opposition arose against two Reagan nominees, Interior Secretary James Watt and EPA Administrator Anne Gorsuch, because of extreme environmental positions.[17] While all of these controversial appointments were ultimately confirmed, Clinton's designate for Assistant Attorney General for Civil Rights, Lani Guinier, one of the few transition appointments to fail over the period of our study, was withdrawn due to intractable opposition to her backing of court-ordered electoral systems designed to maximize minority representation.[18]

While these controversies illustrate the importance of policy conflict, even more compelling evidence comes when we examine the "dogs that did not bark" due to the new administration's rational anticipation. One of President Kennedy's main goals during his transition was to appoint a "Wall Street" Republican to head the Treasury Department.[19] This represented the administration's clear anticipation of opposition stemming from the fact that many of Kennedy's other economic advisers, such as John K. Galbraith, were noted economic liberals.[20]

Rational anticipation often precludes an attempt to replace an incumbent. Richard Nixon was quite anxious to replace Robert Ball as Commissioner of Social Security. However, Ball, considered one of the program's architects, had such support on the Senate Finance committee that Nixon expected any replacement to meet substantial opposition.[21]

Clearly, strategic anticipation should also play an important role in decisions about when particular nominations should be made. Early in their terms, presidents should be frugal with important political resources on controversial nomination fights. Such fights invariably distract from formulation of the president's program and potentially compromise support for the hundreds of other nominations. All things being equal, the president should confront opponents with difficult nominations later rather than sooner.

THE CONFIRMATION PROCESS

To examine our hypotheses about strategic delay in appointments, we needed a reasonable measure of both expected opposition and the resources that must be expended to secure confirmation. This required that we understand how opposition to presidential appointments is typically manifested.

Under most circumstances, presidential nominations are read while the

Senate is in executive session. Occasionally, the Senate will immediately confirm a nomination without referring it to committee, but normally nominations are referred to one or more standing committees to hold hearings. Once the committees complete their work, they report back to the Senate in executive session where the nominee is typically confirmed on a voice vote.[22]

Both the use of executive session and reliance on committees to vet nominees gives leverage to opponents to introduce obstacles. Decisionmaking in executive, as opposed to regular session, depends crucially on unanimous consent agreements. Under Senate standing rules, a nomination cannot be considered on the same day the committee reports without unanimous consent. Furthermore, a prolonged "hold" by a single senator can prevent the consideration of a nominee in an executive session.

The use of committees to examine nominees' qualifications also provides opportunities for recalcitrant Senators to engage in institutional heel-dragging. Only in the case of sequential referrals is a time limit placed on committee deliberations. While nominations can be formally discharged from committee, this procedure occurs very infrequently and usually after the process has been long delayed.

Because of these hurdles, a timely confirmation requires one of two conditions. The first is that the nominee does not stir opposition in any significant quarters. The second is that the nomination is important enough to a majority (or more realistically three-fifths, for purposes of cloture) of senators that they choose to circumvent typical procedures. As these conditions are increasingly hard to meet, delay tends to be an integral part of the confirmation process.[23]

THE DURATION OF THE CONFIRMATION PROCESS

Given our argument about presidents avoiding drawn-out confirmations early in their administration, we turn now to a discussion of the determinants of the duration of the confirmation process. First, since substantial opposition to the president and his program should be an important factor in the confirmation process, we predict that the committee to which the nomination is referred can have a significant impact on the length of delay. We expect that the greater the divergence in the president's and the relevant committee's preferences, the longer the confirmation process will take.

Second, the president's stature with the public may also provide an important resource which can be used to mitigate Senate opposition and ease the confirmation process. Therefore, we suspect that nominations from presidents with high levels of public support will tend to take less time to confirm.[24]

Finally, there are a number of other variables that should affect confirmation delay.[25] The particular policy jurisdiction of the appointee's agency is likely to have an impact on the duration of the process. Agencies with jurisdictions that are venues for partisan and ideological conflict should be more prone to delays than those that are essentially administrative.

We also expect the Senate's expediency on any nomination to vary with the level of the position in question. High-level positions that are the first steppingstones to political control of the bureaucracy are the most important. We suspect that Senate majorities will be less tolerant of delay tactics on very salient nominations such as those on the level of cabinet Secretary or Attorney-General. In fact, there is an informal norm against using holds against high-level nominees. However, lower level nominations may be more vulnerable because they may lack the necessary stature to prompt the majority to circumvent normal procedures. Lower level nominations may also be more vulnerable because they often deal directly with controversial policy matters.

A Model of Rational Anticipation

While the preceding qualitative evidence shows that rational anticipation is suggestive, it is important to subject the theory to a rigorous quantitative test. Our theory, as we have sketched it above, is represented schematically in Figure 15.1.

In our model, nomination delay is positively related to expected confirmation delay while the confirmation delay is a function of nomination delay. Given the reciprocal causation of nomination and confirmation delay, we must be concerned with "simultaneity bias" that would occur if we did not control or adjust for the theoretically possible reverse effects. Uncorrected simultaneity bias may distort the effects of certain variables on nomination delay. For example, the effect of any variable on nomination delay would be double counted, once for its direct effect on nomination delay and again for its effect on confirmation delay, which feeds back into nomination delay.

To deal with these problems, we employ a two-stage estimation strategy. First, we estimate confirmation delay as a function of only exogenous variables such as committee opposition and public approval, but not of nomination delay. Then we use the predicted values derived from the equation for confirmation delay and estimate nomination delay. These predicted values are proxies for confirmation delay, but they are "purged" of the reciprocal effects of nomination delay.

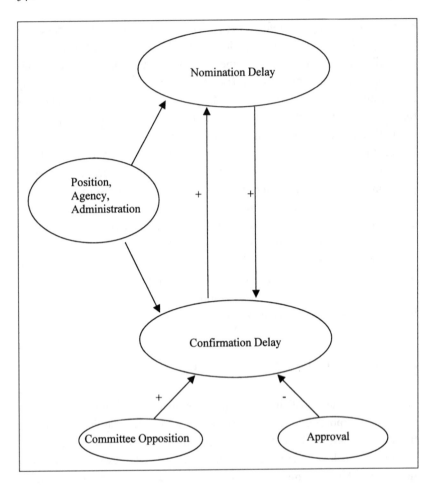

FIGURE 15.1.   Transition Nomination Model

Therefore, as long as some of the variables used to estimate confirmation delay are not included in the equation estimating nomination delay, the effect of confirmation delay on nomination delay will be appropriately measured.

DATA

To test our model of presidential anticipation of confirmation battles, we have collected information about 987 transition nominations to positions in domestic executive branch agencies. We have not collected data on the Departments of State or Defense nor have we collected data on nominees to head regional offices such as United States attorneys or marshals.[26] Our study spans presidential transitions from 1961–1993, but excludes second terms and the transitions of Lyndon Johnson and Gerald Ford because the factors at work during these transitions are quite different than those that resulted from elections. From the *Congressional Record*, the *Journal of the Executive Proceedings of the Senate of the United States*, and the *United States Government Policy and Supporting Positions (The Plum Book)* we have attempted to reconstruct the universe of nominations that meet our criteria. From these documents, we collected our main endogenous variables *nomination duration* and *confirmation duration* by recording the dates of inauguration, nomination and confirmation and then computing the number of intervening days.[27] To avoid any complications arising from second presidential terms, we do not measure nomination durations beyond the first term publication of the *Plum Book*, which tends to occur between September and November of the reelection year.[28] Use of the *Plum Book* for this purpose was crucial in identifying eligible positions for which the president did not field any nominations. In 54 cases, we were forced to censor the nomination duration. In theory, confirmation durations could have been censored at this point as well, but there were no transition nominations pending confirmation at the publication dates.

To estimate our model, we need to identify factors affecting the delay of confirmation but only indirectly affecting the timing of nomination.[29] We have identified two variables for this purpose. The first is what we call *committee opposition*. This is a measure of the differences in policy preferences between the president and the mean member of the committee handling a particular nomination. We measured this as the difference between the president's Nominate score and the Nominate score of the median member of the relevant committee at the time the nomination was made.[30] Our expectation is that *committee opposition* will clearly lead to longer confirmation delays. However, we anticipate that its effect on nomination times will be through greater expected confirmation delays.

Our second variable, intended to explain confirmation delay but not nomination delay, is the president's public approval rating as measured by Gallup at the time of the nomination. We argue that the president's standing with the public is a resource that can be used to mitigate senate opposition and lead to quicker confirmations. However, it is not clear that approval should directly affect the timing of the nomination.

We include several variables designed to capture other variations in confirmation and nomination times. First of all, we use agency indicator variables to capture any effects attributable directly to the agencies themselves or their policy domains. We include variables for the following departments: *Agriculture, Commerce, Justice, Labor,* and *Treasury*. For reasons of historical continuity and sample size, we combine a number of departments into a single indicator. We define Education; Housing and Urban Development; Health, Education, and Welfare; and Veterans Affairs as *Social Welfare* departments. Additionally, we combine Interior, Energy, and Transportation into an indicator for *Infrastructure* departments. Our omitted category includes the positions in the Executive Office of the President requiring Senate confirmation.

To capture the possible effects of the executive branch hierarchy, we create three indicators. The *first-tier appointments* variable indicates secretaries, attorneys-general, and the administrator of the Environmental Protection Agency. *Second-tier appointments* include the under and deputy secretaries, the associate and deputy attorney general, and the associate and deputy administrator of the Environmental Protection Agency. The *third-tier appointments* comprise the assistant, deputy assistant, and deputy under secretaries, as well as the assistant attorney general. We expect that the first two tiers have faster confirmations but that first-tier confirmations will be much more expeditious.

Finally, to capture differences across individual presidents, we include indicators for each presidential administration in the sample except Kennedy, who serves as the baseline. Unfortunately, isolating administration-specific factors from secular trends in the average nomination and confirmation duration will prove difficult as these indicators will pick up all variation specific to each president including their standing in secular time. Table 15.1 contains summary statistics for many of our variables.

To estimate the full model shown in figure 15.1, including the effect of nomination delay on confirmation delay, we would need to identify measurable factors that directly affect nomination delay but not confirmation delay. However, since such indicators are not readily available, we are unable to estimate the true confirmation model.[31] Fortunately, our main hypotheses about rational anticipation only require estimation of the effects of the nomination model.

Since our dependent variable is the duration of the confirmation process, the appropriate statistical approach is duration analysis. The goal is to model the duration of the nomination and confirmation processes as a function of our independent variables. Since our dependent variables are censored at zero and the end of the congressional session, we have employed the Weibull duration model.[32]

TABLE 15.1   Descriptives

Variable	Mean	Median	Standard Deviation
Nomination Duration	224.62	105	324.82
Confirmation Duration	45.42	27	84.40
Distance between President			
and Committee	0.398	0.456	0.181
Approval Rating	57.99%	59%	10.30
	Frequency		*Frequency*
First Tier Executive Appointments	64	Agriculture	65
Second Tier Executive Appointments	98	Commerce	133
Third Tier Executive Appointments	385	Justice	105
Kennedy	75	Labor	71
Nixon	114	Treasury	90
Carter	151	Social Welfare	201
Reagan	196	Infrastructure	214
Bush	215	White House Personnel	108
Clinton	236		

In our two-stage model, we use the Weibull model to estimate the expected confirmation time which is then used to estimate the expected nomination time. Since the estimated coefficient of each variable represents the percentage increase in expected duration given a unit increase of that variable, the prediction of our rational anticipation model is that the coefficient on confirmation time in the second-stage model should be positive, indicating that higher expected confirmation times lead presidents to delay nominations.[33]

STATISTICAL RESULTS

We turn first to the estimates of our first-stage model, which relates all of the exogenous factors to the duration of the confirmation process. The results of this model are given in table 15.2. While it should be acknowledged that these reduced-form estimates are not valid for making specific inferences about the causes of confirmation delay,[34] the results are important in validating the use of committee opposition and presidential approval as instruments for expected confirmation delay. We find that both of these variables are statistically signifi-

TABLE 15.2   First Stage Confirmation Model
(dependent variable: length from nomination to confirmation)

Explanatory Variable

Constant	3.575	Treasury	0.032
	(11.437)		(0.228)
Approval Rating	−0.017	Social Welfare	0.029
	(−4.420)		(0.243)
Distance between President	0.552	Infrastructure	0.126
and Committee	(2.278)		(1.092)
First Tier Executive	−1.931	Nixon	0.532
Appointments	(−15.324)		(3.601)
Second Tier Executive	−0.795	Carter	0.867
Appointments	(−7.513)		(6.183)
Third Tier Executive	−0.116	Reagan	0.775
Appointments	(−1.638)		(5.716)
Agriculture	0.083	Bush	1.468
	(0.547)		(11.378)
Commerce	0.727	Clinton	1.447
	(5.687)		(9.168)
Justice	0.273	Duration Dependence[a]	1.110
	(2.076)		(4.326)
Labor	−0.063		
	(−0.432)		

Note: Entries are maximum likelihood estimates. t-statistics appear in parentheses. N=933.
Log likelihood = -1289.34.
[a]H_0: $\sigma = 1$.

cant in the predicted directions. Committee extremity has substantial effect on
confirmation delay. A committee located at the mean distance delays nominations 20 percent longer than committees sharing the president's preferences.
Similarly, the president's approval rating reduces the time of Senate deliberation. A one standard deviation increase in the approval rating (about 10 points)
decreases the time of confirmation by about 17 percent.

The other first-stage estimates show that higher positions are clearly confirmed more quickly, with secretaries confirmed more than twice as fast as
their deputies who are confirmed 60 percent faster than assistant secretaries.

The effects of individual presidents mostly reflect a secular increase in confirmation times; however, it should be noted that Reagan was more successful than Carter and that Clinton was more successful than Bush.[35] Unfortunately, it is impossible to discern whether these deviations from trend are due to peculiarities of Republican administrations, divided government, or simply personal differences across presidents.[36]

In table 15.3, we present our main results derived from the model of nomination delay corrected for the endogenous effects of confirmation expectations. We find strong support for our main hypothesis. The expectations about confirmation delay lead presidents to hold back on more difficult nominations. Our statistically significant estimates imply that each additional day of

TABLE 15.3 Second Stage Nomination Model
(dependent variable: time until nomination)

Explanatory Variable

Constant	4.540	Treasury	0.400
	(22.038)		(1.986)
Predicted Confirmation	0.009	Social Welfare	0.410
Duration	(2.888)		(2.435)
First Tier Executive	−2.783	Infrastructure	0.347
Appointments	(−9.983)		(2.120)
Second Tier Executive	−1.392	Nixon	0.006
Appointments	(−7.254)		(0.032)
Third Tier Executive	−1.118	Carter	0.198
Appointments	(−10.527)		(0.929)
Agriculture	0.294	Reagan	0.487
	(1.346)		(2.375)
Commerce	0.404	Bush	1.057
	(1.865)		(3.779)
Justice	0.611	Clinton	0.503
	(3.175)		(1.841)
Labor	0.302	Duration Dependence[a]	0.780
	(1.414)		(−11.407)

Note: Entries are maximum likelihood estimates. t-statistics appear in parentheses. N=987.
Log likelihood = −1724.73.
[a]$H_0: \sigma = 1$.

expected confirmation delay translates into a 1 percent increase in the time before the nomination is made. Since the median time of nomination is slightly more than 100, this means that the estimated effect is approximately one day of nomination delay for each day of expected confirmation delay around the median. Since the standard deviation of confirmation delays is over 80, substantial variations in time prior to a nomination can be accounted for by expectations about confirmation. These results suggest that presidents are highly responsive to the Senate during the transition opposed to acting more or less unilaterally during some kind of "honeymoon" period. In fact, any simple relationship between presidential success and newness of the administration must be questioned because of the bias induced by the fact that presidents are delaying the most difficult nominations.

Table 15.3 also provides other information about presidential strategies during the transition. Not unexpectedly, we find that presidents tend to appoint down the agency hierarchy beginning with the cabinet, moving to deputies, and ending with assistant secretaries. Note that this effect is present once confirmation expectations are controlled for, indicating that this process is not a reflection of confirmation politics but rather the internal politics of the administration whereby cabinet secretaries often appoint their own subordinates. The results suggest that there is not much variation across agencies with the exception that turnover in the White House, our baseline, is much faster during the transition than all of the agencies, while the Justice Department is the slowest.

The estimates of the administration specific effects are also interesting. For each subsequent administration, they tend to show a gradual increase in the time until nomination. However, the Bush administration stands out as by far the longest. This confirms our intuition about the differences between an interparty transition and an intraparty transition. Because Bush faced a hostile Congress, he was able to leave the holdovers from the Reagan administration in office for a longer time.

A liability of the results presented in tables 15.2 and 15.3 is that they are based on "pooling" the data from all of the presidencies together. This is probably not a justifiable assumption either statistically or substantively given that presidents faced very different strategic situations. For example, Bush's strategy of continuing the Reagan agenda is very different from the strategies of any of the other new presidents. Therefore, table 15.4 shows the estimates of our model for each presidential administration.

We do in fact find that extent of rational anticipation differs somewhat across administrations. For three of the six transitions, we find significant

TABLE 15.4 Second Stage Nomination Model
(dependent variable: time until nomination)

Explanatory Variable	Kennedy	Nixon	Carter	Reagan	Bush	Clinton
Constant	0.164	5.302	4.282	4.603	7.264	6.236
	(0.213)	(6.938)	(16.657)	(5.450)	(23.326)	(21.841)
Predicted Confirmation Duration						
	0.096	−0.003	0.031	0.037	−0.033	−0.003
	(2.263)	(−0.164)	(7.899)	(1.883)	(−6.729)	(−0.774)
First Tier Executive Appointments						
	−4.476	−5.643	−2.619	−2.934	−1.904	−6.149
	(−5.593)	(−6.009)	(−7.843)	(−3.942)	(−4.654)	(−19.300)
Second Tier Executive Appointments						
	−3.009	-3.594	−0.505	−0.582	−2.363	−1.199
	(−4.749)	(−4.525)	(−2.007)	(−1.087)	(−7.267)	(−5.511)
Third Tier Executive Appointments						
	−3.144	−1.774	−0.638	−0.282	−0.567	−0.705
	(−5.836)	(−2.941)	(−4.412)	(−0.954)	(−2.973)	(−3.879)
Agriculture	4.444	0.618	0.049	−0.880	1.846	0.153
	(4.391)	(0.925)	(0.144)	(−2.008)	(4.458)	(0.487)
Commerce	3.785	0.718	−1.278	−0.210	1.944	0.314
	(3.466)	(0.845)	(−3.699)	(−0.565)	(4.854)	(1.173)
Justice	4.445	0.883	−0.033	−2.253	1.518	0.011
	(4.912)	(1.630)	(−0.111)	(−2.161)	(4.349)	(0.035)
Labor	4.333	−0.670	−0.347	0.363	0.965	−0.230
	(4.638)	(-1.023)	(−1.067)	(0.816)	(2.482)	(−0.751)
Treasury	3.057	0.142	-0.712	−0.893	0.620	-0.131
	(2.887)	(0.237)	(−2.332)	(−2.036)	(1.731)	(−0.443)
Social Welfare						
	4.603	0.672	−0.158	−0.767	0.715	−0.309
	(4.698)	(1.226)	(−0.597)	(−2.081)	(2.419)	(−1.273)
Infrastructure						
	4.736	0.439	−0.326	−0.619	1.068	0.154
	(5.271)	(0.852)	(−1.139)	(−1.886)	(3.591)	(0.675)
Duration Dependence[a]						
	0.787	0.780	1.389	0.959	0.995	1.131
	(−2.778)	(−3.695)	(4.139)	(−0.801)	(−0.084)	(2.273)

Note: Entries are maximum likelihood estimates. t-statistics appear in parentheses.
Model 1: N=75. Log likelihood = −136.11. Model 2: N=114. Log likelihood = −206.68.
Model 3: N=151. Log likelihood = −190.54. Model 4: N=196. Log likelihood = −305.24.
Model 5: N=215. Log likelihood = −338.29. Model 6: N=236. Log likelihood = −341.04
[a]H_0: $\sigma = 1$.

positive coefficients on the expected confirmation delay. We find especially large effects for the Kennedy transition where the effect of an additional day of confirmation delay leads to about a 10 percent increase in nomination delay. The Reagan and Carter transitions exhibit about 3 percent increases per day. The effect of confirmation delay is not statistically significant for either Nixon or Clinton. However, during the Bush transition, we find that expected confirmation *decreased* the prenomination delay. However, we think that this result is quite consistent with the unique circumstances of the Bush administration. Bush inherited both the personnel and the policies of the Reagan administration; in fact, Bush was the first new president since Taft not to appoint every member of his cabinet upon entering office.[37] It is quite conceivable that given his intention to continue the Reagan agenda, a priority was put on fighting the remaining battles rather than making the easier personnel adjustments.

The weaker effects for Clinton and Nixon are somewhat more puzzling. It is not clear what similarities either in strategic circumstances or personal styles would explain their distinctiveness in this regard.[38]

CONCLUSIONS

While the president may appoint the most important officials of the federal government, scholars have repeatedly found that presidential control of the bureaucracy is somewhat illusive. However, the problem lies exactly where Richard Neustadt claimed it would be found: ours is a system of separated institutions sharing power.[39] Whether we focus on persuasion and bargaining as Neustadt did, or emphasize strategic interaction as we do, the presidency cannot be adequately studied without references to the broader political environment. Presidential personnel decisions cannot be made in isolation from the preferences of other relevant political actors.

This chapter attempts to examine broadly the strategies employed by new administrations to overcome certain institutional hurdles to gain control of the administrative state. While our focus has been on the Senate confirmation process, we think that many of the lessons may carry over to other areas of presidential decisionmaking.

First of all, we find evidence that presidents strategically anticipate opposition to their appointments and make adjustments accordingly to avoid confirmation battles early in their administrations. This result clearly calls into question any inferences that might be drawn from the ease with which early nominations tend to be confirmed. Rather than enjoying the "honeymoon" period, presidents may be simply avoiding early battles for strategic reasons. Similar explanations may well explain the dynamics of other presidential decisions, such as those pertaining to an administration's early versus its subsequent legislative programs.

We think that specific attention should be paid as well to strategic interactions involving other actors in the presidential transition environment. While the appointment/confirmation process for new presidents is certainly one of the biggest hurdles to maneuver effectively, we do not want to minimize the role of partisan, bureaucratic, media, and interest group actors. Any theory of the presidency must account for the strategic behavior of all of these groups.

This chapter, however, has also uncovered some anomalous behavior. In spite of the predictive success of our theoretical framework which is presidency specific not *president* specific, and the demonstration of secular trends potentially indicative of changes in the institutional environment of the presidency, we still find substantial variation in behavior across individual presidents. We are at our methodological limit in terms of explaining these differences: too many theories of individual differences and too few observations.[40] Solving these types of problems will continue to challenge presidency scholars for years to come, as new presidents face transitions into power.

NOTES

1. See Hugh Heclo, *Government of Strangers: Executive Politics in Washington* (Washington D.C, Brookings Institution, 1977).

2. Heclo, *Government of Strangers*. See also Richard Nathan, *The Administrative Presidency* (New York: Wiley, 1983); Terry M. Moe, "The Politicized Presidency," in John Chubb and Paul Peterson, eds., *New Directions in American Politics* (Washington D.C: Brookings Institution, 1985); Terry M. Moe and Scott A. Wilson, "Presidents and the Politics of Structure," *Law and Contemporary Problems* 57 (2) (1994):1–45; Thomas J. Weko, *The Politicizing Presidency* (Lawrence: University of Kansas Press, 1995); and Kenneth Mayer and Thomas Weko, "The Institutionalization of Power" (chapter 9, this volume).

3. See Heclo, *Government of Strangers*, and Weko, *The Politicizing Presidency*.

4. James P. Pfiffner, *The Strategic Presidency: Hitting the Ground Running* (Chicago: Dorsey Press, 1988).

5. Pfiffner, *The Strategic Presidency*, p. 70.

6. Richard E. Neustadt, *Presidential Power and the Modern Presidents* (New York: The Free Press, 1990).

7. See Matthew J. Dickinson, "Staffing the White House, 1937–96: The Institutional Implications of Neustadt's Bargaining Paradigm," (chapter 10, this volume), for study of the institutional response to "atomization." See also Hugh Heclo, "Issue Networks and the Executive Establishment," in Anthony King ed. *The New American Political System* (Washington: American Enterprise Institute, 1978).

8. See Nolan McCarty and Rose Razaghian, "Advise and Consent: Senate Responses to Executive Branch Nominations 1885–1996," *American Journal of Political Science* 43(3):1122-43.

9. See the earlier essays by Charles Cameron (chapter 5, this volume), David Epstein and Sharyn O'Halloran (chapter 15), Matthew Dickinson, and Kenneth Mayer and Thomas Weko. Also see Terry M. Moe, "Presidents, Institutions, and Theory," in George Edwards, John Kessel, and Bert Rockman, eds., *Researching the Presidency* (Pittsburgh: University of Pittsburgh Press, 1993).

10. See Weko, *The Politicizing Presidency*, and Mayer and Weko, "The Institutionalization of Power."

11. See Weko, *The Politicizing Presidency*. On the other hand, Heclo, *Government of Strangers*, points out that declining political parties have exacerbated the problem of identifying political executives due to the lack of partisan cadres of executives and administrators ready to enter each new administration.

12. Bush's nomination of John Tower for Secretary of Defense failed confirmation due to charges of womanizing and alcoholism, while Clinton's Attorney-General designate Zoe Baird and potential nominee Kimba Wood were both doomed after allegations of failing to pay social security taxes on domestic servants.

13. Sometimes these concerns for balance reached almost comical proportions. George Schultz was passed over for Secretary of State because he and Secretary of Defense-designee Caspar Weinberger were both executives for the same company. Nixon allegedly chose David Kennedy to head the Treasury Department because he was a Chicago banker rather than one from New York or Boston. See Carl M. Brauer, *Presidential Transitions: Eisenhower through Reagan* (New York: Oxford University Press, 1986).

14. Attorney General Griffin Bell was criticized as being insensitive to civil rights, HEW Secretary Joseph Califano did not support federal abortion funding, and Labor Secretary Ray Marshall supported right-to-work laws (*Congressional Quarterly Almanac*, 1977).

15. Ibid., 1969.

16. Ibid., 1961.

17. Ibid., 1981.

18. Ibid., 1993.

19. Brauer, *Presidential Transitions*.

20. Kennedy eventually settled on C. Douglas Dillon who has served as Undersecretary of State in the Eisenhower administration and had supported Nixon in the 1960 election.

21. See Weko, *The Politicizing Presidency*, and Martha Derthick, *Policymaking for Social Security* (Washington, D.C: The Brookings Institution, 1979).

22. For an excellent discussion and history of the Senate's confirmation procedures, see Joseph P. Harris, *The Advice and Consent of the Senate: A Study of the Confirmation of Appointments by the United States Senate* (Berkeley: University of California Press, 1953).

23. McCarty and Razaghian, "Advise and Consent."

24. While many presidents have tried to use the resource of favorable opinion for prominent nominations, President Clinton resorted to "going public" to try to break the Senate Judiciary committee's stranglehold on lower level judicial appointments (Weekly Radio Address, September 27, 1997).

25. See McCarty and Razaghian, "Advice and Consent."

26. These regional offices are often subject to senatorial courtesy in which the senior senator of the president's party in that state often makes the nomination.

27. In prior work on confirmations, which covered a much longer historical period, we excluded days in which the Senate was in recess. However, in the modern period, recesses are so short as to be inconsequential for our purposes.

28. In the analysis that follows, we treat these observations as *censored*. That is, our model only incorporates the information that a nomination did not take place before a given date rather than the actual date of nomination.

29. That is, the only effect of these variables on nomination times is through their effect on confirmation times.

30. For a general discussion of Nominate scores for members of Congress, see Keith T. Poole and Howard Rosenthal, *Congress: A Political-Economic History of Roll Call Voting* (New York: Oxford University Press, 1997). For the application to presidents, see Nolan McCarty and Keith T. Poole, "Veto Power and Legislation: An Empirical Analysis of Executive and Legislative Bargaining from 1961–1995," *Journal of Law, Economics, and Organization* 11 (1995): 282–312.

31. In our previous work, we ignore the endogeneity of nomination time which is a far more valid assumption in the context of the analysis of all nominations, not just transition nominations.

32. There are numerous problems associated with linear models such as OLS in this context. First, the dependent variables for both models, length of confirmation and time until nomination, are censored at zero. Furthermore, when the President

does not make a nomination, either the position remains vacant or the appointee from the previous administration is still holding the post, the time until nomination is censored at the end of a congressional session, as well. Secondly, while the censoring problem can be solved using log-linear or censored regression models, the problem of duration dependence cannot be. Duration dependence occurs when the probability of confirmation at a given time depends on how long the process has survived. Failing to account for duration dependence leads to a number of problems of inference.

Our choice of the Weibull model was based on a preliminary investigation of our data which showed that its properties closely matched those of our data. While in many applications of this model, researchers present their results in terms of hazard rates (the probability that an event will occur at time t given that it has not occurred), we have parameterized the model in terms of the expected duration so that a positive coefficient reflects a positive association with expected duration (but a negative relationship to the hazard rate). Each estimated coefficient represents approximately the percentage increase in expected duration given a one unit increase in an independent variable. For an extensive review of the application of survival analysis in political science, see Janet M. Box-Steffensmeier and Bradford S. Jones, "Time is of the Essence: Event History Models in Political Science," *American Journal of Political Science* 41 (1997): 1414–61.

33. Since there were positions for which there was no new nomination over the president's first term, the confirmation model is estimated on fewer observations than the nomination model which treats those cases as censored. Therefore, we were able to use our estimates of the first stage to estimate expected confirmation times even for those nominations that were not made. Therefore, the second-stage model could be estimated on all observations.

34. As we explained above, estimation of the confirmation model requires variables that directly affect confirmation delay but not nomination delay.

35. Again not too much weight can be placed on these estimates as they do not account for the timing of nominations.

36. Even the large number of appointments does not completely eliminate the "small N" problem that has plagued presidency research. See Gary King, "The Methodology of Presidential Research" in George Edwards, John Kessel, and Bert Rockman, eds., *Researching the Presidency* (Pittsburgh: University of Pittsburgh Press, 1993).

37. Richard Thornburgh at Justice, Nicholas Brady at Treasury, and Lauro Cavasos at Education were all confirmed in September 1988. The role that Bush played in these choices is uncertain. Certainly, however, it must have been a relief to have these three positions locked given the ensuing difficulties surrounding John Tower and others.

38. Because we were concerned about the effect of the smaller administration-specific samples, we reestimated all of the models dropping the agency dummy variables. The results tended to be somewhat more favorable to our hypotheses with the relevant coefficient in the Clinton administration estimated as positive and significant at the 10 percent level. However, we are choosing to focus on the more conservative set of estimates.

39. Neustadt, 1990, *Presidential Power and the Modern Presidents.*

40. See King "The Methodology of Presidential Research," 1993.

PART 5

The Potential for Leadership

CHAPTER 16

Presidential Power and the Potential for Leadership

Mark A. Peterson

The American presidency is not a sideshow, despite the salacious allegations that encumbered President Bill Clinton during his second term. Whether as scholars or citizens, we are drawn to the presidency because of what we anticipate, believe, or simply hope the president can do. Richard Neustadt put it forthrightly in *Presidential Power*: "Everybody now expects the man inside the White House to do something about everything."[1] Subsequent students of the institution have noted that "[t]he hallmark of modern U.S. government is presidential leadership [and a] creeping presidentialization of the system," or even more emphatically, that we have entered a period of "presidential government."[2] The spotlight falls upon presidents at center stage because we expect them to exercise leadership and to make a conscious difference in the life of the nation and even our personal welfare. Indeed, we know that "at times strong leadership does get exercised."[3]

EVALUATING LEADERSHIP

But what is leadership? It would seem both obvious and intuitive. Leadership must mean something, and in some way impart a tangible marker. Franklin Roosevelt, slayer of the Great Depression and vanquisher of fascism abroad, seemed to embody it. Certainly the disparate supporters of Lyndon Johnson, architect of the Great Society, and Ronald Reagan, vanguard of the conservative counterrevolution, thought these presidents had it at crucial times. Jimmy Carter and George Bush were often denigrated for failing at it. The country appears to be divided over whether Bill Clinton has demonstrated it. The "it," presumably, is a verifiable capacity to have a designed and instrumental impact on politics and policy. It is more than "status" or formal authority.[4] Possession of titles and airplanes does not assure its presence. It is closer to "direction," "navigation," and, perhaps, establishing a "culture of cooperation."[5] For leaders to make a difference, their actions must be one cause, perhaps among many, of a particular course of events.[6] Or by their actions (or lack thereof) they bear some measure of responsibility for what transpires.[7] Stated somewhat more concretely, for our purposes here "[l]eaders are those who make things happen that otherwise would not come about" in a way that "involves moving (others, the group) toward an objective or goal."[8] In the reverse formulation, the potential of leadership is manifest when the outcome would have been different had the leader—the president—decided to act.

This relatively straightforward statement of leadership and its applicability to the American presidency, however, is immediately bogged down in the substantive complexity associated with leadership and dissension about how to interpret it. Congressional scholar Barbara Sinclair suggests that "none [of the definitions of leadership] tell us how to identify leadership with sufficient clarity that trained observers will agree on what is and is not leadership."[9] Such clarity is not advanced by the fact that contemporary observers of the presidency—peering into the same institution—offer such divergent images of its potency. It is at once "imperial" and "fettered," "strong" and "tethered," a source of "energy" and a "prisoner," potentially "order-shattering" yet "beleaguered" and caught in a "no-win" bind.[10] The jacket of one volume on the modern presidency laments that "[t]he question is not whether there is an imperial presidency, but whether there still is a presidency," while the author of another proclaims that "the executive has in effect become the first branch of government . . .[achieving] executive hegemony."[11]

Understanding the potential and realization of presidential leadership requires developing a perspective that can make sense of these clashing impressions by specifying the assumptions and empirical vantage points motivating work on the subject. Figure 16.1 depicts two core conceptual dimensions associated with the study of leadership generally, which generate alternative images of leadership opportunities. Each dimension has two extremes where leadership as a collective act is not possible—leaders and followers are not both capable of independent action—but at their intersection they demarcate a zone,

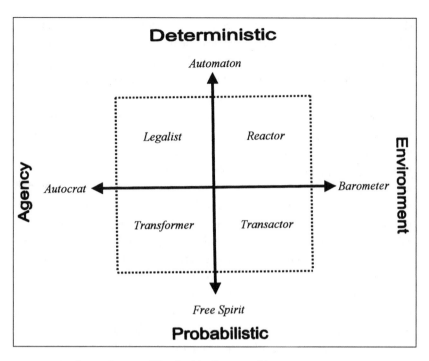

FIGURE 16.1.   Images of Leadership Opportunities

indicated by the box in the figure, in which different forms of leadership may occur or different expectations of leadership may be best understood.

The first dimension poses the age-old empirical question of whether the outcomes of events and interactions occur because of *agency* or *environment*. Agency denotes results dominated by an individual's efficacious choices and actions distinct from the pressures of the contexts in which she acts.[12] An autocrat enjoying complete control over all decisions and outcomes marks the polar extreme of agency. Here, as with "brute force" and "tyrants," there is no requirement for leadership, as the autocrat accomplishes objectives without the need to secure the support of followers or other participants.[13] Extolling the accomplishments of heroes or great men seemingly in command of their surroundings and changing the course of history, Thomas Carlyle suggests a characterization of potent agency that falls within the domain of leadership.[14] These are the accomplishments consistent with the "action theory" of heroic leadership, which "emphasizes decisive deeds by extraordinary men."[15] In contrast to agency, environment means situations dominated by the cumulation of external social, political, and institutional forces that overwhelm the impact of leaders who exist in name only.[16] In the extreme, the behavior of the leader is not leadership but rather a barometer of environmental parameters. Unlike Carlyle, Herbert Spencer finds leaders defined by their opportunities and portrays them with little independent room to maneuver within their environments.[17]

The second dimension captures variation in the methodological assumptions associated with explaining leadership behavior or possibilities. It ranges from viewing the act and consequence of behavior as *deterministic*—products of rational reactions to either law-like incentives or explicit and fixed rules—to considering it a *probabilistic* enterprise in which the decisions of individuals and their effects are subject to the more ambiguous influence of complex motives, interpersonal relationships, and chance sequences.[18] Bryan Jones dubs this a distinction between Newtonian and organic (or biological) views of leadership.[19] For example, from the deterministic perspective, leaders are self-interested actors who respond in predictable ways to tangible incentives in the decision-maker's environment.[20] In the extreme, they do not lead at all; their actions reflect the accumulation of incentives. Alternatively, an individual's behavior may be equally deterministic when it responds automatically to rigidly internalized rules and procedures, such as theological dictates. Either way, those whose actions are fully determined are automatons rather than leaders. A probabilistic approach treats individuals as influenced or constrained by the external or internal contexts in which they operate, but variations in their actions reflect differences in their own perspectives, talents, and other personal traits, as well as the evolving contours of a policy process buffeted by external events.[21] The entirely unconstrained individual is a proverbial free spirit.

In combination these two dimensions of leadership context identify various possible images of leadership. Because the extremes of the two dimensions— the autocrat, automaton, barometer, and free spirit—are not engaged in leadership, they do not interest us here. What we care about is the boxed area in the figure, where meaningful acts by leaders can take place. The instances in which leaders actually make decisions and act will fall somewhere in the space among the polar extremes, and the tendencies along each dimension suggest the four general images of leadership opportunity shown in the figure. They offer a means for sorting through the diverse assessments that have been made of presidential leadership.

We start with the "transactor," because Neustadt's effective chief inhabits this quadrant of the figure. The term is based on what James MacGregor Burns defines as "transactional" leadership—taking "the initiative in making contact with others for the purpose of an exchange of valued things."[22] As "event-ful" leaders, these individuals have an impact on outcomes without influencing the character of the environment itself.[23] Thus, bargaining and exchange promoted within a firmly rooted set of environmental constraints are at the core the *transactor* leadership opportunity. In Neustadt's view, presidential power is the power to persuade, and "the power to persuade is the power to bargain."[24]

Why is this so? Neustadt's presidents, working in a world of "separated institutions *sharing* power," in which fulfilling their goals depends upon the actions of myriad others who share legitimate authority with the president, are backed up against the wall. Environmental factors can easily dominate. The only real hope for success is for individual presidents to exploit their individual skills to develop and sustain informal sources of influence beyond those of formal authority, which give other actors in the system reason to take notice of and abide by the president's wishes. Neustadt latches on to two important resources: prestige with the public and reputation within the Washington community. But securing these resources takes skill, awareness, and the wisdom necessary to judge how each decision today will affect these "power stakes" in the future. This behavior is not a simple responsiveness to rules or incentives, but rather far more personal, idiosyncratic, and imprecise: "[t]he keys to success, by Neustadt's reckoning, are almost entirely personal."[25] Others echo this view as well. In her book on the "practice of leadership," Barbara Kellerman suggests that "the president's success as a directive leader—the degree to which he accomplishes what he set out to accomplish—seems to depend to a considerable degree on his own personal capacities. . . . (1) the vision and motivation to define and articulate his agenda so as to broaden his base of support; and (2) some considerable ability to perform effectively in those interpersonal interactions necessary for bringing about his most important goals."[26]

It is fair to say that most of the literature on presidential power and leadership has grappled with these issues both within the context of the transactional leadership domain in figure 16.1 and in direct, if not always explicit, response to Neustadt. The decades-long endurance of *Presidential Power* is testament to the inherent appeal of Neustadt's core empirical claims. A number of more recent studies, examining in different ways myriad presidential actions during multiple presidential administrations, often analyzing extensive quantitative data in contrast to Neustadt's case studies, have generated results that only confirm just how bound the effectiveness of presidential leadership is to the broader social, political, and institutional context.[27] Even George Washington, the president with the greatest opportunity to act as a "director" of change, the leader of popular imagination, could only function as a "facilitator," like his modern successors working "at the margins" to affect the course of policymaking.[28] U.S. presidents from one century or another have confronted, in Bert Rockman's nice turn of phrase, "the dilemmas of generating leadership in a system not designed to endure much of it."[29] The only point of disagreement is just how much presidents can affect outcomes at all.

Despite the resiliency of Neustadt's formulation, it has nonetheless sustained three sets of critical challenges. The first involves a large body of work conducted within the broad frame of transactional leadership. Although these studies embody a wide range of methodological approaches and differ in the breadth of their historical sweep, they have in common a concern for variations in the contexts in which presidential leadership is attempted and the impact of environmental factors on presidential performance. Some of these changes over time transpire within a single presidential term, such as the patterns Paul Light characterizes as the concurrent cycles of increasing effectiveness (learning the ropes) and decreasing influence (depleted political capital).[30] Others fit the rhythm of longer-time development and decline of party regimes, the dynamic that, in Stephen Skowronek's analysis, has widely separated presidents sharing and sequential presidents experiencing contrasting moments in "political time."[31] That is a theme picked up by Robert Lieberman in chapter 13. Either way, the environment of presidential leadership is in flux, offering different mixes of opportunities for and constraints on influence.[32] They are often far more important in explaining fulfillment or denial of presidential objectives than anything that presidents themselves do. Consider what would seem to be the obvious differences between the legislative mastery of Lyndon Johnson and the congressional clumsiness of Jimmy Carter. By my count, about 70 percent of LBJ's domestic legislative initiatives were enacted in some form by Congress. For Carter the figure is 33 percent, although both presidents had large Democratic majorities in Congress. But if one controls for all of the institutional, political, and economic differences between the periods of the two administrations, each president was about as successful legislatively as one would have expected before knowing anything about either president or what they did to advance his legislative program. Johnson would have suffered cruelly had he been chief executive in 1977 instead of 1965.[33]

The contrast between the experiences of Johnson and Carter also illustrates a theme replete in the presidential literature—social, political, and institutional transformations begun in the 1960s and brought to full fruition by the 1970s have elevated the environmental barriers to effective leadership or at least the achievement of presidential objectives. The emergence of a more egalitarian culture, the fragmentation of governing institutions embodied in an independent and entrepreneurial Congress, the vast mobilization of divergent and competing organized interests, the weakening of partisan ties within the mass public, the ascendancy of broadcast media focused on conflict and scandal, the excessive focus on the person of the president and his words instead of substantive actions, the disruption of previous economic patterns and budgetary norms, the expansion of the welfare state and its associated bureaucracy, and globalization have all been linked to a rising tide of trouble for presidents.[34] In this altered environment, fragmented electoral coalitions have forced upon presidents that difficult imperative of building multiple, successive, and narrow coalitions for each policymaking task.[35] Richard Rose concludes that "[t]he biggest problem for the postmodern President is: *What it takes to become President has nothing to do with what it takes to be President....* An even more troubling prospect must be faced: *What it takes to become President actually makes it more difficult to be a successful postmodern President.*"[36] Calibrations of presidential power and its effective application, even in a transactional setting, must take these variations into consideration.

An even more formidable challenge is posed by those scholars who have concluded that presidents have more "agency" than previously admitted by Neustadt and others, largely due to their capacity to shape the environment itself. In addition to the transactional leader, Burns describes "transforming leaders [who] *engage* with others in such a way that leaders and followers raise one another to higher levels of motivation and morality."[37] Related to Max Weber's original characterization of "charismatic" leaders and similar to Sidney Hook's "event-making" leaders, who both find and create "forks in the historical road," these pioneers—through their considerable agency and freedom of action—can rearrange old or create new preferences, alter values, reconstitute institutions, shift paradigms, and personally redirect the trajectory of policymaking.[38] Following Burns, I call this image of leadership opportunity a *transformer*. The most influential recent work of this sort is Stephen Skowronek's book, *The Politics Presidents Make*, which notes critically that "Neustadt's presidents do not change the political system in any significant way. The political and institutional parameters of the system appear impervious to the exercise of presidential power." In contrast, Skowronek's presidents not only have their leadership possibilities influenced by their place in "political time," but also are themselves a "blunt disruptive force," even more significant in transforming the political terrain than social and economic factors. As "order-creating," "order-affirming," or "order-shattering" actors, "in their most precise signification, presidents disrupt systems, reshape political landscapes, and pass to successors leadership challenges that are different from the ones just faced."[39] Taking a longer historical view than Neustadt, and most other scholars who emphasize the environmental parameters of the modern (and postmodern) presidency, Skowronek in many respects shares Neustadt's focus on individual presidents, but argues that they often have more independent, personal impact on politics writ large than Neustadt recognizes.

The third challenge to Neustadtian perspectives on presidential leadership seeks to shift away from the concentration on the person of the presidency and all its prescriptive and explanatory baggage. It has two distinct streams. One is a normative reaction to the perceived personalization of the constitutional office of the presidency. The complaint is proffered vigorously by Theodore Lowi, who suggests that the great expansion of the federal government's role since FDR's New Deal has led us into a "Second Republic of the United States" that is "presidency-centered." It is "a plebiscitary republic with a personal president" but is predicated on what turns out to be a failed relationship between the public and the chief executive.[40] The argument reinforces concerns raised by Jeffrey Tulis, who sees a second "constitutional presidency" emerging even earlier in this century. In his analysis, Woodrow Wilson conceptually ratified, in his search for instruments of influence over other policy makers, the beginning practice of twentieth century Presidents to forge direct ties to the public using rhetorical appeals. This practice broke what Tulis argues was the nineteenth-century norm established by the founders of promoting deliberation in policymaking and avoiding demagoguery.[41] Although Samuel Kernell posits that "going public" on the part of presidents supplants traditional bargaining, Neustadt would accept it as merely a variant of the methods of persuasion he discusses.[42] The point again is that the formal authority possessed by the president is not sufficient to wield effective leadership. By its nature, then, the search for the basis of presidential power can lead to the focus on the individual rather than the institution of the presidency.

That is the fear. In what he poses as a "*constitutional* corrective to *Presidential Power*," Terry Eastland wishes to reintroduce the importance, indeed the centrality, of formal authority. In his view, Neustadt's core assumption is incorrect. The Constitution did in fact create a system of government with a separation, *not* an encompassing sharing, of powers "that at their core are different in nature."[43] Presidential leadership, "energy in the executive," is both possible and necessary to bring energy to government, but it must to done in accordance with the precepts—the rules and arrangements—of the Constitution. According to figure 16.1, the president can also be a leader who has some measure of agency—a capacity for producing an independent impact on outcomes—but pursues a path consistent with a prescribed set of rules or beliefs. This is a "legalist" leadership image. The leader makes choices of some consequence, but they are rooted in guiding principles that specify correct and incorrect courses of action. One might also think of military officers in these terms, following explicit standard operating procedures, such as those found in the *Manual of Naval Operations*.

The second intellectual assault on Neustadt's "personal" president is deeply analytical rather than normative. From this vantage point, the problem is how to understand, explain, and develop enduring theories about presidential behavior and leadership. Terry Moe has been the main provocateur of this line of reasoning.[44] Moe accepts as correct two central themes of Neustadt's work and much that has followed it: the president is highly constrained and motivated by environmental pressures, to the detriment of individual agency; and the full characterization of presidential behavior in any one instance would require consideration of intricately related personal as well as more systemic factors. But this latter recognition does not take us very far, according to Moe, because it does not permit a systematic study of the presidency that yields real theory building. Instead, presidency studies should "move toward a methodology that values simplicity and parsimony rather than complexity and comprehensiveness" and that we should "think of presidents generically as institutional actors."[45] Starting from this perspective, one can turn to conceptual tools derived from rational models of individual and organizational behavior to construct theories of presidential strategies and choice. Empirically the real presidency—what presidents do and what outcomes they generate—may be a probabilistic enterprise, but explanations of core behavior can be better derived by imposing a more deterministic approach based on the assumption of rational action in response to environmentally induced incentives and the identifiable influence of other participants.[46]

These challenges lead to the final quadrant of Figure 16.1 and a fourth image of presidential leadership. When the role of environmental factors is dominant and there are external incentives with predictable courses of action that leaders choose, the leader acts as a *reactor*, behaving strictly in accordance with those incentives or pressures. The growth and elaboration of the institutions surrounding the president, for example, is not the idiosyncratic creation of the particular individuals who served in this presidency in modern times. Rather, according to Moe, it reflects the efforts of presidents qua presidents striving to gain some mastery over a political system that imposes demands that exceed their capacity to address them. Operating with relatively few degrees of freedom, presidents focus on the attributes of policymaking over which they have most control—their immediate institutional surroundings—and seek changes that will enhance the "responsive competence" of these organizations to meet the president's specific political needs.[47]

A very different level of analysis that also fits into this part of figure 16.1 is one in which the focus is on the capitalist state, the "privileged position" of business, and the capacity of business leaders to inhibit—even to imprison— the president.[48]

THE NEXT GENERATION

The three essays on presidential leadership that follow contribute to filling out the mechanics and understanding of the images of leadership I have just presented. Diane Heith's chapter, "Presidential Polling and the Potential for Leadership" (chapter 17) continues the convention of viewing the presidency in transactional terms and builds further on research stimulated by a central element of Neustadt's argument in *Presidential Power*. A crucial informal source of influence with other policymakers for Neustadtian presidents is the public's substantive image of them and their performance. An incumbent's standing with the public is part of the president's "political capital."[49] The electorate's views of the resident of the White House, of course, do not come out of the blue. "[T]he American people form and revise their impressions of the quality of presidential performance on evidence contained in reports of politics and policy outcomes—political news—in the news media."[50]

Chief executives, of course, know the presumed value of their popular support and the role of the media, and strive to mobilize a favorably inclined public to support their actions at home and abroad, especially to sway the decisionmaking of Congress.[51] To this end, representing a "superpersonalization of the American presidency," chief executives made nearly 10,000 public speeches of some kind between 1945 and 1985. In 1976, President Gerald Ford made public pronouncements just about every six hours.[52] Renee Smith in chapter 6 shows the strategic imperative of these public activities. If public approval provides an advantage to the president, and if presidents have the capacity to mobilize supportive constituencies on their behalf, then it would seem that chief executives would be most effective as leaders if they thoroughly understood the sources of public opinion and could engage in practices that would bring more people into agreement with their positions.[53] There is evidence that popular presidents do have the capacity to shift public opinion on an issue by as much as ten percentage points.[54] Transactional presidents thus seek to know public opinion, not just in terms of popular support for the administration, but also, as Heith emphasizes, in response to substantive issues. They do so not necessarily to put their fingers to the wind and follow—or pander to—popular views, but rather to design effective strategies for leading and persuading the public on the merits of their policy designs.[55]

Using archival material from several administrations, Heith observes the mechanics of how presidential staffs have developed for leadership purposes the connection between the president and public. First, successive administrations both have become more open about and have refined the technology for measuring public opinion. They want to know far more than simply whether or not the public generally approves of the president's job performance. They use survey research to delve into the details of what particular categories of individuals, what specific constituencies, support or oppose the president and why. As Heith then shows, these data are utilized by presidential advisers, with some variations across different administrations in actual approaches, to lend greater precision to the president's rhetorical efforts to gain influence with the public and thus in American governance. The chief executive in the original edition of *Presidential Power* would barely recognize the infrastructure that has developed around the president to pursue these activities. Neustadt would worry about the difficulty of overseeing such an expansive White House enterprise and ensuring that it serves presidential interests. But emergence of this apparatus in response to the demands of transactional leadership would be easily comprehended by the Neustadtian president.

It is not possible to assess accurately the president's efforts to influence the public and ongoing politics without examining the president's interactions with the mass media. This is the subject of Martha Kumar's chapter, "The President as Message and Messenger: Personal Style and Presidential Communications" (chapter 18).

White House institutions and organizations dealing with the press and presidential communications long preceded the public opinion apparatus Heith emphasizes. How presidents interact with the mass media can affect their potential for public leadership of any sort, and in this relationship as Kumar describes it, we can see the importance that Neustadt attached to the mix of personal and institutional factors influencing presidents' prestige and ability to govern. Political observers and the public alike were attentive to how the Clinton Administration dealt with the mass media during the entire scandal and impeachment ordeal.

In the case of the president' relations with the media, personal factors—presidential style—are central for two reasons: presidential style is a characteristic of the message and also the messenger. Kumar emphasizes the media's audience and business motivations for focusing on a president's personal qualities, in which television and newspaper audiences have shown deep and wide interest. And, most important, apart from the public's interest in these personal factors, how presidents communicate with and through the media depends on their personal styles (as related to their past experiences to be sure). Kumar suggests that the effectiveness with which presidents deal with news organizations is likely to be indicative of their relations with Congress, the components of their administration, and other institutions.

Russell Riley in "The Limits of the Transformational Presidency" (chapter 19) returns to the question of whether presidents can in fact have greater agency than Neustadt's transactional leaders. Were the great presidents of popular lore—such as Lincoln and Franklin Roosevelt—individuals of effective agency and independent bearing? Were these "order-creating" presidents "making politics" in Stephen Skowronek's terms?[56] By ending slavery and saving the Union, by rebuilding the nation's economy and defeating the Axis powers, were these presidents and others like them transformers?

Riley argues, on the contrary, that close examination of presumably transformational presidents reveals a number of paradoxes that must alter our image of their leadership. They took bold action, but it was circumstances that "impelled" that action. Their decisiveness involved policy changes, to be sure, but those were typically launched by others. Further, these presidents acted in the mission of preserving, not transforming, the larger social order in the face of severe threats to the political system. These were leaders who reacted to the state of affairs they confronted, forced into action by the failure of predecessors to meet the exigencies generated by the political and social environment, and often more content with maintaining the status quo than disrupting it. Rather than transformers, they were "conformers." According to Riley, they were much like the presidents that Neustadt described, highly bound and constrained by the environments in which they served. But because they were reactive to circumstances much in the way Moe characterizes presidents as institutional actors responding to a defined set of incentives, I would treat Riley's conformers as fitting in with the less personal, more predictable "reactor" leadership image in Figure 16.1.

When Neustadt began to study the presidency and presidential leadership, the core text was Edward Corwin's volume, *The President: Office and Powers*, initially published in 1940. As Corwin highlighted in the preface to the fourth edition, "It is primarily a study in American public law."[57] Consistent with the "legalist" image of leadership offered in Figure 16.1, the president from this perspective was a holder of formal powers and prescribed roles. Neustadt, based on both personal experience as an assistant in the Truman White House and his own scholarship, found presidents much too overwhelmed by institutional complexities, divided authority, and environmental pressures to be effective, if they relied solely on formal authority. Presidents had to become effective bargainers, transacting exchangers with multiple players. The subsequent literature on the presidency has substantiated those constraints on presidential influence, expanded dramatically our understanding of the transactor's variegated contexts for leadership, and proffered competing images of leadership opportunities and paths of explanation. Heith, Kumar, and Riley continue that tradition, together reinforcing the Neustadtian imperatives facing modern American presidents while also demonstrating the utility of reaching beyond the analytical approach taken in *Presidential Power*.

NOTES

1. Richard E. Neustadt, *Presidential Power and the Modern Presidents: The Politics of Leadership from Roosevelt to Reagan* (New York: Free Press, 1990), p. 7.

2. Terry M. Moe and Scott A. Wilson, "Presidents and the Politics of Structure," *Law & Contemporary Problems* 57 (2) (Spring 1994): 1, 3; and Theodore J. Lowi, *The Personal President: Power Invested, Promised Unfulfilled* (Ithaca: Cornell University Press, 1985), p. 11.

3. Barbara Sinclair, "Studying Presidential Leadership," in George C. Edwards III, John H. Kessel, and Bert A. Rockman, eds., *Researching the Presidency*, pp. 203–232 (Pittsburgh: University of Pittsburgh Press, 1993), p. 205.

4. John W. Gardner, *On Leadership* (New York: Free Press, 1990); and Neustadt, *Presidential Power*.

5. Robert C. Tucker, *Politics as Leadership* (Columbia: University of Missouri Press, 1981), p. 15; Frank R. Baumgartner, *Conflict and Rhetoric in French Policymaking* (Pittsburgh: University of Pittsburgh Press, 1989), p. 3; Erwin C. Hargrove, "Two Conceptions of Institutional Leadership," in Bryan D. Jones, ed., *Leadership and Politics: New Perspectives in Political Science* (Lawrence: University of Kansas Press, 1989), quoting Gary Miller, p. 61; see also Philip Selznick, *Leadership in Administration: A Sociological Interpretation* (New York: Harper, 1957).

6. Andrew S. McFarland, *Power and Leadership in Pluralist Systems* (Stanford: Stanford University Press, 1969); and Aaron Wildavsky, "A Cultural Theory of Leadership," in Bryan D. Jones, ed., *Leadership and Politics: New Perspectives in Political Science* (Lawrence: University of Kansas Press, 1989).

7. Dennis F. Thompson, *Political Ethics and Public Office* (Cambridge: Harvard University Press, 1987).

8. Wildavsky, "A Cultural Theory of Leadership," p. 94; Sinclair, "Studying Presidential Leadership," p. 205; also James MacGregor Burns, *Leadership* (New York:

Harper, 1978); Fred I. Greenstein, "The Impact of Personality on Politics: An Attempt to Clear Away Underbrush," *American Political Science Review* 61 (3) (September 1967): 629–641; McFarland, *Power and Leadership*; and Thompson, *Political Ethics and Public Office.*

9. Sinclair, "Studying Presidential Leadership," p. 205.

10. Arthur M. Schlesinger, Jr., *The Imperial Presidency* (New York: Houghton Mifflin, 1973); L. Gordon Crovitz and Jeremy A. Rabkin, eds., *The Fettered Presidency* (Washington, D.C: American Enterprise Institute, 1989); Ryan J. Barilleaux, *The Post-Modern Presidency* (New York: Praeger, 1988); Thomas M. Franck, ed., *The Tethered Presidency: Congressional Restraints on Executive Power* (New York: New York University Press, 1981); Terry Eastland, *Energy in the Executive: The Case for a Strong Presidency* (New York: Free Press, 1992); William F. Grover, *The Presidency as Prisoner: A Structural Critique of the Carter and Reagan Years* (Albany: State University of New York Press, 1989); Stephen Skowronek, *The Politics Presidents Make: Leadership from John Adams to George Bush* (Cambridge: Harvard University Press, 1993); Aaron Wildavsky, *The Beleaguered Presidency* (New Brunswick, N.J.: Transaction Publishers, 1991); Paul C. Light, *The President's Agenda: Domestic Policy Choice from Kennedy to Carter* (Baltimore: Johns Hopkins University Press, 1982).

11. Franck, *The Tethered Presidency*; and Robert J. Spitzer, *President and Congress: Executive Hegemony at the Crossroads of American Government* (Philadelphia: Temple University Press, 1993), p. xiv.

12. Jean Blondel, *Political Leadership: Towards a General Analysis* (Beverly Hills: Sage Publications, 1987); Greenstein, "The Impact of Personality;" Sidney Hook, *The Hero in History: A Study in Limitation and Possibility* (New York: John Day, 1943); Bryan D. Jones, "Causation, Constraint, and Political Leadership," in Bryan D. Jones, *Leadership and Politics: New Perspectives in Political Science* (Lawrence: University of Kansas Press, 1989); and Barbara Kellerman, *The Political Presidency: Practice of Leadership from Kennedy Through Reagan* (New York: Oxford University Press, 1984).

13. Burns, *Leadership*, pp. 3–4.

14. Thomas Carlyle, *On Heroes, Hero-Worship, and the Heroic in History* (London: Chapman and Hall, 1840).

15. Kenneth E. Morris and Barry Schwartz, "Why They Liked Ike: Tradition, Crisis, and Heroic Leadership," *Sociological Quarterly* 34 (1) (Winter 1993): 133–152.

16. Blondel, *Political Leadership*; George C. Edwards III, *Presidential Influence in Congress* (San Francisco: W. H. Freeman, 1980); George C. Edwards III, *At the Margins: Presidential Leadership in Congress* (New Haven: Yale University Press, 1989); Jones, "Causation, Constraint, and Political Leadership;" and Wildavsky, "A Cultural Theory of Leadership."

17. Herbert Spencer, *The Study of Sociology* (New York: D. Appleton, 1874).

18. Margaret Weir, *Politics and Jobs: The Boundaries of Employment Policy in the United States* (Princeton: Princeton University Press, 1992), pp. 18–19.

19. Jones, "Causation, Constraint, and Political Leadership;" also Frank R. Baumgartner, "Strategies of Political Leadership in Diverse Settings," In Bryan D. Jones, ed., *Leadership and Politics: New Perspectives in Political Science* (Lawrence: University of Kansas Press, 1989).

20. For an excellent summary of this perspective, Morris P. Fiorina and Kenneth A. Shepsle, "Formal Theories of Leadership: Agents, Agenda Setters, and Entrepreneurs," in Bryan D. Jones, ed., *Leadership and Politics: New Perspectives in Political Science* (Lawrence: University of Kansas Press, 1989).

21. Jones, "Causation, Constraint, and Political Leadership."

22. Burns, *Leadership*, p. 19.

23. Hook, *The Hero in History*.

24. Neustadt, *Presidential Power*, p. 32.

25. Terry M. Moe, "Presidents, Institutions, and Theory," in George C. Edwards III, John H. Kessel, and Bert A. Rockman, eds., *Researching the Presidency*, pp. 337–385 (Pittsburgh: University of Pittsburgh Press, 1993), p. 339.

26. Kellerman, *The Political Presidency*, pp. xi, 21; see also James David Barber, *The Presidential Character: Predicting Performance in the White House*, 3rd Ed. (Englewood Cliffs, N.J.: Prentice-Hall, 1985); and Dean Keith Simonton, *Why Presidents Succeed: A Political Psychology of Leadership* (New Haven: Yale University Press, 1987).

27. Jon R. Bond and Richard Fleisher, *The President in the Legislative Arena* (Chicago: University of Chicago Press, 1990); Edwards, *Presidential Influence*; Edwards, *At the Margins*; Grover, *The Presidency as Prisoner*; Mark A. Peterson, *Legislating Together: The White House and Capitol Hill from Eisenhower to Reagan* (Cambridge: Harvard University Press, 1990); Mark A. Peterson, "The President and Congress," in Michael Nelson, ed., *The Presidency and the Political System*, 5th Ed., 469–498 (Washington, D.C.: CQ Press, 1998); Bert A. Rockman, *The Leadership Question: The Presidency and the American System* (New York: Praeger, 1984); and Jean Reith Schroedel, *Congress, the President, and Policy Making: A Historical Analysis* (Armonk, N.Y.: M.E. Sharpe, 1994).

28. George C. Edwards III, "George Washington's Leadership of Congress: Director or Facilitator?," *Congress & the Presidency* 18, (2) (Autumn 1991): 163–183; and Edwards, *At the Margins*.

29. Rockman, *The Leadership Question*, p. xv.

30. Light, *The President's Agenda*.

31. Skowronek, *The Politics Presidents Make*.

32. Charles O. Jones, *The Presidency in a Separated System* (Washington, D.C.:

Brookings Institution, 1994); and Peterson, *Legislating Together*; Rockman, *The Leadership Question*.

33. Peterson, *Legislating Together*.

34. Samuel Kernell, *Going Public: New Strategies of Presidential Leadership*, 2nd Ed. (Washington, D.C.: CQ Press, 1993); Light, *The President's Agenda*; Lowi, *The Personal President*; Charles O. Jones, *The Trusteeship Presidency: Jimmy Carter and the United States Congress* (Baton Rouge: Louisiana State University Press, 1988); Peterson, *Legislating Together*; Peterson, "The President and Congress;" George E. Reedy, *The Twilight of the Presidency: From Johnson to Reagan* (New York: New American Library, 1987); Richard Rose, *The Postmodern President: George Bush Meets the World*, 2nd Ed. (Chatham, N.J.: Chatham House, 1991); and Lester G. Seligman and Cary R. Covington, *The Coalitional Presidency* (Chicago: Dorsey Press, 1989).

35. Seligman and Covington, *The Coalitional Presidency*.

36. Rose, *The Postmodern President*, p. 6 (italics in the original).

37. Burns, *Leadership*, p. 20.

38. Max Weber, *The Theory of Social and Economic Organization*, edited by Talcott Parsons (New York: Free Press, 1947); Hook, *The Hero in History*; James G. March and Johan P. Olsen, *Rediscovering Institutions: The Organizational Basis of Politics* (New York: Free Press, 1989), p. 163.

39. Skowronek, *The Politics Presidents Make*, pp. 5, 6, 20.

40. Lowi, *The Personal President*, p. xi.

41. Jeffrey K. Tulis, *The Rhetorical Presidency* (Princeton: Princeton University Press, 1987). For an alternative analysis that finds presidents using "public" strategies from the beginning of the republic, see Melvin C. Laracey, "Constitutionally Speaking: The Evolution of Going Public," unpublished Ph.D. dissertation, University of Michigan, 1997.

42. The connection between traditional bargaining and going public is explored by a former student of Richard Neustadt, Marc Bodnick, " 'Going Public' Reconsidered: Reagan's 1981 Tax and Budget Cuts, and Revisionist Theories of Presidential Power," *Congress and the Presidency* 17 (1) (Spring 1990): 13–28.

43. Eastland, *Energy in the Executive*, pp. 8–9 (italics in the original).

44. Terry M. Moe, "The Politicized Presidency," in John E. Chubb and Paul E. Peterson, eds., *The New Direction in American Politics*, pp. 235–271 (Washington, D.C.: Brookings Institution, 1985); Moe, "Presidents, Institutions, and Theory;" and Moe and Wilson, "Presidents and the Politics of Structure."

45. Moe, "Presidents, Institutions, and Theory," p. 338; and Moe and Wilson, "Presidents and the Politics of Structure."

46. See also Sinclair, "Studying Presidential Leadership," as well as Charles Cameron, "Presidents, Vetoes, and Bargaining," and David Epstein and Sharyn

O'Halloran, "The Institutional Face of Power: Congressional Delegation of Authority to the President," in this volume.

47. Moe, "The Politicized Presidency." An alternative analysis of White House staff growth and the use of staff to facilitate presidential bargaining is provided by a former doctoral student of Richard Neustadt's, Matthew J. Dickinson, *Bitter Harvest: FDR, Presidential Power, and the Growth of the Presidential Branch* (New York: Cambridge University Press, 1997).

48. Grover, *The Presidency as Prisoner*.

49. Light, *The President's Agenda*; Richard A. Brody, *Assessing the President: The Media, Elite Opinion, and Public Support* (Stanford: Stanford University Press, 1991); George C. Edwards III, *The Public Presidency: The Pursuit of Popular Support* (New York: St. Martin's Press, 1983; see also Edwards, *Presidential Influence in Congress*; and Edwards, *At the Margins*. Many other authors have also studied the relationship between public support of the president and presidential success in Congress, producing divergent results. See, for example, Bond and Fleisher, *The President in the Legislative Arena*, and Peterson, *Legislating Together*.

50. Brody, *Assessing the President*, p. 4; see also Elmer Cornwell, *Presidential Leadership in Public Opinion* (Bloomington: Indiana University Press, 1965); and Michael Baruch Grossman and Martha Joynt Kumar, *Portraying the President: The White House and the News Media* (Baltimore: Johns Hopkins University Press, 1981).

51. Kernell, *Going Public*; Tulis, *The Rhetorical Presidency*; Barbara Hinkley, *The Symbolic Presidency: How Presidents Portray Themselves* (New York: Routledge, 1990); and Craig Allen Smith and Kathy B. Smith, *The White House Speaks: Presidential Leadership as Persuasion* (Westport, CT: Praeger, 1994).

52. Roderick P. Hart, *The Sound of Leadership: Presidential Communication in the Modern Age* (Chicago: University of Chicago Press, 1987), p. 208.

53. Edwards, *The Public Presidency*.

54. Benjamin I. Page and Robert Y. Shapiro, *The Rational Public: Fifty Years of Trends in Americans' Policy Preferences* (Chicago: University of Chicago Press, 1992).

55. Lawrence R. Jacobs and Robert Y. Shapiro, "The Politicization of Public Opinion: The Fight for the Pulpit," in Margaret Weir, ed., *The Social Divide: Political Parties and the Future of Activist Government*, pp. 83–125 (Washington, D.C: Brookings Institution Press, Russell Sage Foundation, 1998).

56. Skowronek, *The Politics Presidents Make*.

57. Edward S. Corwin, *The President: Office and Powers*, 4th Ed. (New York: New York University, 1957), p. vii.

CHAPTER 17

Presidential Polling and the Potential for Leadership

Diane J. Heith

INTRODUCTION

The public has long been considered a source of strength and support for the president. Richard Neustadt claimed "public standing is a source of influence for him, another factor bearing on . . . [the] willingness to give him what he wants."[1] Elmer Cornwell further observed that "the leverage the President has acquired in the lawmaking process has been indirect, based on the use of the arts of persuasion, and ultimately grounded in the popular support he can claim or mobilize."[2] From Neustadt and Cornwell's perspective, the public represents a strategic, albeit oblique, tool which helps achieve presidential goals.

Samuel Kernell also argues that presidents indirectly use the public as a political resource whenever they undertake "going public" efforts.[3] "Going public is a class of activities that presidents engage in as they promote themselves and their policies before the American public . . . . in a way that enhances . . . chances of success in Washington."[4] While Kernell argues that presidents increasingly rely on White House public relations efforts in order to translate approval of presidential performance into support for presidential policies, he also observes that "a strategic president must answer for himself two kinds of questions. First, what does the public want . . . . [and] how much popular support he is willing to give up to secure his policy goals."[5]

Despite Neustadt's warning that "professional reputation is not popularity," a great deal of interest and scholarly research developed around the notion that a popular president is a successful president.[6] Popularity, not the public, became the "political resource that can help him achieve his program, keep challengers at bay and guide his and other political leaders' expectations about the president's party prospects in presidential and congressional elections."[7] Certifying public opinion as a presidential resource implies a level of control or strategy in its application. However, scholars found that "presidential" factors (i.e., actions or utterances) could explain only some of the up and down fluctuations in presidential popularity ratings as measured typically in Gallup poll results.[8] Media coverage, macroeconomic factors and world events exert greater influence on presidential approval ratings than presidential actions.[9] Moreover, without a mechanism for direct control, presidential efforts seem only to improve approval ratings "at the margins."[10] Presidents' attempts to boost popularity have quite transitory effects.[11] Furthermore, translating popularity into a legislative victory is problematic at best. The multitude of scholarly evaluations on the effect of presidential popularity in Congressional outcomes is ambiguous and contingent.[12] Recent scholarly efforts demonstrate, however, that presidents have greater influence on the nation's agenda and the "national mood" (the public's general orientation to all policies and issues) than on legislative success or even their own popularity.[13] The conflicting evidence connecting popularity ratings with presidential success underscores the lack of systematic strategic value of these ratings. If a president cannot control or consistently influence popularity ratings, and if the effects of improving these ratings are uncertain, then popularity alone can never be a useful leadership tool for the president.

The unreliability of popularity as such a tool, however, does not preclude the value of public opinion to the president. Since the publication of *Presidential Power*, presidents and their staffs have successfully utilized a more reliable and direct connection with the public. In the midst of the scholarly focus on a president's popularity, the national party organizations increasingly obtained private public opinion polls not only for use by presidential candidates but also by presidents between elections.[14] This has led to important new research on presidents and public opinion.[15] Specifically, all White Houses since 1969 sought to determine public attitudes about policy, presidential performance, and personal socioeconomic status.[16] Based on archived documents from the Nixon, Ford, Carter, and Reagan administrations, this chapter reconstructs presidential efforts to utilize public opinion (and not just popularity) in the governing arena, and in constituent and rhetorical efforts in particular, to improve the president's potential for public leadership.[17] These four administrations viewed public opinion as a strategic and purposeful tool, not simply as a barometer of the policy environment. Public opinion appeared to encourage and aid leadership from a presidency-centered perspective as these presidents used polling results to identify constituents and their desires, and to design the rhetoric of public appeals on policy issues.

POLLING AS A CONSTITUENCY BUILDING TOOL

In the past, public opinion and the polling consultant were not critical either to presidential campaigns or to presidential governing efforts. As late as the 1960s, polls played a secondary role in campaign strategy. Kessel contends that older candidates did not trust the data and that the surveys and analysis were relatively simple.[18] By 1976, however, pollsters and surveys were clearly crucial to campaign structure and strategy. During this period, polling consultants increased their expertise to produce sophisticated levels of analysis, moving from "simple cross-tabulations to multidimensional scaling and simulation . . . but having knowledgeable pollsters sitting in on strategy discussions is more important in making effective use of these data."[19] Since Nixon, all presidents have recognized the benefits of public-opinion polling from their campaigns and translated that knowledge, and their consultants, to the governing era.[20]

The Nixon administration retained several polling consultants, Professor David Derge, Robert Teeter, and Richard Wirthlin. By 1972, Nixon had replaced Derge with Teeter (who also worked for Presidents Ford and Bush). President Ford primarily employed Robert Teeter and his firm, Market Opinion Research (MOR). While working for the Ford administration, Teeter subcontracted regional polls to Richard Wirthlin and his firm Decision Management Information (DMI). Apparently pleased with Wirthlin's expertise, the Ford White House considered switching from Teeter to Wirthlin. January 27, 1975, Wirthlin detailed a proposal to the White House and subsequently received a contract for the purchase of poll data and analysis.[21] The Ford White House continued to discuss the possibility of hiring Wirthlin's firm and continued to purchase polls and analysis until September 1975. In a memo to Donald Rumsfeld and Richard Cheney (both Assistants to the President in the White House Operations Office), Jerry Jones, (White House Staff Secretary) informed his superiors that Wirthlin agreed to poll for Ronald Reagan from September 1975 to January 1976 to determine the viability of a run for the Republican nomination.[22] Upon receiving that news, the Ford White House quickly terminated the relationship with Wirthlin and his firm. Presidents Carter and Reagan each retained only one polling consultant, Patrick Caddell and Richard Wirthlin, respectively. In terms of the depth of relationship between pollster and president, Caddell was in a league of his own, providing surveys, analysis, advice, and a personal agenda.[23]

Changes in modern presidential campaigns and the party system also significantly influenced the use of polling in the governing arena. The national Republican and Democratic party organizations have primarily existed to field candidates and mobilize voters during elections. However, party loyalty, party support, and voter turnout have all been declining.[24] The increasing number of independent voters and the decentralized party system as a whole ensures that political parties cannot consistently turn out voters in support of presidential candidates. As a result, presidential candidates have gradually abandoned party strategies and deployed presidency-centered campaign strategies to take advantage of changes in participation and nominating procedures.[25] Since FDR, presidents and candidates have minimized links with party connections and maximized direct links between themselves and their supporters. Modern presidents have forged direct, personal connections between themselves and constituents in both the electoral and governing arenas.[26] Split-ticket voting, split electoral outcomes, the rise of independents, and the spread of insurgent groups and candidates have all combined to produce a personal, mass constituency for the presidency.[27]

The presidential constituency is highly fragmented. It is united only by a single act of voting. By virtue of the disparity between nominating and general election constituents, the presidential electoral coalition has inevitably become a conglomeration of party ideology, short-term, campaign-driven attitudes and single-issue supporters. Presidential candidates attempt to successfully mobilize these blocs of voters based on political and socioeconomic factors using sophisticated polling techniques.[28] Upon election, presidents must attempt to translate this divergent multitude into stable coalitions from which to govern. Moreover, all first-term chief executives want to be reelected, so the president must not only translate an initial electoral coalition into a governing coalition, but also maintain and even expand this personal coalition into the next election cycle. Due to the decline of party identification, presidents must discover from their unique presidential, and not party, perspectives who their supporters are, who their opponents are, and who languishes in the middle. Presidents Nixon, Ford, Carter, and Reagan adapted their campaign polling strategies to the White House and learned to use public opinion polling by the end of their first year in office to classify the electorate into traditional and nontraditional categories.[29] The classifications provided detailed definitions beyond age, gender, geography and employment, as these administrations used polling to classify individuals by their support for presidential issues.

IDENTIFYING PRESIDENTIAL SUPPORTERS

All four administrations undertook extensive efforts to monitor and evaluate the president's electoral coalition. The electoral coalitions were conglomerations of party members, and short-term campaign-driven and single-issue supporters whose depth and breadth of support varied considerably.[30] These presidents moved beyond tracking presidential approval and traditional Democrat or Republican demographics; instead, the polling apparatus helped their administrations isolate constituencies by focusing on what linked individuals to the president and the administration's policies.

The first to utilize polling consistently, the Nixon administration initially employed polling to construct traditional classifications (e.g., party and group supporters).[31] Nixon's polling advisers cautioned that tracking group support and desires was not always sensible. For example, "farmers always constitute such a tiny part of a national sample that results which are extrapolated from a national sample are often misleading."[32] Age, religion, race and geography were common distinctions catalogued to constitute groups thought to vote together. Despite the commonly held view that the president represents a national constituency, presidents and their staffs recognized that different parts of the country have different desires and different characterizations of the president. President Nixon even directed H. R. Haldeman to cease all national polls "because he doesn't feel they will be meaningful—RNC [Republican National Committee] may have some argument with this."[33] Nixon's targeted efforts also centered around American youth. With the passage of the 26th amendment, which reduced the voting age from 21 to 18, the youth vote was a potential ally or threat. Since young people had never voted, the Nixon administration did not "really know anything about the voting probabilities of kids who are now 17 or 19. But there are a great many of them and it behooves us to find out whatever we can."[34] The Nixon and Ford White Houses also closely tracked the liberal-conservative spectrum, believing that a vast bastion of conservative support existed and endorsed Republican presidents.[35]

The geographic classifications gradually became more detailed. Former Census director Richard Scammon informed the Nixon administration that in the "1970s political power will shift to the suburbs . . . . The constituency is relatively affluent, essentially middle-aged . . . . These people are less committed to parties as an electorate. They are drawing their knowledge from television, and can be reached much more so than 25 years ago."[36] Scammon unwittingly provided the heart of the modern presidency-centered strategy: less reliance on parties and party ideology than in the past, and greater use of television to target individuals by demographics.

Although personal attributes are easily discernible utilizing polling, the Carter administration had another reason to turn to socioeconomic (SES) data. According to Patrick Caddell, "Jimmy Carter managed to garner the 'traditional' majorities from a number of 'New Deal Coalition' groups. Unfortunately, the size of many of those groups is shrinking in the general populace. . . . To make up the difference—and to win the election—Jimmy Carter did far better than is 'traditional' among a number of groups that did not participate in the old coalition."[37] Carter won traditional Democratic support from Catholics, Jews, Blacks, labor, the poor, and traditionally Democratic geographic areas, like Chicago. It was "clear that while Carter benefited from their support, he may owe his election more to the non-traditional groups that helped him to do better in unexpected places."[38] Those supporters were white Protestants, the better educated, white collar, and rural, small-town voters. Poll data also revealed problem constituencies for Carter upon entering the White House, including voters age 25–35, in particular nonworking housewives, and those residing in the West.[39] In short, the Carter White House believed it owed its campaign success and future presidential success to independent issue voters and segmented portions of the population. Other explanations for Carter's narrow victory, such as Nixon and Watergate issues, and Ford's debate gaffe where he claimed Eastern Europe was not under Soviet control, did not factor into Caddell's poll-produced constituency assessments. Instead, the administration tracked the support (or lack thereof) flowing from the nontraditional Carter constituency during the administration's four-year tenure because "relatively small changes in the popular vote totals [in the 1976 election] could have changed the Electoral College outcome dramatically."[40]

The process of identifying and tracking presidential support continued to evolve. By Ronald Reagan's tenure, strategists not only identified the Reagan constituency, but also used polls to gauge the intensity of the connection between Reagan and his supporters. The White House analysts distinguished Reagan supporters and opponents in terms of what they defined as the core and periphery of both American society. The strong support group, they found, "represents the core of American society and . . . support for the President weakens as one moves away from this core."[41] The White House staff's characterization of the Reagan constituency is shown in Table 17.1.

TABLE 17.1   Reagan Supporters

Strong Support Group	Mixed Support Group	Low Support Group
35-54 Years Old	55-64 Years Old	65+ and non-affluent
College Educated	25-34 Years Old	24 and Under
$20,000+ income earners	Postgraduates	Union Members
White, Anglo Saxon Protestants		
(Teutonic and Scandinavian)	High School Graduates	Less than High School Graduates
Non-Union Workers,	$10,000-$20,000 income	Less than $10,000 income earners
professionals, managers,	earners	
owners, farmers and white		
collar (clerical/sales) workers		
	Blue Collar Workers	Ethnics: Southern/Eastern Euro
		pean, Jews, Non-Anglo Catholics,
		Blacks
	Some Ethnics: Hispanics	
	and Anglo Catholics	Women

Source: Memo to the Senior Staff from Beal 12/21/81 in PR 15 050001-056000 doc # 0533818

The Reagan staff tracked the administration's constituency almost reli-
giously, receiving monthly updates on the distribution of its supporters. Like
those in the Carter administration, the Reagan strategists were very concerned
with the fringe of Reagan's support. Substantial time and effort was also
devoted to watching the newly identified "gender gap." Polling revealed that
Reagan suffered on "[the] war issue . . . [his] personal style. . . [and the] economic issue among working women."[42] The Reagan White House was very
concerned about the creation and persistence of this gap, and therefore monitored it regularly.

IDENTIFYING SUPPORTERS' ISSUES

Although constituents' support continued to be classified by region, gender,
age and education,[43] all administrations experimented with associations
beyond routine SES data. This electoral monitoring essentially represented
efforts to answer the "who" question: *who* supported the president. In addition,
the White House needed to know *why* individuals supported the president.
Specifically, the White House needed to understand its electoral coalition so

that coalitions could be rebuilt across issues.[44] In order to lead, follow, respond to, or ignore public opinion, the president needed to know what drove his personal and policy support.

Upon coining the phrase, " Silent Majority," and receiving so much support from self-identifiers, the Nixon administration went to great lengths to capture the Silent Majority in surveys. The administration used its poll apparatus to identify supporters not by party or group affiliation, but by identification of attitudes contrary to those of the students protesting against the Vietnam War. The Nixon administration also undertook a serious campaign to identify the "forgotten American," a profile the staff wanted to develop in order to assess "the impact of existing Federal programs on the forgotten American. . . . Careful definitions, followed up by this kind of analysis, must be obtained before the forgotten American can become a serious subject for governmental programming."[45]

In keeping with the focus on demographics, the Nixon White House closely examined its suburban supporters, but not simply by geographic locale. Nixon noted to John Ehrlichman that from poll results "people who live in homes that they own tend to take a much more conservative view on public issues than people who rent. I think this has significant consequences as far as our own programs are concerned. . . . I would like you to follow through in any way that you think would be appropriate to reach our homeowner constituency."[46] Thus, Nixon's staff disaggregated support not only by urban, suburban, and rural, but also by lifestyle, with home-ownership as the prized attribute.

The Carter administration continued this disaggregation of presidential support by lifestyle choices. On energy policy, an area which the administration polled extensively, in addition to traditional socioeconomic factors, the White House sought out the opinions of individuals based upon the type of heating used in their homes. Caddell would cross-tabulate answers to questions on Carter's energy policy with traditional respondent characteristics and the type of home heating utilized by the respondent. The White House believed that the type of home heating would indicate support for various energy programs and options for conservation.[47] However, no significant levels of support for the president's energy program were discovered in the public as a whole or in any segment of home heating users. As such, no "home heating" constituency was discovered when the opinions of homeowners were compared by their oil, gas, coal, or electricity usage and by their answers to questions such as, "how serious do you think the problem of real shortages of natural fuels—such as oil and gas is," and "do you favor or oppose a tariff (tax) on imported oil that would raise the price of gasoline 10 to 15 cents per gallon if it would end our dependence on foreign oil."[48] The extra classification simply revealed more of the same—that the public did not believe the oil shortage was a crisis requiring sacrifice.[49]

The Reagan White House extended the effort to segment and identify further which factors affected support for the president and his policies. Both Jack Burgess, Deputy Director and Special Assistant to the President, and Elizabeth Dole, Assistant to the President in the Office of Public Liaison, worked on a coalition-building program targeted at "ethnics." Dole and Burgess wanted to break down ethnicity further in a way "which would enable us to track the opinions of Italian-, Polish-, Lithuanian- Americans, etc."[50] The Reagan administration also tracked more detailed religious categories than any other administration, distinguishing among Presbyterians, Methodists, Lutherans, Baptists, Other Protestants, Catholics, Jews and agnostics; while there was no direct reference to Islam, a follow-up question inquired into born-again status.[51] These categories were used frequently to classify supporters on the social issues of abortion, school prayer, gun control, a balanced budget, and tuition tax credits. Interestingly, the Reagan administration believed that "even when we are on the 'wrong' side of some of these issues from a [general] public opinion standpoint, they still may be politically positive. For example, there is little doubt that the Democrats are suffering greatly among urban Catholics because they have been associated with abortion on demand. They [sic] President ran extremely well among this group in 1980."[52] Like Nixon's and Carter's strategists, Reagan's advisers clearly distinguished between general and segmented levels of public support. Moreover, the Reagan strategists recognized the value of specific single issues to certain supporters regardless of party affiliation. Information about public opinion empowered presidents to reframe their actions and decisions based on the possibly shifting constituent support found in survey data.

The innovation of private White House polling aided presidents' coalition balancing acts by providing detailed descriptions of supporters and the issues important to them. Presidents must maintain their initial base of support and also attempt to expand or adjust their electoral coalition in order to govern effectively.[53] Nixon, Carter, and Reagan assessed the depth of their support across numerous presidential policies. Moreover, the Nixon and Reagan administrations used polling to define, identify, and track supporters in terms of the core and periphery. Peripheral support required the constant monitoring that only public opinion polling can provide since support from weak-identifiers is transitory: "Peripheral supporters can be appealed to only on the issues of concern to them, and their demands may constrain a president's option and even conflict with the preferences of the president's core coalition."[54]

The Ford administration represents an interesting dilemma for this line of inquiry. Seemingly the lack of an electoral constituency posed a problem, or at least a lack of continuity, for research into leadership via poll-produced constituency building. Unlike the other presidents, Ford did not enter office with an electorally produced constituency, and thus it was difficult to trace support for Ford himself to the behavior of voters in the last presidential election. The lack of an electoral coalition resulted in the absence of a constituency which was attached to Ford personally. To overcome the appointment problem, Ford's staff attempted to create a baseline for comparison by employing a standard, almost stereotypical, Republican measure for comparison. Robert Teeter, Ford's pollster, noted, "the President has not created any Ford constituency unique from that of any Republican President. The one exception to this is that he does show unique strength with young voters for a Republican."[55]

Teeter's lament that Ford lacked a unique constituency only underscores the presidential transition from party leader to personal leader and the role of polling in that transition. If President Ford represented the Republican party as nineteenth-century presidents did, then personal attraction would not matter. Teeter highlighted the evolution from candidate-centered campaigns to presidency-centered governing, and demonstrated that the modern president requires his own individual base of support in order to lead. Moreover, Teeter indicated the importance of polling for coalitional governing. The Nixon, Carter, and Reagan administrations used exit poll information as a baseline for subsequent constituent assessments. Without an electoral coalition for comparison, the Ford administration used the polling apparatus to produce an artificial electoral coalition baseline so that they too could compare current coalition composition.

Presidents have used public opinion polls to define and redefine their audience into useful associations for presidential appeals. The highly fractured approach to the president's constituencies challenges traditional perceptions of the presidential audience, that is, the common, constituent, and partisan approaches to determining president's audiences.[56] In this typology, the common audience refers to the president's unique relationship with the entire country. Constituent patrons are "specific groups within the broader national community," such as the American Association for Retired Persons, while partisan audiences, by definition, stem from the president's party.[57] However, as demonstrated above, the president and his staff rarely view the nation as "a common audience," focusing instead on increasingly narrow conceptions of the president's audience. Popularity ratings represent the most frequently utilized reference to the president's common audience. The Nixon, Ford, and Reagan administrations did track presidential popularity, but they rarely referenced the findings in White House memoranda. The Nixon, Ford, and Reagan administrations kept approval data in binders chronologically, in order to establish trends and to relate dips or rises in popularity to events. This tracking of presidential approval allowed Richard Cheney, Assistant to the President, White House Operations, to inform President Ford, for example, that "a Gallup poll published today shows your approval rating stable at 47%, with 37% disapproval. These findings agree with the last three surveys conducted since August by Gallup."[58] President Nixon even wanted to know how his popularity ranked against the past four presidents. According to one White House memo, "studying the change in popularity . . . over a comparable first-11-month period, we see Eisenhower dropping 8% and Johnson 10%, and Kennedy rising 6% and Nixon 9%. As a result, Nixon is now well ahead of Eisenhower at this stage of his term in office, about equal to Johnson, well behind Kennedy."[59] When I examined the Carter archives, I was unable to discover any separate tracking of presidential popularity, in contrast to the three Republican administrations. Caddell provided the administration with popularity figures without segregating the information from the rest of the public opinion data. Information from the common audience represented by approval ratings lacks both the "who" and the "why" necessary for strategic application. As such, in order to utilize public opinion as a strategic tool, "constituent" patrons were increasingly disaggregated within the White House memoranda into narrower definitions of "specific groups" such as homeowners, born-again Christians, and types of heating users.

Presidents, then, apparently seek support for themselves and their own policy positions rather than support for their party and its positions. Table 17.2 shows that Presidents Nixon, Carter, and Reagan devoted significantly more attention, through public appearances, to their common and constituent audiences than to partisan audiences; Ford had only slightly more common and constituent appearances than total partisan appearances. These presidents did not appeal to partisan audiences as often as they appealed to other stylized audiences. Across the four administrations, constituent appearances increased. Moreover, the yearly average number of partisan appearances revealed that these presidents made 4.5 times more partisan appearances in election years than in nonelection years.[60] Outside of election years, these presidents spent

TABLE 17.2   Presidential Public Activities

Type of Appearance[a]	Nixon	Ford	Carter	Reagan
Common (Major Speeches, News Conferences)				
	12.5%	6.4%	11.8%	6.3%
Constituent				
(Minor Speeches, Non Political Appearances)				
	63.5%	44.3%	52%	63.5%
Partisan				
(Political Appearances)	24%	49.3%	36.2%	30.2%
Number	425	829	646	680

[a]From First Terms only
Source: Gary King, and Lyn Ragsdale, *The Elusive Executive: Discovering Statistical Patterns in the Presidency* (Washington, DC: Congressional Quarterly Press) 1988, pgs. 262-275.

the majority of their time appealing to individuals for their support based on demographic and issue factors rather than partisanship or mass membership. The polling apparatus, which could disaggregate individuals limited only by the questions asked, permitted a continuation of the leadership strategy that presidents (except Ford) learned on the campaign trail: connect individuals to the president based not on party affiliation but on disconnected affiliations ranging from individual attributes, to lifestyle choices, to presidential policy positions.

POLLING AS A RHETORICAL TOOL

The Nixon, Ford, Carter, and Reagan administrations used public opinion polls to identify and classify individuals by the characteristics engendering support for the president. This kind of extensive classification system can aid the understanding of who supports the president and why. Gathering information on constituent support, however, is meaningless if the White House does not translate the data into activities directed at the public. Speeches are the rhetorical mechanism by which presidents relate to the public: "presidents have a duty constantly to defend themselves publicly, to promote policy initiatives nationwide, and to inspirit the population."[61] Moreover, a president who seeks to lead by promoting his policies with the public must communicate with that public. By understanding his customers' wants and desires, a savvy salesman improves the potential for success. Not surprisingly, those in charge of design-

ing the president's pitch have dominated the use of the president's public opinion apparatus as a means of enhancing the president's prospects to lead public
opinion.[62]

POLLING FOR RHETORICAL CONTENT

Presidential staffs have honed presidential rhetoric by testing phrases for
unwanted reactions. Nixon, for example, wanted to be recognized for containing perceived lawlessness during the 1960s; but he did not want to appear racist.
Thus, the administration tested phrases for heightened constituent responses:
"When asked whether the phrase 'law and order' is nothing more that a code
word for racism, 70.5% of the persons polled disagreed and only 20% agreed
with that statement."[63] The poll data reassured the administration that they
could use "law and order" in speeches without fear of a negative response.

In addition to testing for inflammatory rhetoric, presidents have also polled
for understanding and clarifying terminology. In a briefing to the National
Governors on energy policy, the Carter administration revealed that Americans expressed "widespread cynicism and skepticism regarding the nature of
the energy problem," as well as "poor knowledge of how to actually save
energy" despite intense White House efforts .[64] The White House incorporated
"educational" efforts into speeches to combat that lack of knowledge, such as
"lowering the temperature from 72 to 68" actually saves energy.[65] President
Carter delivered four major energy speeches and six other major addresses to
the nation which targeted the energy problem.[66] By saturating presidential
messages with the energy agenda, Carter was able to convince the public that
there was an energy shortage by March of 1979. However, the public still preferred increased production over sacrifice through conservation (58% to 29%).
In 1979, Lou Harris reported to Vice-President Mondale's assistant Gail Harrison that "anything we [the administration] can do to increase [oil] supplies
from Alaska, Canada and Mexico would be strongly supported."[67]

President Ford's staff linked poll data directly to speech content, particularly
for the State of the Union address. In December 1975, Teeter gave the administration a laundry list of poll results which begged for attention in the State of
the Union. For the upcoming election year address, Teeter recommended
specifically addressing the following issues: inflation and unemployment,
crime, energy, health care, increased aid to the elderly, and education. Every
item appeared in the January 19, 1976, State of the Union address to the
nation.[68] However, despite the State of the Union's traditional emphasis on
programs, Teeter also recommended a message to counter the negative mood
of the nation, as revealed through polls.[69] He emphasized that "our most

important job is to repair the President's perception so that he is seen as a decisive, forceful leader with a plan for the country."[70]

Perhaps the most infamous use of poll data to determine the timing and content of a major presidential address was President Carter's "Crisis of Confidence" speech. Caddell urged First Lady Rosalynn Carter and Press Secretary Jody Powell that the alarming state of the national mood, discovered in the poll data, demanded a presidential address.[71] Caddell informed Carter's White House staff that "on a broad front of social, political and economic issues we find a deep, significant, and accelerating decline . . . . we find a unison of negative movement at a velocity that raises doubts not only of political survival but of national cohesion . . . . If this process continues at the current rate and direction, you . . . inadvertently run the risk of being identified as the President who presided over the dissolution of the American political society."[72] Who would not have given a speech alluding to a fundamental malaise when provided with Caddell's advice?

In addition, as part of rhetorical content, all four administrations included public opinion data within public discourse rather than confining its use to providing a genesis for content. These White Houses used polls as their own representatives by allowing "public opinion" to make a statement about the president or his actions with a voice that did not involve a member of the White House staff. Nixon used the results from Gallup polls, (of which he had advanced notice of content) as well as other polls that he commissioned himself, to demonstrate support for his policies. After a major presidential address to the nation on Vietnam given November 3, 1969, a Gallup poll found that the "President's popularity increases 12% over last poll."[73] The administration decided to take that positive approval increase and "disseminate widely and tie in with the President's Vietnam policy."[74]

This tactical, if not strategic, use of poll data helped promote Nixon's Vietnam policy with little administration effort. H. R. Haldeman, President Nixon's Chief of Staff, recommended no references to the 12 percent increase in the President's popularity rating, but the Press Secretary was to refer to the poll if asked. Disseminating poll results allowed Nixon to celebrate improvement without appearing to rejoice. In a thirteen step program, the Nixon staff took every opportunity to communicate this information to national and state elites. A memo entitled "Gallup Poll Game Plan" urged circulation of the 12 percent popularity increase and the relationship to Vietnam policy on the "Hill." The poll information was distributed to all staff and personnel, to all editors, selected columnists, and radio and TV commentators, as well as executive directors of every business group or association in Washington. All GOP governors were informed and the Vice President was asked to mention it. The memo recommended asking H. Ross Perot (head of United We Stand) to tie the increase to Nixon's policies. Nixon and Haldeman even directed the Paris negotiators to "push this as a sign of unity," and the "South Vietnam Government should be asked to push this as a sign that Americans back Nixon policy." Such public opinion data sold success and confidence in a manner no official could.

Perhaps due to the aftermath of Watergate and the distrust of overt public relations, Ford, Carter, and Reagan did not disseminate their supportive poll data as blatantly as did President Nixon.[75] However, some of their rhetoric was heavily seasoned with favorable poll results. During the government reorganization effort, which was a centerpiece of the Carter campaign, the administration obtained poll data to derive solutions specifically from survey results that identified constituent problems. In a manner reminiscent of Nixon, Carter actively highlighted the use of the poll data both to sell the public on reorganization solutions and to celebrate the public's input into the reorganization effort. In particular, the administration pointed to poll data bearing on "those federal activities which cause the most constituent complaint regarding inefficiency, confusion, excessive paperwork requirements and general program failure."[76] The Carter administration believed the survey gave President Carter the means to stress that he was "involved personally in an effort to make government work better for people."[77]

The Reagan administration occasionally used polling to provide rhetorical peer pressure. Interspersed with rhetoric such as "but who can deny that we face a crisis; that no more that a thin wall of wavering willpower stands between us and ruin by red ink," Reagan incorporated poll results into his speech for the kickoff rally (July 19, 1982) for his balanced budget amendment plan.[78] Reagan's rhetoric and goal (the desire to add an amendment to the constitution) took a lofty, broad tack, artfully drawing his audience toward support. However, he suddenly abandoned his inspirational rhetoric and abruptly informed the public, "nor should ratification be difficult. Thirty-two States have already taken a separate initiative of their own in favor of an amendment, and recent surveys show 4 of 5 Americans want a constitutional check on red-ink spending."[79] However, only one survey by Market Opinion Research was cited in the talking points prepared for the administration and used in drafting the speech.[80]

POLLING FOR RHETORICAL STRATEGY

Planning, limiting priorities, and controlling the agenda are the tools of the "strategic presidency."[81] Moreover, successful articulation of "the policy direction of the administration" can maximize the strategic president's time in office.[82] The Nixon, Ford, Carter and Reagan administrations focused their thematic messages by using information about public opinion to evaluate presidential leadership efforts and to measure the strength of those efforts.

Poll results helped determine the timing and the necessity of speeches by providing evidence of what the public wanted or needed to hear. The troubling political aftermath of the Nixon administration represented a unique problem for President Ford's effort to go public. In November of 1975, Ford's staff came to the conclusion that a major address to unite "legislative, diplomatic and executive initiatives" was necessary. From their data, Ford's pollsters detected anomalous support from the public: "Almost like jilted lovers, the American public seem reticent to give their whole-hearted support to the President. . . . The President has a high rating on foreign policy and personality, and a low one on domestic policy and strength of decisiveness needed to achieve results."[83] To reconcile these conflicting findings, the staff decided President Ford needed a speech to demonstrate how his policies tied together.

In addition, poll data helped determine how constituencies responded to presidential messages before and after delivery. Ronald Reagan's September 24, 1981 speech on his Economic Recovery Program favorably impressed 57 percent of his audience. However, it was found that those "least likely to be impressed include: 25–34 year olds . . . Blue collar workers and retirees . . . [and] minority respondents."[84] For the Ford administration, post-speech polls revealed how the public responded to the message as well as the chosen rhetorical style. Teeter reported that the administration received a "large pay-off with men resulting from the President taking a tough stand in the area of international problems and incidents."[85]

Polling also aided efforts to determine the effectiveness of public relations. With regard to thematic policy messages, the Nixon administration tested simple phrases which painted a picture of America; for example, "positive themes which came through in the first year (for example) . . . . identify with Middle America . . . orderliness and calm restored . . . ending the war honorably." Some cases of themes which did not work were: "dealing with the problems of the poor . . . the new federalism . . . the streamlining of government decision-making." Sensitive to negative media and partisan views, the Nixon administration examined what negative themes resonated with the public, including: "doing the right thing for the wrong reason . . . [and] the president cannot handle Congress."[86] Thus, Nixon's staff relied on the public opinion apparatus to measure public relations successes and failures.

Similarly, the Ford, Carter, and Reagan administrations tested presidential themes using polling methods. The Reagan administration raised the bar for measuring message evaluation by asking open-ended survey questions after major addresses. Open-ended questions, such as "tell me what some of the major points of the speech were"[87] required real understanding by the respondent, since the respondent was asked not simply to choose among stated options, but to remember content without prompting or specific cues. The responses to such open-ended questions, especially the responses about the "most important problem facing the nation" were tabulated and tracked for changes over time.[88]

In addition to evaluating ideas, presidents also polled to evaluate reactions to planned and unplanned events. As noted earlier, the Nixon, Ford, and Reagan administrations tracked their president's popularity ratings to understand the influence of events. These administrations firmly believed that poll results were both directly dependent on and stemmed from news events and presidential actions. The Nixon and Ford staffs designed elaborate mechanisms to identify trends in the area of presidential popularity and events. In particular, they compared: "major (and non-sensitive) daily Presidential activity record of the President . . . major daily news events . . . Presidential news conferences and speech record and . . . Nielsen ratings for nationally televised Presidential news conferences and addresses."[89] Public opinion polls revealed any weak responses and positive reactions. For example, the Ford administration found that although "conventional wisdom holds that Presidential summitry should be a significant plus for the president . . . President [Ford] suffered a three-point drop in his Gallup approval ratings."[90]

Television coverage was an important factor in evaluating planned and unplanned events for the Reagan administration. Following a dip in Reagan's August 1983 job approval ratings, David Gergen reported that "as the total percentage of coverage (measuring TV nets, major newspapers and magazines) went up for foreign policy/ Central America, the president's rating went down—and vice versa. . . [due to the] tension in Central America and the possibility of greater US involvement"[91] In essence, the more television covered foreign affairs, the worse Reagan appeared to the public. Thus, the natural conclusion drawn from Gergen's memo was to keep foreign policy off the national news. The memo went on to explain how the numbers were not yet in for September, "but the experts feel that the Korean Air Lines disaster (the Soviet Union shot down Korean Air Line flight 007 on September 1, 1983) will be the biggest story of the year and will help the President's standing in job approval polls."[92] The "experts" were correct; by the end of 1983, Ronald Reagan's popularity figures and foreign policy job approval ratings were both over 50 percent.[93]

Public opinion findings also helped these four administrations plan legislatively significant rhetorical efforts. Planning the President's "Moral Equivalent of War" strategy for energy legislation before Congress, President Carter and his staff used polls to determine reception for particular themes and strategies. "The public will probably not be receptive to the argument that we need energy legislation because we are running out of fuel . . . Pat's [Caddell] figures show 'real energy shortages' running a poor third (38%) to 'the way oil companies act' (58%) and 'high fuel prices' (65%)."[94] However, Caddell's figures did show that the public was concerned with inflation, so the staff tried to tie energy to inflation by using the trade deficit and energy price arguments.[95] Carter's staff employed a strategy that was designed not to convince the public the president was right because he was a "leader," but rather to convince the public that the administration presented the "real" version of the energy crisis. A poll commissioned to evaluate the public's energy knowledge and concerns found that "the public is preoccupied with the economy, particularly high prices, while the energy crisis is remote and unreal."[96] Moreover, polling identified for the Administration where "education" was required to improve the prospects for a successful policy outcome of Carter's energy bill: "One viewpoint is that as energy prices continue to increase, consumers will engage in self-help. [Thus] . . . government-funded public education efforts are a waste of money, and perhaps even counter-productive. . . . The other viewpoint is that a concerted public education campaign must be developed to overcome these barriers . . . . Once that new ethic is widely adopted, people will eschew gas guzzling autos, needless driving, overheated and overcooled homes, etc."[97]

Similarly, the Reagan staff utilized poll data to define the terms of debate prior to legislative discussion of an issue. For example, they commissioned polls on the 1981 Social Security proposals in order to "draw out those conclusions which you think are most relevant and important to the emerging [1982] debate on social security."[98] In addition to the questions on policy alternatives such as tax increases to pay for cuts and support for eliminating earnings tests on the elderly, staffers examined issues of trust in the administration.

Part of the rhetorical focus of these administrations included details and alternatives to their policy programs. In 1970, a Republican National Committee poll revealed that of the 48% of poll respondents aware of President Nixon's environmental program "26% said it was inadequate . . . . 21% (of the 48% who had heard of it) said it was too lenient on industry." The environmental poll data were included in a memo which stated that Nixon's objective on the environment should be to "maintain and expand [our] lead on [the] pollution issue."[99] To accomplish this objective, the White House staff recommended attacking the "major hurdle . . . air and water pollution caused by industry" with several options ranging from continuing on the present course, to new environmental taxes and research and monitoring.[100] In a time of deep recession, deficits and inflation, Ford decided to limit his domestic agenda to budgetary restraints and blocking Congressional legislation.[101] For the Ford administration, poll data helped determine which unfortunate alternative to stress with the public. "More than half the people still regard Inflation as Public Enemy No. 1 . . . . The idea of a one-year moratorium on new Federal spending is approved by more than two-thirds of the people and, even though a negative thing, should be stressed more as an integral part of your economic program."[102]

By the Reagan administration, however, polling used explicitly for policy-making fell out of favor. In a 1982 memorandum, Ken Clarkson, of the Office of Management and Budget argued to Deputy Chief of Staff Richard Darman that poll data were not always useful for designing policy: "The poll data compiled by Dick Wirthlin demonstrates some of the pitfalls in trying to gauge how citizens feel about extremely complex and emotional issues like social security. On their face, many of the responses appear inconsistent: "respondents generally indicate support for the status quo, but provide seemingly contradictory answers."[103] Yet, despite the caveat, Clarkson still recommended that the administration utilize polls to determine whether or not the president should get involved in social security, "design an initial solvency package," work with Congress, or provide a "menu of solvency proposals from which the Congress can select."[104] However, usage of White House polls across these four administrations essentially supports Clarkson's argument that poll data were useful mainly for general agenda development and not specific policy selection.[105]

To sum up, presidential leadership efforts depend on the ability to inspire, or at least communicate successfully with, the public. Rhetorical efforts require carefully crafted phrases designed to impart knowledge clearly and concisely. Moreover, the media scrutinize every presidential utterance for style and meaning. The polling apparatus provided these presidents with the ability to design rhetoric and, in essence, help design leadership by tapping into disparate presidential constituencies.

The Nixon, Ford, Carter and Reagan White Houses incorporated public opinion information into all aspects of rhetorical leadership from the content of speeches, to the planning and prioritizing of issues. More important, these administrations' use of public opinion in rhetorical leadership represents a change in thinking about the role of the public within the presidency. Neustadt, Cornwell, Kernell, and the myriad scholars exploring the importance of popularity ratings, all implicitly begin with the assumption that the public is an indirect tool. In Kernell's case, influencing the public is thought to affect congressional outcomes. Others who have focused on presidential popularity note the indirect effect of altering actions based on fluctuations in approval ratings. In contrast, the incorporation of polling into presidential rhetorical efforts provides a direct connection between public beliefs and attitudes and leadership endeavors.

PUBLIC OPINION AND THE POTENTIAL FOR LEADERSHIP

Presidents Nixon, Ford, Carter and Reagan all created and utilized a public opinion apparatus in constituency building and rhetorical efforts. Although awareness of presidential interest in polls can be traced back to studies of FDR, the analysis of presidential leadership traditionally ignored opinion polling as an effective tool of leadership in policymaking. Most presidency scholars have made the assumption "that concerns about policy take second place to maximization of public support. The reason for this particular ranking is that politicians need the public's support before they can effectively pursue policy."[106] A popular president is a successful president, in other words, a popular president has a conducive environment for effective leadership. Moreover, "public opinion is generally too ambiguous to be of help in framing specific programs and the levels of public awareness are often low."[107] However, there is substantial evidence presidents and their staffs *believe* public opinion is a useful leadership tool, and not just for producing a positive working environment.

Using public opinion enables presidents to bridge the gap of understanding between elites and masses, and to create rhetoric which appeals to a supportive audience for proposed policies. Polling not only aids rhetorical outcomes and constituency building, but also is now necessary for presidential leadership. Although public opinion is but one source of information for the president, it has become an essential source for the modern president. Presidents cannot lead without consideration of public opinion.[108]

Specifically, as others have emphasized, presidents need tools to improve the opportunities for leading across fractured groups and issues. The decline of party voting, the fracturing of the president's audience, and the rise of candidate-centered campaigns also affect issues.[109] Wattenberg argued that "policy and performance were tied together in the public's mind because of the central role of partisanship in political behavior."[110] Therefore, the decline of partisanship inevitably alters the links between policy, performance, and public support for the president and his agenda. The partisan connection between citizens and elites rests on a commonality of issues and beliefs. Until the mid-twentieth century, identification with either party connected an individual to a set of issue positions. Due to the decline in partisanship, there has increasingly been no definitive commonality of issue positions on which any president can rely on for support. In short, neither a Republican nor Democratic president can automatically assume Republican and Democratic citizens will support his issue stances.

To discover the linkages between policy attitudes and public support for the presidential agenda, the four White Houses described here used their polling apparatus to query the public. In the modern political environment (of split-ticket voting and single-issue voters) presidents have no way of identifying what has influenced their approval levels without delving into public policy preferences. Presidents have turned to polling on public policy precisely because presidency-centered coalitions must still produce majorities in Congress or implement policies in the bureaucracy. Presidents cannot govern or lead without understanding the policy environment in which they function. Without political parties to provide a common and strong ideological framework, presidents need policy-based opinion polls for building and rebuilding support for the presidential agenda.

Moreover, presidents have to build and rebuild coalitions across groups and issues more frequently.[111] As the frequency of metamorphosis continues, so must the dependence on polling. Tracking presidential support on policy issues necessitates the in-depth questioning and analysis provided by the polling apparatus. A public opinion apparatus allows the president to make sense out of the increasingly fragmented mass audience and helps to provide some order to the chaotic issue environment. For effective presidency-centered leadership, tracking and monitoring public opinion is critical to White House efforts to effectively mobilize the president's audience toward the president's policy concerns, ideology and goals.

NOTES

1. Richard E. Neustadt, *Presidential Power and the Modern Presidents: The Politics of Leadership from Roosevelt to Reagan*, rev. ed. (New York: Free Press, 1990), p. 73.

2. Elmer E. Cornwell, Jr., *Presidential Leadership of Public Opinion* (Bloomington: Indiana University Press, 1965), p. 4.

3. Samuel Kernell, *Going Public: New Strategies of Presidential Leadership*, 3rd ed. (Washington, DC: Congressional Quarterly Press) 1997.

4. Ibid., p. ix.

5. Ibid., p. 225.

6. Neustadt, *Presidential Power*, p. 78.

7. Richard Brody, *Assessing the President: the Media, Elite Opinion and Public Support* (Palo Alto: Stanford University Press, 1991), p. 3.

8. Richard Brody, and Benjamin Page, "The Impact of Events on Presidential Popularity: The Johnson and Nixon Administrations," in Aaron Wildavsky, ed. *Perspectives on the Presidency* (Boston: Little, Brown, 1975); John Mueller *War, Presidents and Public Opinion* (New York: Wiley 1973); Samuel Kernell, "Explaining Presidential Popularity," *American Political Science Review* 72 (1978): 505–522; Paul Brace and Barbara Hinckley *Follow the Leader: Opinion Polls and Modern Presidents* (New York: Basic Books 1992).

9. Brody and Page, "The Impact of Events on Presidential Popularity"; Michael MacKuen "Political Drama, Economic Conditions and the Dynamics of Presidential Popularity," *American Journal of Political Science* 27 (1983): 165–192; Charles Ostrom and Dennis Simon, "Promise and Performance," *American Political Science Review* 77 (1985): 175–190; George Edwards, *At the Margins: Presidential Leadership of Congress* (New Haven: Yale University Press, 1989); Brody, *Assessing the President*; Shanto Iyengar and Donald Kinder, *News That Matters: Television and American Opinion* (Chicago: University of Chicago Press, 1987), Shanto Iyengar and Donald Kinder, *Is Anyone Responsible: How Television Frames Political* Issues (Chicago: University of Chicago Press, 1991); Todd Schaefer, "Picking on the President: News Sources' Effects on Mass Opinion About Presidential Performance," Presented at the Annual Meeting of the American Political Science Association, September 1–4, 1996.

10. Edwards, *At the Margins*.

11. Edwards, *At the Margins*; Lyn Ragsdale, "The Politics of Presidential Speechmaking 1949–1980," *American Political Science Review* 78 (1984): 971–984, Lyn Ragsdale, "Presidential Speechmaking and the Public Audience: Individual Presidents and Group Attitudes," *Journal of Politics* 49 (August 1987): 704–736; Brace and Hinckley, *Follow the Leader*.

12. Edwards *At the Margins*; Jon Bond and Richard Fleischer, *The President in the Legislative* Arena (Chicago: University of Chicago Press, 1990); Mark Peterson, *Legislating Together: The White House and Capitol Hill from Eisenhower to Reagan* (Cambridge: Harvard University Press, 1990).

13. Jeffrey E. Cohen, "Presidential Rhetoric and the Public Agenda," *American Journal of Political* Science 39 (1995): 578–599; Jeffrey Cohen and John Hamman, "Beyond Popularity: Presidential Ideology and the Public Mood, 1956–1989," Presented at the Annual Meeting of the American Political Science Association, September 1–4, 1996.

14. The Democratic and Republican National Committees paid for all presi-

dential polls since public funds cannot be used for political purposes. However, as Nixon, Ford, Carter and Reagan routinely denied members of their own party access to the data, we can consider the data and the pollsters as essentially the president's (See Diane J Heith, *Polling for Policy: Public Opinion and Presidential Leadership*, Ph.D. dissertation, Brown University, 1997 and Diane J. Heith, "Staffing the White House Public Opinion Apparatus: 1969–1988," *Public Opinion Quarterly* 63 (Summer 1998).

15. See Lawrence R. Jacobs and Robert Y. Shapiro, "Presidential Manipulation of Polls and Public Opinion: The Nixon Administration and the Pollsters," *Political Science Quarterly* 110 (Winter): 519–538.

16. Heith, *Polling for Policy*.

17. For each administration I assembled materials which included formal and informal memoranda, handwritten notes, polling reports and other written documentation. These memos provided first-hand accounts of polling usage. Scholars generally consider archival records to be reliable, primary sources of information on presidential processes. As my sample encompassed a wide continuum of issues and events, from the significant to the trivial, I minimized the dangers from "memo writers whose purposes run counter to those of the researcher" experienced when researching only a narrow topic. (Martha Kumar, "Presidential Libraries: Gold Mine, Booby Trap or Both" in George Edwards and Stephen Wayne eds. *Studying the Presidency* (Knoxville: University of Tennessee Press, 1983), p. 211. I do not include phone calls, or White House conversations. However, the absence of verbal exchanges does not preclude the discussion that follows. To incorporate public opinion into leadership endeavors, staffers would need to identify who they worked with, and what information was discussed whenever public opinion was employed. It is without question that there were verbal exchanges concerning public opinion within the White House. Given the expansive public opinion usage, it is unlikely that the inclusion of verbal communication would have altered the patterns found in the written flow of information.

18. John H. Kessel, *Presidential Campaign Politics: Coalition Strategies and Citizen Response*, 3rd ed. (Chicago: Dorsey Press, 1988).

19. Ibid., p. 141.

20. Lawrence R. Jacobs and Robert Y. Shapiro, "The Rise of Presidential Polling: The Nixon White House in Historical Perspective," *Public Opinion Quarterly* 59: 163–165.

21. Proposal, Presidential Survey Research, A National Listening Post—Plus Brushfires, January 23, 1975, in Hartmann box 34 Presidential Survey Research Proposal, Gerald R. Ford Library.

22. In Cheney, Box 17 Polling Gerald R. Ford Library.

23. Heith, "Staffing the White House Public Opinion Apparatus."

24. Frank J. Sorauf, *Party Politics in America* (Boston: Little, Brown, 1984); Martin Wattenberg, *The Rise of Candidate-Centered Politics: Presidential Elections of the 1980s* (Cambridge: Harvard University Press, 1991).

25. James R. Beniger, and Robert Guiffra Jr., "Public Opinion Polling: Command and Control in Presidential Campaigns" in Alexander Heard and Michael Nelson eds. *Presidential Selection* (Durham: Duke University Press, 1987); Wattenberg, *The Rise of Candidate-Centered Politics*.

26. Theodore J. Lowi, *The Personal President: Power Invested, Promise Unfulfilled* (Ithaca: Cornell University Press, 1985); Sydney Milkis, "The Presidency and Political Parties," in Michael Nelson ed. *The Presidency and the Political System* (Chapel Hill: University of North Carolina Press, 1995).

27. Lowi, *The Personal President*.

28. Beniger and Guiffra, "Public Opinion Polling."

29. Other presidents were interested in polling before 1969. Cornwell notes that FDR and Eisenhower were interested in polling, but Truman was not (1965). However, I excluded administrations prior to Nixon's as this analysis focuses on the routine employment of public opinion. The Kennedy and Johnson administrations did purchase surveys between election cycles but only obtained partial, piggybacked control over their poll questions and surveys, while subsequent presidents achieved complete control (Jacobs and Shapiro, "The Rise of Presidential Polling). Moreover, marked by infrequent poll usage, Jacobs and Shapiro argue that the Kennedy and Johnson administrations were quantifiably different than the institutionalized efforts evident in the post-Johnson presidencies. See Heith for examples of polling usage between elections in the Nixon, Ford, Carter and Reagan administrations (Heith, *Polling for Policy*, and Heith, "Staffing the White House Public Opinion Apparatus").

30. Lester Seligman, and Cary Covington, *The Coalitional Presidency* (Chicago: The Dorsey Press, 1989).

31. Heith, *Polling for Policy*, and Heith, "Staffing the White House Public Opinion Apparatus."and Lawrence Jacobs and Robert Y. Shapiro, "The Rise of Presidential Polling: The Nixon White House in Historical Perspective," *Public Opinion Quarterly* 59 (Summer 1995): 163–195.

32. Memo to Higby from Strachan 6/8/71 in WHSF Haldeman box 334 Nixon Presidential Papers.

33. Memo to Higby from Haldeman 7/31/70 in WHSF Haldeman box 403 in Derge Poll File, Nixon Presidential Papers.

34. Memo to Haldeman from Moore 12/20/70 in WHSF Haldeman box 141, Nixon Presidential Papers.

35. Memo to Ehrlichman from Butterfield 7/15/69 in Polls, Nixon Presidential Papers.

36. Memo to Dent from Fisher 11/1/69 in WHSF Dent box 8 in Middle America, Nixon Presidential Papers. Joel Fisher summarized Scammon's comments from a meeting earlier that day in this memorandum to Harry Dent.

37. Memo to Carter from Caddell 12/7/76 Cabinet Selection, Political Problems, in 11n6–1l77 Box 1 Handwriting File, p. 11, Jimmy Carter Library.

38. Memo to Carter from Caddell 12/7/76 Cabinet Selection, Political Problems, in 11176–1/77 Box 1 Handwriting File, p. 13, Jimmy Carter Library.

39. Memo to Carter from Caddell 12/7/76 Cabinet Selection, Political Problems, in 11176–1177 Box 1 Handwriting File, p. 15, Jimmy Carter Library.

40. Herbert B. Asher, *Presidential Elections and American Politics: Voters, Candidates, and Campaigns Since 1952*, 5th ed. (Pacific Grove: Brooks Cole, 1992), p. 168.

41. Memo to the Senior Staff from Beal 12/21/81 in PR 15 050001 -056000 document # 0533818 Ronald Reagan Library.

42. Memo for File from Harper 6/24/82 Pr 15 068001 -073000 document # 072629 Ronald Reagan Library.

43. Letter to Hartmann from Baldwin 2/19/75 in Hartmann Papers box 163 Public Opinion Polling General (1) Gerald R. Ford Library.

44. Seligman and Covington, *The Coalitional Presidency*.

45. Memo to Cashen from Nathan 11/3/69 in WHSF Dent box 8 Nixon Presidential Papers.

46. Memo to Ehrlichman from Nixon 3/10/73 in WHSF box 18 Ehrlichman Nixon Presidential Papers.

47. Cambridge Report—First Quarter 1977, in Pat Caddell Energy Material—2 in Rafshoon box 24 Jimmy Carter Library.

48. Cambridge Report—First Quarter 1977, in Pat Caddell Energy Material—2 in Rafshoon box 24 Jimmy Carter Library.

49. Heith, *Polling for Policy*.

50. Memo to Wirthlin from Burgess 7/22/81 in PR 15 document # 034283 Ronald Reagan Library.

51. Memo to Wirthlin from Burgess 7/22/81 in PR 15 document # 034283 Ronald Reagan Library.

52. Memo to Harper from Bauer 3/29/82 in PR 15 document # 093915 Ronald Reagan Library.

53. Seligman and Covington, *The Coalitional Presidency*.

54. Seligman and Covington, *The Coalitional Presidency*, p. 13.

55. Memo to Cheney from Teeter 11/12/75 in Hartmann Papers box 163 Public Opinion Polling General (1) Gerald R. Ford Library.

56. Gary King, and Lyn Ragsdale, *The Elusive Executive: Discovering Statistical Patterns in the Presidency* (Washington, DC: Congressional Quarterly Press, 1988).

57. King and Ragsdale, *The Elusive Executive*.

58. Memo to President Ford from Cheney, 10/23/75, Cheney Box 17: Polling. Gerald R. Ford Library

59. Memo to Haldeman from Safire via Keogh 12/8/69 in WHSF Haldeman box 141. Nixon Presidential Papers.

60. King and Ragsdale, *The Elusive Executive*, p. 274.

61. Jeffrey Tulis, *The Rhetorical Presidency* (Princeton: Princeton University Press, 1987), p. 4.

62. Heith, *Polling for Policy*.

63. Memo to Nixon from Dent 1/9/70 in WHSF Haldeman box 403 Nixon Presidential Papers. This poll was of Minnesota voters and not the nation.

64. Briefing Book—White House Conference on Energy, 718177–9177 in box 43 Rafshoon Jimmy Carter Library.

65. Briefing Book—White House Conference on Energy, 718177–9177 in box 43 Rafshoon Jimmy Carter Library.

66. King and Ragsdale, *The Elusive Executive*, Table 5.3.

67. Memo to Mondale from Harrison in PR 15 3/17/79 Jimmy Carter Library.

68. Memo to Cheney from Teeter 12/24/75 in Chanock box 4 Teeter Memo Public Opinion Data (2) Gerald R. Ford Library; Ford, Gerald *Papers of the President,* 1976.

69. Tulis *The Rhetorical Presidency*.

70. Memo to Cheney from Teeter 12/24/75 in Chanock box 4 Teeter Memo Public Opinion Data (2) Gerald R. Ford Library.

71. Caddell originally pitched his tale of woe to President Carter in a January memo. Receiving no presidential response, Caddell related his information to sympathizers with the President's ear in April of 1979 (Robert Strong, "Recapturing Leadership: The Carter Administration and the Crisis of Confidence," *Presidential Studies Quarterly* 16 (Fall 1986): 636–650.

72. Memo to Carter from Caddell 1/1/7/79 in CF O/A 743 box 1 Eizenstat Jimmy Carter Library.

73. Andrew Z. Katz, "Public Opinion and Foreign Policy: The Nixon Administration and the Pursuit of Peace with Honor in Vietnam," *Presidential Studies Quarterly* 28 (Summer 1997): 496–513. See also, Jacobs and Shapiro, "The Rise of Presidential Polling.

74. Gallup Poll Game Plan in WHSF Chapin box 22, Nixon Presidential Papers. This memo has no date provided; however, based on Haldeman's notes, the memo was written soon after the Silent Majority Speech, (Address to the Nation on the War in Vietnam, November 3, 1969) most likely as soon as these Gallup figures were known.

75. However, the blatant distribution of positive poll data was also found in the Johnson administration. Jacobs and Shapiro note that "Johnson suspended his

links" to his pollster due to overexposure. (Jacobs and Shapiro, "The Rise of Presidential Polling"). Haldeman noted in his diary, February 3, 1969, that Nixon wanted to avoid LBJ's boasting of positive poll results [H. R. Haldeman., *The Haldeman Diaries: Inside the Nixon White House* (New York: Berkeley Books, 1995), p. 35]. The concern for poor publicity apparently faded nine months later when the Nixon administration worked so diligently to release its own positive popularity figures.

76. Survey of Congressional Case Work Fact Sheet, October 1977, in PR 15 Jimmy Carter Library.

77. Memo to Powell from Pettigrew 10/6/77 in PR 15, Jimmy Carter Library.

78. Memo to Senior Staff from Darman 7/15/82 in SP 644 document # 085240PD Ronald Reagan Library.

79. Memo to Senior Staff from Darman 7/15/82 in SP 644 document # 085240PD Ronald Reagan Library.

80. Memo to Senior Staff from Darman 7/15/82 in SP 644 document # 085240PD Ronald Reagan Library.

81. James A. Pfiffner, *The Strategic Presidency: Hitting the Ground Running* (Chicago: Dorsey Press, 1988).

82. Pfiffner, *The Strategic Presidency*, p. 158.

83. Memo to Cheney from Chanock November 26, 1975 in Chanock box 2 polls general (2). Gerald R. Ford Library

84. Memo to Richards from Wirthlin 10/7/81 in Box 1 PR 15 044601 -050000 document # 045132 Ronald Reagan Library.

85. Memo to Callaway from Teeter 12/5/75 in Chanock box 4 Teeter Memoranda (3) Gerald R. Ford Library.

86. Memo to HR Haldeman from Safire in WHSF Haldeman box 141, Nixon Presidential Papers.

87. Memo to Richards from Wirthlin 10/7/81 in Box 1 PR 15 doc # 045132 Ronald Reagan Library.

88. Initial Aggregate Results, Eagle IX, July 1981, in box 1 PR 15 doc # 044601–05000 Ronald Reagan Library.

89. Memo to Jerry Jones from Slight 1/28/75 in Chanock box 2 polls general Gerald R. Ford Library.

90. Memo to Cheney from Gergen June 21, 1976 in PR 15 box 42 Public Relations Public Opinion Polls Ronald Reagan Library.

91. Memo to Baker, Deaver, Duberstein, Darman and Fuller from Gergen 9/12/83 doc # 171615 Ronald Reagan Library.

92. Memo to Baker, Deaver, Duberstein, Darman and Fuller from Gergen 9/12/83 doc # 171615 Ronald Reagan Library.

93. James W. Ceaser, "The Reagan Presidency and American Public Opinion," in

Charles O. Jones ed. *The Reagan Legacy: Promise and Performance* (Chatham: Chatham House Publishers, Inc., 1988).

94. Memo for Distribution from Rafshoon in Public Support for the President's Energy Plan in box 44 Rafshoon Jimmy Carter Library.

95. Memo for Distribution from Rafshoon in Public Support for the President's Energy Plan in box 44 Rafshoon Jimmy Carter Library.

96. Memo to the President from Hutcheson 6/10/77 in PR 15 Jimmy Carter Library.

97. Briefing Book, White House Governors Conference on Energy, July 8–9, 1977, in Rafshoon box 43 Jimmy Carter Library.

98. Memo to Ferrara from Harper 11/18/82 in PR 15 doc # 105906 Ronald Reagan Library.

99. White Paper on the environment in White House Central Files box 4 Anderson Nixon Presidential Papers.

100. White Paper on the environment in White House Central Files box 4 Anderson Nixon Presidential Papers.

101. Peterson, *Legislating Together*, p. 253.

102. Memorandum in Hartmann box 34 Presidential Survey Research (2). February 1975 Gerald R. Ford Library.

103. Memo to Darman from Clarkson 11/17/82 in doc # 098467SS Ronald Reagan Library.

104. Memo to Darman from Clarkson 11/17/82 in doc # 098467SS Ronald Reagan Library.

105. Heith, *Polling for Policy*.

106. John Geer, *From Tea Leaves to Opinion Polls: A Theory of Democratic Leadership* (New York: Columbia University Press, 1996), p. 37.

107. Paul Light, *The President's Agenda: Domestic Policy Choice From Kennedy to Reagan* rev. Ed. (Baltimore: Johns Hopkins University Press, 1991), p. 93.

108. Lawrence R. Jacobs and Robert Y. Shapiro, *Politicians Don't Pander: Political Manipulation and the Loss of Democratic Responsiveness*. Chicago: University of Chicago Press, 2000.

109. Wattenberg, *The Rise of Candidate-Centered Politics*.

110. Wattenberg, *The Rise of Candidate-Centered Politics The Rise of Candidate-Centered Politics*, p. 163.

111. Seligman and Covington, *The Coalitional Presidency*.

CHAPTER 18

The President as Message and Messenger: Personal Style and Presidential Communications

Martha Joynt Kumar

Richard Neustadt observed the importance of the mix of personal factors and institutional forces influencing a president's prestige as well as his ability to make the most effective use of the formal powers accorded him.[1] Through the choices he makes, the president affects his own reputation and the ability to achieve his policy ends. According to Neustadt: "His choices of what he will do and when and how—his choices, also, of whom he will tell and in what way and words—are his means to protect this source of influence, just as they are his means to guard those other power sources: formal powers or status and professional reputation. . . . But whether his choice making actually is usable and whether it proves useful or does not, the fact remains that for the human being in the White House choices are the only means in his own hands by which to shield his sources of each power, prestige no less than the rest."[2] His choices are based on a mixture inherent in his personal style, all defined by his own experiences and knowledge, the surrounding environment and how he construes it, his natural ways of expression, and his goals. No area better illustrates this mixture than does the relationship the president has with news organizations and how he uses it to communicate his goals, his policies, and himself.

For a president to lead effectively, he must sense the link between communications and governing, then act upon that knowledge. While those involved in White House operations sometimes perceive as commonplace the ability to communicate, presidential actions often belie their words. For example, when President Bill Clinton took office, he demonstrated that presidents do not enter the White House with a native sense of effective communications. Once in office and after becoming aware of its importance, presidents often find it difficult to incorporate communications into their methods of governing and the personal conduct of their office.

Effective presidential communications do not occur by chance, evolving instead from presidential direction, an able communications staff operation, the political climate in which a president is operating, and especially, a set of administration goals congruent with the public's aims and interests. How a president chooses to publicize his aims, the staff system he creates, and whom he hires to work for him, are all elements constituting the president's personal style. While a president is limited in how much he can influence his immediate environment, his understanding of both that environment and his limits and opportunities may either work to his benefit or detract from his ability to influence outcomes. In their relations with news organizations, personal style is important to a president and his staff in two central ways: the president as the message and messenger. As the message, a president's personality, habits, and personal life are the focus of news organizations' attention, compelling him to positively use that interest to develop public interest in his policies and objectives. As the messenger, a president must integrate into his leadership a capacity to articulate his programs to an audience beyond Washington. Clearly, an ability to draw the news media's interest and attention is important to his eventual success in realizing his policy goals.

Rarely does a president find himself in a situation where personal and political elements are in harmony. Yet all of these forces, for example, worked in President Ronald Reagan's favor with Reagan regularly enjoying the opportunity to speak directly to the public without being preceded by a noisy opposition. Confronting Bill Clinton, however, was a Washington political climate that could be characterized as partisan poison, with his motives publicly questioned by opposition party leaders, even when military operations were involved. While opposition leaders like House Speaker Tip O'Neill may have thought Reagan initiated the Grenada invasion to draw attention away from the disastrous military operation in Lebanon resulting in the bombing death of 251 Marines, he did not publicly question the president's actions or motives. When Clinton ordered the bombing of Iraqi military targets on the eve of the House vote on the Articles of Impeachment, the Senate Minority Leader, the House Majority Leader, and the chairman of the House Rules Committee all publicly expressed doubt about the President's motives, and some characterized the action as unwise. Senate Majority Leader Lott went further than others, criticizing the action before military operations were underway.

Not only was Reagan's charming manner a valuable complement to his policies, but he also had regular opportunities to showcase this talent. In addition to being regularly featured on the evening news, he spoke to groups, met with leaders in the Oval Office, and addressed members of Congress. What is more, Reagan's appearances were particularly powerful since Americans saw and heard him personally convey his message. After her piece about the drastic impact of Reagan's policies on America's powerless appeared on the CBS Evening News, Leslie Stahl awaited a call of complaint from the White House staff. When the call finally came, the reaction was not what Stahl had anticipated. "Great piece," the aide said, and elaborated, "We're in the middle of a campaign and you gave us four and a half minutes of great pictures of Ronald Reagan. . . . And that's all the American people see."[3] The staff simply wanted President Reagan to speak directly to the public in his own words. Presidents today are not accorded this opportunity unless there is a crisis, especially one involving their tenure in office.

Martin Schram, a correspondent and long time observer of presidents from just about every beat in Washington, summed up Reagan's ability to use the media, particularly television, to suit his purposes. He was able to bypass television anchors, Schram pointed out, "by making America's most famous television stars irrelevant. He stepped right past these stars and took his place alongside the Americans in their living rooms, and together they paid no great mind to what these media elites were saying."[4] Other presidents have not been so lucky. Of the four most recent presidents—Jimmy Carter, Ronald Reagan, George Bush, and Bill Clinton—only Reagan successfully used the media as his natural ally. His administration understood the media's routines, had an appreciation for the president's strengths, and knew how to make the two intersect in new ways involving reputation as well as developments in the news media and elsewhere. The other three presidents viewed the media as predators. In Neustadian fashion, the way the messengers and their administration manage the messengers' interactions with the media have come to matter more than ever before for the American presidency.

PERSONAL STYLE: THE PRESIDENT AS THE MESSAGE

On a day when President Reagan spoke publicly, correspondents typically covered how the speech was received. The emphasis, however, remained on the speech itself and the situation, problem, or event Reagan was addressing, while the reaction of opponents was merely one aspect of the story. In the tradition of the late twentieth century, stories are often built around the person of the president, and the event or situation he is addressing is pictured directly through the eyes of his critics. While not necessarily by design, these stories may inflict some damage to the president's reputation, particularly if they appear early in his tenure.

More than ever, the media play a powerful role establishing a president's reputation and its impact. Reputation is not just titillation, but a fungible resource used by a president to reach his political goals. Further, how a president is portrayed is a critical factor in his success building and consolidating support. Unfortunately, just as the reputation stakes have increased, the president's ability to control how he is perceived has decreased. The news media have actually reduced presidential opportunities to talk directly to the public while opponents have found the means to get more coverage. The reason the press has narrowed its presidential focus, as well as that of other elected officials, has to do with a confluence of factors coalescing in the 1980s and 1990s. The reasons are rooted, at least partially, in the natural suspicion with which the public currently approaches elected officeholders of all stripes, the increased sophistication of the president's critics, and in the business orientation of the media.

REPUTATION AND RECTITUDE

A president's reputation serves as a cornerstone of his ability to influence his government and public supporters. While many elements of a presidency are shaped by institutional forces, a president's reputation is one area where he can affect the views of others and his ability to lead. "A president's decisive role in reputation building is a source of opportunity as well as risk," observed Neustadt.[5] "No one can guard it for him; no one can save him from himself." President Clinton provides the example. While for most presidents reputation serves as a risk or an opportunity, Bill Clinton demonstrated that reputation can simultaneously operate both for and against a president. During his presidency, the general public and the Washington community peered at his conduct through a different lens. The public looked approvingly at his role as a leader handling institutional tasks while the Washington political community observed him in more personal and unfavorable terms—how he handled his office. The public viewed the public presidency while the political community observed the individual who was president. How he behaved became more significant than what he did.

In recent years, news organizations through their words and pictures have had a significant impact on the president's reputation. The media's decisions about what events to cover and how to interpret them have made them important purveyors of political reputations. Jimmy Carter was viewed as a nice guy not up to the job, while Ronald Reagan was perceived as understanding the essence of leadership. George Bush, was portrayed as out of touch with the daily realities of American life, and Bill Clinton as someone lacking ethical or political moorings. Once formed, these reputations are hard to recast. Initially, these characterizations were developed by key Washington policymakers and power brokers, including those inside government and in such elite power centers as interest groups, law firms, and political parties. But the news media solidified and amplified these character judgments and made them much more difficult to alter.

Events and actions affecting reputation have become the stuff of which presidential stories are made. Stories dovetailing with formulated judgments have been the ones most likely to find their way into the news.[6] When Clinton took office, the unresolved questions related to flaws in his character, not his programs or agenda. From early in his presidency, the stories appearing in prominent news venues focused on his character failings and lack of experience. While at first the stories of illicit sex were confined to tabloids, once governmental institutions became involved in tracking the president's actions, mainstream news organizations followed the path of their tabloid cousins. Whether leaks originated with committee staff, members of Congress, or people working in offices charged with investigating presidential misconduct, all became sources of information for news organizations.

Other presidents have observed the same pattern of press coverage of presidential uncertainty or perceived weakness. George Bush once complained bitterly about the treatment he received from the *New York Times*. Their reporter, Andy Rosenthal, was quick to go with any story about Bush demonstrating his distance from the realities of every day life. This was a snap judgment made earlier and repeated whenever the president unwittingly provided an occasion. Rosenthal wrote a piece stating that when visiting a technology exhibit, Bush was startled by a supermarket device which reads prices when an item is swept over the checkout counter detector. "The fact was, I had been shown something else, some mind-boggling new technology, and that was what I referred to, not a routine checkout counter. The company that displayed the technology pointed that out, and a CBS reporter looked into the facts and reported that what I'd said was true. But the myth had been created by the *New York Times*," said Bush.[7] Even today people continue to cite the example to illustrate the point that Bush was out of touch with the realities of the everyday lives of Americans.

In keeping with a general fascination for famous athletes, movie stars, or governmental figures, there has been great interest in the president as a celebrity. Many stories have come to stress the personal side of the president, focusing on how he undertakes his tasks rather than emphasizing his policies. "Policy problems lack the novelty that the journalist seeks," commented Thomas Patterson.[8] "A new development may thrust a new issue into the campaign, but problems tend to be long-standing." Once a president assumes office, the difficulty remains of acquiring coverage of issues and policies. The problems landing on a president's desk are inevitably ones that could not be solved elsewhere, but, the press seldom reveals in full the challenging questions confronting the president, while usually denying him extra points for difficult situations. Reagan got as much acclaim for his victory persuading Congress to pass a cut in the personal tax rate as Clinton did for getting congressional approval of the North Atlantic Free Trade Agreement (NAFTA). In fact, persuading the public to accept a tax cut was far easier than convincing Congress to pass NAFTA, which could threaten jobs in some sectors. News organizations reporting on policy victories, however, routinely give equal weight to a win. "It is as if winning against the Minnesota Twins is the same as a victory against the New York Yankees," commented Francis Rourke, a shrewd observer of the games of politics and baseball.[9] The president gets no extra credit for the tough score.

Such an environment makes it difficult for a president to develop the positive image he needs to build faith in his leadership. "Personal traits of the incumbent are likely to be granted more latitude for influence when presidential success is evaluated by performance rather than by reputation with the public," commented Dean Simonton in his *Why Presidents Succeed*.[10] With constant interest in presidential shortcomings, it is difficult to mobilize support for the president's programs. From the beginning, Clinton complained that news stories focused on his weaknesses rather than his programs, even while dutifully providing news organizations with the evidence they sought.

"His problems in maintaining public confidence are rooted in the record of his life," declared the *New York Times Magazine* in 42 point type. "They do not arise because Bill Clinton was a cheap political hack—but precisely because he was not."[11] Michael Kelly, then a staff writer for the magazine, focused on Clinton's Arkansas years and where he fell short as a political figure. There were no successes here, only failures relating to Clinton's character. When presidential character is scrutinized, presidents have almost always come up short in recent years. Underlying Kelly's article and others like it is a view of politics shared by many reporters: that politics is a corrupt business and politicians are masters of the trade. In his book on the role of the press in presidential campaigns, Thomas Patterson discussed the antipolitics bias of reporters and its impact on campaigns: "The poisonous effect of Vietnam and Watergate on the relationship between journalists and politicians has not dissipated. The antipolitics bias of the press that came out of the closet two decades ago has stayed out."[12] He continues: "If most journalists today would hesitate to call themselves reformers, they take pride in unmasking politicians' images and refuting their claims."

For many reporters, compromise is regarded as betrayal. One example provided by Kelly of Clinton's public betrayal concerned his alleged personal promise to chicken magnate Don Tyson to raise the highway weight limit on trucks.[13] He came through on the promise only after winning office following his first term. "Almost immediately after taking office again in 1983, Clinton maneuvered the 80,000-pound limit through the Legislature by linking it to a special tax on the heavier trucks, to pay for potential road damage," Kelly writes.[14] But instead of crediting Clinton with brokering a compromise between truckers and environmentalists, he charged him with selling out. Good politics does not allow for compromise.[15]

DWINDLING INK AND AIR TIME

In the spring of 1998, Clinton held a news conference with Leonid Kravchuk, the president of the Ukraine. Together they discussed the provisions to be made for the destruction of nuclear weapons in the Ukraine. The topics were critical but apparently not so significant from the television or network viewpoint to warrant full coverage. In fact, the only network to cover the press conference live in its entirety was C-Span. Even newspapers failed to publish the full transcript of the news conference. In contrast, as recently as the Reagan administration, full coverage by newspapers and the networks was taken for granted. Barring issues of presidential scandal, as there was for most of 1998, it has become rare for press conferences to receive coverage of any sort. This lack of press coverage denies to the president the time honored right to regularly explain to the public his actions, programs, and goals. When scandal arises, then it is the president who is reluctant to bring in reporters. President Clinton held only one press conference in the year following press reports of his improper sexual relationship with a White House intern, Monica Lewinsky. This relationship ultimately played an integral role in Clinton's impeachment by Congress (for a discussion of the impeachment scandal, see the essays by Hritzuk (chapter 21) and Pious (chapter 22) later in this volume).

THE WHITE HOUSE LOSES THE COPYRIGHT ON THE PRESIDENT'S IMAGE

For decades as television developed as an institution, presidents had a corner on their own images. They released information as they saw fit through people of their choosing. News organizations relied upon the White House to shape the president's image. The president and his staff conceived his activities and the implementation of his plans. The Press Secretary's daily briefing was important in the areas reporters chose to highlight. To some extent this has remained true, but the opposition has an unprecedented opportunity to shape the presidential story. In this vein, Clinton received torrents of criticism for his behavior with Lewinsky, but could not stanch the flow of negative stories about him.

Reporters have been interested in defining a president's term and what problems lie ahead. While members of the president's own party are reluctant to discuss his problems, the opposition is more than interested in providing its viewpoint. During the process leading up to Clinton's impeachment, House Majority Whip Tom Delay (R-Texas) regularly appeared on major television news programs to push his agenda for impeachment proceedings and to condemn the president's conduct. Always looking for experts to discuss White House operations, reporters often contact individuals from previous administrations to give their expert opinion on how the White House is running. For the Clinton administration, this meant reporters were seeking out people from the Reagan and Bush administrations to evaluate Clinton's job performance.

When legal questions surfaced, as they did for almost all of 1998, news organizations regularly sought out C. Boyden Gray, White House Counsel during the Bush years, for his observations on Clinton's legal problems. In Clinton's first term, the media also featured analysis from members of Bush's White House staff. "This is the crucial 100 days of the Clinton presidency," Kenneth Duberstein, White House chief of staff in the Reagan years, told Ruth Marcus of the *Washington Post*.[16] "This is the time we check not only what the temperature of health care is but also the general health of Bill Clinton. The country and the world will see if he measures up," Duberstein declared. In the same article, Marcus also talked with William Kristol, chief of staff to Vice President Quayle during his years in the White House. Kristol was called upon to comment on the Paula Jones lawsuit and the anticipated refusal of the president to provide information until after his term has expired. The argument of presidential immunity found no ally in Kristol. "A party that has spent 20 years proclaiming that the president cannot be above the law, I think, is going to have a tough time arguing that this president should be above the law." Within the article, the three people quoted on the record, Duberstein, Kristol, and a Democrat, Will Marshall, of the Democratic Progressive Institute, had nothing nice to say. "This year started with great promise and is threatening to end in a muddle," Marshall told Marcus. "It's up to the president to turn this around" With no named supporters of the president offering their endorsement, the critics defined the tone of the article. Kristol and Duberstein were good examples of critics who sensed reporters' needs and shared an awareness of how long a quote should be and what makes it sing.

Opponents have gained particularly good opportunities to define a president because today's news organizations have lowered their standards of proof and attribution of sources. Larry Sabato observed the problem as it affected presidential candidates: "The press itself has aided and abetted the lowering of the evidentiary standard held necessary to make a charge stick."[17] Further, he remarked that "In addition to the publication of rumor and the insinuation of guilt by means of innuendo, news outlets are willing to target indiscriminately not just ethical problems, but possible problems and the perception of possible problems." With opposition groups and individuals ready to provide grist for the news mill, presidents have difficulty shaping their own image. The low bar of proof prior to airing or printing information was an issue early in the sex scandal involving Clinton and Lewinsky. With fierce competition among news organizations to be the first to air or print a new development, the standards of proof dropped substantially, especially for those with rolling deadlines. Neither reporters, editors, nor their publishers wanted to be left behind.

ATTACK BY TALK SHOW

Other changes in the Washington news media have worked against the president. Political talk shows have come into vogue as a place to express opinions no matter how uninformed the judgments. Such programs began on television in 1967 with the appearance on Public Broadcasting of *Washington Week in Review*. The featured print journalists found they had become better known among members of Congress, the White House staff, and officials in the bureaucracy for their television appearances than for their newspaper stories. Since most of the reporters appearing on the program wrote for out of town papers, they were not read in Washington. Jack Nelson, when he was bureau chief of the *Los Angeles Times*, for example, became well known for his Friday night presence on the program. Appearing on television helped him and others make needed Washington connections. "I am better known for being on

'Washington Week in Review' than for being bureau chief of the *LA Times*," he once said.[18] The number of such programs has since increased, as has the group of reporters wanting to make such appearances. Today, Washington political talk programs span the weekend from Friday evening through Sunday afternoon. The staple of the shows is the same: judgments and opinions. Panelists have become "high practitioners of the art of assertion," observed Thomas Rosenstiel, media critic for the *Los Angeles Times*.[19] "Taken together, the talk-show culture is changing print journalism, downgrading the traditional skills of reporting and a devotion of neutrality and objectivity while rewarding the skills that win talk-show audiences—a knack for asserting opinions, thinking in sound bites, and honing an attention-getting public persona," said Rosenstiel.[20] The focus of these judgments and opinions is commonly the president.

For Clinton the importance of talk shows in shaping the views of his Washington political audience proved particularly onerous. He was criticized every weekend on the Washington talk shows and daily on those from out of town. In both, the focus became what his critics said about him. His opposition in Congress, among interest groups, and in the Republican party all defined his presidency. While Senate Majority Leader, Robert Dole was particularly resourceful and persistent in criticizing the president's every action, motive, and program. Dole targeted Clinton's Achilles heel, making sure reporters and news organizations remembered Clinton's lack of a strong electoral base in the 1992 election. Through carefully contrived rebuttal from the floor of the Senate, Dole often usurped news coverage, infiltrating prime news time to Clinton's disadvantage during his first term.

CHASING THE DOLLARS

For strong business reasons, the personal style of the president has also become a media focus. In the last decade, traditional news organizations, whether print or network television, have seen their readers and viewers dwindle. With the rise of cable television, networks have seen their monopoly over news vanish; concretely, between 1980 to 1994, households with cable increased from 19.9% to 62.4%.[21]

With an increase in the variety of news channels, individuals can tailor their viewing to fit their schedules and preferences. No longer limited to evening network news programs, people can tune in earlier or later than the traditional evening hour—in fact, 24 hours a day. Network news executives feel the pressure. David Gergen recounted a conversation with Larry Grossman, an executive who worked at all three major networks during the 1960s, 1970s, and 1980s:

"When Larry Grossman became president of NBC News he told me that his greatest challenge was figuring out how to make the news fresh when so many people had already seen the national and international news stories that the network provided to local stations."[22] In addition, Grossman and other network executives faced competition from other sources. Since 1981, CNN has delivered news throughout the day on an up-to-the-minute basis, while people seeking news with an emphasis on religion can choose the Christian Broadcasting Network with its 100 Club. New arrivals in television news programming, CNBC, MSNBC, and the Fox Cable Network provide regular news updates and offer talk programs all evening, most of which focus on the president. If, on the other hand, one wants direct news, unfettered by anchors, close-ups, and bromides, C-Span broadcasts 24 hours a day. The result is a falling number of viewers for the network news, especially among younger cohorts who have grown up with cable television.[23]

Newspapers have also seen their readership diminish. From a twentieth-century high of 2,600 in 1909, daily newspapers fell to 1,556 in 1993, with these remaining newspapers aggressively searching for an audience. When Harry Truman was President, newspapers reached 37% of the population. By Clinton's term, newspaper readership was reduced to only 22.6%.[24] Both network television and newspapers have had to search for new audiences in an effort to stabilize their financial picture.

Newspaper coverage in Baltimore provides an example of this problem and how it is being addressed. Fifteen years ago the city had two strong dailies, the *News American* and the *Baltimore Sun*, each with a morning and evening paper. Today it has only the morning *Sun*. Lyle Denniston, the Supreme Court correspondent for the *Sun* and a veteran reporter of several newspapers, spoke about the challenge of searching for new readers:

> But the reality is that the *Sun* is declining in circulation and the Board of Directors . . . is concerned that our profit ratio is dropping . . . so the editorial side is constantly confronted with what do we do now to try to get readers and what that usually resolves itself into is a question, 'What do we do to get young readers?' Because people under the age of 25 don't read newspapers but they spend money like crazy. And so advertisers want you to appeal to the young audience, the young audience which has been nurtured on television supposedly wants more celebrity or personality journalism.[25]

The *Sun* is no different from most daily newspapers in search of paying customers. Readers are regularly polled for their preferences with an eye to directing attention to increasing readership among young people. Just as on television, this has led to sustained attention to the president's personal style.

PERSONAL STYLE: THE PRESIDENT AS THE MESSENGER

The second way personal style is significant and time-honored is by guiding a president's choices in communicating his themes and providing rationale for his actions. It influences how he speaks to his national constituency and to members of institutions involved in the development and implementation of policy.

COMMUNICATIONS CHOICES

In delivering their messages through the media, presidents have done so in ways that reflect their own unique style. Presidents have varied in the public forums they use, the frequency of their contacts, and the general atmosphere around their dealings with the media. Generally, presidents have done what makes them comfortable, which may be as simple as choosing a formal speech over a press conference to provide policy information. Or it may involve a more complicated decision about whether to surround oneself with old associates from earlier political experiences or to hire people with Washington experience but lacking direct, personal ties to the president.

Variations in communication style have been as numerous as presidents. President Kennedy liked reporters, enjoying them as verbal sparring partners. Lyndon Johnson saw reporters frequently because he liked having people around him who listened and would mark his words. He met formally and informally with the media, hoping either personally or officially to persuade reporters to be his friends. Gerald Ford also enjoyed the company of reporters and was very responsive to their requests for time with him. He invited reporters in to the White House for social occasions, including meetings with the "Sperling group" who regularly convened for breakfast with public officials. Even Bush sought out reporters, calling them over for a spur of the moment lunch or making an unannounced visit to the Press Room to see if they might like to field a few questions. Each was comfortable with reporters and chose to spend time with them.

Other presidents such as Carter, Reagan, Nixon, and Eisenhower preferred to keep their distance from reporters. Clinton joined their company, also restricting his interaction with the media. Their reasons for doing so may have varied, but the fact remained that there was a distance between these presidents and the press. Reagan was, in fact, more willing to meet with reporters and answer their questions than his campaign and White House staff wanted. Their efforts were aimed at minimizing his informal media contacts. They preferred instead to present him in formal settings where his talents were displayed to best advantage. In contrast, Carter only met infrequently with reporters on an informal basis because of his personal antipathy for small talk. His personal style was partially defined by his discomfort with making light, easy conversation with anyone, including reporters. Suspicious of reporters' true interests, Nixon was tentative shaping his contacts with them. He kept them at arms length as had Eisenhower. Clinton came to view the press in a similar manner: as the president's natural predator.

Like a dowser looking for water, former presidents and their staffs have traced the wellspring of their disappointments to their relations with the media. For nearly every modern President, the divining rod dips with unfailing regularity at this soft spot. Some blamed the press outright for their failures. Others admitted an inability to effectively use the media to channel messages to their constituents. Bush did both: "I wasn't articulate enough to overcome the politically-driven, press-driven perception that the economy in 1992 was in deep recession." In this first interview after leaving the presidency, Bush continued: "In the third quarter of '92, and indeed the beginning of the fourth quarter, during the campaign, things were going better. But when I tried to point that out, the perception was that I was totally out of touch. I just wasn't a good enough communicator."[26] Bush believed this was not due to a lack of a political base or a failure to present a coherent agenda dealing with mounting economic and social problems. It was the press and his inability to communicate through it. Bush felt that had he possessed Reagan's communications talents, he might have won the 1992 election. "If he [Ronald Reagan] had been in my place, he'd have cut through the opposition fog that everything was going to hell. He'd say, 'Wait a minute, here are the facts, the reality.' " Bush continued, "the last two quarters of 1992 were better than what the economy has done under President Clinton, but I failed as a communicator."[27]

To accept the notion that Bush puts forward is to accept the belief that a presidency rests on an ability to communicate. In fact, what it does rest on is what a president is communicating and whether that agenda fits with the perceived needs of the public. Reagan succeeded in moving forward his agenda early in his first term because the public knew just what he stood for and supported several of his proposals. He called for reducing government regulations on private enterprise, cutting the size of government and the social programs it was implementing, and strengthening our defenses in the face of a hostile Soviet Union.

He sold the same message he had been promulgating since speaking on behalf of Barry Goldwater's 1964 presidential bid. All of the elements of the Reagan agenda were in his speech then and continued to be included in his own presidential campaigns in 1976 and 1980. A staff member in the Bush White House explained from his perspective the place of policy in the two administrations:

> In a White House motivated at least in part by ideas—as the Reagan administration was, and as the Johnson administration was—every staffer could feel he was a part of the policy process because he understood the philosophical and theoretical outlines of administration policy. In the Reagan White House, the outlines were quite simple: Reagan was philosophically opposed to the growth of government, the growth of taxation, and the spread of Communism. He was prolife, anti-gun control, opposed to judicial activism. With this ideological outline in mind, White House staffers from assistants to the president to secretaries in the New Executive Office Building could go about their business with little confusion. But in the Bush White House, it was very difficult to feel a part of things in the same way, because staffers had no idea from one day to the next where the administration stood on *anything*. Policy was an ever evolving thing, always under negotiation.[28]

If the president's staff members had difficulty knowing his policy positions, the public had no hope of knowing them. In addition to Reagan's ideological consistency, he had a group of constituents supportive of him and his message. His backers among the public and Washington elite, including members of the press, rallied to his side when attacks were leveled against him or his message. Bush never had such a group of loyal supporters. People liked him, but his support was never deep or wide. Unfortunately for his candidacy, his support was more personal than political. People felt comfortable with him as President even if they tended not to associate him with an agenda. When the economy worsened and no one had a clear idea of where Bush was headed, the lack of a permanent coalition of supporters proved fatal. His electoral failure in 1992 was not, as Bush would have us believe, really a failure of communications. Yet communications was not insignificant either, proving to be a limiting factor in his administration. This shortcoming can also be traced to his personal style as a leader.

LIMITATIONS ON PERSONAL CHOICE: THE NEED FOR THE PRESS

The relationship between a president and press has permanent contours shaping their interaction.[29] Basically, a president needs news organizations to govern. It is through the media as an intermediary that a president channels his views, priorities, explanations, and interests to an attentive, and sometimes not so attentive, public. With fewer actual opportunities to personally contact the citizenry, he must rely on a communications link to provide that contact. No matter who occupies the presidency or serves on his staff, news organizations remain a vital link. In his first term, Clinton was especially resourceful controlling his interaction with the media and expanding the number of choices to get in touch with citizens. His range extended from person-to-person interactions when he was out for his daily run to popular radio and television programs aimed at specific audiences. From appearing on *Larry King Live* to talking on WFAN radio with Don Imus, Clinton targeted a broad group of media outlets to direct his comments and explanations. He used these venues to establish a dialogue with the public, speaking with them directly and listening to their concerns. Once Mike McCurry came on to the White House staff as the presidential press secretary, such appearances ended and the more familiar White House venues again took center stage. Highly unstructured events such as the ones in which Clinton chose to participate early in his term sometimes led to unanticipated problems. In a question and answer session on MTV, for example, the president responded in surprising detail to an embarrassing query from a young questioner about his underwear choices.

While some practices may have changed, news organizations remain equally dependent on the president for the news their readers and viewers want. News organizations must satisfy their audiences, no matter how fickle, and regardless of who the president happens to be. Minor shifts in the electoral winds do not alter this dictum. The fortunes of White House correspondents remain tied to the luster of the presidency, with network correspondents often moving from the White House to anchor positions on evening news programs. In the newspaper world, it was common for a tour of duty at the White House to be the stepping stone for a move to a bureau chief position or to writing a column. During the Bush years, when the public showed less interest in following the president, the White House did receive less attention from news organizations. Yet the president remains a central figure even in a post-Cold War era. "As Lyndon Johnson said, we only have one president at a time," commented James Deakin, a long time White House correspondent.[30] "If he succeeds, we succeed. If he fails, we fail." The stakes continue to be high for both sides, but failure has become the basis for successful stories. Reporters' reputations can be made through detailing the shortcomings of the president. In Clinton's case, entire networks grew as his failings became clear. MSNBC, Fox News, and CNBC all advanced as networks as did the personnel associated with their shows.

COMMUNICATION CHOICES AND PERSONAL STYLE

Overall, what flexibility does a president have in choosing the venues and vehicles of communications? Here, especially, personal style acts as a barometer providing a reading of the president's opportunities to communicate with the public. At the same time, there are limits to his choices. "The president brings into the White House a definite disposition that unfolds during the course of his administration, but he does not have a free hand to indulge in self-expression," observed Simonton.[31] "Rather, a host of situational factors set the boundaries and opportunities for the projection of presidential personality on the world of political action. Any given presidential behavior may be the result of individual characteristics, political setting, and the subtle interaction between the two." And so it is with presidential communications. His personal style may represent only a part of his success or failure in the presentation of himself and his programs. The strength of his party in Congress, his own political strength, the intractable quality of the programs he designs, the state of the economy are all variables determining his success in reaching his goals. A winning personal style will nevertheless facilitate his goal attainment, even if communications alone fail to determine success or failure.

Personal style is the product of past experience, personality, and a president's philosophy about the role of communications in governing. His past experience, what he knows and does not know about communications, influences the choices he makes in the White House. Both the skills developed in his earlier public offices and the relationships established in the pre-presidential years are indicators of how he will approach news organizations and their representatives. Personality also characterizes a president's communications choices. Quite naturally, a president gravitates to those activities and adopts those strategies that fall within his comfort zone. Personality draws some presidents, as it did with President Reagan, toward strategies that emphasize persuasion through personal charm. Others select approaches featuring institutional skills, as did President Johnson. The third element of personal style—the president's philosophical belief in the media's role in government—is shaped by the constraints of experience and personality. Recent presidents have had different views of where the media fit into their efforts to reach their personal and policy goals during their term in office. These range from President Reagan, who saw the media as a natural element in building public support to Presidents Carter and Clinton, who regarded the media as more foe than friend.

Shaping Communications Policies: Experience

There is no place to acquire the experience to be chief executive. Instead our presidents come to office with a broad range of exposures, some at the national and some at the state level. They have all previously held public office, but these posts are essentially diverse and often diffuse. Each would-be President has been taught a different lesson. Nowhere is this disparity more obvious than in their communications choices. Yet each background hones a variety of skills, strategies, and strengths that affect who and how a president will tend to choose.

Carter and Clinton: the Impact of Inexperience

One may learn new things ensconced in the White House but new skills are rarely developed there. The White House is not a place where circumstances foster the acquisition of on-the-job skills. "When a person becomes President, they travel on what they bring with them to office," noted Jody Powell about President Carter's lack of interest in developing the communications skills that could have helped him sell his programs once he arrived in Washington.[32] "You don't take someone who's basically good at answering questions and that sort of discussion and explaining and synthesizing and so forth, and turn them into a rhetorician while they're trying to run the country at the same time."

Nor have modern presidents found the White House a place to make friends. "He is no longer a person," observed Jody Powell.[33] "He is but he is something else. He can't be a friend primarily to anybody anymore. His job, his responsibilities, and so forth require that he subordinate to some extent those things. He can't say things, except to a very small number of people, that a normal person can say. In terms of talking about what he thinks, and how he feels, and when he has doubts, and what he's worried about and that sort of thing."[34] If the president has no close Washington friends, it is rare for him to acquire them after he comes to town. To be without friends is to open the door to more enemies. At its core, a network of Washington friendships can be essential for a president to glean information about others and to ascertain others' orientations to him.

Significantly, when Jimmy Carter entered office he lacked interactive experience. The people he did not know and the network of people he did not have below him lurked like a phantom opposition force. Without friends to catch his errors and explain his actions to those in news organizations, there were no intermediaries to interpret and ameliorate Washington's assessment of him and his administration. Other than in his presidential campaign, he had little experience dealing with the national press corps. The White House is simply no place to begin spinning the web of relationships with media barons that a president needs to explain himself. Alfred Friendly, who worked for National Security in the Carter White House, observed the impact of not having relationships with individuals in the media and elsewhere in Washington: it was "impossible in those first months to make the town Carter's Washington and it hurt from then on because you didn't have and never could get, from the twelve opinion leaders in the White House, a ripple effect where each one has twelve people on the Hill who in turn have twelve editors in Arizona whom they call," said Friendly.[35] "That's how you mobilize a sympathetic network," he added.

The absence of a support network was sharply felt when it came to explaining the President's financial rectitude. Moreover, Carter had few defenders when charges arose in the media that he had illegally laundered loan funds through his peanut warehouse and spent them in his campaign. Today there are few in America today who would believe such a charge. But when Carter entered the presidency, he was an unknown quantity, and the charges swirled around him for several months. In the end, a special prosecutor was brought in to investigate the loan transactions and gave the President a clean bill. "Every nickel and every peanut have been traced," Paul Curran, the special prosecutor, said in his report to the Attorney General.[36]

President Clinton had a weak start to his presidency. By frittering away the early months with initiatives such as allowing gays in the military, he ultimately divided his supporters and gave ammunition to his critics. However, where Clinton differed from Carter was in his ability to shift course. After the first three months, he saw when his administration was in trouble and reached out for help from established sources. While Carter eventually made the same move, he did so after his administration's reputation as an amateur operation was frozen in minds of the Washington community. By the end of his first two years, Clinton replaced inexperienced White House staff with Washington insiders beyond his circle of associates, such as Lloyd Cutler, David Gergen, and Abner Mikva. He shifted the form of his White House staff organization from the loosely structured ten-people-in-a-room style with no central organizational focus to a system with a strong Chief of Staff. A Washington veteran, former Congressman Leon Panetta, took the newly constituted chief's job and made it the center of White House organization, creating an administration characterized by its structure, rules, and discipline. Further, the communications team was restructured to ensure that the people explaining policy were not involved with making it and that those speaking for the President enjoyed walk-in access to the Oval Office. It did not take Clinton long to discover the ineffectiveness of the George Stephanopoulos–Dee Dee Myers communications combination. However, figuring out a way to revamp the system was more time-consuming than discovering and acknowledging the old system's faults.

BUSH: MORE IS LESS

No president in the twentieth century came to the White House with more national government experience than George Bush. He served in the House of Representatives, ran for Senate, headed the Central Intelligence Agency, served as the first consul to China, was the United States representative to the United Nations, headed the Republican National Committee, and served as vice president for eight years. The only significant part of government unknown to him was the judicial branch. Yet this wealth of experience could not deliver a second term for George Bush.

President Bush established a friendly relationship with White House reporters, most of whom he recognized by name, and with the columnists, editors, and publishers he knew from his years on the national scene. In short, Bush was generally acknowledged as someone familiar with the levers that make Washington work. Despite this solid Washington background, Bush's career experiences were not all successful. According to a former White House aide closely affiliated with Bush: "He had always excelled in those roles that had little to do with politics and instead had to do with governing." Moreover, this aide noted: "As vice president he didn't have to set the agenda. As President he had to set his own political agenda. As President, he tried to divorce politics and policy." This separation did not work for anything the President was trying to accomplish.

Most important, the Washington of Bush's presidency was not the Washington of 1989, his aide felt, but the Washington he knew as a youth when his father served as a United States Senator from Connecticut. "It was no accident that Eisenhower was his favorite President," observed the same aide.[37] "He would have loved to have governed as Ike did. Would have loved to have had the America of the 1950s. Would have loved to have had Sam Rayburn in the House and Lyndon Johnson in the Senate." But the Washington of those days has been replaced by a "government that is more fractured, much more partisan, and much more mean than it was," his staff member observed, "These facts bore to the president's disadvantage." In Bush's ideal Washington, a president could make policy working in conjunction with those in key positions of power. Instead, he confronted a different Washington, where policy had to be sold to the public to win congressional support.

Personal Style: a Force in Communications Choices

George Bush's personal style also worked against him when it came to selling programs on the national stage. "His style is direct, honest, forward, home spun and non-theatrical," commented a person who wrote for President Bush.[38] "He would rather quote Yogi Berra than Thomas Jefferson." Unfortunately, selling a policy to the public was not something that particularly interested him. "I don't think he enjoyed it and he wasn't especially successful at doing it," he commented. "But it is a required part of the presidency and in the end it was a serious weakness of his presidency."[39]

George Bush: a Critical Gap

Personal style is also important in a secondary way, determining the coverage a president will receive. For instance, when a president gets involved in a public conflict, he leaves himself open to more negative stories. Bush's appearance before a conference of the National League of Families of POW/MIA's provides such an example. The organization, representing parents and siblings of those missing in action in the Vietnam War, gathered for its annual meeting with approximately 600 present for the President's speech. Some relatives of American servicemen lost in Vietnam heckled the President, while other group members chanted: "No more lies, no more lies."[40] Bush protested that it was difficult speaking under these conditions. The audience continued to challenge the President, wanting to know what was being done to track recent stories of sightings of Americans in Vietnam. Just as Bush thought the crowd was under control, disruptions erupted again. An exasperated Bush responded by asking the crowd to "please shut up and sit down."[41] Matters furthered deteriorated when Bush got into a finger pointing exchange with one of the organization's board members, Jeff Donahue, culminating in Bush asking Donahue: "Are you calling me a liar?" There were no winners here. The exchanges stood in direct contrast to the presidential personality his aides were trying to project. "His qualities are decency, civility, and honor," said one of his speechwriters who worked with him during his presidential years.[42] The scene demonstrated that civility depends on which side of the fence the president stands.

A president limiting himself to public presentations, showcasing the command aspects of his job and not becoming carried away by emotions, is more likely to get beneficial news coverage. Favorable coverage seldom occurs for presidents relying on serendipity to govern appearances. For this reason, President Reagan rarely walked into situations that were not carefully scripted. The set speech is generally safe and remains the method of choice for presidents interested in presenting a policy and all its technical aspects. There is minimum risk of personal presidential exposure and reporters are likely to cover the speech and comment afterward.

CONTRAST REAGAN: PERSONAL STYLE COMPLEMENTS POLICY

No president in modern times was as successful with the set speech as Ronald Reagan. From the Oval Office, he was a picture of a leader in command. In his appearances, he combined a tailored message with an engaging personality, with each enhancing the other. His warm personality was often used to offset the sharp nature of his policies, subtly blending his personal style and message. In this vein, there must be consonance between the message and the president. For example, when Reagan made public his hard-edged civil rights policies, his aides arranged a presidential visit to the home of an African-American couple living in Prince George's County, Maryland, who had a cross burned on their lawn. The subtext of the visit was: how could a nice and caring man institute harsh civil rights legislation?

During his reelection campaign, his genuine concern for individuals was a spontaneous force. To counter Democratic charges that his budget cuts harmed the lives of ordinary Americans, the President appeared in a sympathetic frame at just about every campaign stop. A typical example occurred at Millersville State University in Pennsylvania where a young woman with leukemia was in the audience. The student had written Reagan the previous year, eliciting a response filled with support and encouragement. After his speech, the young woman appeared, her illness in remission, to thank him. The President warmly hugged her and told her how happy he was at her improvement—his genuine concern was there for all to see. Bush suffered because he followed a president with a keen nose for using his personality to soften his policies. Bush's actions were often unconnected to programs under consideration. For example, during the Persian Gulf War preparations, Bush vacationed in Maine and sported about in his cigarette boat. An image of a president at play contrasted with the somber mood leading up to the impending war.

Personality was also an important element in Reagan's staff choices. In this, he parted company with not only most of his predecessors, but with his successors as well. Most presidents come into the White House with their campaign team in place, bringing in the group who guided them to victory. However, during his first year at the White House, the president usually learns a very hard lesson about the differences between campaigning and governing. And in the process, valuable time is lost on the policy front. Of the last four administrations, Reagan's was the only one to staff its White House with people other than its campaign group. Reagan's ability to hire James Baker as his chief of staff, despite Baker's role organizing Ford and Bush's campaigns, rested in his personality. Reagan was so comfortable with himself that he didn't worry about employing those whose work he knew only from their reputations working for opponents. A further mark of his confidence was that, once hired, Reagan allowed his appointees a fairly free rein. That propensity caught up with him in the national security area, however, with the actions taken in his name by Robert McFarlane, John Poindexter, and Oliver North.

In the communications area, Reagan's willingness to reach outside his personal realm of experience created at least two distinct advantages. First, he acquired people capable of managing successful communications strategies, including knowing what strategies worked and who to pick for selected jobs. In addition, Reagan's outside reach created a group of Washington people predisposed to see his side, thanks to his staffs' efforts to build up trust on his behalf. He may not have known official Washington, but those he hired did. Clinton sought to take a leaf from this book by adding to his staff the expertise of David Gergen, a veteran of three Republican administrations. While he and the President had known one another, Gergen had no history with the Clinton White House staff—he had not campaigned for the president or even publicly declared his support for Clinton. Later in his first term, Clinton changed press secretaries, replacing Dee Dee Myers, a campaign experienced aide unfamiliar with the workings of Washington, with Mike McCurry, a Washington veteran who had held posts in the city since 1972.

CLINTON: AMBIGUITY AND PERSONAL STYLE

Other than Ronald Reagan, no president in recent times has exhibited the political strengths of Bill Clinton. "The fact is that with Clinton we have one of these natural phenomena like a typhoon or a hundred year flood," observed Washington lawyer Harrison Wellford in 1997.[43] "Clinton is the most naturally exuberant and charismatic politician that I have seen." While his personality and brand of charm served as a political strength, it also resulted in the conduct precipitating his impeachment by the House of Representatives. Ultimately, Clinton's lack of discipline and failure to take responsibility for his actions caused his presidency to come to the cliff's edge.

His strengths and weaknesses sometimes intertwined, leading to confusion about his commitments. For example, during the December 1998 Middle East peace discussions with then Israeli Prime Minister Benjamin Netanyahu and PLO leader Yasir Arafat at Wye River, Clinton left participants with conflicting interpretations of his commitment to release convicted spy Jonathan Pollard. John Harris, senior *Washington Post* White House correspondent, noted the importance of ambiguity in the Clinton political style. As Harris observed, Clinton occasionally uses ambiguity to coalesce divided factions: "As on so many prior occasions, Clinton relied on a personal style of charm, persistence, and language that could be artfully imprecise, but managed in the end to bring antagonistic sides together."[44] Similarly, Netanyahu praised Clinton for his "flexibility," which some would characterize as waffling. Netanyahu said Clinton's flexibility gave him the opportunity to "truly explore the possibilities of both sides, and never just on one side." As Harris notes, what appears to be disorganization in one setting can, under different circumstances, generate fruitful results. In his words: "Clinton, after a lifetime of getting himself out of jams with last-minute heroics, is chronically disorganized and crisis-prone, say the critics. . . . But the Wye River summit, with its all-night sessions and constant brushes with disaster, was a setting in which Clinton's penchant for keeping all the balls in the air at once seemed to thrive."[45]

CARTER: ENGINEER, PREACHER, AND TEACHER

President Carter's personality shaped his relations with reporters and other Washington institutions, leading him to approach news organizations in much the same way he would Congress. He summarized his own style:

> As an engineer and as a governor I was much more inclined to move rapidly and without equivocation and without the long, interminable consultations and so forth that are inherent, I think, in someone who has a more legislative attitude, or psyche, or training, or experience. So for all these reasons, I think there was a different tone to our Administration.[46]

Carter was comfortable explaining what his decisions meant. Jody Powell pointed to Carter's personal makeup as key to the command and ease he exhibited during press conferences. "One of the reasons he enjoyed press conferences and liked to do them was that he has that combination of preacher and teacher," Powell said.[47] "It's part of his basic makeup. And he takes it very seriously and likes to do that sort of thing, of explaining to someone what's going on and why and the various nuances and complications thereof and to give a very informed and well thought out answer." Carter's enthusiasm resulted in regular news conferences with White House correspondents, alternating between question and answer sessions with the editors and correspondents from out of town newspapers. After he cut back on his Washington press conferences in 1979, Carter continued sessions with out of town editors until the end of his administration.

The Media in Governing: The President and His Message

Communications strategies are one area where the president as messenger has real flexibility in delivering his message. It is less important whether the president communicates through press conferences or speeches from the Oval Office than that the communications take place at the appropriate time and under favorable circumstances. He must be able to get directly to the people with his message in a comfortable manner and without interruptions, though he need not do all of the selling himself, but can rely on the assistance of others.

Overall, the president's communications choices include three possible routes: personal contact, surrogates, and institutional operations. While there is flexibility within each route, the president must be comfortable using all three. Personal contact strategies include public presentations such as press conferences, interviews with selected journalists, editorial boards, and personal noodling. The latter consists of having reporters for lunch or dinner with off-the-record events designed to portray the president as a person working hard on the public's behalf. A president needs to also have people regularly speaking on his behalf. The mix, however, can vary with the president and the nature of his agenda. Surrogate stand-ins include four groups: White House staff, administration figures, congressional party members, and journalists willing to see and write about the president's point of view. Each is important, representing the president through appearances on Sunday and evening television talk shows, radio interviews, and in speeches outside of Washington. Institutional operations round out the choice of presidential settings, and include internal White House resources like the Press Office and the Office of Communications with its subsidiary institutions—Media Liaison, Public Affairs, and the Office of Public Liaison. A president can emphasize long-range planning or the daily release of information, but either way the operation must be competent. The institutional resources provide continuing benefits through a routine established to disseminate information at the national, state, and local levels. In sum, a president can choose freely within each of these three communications groups for strategies to advance his personal and policy goals. Yet all three are necessary and must be strong.

Ultimately, presidential communications are central to governing. If a president cannot communicate, he cannot lead. On the other hand, if a president can effectively communicate his goals, programs, actions, and character, he can generate influence through the use he makes of the personal and institutional tools at his command. How a president uses news organizations to communicate with his public is an important element in his personal leadership style. Rather than condemning a president and his White House staff for the time and energy spent shaping public perceptions of the chief executive, presidential scholars should instead use a president's ability to communicate as an element in evaluating how a president handles power and what influence he generates.

NOTES

1. Richard E. Neustadt, *Presidential Power and the Modern Presidents: The Politics of Leadership from Roosevelt to Reagan* (New York: Free Press, 1990), p. 90. This chapter draws on material to be found in my forthcoming book, *Wired for Sound and Pictures: The President and White House Communications Policies* (Johns Hopkins University Press), and a paper of the same title presented in 1994 at the annual convention of the American Political Science Association.

2. Neustadt, *Presidential Power and the Modern Presidents.*

3. As quoted in Martin Schram, *The Great American Video Game: Presidential Politics in the Television Age* (New York, William Morrow, 1991), p. 26.

4. Ibid. p. 27.

5. Neustadt, *Presidential Power and the Modern Presidents,* p. 69.

6. For a thorough discussion of the way in which the press uses stories that emphasize a previously defined image of a presidential candidate see: "The Search to Validate the Subtext," Larry J. Sabato, *Feeding Frenzy: How Attack Journalism Has Transformed American Politics* (New York: The Free Press, 1991), pp. 71–79.

7. Victor Gold, "George Bush Speaks Out on Bill Clinton," *Washingtonian* 29 (5) February 1994): 124.

8. Thomas Patterson, *Out of Order* (New York: Knopf, 1993), p. 61.

9. In conversation, August 25, 1994, Baltimore.

10. Dean Keith Simonton, *Why Presidents Succeed: A Political Psychology of Leadership* (New Haven: Yale University Press, 1987), p. 163.

11. Michael Kelly, "The President's Past," *The New York Times Magazine*, July 31, 1994, p. 20.

12. Patterson, *Out of Order*, p. 19.

13. Ibid., p. 22.

14. Kelly, "The President's Past," p. 20.

15. For a discussion of the antipolitics bias of the news media in presidential campaigns, see Patterson, *Out of Order*, pp. 16–25.

16. "Clinton Confronts Series of Make-or-Break Tests," Ruth Marcus, *The Washington Post*, June 12, 1994, p. A16.

17. Sabato, *Feeding Frenzy*, p. 209.

18. Michael Baruch Grossman and Martha Joynt Kumar, *Portraying the President: The White House and the News Media* (Baltimore: The Johns Hopkins University Press, 1981), p. 220.

19. Thomas Rosenstiel, "Talk-Show Journalism," in Philip Cook, Douglas Gomery, and Lawrence Lichty, eds., *The Future of News: Television-Newspapers-Wire Service-Newsmagazines* (Baltimore: The Johns Hopkins University Press, 1992), p. 73.

20. Rosenstiel, "Talk-Show Journalism," p. 74.

21. Harold Stanley and Richard Niemi, *Vital Statistics on American Politics*, 4th ed. (Washington, D.C.: Congressional Quarterly, Inc., 1995), p. 47.

22. David Gergen, "Commentary," in Cook, Gomery, and Lichty, *The Future of News: Television-Newspapers-Wire Service-Newsmagazines*, p. 207.

23. A survey of the ways in which people acquire news demonstrated the weakness among young people of both the network news and newspapers as a group.

TV Viewers and Newspaper Readers, By Age

	TV Viewers		Newspaper Readers	
		Network		
Age	Cable TV	Evening News	Daily	Sunday
18–24	61.4%	10.3%	45.9%	57.0%
25–34	58.1	10.5	54.6	64.5
35–44	63.7	13.4	61.6	69.1
45–55	63.7	15.9	69.0	73.3
56–64	61.6	18.3	67.2	69.5
65+	49.7	18.9	66.5	66.3

Source: Stanley and Niemi., *Vital Statistics in American Politics*, p. 56.

24. Stanley and Niemi, *Vital Statistics on American Politics*, p.50.

25. Elliott E. Slotnick, "The Media and the Supreme Court," *Political Communication Report*, a newsletter of the Political Communications Division of the American Political Science Association, Volume 5, Number 1, February/March 1994, p.11.

26. Victor Gold, "George Bush Speaks Out," *Washingtonian* 29 (5) (February 1994): 41.

27. Ibid., pp. 41 and 124.

28. John Podhoretz, *Hell of a Ride: Backstage at the White House Follies 1989—1993* (New York: Simon and Schuster, 1993), p. 129.

29. For a discussion of the nature of the relationship see Grossman and Kumar, *Portraying the President*, pp. 19–35.

30. Kenneth Thompson, ed., *White House Press on the Presidency: Management and Co-option* (Lanham, MD: University Press of America, 1983), p. 221.

31. Simonton, *Why Presidents Succeed: A Political Psychology of Leadership*, p. 165.

32. Session with Jody Powell and the Press Office staff, Carter Presidency Project, White Burkett Miller Center of Public Affairs, University of Virginia, December 17–18, 1981, p. 81.

33. Powell and the Press Office staff, Carter Presidency Project, p. 29.

34. Ibid., pp. 28—29.

35. Ibid., p. 30.

36. *Congressional Quarterly, Congress and the Nation, 1977–1980*, Volume 5 (Washington, D.C.: Congressional Quarterly, Inc., 1981), p. 975.

37. Ibid.

38. Background interview, Martha Joynt Kumar, January, 1992, Washington, D.C.

39. Ibid.

40. Maureen Dowd, "The 1992 Campaign: The Republicans; Kin of Missing G.I.'s Heckle the President," *The New York Times*, July 25, 1992, p. 1.

41. Ibid.

42. Background interview, Martha Joynt Kumar, January, 1992, Washington, D.C.

43. Interview with Harrison Wellford, Martha Joynt Kumar, August 26, 1997, Washington, D.C.

44. John Harris, "Clinton Ambiguity Proves a Strength in Summit Role," *Washington Post*, October 25, 1998.

45. Ibid.

46. Jimmy Carter interview, Carter Presidency Project, White Burkett Miller Center, November 29, 1982, p.

47. Powell and the Press Office staff, Carter Presidency Project, p. 81.

CHAPTER 19

The Limits of the Transformational Presidency

Russell L. Riley

INTRODUCTION

The purpose of this essay is to examine transformational leadership in the presidency, or more precisely the extent to which presidential leadership and transformational leadership are harmonious—or antithetical—concepts. By transformational leadership, I mean initiatives that help induce others to generate intended, fundamental change in social structures, including, especially here, political institutions and their basic configuration.[1] I examine a series of cases of social and political transformations in America to search for clues about patterns of behavior characteristic of the presidential office over time. What emerges is a portrait of a complex institution, programmed by nature and nurture—that is, by constitutional design and by the evolving political realities of the office—to see transformation as auxiliary to the more fundamental institutional imperative of constitutional maintenance.

I propose here to make two primary contributions to the study of presidential leadership and transformation. First, I offer what might be called a Neustadtian characterization of transforming leadership in the presidency. This characterization may, at the outset, seem a bit counterintuitive. Neustadt's president is burdened by a host of institutional and political constraints, and is thus typified by a prevailing weakness. Conversely, the transforming leader is commonly thought of as a figure of enormous strength, who has managed to break free from conventional constraints in service of some transcendent end. Neustadt finds the essence of the presidency revealed in Harry Truman's lampooning of his successor in the White House: "Poor Ike, . . . He'll sit here and he'll say, 'Do this! Do that!' *And nothing will happen.*"² This depiction differs dramatically from shorthand perceptions of such transforming figures as Abraham Lincoln, who ordered and executed an emancipation policy once judged the most "stupendous act of sequestration in the history of Anglo-Saxon jurisprudence."³ Thus, there are tensions in these two conceptions of the presidency, which I reconcile in the following pages. I do so by focusing, as does Neustadt, on constraints on presidents, but on those rare constraints that impel bold action rather than on those common ones that obstruct it.

This essay's second contribution concerns the scope of my inquiry. I hold that in order to understand fully the role of the presidency in relation to transformational change, we need to examine carefully not just those epoch-making figures who brought such change to fruition, but also those presidents who served in the institution *before* transformation occurred. How those pre-change occupants of the White House dealt with transforming forces in the polity, in the form of social and political movements, is instructive about the essential nature of the presidential institution. The logic here follows that of Justice Oliver Wendell Holmes in his *Northern Securities* dissent: "Great cases like hard cases make bad law."⁴ What is true of constitutional law is also true of the laws of political science. There is something fundamental about transformation and the presidency that can be learned only by looking at figures other than those presidential giants who ushered in great change.

Transformational leadership, by any conventional definition, is *not* a commonplace of presidential behavior. Indeed I will argue that except under a very narrow set of conditions, transformational leadership is inconsistent with what Stephen Skowronek calls the "institutional logic" of this office.⁵ Of course, there have been prominent episodes in the nation's social and political development in which presidents have clearly played indispensable roles in dramatic, transformative outcomes. Our common conceptions of institutional performance and possibility rely heavily on such icons as Washington, Lincoln, and Franklin Roosevelt, who were individuals at the very center of some of the most profound transformations in American history. In examining the *institutional* role in such transformations, however, it is necessary to consider the forces giving shape to the actions of these actors, and how the institution responded to these forces as other incumbents filled the office before and after.

My consideration of these contextual factors suggests three paradoxes about the presidential role in the production of transformational change. I describe these here and then turn in conclusion to a brief discussion of the twenty-first-century presidency.[6]

THREE PARADOXES

Paradox 1. What we typically call transformational leadership in the presidency is not, essentially, about transformation, but about preservation.
The archetype of transformational leadership in the presidency occurs in the case of the centralized defense regime erected under conditions of total war. Here, the preservationist aspect of the first paradox is clearly revealed.

During system-threatening crises, such as the Civil War and the two world wars, the American people have demonstrated a willingness to transform their usually dispersed political and economic structures into more centralized forms for the purpose of defeating the enemy and thereby *preserving* the fundamental way of life prevailing before the emergence of threat. Under these conditions, George Washington (acting as a presidential equivalent), and Presidents Lincoln, Wilson, and Franklin Roosevelt, were given license to escape the usual constraints imposed on presidential action by a wary public and jealous national policymakers. Here the barriers to centralized direction, which were erected in a political culture suspicious of it and encoded in the legal forms of the Constitution, are temporarily taken down. Such conditions reveal a presidential role as *nation-keeper*. The president is charged with conceiving, organizing, and executing a national response to system-threatening crises.[7] Profound changes are accepted because they are necessary to fight off a threat that would result in even greater, and less desirable, change in the nation's political and social structures. In the way of inoculation, a small dose is administered to the system to fight off the adverse consequences of an uncontrolled contagion.

These same preservative elements have been present in other episodes of transformational change, beyond, or as an adjunct to, presidential direction to fight off a common military enemy. The abolition of slavery proceeded directly from Lincoln's conclusion that Union victory could not be secured without converting the northern effort into a moral crusade. After the attack on Fort Sumter, the American Union transformed itself into a more centralized war-making apparatus, largely under Lincoln's direction. Yet well into 1862, Lincoln sought to restore the Union to the *status quo ante-bellum*, without enforcing changes in the status of slavery on a reluctant South. He held firm to a pledge frequently made during the 1860 campaign and reiterated mere seconds after taking the oath of office: "I have no purpose, directly or indirectly, to interfere with the institution of slavery in the States where it exists. I believe I have no lawful right to do so, and I have no inclination to do so."[8]

Only when he became convinced that his primary project of restoring the United States could not succeed without emancipation did Lincoln take extraordinary executive action to end American slavery. He sought the energizing effect emancipation would have on northern publics whose enthusiasm had evidently dimmed in the prosecution of a war intended only to reunite the states; he sought the subversive effect that a liberated army of black contributors to the war effort would cause among southern confederates; and, he sought the neutralizing effect a clear call for emancipation would exert on European powers, whose moral disdain for slavery was giving way to the self-interested realization that their textile industries were starving without southern cotton. Diplomatic recognition of the confederacy by England or France might have ended any chance of bringing the South back into the Union.[9]

Civil war alone, then, had been an insufficient condition for Lincoln to embrace a change in the nation's most vexing socioeconomic institution. He pressed to end slavery only when he became convinced that the sole way back to Union was down that avenue. This Lincoln plainly announced to Horace Greeley in August 1862.

> My paramount object in this struggle *is* to save the Union, and is *not* either to save or to destroy slavery. If I could save the Union without freeing *any* slave I would do it, and if I could save it by freeing *all* the slaves I would do it; and if I could save it by freeing some and leaving others alone I would also do that. What I do about slavery, and the colored race, I do because I believe it helps to save the Union; and what I forbear, I forbear because I do *not* believe it would help to save the Union.[10]

Similar aims for preservation by presidents have been central in other episodes of political and social transformation. Franklin Roosevelt adopted as his central task during the early years of his administration economic *recovery*, much to the dismay of many New Dealers who preferred to use the centralized powers invested in the president to advance permanent, fundamental restructuring of the nation's social and economic institutions.[11] Roosevelt, however, saw the structural reforms he offered as temporary necessities for rehabilitating a badly deteriorating national economy. He persistently goaded his lieutenants to quick action, with the intention of restoring a sound economy and then removing the administrative scaffolding, as it was no longer needed.[12]

The more permanent structural changes of Roosevelt's presidency were those commonly associated with the so-called Second Hundred Days or the Second New Deal. As Alan Brinkley and Arthur Schlesinger, Jr., among others, have demonstrated, the president's efforts to move these later transformations occurred against a backdrop of increasing national anxiety fueled by fascist and communist advances abroad, and exploited domestically by Huey Long, Charles Coughlin, and Francis Townsend. After he made the decision to move more aggressively on a number of significant reforms in 1935—the Social Security bill, the Wagner Act, and a more progressive tax program—Roosevelt reportedly identified his impulse to preserve. "I want to save our system, the capitalistic system; to save it is to give some heed to the world of thought of today." His program of change was intended to undermine those pushing for even greater change, whose power threatened the nation's political and economic fabric. He thus sought to "steal the thunder" of those who wanted more change than he was willing to accept.[13]

Preservation was also crucial for the civil rights revolution of the 1960s. John Kennedy's behavior in office before 1963 betrayed a marked reluctance to embark on any significant civil rights initiatives. The environment of his presidency, however, was substantially changed by the success of civil rights activists in provoking violent reactions to their protests in the South, most prominently in Birmingham, Alabama.[14] That experience sparked similar episodes across the nation, imperiling domestic tranquility with no end in sight. In a ten-week period after calm was restored in Birmingham, law enforcement agencies recorded 758 racial demonstrations in 186 communities, with almost 15,000 arrests.[15] Moreover, the nation's international security position suffered as a result of these events. In the Cold War competition for clients among developing African and Asian nations, the United States found itself at a severe disadvantage vis-à-vis the Soviet Union, as televised pictures crossed the globe of police dogs and fire-hoses turned on black protesters. A nation-keeping president could not long ignore these developments. Kennedy moved to make common cause with the protesters, but only after they had successfully cultivated the soil of American public opinion to make the nation relatively more receptive to their demands, and only after they had revealed to the president a willingness and ability to promote a continuing disequilibrium that might explode further into unrestrained violence.

These same factors later played a crucial role in Lyndon Johnson's belated embrace of the 1965 Voting Rights Act, after the violence at the Edmund Pettus Bridge in Selma, Alabama recapitulated Birmingham's unrest. In December 1964, the president had informed Reverend Martin Luther King, Jr. directly that no act would be forthcoming in the near future. Only three months later, however, Johnson dramatically reversed course in an attempt to stay ahead of events in Alabama.[16] Presidential embrace of transformational change in the nation's racial structures came when it became evident that the nation's peace could not be restored without it; the protesters showed no signs of relenting in their efforts to spark a violent racial backlash that would undermine national confidence at home and prestige abroad.[17]

Emancipation, economic and social reform, and advances in black civil rights—in each context, presidents embraced transforming change as a means of preservation.[18]

Paradox 2. What we typically call transformational leadership in the presidency is a mark of institutional failure—as well as success.
The system-threatening crises described above arose despite vigorous presidential attempts to avoid them. Presidential failure, then, has been a crucial ingredient in the signature transformations of American political development.

Again, it is useful here to consider first the defense regime as an archetype. In the three most notable instances of United States' mobilization for wartime purposes, the nation's presidents labored vigorously in advance to avert the conflict that eventually erupted.

Pre-Civil War presidents, at least as far back as James Monroe, sought to manage pressures between northerners and southerners on the issues of slavery and states' rights. The great compromises brokered in 1820, 1833, and 1850 bought time, but did not resolve the root conflicts that eventually detonated in 1861. Indeed, the final months of James Buchanan's presidency were devoted to reversing in substance the election of 1860, by erecting constitutional barriers to put slavery permanently beyond the reach of Lincoln's meddling Republicans, who Buchanan saw as causing secession through their insensitivity to southern rights. Buchanan was neither successful in this effort at constitutional reform nor the more general one to avert the impending war.

Later, as the European continent floundered in inconclusive warfare after 1914, President Wilson spent every effort to sustain an official isolation with a policy of strict neutrality. He sought to negotiate a halt to European hostilities, only to find this beyond his powers. In the end, the resumption of U-Boat warfare (in the unsettled aftermath of the *Lusitania* disaster), and the evidence of the Zimmermann telegram, unavoidably brought World War I to American shores.[19] This same general pattern describes Franklin Roosevelt, who isolated the United States as best he could from the onrush of events in Europe in the 1930s, and then did what he could to tilt the conflict with the use of American economic rather than military power. In the end, all these efforts to avoid war—

and its transformations—succumbed to uncontrollable events. Presidents tried vigorously to avert what came. Transformation arose from those failures.

Similar patterns of presidential behavior—first aversion, then empowerment and change—characterize those transformations in racial and socioeconomic structures described above. In each case, presidents became agents of change only after their predecessors—*and they themselves*—failed to arrest efforts by social and political agitators to wrest transformation from a reluctant polity. Before the conversions of Lincoln and Franklin Roosevelt, Kennedy and Lyndon Johnson, the presidency was not merely a benign institution on the political landscape, awaiting the ripening of time to play a positive role. Rather, the history of the presidential institution in each instance was one of incumbents actively working to suppress the advanced efforts of movements and transformational leaders mobilized against the status quo.[20]

As early as Andrew Jackson's tenure, an organized movement for abolishing slavery encountered a presidency deployed actively against it. Among other things, antebellum presidents used their powers to deny antislavery publishers access to the United States mails and worked to convince the United States Supreme Court—behind-the-scenes—to undermine antislavery efforts by constitutional decree.[21] As the new industrial order developed in the aftermath of the Civil War, those working to advance the interests of common laborers and to establish more equitable treatment of society's disadvantaged found that when their efforts to organize became too potent or too threatening, the office of the presidency was available for the provision of legal support and federal troops to aid those defending the status quo.[22] And those pressing for equal civil rights for African Americans encountered a long train of presidents manipulating their internal affairs so as to diminish prospects for transformational change, including the elevation of Booker T. Washington over more aggressive movement figures, and the deployment of agents of the police state to undermine the credibility of activists from Marcus Garvey to Martin Luther King, Jr.[23] In each of these instances, institutional failure preceded transformational success.

Yet these latter episodes share something elemental that distinguishes them from the defense-regime archetype: *a domestic cause of intended transformation*. This difference has important consequences for how we conceive of the presidency, leadership, and transformation. Indeed, while it seems appropriate to retain the term transformational leadership to describe presidential behavior in mobilizing a defense regime, a careful examination suggests that the term should *not* be applied to the institution in these other instances.

Usually inherent in definitions of political leadership are the notions of "initiative" and "intent." Leadership commonly means taking the first meaningful steps toward some intended goal. Both of these requirements—initiative and intent—have been met by presidents in the defense-regime archetype, as the presidency served as the locus of activity for initiating national mobilization to fight total war against aggressors bent on disabling the United States.[24]

The application of the term to the presidency in the second set of cases is objectionable, however, because in those instances initiative *and* intent arose from sources *other than the presidency*. An organized movement for emancipation existed at a national level beginning in the early 1830s, struggling to obtain precisely the results Lincoln achieved in 1863–65. Many of the socioeconomic transformations of the 1930s had been advocated by a succession of labor, populist, and progressive organizers reaching back into the late nineteenth century. And the civil rights revolution of the 1960s can be traced back to organized efforts pursued for almost three-quarters of a century by such varied figures as W. E. B. DuBois and Charles Houston. In these cases, we can find transformational leadership, but not, if we remain true to our definitions, by looking in the White House. In these cases, the nation's transformational leaders were extrainstitutional, or what Robert C. Tucker calls "nonconstituted."[25]

The absence of transformational leadership from the White House in these circumstances does *not* mean, however, that our so-called "transformational" presidents exercised no leadership on these major issues. Rather, *presidential leadership was of a different sort*. These presidents served as crucial completers of social transformation, as successful channelers through the political system of the transformational forces others mobilized. This is a very refined role, exercised within rare transformational contexts that are largely the product of organized efforts by purposeful movements to institute major change in the American polity.

There are several distinguishing features of a transformational context. Typically there is a recognizable increase in popular support for the cause advocated by the relevant movement(s). There is also an altered institutional environment in Washington. Usually, at least one of the nonpresidential branches of the government exhibits a recently elevated level of support for the movement in question. Congress, for example, took a more advanced position on slavery than did Lincoln, and the Warren Court (and lower federal courts) often pushed Dwight Eisenhower further than he wanted to go on civil rights.

Also, transformational contexts feature enlarged presidencies, although not necessarily presidencies enlarged expressly for purposes of dealing with a domestic social conflict. Presidential leadership in transformational contexts has been derived, in no small measure, from the possession by presidents of enlarged powers associated with emergencies to which they have successfully tied transformation. Lincoln's own creatively expanded war powers made emancipation possible; Roosevelt's emergency economic powers during the Depression allowed him to advocate change that might otherwise have been challenged as overreaching; and the enlarged Cold War presidency, responsible for keeping America secure in a perilous world, aided Kennedy and Johnson in making use of the office to secure for the civil rights movement the legislative reforms of the 1960s.[26] In each case, the American people were already disposed, because of preexisting conditions, to look to the presidency as a nation-keeping institution.

That nation-keeping role took on special relevance, however, in cases of domestic transformation, because of the destabilizing influence of social and political movements. Presidents routinely encountered majority populations or powerful entrenched interests who were agitated and prepared to avail themselves of all manner of action, including force, to repel change. Accordingly, transformational contexts are inherently periods of severe instability. A president can remedy this by use of the enlarged powers of persuasion to tip a destabilized polity into adopting transforming change, in part by explaining *why* transformation is needed to preserve the nation's basic commitments.[27] Above all, as Lincoln and Roosevelt and Kennedy and Johnson discovered, a failure to exercise presidential power toward this end merely produces continued instability along with renewed efforts by nonconstituted leaders to bring about presidential conversion. Ultimately, then, the only way presidents have successfully transcended the constraints of a transformational context has been to yield to them.

What emerges from this examination is a reactive presidency, which is less a potent initiator than a manager of the disruption others have wrought. Thus, assigning the term transformational leadership to such presidents claims too much. The term *conformative leadership* is more apt. The Oxford Universal Dictionary defines the root "conform" as "to form according to some model" or "to bring into harmony." Both seem about right. The models of social structure and political action that Lincoln, Roosevelt, Kennedy, and Johnson embraced originated with others, but the circumstances of transformational contexts led them to conform their actions, and those of the nation's government, accordingly. The motive in each instance was "to bring into harmony" that which had become increasingly dissonant because of the demands of those who can accurately be called transformational leaders.

The portrait of the presidency that emerges from this description of transformational contexts is—unlike typical accounts of the transforming presidential hero—quite Neustadtian. This presidency is ultimately a constrained institution, but one constrained toward boldness, not away from it. As we have just seen, in a transformational context, Neustadt's two contingent components of presidential power—public prestige (in the form of receptivity by public opinion to presidential direction) and professional reputation (in the form of a relative ascendancy among Washington policymakers)—are aligned for major presidential action. Moreover, the president finds himself pushed to act not so much because he freely chooses to do so, but because others "find his actions useful in [completing] their business."[28]

A particularly illuminating instance of this dynamic in the processes of transformational change occurred in the early 1960s, with the Freedom Ride through the Deep South. James Farmer, a chief organizer, later explained that "We planned the Freedom Ride with the specific intention of creating a crisis. We were counting on the bigots in the South to do our work for us. We figured that the government [especially the Kennedys] would have to respond if we created a situation that was headline news all over the world, and affected the nation's image abroad. An international crisis, that was our strategy."[29]

Farmer's view of American politics was, then, quintessentially Neustadtian. He and other civil rights activists "found it practically impossible to do their jobs without assurance of initiatives from" the president.[30] Thus, what I have called here conformative leadership might also be called by a more Neustadtian term: a transformative clerkship. These presidents found their jobs largely dictated to them by those who could not succeed in pushing social transformation absent White House involvement.

The president's role as a conformative leader is derived from the unique position the president holds as a nation-keeper, the chief guarantor of the nation's domestic tranquility, who is pledged "to preserve, protect, and defend the Constitution of the United States." That pledge also extends in practice to the small-c constitution of the United States, that is, to the fundamental social structures and cultural institutions upon which formal political arrangements are constructed. In the cases described here, preservation, protection, and defense could be reestablished with some permanence only by the vigorous application of presidential powers to construct a new, changed social model.[31] The directed application of these powers has led to some of the most celebrated political success stories in American history. That celebrity, however, tends to blind us to the full implications of what always preceded it: presidential failure.

Paradox 3. Many exercises of leadership in the presidency, especially on transformational issues, are not exercises of "leadership."
This apparently nonsensical claim is rooted in a definitional bias common to some of the most prominent texts on leadership in political science. Those definitions focus on *change*. In short, leaders are those who produce change

toward some preferred end.[32] By that common standard, the presidential institution is, considering the evidence discussed above, routinely hostile to the exercise of "leadership."

Consider the following definitions, crafted by some of the most authoritative scholars working in the field:

- Barbara Kellerman: "[P]olitical leadership implies some kind of partisan (or ideological) leadership, *a personal push for particular changes* in group goals, activities, or structure."[33]
- Bert A. Rockman: "A natural way of thinking about leadership is to see it as relevant to the process of producing significant change—that is, intended adaptations meant to lead to a significant alteration in the status quo."[34]
- James MacGregor Burns: "For me the leader is a very special, very circumscribed, but potentially the most effective of power holders, judged by the degree of intended 'real change' finally achieved . . . The test of [the leaders'] leadership function is their contribution to change. . . . "[35]

Also, in his edited volume on leadership, Dankwart A. Rustow wrote that "Both for the leader himself and for his followers or antagonists, leadership is a process of change, often drastic and discontinuous change." Albert O. Hirschman, in his essay for Rustow's volume entitled "Underdevelopment, Obstacles to the Perception of Change, and Leadership," concluded that "the ultimate function and justification of the leader [is] to improve on the *average* prospects for the advance of those whom he leads," fostering change (incrementally or drastically) for the better. Ultimately, leadership "is precisely the ability to perceive change when most of one's contemporaries are still unable to do so," enabling "a leader to take advantage of new opportunities [for change] as soon as they arise."[36]

Perhaps the most elaborate, and surely the most prominent, exegesis of this basic argument in relation to presidential leadership appears in Stephen Skowronek's *The Politics Presidents Make: Leadership from John Adams to George Bush*. The change orientation is the very hub of Skowronek's theory of presidential function in the nation's polity. Skowronek styles his work as "a general study of presidents as agents of political change," an examination of "faith in the transformative capacities of the presidency."[37] His central argument is that the presidency is "a prominent institution intimately and regularly engaged in changing things, one whose routine impulse is to *reorder* things."[38] It is an office that "routinely jolts order and routine elsewhere, one whose normal activities and operations alter system boundaries and recast political possibilities."[39]

The orientation toward change in each of these works may, in fact, be justified to the extent that such change is confined to the routines of politics. Yet these limits are seldom explicitly acknowledged, and sometimes they are implicitly rejected by these authors. To Burns, leadership is judged by "actual *social* change." And, the title of his book notwithstanding, Skowronek does not consistently limit the scope of his claims for presidential disruption to the political arena, that is, to the "*politics* presidents make." Those "system boundaries," which Skowronek claims presidents routinely alter, evidently include the frontiers where politics meets more basic social and economic structures. His presidency is "an office that routinely disrupts established power arrangements and continually opens new avenues of political activity for others."[40] There is an inference, then, that an institution that transforms those "arrangements" and "avenues" does so by changing the character of the more fundamental social structures to which political life commonly conforms.

These change-oriented definitions of leadership are problematic, for two reasons. First, they prompt us to expect behavior in the presidency that does not, by and large, occur naturally. Americans expect presidents to be leaders. To the extent, then, that we are conditioned to associate leadership with change—especially with "social" change or change in "established power arrangements" and "avenues of political activity"—we are bound to be disappointed. There may be powerful incentives, which Skowronek well identifies, for every president to generate some kind of *political* change, but that disruption seldom disturbs such fundamental social realities as racial or gender inequality or the distribution of economic and political resources. Indeed, presidents may promote *political* disruption in service of shoring up existing institutions, as did John Tyler when he annexed Texas to secure more firmly southern slavery.[41] It is the *limits*, then, of that disruption that are profound.

Second, change-oriented definitions of leadership leave us without a ready term to describe much of what even activist presidents do. What are we to say of the aggressive, creative, suppressive, anti-change initiatives many presidents have pursued to preserve the polity from those with transforming visions of America? Deprived, by definition, of the term "leadership," what ought we to call this? Is it indeed "anti-leadership" behavior?[42] If so, the very phrase "presidential leadership" is more often than not an oxymoron.

These problems suggest a turn—perhaps a return—to more utilitarian definitions of leadership, which assert the simple centrality of mobilizing others toward some common purpose, whether in the direction of change or preservation. Such definitions—common in sociological studies of leadership—are not premised on change, but allow, too, for the protection of "social order and stability."[43] Although American institutions (including the presidency) have played crucial roles in the production of transforming change, the routines of institutional behavior recommend more austere definitions of leadership, with the change orientation pared away. Not every president exercises leadership, but those who do, do not always have change in mind as the ultimate intent of their initiatives.

THE 21st Century Presidency

The immediate prospects for transformational (or conformative) leadership in the presidency do not at present appear auspicious. Indeed, the absence of opportunities for the exercise of grand leadership have frustrated the expansive ambitions of Bill Clinton, whose own efforts to transform the nation's health care systems signally failed. "I would have much preferred being president during World War II," the twentieth century's final president reportedly confided to one intimate. "*I am a person out of my time.*"[44] He elsewhere confessed, only partially in jest, "Gosh, I miss the Cold War," directly confirming Neustadt's 1990 prediction that future presidents would "yearn for the simplicity they see in retrospect, and also for the solace" of that presidency empowering bygone era. It is unsurprising that the "stability, authority, and glamour" of the Cold War would appeal to a figure beset by the characteristic forces of presidential repudiation typical of postwar regimes in American politics.[45]

Clinton may have aspired to the heights of a Roosevelt or a Lyndon Johnson, but he governed in the decidedly hostile environment of an Andrew Johnson or a dying Woodrow Wilson.[46] Leadership of any form, but especially that of the transforming variety, does not easily flow from a president who confronts a polity disinclined to follow, one unwilling to sustain the heightened sense of public purpose that wartime presidents may invoke. And as Andrew Johnson, Wilson, and Clinton discovered, whether transforming or conformative, leadership from the president becomes nearly impossible when that polity opts for a Congress rejuvenated by those intent on reasserting legislative primacy in national policymaking.[47] This is not so much the stuff of transcendent presidential leadership as of impeachment politics in the case of Johnson and Clinton or grand renunciation on the scale of America's rejection of the League of Nations.

Is, then, transformational (or conformative) leadership in the presidency still conceivable? The burden of proof actually falls on those who would argue for its demise. The historical ebb and flow of change and preservation—and of aggregation and disaggregation of centralized power—suggests great risks in projecting current practices indefinitely into the future. Institutional infirmity, sometimes of the most severe sort, has been a distinguishing feature of the presidency in almost every instance just before bursts of major transformation. A composite portrait of contemporary impressions of Presidents James Buchanan, William Howard Taft, and Herbert Hoover, for example, would not provide a very reliable basis for an unknowing observer to predict what the White House was able to accomplish shortly following their departures. Few could predict the institutional resurrections performed by Lincoln, the vigorous Wilson, and FDR respectively.

Moreover, the sophisticated tools available to present-day presidents—especially those related to polling and reading popular opinion—create possibilities for divining and manipulating public attitudes to an extent unimaginable in prior eras. Perhaps prospects for transforming leadership have been enhanced, then, by the modern president's ability, to an unprecedented degree, to know what Americans are thinking and to shape his or her presidency accordingly. A greater mastery of why Americans are attached to their existing social structures, and of their perceptions of which arguments might ease them into accepting change, *may* make the exercise of transforming leadership from the White House more possible into the future.

Yet the realities of twenty-first-century life, which will provide the context within which future presidents must operate, probably will in fact complicate the processes of mobilizing the nation for transformational purposes in the decades to come. The future of transformational leadership—indeed of presidential leadership of any variety—is intimately linked to the processes of social, technological, and political dis-integration which were a hallmark of the late twentieth century, and evidently are accelerating in the new one.

The defense-regime archetype as we have known it, with national mobilization under presidential direction, may well be a thing of the past. The vast proliferation of broadcast news sources, for example, which give every television watcher-as-citizen a sense of information (if not real knowledge) about dramatic events worldwide, has the potential to change how the nation responds to war or rumors of war. It is not clear that a sense of popular deference to presidential direction can survive when the president's presumed monopoly of relevant information has crumbled.

Prospects for conformative leadership from the White House may be equally undermined if an advancing individualism some see as endemic at the century's turn diminishes further possibilities for mobilizing mass publics toward some common purpose. Perhaps, as some have suggested, a nation of increasingly isolated individuals—those who "bowl alone"—has insufficient social capital to invest in common political enterprises if and when the need arises.[48] We do not now know whether the communications revolution associated with advancing computer technologies and the Internet, and which can help overcome many collective action problems by putting people with common purpose in touch with one another, is on balance an atomizing or integrating political force. Yet it is undeniable that advanced polling and communications technologies are available not only to the White House, but also to a host of private and public interests whose agendas may be at cross-purposes with the president's. Thus, the voice from the bully pulpit is increasingly drowned out by a cacophony of voices from competing pulpits, each with its own specially tailored message and audience. These complex contextual developments have major implications for how the political order functions, inasmuch as they help determine how the nation's institutions see problems of public policy, and how they feel political pressure. In sum, the future of conformative leadership in the presidency is contingent on the now-uncertain ability of others to create anew transformational contexts.

There remains one additional possibility, however, for using the presidency for transformational purposes. The accrued legacy of past movements—including those for racial, ethnic, economic, and gender equality—has opened the doors for the aggrieved directly into the normal channels of political action, diminishing the necessity of using the less efficient and more time-consuming processes of mass mobilization. The political mainstream is no longer completely closed to them, although their voices remain significantly muted because of a host of accumulated inequalities that mere access cannot remedy in a majoritarian political culture.

These uncompleted advances toward full inclusion by past movements and presidents, then, offer the presidency of today and tomorrow the opportunity to participate in a continuing process of evolutionary transformation, by working to complete the revolutionary changes of the past. Politics, as Max Weber declared, is the slow boring of hard wood; not a very glamorous job, certainly without the intensity—and the associated psychic rewards—of taking charge in historic moments, of rallying the nation to some higher purpose, of setting a course to victory against a common enemy. But, given a deficiency of power to manufacture historically favorable, empowering moments (and given a presumed unwillingness by presidents to provoke system-threatening crisis for such purposes); given common popular resistance to centralized direction; and given the absence of an easily recognized national foe, a president with transformational aspirations must be satisfied to serve these more modest, yet no less consequential, ends—or to await changing times. That transformational prospects might spring from the routines of transactional leadership—from the purposive use of the ordinary presidential power to persuade—may be the ultimate legacy the twentieth century leaves to the twenty-first century presidency.

ACKNOWLEDGMENTS

I am indebted to Professors Betty Glad, Lawrence Jacobs, Jack Nagel, Richard E. Neustadt, Mark Peterson, Robert Y. Shapiro, Theda Skocpol, and James Sterling Young for comments on earlier versions of this work.

NOTES

1. James MacGregor Burns offers a more elaborate, purposive definition in *Leadership* (New York: Harper & Row, 1978).

2. Richard E. Neustadt, *Presidential Power and the Modern Presidents: The Politics of Leadership from Roosevelt to Reagan* (New York: The Free Press, 1990), p. 10.

3. Charles A. and Mary R. Beard, *The Rise of American Civilization* (New York: MacMillan, 1930), vol. II, p. 100.

4. 193 U.S. 197 (1904).

5. The term is borrowed from Stephen Skowronek, although, as will become clear below, I have some points of disagreement with him over what the nature of that logic is. See Skowronek, *The Politics Presidents Make: Leadership from John Adams to George Bush* (Cambridge: Harvard University Press, 1993), p. 15.

6. I term these paradoxes because each statement embodies concepts that, given common notions of leadership and followership, change and preservation, seem self-contradictory.

7. The distinctly American way of responding to such incidents is explored in Clinton Rossiter's *Constitutional Dictatorship: Crisis Government in the Modern Democracies* (New York: Harcourt, 1948). See also Russell L. Riley, *The Presidency and the Politics of Racial Inequality: Nation Keeping from 1831–1965* (New York: Columbia University Press, 1999).

8. "First Inaugural Address," reprinted in Don E. Fehrenbacher, ed., *Abraham Lincoln: Speeches and Writings, 1859–65* (New York: The Library of America, 1989), p. 215. This is not the Lincoln of popular memory. Only the second inaugural address, with its antislavery overtones, joins the Gettysburg Address on the walls of the Lincoln Memorial.

9. Riley, *The Presidency and the Politics of Racial Inequality*, ch. 3; James M. McPherson, *Battle Cry of Freedom*, chs. 12, 16, 18.

10. Fehrenbacher, ed., *Speeches and Writings*, pp. 357–58.

11. A contributing factor here was the administration's need to have the nation's most experienced experts in commercial activity—the business interests—involved in crafting and executing the government's response to depression. As Arthur Schlesinger, Jr., observed of the early New Deal, "The very moneychangers, whose flight from their high seats in the temple the president had so grandiloquently proclaimed in his inaugural address, were now swarming through the corridors of the Treasury"—among other buildings. *The Age of Roosevelt: The Coming of the New Deal* (Boston: Houghton Mifflin, 1960), pp. 4–5.

12. See Roosevelt's Fireside Chat, in Rosenman, ed., *The Public Papers and Addresses of Franklin D. Roosevelt* (13 vols, New York, 1938–50), June 28, 1934, p. 317.

13. Arthur M. Schlesinger, Jr., *The Age of Roosevelt: The Politics of Upheaval*, pp. 325–26, *passim*. See also Alan Brinkley, *Voices of Protest: Huey Long, Father Coughlin, and the Great Depression* (New York: Vintage Books, 1982); Robert S. McElvaine, *The Great Depression: America, 1929–1941* (New York: Times Books, 1984), chs. 10–11.

14. Kennedy's conversion is recorded in numerous places. One valuable treatment is Carl M. Brauer, *John F. Kennedy and the Second Reconstruction* (New York: Columbia University Press, 1977).

15. Taylor Branch, *Parting the Waters: America in the King Years, 1954–63* (New York: Simon and Schuster, 1988), p. 825. See also Brauer, *Second Reconstruction*, p. 238.

16. See David Garrow, *Bearing the Cross: Martin Luther King, Jr., and the Southern Christian Leadership Conference* (New York: Vintage Books, 1988), ch. 7.

17. Riots in Watts soon after the enactment of the voting rights act indicated that such action was a necessary but not sufficient condition to halt racial unrest.

18. The same trends also applied to Theodore Roosevelt, as he met the excesses of a new industrial order with growing state power. Henry Steele Commager and Richard Brandon Morris have written of the elder Roosevelt: "He was in a sense an orthodox heretic, a respectable agitator, . . . a conservative revolutionist, and his sponsorship was a guarantee that the revolution would be conducted under the most high minded auspices, in the most orderly fashion, and to the most respectable ends. What this meant was that the United States would escape those convulsions which attended the social revolutions in so many other countries, and that this revolution—like earlier American revolutions—would be essentially conservative in character." "Editors' Introduction," to George E. Mowry, *The Era of Theodore Roosevelt and the Birth of Modern America* (New York: Harper Torchbooks, 1958), p. x.

19. The Zimmermann telegram was an encrypted diplomatic message from

Germany to Mexico, intercepted by the United States, inviting Mexico's alliance in the war effort. In return, Mexico would receive the southwestern part of the United States upon successful conclusion of the conflict.

20. Included within the general rubric of suppression are those efforts by some presidents to coopt their challengers by steering protest activity into more benign channels. An example was Robert Kennedy's aggressive attempt, as attorney general on behalf of his brother, to halt southern black street demonstrations and freedom rides by advocating in 1961 a government program to subsidize movement efforts to register voters. Kennedy personally sought tax-exempt status for the Voter Education Project, and pledged to secure favorable draft status for young African American leaders who turned away from more disruptive behavior toward registration. See Mark Stern, *Calculating Visions: Kennedy, Johnson, and Civil Rights* (New Brunswick: Rutgers University Press, 1992), pp. 63–67; Branch, *Parting the Waters*, pp. 478–82.

21. These (and related) activities are detailed in Riley, *The Presidency and the Politics of Racial Inequality*, ch. 2.

22. The clearest example of this trend was in relation to strikes and other protests initiated by labor organizers. Presidents Hayes and Cleveland took vigorous steps to deploy the power of the national government to undermine the use of the strike as a weapon of an infant labor movement. See Bennett M. Rich, *The President and Civil Disorder* (Washington: The Brookings Institution, 1941); Grover Cleveland, *Presidential Problems* (New York: The Century Company, 1904), ch. 2. The national government took a more sympathetic approach to granting pensions to those responsible for keeping the Union together through civil war. See Theda Skocpol, *Protecting Soldiers and Mothers: The Political Origins of Social Policy in the United States* (Cambridge: Harvard University Press, 1992).

23. Riley, *The Presidency and the Politics of Racial Inequality*, chs. 4–6. See also Kenneth O'Reilly, *Nixon's Piano: Presidents and Racial Politics from Washington to Clinton* (New York: The Free Press, 1995), *passim*.

24. Some might object that, even in the defense-regime archetype, presidents were essentially reactive agents, responding to the initiative of others. However, the *intent* of those firing on Fort Sumter, the *Lusitania*, and Pearl Harbor, clearly was contrary to the purposes for which these presidents mobilized the polity. The effect, in the long run, was not to weaken the foe, but to cause its citizens to rally to the flag.

25. Tucker, *Politics as Leadership*, revised ed. (Columbia: University of Missouri Press, 1995), pp. 71–76.

26. The notion that the president (or, for that matter, the national government in *any* form) might possess the power to confiscate slave property was for most Americans a ludicrous proposition before the advent of civil war. However, the

"war power," as Lincoln called it, allowed him to "do things on military grounds which cannot be done constitutionally by Congress." For more on this question in a comparative context, see Arthur M. Schlesinger, Jr., "War and the Constitution: Abraham Lincoln and Franklin D. Roosevelt," in Gabor S. Borritt, ed., *Lincoln, the War President: The Gettysburg Lectures* (New York: Oxford University Press, 1992), pp. 145–78 (above quote appears on p. 157).

27. Here my argument dovetails with Skowronek's. See note 39 below.

28. Neustadt, *Presidential Power*, p. 7.

29. Quoted in David Garrow, *Bearing the Cross*, p. 156.

30. Neustadt, *Presidential Power*, p. 7.

31. These same factors usually lead presidents into a vigorous protection of the nation's fundamental social structures, of the status quo in its deepest sense. There is thus a duality to conformative leadership, as the nation-keeping role in one context constrains a president to work against change, and in another promotes pro-change behavior. Riley, *The Presidency and the Politics of Racial Inequality*, Introduction, ch. 8.

32. The public choice literature seems to me ambiguous on this point. To the extent that its focus is on maintaining equilibrium, the change-orientation seems absent. Yet much of its leadership literature is devoted to the examination of "political entrepreneurs," whose goals *are* change oriented; leaders move followers from one equilibrium to another. For more on this subject, see the essays in Bryan D. Jones, *Leadership and Politics: New Perspectives in Political Science* (Lawrence: University Press of Kansas, 1989).

33. Barbara Kellerman, "Leadership as a Political Act," in Kellerman, ed., *Leadership: Multidisciplinary Perspectives*, p. 71. Emphasis in the original.

34. Bert A. Rockman, *The Leadership Question: The Presidency and the American System* (New York: Praeger, 1984), p. 20. Rockman admits that this "natural way" is not without complications—especially in how change is conceived—but the emphasis throughout is on how leadership can provide direction. He is more sensitive than many others to the preservative component of presidential action, but the emphasis in his work is more on leadership as an act of mobility than of stasis.

35. James MacGregor Burns, *Leadership*, pp. 3, 19, 413–21, 427.

36. Dankwart A. Rustow, "The Study of Leadership," and Albert O. Hirschman, "Underdevelopment, Obstacles to the Perception of Change, and Leadership," both in Rustow, ed., *Philosophers and Kings: Studies in Leadership* (New York: American Academy of Arts and Sciences, 1970), pp. 27, 362, 365. It is instructive that of the twelve other essays on political leadership in that volume, nine deal with founders of new orders, revolutionaries, or prophets. Indeed, Bruce Mazlish began his essay by remarking, critically, that "Most studies of leadership tend to center on dramatic and revolutionary figures, guiding powerful mass movements." Yet his own study of

intellectual leadership ironically focused on the utilitarians and their contributions to political and social change in the England of the early 19th century. Mazlish, "James Mill and the Utilitarians," p. 465.

37. Stephen Skowronek, *The Politics Presidents Make*, p. vii.

38. Skowronek, "Response [to Peri Arnold, Sidney Milkis, and James Sterling Young]" *Polity* 27 (3) (Spring 1995): 521 (emphasis in the original).

39. Skowronek, *The Politics Presidents Make*, pp. 4, 21, 49. In places, Skowronek does make claims for an "order affirming" aspect of presidential activity, but this part of his argument emphasizes the need for some presidents to *justify* their routinely disruptive behavior. Skowronek's presidency is "an *order-affirming* institution in that the disruptive effects of the exercise of presidential power must be justified in constitutional terms broadly construed as the protection, preservation and defense of values emblematic of the body politic" (p. 20). This accords with the argument I make here about the special rhetorical role present among pro-change, conformative leaders, for whom change is an institutional necessity. But few presidents fit this description, and justifying change through the language of preservation is not the same thing as actually taking action to retard change. Skowronek tellingly quotes Machiavelli: "He who desires to reform the government of a state, and wishes to have it accepted and capable of maintaining itself to the satisfaction of everybody, must at least retain the semblance of old forms; so that it may seem to the people that there has been no change in the institutions, even though they are entirely different from the old ones." Skowronek begins with the premise that the ruler seeks change; order affirmation is voiced in service of reform.

40. Skowronek, *The Politics Presidents Make*, p. 15.

41. William W. Freehling, *The Road to Disunion: Secessionists at Bay, 1776–1854* (New York: Oxford University Press, 1990), chs. 20–25.

42. Robert C. Tucker writes that "Repression . . . can be seen as leadership for non-change," a characterization that is consistent with my argument. *Politics as Leadership*, p. 83.

43. Arnold S. Tannenbaum, "Leadership: Sociological Aspects" in the *International Encyclopedia of the Social Sciences* (New York: MacMillan-Free Press, 1968), 9: 101. In examining sociological studies of the subject, Tannenbaum claims that "most theories of leadership are conservative in that they are addressed to the maintenance of social systems rather than to their change." There is thus a striking contrast to studies in contemporary political science.

44. Bob Woodward, *The Choice* (New York: Simon and Schuster, 1996), p. 65. The emphasis is Woodward's. Another *Washington Post* reporter, David Maraniss, notes that "Clinton has long lamented that he was born into the wrong era." "First and Last," *The Washington Post Magazine*, October 27, 1996, p. 13.

45. Clinton is quoted in John Kenneth White, *Still Seeing Red: How the Cold*

War Shapes the New American Politics (Boulder: Westview, 1997), p. 256; Neustadt, *Presidential Power*, p. 318.

46. For a time, Clinton turned to Theodore Roosevelt as a model for his own presidency, asserting that the elder Roosevelt "made a major change in the way people worked, lived and related to each other . . . without a major war catalyzing it." Clinton recognized that the end of the Cold War was a definitive historical force on his presidency. Yet rather than read his time as analogous to the end of other wars (and thereby accept the sobering lessons of history such a reading conveyed), he instead sought parallels that comported with his own preferences for strong presidential direction. He announced his frame of mind shortly after his 1996 reelection: "I'm very mindful of history's difficulties and I'm going to try to beat them." Interview transcript, "My Election Will Be Overwhelmingly Focused on the Future," *The Washington Post*, August 25, 1996, p. A19; "Excerpts from President Clinton's News Conference," *The Washington Post*, November 9, 1996, A17. On Clinton's choice of Theodore Roosevelt as a role model, see Edmund Morris, "The Rough Rider and the Easy One," *The New York Times*, October 6, 1996, E15.

47. In 1866 and 1918, congressional midterm elections provided Johnson and Wilson with an extraordinarily hostile institutional opposition controlling the nation's capitol. In each case, the American people sent to Washington a Congress energized to bring a war-enlarged presidency back down to size. I liken the 1994 "Republican Revolution" to those earlier plebiscites. In Clinton's case, his failure to understand his historic context actually helped create the electoral climate that empowered his opposition in 1994. (I might add here that the 1946 election conforms also to this general pattern, although the postwar decommissioning of that leadership regime was interrupted by the ongoing emergencies of the Cold War that soon broke out.)

48. Robert D. Putnam, "Bowling Alone: America's Declining Social Capital," *Journal of Democracy*, January, 1995.

PART 6

Conclusion: Forging the Presidency
for the 21st Century

CHAPTER 20

A Preachment from Retirement

Richard E. Neustadt

As a politician might say: It is good to be back at Columbia again. It really is! I taught here for 10 years, from 1954 to 1964, in the then wholly civilized, collegial, friendly atmosphere of the Department of Public Law and Government. Those adjectives, I trust, apply to its successor, the Department of Political Science. Alas, they fled the scene for a time, after the troubles of 1968. But I was gone by then. My memories are all good ones. And appreciative. It was here that I wrote *Presidential Power* on an 18-month paid leave of absence arranged by Schuyler Wallace and David Truman—junior faculty members present should take note, and let their seniors blush! David Truman, indeed, as adviser to a new political science list then being undertaken by the editors at John Wiley and Sons, persuaded them to publish that book after four other publishers had turned it down. Junior authors, I hope, will be encouraged!

Martha Joynt Kumar asked me to address three questions here. First, whether I think it appropriate to integrate scholarship—more precisely its product—into decisionmaking. Second, should relevance be our goal? And third, what do we, as scholars, need to learn that is hard to see from outside? These questions I shall simpify to two, Can what we do as students dealing with the presidency be relevant to sitting presidents? My answer is yes, sometimes, though with difficulty often and uncertainty always: There are at least five hazards in the way. And how hard should we try? My answer is, harder than we do now.

Let me elaborate, starting with those hazards. Presidents newly in office—by that I mean during their first two years, at least—will not yet have lived through enough to recognize the relevance of many things we possibly could tell them. Experience is by far their best teacher; its lack, frequently, can be made up by nothing they have done before. If they cannot recognize our nugget for themselves, its relevance becomes irrelevant. Let me offer an example, involving Brewster Denny.

In 1960, Brewster was a full-time consultant to Senator Henry "Scoop" Jackson's Senate Subcommittee on National Policy Machinery, after recent experience in the Central Intelligence Agency, while I was a part-time consultant, more remotely experienced, on President Truman's White House staff. Late in the summer of 1960, Jackson asked me for a memo on the possible presidential transition, then took it and me to Senator John F. Kennedy, who requested more of the same.

While preparing those subsequent memos that October, I discussed one idea with Brewster on which I had views but no recent information, namely that the incoming president should be briefed, well in advance of his inaugural, on preparatory processes behind the intelligence reports he would receive and also on preparatory work for actions in the pipeline.

The upshot of our discussion was this: I included in my memos a proposal for a "Special Assistant to the Commander-in-Chief-Elect," to be chosen for a temporary period from among career officials in the intelligence community—someone in whom the president-elect had personal confidence. I also included a brief, discreet memo from Brewster, outlining that person's functions, albeit in a rather coded, relatively undescriptive manner, since these were not classified communications.

A week after his election, JFK had me down to his family's house in Palm Beach where he was vacationing to discuss a number of "what next" issues growing out of his situation, most of them touched on in my pre-election memos. Among them was this bit, associated with Brewster. Kennedy couldn't get it. He simply didn't understand the need that we were trying to address. I could not enlighten him with vivid enough illustrations, having left the White House eight years earlier, and not having been on that action-channel anyway. Finally I said, "There must be someone in the intelligence community you trust. Let me take this to him, get him to vet it and bring his own views back to you." "Ok" said Kennedy, "take it to Dick Bissell. He's the one man I know well enough to trust."

So, I went to Bissell the next week. He professed himself in favor of the idea, said he himself might be the right man to do it, and promised to discuss it with

Kennedy when he saw him; they had a date in the next few days. I heard no more about it from either of them.

The next April, of course, I discovered with the rest of the world that Bissell had been charged by the Eisenhower Administration to plan and oversee a covert action against Fidel Castro—eventuating in Kennedy's first disaster, at the Bay of Pigs. Bissell was among the last men to be trusted in this staffing matter, for it was in part directed against the likes of him. But I did not know that, and Kennedy did trust him.

They may not know what you know, and there may not be a practicable way to tell them. That is one hazard with relevance.

A second hazard is that they may share your understanding, appreciate the meaning of your nugget, but in a different time-dimension where what is to you the future is for them the past. If so, they weigh it differently.

I still recall the first time my attention was drawn forcibly to this phenomenon. For some reason I no longer recall, it fell to me to present President Truman a letter from Lindsay Rogers, a very senior professor at Columbia, whose White House credentials ran back to FDR's original brains trust. The date was late September 1950, some 10 days after General MacArthur's splendid victory at Inchon in Korea where he almost succeeded, but not quite, in rolling up the North Korean army. Rogers wrote, in thoughtful terms, to argue against pursuing what was left of it across the 38th Parallel, the prewar boundary. This was not a popular view, just then, but certainly defensible (especially as things turned out), and shared by some inside the government, notably George Kennan.

But the President was irritated and dismissive. His attitude was: why does he argue now? That's over and done with. From his personal perspective, so it was. Some days before, he had approved Dean Acheson's wording of a UN General Assembly resolution to be introduced by our allies. It authorized MacArthur, as UN Commander, to go north, looking toward an old UN objective, reunification of Korea.

When Rogers wrote, this resolution had not yet been introduced at the UN, much less approved, but in Truman's mind it represented a decision taken, a case closed, yesterday's business, while his job now was to get on with today's or prepare for tomorrow's. Considering the extent to which the Presidency presents itself to Presidents as a decision-machine, this too is defensible. So their time-frame, very often, is not ours, which, as in the Rogers case, can disguise or belie the relevance of what we have to say.

A third hazard for relevance is similar. It is that Presidents may see themselves still weaker, more beset, less masters of their fate, even than political sci-

entists do! "He'll sit here and say 'do this . . . do that' and nothing will happen."
That was Truman on Ike—but it also was Truman on Truman.

Henry Kissinger once told me that he last saw President Kennedy during the
Berlin crisis in the summer of 1961. Henry had elaborate views about Berlin
and novel plans he thought the president should implement.. These he set
forth, to which the president replied, 'That's fine, Henry, now can you convince
the government?"

Changing the example, we now know that in the spring and summer of
1965, Clark Clifford, then a private citizen and informal adviser, argued vigorously with President Johnson against Americanizing the Vietnam war. Unchar-
acteristically, LBJ ignored Clifford's advice. It isn't that he mistrusted him, or
didn't respect his political acumen. Rather, it seems to be that he felt Clifford
couldn't give him any cover against all the specters haunting him should
Saigon fall.

There was the specter of the Senate after Truman "lost" China! There was
the specter of MacArthur, sabotaging the administration and complaining to
Congress when he couldn't have his way on warfare with the Communist Chi-
nese! There was the specter of FDR, committing an imprudent act in 1937,
"court-packing," which cost him his outsized congressional majorities, hence
his chance at a third New Deal (for which the Great Society was to be a bigger,
if belated, substitute)! Finally, perhaps worst, there was the specter of Robert
Kennedy, newly elected from New York, rising in the Senate to read the roll of
martyred Roman Catholic nuns in Saigon (I made that up, but think the
spirit's right)!

Could private-citizen Clifford protect the president from these? If not, the
latter evidently felt he had to go a different way, "prudently" settling for the
least extreme expansion of the war his military chieftains would sign onto,
while disguising the effects from Congress as it concentrated on the Great Society. Clifford was a political practitioner, not a political scientist. Had he been
the latter, his influence would have been the less.

This brings me to my fourth hazard, the standing of our profession with
politicians. It is not high. That is partly because so many of us cease to discipline ourselves to write in accessible language—a harder task, to my mind,
than writing in professional code, to say nothing of mathematics. Partly our
standing is not high because so many of us nowadays appear to dislike politics,
a common American attitude, not least in the professional middle classes, but
offputting to politicians when combined with an ostensible commitment to
the subject of their profession. Partly our standing reflects the hopeful commitment of so many to pursuing regularities in political behavior that serve

theory-building which, in time, may produce tightly useful predictions. With something as irregular as successive presidencies, the time won't be short. That makes the effort seem quixotic to practitioners. But the hope is that if the pot of gold at the end of the rainbow finally can be gained, the politicians will sit up and notice, despite themselves, because the predictions work! I admire the faith, but confess to some doubt of the outcome, at least in spheres where Presidents have greatest need.

The fifth hazard is bound up with that need. I do not mean a crystal ball for policy and politics, however wonderful (if always accurate), but something more nearly achievable by human effort, and more nearly within the compass of our professional skills. To me it now appears to be a narrowing of the great gap, which seems to widen, president after president, in the institutional memory available to them about the presidential office. In most of my writings I have shied away from trying to fill that gap, although I did begin by assaying one corner of it. I now think staying away was a mistake. My thinking is informed, watching from afar, as one president after another exacerbates his troubles by errors in the staffing and procedures of his office, which an empathetic knowledge of the past would have allowed him to avoid. The trouble is compounded both of lack of empathy and lack of knowledge.

This was not always true, at least not to the same degree. FDR, for instance, knew a great deal about the White House as a nascent—very nascent—organization from the time he first stepped into it. As recently as Ronald Reagan's time, James Baker and his chief aide, Richard Darman, knew a lot about that place as it had worked since Nixon's days, while their associates, Edwin Meese and Michael Deaver, knew all about how Reagan had worked previously in Sacramento. They put what they knew together. As guidance it was largely accurate enough to suffice for his whole first term..

But what are we to make of the two Southern governors, Misters Carter and Clinton, who had neither the experience nor the likes of a Baker to guide them, yet seemed to think that no lack? It is well-known now that the first of these presidents made every mistake in the book during his transition into office. The second, determined not to repeat Carter's mistakes of substance, replicated all his mistakes of staffing and process, along with more besides.

Clinton's reelection (in 1996) after the great shock of losing Congress, just two years before, demonstrates his learning and adaptive capabilities. So do his relatively stabilized and regularized staff arrangements, and the relative good order in his present use of time. But history will record, I believe, that the months after his first election represented the worst presidential transition, most chaotic, most disorderly, and least effective in preparing him to govern, of any known up to that time. Carter becomes a mere runner-up, yards behind. Yet Carter's misadventures were well known to those of us who keep up with the Presidency, and known best of all to Carter's people. Why then not to Clinton and his people? There's the rub.

For reasons about which I know nothing, the relations of the White House, in Carter's time, with the then Governor of Arkansas were such that Clinton wished for none of "them" around him—and got his wish. There goes one source of memory. As for the other, those who "keep up" with the Presidency, who are they? A grab-bag of professors, journalists, and former White House aides, whose views are integrated nowhere in a neutral setting and who individually are capable of offering quite contradictory advice.

Clinton is said to have checked early with a Bush White House adviser, whom he had good reason to trust. That person reportedly told him: Concentrate on your Cabinet appointments; if you don't you'll face later embarrassment. Others volunteered advice to focus on the staffing of the White House, letting the new staffers cut their eye-teeth on such things as Cabinet selections. In the hurly-burly of post-election excitement, adrenaline flowing, hubris showing, haste necessitated by the calendar, whom to believe? And why bother? After nomination and election, "we"—the victorious band of brothers—scarcely need to be told how to govern.

Clinton and his entourage are neither the first nor likely to be last among those led astray by such sentiments, just after winning the White House from the opposition party. Historically, that pales into insignificance compared with the record a man makes in eight years. Politically and operationally, however, Clinton's early scars still showed until his fourth. So may the next person's.

But their need for institutional memory and the lack of it applies not only at the outset of a new administration embodying a change of party. Matt Dickinson has reminded us that the entire logic of presidential staffing for the longest-serving of our presidents dropped so far out of sight of his successors as to literally disappear. More particularly, even those of us who "follow" presidential matters would be hard put to remember just how Reagan used staff changes in his second term to help him ease the Iran-Contra scandal. Yet, in anybody's second term, that might well become relevant to know. And so forth, ad infinitum.

The most thoroughgoing, sensible, and relatively successful effort to shrink the size of White House staff was made not in Carter's time, nor in Clinton's—both made highly publicized efforts, both wrong-headed, cutting service personnel instead of policy wonks—but rather, unpublicized, in Gerald Ford's time, associated with an aide of his who once taught here, Jim Connor. Who recalls that? Probably not even Connor!

The fifth hazard for relevance, then, is that no regular, reliable, acceptably neutral source provides a president and his associates with what they recurrently require through their times in office. Nobody's at hand to trace for him (or someday her) the origins and possibilities and pitfalls of the institutional arrangements he inherits, to say nothing of the changes he may put in place in ignorance of what was tried before. Or rather, all too many are at hand, with partial knowledge and imperfect recollection.

We have, in short, no substitute for that extraordinary British institution, Cabinet Office. OMB once aspired to be such, and forty years ago, or so, came close to making it. But the career staff there is now pushed down so many levels that it cannot serve, with accuracy, for the presidential office as a whole. Nor, of course, can the Executive Clerk in the White House proper, whom Nixon's people pushed down out of sight.

So how is any president to know your nugget is the best one? How, indeed, are you?

How indeed are you to know your notion, idea, proposition is the best afforded by the whole of White House history? This brings me to the heart of the second question to be addressed: how hard should we, political scientists studying the Presidency, strive to be relevant? By the logic of what I've said thus far, that means, above all, striving to repair the lack of institutional memory. Before I come to whether that ought to be done by us, let me pause, for a moment, over how it could be done at all.

In such a cause, the underlying resource is the ever-widening array of presidential "Libraries." They are treasure-houses for this purpose, as Fred Greenstein keeps reminding us. They have the drawback that there are so many of them, and will be more, scattered throughout the country. For scholars, this is a matter of money and time, inconvenient but not unmanageable, I hope, and with more than a few compensations.

A more serious limitation is that what those buildings house are archives, written records, or now disks and the like, in a few cases tapes (unlikely to be seen again for a while). These, all too often—more now than in the past and in the future more than now—disguise or distort the living purposes, the interchanges, struggles, and reactions of the people involved, and their outlooks on the world at the moment. The only way to partially make up those lacks is by interviewing, where the interviewer knows the record and can conjure up the atmosphere, while the interviewee still fully commands memory, inevitably imperfect, and both are eager for a genuine reconstruction. (Once upon a time, one could have added memoirs, but no longer. Presidential memoirs, while obligatory, are formulaic, and in Washington scarcely anyone else except sex-objects writes them at all.)

This implies an enormous, orchestrated effort, an effort larger and more focused even than those Greenstein urges. It would have to focus on construction of the action-channels which, for any length of time, have fed recurrent tasks through presidency to president. The object could not be the general histories of such pathways, though these become a start, but, more particularly, detailed reconstructions of their major alterations—change-points, if you will—and no less detailed looks at entrant-points, where new officials, critically astride a channel, alter some significant aspect of its procedures, either for their own comfort or for their President's.

That charge, I think, goes far beyond what the "new" institutionalists seem to mean by institutionalism. If I'm wrong, Terry Moe can correct me. I hope he will, if not now, later. As I understand them, they seek identifiable regularities over time in the work-product of presidential agencies, on which to base theory-building. More power to them. But that search will scarcely bring them to the detailed histories I have in mind, the histories of actual development at changeful moments in the lives of institutions. Yet nothing less, it seems to me, can fill the gap I have described, the gap in institutional memory—for nothing else, if neutrally presented by a creditable source, can offer information relevant precisely to those things a President most needs to know about his institutional surroundings.

Why make such an effort to fill the gap? First, because it is there. Second, because we would so much enrich our understanding, our capacity to theorize from an inductive base, and our ability to test hypotheses against a wealth of all-but-real experience. And third, because as we succeed we meet a need of presidents, thus we contribute, we can hope, to more effective government. The argument can be made that as scholars we are not obliged to care, one way or the other. Perhaps so, though as heirs to Tudor universities, which we all are, I wouldn't press the point. Even so, as citizens we're bound to care. In my time, that might have sufficed; I cannot speak for yours.

To mount a long-term project adequate to the purpose seems a formidable task. No doubt it is. Yet tasks as comprehensive have been undertaken in the past. I think of David Truman, from this university, nearly fifty years ago, working with a small group of inspired souls assembled through the Social Science Research Council, to energize the study of congressional behavior, and more, to put upon a cumulative footing the study of voting behavior. Something like their effort is needed now, I judge, from senior members of our discipline. Senior, I stress, but working, not retired!

But why political science? Why not history, whence political science came a century ago? The skills required start with archival research and complex interviewing—after all, are these not historians' skills? But when we broke away from them it was not on account of separate skills—we had none then, except for lawyers' skills which we've now mostly shed. We broke away to pursue different questions. Ours concerned power and polity, their inner workings and philosophical justification. These still are not the questions asked by most historians, except as they impose themselves upon their narratives. Besides, we have an asset here, in you, by whom I mean especially the young among you. Here is a ready-made array of energetic scholars, already deeply interested in aspects of the presidency.

Finally, institutional history of the sort and at the level I suggest keeps us engaged with what has always fascinated me, I daresay also some of you, in studying the presidency—namely its relation to the mysteries and tragedies of human governance. Whatever the limitations on an American President's powers and power alike, and those are severe, the Office holds enough of both, exercised on a sufficiently personalistic basis, so we know that what we study has affinity to ancient kings, to Shakespeare's Henrys, as to modern counterparts. We work on a subject which keeps us in touch with terrible human dilemmas, as old as the first society to succeed the hunter-gatherers. For me that adds an irresistible dimension.

Should there be no place in political science for the work I here propose, those who care to pursue it may have to return to history, lugging our questions back with them. The historians won't have jobs, alas, but at least they cultivate the skills, and some appear to share that fascination. I hope, however, that our discipline is broad enough to keep hold of those founding questions. If so, it ought to tackle what I urge here.

ACKNOWLEDGMENTS

This essay is a revised version of an address to the conference at Columbia University, November 15, 1996.

CHAPTER 21

The Impeachment of President Bill Clinton: Background

Natasha Hritzuk

Spanning five years and multiple scandals, the events leading to President Bill Clinton's impeachment and eventual acquittal began in 1994 with an independent counsel investigation into the diversion of funds from a failed savings and loan company into Clinton's 1984 Arkansas gubernatorial campaign. Over the next three years, the investigations into financial wrongdoing expanded into a broader inquiry stemming from a sexual misconduct lawsuit brought against the president by a former Arkansas state employee, Paula Corbin Jones. Spearheaded by Independent Counsel Kenneth Starr, originally appointed to investigate Clinton's alleged financial transgressions, the inquiry turned on evidence that the president misrepresented a sexual relationship with White House intern Monica Lewinsky in the Jones lawsuit deposition. On the basis of these findings, Starr recommended that the House initiate impeachment proceedings against the president on charges of obstruction of justice and perjury. Despite an affirmative vote in the House to impeach Clinton on two impeachment articles, the Senate ultimately acquitted Clinton of all charges. Voting in both instances occurred primarily along party lines, with the majority of Republicans supporting Clinton's impeachment and removal from office while Democrats sought to keep the president in power.

Particularly striking during the impeachment hearings and trial was the disjuncture between elite and public opinion concerning Clinton and the scandals threatening to end his presidency. While many political leaders and members of the media expressed outrage over Clinton's misdeeds, polls indicated that the public continued to stand behind the president throughout the entire process, even while condemning his personal behavior.[1] Americans not only supported Clinton's leadership in surprisingly high proportions, but also elected a greater than anticipated number of Democrats to the House of Representatives on the eve of the House impeachment hearings. At the same time, Americans' orientations toward Congress took a negative turn, with majorities consistently expressing concern that Congress was excessively focused on impeachment at the expense of the nation's day-to-day business.[2]

What follows is a more detailed discussion of the events leading to President Clinton's impeachment and acquittal.

Act I: The Stage is Set

The August 1994 renewal of the Independent Counsel Act, signed by Bill Clinton, and the appointment of Kenneth Starr as Independent Counsel revived inquiries into connections between the president, the Madison Guaranty Savings and Loan Association of Arkansas, and the Whitewater Development Company. Picking up where his predecessor Robert Fiske left off, Starr set out to uncover whether James MacDougal, the head of Madison, illegally siphoned money into Clinton's gubernatorial campaign and the Whitewater vacation home development, co-owned by the Clintons and MacDougal. In these early stages of the Starr investigation, the focus remained on alleged financial improprieties, none of which arose as sufficiently concrete to challenge Clinton's presidency.

Instead, the presidential crisis evolved from a 1994 lawsuit brought against Clinton by former Arkansas state employee Paula Corbin Jones.[3] Initially a backdrop to the Whitewater inquiry, Jones' sexual harassment suit against Clinton set in motion the scandal that eventually became the driving force behind Starr's presidential misconduct investigation. At the outset, Jones's allegations that the president sexually propositioned her while Governor of Arkansas did not seem destined to bring down the Clinton presidency. Not until the start of Clinton's second term in office when the Supreme Court rejected the administration's effort to delay the lawsuit, did it become clearer that Jones's lawsuit could be more pernicious than anticipated.

Act II: Presidential Crisis

Launching the chain of events leading to Clinton's impeachment, a former White House intern, Monica Lewinsky, was called in January 1998 to testify in

the Jones lawsuit deposition. Initially denying an improper relationship with
the president, Lewinsky was forced to revise her story when a former colleague
and friend, Linda Tripp, presented Ken Starr with taped telephone conversations of Lewinsky documenting her affair with Clinton. Repudiating this evidence publicly and in his deposition, the president adamantly rejected accusations of a sexual relationship with "that woman, Ms. Lewinsky." Despite these
denials, a court panel authorized Starr's investigation of the Lewinsky-Clinton
relationship.

Starr first raised the possibility of charging Clinton with perjury and
obstruction of justice in August, following Lewinsky's grand jury appearance.
Confronted with Lewinsky's detailed testimony, Clinton finally conceded his
"improper" relationship with the White House intern to Starr's grand jury,
offering a public apology for his behavior. But he flatly refused to accept Starr's
charge that he falsely characterized his relationship with Lewinsky in his Jones'
lawsuit deposition, arguing that he employed a more narrow definition of "sexual" than that used by prosecutors. In response to the obstruction of justice
charges, Clinton denied that he pressured administration staffers to lie or
destroy evidence of his affair, including doing away with gifts he had given
Lewinsky. Starr nevertheless deemed the evidence sufficiently substantial to
recommend that House leaders consider impeachment proceedings against
President Clinton. Representatives were provided with 36 boxes containing
copies of Starr's Independent Counsel report graphically detailing Clinton's
sexual relationship with Lewinsky, grand jury testimony, and other critical evidence. The Starr report was also released to the public on the Internet and in a
monograph, provoking much debate over whether the lurid descriptions of the
president's affair should have been kept private.

Act III: Impeachment and Trial

After considering the assembled evidence, House members voted 258–176
along partisan lines to investigate grounds for impeaching the president on
charges of perjury, obstruction of justice, and abuse of power. While the Judiciary Committee considered Starr's case against Clinton, the House recessed to
prepare for the November midterm elections. Despite Republican efforts to
increase their majorities in Congress, voters unexpectedly gave Democrats five
more House seats and left unchanged the Senate's partisan balance in a marked
departure from most midterm elections where the president's party generally
loses seats. Widely regarded as a repudiation of Congressional Republicans'

support for impeachment, the election seemed to signal public exhaustion with scandals and partisan conflict. This sentiment was confirmed when exit polls indicated opposition to House impeachment hearings, with voters supporting the president's retention of power and voicing disapproval of Congress' administration of the impeachment proceedings.[4]

Although lacking a clear public mandate for impeachment, the House Judiciary Committee voted on December 12 to approve all four articles of impeachment. By a vote of 21 to 16 along party lines, committee members endorsed Article I, charging the president with giving "perjurious, false, and misleading testimony" in his August grand jury testimony. A slightly smaller margin of 20 to 17 members voted for Article II, alleging Clinton committed perjury in his Jones deposition testimony. In two separate votes of 21 to 16, the Judiciary Committee sanctioned Articles III and IV, accusing Clinton of manipulating witness testimony and abusing his power by falsely or incompletely responding to 81 questions posed by the committee about his extramarital affair.

Four days later on December 16, 1998, the full House, in defiance of public sentiment, voted to impeach President Clinton on two of the articles. A slim majority of 228 to 206 representatives voted to impeach Clinton on Article I, accusing him of lying under oath in his grand jury testimony. An even smaller margin of 221 to 212 house members supported Article II, impeaching the president for tampering with witnesses and obstructing justice. House members rejected charges that Clinton perjured himself in the Jones deposition and abused his power by inaccurately responding to Judiciary Committee questions. Illustrating the depth of the disjuncture between the public and their elected representatives, a New York Times/CBS poll found that on the eve of Clinton's impeachment, 72 percent of Americans approved of his job performance, up from 66 percent the previous week.

After the Christmas recess, the Senate prepared to go to trial to decide President Clinton's fate, with Chief Justice William Renhquist swearing in 100 senators as jurors. Lacking a solid precedent on how to proceed with the trial, senators spent over two weeks arguing the merits of reintroducing witnesses to testify and calling an early vote to censure rather than dismiss the president. Determined to avoid the rancorous partisanship marking House impeachment proceedings, the Senate focused on securing bipartisan support for the trial procedures. After much debate, senators finally agreed to a trial lasting two weeks, allowing arguments from both House managers (i.e., prosecutors) and Clinton's defense team.

After almost five years of Independent Counsel investigations and scandals clouding the Clinton presidency, the Senate trial concluded on February 12.

Along primarily party lines, the Senate voted to acquit President Clinton on both articles of impeachment, failing to muster the 67 member plurality required by the Constitution to remove a president from office. In a 55–45 vote against Article I, senators dismissed the perjury charges and in an even split, rejected the obstruction of justice accusations laid out in Article III. Significantly, the Senate's acquittal of President Clinton served to narrow the perceptible gap between political elites in Congress and the public on the question of Bill Clinton's fate by preserving his presidency and freeing Congress to return to governing the nation.

NOTES

1. Polls reporting these results include The Gallup Poll, January 1999, The Gallop Organization; *The New York Times*/CBS News Poll, December 20, 1998; and in an analysis of an ABC News/*Washington Post* poll by Gary E. Langer, "Clinton Support Intact: Public Opinion Backs President, Opposes Calling Witness," January 11, 1999, ABC News Polling Unit, ABCNews.Com.

2. See analysis of ABC News/*Washington Post* poll by Gary E. Langer, "Public Yearns for Trial's End: Clinton Support Strong Despite Trial," February 8, 1999, ABC News Polling Unit, ABCNews.com.

3. On November 13, 1998, Clinton and his legal team agreed to pay an $850,000 settlement to Paula Jones to put an end to the lawsuit. While still denying the charges leveled against him, Clinton was advised by his legal team to settle with Jones to avoid disclosure of any more incriminating information, particularly on the eve of a possible impeachment trial.

4. See analysis of exit poll results from the November 1998 midterm elections in R. W. Apple, "Analysis: In the End, Voters React to Issues," November 4, 1998, *The New York Times* On the Web, www. NYTimes.com.

CHAPTER 22

The "Hard Case" for Presidential Power: Impeachment Politics and Law

Richard M. Pious

Can Neustadt's concepts help us analyze the Clinton impeachment? Neustadt will speak for himself in any future edition of *Presidential Power*, but what about the rest of us? Are his concepts a useful addition to our analytic tool kits? At first glance one might think not. For one thing, Neustadt offered his analysis for practitioners rather than as a method for scholars.[1] For another, he observed in revised editions of his work that with "power obsessed individuals" such as Johnson and Nixon, power stakes theory might need to be supplemented by individual and institutional constraints.[2] Finally, in Neustadt's phrase, the impeachment of Clinton is a "hard case," unlike Iran-Contra, which clearly illustrated the problems faced by an inattentive president dealing with zealous aides. Does not Clinton's affair and coverup—the alleged perjury and obstruction of justice—illustrate precisely the pathological behavior Neustadt's critics have advanced against his supposedly Machiavellian and amoral analysis of presidential power?

Neustadt's concepts have twofold use here: first, prospectively their use would have constrained Clinton had he only thought about power stakes, reputation, and the Washington Community; second, retrospectively these concepts can help presidency scholars analyze what went wrong and why. I also want to point out how Neustadt's methods can be integrated into some of the other methodological strands of presidential studies. Finally, I want to suggest, in the spirit of Neustadt's work on the presidency at mid-century, the impact on the presidency of the Clinton scandal.

SCANDAL AS A HARD CASE

At first glance this case seems to be about scandals and constitutional law. What does it have to do with Neustadt's concepts? A lot, as it turns out, because Neustadt was primarily concerned with the president more than the presidency, with the man more than the office, with individual choice more than institutional decision. In this case, as in Watergate and Iran-Contra, Neustadt's observation holds true that accomplices or adversaries take confidential matters public at great cost to the president. The incumbents mortgage themselves to those involved in their affairs, whether official or personal, and they pay interest on the mortgages to maintain confidentiality. Coverups expose presidents to political and legal costs, and become more serious than the original affairs.[3]

Clinton failed to understand his power stakes, and consequently jeopardized and destroyed his reputation within the Washington Community.[4] As Neustadt put it about Nixon's decision to cover up the Watergate burglary: "the short-run intangibles again seem to have overshadowed long-run risks."[5] The Clinton scandal demonstrates the limits of presidential power and influence even—or especially—in private matters. There are limits to the presidential power to persuade.[6] Clinton could not order Monica Lewinsky's silence, nor command her to return gifts and conceal the existence of the affair. He could offer inducements to encourage her to lie low, such as the possibility of using presidential contacts (e.g., Vernon Jordan) in her job search. But there were limits on presidential influence: as the scandal developed, Lewinsky was influenced far more by her own legal team than by the White House. As in most instances of presidential failure, influence (and even command) is eventually trumped by law and by individual interest. So it was in the steel seizure and desegregation cases that began Neustadt's analysis; so it was with the Clinton scandals.

Neustadt described a system of separated institutions sharing power and competing for the power of decisionmaking, an insight known well to public law practitioners and dating from Madison's theory of partial separation of powers.[7] The president is not prosecutor-in-chief: his law enforcement powers are shared with Congress and the courts. Clinton did not control Attorney General Janet Reno's decisions about an independent counsel, and had neither power nor influence with the Special Division of the Court of Appeals for the District of Columbia, the unit that supervised the work of the Independent Counsel.

And so, in many respects the Clinton caper illustrates the failure of presidential influence with which Neustadt's work began. There were initial flawed decisions by a president who did not look ahead, did not calculate where and when he would be vulnerable, and did not understand the limits of persuasion and influence in a complex constitutional system. As with many of Neustadt's cases, this one involves the failed deployment of prerogative power: attempts to assert presidential immunity from civil suit in the Paula Jones case; attempts to "stonewall" the Independent Counsel with claims of executive, protective, and attorney-client privilege; attempts to avoid subpoenas and testimony before congressional bodies, all of which prolonged the proceedings but did not ultimately prevent the gist of his extramarital affair from being investigated and reported. In some respects, the case also seems to fit neatly into an "overshoot and collapse" model of prerogative power. The president was overruled on most of his legal claims (all but attorney-client privilege applying to the deceased Vince Foster). He ultimately settled with Paula Jones on the sexual harassment suit she initiated against him, having lost his immunity bid and facing a revival of the case after the initial dismissal was overturned by the Court of Appeals. His answers to the 81 questions asked by the House of Representatives and his unwillingness to admit that he perjured himself ignited a firestorm in the House leading to his impeachment.

And yet, for both the Neustadt and the prerogative power approaches, this case is harder to analyze than it initially seems. Unlike the Watergate and Iran-Contra scandals, the White House was not paralyzed, either in its public relations or governmental functions. Consider issues of approval and prestige outside of the Washington Community. Clinton did not drop in approval ratings: on the contrary, he rose in the polls to the high 60s after his 1998 State of the Union Address, remained in the 60s through all the revelations of the Starr Report and the House release of his videotaped grand jury testimony, rose close to 70 percent after being impeached by the House, and wound up with approval ratings over 70 percent after his 1999 State of the Union Address.[8] Bill and Hillary Clinton were voted, once again, the "most admired" man and woman in the U.S. in a Gallup Annual Survey: Clinton's own vote rose from 14 percent of respondents the previous year to 18 percent in 1998.[9] Asked in an ABC News Poll, "Which President in your lifetime do you think did the best job, worst job" Clinton came in second on "best job" (22%) to Reagan, and third (after Nixon and Reagan) on "worst job (14%)."[10] An Andrew Johnson or Richard Nixon he was not.

Unlike his predecessors, Clinton's presidency was not rendered impotent. Clinton gained room to maneuver with both the 1998 and 1999 State of the

Union Addresses. Perhaps because the Republicans hoped for a "pure play" on impeachment, they sidestepped the traps he set for them in budget negotiations in the Fall of 1998 and gave Clinton more than half of the administration's budget requests, preventing a budget shutdown but allowing the White House to retain much more influence than one would have expected in governance.

Clinton continued to demonstrate his mastery of spatial positioning in setting the public agenda. After his 1999 State of the Union Address, 77 percent of the public approved of his speech, and 50 percent trusted Clinton more than the Republicans to deal with issues (32 percent favored the Republican Congress), including the Republican perennial, cutting taxes.[11] Clinton made Kenneth Starr and the Republicans as much of an issue as his own conduct, portrayed his administration as moderate and pragmatic and the Republicans as extremists engaged in reckless conduct, and forced his opponents to do most of the explaining and apologizing. His own party, however reluctantly, united behind him; Republicans splintered, costing a Speaker (Newt Gingrich) and Speaker-designate (Robert Livingston) their careers, and pitting hardliners against moderates, governors against legislators, and corporate constituencies against the religious right. If he had no sense of power stakes at the beginning of this affair, Clinton was blessed with opponents who had no such sense at the end.

CONGRESSIONAL POWER STAKES

Neustadt's concepts are also useful if we turn the case around and focus on congressional decisions. Initially Gingrich as House Speaker thought of establishing a special committee to receive the referral from the Independent Counsel that might well have buried the Starr report. The Judiciary Committee mobilized its conservative constituencies, and put enough pressure on Gingrich so that it retained jurisdiction. Mobilized (or intimidated) by its rightwing base, the leadership decided on a different tack: release the Starr report, dump the documents, roll the videotapes of Clinton's grand jury testimony. Starr and the House Republicans lost reputation and prestige immediately: they were framed by their Democratic opponents as partisan, vindictive, unfair, and overzealous. Starr was compared to Victor Hugo's Javert in *Les Miserables*, and portrayed as relentlessly hounding his president unto death; he was conducting a star chamber, intimidating witnesses (the president's secretary Betty Currie and Monica Lewinsky's mother). Ultimately, Starr became (for those who remember their constitutional history) a modern-day Edmund Burke, pursuing Warren Hastings on "widows and orphans" charges; he was not perceived as a Special Prosecutor but at one point was viewed as a pornographer, providing salacious materials for release by Congress on the Internet. The House actions fed into the public's general suspicion of government prosecutions: 69 percent of the public said a tape of grand jury testimony should not be released; 59 percent believed releasing the tape had more to do with embarrassing the president than anything else. Congress's approval ratings dropped sharply, from 56 to 44 percent after the release.

There was no evidence that House managers were thinking ahead, or that they understood their power stakes as the Judiciary Committee moved forward with articles of impeachment. If the House voted to impeach, members feared developments would move beyond their control, and since the Senate was not likely to convict, the House would eventually face repudiation, in a classic "backlash" situation. If the House decided to censure the President or invoke another type of rebuke, however, it would have retained control over the language of its denunciation (rather than cede to the Senate). This tactic would have been in tune with public opinion and with the results of the midterm election. Instead, the House went for a riskier but, in its estimation, not an irrational decision. Not only was impeachment popular with Republican primary and general election constituencies in about 180 House districts, but it also might set in motion events that would topple Clinton. Just before the House vote, a national poll was released that indicated that 58 percent of the public believed that Clinton should not "fight" impeachment but should resign if the House did vote to impeach.[12] Unfortunately the poll wording was misleading: Americans don't like conflict, and when the wording was changed to "defend himself in a Senate trial" support for resignation dropped precipitously into the 30 percent range. At the same time, two-thirds of the public believed that the House impeached the president on political grounds, and as the House approval rating sagged, Clinton's rose.[13]

Senators from both parties seemed to have a much better sense about the intersection of the constitutional and popular law of impeachment. They understood the need to guard their reputation for acting judiciously and with bipartisanship, and the need to focus on perjury or obstruction of justice, not sexual conduct. Even so, the Republican leadership understood it was faced with a classic dilemma: if it voted to convict and won, the Democrats would get Gore in the White House before the 2000 elections, giving him a chance for up to ten years in office; if it voted to convict and lost, Clinton would argue that he had been vindicated; if it voted to do anything less than hold a trial and have a vote on articles of impeachment, it would be taken as a repudiation of the House's vote to impeach (particularly if it voted for censure). Republican leaders settled on a minimal strategy: avoid infighting, prevent a revolt of the backbenchers, and "kick the can down the road" to placate the House managers and the conservative base of the party. Permit at least the semblance of a trial without letting it get out of hand, and minimize losses with the American people by trying to act judiciously and in accordance with the rule of law.

Understanding their power stakes, Republican Senators agreed with their Democrat counterparts on rules that created an incremental process of decision designed to be calibrated as circumstances developed. The Senators would not be passive "jurors" but would be making their own choices and decisions. Members of the House were effectively converted into supplicants (Justice Committee Chairman Henry Hyde implored senators for a "pitiful three" witnesses near the end). The bipartisan agreement took away power from Chief Justice Rehnquist as well. Under the "Rules of Procedure and Practice in the Senate When Sitting on Impeachment Trials," which would have governed deliberations in the absence of the bipartisan agreement, all motions on evidence, including calling of witnesses, would have been decided by the presiding officer. Under the agreement, the Senators themselves voted about deposing witnesses, then about calling witnesses to the Senate floor, and about what evidence would and would not be admissible. Even the final set of procedures, passed by a partisan Republican vote, allowed Minority Leader Daschle a "co-veto" along with Majority Leader Lott over the witnesses and evidence.

Contrast this strategic approach to the rules of the game with the performance of House managers, who were effectively reduced at the end to throwing "Hail Mary" passes on fourth down and long. *Maybe* a witness would implicate the president in obstruction of justice; *maybe* Clinton would provoke a new backlash by refusing to answer ten questions or by refusing to testify; *maybe* after public opinion shifted Clinton would resign; *maybe* after all the evidence was in, the votes for conviction would materialize; *maybe* if the votes were not there in the Senate, the public would rally to the Republican side, limiting the overall damage in the next elections. These were all speculations and long-shots. By the endgame the Republicans had 2–1 unfavorable ratings while Democrats had 2–1 favorable ratings; Republicans were down five House seats, had lost a Speaker and Speaker designate, and had suffered the indignity of having several members "outed" for adultery. The public disapproved of Starr and Barr, of Hyde and Lott, it wanted the trial to end when Republicans insisted it continue, it disapproved of calling witnesses by 55 to 39 percent, and was critical of the manner in which Republicans were conducting the trial, with 37 percent approving and 54 percent disapproving.[14] The stated goal of House managers, to remove the president from office, did not command public support at the endgame: by about two to one in most national polls that option was rejected in favor of simple acquittal or some form of censure and rebuke, which commanded support of three out of five Americans.[15] A significant share of the electorate (around one-fifth) was telling pollsters just prior to the final vote that a vote to convict would have a negative impact on their evaluation of their own senator in the next election, with about one-quarter of Republican rank and file opposed to the congressional party's policies.

RATIONAL CHOICE AND IMPEACHMENT POLITICS

In certain respects formal modeling and rational choice approaches to political power have descended from Neustadt's insights (see Cameron's essay, chapter 5 in this volume). It would be easy to conclude however, that Clinton's behavior and the congressional response are not susceptible to analysis with rational choice methodologies. But techniques and concepts used by its practitioners are helpful in answering certain questions, or at least framing the issues. Why, given the early, consistent, and overwhelming indicators from public opinion polling that pursuing the president was counterproductive, could not Republicans work their way to the apparent middle point of censure early in the proceedings? Why instead would Republicans, in essence, play "kick the can" on railroad tracks with a speeding locomotive bearing down on them? Why would they be willing to pay the costs of dragging things out?

One insight comes from the concept of a decisional heresthetic: just as no one wanted to be the one to allow a red flag over Saigon, in this case no one wanted to hoist a white flag of surrender against the adversary. The decisional rule for Lyndon Johnson in Vietnam and for Gingrich and Senate Majority Leader Trent Lott in impeachment was to do as little as possible consistent with avoiding an unacceptable surrender of position. Particularly in the Senate, these decisional rules bought time, established credibility (and some measure of dignity), and protected legislators with their core constituencies. Even taking losses can be "rational." The U.S. might not win in Vietnam, but it would impress allies and adversaries with the losses it was willing to take. So too with impeachment: Republicans might not win, but they would impress their constituents with their willingness to act in the face of general public opinion. Later they could move beyond their base with a legislative program and make up lost ground. Or so they thought.

Insights about "games of chicken" are useful. Who blinked first, Clinton or
Starr? Clinton or the House? Clinton or the Senate? In each game, Clinton took
not only a tough position, but also an irrevocable public stance, somewhat akin
to a pre-commitment in game theory. He was like the driver who puts on a
blindfold or the scientist who arms a Doomsday machine. Consider the variations of claims Clinton might have chosen during the scandal and how little he
moved from them until he was caught out by forensic evidence: (a) there is a
zone of privacy and the president need not respond to these allegations; (b)
there was no sexual relationship, no inappropriate relationship, and no perjury
or obstruction of justice; (c) there was an inappropriate relationship but no sex
and no perjury or obstruction of justice; (d) there was sex but no perjury or
obstruction of justice; (e) there was sex, perjury, and obstruction of justice but
it isn't an impeachable offense. The president had choices not only in describing facts and law, but also in providing emotional spin. He could have done any
of the following: (a) expressed outrage at invasion of privacy; (b) shown
bemusement or anger at inaccurate and scandalous reports about him and
Monica Lewinsky; (c) apologized for inappropriate actions that hurt him, his
family, and the nation; (d) come out with the strongest possible apology and
remorse for his sexual activities; (e) thrown himself on the mercy of Congress,
Courts, and country for illegal activities. We know that Clinton lied to the
nation about the affair until it could no longer be sustained, he limited his
apologies and remorse, and continued to maintain that he did not perjure
himself nor obstruct justice.

Clinton may have believed these were rational moves. They put supporters
and followers on notice that he would fight to the end, and that either he or his
opponents would remain standing. But there is a "time-weighted" aspect here:
early moves in these games gain value, late moves lose value. Presidential truth-
fulness gains high marks early on, but is worth much less after a period of
deception. Eisenhower found this out with the U-2 affair, Kennedy with the
Bay of Pigs, Johnson with Vietnam, Nixon with Watergate, and Reagan with
Iran-Contra. What seems rational (stonewall and fight with a seemingly irrevocable position) on one dimension becomes irrational and counterproductive
on another, especially when Clinton was forced to concede points about the
nature of his relationship with Monica Lewinsky.

The key question for the rational choice theorist might be: where is the core
or the core agreement? Is there some stable equilibrium point, or some package
deal, that would provide equivalent or greater incentives to a congressional
majority than a final vote on impeachment or the perjury and obstruction of
justice charges? There are several problems with a spatial positioning model

attempting to find such a point on one dimension, where one might expect to determine a solution. One might array the various possible results along a punishment dimension: no referral by the Independent Counsel; no referral by House leadership to Judiciary Committee; no referral by Judiciary Committee to full House; no vote to impeach by House; censure by House; censure plus by House, passage of Articles of Impeachment by House. Similarly one might array the possible results in the Senate: early vote of dismissal; censure or censure plus without trial; truncated trial followed by dismissal, censure, or censure plus; full trial with witnesses in Senate followed by acquittal; full trial followed by acquittal and censure or censure plus; full trial followed by acquittal on charges, but sense of Senate that charges were true; conviction on charges, removal from office, and disqualification to hold public office again. The American people, by a three to two margin, wanted censure from the House, and having failing to get it, wanted censure from the Senate. This was the middle position. They did not want the House to impeach and they did not want a full Senate trial, yet they got both. Why couldn't Clinton, given his popularity and the difficulty from day one of winning a conviction against him, escape impeachment? Why did the micro-rationality of individual members overwhelm the macro-rationality for the legislative parties taken as a whole? Why did Republicans demonstrate 100 percent party cohesion on votes that might well cost them their majority position in the next election?[16]

Republicans departed from a rational spatial choice for several reasons, none of them irrational. For one, they may well have remembered that they never do well when divided on a big-ticket issue when Democrats are united: their splits in 1973–74 and 1985–86 ("Republicans heading for the tall grass," as Pat Buchanan put it) cost both Nixon (Watergate) and Reagan (Iran-Contra) dearly. For another, they may well have remembered that they never do well when their leadership brokers a bipartisan deal in which much of the right-wing rank-and-file base is cut out; the 1990 and 1995 budget debacles provide two examples. They do not like to get taken in by White House compromise positions and have been outmaneuvered each time by Clinton when they moved to the middle. "The power of trying impeachments was lodged in this body as more likely to be governed by cool and candid investigation, than by heats that too often inflame and influence more populous assemblies," explained James McHenry to the Maryland House of Delegates during the ratification debates, and in general the Senate has acted coolly in impeachments.[17] But in this case, it could not be seen to be acting so, at least not by its electoral base.

Another complex element for rational choice theorists is that there is a nested game problem. Clinton's impeachment testimony was nested in a larger legal process, which involved threat of indictment. A censure resolution or statement of facts, depending on how they could have been worded, were also nested in the indictment question. The House and Senate impeachment votes were also nested in electoral games. Yet another complexity for formal theorists is that the spatial positioning is multidimensional. This means not only that no core agreement is likely to be mathematically specified, but also that outcomes were subject to cycling, in which institutional norms and voting rules, or minorities with decisive position, determined the outcome. At least that seemed to be how Majority Whip Tom DeLay could keep the House from an immediate censure vote. Some of the dimensions seemed to involve valences, which collapse policy space from "more or less" into a simple "yes or no, right or wrong, up or down" binary notation, particularly within the extremes of each party. In the end the House leadership constructed the agenda so that censure was not an option, ending the chaos. It came down to "impeach" or "let him go."

There is one fruitful fusion of methods, however, that this case reveals. What William Riker, one of the founders of rational choice theory, called "heresthetics" is based on what public law practitioners know as rules, procedures, and constitutional law.[18] "There is nothing more terrifying," Alexis De Tocqueville observed about American impeachments "than the vagueness of American laws when they are defining political crimes properly so called."[19] In this case, the heresthetics played the determinative role, but they were not known in advance. In this as in many important cases, the rules that determined the results were improvised by the winning coalition as it went along. And in the case of impeachment, improvisation by majority rule is risky: an extraordinary majority is needed to complete an act initiated by an ordinary majority, so a heresthetic rule may bring you close to victory but then be repudiated by a one-third plus one minority at the very end. Who ultimately lost on the heresthetic of defining "High Crimes and Misdemeanors?" One could argue the proposition either way: the House vote would seem to indicate that routine felonies, insofar as the president commits them, constitute a high crime or misdemeanor because they weaken respect for the law. On the other hand, the Senate's failure to provide an extraordinary majority to convict, all the while assuming that the crimes (at least obstruction of justice) had been committed, would seem to constitute a rebuke to the House's position, leaving the constitutional precedent indeterminate.

Still a final fusion should be considered: one of Neustadt's theory with critical path theory. In presidential business not all choices are open at all times. The game is not like a possibility frontier or a smooth policy space in which infinite calibrations of position are possible to achieve a desired outcome. Policy space (or a possibility frontier) is not frictionless but lumpy. Discrete options emerge out of discrete processes. Presidential decisionmaking follows paths akin to a set of native-American trails in the wilderness or the swampy waterways of the Everglades. One gets to a destination by choosing paths that intersect with or diverge from others. One may have to retrace one's steps, go back to an earlier position, or adopt a previously rejected process in order to recalibrate for a desired result. Resilience, navigational skills, and a certain amount of backwoodsman's luck count for a lot.

And so we are back to Neustadt's insights, which may be useful in rethinking rational choice methodology so that it can be helpful in presidential hard cases. Game moves are analogous to the moves and countermoves developed through power stakes analysis. But these moves are subject to valences, akin to the reputational problems outlined by Neustadt. How do you make moves that enhance your reputation rather than detract from it? How do you shift position without looking as if you are waffling, retreating, giving up your principles? Bush could not do it successfully in the budget summit of 1990. Neither could Republicans in the House in 1998. Then there is the problem of prestige, of public opinion and approval ratings. In an anti-political culture, it is difficult to retreat, difficult to compromise (i.e., move laterally on the "more or less" spatial dimension) without losing public support for acting like a politician rather than a person of principle. Ultimately there are so many dimensions involved, and so many valences, it is better for the president to calibrate and navigate than to calculate mathematically, especially when the mathematics are unlikely in any event to provide a valid core agreement. If there is a methodology to be used, it is more likely to be risk management using decision-trees, than it is to involve spatial positioning or game matrices.

Last, after analyzing the Watergate and Iran-Contra models, Neustadt observed that power stakes analysis needed to be supplemented by other approaches to calculation. His conclusion was that backward mapping—backward induction in game theoretic language—was required: one needs to determine the final thing that must be done to complete a successful policy initiative, and then ask: what is the sequence of events by which the final act takes place? What should precede it? And what should precede that act? This regress to the initial decision point, this reversal of perspective, supplements power stakes analysis: Neustadt believes that both the prospective and the retrospective methods should be employed.[20] In more formal terms, the techniques of critical path analysis, critical event analysis, high reliability theory, normal accident analysis, rare event analysis (and walk back the cat techniques adapted from the intelligence community) might well be used by presidential scholars.

THE PRESIDENCY THE END OF THE CENTURY

After Andrew Johnson's Impeachment, there was no backlash against the assertion of irresponsible congressional power, but rather a weakening of the presidential office. To save himself, Johnson not only gave up all pretense at having the prerogatives of the commander-in-chief, but also gave up control of the War Department and his influence on Reconstruction. The aftermath of the Johnson impeachment until the McKinley and Theodore Roosevelt presidencies was a system of congressional government, as chronicled by Woodrow Wilson. During and after Watergate, a period of ethics reform (Campaign Finance Amendments of 1974, Ethics in Government Act of 1979), collaborative government (War Powers Act of 1973, Budget and Impoundment Act of 1974, Intelligence Oversight Act of 1980), and congressional micro-management (Clark Amendment of 1976, Boland Amendments of 1984–85), and what some have seen as the criminalization of politics (eighteen independent counsels authorized, five in the Clinton administration alone) ensued. Can we predict any patterns of governance emerging from the Clinton scandals? And do they comport with, or undercut, the thrust of Neustadt's argument?[21]

An answer to that question inevitably brings us to issues of political time and regime formation. Dealignment theorists suggested that political time as we know it might be ending, given the instability of voting patterns, the lessening of voter and other political participation rates, the public's lack of political knowledge and attentiveness, and the weakening of political parties. But perhaps new realignments are in the offing as a result of the Clinton scandal. Each party went to its base. Ideological divisions hardened, and if anything the "culture wars" became more salient. Perhaps in the next election some of the disaffected Republicans will defect, or even realign; or perhaps some of the more culturally conservative Democrats will finally abandon their party. Herewith three alternative scenarios for the post-Clinton scandal and impeachment, depending on which party benefited from such a realigning election.

In scenario I, involving a surge toward the Democrats, we would (retrospectively) say that public had divorced the personal and private from the political. The Democratic position on impeachment would have been validated. The White House effort to dominate public opinion and to use that domination to induce Democrats to remain on board would have moved the nation further toward a plebiscitary presidency. Neustadt's analysis in *Presidential Power* gave shorter shrift to public opinion and prestige than he and other analysts did later (see Smith's and Heith's essays [chapters 6 and 17] and Jacobs and Shapiro's concluding chapter); he saw it at the time as primarily a means to influence Washington elites. In the Clinton scandal we come full circle, for "going public" was exactly how Clinton could influence the Washington Community. A president who once intended to move past Congress and mobilize the public by direct action wound up in this instance going back to the original Neustadt model to parley public support into party cohesion. Although the Independent Counsel defeated the White House in the courts on many issues of evidence (executive privilege, protective privilege, and attorney-client privilege all being denied, as well as a civil immunity claim), in this scenario a Democratic Congress might be expected to look long and hard at the provisions of the Ethics in Government Act that deal with the independent counsel, and if it were ever revived, it might well be as an appendage to the Justice Department. It might also overturn some of the adverse court decisions.

In this scenario Clinton's escape from the noose would lead to a new kind of presidential image, uneasily coexisting with all the other "hats" worn by the president: now the black hat of the "outlaw" president, carrying all the resentments of the popular culture against the media, against elites, against the hall monitors and principals, against everyone that creates and enforces "the Rules." We could be in for another period, much like the Jacksonian period, in which the presidency infuses a stuffy meritocratic political culture with some celebrity, transgression, sin and redemption. While the Jesse James presidency is a logical cultural offshoot of a Clinton acquittal, it is difficult to see how either of the 1999–2000 Democratic contenders (Al Gore? Bill Bradley?) would advance that kind of image. And Republicans (other than John McCain) do not seem to be into cultural transgression either. So the impact of acquittal on the political culture (and American morality) could easily be overstated.

The second scenario posits a Republican realignment. This could be based on a "hangover" syndrome (some shame about Clinton's acquittal), the possibility of some new scandal or a successful criminal suit brought against the president by Starr, or a weakening of the economy, or some foreign crisis poorly handled. In this scenario, a Republican realignment (retrospectively), would lead to the fusion of the personal and private with the public responsibility of office. It would reinforce the anti-political atmosphere in Washington, in which movement to the center and willingness to compromise would be taken as moral weakness. Such a realignment would vindicate the scorched earth strategy of the more extreme Republican right. In this scenario we would move into uncharted territory, into new political time, in which new forms of religio-political governance were attempted by a nascent regime unlike any other in American political history.

A third scenario, perhaps most likely, is another flipflop in party control back to 1969–1993 patterns. George W. Bush or some other Republican assumes the presidency, as Gore or Bradley reenact the failed Walter Mondale campaign of 1984 (proving once again that boring the public, given the public's past percep- tions of Gore and Bradley, is not a good strategy). The Democrats regain control of Congress as a sliver of voters in individual states and districts cross over in retrospective voting against the Clinton impeachment. In this scenario, there really are no long-term implications of the Clinton scandal other than the bits of constitutional case law that emerge from the federal courts. Patterns of stale- mate punctuated by policy breakthroughs resume in pre-Clinton patterns.

Whichever scenario holds, there is one long-term development that will come out of this scandal, and it will weaken the office of the president. "I love dish! I live for dish!" exclaimed Lucienne Goldberg, in talking about her role in encouraging Linda Tripp to get the goods on Clinton.[22] A scandal- industrial complex now serves up infotainment about politicians' peccadil- loes. Agents market proposals by authors, columnists, investigators and jour- nalists for books, cable and network mini-series, and other projects; bounties are offered for the scalps of leading players. In the new economics of scandal, information and revelations fetch the most just at the point when a pol has gotten near the top. The result is an inversion of the traditional norms: those who were once protected from all inquiry (and who enjoyed their own version of *droit du seignior*) are now the top quarries. Neustadt recently pointed out that politicians have become increasingly sophisticated in manipulating the public with public relations and spin, and yet have ended up with a citizenry that knows it is being manipulated and has less and less respect for the politicians doing it.[23] The scandal market can only make that irony worse.

In talking about impeachment and of the possibility of legislative tyranny, de Tocqueville warned that if American democracy degenerated, we would know it when "the number of political judgments increases."[24] This is one of the dangers we now face as a result of the Clinton impeachment.

NOTES

1. Richard Neustadt, *Presidential Power and the Modern Presidents* (New York: John Wiley and Sons, 1990), p. 293.

2. Ibid., pp. 292–93.

3. Ibid., p. 212.

4. Ibid., pp. 50, 150–51.

5. Ibid., p. 212.

6. Ibid., p. 30.

7. James Madison, *Federalist* No. 51, in Alexander Hamilton, James Madison, and John Jay, *The Federalist Papers* (London: Bantam Books, 1982).

8. NBC News Poll, January 19, 1999 had Clinton at 76 percent approval; ABC News Poll of January 19, 1999, at 66 approval.

9. Gallup Annual Survey, January 2, 1999.

10. ABC News Poll, Sept. 11–15 1998.

11. ABC News Poll, January 19, 1999.

12. ABC/*Washington Post*, December 12–14, 1998.

13. Pew Poll, December 19–21, 1998.

14. Robert Barr, Republican Representative from Georgia, filed the first impeachment resolution against Clinton in November, 1997, over campaign finance charges. On witnesses, ABC News Poll, January 19, 1999; on approval of the trial, CNN/TIME, January 21–22. Democratic handling of the trial gained a 49 to 40 percent approval rating.

15. ABC/Washington Post Poll, January 8–10, 1999.

16. This is a classic collective action problem, which is the subject of a large literature on the importance of institutions, including parties (see John H. Aldrich, *Why Parties? The Origins and Transformations of Party Politics in American* (Chicago: University of Chicago Press, 1995).

17. Max Farrand, *Records of the Federal Convention* (New Haven: Yale University Press, 1966), p. 148.

18. William Riker, "Heresthetic in Fiction," *The Art of Political Manipulation* (New Haven: Yale University Press, 1986), p. 58.

19. Alexis de Tocqueville, *Democracy in America, Volume 1* (New York: Knopf, 1945), p. 109.

20. Neustadt, *Presidential Power and the Modern Presidents*, p. 214.

21. Although most of Neustadt's work dealt with the personal presidency, he was also interested in institutional analysis, both temporally and cross-nationally. See his two classic articles: Richard E. Neustadt, "The Presidency at Mid-Century" *Law and Contemporary Problems* 21 (3) (Autumn 1956): 609–645; Richard M.

Neustadt, "Shadow and Substance in Politics: The Presidency and Whitehall" *The Public Interest* 2 (Winter 1966): 55–69.

22. Jane Mayer, "Department of Accomplices," *The New Yorker*, February 2, 1998, p. 25.

23. Richard E. Neustadt, "The Politics of Mistrust," in Joseph Nye, et. al., eds., *Why People Don't Trust Government* (Cambridge: Harvard University Press, 1997) pp . 179–202.

24. Alexis de Tocqueville, *Democracy in America*, p. 111. Another translation of this section of de Tocqueville states this as "the number of political impeachments is increased" (Alexis de Tocqueville, *Democracy in America, Volume I* (The Henry Reeve Text, as revised by Francis Bowen and edited by Phillips Bradley), (New York: Vintage Books, 1945), p. 115.

CHAPTER 23

Conclusion: Presidential Power, Institutions, and Democracy

Lawrence R. Jacobs and Robert Y. Shapiro

INTRODUCTION

The essays in this volume, *Forging the Presidency*, show how the study of the presidency is unmistakably, though not exclusively, moving away from the direction charted by Richard Neustadt's *Presidential Power*. While Neustadt's classic work remains still, in effect, a beacon for the study of the presidency, it no longer offers a reliable roadmap embodying the consensus among contemporary scholars. The current study of the presidency is motivated by different concerns and is pursuing new theoretical and substantive research questions. Reevaluating Neustadt's place in presidential studies helpfully identifies future challenges both for presidents and scholars. New developments have also kindled further interest in particular aspects of American democracy.

In his own essay (chapter 20), Neustadt himself laments that today's presidency researchers are no longer motivated by the same concerns that prompted him to write *Presidential Power*. Neustadt had been motivated by a drive to *instruct* sitting presidents and to teach them the means and strategies for exercising genuine influence and power. Neustadt concludes, however, that today's students of the presidency fail to deliver research that politicians find pertinent, because they "dislike politics" and "pursu[e] regularities in political behavior. . . . [that] seem quixotic to practitioners." Tailoring research explicitly to produce advice that sitting presidents would consider useful now takes a backseat to more insular professional disputes over theory and methodology. Richard

Pious's essay (Chapter 22) engages this critique and examines the usefulness of *Presidential Power* and the approaches of today's students of the presidency in analyzing political power and politics in the impeachment of Bill Clinton.

The contemporary study of the presidency is also characterized by two additional departures, which we explore further here. First, most of the chapters in *Forging the Presidency*, and a growing proportion of research more generally, replace Neustadt's emphasis on the personal attributes of presidential power—bargaining skill, individual choices, and personal attributes—with a sharper emphasis on *institutions and political structures*. Second, whereas Neustadt largely focused on elites, current presidential studies devote increasing attention to the direct and institutionally induced relationship between presidents and public opinion. This latter departure makes more visible than in the past certain dilemmas of democracy. In reassessing *Presidential Power*'s place in presidential studies, we avoid replacing Neustadt's arguments with implausible extremes and caricaturing Neustadt's arguments, which still remain prescient decades after publication.

I. Toward an Institutional Analysis of the Presidency

Government institutions have never been altogether absent from presidential studies. The longstanding debate over whether America had a "government of men or institutions" assured that the topic was never ignored.[1] Indeed, historically, the longstanding tradition in scholarship on government and the executive branch has been to study the formal and legal characteristics of institutions.

Nor were institutions missing from Neustadt's analysis. The third chapter of *Presidential Power*, "The Power to Persuade," opens with an institutional analysis of the competitive sharing of powers created by the Constitution and the structural features of political parties and other political forces. Indeed, Neustadt built his theory of presidential power on this institutional analysis. However impressive the president's constitutional powers, chief executives still lacked the institutional capacity to master their political environment; whereas other members of the Washington political establishment possessed the constitutional and informal powers to resist successfully.

A. Neustadt's Presidency

If institutions were never exiled from presidential studies, it is nonetheless true that Neustadt's theorizing and analysis focused on the personal choices of presidents and on the variations in the skills and temperament across individual presidents. Neustadt, in effect, held institutions constant by assuming that the president's constitutional powers and institutional capacity were fixed and that variations in presidential power were a function of differential skills in bargaining. The importance of institutional context—"the separateness of institutions and the sharing of authority," was that it "prescribes the terms on which a President persuades."[2]

According to Neustadt, the power-conscious and skilled president would enter into reciprocal exchanges with Washington influentials. The effective president would take advantage of Washingtonians' dependence on his formal authority in order to persuade them that "what the White House wants of them is what they ought to do for their sake and on their authority."[3] In short, Neustadt and the paradigm associated with *Presidential Power* analytically treated presidential influence as an outgrowth of the personal ability of individual officeholders rather than as an attribute of institutional capacity.

B. INSTITUTIONAL ANALYSIS OF THE PRESIDENCY

Much recent research—as reflected in several of this volume's essays—has rejected Neustadt's emphasis on the personal basis of power in favor of an analysis of institutions and political structures.[4] Scholars have redirected analytic attention from the individual attributes of specific presidents to factors and patterns of behavior that transcend any one president. Presidential studies have been increasingly defining the problems that presidents face, the resources that they possesses, and the decisions made in the president's name within the context of the institutions and political structures in which the executive operates.

Presidential studies have devoted greater attention to institutions for two reasons. First, this shift reflects real-world developments. Since the 1930s, the national government and presidents in particular have been inundated not only by a growing number of demands from constituents and pressure groups for economic, legal, and other sorts of traditional assistance, but also by a qualitative change in the nature of these demands. Ever since the early 1990s, presidents have faced rising expectations to manage ever more fluid world markets and complex military and diplomatic challenges that no longer fit into a simple East-West or North-South divide. Added to this has been the press's increasing scrutiny of government and especially the president. Thus the politics as well as the problems facing the presidency have become increasingly complex. To the extent that presidents have fallen short in handling these complexities (far more consequential than Bill Clinton's private behavior for the presidency), they have contributed to the unprecedented public cynicism toward politics and government that arose during the 1960s and 1970s and that has continued to characterize public attitudes at this writing.[5]

As far back as 1937, the growing demands on presidents prompted the Brownlow Commission to recommend that "the President needs help."[6] The effort to meet these growing demands contributed to a genuine "swelling of the presidency," characterized by an expansion in the executive branch and the institutional arm of the presidency (the Executive Office of the President [EOP]). The growing demands on the president to take responsibility for foreign policy and domestic issues (such as the budget process) fuelled an accelerated rise in the number and responsibilities of his staff, offices, and agencies.

In this new century, the reality is that this executive office is a corporate body; many actions taken in the name of the president are made with little personal involvement by the president and are implemented by other agencies and individuals. "Presidential action" is generally not the product of the chief executive's behavior but of the interactions of many individuals and organizations within the EOP. The essays in this volume that examine the White House staff and staff agencies (such as the Office of Management and Budget [OMB]) simply reflect, on one level, the fundamental reality that the size, complexity, and organizational capacity of the modern presidency has grown dramatically. Presidential behavior can no longer be understood, if it ever was, in mainly personal terms.

Second, the gravitation of presidential studies toward institutions has reflected a wider shift within the social sciences. Researchers in history, economics, sociology, and political science have all devoted greater attention to political, economic, and social institutions. Within political science, analyses of positive theory, the new economics of organizations, and political history have all assigned the highest theoretical significance to institutions. One need only review recent issues of academic journals such as the *American Political Science Review*, *American Journal of Political Science*, *Journal of Politics*, *Political Science Quarterly*, or *Studies in American Political Development* to see clear evidence of the wider professional interest in institutions that presidential studies have also come to reflect (though perhaps belatedly). The new scholarly interest in institutions as agents or explanations of change contrasts with Neustadt's perspective.

1. Types of "Institutional Analysis"

The contributors to this volume as well as other presidential scholars use the term "institutional analysis" to describe what are actually different alternatives to Neustadt's emphasis on individual traits and capabilities. At a general level, the focus of analysis is on the impersonal characteristics of institutions and structures which exist independently of particular individuals. In reality, the term encompasses different theoretical approaches and substantive interests. The variations of institutional analysis presented in *Forging the Presidency*, and more generally in presidential studies, involve at least two different types of approaches.[7]

The first type of analysis involves the identification of organizational characteristics and rules associated with specific government entities as well as the analysis of their impact on political decisionmaking. For example, Lyn Ragsdale's and John Theis's *American Journal of Political Science* (1997) article, "The Institutionalization of the American Presidency, 1924–92," emphasized the importance of the stable development over time of four distinct dimensions of the institutionalization of the presidency.[8] The first of these was the presidency's organizational capacity to use its budget, personnel, and authority to act autonomously from its environment and other organizations. The second was the office's adaptability to the changing environment as evidenced by the longevity of EOP units and by the functional changes of these units as they were created, modified, or eliminated. The third dimension was the increased specialization (due to the increasing complexity observed above) of subunits within the EOP to create functionally distinctive roles and compartmentalize tasks. For instance, until the 1940s top-level White House staffs were generalists, but by the late 1970s they received explicit titles and responsibilities for the specific tasks of congressional affairs, national security, and other areas. The fourth dimension concerned the coherence in managing the volume of work; the EOP operated according to universal criteria that routinized work and produced a predictable handling of the workload.

Part 3 of *Forging the Presidency* devoted to "Organizing and Institutionalizing the Presidency" directly examines organizational characteristics bearing on dimensions of institutionalization, including those affected by political appointments and the staffing of the White House. Matthew Dickinson's essay (chapter 10) analyzes the increasing institutionalization of the White House staff. He defines this institutionalization in terms of not only increases in staff size but also specialization and hierarchy, which provides presidents with a resource to offset sources of uncertainty in their environment—especially in processes of bargaining with Congress and the rest of the bureaucracy.

In his chapter on presidential advisory networks, Michael Link (chapter 11) suggests that particular patterns of interractions with advisers coincided with the institutionalization of staffing. He finds that during the Nixon and Carter White Houses, these patterns of interaction reflected an increasing institutionalization of unified and centrally directed networks of advice.

Kenneth Mayer's and Thomas Weko's chapter (9) on "The Institutionaliza-tion of Power" examines how twentieth-century presidents added substantially to this office's structural capacity for power through institutional control over political appointments, budgeting, and regulation. Comparing Presidents Tru-man, Kennedy, Johnson, and Carter, they show how these presidents probed and sought to establish institutional arrangements that would make presiden-tial leadership more effective than existing arrangements. They found that the cumulative results of these presidents' efforts, through different ways of orga-nizing their staffs into screening or personnel committees, made the political appointment process far more a presidential process by the end of the twenti-eth century than it had been at mid-century—independent of the skill of indi-vidual presidents.

In the case of budgeting, the creation and expansion of the Bureau of the Budget (BOB), now the Office of Management and Budget (OMB), was the epitome of institutional dynamics central to presidential power. From the start, the BOB took on more than simple budget preparation and by the Coolidge administration required central clearance of all legislation having budgetary implications. Franklin Roosevelt expanded this clearance authority to include executive orders, all agency legislation proposals, and coordinating agency rec-ommendations on bills; later expansion of this process included specific proce-dures, such as the the development of the OMB-established deadlines and guidelines for processing executive orders and bills that passed Congress.

In the area of regulatory policy, presidents beginning with Nixon asserted control over new institutions, processes, and procedures through a series of executive orders which imposed increasingly more procedural rules and con-straints on agencies issuing new regulations (e.g., with the Environmental Pro-tection Agency being an important early case).

The second use of the term "institutional analysis" refers to political proper-ties and relationships, especially those involving the partisan and ideological composition of Congress and the patterns of interbranch relations. Institu-tional developments like regulatory review and the national budget process played a part in institutional struggles for control between the president and Congress. For instance, important works by George Edwards and Jon Bond and Richard Fleisher indicate that congressional composition largely deter-mines the president's legislative success in Washington.[9] Indeed the kind of political polarization in Congress that helped drive the impeachment of Bill Clinton appeared to be the logical extension of the increase in ideological par-tisanship that had occurred over the last thirty years.

The second type of institutional analysis is evident in part 4 of *Forging the*

Presidency. David Epstein's and Sharyn O'Halloran (chapter 14) explicitly study the "institutional" rather than the personal side of presidential power. O'Halloran and Epstein focus on the policy goals of members of Congress in order to explain the degree and type of legislative delegation to executive branch officials. They find that congressional delegation of powers to the executive and the extensiveness of these delegated powers can best be explained by whether the same party controls the legislative and executive branches as well as by the partisan leanings of Congress and its committees. By tending to limit the powers delegated to the executive branch when it is in the hand of the opposition party, Congress is anticipating how the executive (as member of that party, not as a consequence of personal behavior) would use such powers.

By the same token, Nolan McCarty and Rose Razaghian's chapter (15) on presidential transitions and appointments shows how presidents are influenced by the partisan or otherwise ideological composition of Senate committees. In determining if and when to put forth particular nominations to executive branch agencies, presidents go through a similar process of strategic anticipation of how committee members will react to particular transition nominees.

Robert Lieberman's "Political Time and Policy Coalitions: Structure and Agency in Presidential Power" (chapter 13) adopts a still broader notion of political structures by borrowing from Stephen Skowronek's concept of "regimes."[10] Lieberman's "structural" account focuses on Madison's constitutional framework as well as political parties, patterns of interest representation, prevailing beliefs and norms, and commitments to particular policies. Rather than emphasizing the similar political and institutional situations of presidents within the modern era, Lieberman confirms Skowronek's case that changes in the political regime pose both dramatically different challenges for presidents even within one era and similar challenges for presidents from different eras. His examination of Presidents Eisenhower through Nixon shows how they confronted a similar set of coalition-forming possibilities; although they viewed these options from different regime perspectives, institutionally speaking their situations had much in common. At the same time, the differences in domestic policymaking between Eisenhower and Nixon (part of one regime) and between Kennedy and Johnson (part of another) were much greater than the regime perspective might suggest.

2. Theories of Change

The analyses of institutions and political structures in *Forging the Presidency* develop two distinct theoretical propositions regarding the behavior of presidents and other Washingtonians. The first emphasizes stability in political behavior; it posits that enduring institutional features such as the constitutional system, the organizational development within the EOP, and weak political parties produce regularities across individual presidencies.[11] Despite great differences in individual political skill and temperament, the behavior of individual presidents is largely stable because of the regularity and continuity of institutions, which create incentives that condition the choices of individual presidents in similar directions. Stable institutions, then, produce predictable and stable behavior.

For instance, as noted above, Link argues that institutional arrangements for presidential advice have become standard features of the presidency and now transcend individual chief executives. Although each new president tries to introduce his own style of interactions, the established institutional arrangements pattern these contacts and produce a significant degree of stability across presidencies in their systems of information gathering, decisionmaking, and implementation.

There are also elements of stability in the institutional competition found in the nature of regimes and the coalition-building options confronted by presidents, as Lieberman emphasized; in the options available regarding the delegation of power, which Epstein and O'Halloran analyzed; and in the factors that affect presidential appointments to the bureaucracy, which McCarty and Razaghian discussed. This clearly poses a challenge to Neustadt's emphasis on the direct intervention of the president himself. Institutional development has ostensibly expanded the area of routine behavior and compliance by Washingtonians without the need for direct presidential bargaining.

The second proposition is that changes in institutions and political structures produce recognizable and clearly connected variations in the behavior of the president and executive branch officials. As Terry Moe suggests, frustration with institutional arrangements that fail to respond to presidents' needs prompts presidents to use their available resources to initiate institutional changes (often over congressional opposition), which subsequently define new behaviors for executive branch officials and enhance the president's institutional position.[12]

For instance, Mayer and Weko argue that presidential alterations of institutions (in the face of congressional resistance) influence the behavior within the executive branch of civil servants, political appointees, and agency heads making budgeting decisions. These institutional changes alter the executive branch's conduct of budget making, rulemaking, and appointment selections, and thereby boost presidential power in relation to Congress. Further, Dickinson suggests that presidents have adapted to high political uncertainty by initiating new institutional arrangements within the White House, specifically, an enduring White House staff system.

Clearly, it is not easy for presidents to alter or build institutions to their advantage due to legal and political constraints. In part 5 of *Forging the Presidency*, Russell Riley (chapter 19) on "The Limits of the Transformational Presidency" argues that the president's "institutional infirmity" in the face of rising demands and responsibilities produces paradoxical transformations: presidential leadership can occur without change; and presidents can oversee change without leading. Alterations in presidential institutions do not necessarily lead to changes that presidents wish to effect.

Diane Heith's chapter (17) describes how presidents have attempted to develop their institutional capacity for using public opinion through a "public opinion apparatus."[13] Neustadt had acknowledged that public opinion could constitute a political resource, though not necessarily the most important one. What is different is that the presidency's capacity to manage public opinion has been institutionalized in an effort to regularize and extend White House control and influence. The presidency's institutionalized capacity to "go public" through public speeches is analyzed in Renee Smith's chapter (6) in part 2. This capacity of the president to turn to the public clearly represents an important institutional development that could be used to facilitate presidential power and change.

3. The Contradictory Impact of Institutionalization on Presidential Power

The analyses in *Forging the Presidency* suggest that the institutionalization of the presidency has had a contradictory impact on presidential power: although it has enhanced the president's power to get things done, it may have eroded his ability to exert decisive individual initiative.

On the one hand, institutional developments enable presidents to exert greater influence within Washington than previously possible. Within the executive branch, the White House has used its organizational capacity through such offices as the OMB to centralize the decisions of the departments and agencies within the White House, as well as to screen potential appointees to select officials who share the president's political philosophy or have demonstrated political loyalty.[14] The president's ability to influence decisions is enhanced by these institutional changes that have centralized and politicized executive branch operations.

Mayer and Weko, for instance, argue that modern presidents have outmaneuvered Congress in their efforts to boost their institutional capacity beyond that of their predecessors to influence budgets, agency rulemaking, and appointments. The institutional development of the presidency has also equipped presidents, as Heith demonstrates, with the ability to orchestrate campaigns to direct public opinion and set the country's agenda.

Institutional changes have also altered the president's relationship with Congress. Presidents now possess the institutional capacity to establish an "administrative presidency," bypassing the normal legislative process of enacting statutes in favor of making policy within the executive branch. Chief executives rely on the White House staff, staff agencies like the OMB, and loyal department heads to make and implement policy that affects the budgets, personnel, and authority of agencies. As President Clinton explained after the Republicans assumed control of Congress in the 1994 elections, "One of the things I have learned in the last two years is that the President can do an awful lot of things by executive action."[15] The institutional development of the presidency has expanded the White House's ability to act without congressional participation, though there are limits to this.[16]

On the other hand, the institutional development of the presidency has produced a paradox: the "swelling" of the presidency's institutional capacity has complicated and eroded the ability of presidents to exercise individual initiative. Six reasons for this stand out. First, the presidency's enhanced institutional capacity has introduced pressures to "program" presidents to serve as predictable components of a bureaucracy. The routinized rules and procedures of the OMB and other staff agencies enhance the uniformity and predictability of executive decisionmaking but also stifle originality and reduce policy differences to the lowest common denominator. Second, the president's reliance on a growing number of staff and agencies "hemorrhages" presidential power. As Hugh Heclo explained, by "becoming more extensive, scattered, and shared," the influence of individual presidents has "decreased by becoming less of a prerogative . . . and less closely held by the man himself."[17]

Third, institutional changes may not operate effectively as intended. For example, the jury is still out on the potency of the institutionalization and use of public opinion analysis that Heith describes. While public opinion was a crucial resource for Clinton and his supporters in Congress in his battle against impeachment and conviction, it is not clear that the White House's institutional capacity to influence and use public opinion was decisive; rather, the public behaved more autonomously—separating Clinton's personal misdeeds from their relevance to impeachment and to their perceptions of the president's governmental performance.[18] Furthermore, the public opinion apparatus may also be unreliable in its effectiveness due to tensions between governing and campaigning, and because of staff turnovers related to each.[19] The presence of an apparatus enabling presidents to respond to and lead public opinion becomes a lightning rod for the dilemmas that leaders face in a democracy: to what extent should they follow or lead public opinion? What factors or circumstances should affect this decision? The result is to further complicate and constrain presidents

Fourth, the "swelling of the presidency" to handle the growing demands on government encourage still greater expectations that no president can satisfy. Developing the presidency to respond to heightened expectations has let loose an avalanche of unrealistic demands on presidents.[20] Fifth, the presidency is now beset by many of the same pathologies that dog other large bureaucracies. Aides and agencies abuse power, distort information, and become enmeshed in debilitating rivalries and intra-staff controversies. Finally, the institutional development of the presidency has been mirrored in Congress and elsewhere in Washington. As Stephen Skowronek argues, the political environment has become more dense, competitive and destructive over time.[21]

The opportunity for effective individual leadership by presidents has declined as presidential behavior has become less the outcome of a single actor and more the result of an expanding corporate entity. There is certainly no evidence that the institutional arrangements that originated as part of an effort to "help" the president, as the Brownlow Commission recommended, have made modern presidents more successful than their predecessors.

C. PRESIDENTIAL PERSONALITY INTO INSTITUTIONAL ANALYSIS

We have observed that presidential studies have unmistakably shifted from Neustadt's emphasis on personal skills and temperament to an emphasis on the durable institutions that stretch across a number of presidencies and are largely beyond the control of any single chief executive. While Neustadt emphasized the differences across individuals, the new institutionalism described above argues that individuals with different personalities will behave alike within the same institutional context.

While institutions may in general induce fairly uniform individual behavior, the personal input of the president still matters and, in specific situations, may well divert the course of presidential behavior and larger political developments from their normal path. What must be avoided is the tendency to replace one extremism—one that gives nearly exclusive emphasis to the personality of individual presidents—with another (one in which institutions dictate presidential behavior).

Presidential studies must avoid the false dichotomy between institutions and presidential personality. For the moment, the challenge is to acknowledge the pervasive influence of institutions and then to map the specific circumstances and personalities under which the personal input of the president, who does enjoy an unparalleled strategic position, is likely to have its greatest impact.

1. Conducive Circumstances for Presidential Impact

Fred Greenstein's masterful book, *Personality and Politics,* persuasively argued that particular circumstances heighten the impact of individuals in altering the course of politics from their normal path.[22] Extending Greenstein's analysis, the probability that individual presidents will have an impact increases when they face an unstable environment that is conducive to political structuring. Consistent with Skowronek's comparisons across historical eras, the chapters by Riley and Lieberman suggest that the underlying conditions enabled relatively modest interventions by individual presidents to produce disproportionately large results, as in the cases of social welfare and racial policies in the 1960s and 1970s.

In addition, ambiguous situations also clear the way for personal differences to be expressed. The behavior of individual presidents is likely to vary quite a bit when they are faced with completely new situations such as the formation of a new political party, complex situations with numerous cues, or contradictory situations stocked with conflicting points of view.

In part 2 Charles Cameron argues in chapter 5 that bargaining is critical in complex and conflictual situations such as successive presidential vetoes of legislation. He offers a striking challenge to conventional wisdom: current research on interbranch relations considers and then rejects bargaining as a significant influence on presidential success after other factors are controlled.[23] Cameron resuscitates bargaining and reputation as theoretically important concepts for analyzing the complexity and conflict inherent in presidential behavior, especially in an "era of divided government," and elaborates upon them theoretically and empirically in a particular of type of presidential activity (i.e., veto bargaining), which is deeply embedded in a context of complexity and conflict, as well as institutions.

Furthermore, a president's performance of the symbolic and ceremonial aspects of his office provide ample room for the expression of his unique personal style. Greenstein's study of Eisenhower emphasizes his skill in performing ceremonial functions to encourage an image of himself as politically detached, which lowered expectations and gave him the freedom to work behind the scenes to pursue his political aims.[24]

Renee Smith's chapter also indicates that individual presidents vary in their exercise of their expressive styles and, specifically, when they decide to deliver major speeches that are not mandated by the Constitution or tradition. The decision of individual presidents to take advantage of an event to deliver a speech is not driven by some factor common to all presidents such as falling approval ratings; rather, it appears to reflect the individual president's own unique temperament, style, and set of values.

2. Differences in Presidential Personality

The personality of individual presidents may lead them to misread or deliberately defy their objective institutional context. Jimmy Carter, for instance, took the politically self-destructive decision to veto a popular bill loaded with pork projects that his fellow Democrats in Congress had passed. Decisions that are incongruous with the institutional context may result from presidents who were not socialized in Washington's assumptions, who harbored an intense disposition to buck established norms, or were driven by intense inner feelings, values, and dispositions regarding politics.

The growth of the specialization in political psychology as a discipline has contributed a variety of theories and empirical research on just these sorts of issues. Thomas Preston's chapter (7) in part 2 illustrates the importance political psychologists attached to the individual characteristics and qualities of presidents. He concludes by suggesting that the president's personal characteristics are especially influential when the president is inexperienced and therefore not fully socialized in the norms of politics.

3. Moving Beyond the Institution-Personality Dichotomy

Moving presidential studies beyond the Neustadtian paradigm makes it imperative to design theoretical frameworks that avoid the false dichotomy between personality and institutions and, instead, incorporate both. For instance, Susan Fiske argues that the goals of presidents do not result from a detached, computer-like calculation of what is "rational" in their institutional context but rather evolve from evaluations of particular situations that are immediately before them. Fiske notes that the process by which individual presidents evaluate their environment can be distorted by biased samples of information, faulty estimates, and flawed assumptions about causality.[25] In particular, the president's motivation and goals affect his style of evaluation. Careful decisions are more likely when the president lacks extensive prior knowledge of the issue area and is able in a more balanced manner to weigh alternative courses of action and the competing arguments of his advisers.[26]

II. Presidential Leadership in American Democracy

Neustadt's argument that the public's perceptions of the president's personal qualities and, especially, his job performance affects his bargaining with Washingtonians has given rise to a burgeoning subfield in presidential studies, the public presidency.[27] The chapters in this volume by Heith and Smith are good cases in point. The debate sparked by Neustadt's arguments have raised fundamental issues relating to representative democracy and the relationship between the governed and the governors.

In analyzing the president's standing with the public, Neustadt focused on elites in Washington and on the president's personal choices. Neustadt argued that Washingtonians take into account the president's public approval when bargaining with him: they accord him more leeway when he enjoys public support and less when he lacks it. The president's personal choices over his actions and statements are essential in guarding his popular prestige. Adverse events dog all presidents; the power-conscious and skilled president will minimize the drain on his approval by teaching realism and fending off unrealistic expectations and hopes.

Research that has critically examined Neustadt's claims regarding the political consequences of public approval has continued to focus on the calculations of Washington elites.[28] Research by Samuel Kernell, Jeffrey Tulis, George Edwards,[29] Smith in her chapter, and others have essentially modified (rather than rejected) Neustadt's connection between public approval and Washington politics. The newer research emphasizes far more than did Neustadt the modern president's establishment of a direct relationship with the public, and the greater frequency and acceptance among politicians of presidents "going over the heads" of Washingtonians to make routine appeals for public support of themselves and their policies.

A third generation of research on the public presidency has departed still further from Neustadt's claims by nesting analysis of presidential public appeals in the institutional development of a public opinion apparatus (elaborated upon by Heith) geared toward tracking and directing public opinion. While addressing Neustadt's relative neglect of presidential appeals to the public, both Tulis and Kernell remain committed to viewing presidential actions in individualistic terms. Kernell, for instance, stresses the "personal character of the office" and suggests that independent actions by presidents "largely reflect the skills and experiences of the person in office."[30] Absent is a systematic focus on the institutional developments relating to "going public."

Heith's essay builds on work by Lawrence Jacobs (and our collaborative work) by demonstrating that presidential appeals to the public are an attribute of institutional capacity and not simply the personal ability of individual officeholders.[31]

Although no modern president can achieve the unattainable standard of mastering the existing political universe, the president inherits the institutional capacity—no matter who the individual is—to have some (not insignificant) impact on public debate. The institutional capacity to conduct both public opinion research and public relations campaigns has provided presidents (beginning in earnest with Kennedy) with additional means to exert influence on their political environment.

The institutional development of the public opinion apparatus shapes the specific nature of a president's strategies and actions. The growing incidence of public appeals over time that Kernell and others have detected is partly a reflection of institutional pressures within the EOP to rely upon the White House's public relations capacity and to use the presidency as a "bully pulpit" to lead public opinion.

In addition to encouraging greater public appeals, the public opinion apparatus affects the *content* of presidential appeals—it contributes significantly to identifying the specific policy issues and arguments that presidents visibly promote in their appeals to the public.[32]

Presidents' public appeals are motivated by political struggles within Washington, but they also profoundly affect the dilemmas of democratic governance—to what extent politicians choose to *respond to* versus *direct* public opinion. The public opinion apparatus's identification of policy issues that have public support, as noted by Heith and others, can contribute to heightening presidential responsiveness to public opinion.[33] It highlights positions that may enable presidents to enhance their opportunities to win public support and outflank their opponents.

Conversely, this new institutional capacity also inflates the confidence of White House officials regarding the president's ability to successfully "win" public support and augment his scarce political resources. Officials overestimate their capacity to dominate public debate by launching elaborate public relations blitzes and crafting their political communications based on their public opinion research. Research on the Kennedy, Johnson, and Clinton presidencies suggests a fairly predictable cycle of responsiveness and direction: responsiveness rises and White House efforts at direction drop as presidential elections approach, while direction rises and responsiveness drops after elections.[34]

The institutional capacity of presidents to conduct sophisticated public relations campaigns does not occur in a vacuum. While Martha Kumar's chapter (18) focuses explicitly on the president as both the message and messenger in political communications and on the president's relations with the press, presidents' use of their "bully pulpit" is no longer (if it ever was) their exclusive prerogative. Congressional leaders and interest groups are increasingly acting "presidential" by recognizing the utility of going public as a means to augment their political resources and build their organizational capacity to make these appeals routinely and effectively.[35] Journalists highlight the battle for public support by flagging politicians' conflict and strategies. Focusing on the single person with the loudest voice (the president) ignores the potentially deafening and sustained chorus of an army of other speakers.[36]

The emergence of the presidency's institutional capacity to track and manipulate public opinion raises important normative questions central to theories about representative democracy. The presidency's capacity to manipulate public opinion has spurred competing Washingtonians to develop their own ability to track public opinion and launch orchestrated campaigns to swing Americans behind their desired positions. The result has been to create incentives for political elites in Washington to discount public preferences and to avoid responding to public opinion as in the past. Indeed, recent research examining the public's specific policy preferences and the decisions of the national government suggests that there has been a decline in actual policy responsiveness to public opinion since 1980.[37] This clearly warrants further study, since it bears not only on government leadership versus responsiveness to public opinion, but also on Americans' perceptions and evaluations of their government.

CONCLUSION: THE NEUSTADT LEGACY

This chapter began as a discussion of presidential power and emphasized the institutional turn in presidential studies.[38] It ends with an emphasis on the visible role of public opinion in American politics and the dilemmas facing presidents and other political leaders in American democracy. Still, in this new context, presidential studies continue to develop in reaction to the Neustadt paradigm. For an extraordinary period, this framework captured the consensus among scholars of presidential power. This has changed as growing attention has shifted toward institutions and the president's direct relationship with public opinion. For Neustadt, however, perhaps the most important question to ask about this shift in focus is the following: To what extent does this change reflect insight and interest in real politics that can offer sitting presidents useful advice for exercising power on the important issues that swirl around the White House? Thus presidential studies pose dilemmas for political scientists as well as for democracy.

ACKNOWLEDGMENT

An earlier version of this was presented at the 1998 Annual Meeting of the American Political Science Association, September 3–6, Boston, Massachusetts. For very helpful written comments, the authors especially thank Richard Pious, Mark Peterson, and Natasha Hritzuk. They also wish to thank Charles Cameron, Martha Kumar, George Edwards, Richard Powell, and Charles Walcott. They are grateful to the Pew Charitable Trusts for research support. All responsibility for analysis and interpretations remains the authors.'

NOTES

1. James Bryce, *The American Commonwealth*, 2 vols. 3rd edition, New York: MacMillan, 1897 [1893].

2. Neustadt, *Presidential Power* (1980), p. 27.

3. *Presidential Power*, p.27.

4. See Terry Moe, "The Politicized Presidency," in John Chubb and Paul Peterson eds., *The New Directions in American Politics* (Washington: The Brookings Institution, 1985); Charles Walcott and Karen Hult, "Organizing the White House: Structure, Environment, and Organizational Governance," *American Journal of Political Science* 31 (1987): 109–25; Samuel Kernell, *Going Public: New Strategies of Presidential Leadership* (Washington, D.C.: Congressional Quarterly Press, 1986); Stephen Skowronek, *The Politics Presidents Make: Leadership from John Adams to George Bush* (Cambridge: Harvard University Press, 1993); Lyn Ragsdale and John Theis, "The Institutionalization of the American Presidency, 1924–92," *American Journal of Political Science* 41 (October 1997): 1280–1319.

5. But compare our further interpretation of this in Lawrence R. Jacobs and Robert Y. Shapiro, *Politicians Don't Pander: Political Manipulation and the Loss of Democratic Responsiveness* (Chicago: University of Chicago Press, 2000).

6. *Report of the Brownlow Committee [for President Franklin D. Roosevelt], 1937.* Reprinted in *Basic Documents of Public Administration* edited by F.C. Mosher (New York: Holmes & Meier, 1976).

7. In addition to the two notions of institutions discussed here, there are at least three more: economic institutions and their influence on the allocation of material resources; symbolic orders and organization of modes of discourses and socially shared meanings; and legal institutions that regulate legitimate behavior.

8. Lyn Ragsdale and John Theis, "The Institutionalization of the American Presidency, 1924–92," *American Journal of Political Science* 41 (October 1997): 1280–1319.

9. George C. Edwards, III, *At the Margins: Presidential Leadership of Congress* (New Haven: Yale University Press, 1989); Jon Bond and Richard Fleisher, *The President in the Legislative Arena* (Chicago: University of Chicago Press, 1990).

10. Skowronek, *The Politics Presidents Make*.

11. See Moe, "The Politicized Presidency"; Theodore Lowi, *The Personal President* (Ithaca: Cornell University Press, 1985).

12. Moe, " The Politicized Presidency."

13. See Lawrence R. Jacobs, "The Recoil Effect: Public Opinion and Policymaking in the U.S. and Britain," *Comparative Politics* 24 (January 1992)): 199–217; Lawrence R. Jacobs, *The Health of Nations: Public Opinion and the Making of Health Policy in the U.S. and Britain* (Cornell University Press, 1993), Chapter 2.

14. Moe, " The Politicized Presidency."

15. Quoted in Alison Mitchell, "Despite His Reversals, Clinton Stays Centered," *New York Times*, July 28, 1996.

16. As Robert F. Durant writes, "In the end, however, both the Bush and Clinton administrations learned the same lessons that their predecessors did about the administrative presidency. It is neither as politically potent a force in the American political system as its proponents suggest or as its critics fear, nor as Lilliputian in potency under all conditions as its detractors allege." Robert F. Durant, "The Administrative Presidency: Retrospect and Prospect," *PRG Report* 21 (Fall 1998): 1–6.

17. Hugh Heclo, "The Changing Presidential Office" in Arnold J. Meltsner, ed., *Politics and the Oval Office: Towards Presidential Governance*, (San Francisco: Institute for Contemporary Studies, 1978), p. 172–73.

18. See John R. Zaller, "Monica Lewinsky's Contribution to Political Science," *PS Political Science and Politics* 31 (June 1998): 182–189.

19. Kathryn Dunn Tenpas and Matthew J. Dickinson, "Governing, Campaigning, and Organizing the Presidency," *Political Science Quarterly* 112 (Spring 1997): 51–66.

20. Hugh Heclo, "The Changing Presidential Office"; Hugh Heclo, "Issue Networks and the Executive Establishment," in Anthony King, ed., *The American Political System* (Washington, D.C.: American Enterprise Institute, 1978); Thomas Cronin, *The State of the Presidency* (Boston: Little, Brown, 1975); Lowi, *The Personal President*.

21. Skowronek, *The Politics Presidents Make*.

22. Fred Greenstein, *Personality and Politics: Problems of Evidence, Inference, and Conceptualization* (Chicago: Markham Publishing Co., 1969).

23. Edwards, *At the Margins*; Bond and Fleisher, *The President in the Legislative Arena.*

24. Fred Greenstein, *The Hidden-Hand Presidency: Eisenhower as Leader* (New York: Basic Books, 1982). On the symbolic side of the public presidency described below, see Barbara Hinckley, *The Symbolic Presidency: How Presidents Portray Themselves* (New York: Routledge, 1990), and Jeffrey E. Cohen, *Presidential Responsiveness and Public Policy-Making* (Ann Arbor: University of Michigan Press, 1997).

25. Susan Fiske, "Cognitive Theory and the Presidency," in George C. Edwards III, John Kessel, and Bert Rockman, eds., *Researching the Presidency* (Pittsburgh: University of Pittsburgh Press, 1993), pp. 233–266.

26. Fiske, "Cognitive Theory and the Presidency."

27. See George C. Edwards, III., *The Public Presidency: The Pursuit of Popular Support* (New York: St. Martin's Press, 1983); Kernell, *Going Public.'*

28. There is a large literature on the public presidency and the determinants of presidential approval (e.g., Robert Erikson, James Stimson, and Michael MacKuen, *The Macro Polity* (New York: Cambridge University Press, forthcoming). Space limitations restrict our focus to the implications of presidential public appeals on the political process in Washington.

29. Kernell, *Going Public*; Tulis, *The Rhetorical Presidency*; Edwards, *The Public Presidency*; George C. Edwards, III., *Presidential Influence in Congress* (San Francisco: W. H. Freeman, 1980).

30. Kernell, *Going Public*, p. 210, 44.

31. Jacobs, "The Recoil Effect"; Jacobs, *The Health of Nations*, chapter 2; Lawrence R. Jacobs and Robert Y. Shapiro, "Issues, Candidate Image, and Priming: The Use of Private Polls in Kennedy's 1960 Presidential Campaign," *American Political Science Review* 88 (September 1994): 527–40; Lawrence R. Jacobs and Robert Y. Shapiro, "The Rise of Presidential Polling: The Nixon White House in Historical Perspective," *Public Opinion Quarterly* 59 (Summer 1995): 163–195.

32. See Lawrence R. Jacobs and Robert Y. Shapiro, "The Politicization of Public Opinion; The Fight for the Pulpit," in Margaret Weir, ed., *The Social Divide: Political Parties and the Future of Activist Government* (Washington, D.C.: Brookings Institution Press, 1998), p. 83–125; Jacobs and Shapiro, *Politicians Don't Pander.*

33. One pertinent book is Jeffrey E. Cohen's, *Presidential Responsiveness and Public Policy-Making* (Ann Arbor: University of Michigan Press, 1997).

34. See Lawrence R. Jacobs and Robert Y. Shapiro, "Public Decisions, Private Polls: John F. Kennedy's Presidency," paper presented at the annual meeting of the Midwest Political Science Association, Chicago, 1992; Lawrence R. Jacobs and Robert Y. Shapiro, "The Public Presidency, Private Polls, and Policymaking: Lyndon

Johnson," paper presented at the annual meeting of the American Political Science Association, Washington, D.C., 1993; Jacobs and Shapiro, "Issues, Candidate Image, and Priming"; Jacobs and Shapiro, "The Rise of Presidential Polling"; Jacobs and Shapiro, "The Politicization of Public Opinion"; Jacobs and Shapiro, *Politicians Don't Pander.*

35. See Douglas B. Harris, "The Rise of the Public Speakership," *Political Science Quarterly* 113 (Summer 1998): 193–212.

36. See Jacobs and Shapiro, *Politicians Don't Pander.*

37. See Alan Monroe, "Public Opinion and Public Policy, 1980–1993." *Public Opinion Quarterly* 62 (Spring 1998): 6–28; Lawrence Jacobs and Robert Shapiro, "Debunking the Pandering Politician Myth," *The Public Perspective* (April/May 1997): 3–5; Benjamin I. Page, "Who Gets What from Government," paper presented at the 1995 Richard S. and Nancy K. Hartigan Lecture on Politics and Government, Loyola University, Chicago; Jacobs and Shapiro, *Politicians Don't Pander.*

38. Our assessment of presidential studies is clearly consonant with the objective of Mark A. Peterson's, *Legislating Together: The White House and Capital Hill from Eisenhower to Reagan* (Cambridge: Harvard University Press, 1990).

INDEX

Acheson, Dean, 124, 461
Adams, John, 267
Adams, Sherman, 129, 167
Administrative Procedures Act (APA), 53
Advisory networks, presidential: access to president, 241, 244, 253; analysis of, 238; autonomy, 239; chaos in, 240; direct ties, 238; fluidity and complexity of, 251–53; "inner circle" advisors, 245–48, 252; institutional presidency, 239–41, 244–45; interaction style, 245, 249–51, 493; multidimensional scaling techniques, 245; outer core, 252, 253; periphery, 252; personal network of contacts, 238; policy-area differentiation, 247; presidential relationships with, 235, 237; stability and centralization in, 239–241, 244–51; turnover rates, 251, 254, 339; *see also* Appointments, presidential; Staffing of presidency

Index compiled by Kim L. Callihan

Affirmative action, 296
Agency, 203n12, 365, 369, 371, 374
Agricultural Adjustment Act, 277
Aid to Dependent Children (ADC), 290, 291
Aid to Dependent Children for Unemployed Parents (ADC-UP), 290
Aid to Families with Dependent Children (AFDC), 281, 290, 298, 302
Allen, James, 342
Altmeyer, Arthur, 283
American Journal of Political Science, 492
American political science, 23, 436, 449; behavioral movement, 16, 17; formalism, 17; group theory, 18; legal/institutional approach, 16; pluralism, 17–19, 20, 21, 22, 23; Progressive agenda, 17, 24; theory development, 3, 16, 17,18; *see also* Behavioralism
American Political Science Association, 23–24, 25
American Political Science Review, 492